Communications in Computer and Information Science 2958

Series Editors

Rationale

The CCIS series is devoted to the publication of proceedings of computer science conferences. Its aim is to efficiently disseminate original research results in informatics in printed and electronic form. While the focus is on publication of peer-reviewed full papers presenting mature work, inclusion of reviewed short papers reporting on work in progress is welcome, too. Besides globally relevant meetings with internationally representative program committees guaranteeing a strict peer-reviewing and paper selection process, conferences run by societies or of high regional or national relevance are also considered for publication.

Topics

The topical scope of CCIS spans the entire spectrum of informatics ranging from foundational topics in the theory of computing to information and communications science and technology and a broad variety of interdisciplinary application fields.

Information for Volume Editors and Authors

Publication in CCIS is free of charge. No royalties are paid, however, we offer registered conference participants temporary free access to the online version of the conference proceedings on SpringerLink (http://link.springer.com) by means of an http referrer from the conference website and/or a number of complimentary printed copies, as specified in the official acceptance email of the event.

CCIS proceedings can be published in time for distribution at conferences or as post-proceedings, and delivered in the form of printed books and/or electronically as USBs and/or e-content licenses for accessing proceedings at SpringerLink. Furthermore, CCIS proceedings are included in the CCIS electronic book series hosted in the SpringerLink digital library at http://link.springer.com/bookseries/7899. Conferences publishing in CCIS are allowed to use our online conference service (Meteor) for managing the whole proceedings lifecycle (from submission and reviewing to preparing for publication) free of charge.

Publication process

The language of publication is exclusively English. Authors publishing in CCIS have to sign the Springer CCIS copyright transfer form, however, they are free to use their material published in CCIS for substantially changed, more elaborate subsequent publications elsewhere. For the preparation of the camera-ready papers/files, authors have to strictly adhere to the Springer CCIS Authors' Instructions and are strongly encouraged to use the CCIS LaTeX style files or templates.

Abstracting/Indexing

CCIS is abstracted/indexed in DBLP, Google Scholar, EI-Compendex, Mathematical Reviews, SCImago, Scopus. CCIS volumes are also submitted for the inclusion in ISI Proceedings.

How to start

To start the evaluation of your proposal for inclusion in the CCIS series, please send an e-mail to ccis@springer.com

Matteo Adamoli · Domenico Amato ·
Daniele Schicchi · Giovanni Fulantelli ·
Marco Rondonotti · Davide Taibi ·
Alessandro Ciasullo · Flavia Santoianni
Editors

Higher Education Learning Methodologies and Technologies Online

7th International Conference, HELMeTO 2025
Naples, Italy, September 23–25, 2025
Revised Selected Papers, Part I

Springer

Editors
Matteo Adamoli
eCampus University
Novedrate, Italy

Domenico Amato
University of Palermo
Palermo, Italy

Daniele Schicchi
Independent Researcher
Palermo, Italy

Giovanni Fulantelli
National Research Council of Italy
Palermo, Italy

Marco Rondonotti
eCampus University
Novedrate, Italy

Davide Taibi
National Research Council of Italy
Palermo, Italy

Alessandro Ciasullo
University of Naples Federico II
Naples, Italy

Flavia Santoianni
University of Naples Federico II
Naples, Italy

ISSN 1865-0929 ISSN 1865-0937 (electronic)
Communications in Computer and Information Science
ISBN 978-3-032-31849-7 ISBN 978-3-032-31850-3 (eBook)
https://doi.org/10.1007/978-3-032-31850-3

This Springer imprint is published by the registered company Springer Nature Switzerland AG
The registered company address is: Gewerbestrasse 11, 6330 Cham, Switzerland

Preface

These two volumes of Communications in Computer and Information Science (CCIS) contain the post-proceedings of HELMeTO 2025, the 7th International Conference on Higher Education Learning Methodologies and Technologies Online.

The conference took place in Naples, Italy, from September 23–25, 2025 and was hosted by the University of Naples Federico II. The conference focused on learning methodologies and technologies in higher education and featured 147 submissions from more than 325 authors in 18 countries, including Italy, Brazil, Morocco, Ukraine, the UK, Hungary, Nigeria, Croatia, France, Germany, Latvia, Canada, Denmark, India, Slovenia, Spain, Sweden and the United Arab Emirates. This broad international participation showcases the conference's crucial role as a hub for exchanging ideas and best practices in online learning.

The contributions were organized into seven special tracks and two general tracks. Presentations and discussions explored the complex link between technology and teaching, focusing on both established topics and emerging trends like artificial intelligence, augmented and virtual reality, learning analytics, and big data analytics in education.

The conference's main tracks were General Track 1 (GT1), focusing on "Online Pedagogy and Learning Methodologies," and General Track 2 (GT2), on "Learning Technologies, Data Analytics, and Educational Big Data Mining." General Track 1 centered on the strategies and practices for effective teaching and learning in digital environments, exploring how traditional pedagogical approaches can be adapted for online platforms using various digital tools. Meanwhile, General Track 2 investigated how learning technologies, data analytics, and large-scale data are transforming education by enhancing teaching, learning, and decision-making processes.

Special Track 1, titled "Rethinking Education The Opportunities and Challenges of Artificial Intelligence" examined the transformative impact of AI on contemporary pedagogical environments. This track facilitated a critical discourse regarding the strategic integration of AI to reconfigure educational paradigms via adaptive learning, intelligent tutoring systems, and automated evaluative feedback.

Special Track 2, "Formative Assessment in Higher Education Conceptual Framework", explored the dialogue between continuous feedback and summative assessment within higher education. By addressing both conceptual frameworks and practical applications, this track evaluated the impact of integrated assessment strategies on modern instructional delivery.

Special Track 3, "AI-Enhanced E-learning for 'Augmented' Mathematics Education at University Level" investigated the synergy between AI-driven platforms, intelligent tutoring systems, and automated feedback mechanisms. It explored how these technologies can be integrated with conventional pedagogical approaches to establish innovative, hybrid learning ecosystems.

Special Track 4, "The Art of Learning Online Creative Practices in Digital Higher Education" explored the integration of artistic disciplines within digital curricula to foster more dynamic and human-centric learning experiences. It emphasized the adoption of creative practices—such as visual arts, music, creative writing, and performance—not merely as curricular content, but as fundamental pedagogical methodologies

Special Track 5, "AI in Higher Education Empowering Design, Critical Thinking, and Reflective Learning", focused on the strategic integration of AI to augment instructional design, foster critical thinking, and facilitate reflective learning processes. It sought to advance the global scholarly discourse by examining how AI can be leveraged to develop effective, inclusive, and adaptable educational practices.

Special track 6, "UDL and AI in Higher Education and in Pre-Service Teacher Education strategies, experiences, and perspectives for inclusive innovation" examined how the integration of Universal Design for Learning (UDL) principles and Artificial Intelligence can augment accessibility, participation, and academic achievement. The track investigated these dynamics across diverse instructional modalities, including digital, distance, and blended learning environments, to promote inclusive innovation.

Special Track 7, titled "Human rights-based approach and practices for preventing and countering online hate speech: digital strategies and educational challenges in Higher Education", explored how higher education can use digital strategies and technologies to prevent and counter online hate speech.

An international Program/Scientific Committee, consisting of members from 10 different countries (Italy, Brazil, Argentina, Slovakia, Turkey, Spain, Greece, Portugal, France, Croatia) was responsible for reviewing the 147 papers submitted to HELMeTO 2025. After a separate double-blind peer-review process conducted by at least three members of the Program/Scientific Committee, a final set of the best 66 papers (46% of the original submissions) were chosen for publication in this book.

We extend our sincere gratitude to all contributing authors for their valuable research, presentations, and dedication, as well as for their participation in the event. Furthermore, we gratefully acknowledge the committee members, organizers, and contributors for their pivotal role in the preparation and execution of both the conference and this volume

April 2026

Matteo Adamoli
Domenico Amato
Daniele Schicchi
Giovanni Fulantelli
Marco Rondonotti
Alessandro Ciasullo
Flavia Santonianni

Organization

Organizing Committee

General Chairs

Alessandro Ciasullo	University of Naples Federico II, Italy
Flavia Santoianni	University of Naples Federico II, Italy
Davide Taibi	CNR - Institute for Educational Technology, Italy

Program Chairs

Giovanni Fulantelli	CNR - Institute for Educational Technology, Italy
Marco Rondonotti	eCampus University, Italy
Gianluca Giannini	University of Naples Federico II, Italy

Permanent Steering Committee

Daniel Burgos	Universidad Internacional de La Rioja, Spain
Christian Stracke	European Institute for Learning, Innovation and Cooperation, Germany
Pier Cesare Rivoltella	University of Bologna, Italy
Paolo Raviolo	eCampus University, Italy
Pietro Picerno	Sassari University Italy
Riccardo Pecori	eCampus University, Italy
Marta Cimitile	Unitelma Sapienza University, Italy
Gabriella Casalino	University of Bari, Italy
Davide Taibi	CNR – Institute for Education Technology, Italy
Giosuè Lo Bosco	University of Palermo, Italy
Marco Rondonotti	eCampus University, Italy

Publicity and Communication Chairs

Salvatore Calderaro	University of Palermo, Italy
Ilaria Terrenghi	eCampus University, Italy
Anna Vacca	Unitelma Sapienza University, Italy

Publication Chairs

Matteo Adamoli	eCampus University, Italy
Domenico Amato	University of Palermo, Italy
Daniele Schicchi	Independent Researcher, Italy

Web Master

Andrea Nelson Mauro	CNR - Institute for Educational Technology, Italy

Program Committee

Adamoli Matteo	eCampus University, Italy
Amato Domenico	University of Palermo, Italy
Ardimento Pasquale	University of Bari, Italy
Balestra Antonio	Link Campus University, Italy
Baroni Federica	University of Bergamo, Italy
Barpi Fabrizio	Polytechnic University of Turin, Italy
Boninelli Maria Luisa	University of Catania, Italy
Buccini Francesca	University of Naples Federico II, Italy
Calderaro Salvatore	University of Palermo, Italy
Carlomagno Nadia	Suor Orsola Benincasa University of Naples, Italy
Carruba Maria Concetta	Pegaso Telematic University, Italy
Casalino Gabriella	University of Bari, Italy
Ciasullo Alessandro	University of Naples Federico II, Italy
D'Ascenzo Stefania	Pegaso Telematic University, Italy
Dalmazzo Davide	Polytechnic University of Turin, Italy
De Angelis Grazia	Pegaso Telematic University, Italy
Del Gobbo Emiliano	University of Foggia, Italy
Di Fuccio Raffaele	Pegaso Telematic University, Italy
Di Martino Valeria	University of Palermo, Italy
Dimitriadis Yannis	University of Valladolid, Spain
Domingues Andrè Luìs Dos Santos	Tecnological Federal University of Paranà, Brazil
Drlik Martin	Constantine the Philosopher University in Nitra, Slovakia
Emanuel Federica	eCampus University, Italy
Farella Mariella	CNR - Institute for Educational Technology, Italy
Fedeli Laura	University of Macerata, Italy
Finestrone Francesca	University of Foggia, Italy
Fiorentino Michele Giuliano	University of Bari, Italy

Fulantelli Giovanni	CNR - Institute for Educational Technology, Italy
Gama Sandra	University of Lisbon, Portugal
Giuliani Arianna	eCampus University, Italy
González Enríquez Isabel	Complutense University of Madrid, Spain
Gulbay Elif	University of Palermo, Italy
Izgi Ümit	Mersin University, Turkey
Kucina Softic Sandra	University of Zagreb, Croatia
Limongelli Carla	University of Roma Tre, Italy
Lo Bosco Giosuè	University of Palermo, Italy
Lombardo Renato	University of Palermo, Italy
Maggi Daniela	eCampus University, Italy
Marangi Michele	eCampus University, Italy
Marsico Emanuele	Pegaso Telematic University, Italy
Mauro Andrea Nelson	CNR - Institute for Educational Technology, Italy
Miranda Annamaria	University of Salerno, Italy
Monacis Domenico	Pegaso Telematic University, Italy
Monfroy Eric	University of Angers, France
Montano Debora	University of Modena and Reggio Emilio, Italy
Montone Antonella	University of Bari, Italy
Peconio Guendalina	University of Foggia, Italy
Pecori Riccardo	eCampus University, Italy
Pedrochi Junior Osmar	Federal University of Maranhão, Brazil
Piacenza Susanna	eCampus University, Italy
Picerno Pietro	University of Sassari, Italy
Pires Rossetto Hallynnee Hellenn	University Pitágoras Unopar, Brazil
Raviolo Paolo	eCampus University, Italy
Rondonotti Marco	eCampus University, Italy
Rossi Martina	University of Foggia, Italy
Santoro Domenico	University of Foggia, Italy
Sasanelli Lia Daniela	Pegaso Telematic University, Italy
Schicchi Daniele	Independent Researcher, Italy
Scifo Lidia	LUMSA University, Italy
Sgreccia Natalia	National University of Rosario, Argentina
Simone Maria Grazia	eCampus University, Italy
Taibi Davide	CNR - Institute for Educational Technology, Italy
Terrenghi Ilaria	University of Milan, Italy
Triacca Serena	eCampus University, Italy
Zaza Gianluca	University of Bari, Italy

Additional Reviewers

Picariello Luca	University of Salerno, Italy
Del Zozzo Agnese	University of Trento, Italy

Higher Education Learning Methodologies and Technologies Online. HELMeTO 2025 Editorial Introduction to the Scientific Contributions

Matteo Adamoli, Domenico Amato, Daniele Schicchi, Giovanni Fulantelli, Marco Rondonotti, Davide Taibi, Alessandro Ciasullo, and Flavia Santonianni

[1] eCampus University
[2] University of Palermo
[3] National Research Council of Italy, Institute for Educational Technology
[4] University of Naples Federico II

Abstract. The HELMeTO 2025 Conference highlighted the significance of integrating methodology, innovation and technology in the educational landscape, especially in the university sector. The proceedings book that we introduce here contains 66 papers each of which contributes significantly to the field. Rather than providing a detailed summary of each individual article, we have identified six overarching themes 1) Digital Pedagogy, Instructional Design and Creative Practices in Higher Education; 2) Inclusion, Accessibility and Human Rights; 3) Formative Assessment and Innovative Feedback; 4) Learning Technologies and Data Analytics; 5) Artificial Intelligence (AI); 6) AI Literacy. While each chapter may primarily focus on one of these themes, it inevitably intersects with the others, reflecting the interconnected nature of these areas within the broader educational landscape.

Keywords: Higher Education · Artificial Intelligence · AI Literacy · Educational technologies · Instructional Design

1. Digital Pedagogy, Instructional Design and Creative Practices in Higher Education

The first section of the book explores the evolution of digital teaching in higher education, focusing on strategies to improve student engagement and inclusivity. In relation to these strategies, microlearning and mobile learning are examined as methodologies that significantly increase university students' motivation and self-regulation compared to traditional e-learning models, thereby reducing the risk of dropout. Other contributions examine the role of digital technologies in promoting inclusive citizenship for students, transforming digital tools into drivers of social justice. Further contributions explore the lifecycle of MOOCs, proposing hybrid models to ensure economic sustainability without sacrificing free access. Overall, this section proposes an educational paradigm centred on personalised learning, the principle of flexibility and the ethical use of technological innovation.

2. Inclusion, Accessibility and Human Rights

The second section explores the themes of inclusion, accessibility and human rights in relation to the integration of advanced technologies into the contemporary educational landscape. Several papers examine how AI can act as a catalyst for educational equity, and a three-dimensional framework (functional, experiential and equity-based) is proposed to analyse how AI can support students with diverse linguistic, cultural or cognitive needs. Another study analyses the effectiveness of Intelligent Tutoring Systems (ITS) based on Universal Design for Learning (UDL), which adapt to the user's digital skills to compensate for any gaps. The UDL paradigm is a constant reference point for designing flexible learning environments across all school levels it is applied to the creation of screen-free learning pathways for primary school children, aimed at teaching computational thinking and the basics of AI in an inclusive manner, and is used to transform virtual museums into inclusive 'third spaces' in higher education, facilitating participation and critical reflection.

The effectiveness of teaching in terms of quality and engagement is analysed through students' perceptions, highlighting a gap in the use of active and flexible methodologies. Another focus addressed concerns the simplicity paradigm to foster the emotional, cognitive and behavioural engagement of future teachers, especially in hybrid contexts.

The theme of digital citizenship and online safety is considered central to technologically assisted, pedagogically inclusive and critically aware teaching. Among the contributions presented, two projects are highlighted. The first uses advanced linguistic models to map hate speech on social media, analysing the impact of negative stereotypes and intersectional discrimination. The second, meanwhile, concerns an AI platform and an educational toolkit designed to monitor and counter online hate speech and disinformation, promoting media literacy.

3. Formative Assessment and Innovative Feedback

The third section of the volume explores the intersection between advanced technologies, innovative teaching methodologies and assessment processes, with a strong focus on the transformation of higher education and teacher training. The main topics covered can be grouped into the following research areas formative assessment, teacher professional development and instructional design. Assessment incorporating generative AI is treated not merely as a set of measurement tools, but as an integral part of the learning process (assessment for learning). Several studies focus on feedback as a continuous process that must be clear, specific and action-oriented to bridge the gap between current performance and expected objectives. The ways in which peer assessment and self-reflection can foster critical thinking and self-regulation among students are also analysed. Some contributions investigate how trainee teachers perceive the timing and methods of assessment in blended training programmes. The introduction of generative AI is a cross-cutting theme that redefines the roles of teachers and students; it is explored not merely as a tool for process automation, but as a potential cognitive partner capable of enhancing learning processes by supporting instructional design and feedback. The text presents various prototypes of generative AI for personalised feedback and various systems for the automated assessment of open-ended questions. Regarding the issue of ethics and transparency in assessment processes, the text discusses the need for explainable AI models to avoid the 'black box' effect and ensure academic integrity and user privacy. Regarding the professional development of teachers, several contributions focus on preparing pre-service teachers to tackle contemporary educational challenges. The analysis examines teachers' ability to critically manage interactions with AI, filtering algorithmic suggestions through their own professional experience and expertise. With regard to instructional design, innovative and collaborative teaching methodologies based on constructivist models and active participation are explored. One example is the use of digital memes, analysed as a tool for cultural mediation and participatory learning to promote inclusion and critical reflection on social issues such as early school leaving. The potential of intelligent tutoring systems and immersive environments is investigated to enhance student motivation and performance, balancing technological support with student autonomy. The organisation of study pathways is examined using advanced analytical models, validating the internal coherence and progression of competence-based curricula. About specific AI applications, the functionality of immediate feedback provided by AI for open-ended maths tasks is investigated, with the aim of facilitating the transition from intuitive reasoning to formalised explanations. It is also worth noting the use of AI and machine learning for monitoring physical activity, predicting health indicators and virtual coaching.

4. Learning Technologies and Data Analytics

The fourth theme of this volume, Learning Technologies and Data Analytics, explores the increasingly sophisticated intersection between digital infrastructure and the systematic analysis of educational processes. The contributions within this area demonstrate a significant shift in the field moving beyond the mere deployment of digital tools toward the creation of evidence-based, personalized and embodied learning ecosystems. This theme highlights a dual progression on one hand, the refinement of data literacy as a fundamental pillar of scientific citizenship; on the other, the technological expansion into immersive and motion-driven environments that redefine the physical and cognitive boundaries of Higher Education. A central pillar of this thematic area is the reconceptualization of data literacy. Rather than being treated as an isolated technical skill, data science is increasingly integrated into participatory, real-world scientific inquiry. Research in this volume illustrates how "smart" environments and large-scale data projects can serve as living laboratories where students transition from passive consumers of information to active analysts of Big Data. This approach bridges the gap between abstract computational models and tangible observations, fostering a deep understanding of research methodologies and the ethical implications of data-driven decision-making. The consensus is clear data education is most transformative when situated within collaborative, interdisciplinary projects that offer immediate, socially relevant results. Simultaneously, the technological horizon is being expanded through the lens of human motion computing and embodied cognition. The research presented here introduces innovative frameworks for "motion-driven" learning which utilize AI and advanced sensors to provide personalized support in online environments. By analyzing how students learn in, with and about motion, educators can deliver real-time guidance that responds to the learner's physical interactions, overcoming the traditionally sedentary nature of digital learning. This shift toward a more holistic, embodied experience is complemented by critical reflections on the use of immersive technologies like Virtual and Mixed Reality. As these tools become more prevalent, particularly in teacher education, there is a pressing need to address the "challenge of corporeality." Scholars argue for a motor-expressive perspective that preserves the relational and expressive nature of the "Digital Self," ensuring that immersion leads to an ecologically grounded presence rather than a reduction of the human experience to a mere digital abstraction. Finally, the evolution of instructional design within these technologies is moving toward an "activity-centred" paradigm. In the realm of Mixed Reality, for instance, there is a growing emphasis on how students interact with content to enhance long-term retention. By adapting classical mnemonic strategies, such as the "Method of Loci," to modern digital environments, technology can facilitate the creation of virtual "memory palaces" where concepts are anchored to spatial and multimedia cues. This synthesis of ancient wisdom and cutting-edge technology exemplifies the broader trend of this theme the use of advanced analytics and immersive tools to create durable, reflective and deeply human knowledge structures.

5. Artificial Intelligence (AI)

The fifth theme of this volume explores the transformative role of Artificial Intelligence (AI) within the modern educational ecosystem. As reflected in the diverse range of contributions, AI has transitioned from a speculative technological frontier to a multifaceted tool that is actively reshaping pedagogical frameworks, instructional design, and the fundamental nature of the teacher-student interaction. The research presented in this section provides a comprehensive overview of the current state of AI integration, moving from high-level mapping of institutional challenges to granular empirical studies in specialized fields such as mathematics, sports science and psychological support. A significant portion of current scholarship is dedicated to the critical mapping of AI's integration into Higher Education (HE). Systematic analyses of recent literature reveal a pivotal shift in the academic discourse while the technical capabilities of AI are increasingly well documented, there remains a pressing need for clearer conceptual definitions and a more robust focus on the long-term pedagogical implications. A recurring finding suggests that universities, particularly in the European context, are navigating a complex tension between leveraging the efficiency gains offered by automation and mitigating the systemic risks associated with academic integrity and the potential depersonalization of the learning experience. Beyond the institutional level, the success of AI integration is deeply tied to the "human element"—specifically, the perspectives and readiness of the faculty. Research within this theme emphasizes that the adoption of technology is not a uniform process across departments. Instead, it is shaped by a complex interplay of conceptual models, individual attitudes and institutional enabling factors. It is argued that faculty development must evolve beyond basic technical training; it requires a profound shift in how educators perceive their role in a curriculum increasingly co-designed with intelligent systems. Institutional support, therefore, must move from providing tools to fostering a culture of informed experimentation and ethical reflection.

One of the most robust areas of investigation in this volume concerns the application of AI within mathematics education, where technology is being utilized to mediate complex cognitive and epistemological processes. The theoretical contributions in this field suggest that we must move beyond viewing AI as a simple auxiliary support tool. New theoretical models proposed here analyze the interaction between learners and AI through the lens of "covariational instructions." This perspective identifies several distinct modes of participation AI can act as a collaborative participant that mirrors human reasoning, as a "critical friend" providing weak instrumental support, or as a full "design partner" that actively shapes the problem-solving environment. Such distinctions are crucial for educators seeking to understand how AI can activate different cognitive dimensions, particularly in geometry and calculus, where the technology can help students visualize abstract relationships and refine their instructional materials in real time. Furthermore, empirical evidence highlights the potential of hybrid environments that pair Large Language Models (LLMs) with Advanced Computing Environments (ACE). This synergy addresses the inherent limitations of linguistic models in STEM—such as the risk of inaccurate mathematical reasoning—by providing a "dialogic scaffold" for reflection while maintaining the computational rigor of symbolic software. This integrated approach allows university students to engage in a more reliable and reflective form of problem solving, where natural language interaction and computational exploration reinforce each other. The integration of AI also extends into the realms of physical experience and motor learning, directly challenging the traditional notion that digital technology is a purely "disembodied" or sedentary activity. In the context of sports science and physical education, research presented here explores the integration of AI-based simulations into youth training protocols. By comparing traditional prescriptive coaching methods with "ecological-dynamic" approaches supported by high-fidelity simulations, findings suggest that AI can significantly enhance cognitive-motor development. These digital environments provide athletes with complex, simulated scenarios that foster better perception-action coupling, improving agility and decision-making speed in ways that traditional drills may not capture. In a related vein, the role of AI in multisensory immersive environments is becoming increasingly prominent. Experimental studies indicate that when AI is used to adapt immersive settings to the learner's sensory feedback, there is a measurable improvement in memory retention, engagement and motivation. By grounding the digital experience in the body's interaction with the environment, this line of research reinforces the theories of embodied cognition. It suggests that the most effective digital learning occurs when technology facilitates a deeper connection between the student's perceptual systems and the educational content.

Perhaps the most innovative perspective emerging from this collection is the conceptualization of AI as a "reflective symbolic space" for emotional and psychological support. As conversational agents become more sophisticated, their potential to act as a "symbolic mirror" for students—particularly those experiencing school-related distress or bullying—is being carefully scrutinized. Drawing on humanistic psychological principles, several studies evaluate the capacity of conversational AI to demonstrate empathy, congruence and unconditional positive regard. While current systems may not yet replicate the relational depth of a human counselor, they are showing a surprising capacity for providing a safe, non-judgmental space for emotional reflection and acceptance. This is particularly relevant for adolescents who may feel more comfortable expressing vulnerability to a digital interface than to a peer or an authority figure. The pedagogical potential here lies in using AI not as a replacement for psychological intervention, but as a preliminary tool for emotional processing and resilience building. Collectively, the contributions within this theme underscore a pivotal transition in Higher Education. We are moving away from a period of "emergency adoption" and toward a more intentional, theoretically grounded integration of Artificial Intelligence.

The recurring themes—the centrality of faculty development, the evolution of AI into a "design partner," the enhancement of embodied learning and the exploration of AI as an emotional scaffold—suggest that the future of the university will be defined by "Human-AI Collaboration." Rather than rendering the educator obsolete, AI is being re-imagined as a sophisticated pedagogical scaffold that allows for more personalized, interactive and reflective learning experiences. However, this transition requires a commitment to "epistemic vigilance." The research presented here provides the empirical and theoretical foundations to navigate the ongoing challenges of ethics, data privacy and the digital divide. It offers a roadmap for an AI-enhanced pedagogy that remains deeply rooted in humanistic values, ensuring that while the tools may change, the core mission of higher education—the cultivation of critical thought and human growth—remains paramount.

6. AI Literacy

The integration of Generative Artificial Intelligence (GenAI) into educational ecosystems demands a profound redefinition of AI Literacy. The contributions gathered in these proceedings collectively demonstrate that AI Literacy extends far beyond mere technical proficiency, representing a multidimensional competence that encompasses cognitive, ethical and critical dimensions. Empirical evidence interestingly highlights a fascinating paradox, revealing that structured AI education fosters critical thinking rather than consumer behavior, leading trained students to use AI tools more selectively and cautiously than their untrained peers.

To navigate this landscape, the authors in this volume propose a paradigm shift concerning cognitive agency and constructionist theories. AI Literacy requires understanding how machines redistribute cognitive agency within human-technology-world relations.

Adopting a post phenomenological perspective, it is crucial to design learning environments where AI serves a constitutive or complementary role, scaffolding interpretation and reasoning, rather than a substitutive one that risks technologically induced cognitive diminishment. In this vein, constructionist theories are undergoing a modern evolution, marking a transition from the traditional "learning by making" to "learning by prompting". Through intentional mathematical inconsistencies and iterative prompt-debug-refine cycles, the prompt itself becomes the new artifact and an "object to think with".

A critical component of AI Literacy is the development of metacognitive awareness. Integrating AI into problem solving, where students actively compare their own human reasoning with AI-generated responses, significantly enhances their evaluative skills and metacognitive control, as measured by instruments like the Metacognitive Awareness Inventory for Critical AI Use (MAI-C). Consequently, AI shifts from a passive tool to an epistemic collaborator or a dialogic partner. This transformation is evident across various disciplines. In medical education, AI acts as a reflective mirror that allows students to compare their communicative strategies with algorithmic suggestions to deepen empathy and pedagogical care. In teacher training, Socratic AI systems stimulate deeper pedagogical reasoning, instructional revision, and critical engagement by posing reflective questions rather than providing immediate answers. Similarly, in higher education student research, AI serves as an auxiliary resource for generating ideas and structuring text, while highlighting the absolute necessity for students to maintain responsibility for verifying accuracy and avoiding overreliance.

Furthermore, mitigating systemic risks is presented as a fundamental pillar of AI Literacy. The uncritical adoption of GenAI presents challenges such as algorithmic hallucinations, proprietary opacity and the amplification of hegemonic biases. To foster genuine AI Literacy and counter concerns about the impoverishment of expressive richness or procedure standardization, it is imperative to implement Human-in-the-Loop (HITL) frameworks combined with technical grounding like Retrieval-Augmented Generation (RAG). These frameworks ensure that human experts remain the ultimate arbiters of factual truth, content validity and ethical integrity, transforming the educator's role into that of a learning designer and epistemic mediator.

Finally, building a robust AI culture requires systemic, participatory and inclusive approaches. Empowering learners through Youth-Led Participatory Action Research (YPAR) positions students not merely as end-users, but as active co-researchers capable of interrogating AI for fairness, transparency and accountability within a Responsible Artificial Intelligence (RAI) framework. This empowerment must span all educational levels, from primary education, where early exposure demystifies the algorithmic black box and fosters ethical curiosity through adaptive virtual assistants, to complex socio-educational contexts. In the latter, large-scale mapping of professionals' capabilities, affordances-in-practice and sentiments guides a truly human-centered and democratic integration of AI, transforming ambivalent emotions of fear and hope into reflective co-agency. Ultimately, the collective research presented in this volume underscores that AI Literacy is about designing technological entanglements that expand, rather than erode, human agency and critical inquiry.

Contents

Learning Technologies e Data Analytics

Digital Pedagogy, Instructional Design and Creative Practices in Higher Education

Digital Technologies in Physical Education: Insights from Italian Teachers and Implications for Training

Francesca D'Elia[1,2](✉), Tiziana D'Isanto[2], Susana Franco[3], and Gaetano Raiola[2]

[1] University of Salerno, 84084 Fisciano, SA, Italy
fdelia@unisa.it

[2] Research Center for Physical Education and Exercise, Pegaso University, Naples, Italy
tiziana.disanto@istruzione.it, gaetano.raiola@unipegaso.it

[3] Sport Science School of Rio Maior, Polytechnic Institute of Santarém (ESDRM-IPSantarém), Rio Maior, Portugal
sfranco@esdrm.ipsantarem.pt

Abstract. The study examines how Italian Physical Education teachers perceive and use digital technologies in their professional practice. Through a mixed-methods design combining a questionnaire administered to 150 teachers and qualitative open responses, the research explores current uses of digital tools, perceived benefits, barriers, and training needs. Results show generally positive attitudes toward digital innovation, particularly for enhancing motivation, inclusion, and lesson organization. However, actual integration remains limited, with technologies used mainly for planning rather than instruction or assessment. Structural constraints, insufficient training, and concerns about preserving the embodied nature of Physical Education emerged as key obstacles. Teachers expressed a strong need for practical, discipline-specific professional development. The study highlights the importance of targeted training pathways and institutional support to promote meaningful, sustainable, and methodologically grounded digital integration.

Keywords: Teacher Perception · Educational Innovation · Professional Development

1 Digital Integration in Physical Education: Opportunities and Challenges

The digitalization of education has reshaped teaching and learning across all disciplines [1–4]. Physical education, traditionally centered on bodily experience and movement, is now confronted with the challenge of integrating technology while preserving its educational identity. Digital tools offer opportunities for planning, teaching, assessment, and communication, yet raise methodological and ethical concerns [5–7], including balancing screen time with physical activity, ensuring equitable access, and protecting students' biometric data.

M. Adamoli et al. (Eds.): HELMeTO 2025, CCIS 2958, pp. 3–14, 2026.
https://doi.org/10.1007/978-3-032-31850-3_1

Research shows increasing interest among physical education teachers in digital tools, which are perceived as useful for motivation, inclusion, and collaboration. However, actual adoption remains limited and irregular, influenced by structural constraints, teachers' digital competence, and cultural beliefs about the compatibility between technology and the embodied nature of the discipline. This study investigates teachers' perceptions and experiences regarding digital integration, exploring opportunities, barriers, and implications for a sustainable and experience-based physical education.

1.1 Digital Transformation in Schools

Digitalization is transforming educational practices and redefining the teacher's role [10, 11]. Rather than a simple technological upgrade, it represents a cultural and organizational shift requiring strategic planning. As noted by Schmidt and Tang [10], schools often adopt technologies in fragmented ways, relying on tools not designed for educational purposes. Ronzhina et al. [11] emphasize generational changes and the expectations of digital-native students, although the actual penetration of technology in schools remains inconsistent.

Within this scenario, physical education must reconcile the centrality of movement with the potential of digital tools to enhance teaching, assessment, and inclusion. Understanding teachers' perceptions is therefore essential to inform targeted educational and training strategies.

1.2 Physical Education and Digital Technologies: A Complex Relationship

Physical education promotes motor development, socialization, and bodily awareness [12, 13]. The spread of wearable devices, exergames, biometric sensors, and interactive platforms has introduced new possibilities for personalized learning, real-time feedback, and inclusion. National and European initiatives, such as PNRR "Scuola 4.0" and Erasmus+ programs, have further encouraged experimentation with digital tools.

Despite growing interest, the literature remains fragmented, with limited longitudinal studies and few validated tools to assess the impact of digital interventions. Teachers acknowledge the potential of technology to enhance motivation, inclusion, communication, and collaboration [6, 8, 9, 14, 15], yet adoption is often hindered by resource availability, connectivity, and insufficient training. Zhong et al. [5] highlight both the opportunities of data-driven, personalized learning environments and the risks related to digital equity.

Studies indicate that digital tools are frequently used to support motivation and health-related activities rather than to transform teaching practices [15, 16]. This may reinforce transmissive models instead of promoting active, student-centered learning, underscoring the need to understand how teachers use technology and what support they require.

Gamification, Augmented Reality, and Experiential Learning. Gamification has shown positive effects on engagement, differentiated instruction, and motor learning through feedback and goal-oriented tasks [17–19]. Augmented reality enhances understanding of complex movements and supports posture correction [20], strengthening experiential learning when integrated thoughtfully [21]. eSports, particularly digital football, may foster cognitive and motivational development, supporting decision-making and tactical reasoning in line with physical education goals [22, 23].

Systematic reviews confirm that gamified environments increase motivation, participation, and autonomy [17, 18], though the diversity of implementation models calls for further research on conditions that ensure effectiveness and sustainability [19]. Jastrow et al. [14] warn against superficial uses not embedded in curricular processes, while Wohlfart et al. [24] stress the need for specific digital literacy. Sargent and Casey [25] propose appreciative inquiry to valorize teachers' effective practices and promote reflective use of technology.

In summary, the literature converges on several critical issues: 1) the lack of shared methodological references, particularly those tailored to the embodied, interactive, and performative nature of physical education; 2) discontinuity in institutional support, and 3) the need for targeted training that considers the specific features of the discipline. This study fits within this framework, proposing an empirical investigation aimed at bridging the gap between potential and practice.

Limits and Risks of Digital Integration in Physical Education. Despite its benefits, the use of digital technologies in physical education presents several critical issues:

- Risk of reduced physical activity: excessive use of technology may compromise the active component of the discipline: physically, cognitively, and socially, and may shift the focus from embodied experience to screen-based interaction weakening students' kinesthetic awareness and motor autonomy.
- Privacy concerns and biometric data management [5].
- Inequitable access to digital resources across schools [6].
- Cultural resistance from less digitally literate teachers [9].

To overcome these obstacles, it is essential to promote continuous and systemic training that goes beyond digital literacy and develops methodological and educational skills for a critical and creative use of technology. As Sargent and Calderón [15] emphasize, it is crucial to question which aspects of teaching are genuinely enhanced by digital tools, avoiding scenarios where technology merely replaces the teacher instead of transforming education.

In light of these challenges, an empirical investigation is needed to understand how physical education teachers perceive and use digital technologies in their teaching practice, what barriers limit their adoption, and what opportunities may arise for a more inclusive, motivating, and experience-based teaching-learning process. This study therefore aims to:

- Explore how digital technologies are used in planning, teaching, and assessing processes in physical education.
- Analyze teachers' perceptions of the effectiveness of digital tools in promoting motivation, inclusion, and participation.
- Identify structural, educational, and cultural barriers to advance a conscious technology integration.

- Detect training needs and prior experiences to outline targeted professional development strategies.
- Contribute to the definition of educational models that integrate digital tools while enhancing the body, movement, and relational dimensions of physical education.

By addressing these dimensions, the study aims not only to map current practices but also to inform the design of evidence-based training programs, support institutional decision-making, and contribute to the development of educational models that align digital innovation with the core values of physical education.

2 Approach and Evidence on the Use of Digital Technologies in Physical Education

This study adopted an exploratory research design with a mixed-methods approach, aimed at investigating both general trends and the subjective and contextual dimensions of teachers' experiences with the use of digital technologies in physical education. This methodological choice responds to the need to grasp the complexity of the phenomenon, emphasizing the complementarity between quantitative and qualitative data. On one hand, the quantitative approach allows for the identification of recurring patterns, distributions, and statistically significant associations; on the other, the qualitative component enables a deeper understanding of the interpretations, motivations, and narratives that shape teachers' practices and perceptions. This dual perspective was essential to capture not only what teachers do with digital tools, but also how they make sense of their use, what values they associate with technology, and what tensions they experience in balancing innovation with the embodied nature of the discipline.

The quantitative part was conducted through a structured questionnaire consisting of 22 closed and semi-open items, administered to a sample of 150 physical education teachers from various school levels (primary, lower secondary, and high secondary).

The questions explored four main areas: (1) use of technologies in the planning, teaching, and assessment of educational activities; (2) perceptions of educational effectiveness, with particular attention to motivation, inclusion, and participation; (3) structural and training-related obstacles; (4) previous training experiences and future professional needs. Quantitative data were processed using descriptive and inferential statistical functions (Chi-square test, Cramer's V), with Microsoft Excel.

The qualitative component was integrated through the analysis of open-ended responses in the questionnaire, which provided interpretive insights into the subjective logics, resistances, and meaning-making trajectories that accompany the use of digital tools in teaching practice. Several teachers, for example expressed enthusiasm for the motivational potential of gamified activities, while others voiced concerns about the risk of reducing movement to screen-based tasks. Some highlighted the usefulness of digital platforms for inclusive planning, especially when working with students with disabilities, whereas others emphasized the need for more structured training to feel confident in using such tools.

The data analysis enabled the construction of a nuanced and contextualized interpretation of the phenomenon, reflecting the complexity of physical education as an evolving educational space, where technological innovation intersects with embodiment, relationships, and educational reflection.

2.1 Results

The data analysis provided a rich and multifaceted picture of physical education teachers' perceptions, practices, and competencies regarding the integration of digital technologies into teaching. The questionnaire recorded a response rate of 96% (144 valid responses), indicating widespread and cross-cutting interest in the topic of digital innovation within the discipline.

The sample, composed of 144 teachers, showed a balanced age distribution (mean = 45.18 years; SD = 12.65) and a male majority (61.1%), consistent with the gender distribution in the physical education teaching profession, with a significant representation of secondary school teachers (77.8%).

In addition to the statistical trends, the qualitative responses offered valuable insights into teachers' reasoning and lived experiences, helping to contextualize the data and reveal underlying beliefs, concerns, and expectations (Fig. 1).

General Opinions and Attitudes. Most participants expressed a positive attitude toward the use of digital tools in physical education: 40.3% considered it very positive, while 51.4% found it useful, albeit with some reservations. Only a small minority (1.4%) expressed a clearly negative stance, highlighting concerns that digital tools might compromise the bodily essence of the discipline. These findings suggest a growing cultural openness, though accompanied by methodological caution. Several open-ended comments reinforced this trend, with teachers emphasizing the need to preserve the embodied nature of physical education and warning that "technology should support, not replace, movement".

Frequency of Use and Tools Employed. Digital technologies are most frequently used during the planning phase of teaching, with 34.7% of teachers reporting frequent use and 47.2% occasional use. Canva was the most cited tool (52.8%), followed by Moodle (30.6%) and Excel for data analysis (25%). During lessons, 34.7% of teachers reported regular use of digital tools, while 43.1% used them only occasionally. The most common devices were video projectors (76.8%), physical activity monitoring apps (22.2%), and to a lesser extent, exergames (16.7%), artificial intelligence (12.5%), and augmented reality (8.3%).

Assessment was the least digitized area: only 20.9% of teachers reported frequent or consistent use of digital tools to evaluate student performance. The most commonly used tools were digital tests (59.7%) and motor monitoring apps (22.2%), while the use of wearable devices and video analysis software remained limited.

Competencies and Training. Perceived digital competencies were not uniformly distributed: 40.3% of teachers considered themselves "fairly competent," while only 11.1% described themselves as "very competent." A significant portion (38.9%) positioned themselves in an intermediate category, with limited experience but openness to innovation. Training was often informal: 31.9% learned through self-study, while 43.1% had received no training but expressed interest in specific programs. Practical workshops (34.7%) and ongoing professional development (31.9%) were the most desired formats. Teachers who reported no formal training often expressed a desire for "hands-on workshops" and "peer exchange opportunities", suggesting that professional development should be both practical and collaborative. These comments help explain why many teachers, despite limited preparation, show a strong willingness to innovate and experiment with digital tools.

Perceptions of Motivation and Inclusion. The majority of teachers acknowledged the potential of digital technologies to enhance student motivation: 52.8% believed they made lessons more engaging, while 11.1% noted a very positive impact. Similarly, 69.4% considered digital tools useful for promoting inclusion, particularly for students with special educational needs or disabilities. Comments from teachers working with students with disabilities emphasized how "visual feedback and structured digital tasks" helped improve participation and autonomy, especially in the contexts where traditional methods were less effective.

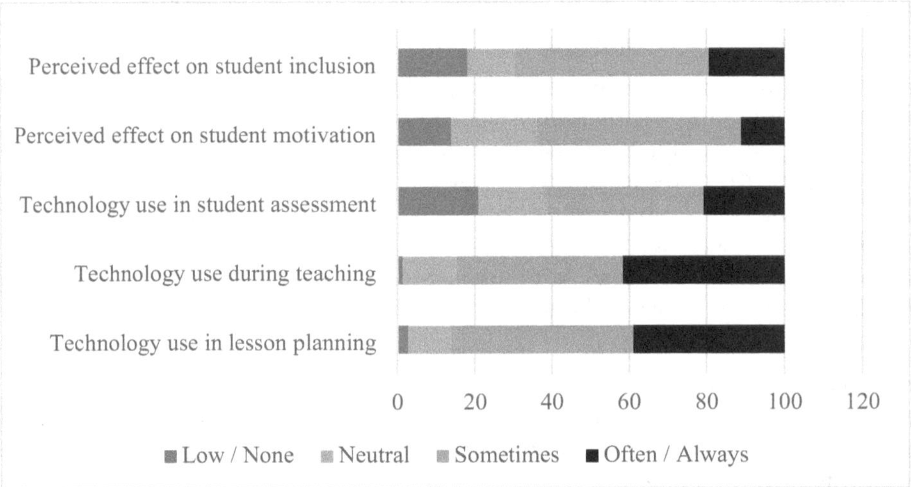

Fig. 1. Distribution of teachers' responses on digital technology use and perceived impact in physical education

Barriers and Challenges. The main barriers to digital integration included limited availability of devices (50.7%), lack of specific training (37.5%), and technical difficulties (25%). Additional concerns emerged regarding reduced physical movement (25%) and the complexity of adapting technologies to physical activities (23.6%). Artificial intelligence, in particular, was seen as promising but still largely inaccessible: only 6.9% used it frequently, while 38.9% did not use it at all. Some teachers also noted that digital tools were often "not designed for physical education", requiring significant adaptation and creativity to be used effectively.

Inferential Analysis. Statistical analyses revealed several significant associations (Table 1):

- *Gender and technology use*: male teachers showed a greater tendency toward frequent use in planning and assessment (Cramér's V = 0.308 and 0.349; $p < 0.01$), while female teachers tended to use digital tools more sporadically.
- *Gender and training*: although not statistically significant ($p = 0.06$), a trend emerged in which women preferred formal training, while men more often relied on self-learning.
- *School level and opinions*: secondary school teachers expressed more favorable opinions toward digital tools ($p = 0.027$; $V = 0.248$), whereas primary school teachers were more cautious.
- *School level and competencies*: in secondary schools, there was greater polarization between highly competent and less competent teachers ($p = 0.024$; $V = 0.279$), while intermediate levels prevailed in primary schools.

Table 1. Summary of inferential analyses

Variables	χ^2 / Fisher	p-value	Cramer's V	Interpretation
Gender × Frequency of technology use (planning)	13.27	0.006	0.308	Moderate association
Gender × Frequency of technology use (assessment)	17.05	0.001	0.349	Moderate–strong association
Gender × Training received	8.82	0.059	0.250	Not significant (trend)
School level × General opinion	8.89	0.027	0.248	Weak–moderate association
School level × Digital competence	11.24	0.024	0.279	Moderate association

Qualitative Insights. The open-ended responses enriched the quantitative findings by revealing a nuanced and context-sensitive understanding of digital integration. Teachers expressed both enthusiasm and caution, often linking their views to personal experience, school context, and student needs. Some described digital tools as "useful for engaging shy students" or "helpful for documenting progress in inclusive settings," while others emphasized the importance of maintaining the physical and relational core of the discipline.

These insights underscore the need for training programs that not only build technical skills but also support methodological reflection and adaptation to diverse educational realities.

3 Educational Implications and Future Perspectives for Effective Digital Integration in Physical Education

The results of this study reveal a clear discrepancy between the perceived value of digital technologies and their actual use in Physical Education (PE), confirming trends already highlighted in the literature [8]. Teachers generally acknowledge the motivational and inclusive potential of digital tools, yet their integration remains sporadic and concentrated mainly in planning activities. Open-ended responses further illustrate this ambivalence: while many teachers express curiosity and willingness to innovate, they also report limited time, insufficient institutional support, and uncertainty in selecting appropriate tools. Structural inequalities, such as uneven access to devices and connectivity, continue to shape these dynamics, particularly in schools located in rural or under-resourced areas.

From an educational standpoint, digital technologies offer opportunities to personalize learning, support formative assessment, and promote inclusion [6, 15]. Wearable devices, monitoring apps, and collaborative platforms can provide real-time feedback and facilitate differentiated instruction. However, their use must remain coherent with the embodied and relational nature of PE and with its broader mission of fostering physical literacy [26]. When technologies are employed merely for visualization or data collection, there is a risk of reducing movement to passive observation, weakening the experiential dimension of the discipline. The findings suggest that meaningful integration requires teachers to make informed decisions about when, why, and for whom specific tools are pedagogically appropriate.

The study also highlights the growing relevance of emerging practices such as gamification and augmented reality. When embedded in coherent instructional designs, these approaches can enhance engagement, clarify complex motor tasks, and support inclusive participation. Teachers' comments indicate that augmented feedback can be particularly helpful for students with motor difficulties, while gamified challenges may foster autonomy and social interaction. Nevertheless, their effectiveness depends on the teacher's ability to integrate them purposefully into curricular goals and avoid superficial or episodic use.

The expanding interest in eSports and simulation-based environments further broadens the landscape of digital integration. Research suggests that these environments can support the development of cognitive, technical, and tactical skills [22], with systematic reviews reporting positive effects on abilities such as cognitive flexibility, memory, and decision-making [23]. For some students, especially those less engaged in traditional PE formats, these tools may stimulate motivation and metacognitive reflection. However, their adoption requires careful consideration of curricular coherence, ethical boundaries, and the balance between virtual and physical activity. Without such alignment, digital innovation risks becoming peripheral or even contradictory to the core aims of PE.

Recent evidence on artificial intelligence (AI) reinforces this complexity. Ayoade Fadare et al. [27] show how machine learning can support performance analysis, injury prevention, and personalized instruction, while also raising concerns about data integrity, ethical issues, and accessibility. Similarly, Bofill-Herrero et al. [27] highlight teachers' and students' mixed perceptions of AI, noting both its potential for personalization and the challenges posed by insufficient training and unequal access to resources. These findings underscore the need for clear frameworks that define the educational role of AI in PE and emphasize the importance of digital ethics and data literacy.

Training emerges as a decisive factor across all dimensions. Teachers consistently report the need for practical, discipline-specific professional development that supports not only technical skills but also pedagogical and methodological decision-making. Aleksieva's study [28] echoes this need, showing that pre-service teacher education often lacks coordinated strategies for developing digital competencies. The findings of the present study reinforce the importance of training pathways that integrate digital education into subject-specific contexts, promote interdisciplinary collaboration, and foster communities of practice where teachers can share experiences and co-construct innovative approaches.

Overall, the results indicate that technology is not neutral: its educational impact depends on how it is interpreted, selected, and integrated by teachers. In PE, this requires recognizing the centrality of movement, embodiment, and relational dynamics, and ensuring that digital tools support, rather than replace, these foundational elements. The study contributes to this perspective by offering empirical evidence on teachers' practices, needs, and perceptions, and by identifying key areas where further research, training, and institutional support are needed to bridge the gap between digital potential and educational reality.

3.1 Toward an Educationally Coherent Digital Transition in Physical Education

The findings of this study show that Physical Education teachers are generally open to digital innovation, yet their practices remain constrained by structural, educational, and cultural factors. Digital tools are perceived as valuable for enhancing motivation, inclusion, and personalization, but their integration into teaching is still partial and uneven. While technologies are more frequently used in planning and instruction, assessment practices remain largely traditional. This discrepancy reflects a broader tension between innovation and disciplinary identity, particularly when digital tools are introduced without adequate pedagogical mediation.

Training emerges as a central issue. Beyond technical proficiency, teachers require a clear educational vision that aligns digital tools with the embodied and relational nature of Physical Education. As noted by Pürgstaller et al. [29], both teachers and student teachers express positive attitudes toward digital media, yet their actual use depends on contextual conditions, confidence, and pedagogical clarity. Similarly, Soegiyanto et al. [30] highlight the importance of digital literacy in the 5.0 era, emphasizing the need for targeted support to ensure ethical and effective use. Qualitative data from this study reinforce these insights: many teachers feel unprepared to select and adapt digital tools to specific learning goals and often rely on informal experimentation rather than structured guidance.

Given the centrality of movement, relationships, and experience in Physical Education, digital tools should enrich, not replace, these foundational elements.

Conscious curricular integration requires targeted training programs, adequate resources, and a shared educational vision. This process also demands institutional commitment, including time for experimentation, access to peer mentoring, and recognition of digital competence as a core professional standard.

Although limited by its cross-sectional design and reliance on self-reported data, this study offers a meaningful snapshot of Italian teachers' perceptions and practices. Future longitudinal, experimental, and comparative research is needed to support a sustainable and inclusive digital evolution of the discipline. Such research should examine how digital tools influence not only teaching strategies but also student engagement, motor learning, and relational dynamics, with particular attention to equity, accessibility, and ethical considerations.

3.2 Perspectives and Recommendations

In light of the findings, several operational recommendations can be outlined to promote effective and sustainable integration of digital technologies in physical education:

- *Targeted and contextualized training*: design programs that consider the specificities of the discipline, focusing on instructional planning, assessment, inclusion, and ethical reflection.
- *Investment in resources and infrastructure*: ensure equitable access to devices, connectivity, and digital environments, overcoming territorial disparities.
- *Integrated teaching models*: promote approaches that combine embodiment and digitality, avoiding the reduction of movement to a secondary content.
- *Ongoing support and communities of practice*: support teachers through mentoring, professional exchange spaces, and hands-on training workshops.
- *Methodological reflection on AI and gamification*: harness the innovative potential of these tools while paying attention to ethical, relational, and educational aspects.

Authentic innovation must begin with people, their needs, and their everyday practices. It is the responsibility of research and university-level training to accompany this process with awareness and rigor.

4 Conclusion

This study examined Italian Physical Education teachers' perceptions, practices, and training needs regarding the integration of digital technologies into teaching. The findings reveal a clear gap between the perceived educational value of digital tools and their actual use in practice. While teachers generally recognize the potential of technology to enhance motivation, inclusion, and lesson organization, digital integration remains partial and mainly limited to planning activities. Structural constraints, insufficient training, and concerns about preserving the embodied nature of Physical Education continue to hinder more systematic adoption.

The results highlight the need for targeted, discipline-specific professional development that goes beyond basic digital literacy and supports teachers in selecting, adapting, and meaningfully integrating digital tools into pedagogical practice. Practical workshops, collaborative design activities, and school-based learning communities emerge as promising formats to strengthen teachers' methodological competence and confidence.

From a broader perspective, the study underscores the importance of aligning digital innovation with the experiential, relational, and movement-based core of Physical Education. Technologies should be used to enrich, not replace, embodied learning, supporting feedback, reflection, inclusion, and differentiated instruction.

The implications extend to Higher Education, where initial teacher education programs should incorporate structured opportunities to explore digital methodologies, critically evaluate emerging tools, and develop reflective and data-literate professional identities. Future research should deepen the analysis of specific digital practices, investigate long-term impacts on learning, and explore how institutional policies can support sustainable and equitable digital integration in Physical Education.

Disclosure of Interests. The authors have no competing interests to declare that are relevant to the content of this article.

References

1. Yadav, N.: The impact of digital learning on education. Int. J. Multi. Res. Arts Sci. Technol. **2**(1), 24–34 (2024)
2. Wang, C., Chen, X., Yu, T., et al.: Education reform and change driven by digital technology: a bibliometric study from a global perspective. Humanit Soc Sci. Commun. **11**, 256 (2024)
3. Aldhafeeri, F.M., Alotaibi, A.A.: Reimagining education for successful and sustainable digital shifting. SAGE Open. **13**(1) (2023)
4. Fischer, G., Lundin, J., Lindberg, J.O.: Rethinking and reinventing learning, education and collaboration in the digital age - from creating technologies to transforming cultures. Int. J. Inf. Learn. Technol. **37**(5), 241–252 (2020)
5. Zhong, Q., Jiang, J., Bai, W., Yin, Z., Liao, Z., Zhong, X.: Application of digital-intelligent technologies in physical education: a systematic review. Front. Public Health. **13**, 1626603 (2025)
6. Martín-Rodríguez, A., Madrigal-Cerezo, R.: Technology-enhanced pedagogy in physical education: bridging engagement, learning, and lifelong activity. Educ. Sci. **15**, 409 (2025)
7. Goodyear, V.A.: Social media, apps and wearable technologies: navigating ethical dilemmas and procedures. Qual. Res. Sport, Exerc. Health. **9**(3), 285–302 (2017)
8. Saiz-González, P., Sierra-Díaz, J., Iglesias, D., Fernandez-Rio, J.: Exploring physical education teachers' willingness and barriers to integrating digital technology in their lessons. Educ. Inf. Technol. **30**, 5965–5987 (2025)
9. Wallace, J., Scanlon, D., Calderón, A.: Digital technology and teacher digital competency in physical education: a holistic view of teacher and student perspectives. Curriculum Stud. Health Phys. Educ. **14**(3), 271–287 (2022)
10. Schmidt, J.T., Tang, M.: Digitalization in education: challenges, trends and transformative potential. In: Harwardt, M., Niermann, P.J., Schmutte, A., Steuernagel, A. (eds.) Führen und Managen in der digitalen Transformation. Springer Gabler, Wiesbaden (2020)
11. Ronzhina, N., Kondyurina, I., Voronina, A., Igishev, K., Loginova, N.: Digitalization of modern education: problems and solutions. Int. J. Emerg. Technol. Learn. (iJET). **16**(4), 122–135 (2021)
12. Aliberti, S., Kaçurri, A., Kasa, A., Giardullo, G.: Stakeholders' opinions on teaching movement education in primary schools: A cross-sectional study. J. Phys. Educ. Sport. **25**(2), 423–431 (2025)
13. Aliberti, S.: Physical education in European primary schools: an up-to-date overview. Sport Sci. **16**(2), 30–34 (2023)

14. Jastrow, F., Greve, S., Thumel, M., Diekhoff, H., Süßenbach, J.: Digital technology in physical education: A systematic review of research from 2009 to 2020. Ger. J. Exerc. Sport Res. **52**(4), 504–528 (2022)
15. Sargent, J., Calderón, A.: Technology-enhanced learning physical education? A critical review of the literature. J. Teach. Phys. Educ. **41**(4), 689–709 (2021)
16. Teutemacher, B., Sudeck, G., Hapke, J.: Pedagogical approaches to health-related physical education (PE) in the context of digitalisation – a scoping review. Phys. Educ. Sport Pedagog., 1–17 (2024)
17. Arufe-Giráldez, V., Sanmiguel-Rodríguez, A., Ramos-Álvarez, O., Navarro-Patón, R.: Gamification in physical education: A systematic review. Educ. Sci. **12**, 540 (2022)
18. Camacho-Sánchez, R., Manzano-León, A., Rodríguez-Ferrer, J.M., Serna, J., Lavega-Burgués, P.: Game-based learning and gamification in physical education: A systematic review. Educ. Sci. **13**, 183 (2023)
19. Fernandez-Rio, J., de las Heras, E., González, T., Trillo, V., Palomares, J.: Gamification and physical education. Viability and preliminary views from students and teachers. Phys. Educ. Sport Pedagog. **25**(5), 509–524 (2020)
20. Chang, K.E., Zhang, J., Huang, Y.S., Liu, T.C., Sung, Y.T.: Applying augmented reality in physical education on motor skills learning. Interact. Learn. Environ. **28**(6), 685–697 (2019)
21. Shekerbekova, S., Kamalova, G., Iskakova, M., Aldabergenova, A., Abdykerimova, E., Shetiyeva, K.: Exploring the use of artificial intelligence and augmented reality tools to improve interactivity in physical education teaching and training methods. Retos. **66**, 935–949 (2025)
22. Ceruso, R., De Cesare, G., Kaçurri, A., Kasa, A., Merati, G.: From pitch to console: exploring the role of football eSports in the development of young footballers. Phys. Educ. Theor. Methodol. **25**(3), 633–641 (2025)
23. Ceruso, R., Esposito, G., Penna, G., Manzi, V., Raiola, G.: The role of eSports in the development of motor and social skills in youth football: A systematic review. Int. J. Hum. Mov. Sports Sci. **13**(4), 996–1002 (2025)
24. Wohlfart, O., Mödinger, M., Wagner, I.: Information and communication technologies in physical education: exploring the association between role modeling and digital literacy. Eur. Phys. Educ. Rev. **30**(2), 177–193 (2023)
25. Sargent, J., Casey, A.: Appreciative inquiry for physical education and sport pedagogy research: a methodological illustration through teachers' uses of digital technology. Sport Educ. Soc. **26**(1), 45–57 (2019)
26. Raiola, G.: Physical literacy, according to the World Health Organization (WHO), in Italian preschool and education for a daily movement routine. Children. **12**, 66 (2025)
27. Ayoade Fadare, S., Beterbo, J.-R.L., Ybanez, F., Abdulrajak Isahac, J.R., Cecilia Fadare, M., Aloy Barahimin, E., et al.: Machine learning in physical education, sports, and recreation: opportunities, challenges, and ethical considerations – A systematic review. Salud, Cienc. Tecnología. **5**, 2251 (2025)
28. Aleksieva, L.: Preparing pre-service teachers for the digital transformation of education: exploring university teacher educators' views and practical strategies. Educ. Sci. **15**, 404 (2025)
29. Pürgstaller, E., Schmeling, J., Barkemeyer, L., et al.: Attitudes of physical education teachers and student teachers regarding digital media in physical education. Ger. J. Exerc. Sport Res. **55**, 541–554 (2025)
30. Soegiyanto, S.A., Rohidi, T.R., Rustiadi, T.: Digital literacy of physical education teachers in the 5.0 era. SPORT TK-EuroAmerican J. Sport Sci. **12**(13) (2023)

Play Experiences with Digital Technologies: Teaching Strategies and Learning Opportunities in Nursery School. The Results of the Systematic Review

Cristiano Zappa(✉)

eCampus University, Novedrate, CO, Italy
cristiano.zappa@studenti.uniecampus.it

Abstract. This study presents a review of the literature using the PRISMA Statement 2020 method. It aims to summarise the results of studies on the topic of gaming with digital devices and technologies in order to investigate the possible effects of multimedia gaming on the learning processes of preschool children aged 3 to 6 years. For these reasons, it is considered important to explore ways of using digital devices, considering that these tools are now an integral part of children's world and experiences [1]. To contextualise the line of research, it should be emphasised that the study is based on three key interrelated dimensions. Firstly, play always activates a range of languages, such as cognitive, relational, social, creative and recreational [2]. Secondly, nowadays every child encounters and is confronted with the media, both as a spectator and as an actor. Thirdly, preschools have the task of helping children become familiar with digital media, resisting two temptations: idealising these technologies or demonising them [3]. In light of this scenario, the research objectives can be formulated as follows: - identifying types of play involving the use of digital technologies; – recognising teaching and learning practices based on digital technologies; – identifying the potential of digital technologies according to the "play to learn" approach. The studies considered highlight how children, through playful experiences using various digital devices, are able to achieve specific educational and teaching objectives, as they require each child to engage cognitively, emotionally and socially, mobilising their mind, body and brain together.

Keywords: Playing · Digital Technologies · Learning

1 The Terms of the Discussion

This study aims to conduct a literature review to investigate how preschools help children become familiar with digital media, and thus to investigate «the uses, transitions, symbolic investments and specificities that always arise when media encounters its audience» [3] , p. 6.

In particular, this survey «seeks ways to introduce digital tools into spaces available to children, given that these tools have now become an integral part of their world and

M. Adamoli et al. (Eds.): HELMeTO 2025, CCIS 2958, pp. 15–33, 2026.
https://doi.org/10.1007/978-3-032-31850-3_2

experiences, but also because citizenship – considered a key skill to be developed at school in order to promote the construction of democracy – also takes on a "digital" form that must be explored and experienced with children» [1]; p. 33.

Along this trajectory, there is an ever-increasing «need for preschools to contribute to the development of digital skills, considering how to incorporate digital experiences into everyday school life» [4]; p. 65. Furthermore, «special attention must be paid to the choice of technological aids (tablets, robots, cameras, video cameras, etc.), which will initially be used by adults and then carefully calibrated for use by children» [5]; p. 25.

For these reasons, «a balanced education on the use of technology, including through discussion with parents, is now an urgent responsibility for educational institutions for children» [5]; p. 25.

2 Digital Resources to Support Play Experiences in Preschools

Before tackling the literature review itself, it is worth contextualising the line of research by pointing out that rapid and pervasive technological development «introduces continuous changes in the ways adults and children learn, relate to each other and experience life. Information and communication technologies, now available in mobile format, bring the world and its events into the daily lives of adults and children in real time; social media are increasing the flow of interpersonal exchanges and giving rise to new group dynamics; web platforms are changing the ways, times and places of work. These changes can create mistrust and concern, especially among parents and educators/teachers, even though they are aware that education cannot remain oblivious to these issues» [5]; p. 12.

In fact, it must be recognised that the global epidemiological emergency has led to a sudden acceleration in the use of digital technologies and the Internet, and that the use of these devices and new forms of communication has made social distancing more bearable and, at the same time, prevented «a drastic interruption of educational connections and learning processes» [6]; p. 59.

With regard to the lockdown period, preschools are also called upon to understand and interpret the meaning of those experiences in a different light, with the use of digital technologies and the Internet. After all, «almost all families own a smartphone, tablet, PC or notebook: these tools, which have always been viewed with a certain degree of suspicion in relation to the age of nursery and preschool children, can be transformed (...) into an opportunity» [7]; p. 2.

From this perspective, when discussing digital media, we can agree that «today, we and our young people [but inevitably also children] are, so to speak, 'permeated by the media'. This means that it makes no sense to discuss whether or not to carve out a space for them in school: if schools want to be contemporary, they must deal with the media, as languages in which youth cultures are articulated and as devices through which everyone's lives are expressed. Dealing with the media does not mean giving in to a fad, but rather achieving the goal of making schools contemporary. The media in schools are an ethical frontier and a space for building citizenship» [8]; p. 1.

Along this path, we also find EU guidelines on preschool education. In particular, these recommendations promote the need to «strengthen the development of early years curricula so that they respond to children's interests, promote their well-being and meet the unique needs and potential of each child, including those with special educational needs, those in vulnerable situations or those from disadvantaged backgrounds» [9]; p. 8.

At this point in the discussion, we can focus our attention on two key dimensions – playing and digital technologies – which will be investigated during the literature review process according to the following combination: playing through/with digital technologies.

The first has deep roots and specific determinations in various fields of research and scientific studies.

Since the last century, in fact, «there has been a proliferation of research on play in the psycho-pedagogical field» [10]; p. 19, aimed not only at implementing «a survey of the types, characteristics, contexts and different manifestations of children's play» [10]; p. 19 but also at recognising «its functionality – and its exploitability – for the purposes of growth, personality development, learning and socialisation» [10]; p. 19.

Based on these beliefs, Francipane [2] specifies that «play, even the simplest form that appears to have no purpose, but is proposed or carried out in an appropriate manner, can: - have a positive impact on personality factors (intelligence and character); – activate and refine certain qualities and consolidate others (dexterity, alertness, common sense, precision, concentration, etc.); – exercise important functions (sensory, motor, psychomotor, intuition, intentionality, logic, observation, reflection, expression, creativity, etc.); – satisfy needs and tastes (sociality, choice, autonomy, self-assertion, risk, comparison, emulation, etc.); – be a valuable training ground on the path that, through tension and effort, leads to serious work (the play-work combination)» [2]; p. 14.

This gives rise to the concept that «teaching today involves the need to relate the complexity of radically new ways of learning to a daily task of guidance, with a focus on methodology, new media and multi-dimensional research» [11]; p. 19.

In light of these statements, it is worth recalling Salati [12] views on play: «play also qualifies as a teaching method, provided that it never loses, even in this respect, its characteristic of manifesting and satisfying a primary need of children. From fully playful activities, the teacher will bring out and consolidate the elements of learning. We can therefore define as *ludomatetico* the teaching intervention (the teacher's action) aimed at the intellectual reconstruction of rewarding and extraordinary events that occur in spaces reserved for them» [12]; p. 255.

The framework outlined above encourages further exploration of *ludomatetiche* strategies in preschools and, in particular, verification of whether the elements that make up the *ludomatetico* model can be applied, either in whole or in part, to play involving new media.

In this regard, it seems reasonable to adopt the definition specified by Chiappetta Cajola [13]: «the *ludomatetico* approach has three fundamental elements: - the active and proactive presence of the adult, but not in a directive role; – the availability of adequate space, time and materials; – the conventional and unconventional use of play. Play-based learning activities are short but intense, which helps keep students motivated to reach their goals. The three aspects of play described above are important for cognitive development because they help kids learn about themselves, others, and the world, encourage discussion and learning, and make work fun» [13]; p. 11.

At this point in the dissertation, we can introduce the second key dimension, consisting of digital technologies, and link it to the dimension of play, since, «(...) every educator must be fully aware that the relationship with the media represents a significant educational event, which intervenes, for better or for worse, in the educational process of every person, starting from the early years of life. The word "educator" should be understood here not only as a profession, but as a broader educational dimension, involving not only those who work in schools or associations, but also every person who has an educational role in everyday life, starting with parents» [14]; p. 11.

According to this approach, schools are called upon to «develop educational programmes that use new technologies and work with them to enable students to learn about them and experience them in a more exploratory and creative way, considering them valuable resources for accessing information and communication and developing awareness and reflection on their multiple uses. This aspect can also become the subject of a shared educational project between the various educational agencies, in particular the family and local structures» [15]; p. 18.

Moreover, Cambi [16] states that the media are increasingly becoming the primary educators: «through them, children discover the world, develop a sense of playfulness, occupy their free time (especially within the family), and are exposed for hours on end to the language of images (...). This is an increasingly intense and global immersion, which has both positive and negative effects. Every educator must be well aware of this. And so they must navigate them together, with two perspectives: a technical one that uses them and makes them be used; and a critical one that interprets them in terms of their structure and function and their grey areas» [16]; p. 17.

3 The Systematic Review Protocol: Methodology and Operational Phases

The overview of the research project presented so far allows us to define the scope and highlight the focal points of the study, which includes all children aged three to six attending preschool.

Consequently, it concerns managers and educational coordinators, as well as teachers who are attentive to the specific needs of these children, parents who are directly and responsibly involved in their educational paths, and the learning environment, including both the physical space and the relationships that are established within it.

In a broader sense, we refer to the context «as an inseparable whole of objects, smells, sounds, colours and people who inhabit and interact in a specific physical environment, which contains it entirely and at the same time is contained by all these elements that are hidden within it and find life in it (...)» [17]; p. 21.

Not only that, but the ongoing research also concerns the accessibility, direct or mediated by adults depending on the age of the children, of digital technological aids, used according to different structures of the teaching activity.

In this regard, Messina [18] states that: «the creation of an effective learning environment (...) goes beyond the confines of the physical or virtual classroom itself and encompasses a connection between physical and digital space, while also requiring a reconfiguration of physical spaces, classrooms and schools, including in relation to preferred learning theories» [18]; p. 179.

Specifically, then, the objectives of the study can be summarised as follows: - identifying types of play involving the use of digital technologies; – recognising teaching and learning practices based on digital technologies; – identifying the potential of digital technologies according to the *ludomatetica* disposition in different school life situations.

To conduct the review, the so-called *The PRISMA 2020 statement: an updated guideline for reporting systematic reviews was identified* [19]. In fact, today, *PRISMA 2020* serves as a reference point for systematic reviews and «includes new reporting guidelines that reflect advances in methods for identifying, selecting, evaluating, and synthesising studies» [20]; p. 3.

At the procedural level, the review was carried out in three stages: 1. overall organisation of the review; definition and registration of the protocol; 2. once the protocol was adopted, analysis of the abstracts and selected texts; 3. analysis and discussion of the results; summary and conclusions.

The entire literature review process was carried out between 1 July and the end of November 2024.

First, an initial form was given to the generative review question in order to «define a scope that could be investigated by the research and to establish a theme around which to draw up a list of keywords for the bibliographic search» [21] , p. 70.

To identify the initial question, the *Population, Context, Outcome* (PCO) tool was used in the version developed by Butler, Hall & Copnell [22] (see Table 1).

Table 1. PCO tool.

Population	Context	Outcome
- Children aged 3–6 years old. - Teachers and educators.	- Experiences of playing with digital devices in different educational situations in preschool.	- Enhancing the value of play as an educational mediator through the use of digital devices. - Defining the characteristics of a *ludomatetico* approach as a learning strategy through the use of digital technologies.

Specifically, the following question was formulated: «What interaction can we consider between play (the playful dimension) with the use of digital technologies and learning (the *matetica* dimension) with preschool children (aged 3–6)?».

The following words were used to combine the search string: *Learning*; *Game*; *Digital*; *Nursery*; *Early Years*.

At this point, in order to search for documents within the bibliographic databases, a search string consisting of four keyword concatenations was created.

The search string for the query is shown below:

«*Learning* AND *Game* AND *Digital* AND (*Nursery* OR *Early* AND *Years*)».

At an operational level, the word "game" was identified in place of "play" for bibliographic research. In this regard, we can assume what Cipriani [23] writes about the two concepts: «We owe to the American psychologist George Herbert Mead (...) a clear definition of the two concepts of play and game, which are useful for a better understanding of the meaning of play in childhood. (...) Play represents the simplest, most elementary form of game. The infant is not yet able to discover its identity. Its self. It may even be able to play different parts, but without splitting itself into each of them. In other words, it is not able to completely control the roles it plays from time to time in a game. Everything becomes more complex in games, when children are able to perceive themselves better and also imagine other roles in relation to themselves. This makes it possible to play multiple roles at the same time, to ask and answer questions, to caress and be caressed, to throw and receive. It is precisely this possibility of splitting that leads to greater complexity in the game, which indicates further maturation. The latter allows for a plurality of roles and the observance of a set of rules» [23]; p. 50.

Furthermore, for one field, Boolean algebra was used with the inclusion of both the "OR" operator to link the two conditions – *nursery* and *early years* – together, and obtain at least one of the words in the result, and the "AND" operator to correlate the two related conditions.

In addition, the formulation of the keywords allowed for a higher level of research, as the duration of children's participation in preschool education in the different countries considered is heterogeneous because it is influenced «by various factors: minimum age of admission, age of commencement of compulsory primary education and rates of participation of children at pre-primary level, which may depend on whether or not pre-primary institutions are free of charge» [24]; p. 2 and, finally, by their prevalence.

The search string identified was placed within two international databases: Scopus and Web of Science (WOS).

Both databases provide a comprehensive overview of global research output, including in the fields of humanities and social sciences, and therefore allow high-quality results relevant to the area of interest for the survey to be found.

The query of the two databases returned the following output: (n = 137) records in Scopus and (n = 123) records in WOS. At the same time, three eligibility criteria were adopted to refine the search.

The first criterion considered was time. The filter used covered the decade 2014–2024. During this period, we can identify at least three factors that have given «a rapid acceleration to the process of global complexity: the digital revolution, population growth and globalisation» [25]; p. 85. In addition, we can consider a fourth factor: the impetus given by the pandemic to the process of digitisation and innovation in education. Furthermore, the *Digital Decade 2024* report, which includes «an assessment of performance, both at European level and at individual country level, in four main areas: digital skills, digital infrastructure, digitisation of businesses, including the use of artificial intelligence (AI), and digitisation of public services» [26]; p. 1, also falls within the time frame considered.

Moreover, the digital revolution of the last decade «has had a profound impact on at least two aspects that are fundamental to any educational activity: access to knowledge and culture, and communication. Above all, they place the student at the centre of the educational process. Thanks to electronic tools, students can become the architects of their own learning path, guided by a teacher who designs a resource-rich, flexible environment that is open to active research and constant monitoring of the teaching and learning process» [27]; p. 13.

Specifically, the time filter applied resulted in the exclusion of (n = 14) records in Scopus and (n = 3) records in Web of Science. The second criterion identified was linguistic. The selection considered the inclusion of documents in English and Romance languages (Spanish and Portuguese). A total of (n = 4) documents in Chinese were excluded: (n = 3) records found in the Scopus search and (n = 1) record found in Web of Science.

The third eligibility criterion was to select documents available through various open access channels. The advantages of this approach can be summarized as follows: - simple and immediate access to international scientific production; – access to full text; – overcoming the so-called academic bait and switch.

Subsequently, duplicate documents (n = 29) were removed, as they were present in both databases.

As a result, (n = 88) documents were extracted.

This was followed by the abstract screening procedure, which took into account the criteria of relevance and type of contribution (articles and conference papers), and which resulted in «reading the title and abstract of each resource found for an initial screening of studies of interest» [28]; p. 125. (n = 57) documents were excluded from the analysis because they were not relevant to the research question (specifically (n = 16) records in Scopus and (n = 41) records in Web of Science) and (n = 5) reviews, since, on the one hand, they did not correspond to the type of contributions considered and, on the other hand, their level of relevance was only partially consistent with the fields related to the research question (heterogeneity of school orders, age of children, forms of learning).

At this stage of the process, (n = 26) documents were identified: (n = 8) in Scopus and (n = 18) in Web of Science.

In the final step, before closing the process, text screening was used. The reports selected so far were subjected to a further analysis phase in order to assess their level of relevance to the research question.

An evaluation rubric was developed for this purpose (see Table 2).

Table 2. Assessment rubric: relevance of selected documents.

Dimension	Levels			
	(4)	(3)	(2)	(1)
Relevance	Representation fully consistent with the fields of the research question.	Representation substantially consistent with the fields of the research question.	Representation only partially consistent with the fields of the research question.	Representation with low congruence threshold with respect to the fields of the research question.

With regard to the research question, two documents were excluded (n = 2) because they had a low level of relevance (level 1) as they examined medical-clinical aspects: in one case, these were related to the cognitive assessment of preschool children; in the other, they concerned a new early biomarker for identifying Autism Spectrum Disorder (ASD).

On the other hand, documents that achieved a level of relevance that was fully or substantially congruent with the research question (level 4 or 3) were included (n = 24).

The *PRISMA 2020* flow chart, outlined in Fig. 1, now provides a graphical representation of the study selection process through three work blocks involving the processes of Identification-Screening-Inclusion of documents. Furthermore, it «contributes to the transparency and reliability of the systematic review» [29]; p. 1.

3.1 Document Analysis

With reference to the corpus of documents (n = 24) included in the review, the analysis initially focused on the following characteristics of the studies: the period of publication, the country/countries of origin, the type of records and the language used.

With regard to the time frame, which covers the decade 2014–2024, we can see in Fig. 2 that the highest number of publications occurred from 2018 onwards, with five contributions. In the following years, up to the present day, this threshold recorded a significant decline in 2019, a progressive growth in 2020, 2021 and 2022, and a further decline in 2023. However, 2024 shows 3 contributions in the first seven months (date of record extraction) of the year.

With regard to the country of origin, the studies extracted were carried out in 15 countries (see Fig. 3), spread across six continents.

Specifically, out of (n = 24) contributions, (n = 16) were made on the European continent; the remaining records (n = 8) were made on the following continents: Asia (n = 2), Oceania (n = 2), North America (n = 2), South America (n = 1) and Africa (n = 1), as shown in Fig. 4.

The type of records identified as useful for the review mainly consists of (n = 22) articles (92%) published in specialised journals; a small number of publications (n = 2) refer to conference papers (8%), as shown in Fig. 5.

The language used in the various contributions by all scholars is English.

The next phase of data analysis continued with the definition «of an analytical framework common to all the documents included: a combination of general information on the study and specific information relating» [21]; p. 46) to the following five categories characterising each article:

- *references*: author(s), title of the contribution, type of document, name of the source and year of publication;
- *abstract*: «a brief and accurate summary of the content of a document, generally without additional notes of interpretation or criticism» [30]; p. 7;
- *terms to consider*: keywords;
- population: the subjects involved in the research;
- objective(s): purpose(s) of the study.

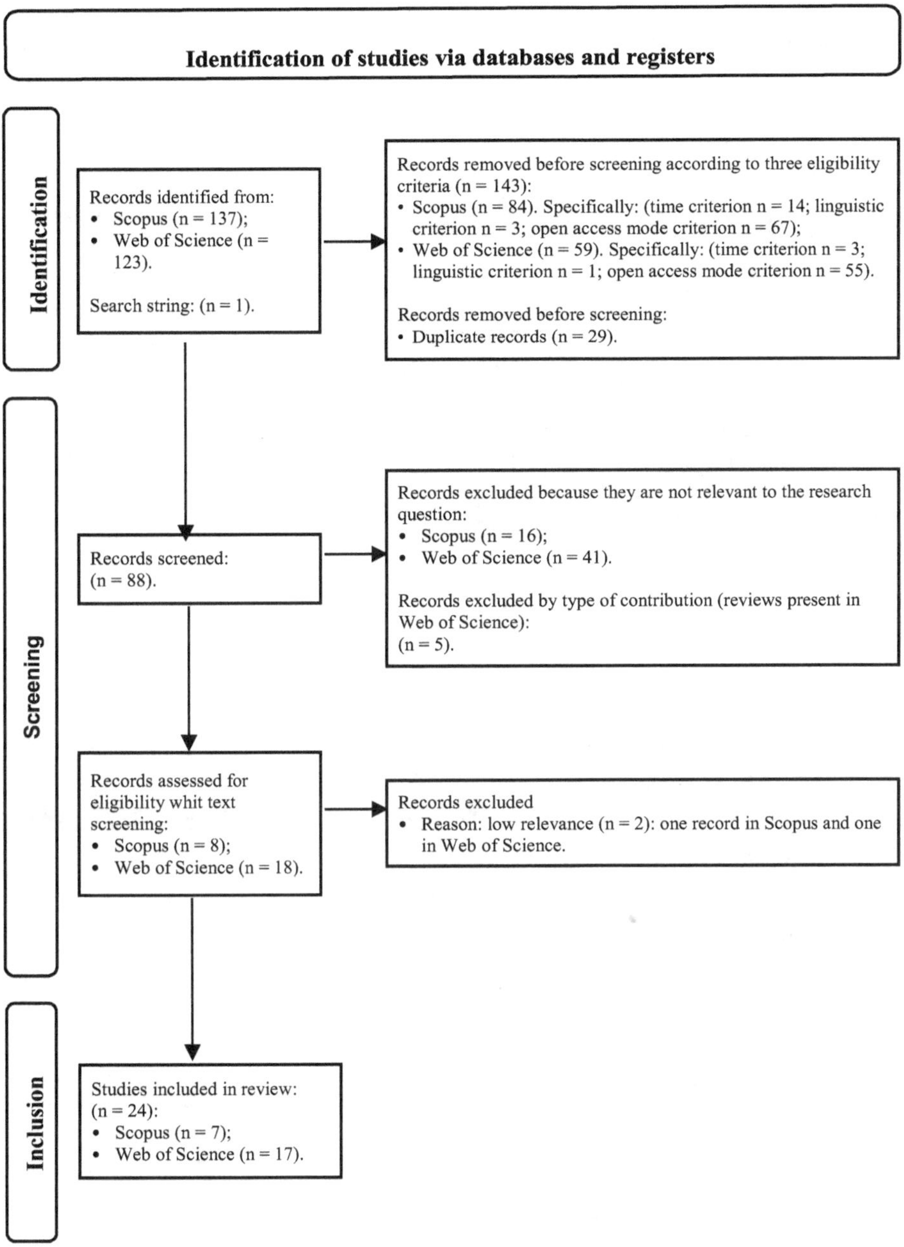

Fig. 1. *PRISMA 2020* flow diagram for systematic reviews

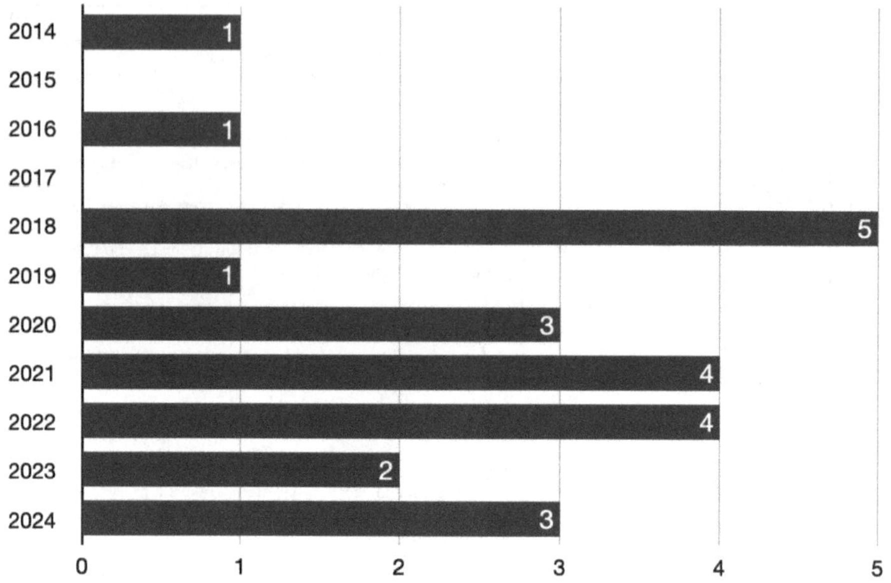

Fig. 2. Publication period 2014–2024.

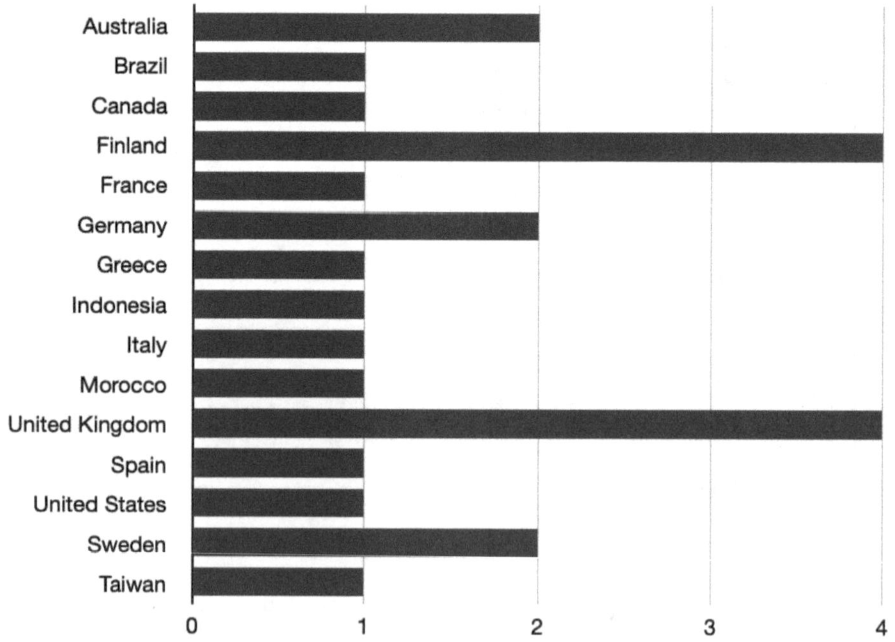

Fig. 3. Countries of origin of studies.

The language used in the various contributions by all researchers is English.

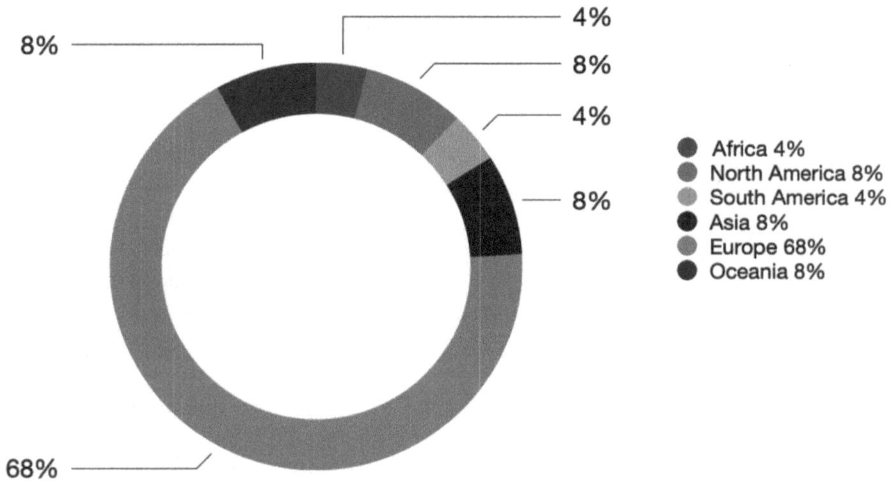

Fig. 4. Geographical distribution (continents) of selected records.

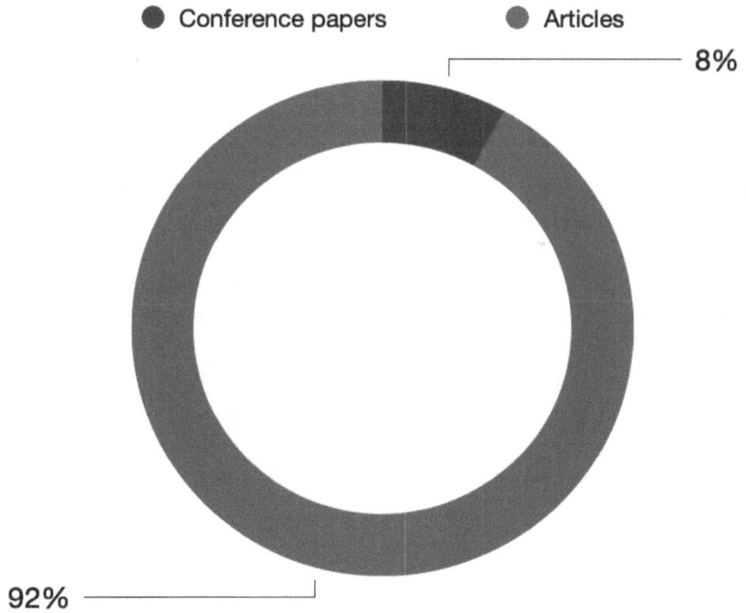

Fig. 5. Record types.

The combination of information resulting from the analytical framework has contributed both to providing a synoptic view of the evidence and to organising punctuation and discourse to give «shape to what emerges from the results of the studies included» [21]; p. 111.

4 Summary of Results: Punctuation and Discourse

To continue with the review process, we refer to the reasons why reviewers may "summarise": «(…) because they want to take stock of the situation, because they want to find generalisations (...) about a phenomenon, because they want to define, improve and resort to effective practices, where effective means practices that are sensitive to the prerogatives of people and contexts, with a view to humanisation». [31]; p. 72.

In this regard, starting from the examination of each document and considering, in particular, the abstracts and keywords included in the extraction framework, a series of emerging themes were identified, based on the assumption that «a theme captures something important in the data, in relation to the review question, and has a certain level of recursiveness» [21]; p. 122.

The themes identified were then grouped into categories according to their relevance to the subject under study. Six main categories were thus established, which «identify concepts at a higher level of abstraction» [21]; p. 130), as specified below:

1) Digital games, learning, neuroscience;
2) Pedagogical implementations based on children's ideas about digital media;
3) Effectiveness of educational interventions based on digital games;
4) Use of digital media in the family environment;
5) Design and evaluation of computer games and videos for children on the YouTube platform;
6) Repertoire of digital games.

At this point, the frequency of the themes was measured «by means of a percentage, dividing the number of studies addressing a given theme by the total number of studies included» [21]; p. 126.

With reference to the categories outlined above, Table 3 below includes topics and studies identified as relevant for exploring the research question in detail.

At this point in the discussion, we can summarise that the categories identified allow us to: - appreciate the richness and complexity of the phenomenon under consideration; – provide guidance for the interpretation and conceptualisation of studies; – position information and data on the digital skills of AMISM pedagogical coordinators and teachers emerging from quantitative research; – outline horizons and perspectives for further investigation.

Table 3. Topics and studies identified as relevant to the research question.

Identification number of documents	Categories	Topics	Frequency of topics
ID: 01 ID: 20 ID: 21	Digital games, learning, neuroscience	- Improving children's skills through play-based learning and gamification. - Learning through Digital Educational Games (DEG). - Re-reading Digital Game Based Learning (DGBL).	(3/24) 12,5%
ID: 18	Pedagogical implementations based on children's ideas about digital media	- Children's ideas on the use of digital media.	(1/24) 4,16%
ID: 05 ID: 13 ID: 17	Effectiveness of educational interventions based on digital games	- Benefits of digital games in reading and writing skills. - Early learning of sonification for the inclusion of children with blindness and low vision. - Early detection of dyslexia and interactivity facilitated by digital technologies.	(3/24) 12,5%
ID: 08 ID: 22	Use of digital media in the family environment	- Relationship between analog and digital environments in home learning. - Impact of digital media in the home.	(2/24) 8,33%
ID: 06 ID: 09 ID: 16 ID: 24	Design and evaluation of computer games and videos for children on the YouTube platform	- Methodology for developing computer games. - Attitudes, perceptions and approaches of educators in supporting children's digital play. - Rubric for assessing the quality of YouTube videos. - Scaffolding features in apps for early childhood learning.	(4/24) 16%

(continued)

Table 3. (*continued*)

Identification number of documents	Categories	Topics	Frequency of topics
ID: 02 ID: 03 ID: 04 ID: 07 ID: 10 ID: 11 ID: 12 ID: 14 ID: 15 ID: 19 ID: 23	Repertoire of digital games	- Digital puzzles. - Digital memory games. - Digital learning games in refugee settings and resource-poor environments. - Mobile touch screen games, particularly Angry Birds. - Digital apps (Daisy the Dinosaur and Kodable) for teaching programming skills to children. - Immersive technology: educational games that incorporate movement interaction. - Digital game to promote learning and use of lighting in preschool settings. - Impact of digital games based on explicit and implicit learning processes. - Digital writing devices (stylus on touchscreen). - Educational computer game (Lola's World) on early numeracy skills. - Interactive game (ABBOT) for exploring outdoor environments.	(11/24) 45,83%

5 Conclusions

The systematic review process has made it possible to focus on a series of avenues for reflection and updating based on the recognition that the spread of digital technology «is an established social fact of the contemporary era» [32]; p. 5 that is increasingly affecting early childhood [33], which, together with adults, is enveloped in a sort of «digital blanket» [32]; p. 5.

According to this framework, the study of the documents leads us to confirm the perspective already suggested by Postman [34] that, faced with the spread of new communication tools, the most effective response may not be to demonise these tools, but rather to initiate a dialogue [34].

This dialogic dimension with the media on the part of schools – in our case, preschools – is, in fact, attested to internationally by several authors [35, 36, 38–41,

43, 45, 46, 52, 58, 59], who agree with the view expressed by Yelland [60] that «digital technologies should be viewed as being complimentary to other resources, rather than alternatives or in competition with traditional modalities» [53]; p. 3 in education. Not only that. If we consider dialogue with digital devices in the family environment, we find dissertations by various authors [49, 53], which argue that «digitally supported learning with very specific, high-quality digital media can support children's learning and development (e.g. Gomez et al., 2013; Berkowitz et al., 2015; Neumann, 2016)» [53]; p. 3.

Since preschools are also called upon to actively participate in the development of digital skills, and considering that play is the preferred educational tool in this type of school, it is essential to focus on the encounter and use of digital technologies by children aged 3–6 in various playful educational situations.

Specifically, the studies just considered [39–46, 50, 52, 59] reveal how children, through play experiences using different digital devices, «have managed to achieve specific educational and teaching objectives and not just pursue generic educational goals» [12]; p. 75.

Moreover, we can agree with Salati [12] that «the transition from a playful to a *matetica* attitude is extremely natural in children, to the point that teachers often find it difficult to assess where one ends and the other begins. This could lead us to believe that the relationship between play and learning – at least in preschool – is neither sequential nor juxtaposed, but much more intimate and interrelated than a theoretical distinction can define» [12]; p. 75.

In addition, within the corpus of documents analysed – which envisage the use of digital technologies in playful situations – we are able to identify and specify certain "seeds" that can be traced back to the *ludomatetica* disposition:

- the teacher's involvement in playing with children on several operational levels (game creator, tutoring guide, support and scaffolding) [37, 38, 45];
- the design of an educational-curricular framework for digital skills that responds to children's cultural-cognitive context [39–46];
- attention to each child through the implementation of high-quality digital learning resources [47–50];
- organising the learning environment to normalise the presence of digital technology [51, 60, 61];
- a workshop approach that focuses on discovery-based learning and mind-body-brain engagement [40, 46, 51–52–60];
- the balanced duration of digital device use [53–55];
- reflection and discussion on the play experience with children (debriefing) [38] aimed at helping them «verbalise and reformulate a series of emotional experiences, observations about themselves and others, and what happened in the play» [48]; p. 22];
- the gratification of children both in terms of learning processes and concrete play products/results [38, 56, 57].

At this point in the discussion, we can reiterate that preschools recognise the promotion of play in all its forms and dimensions as an essential feature of their educational service. On this basis, and in view of rapid and pervasive technological development, we can assert that the media, as allies of contemporary preschools, «are not only tools to be used in the classroom, but also a necessary basic skill» [49]; p. 1] and, as such, it is reasonable to use them in the field of *ludomatetico*, as they require each child to engage cognitively, emotionally and socially, mobilising the mind, body and brain together.

In addition to this, the aspects concerning the *ludomatetico* approach provide a framework that teachers and educators working in nursery schools can implement during play activities using digital devices. Furthermore, these elements constitute useful methodological and didactic resources, both for the academic training of future teachers and for the reflection and professional development of teachers already in service, open to discovering the transformative power of play [62].

After all, we can «be convinced that a school tailored to children should consider play as a normal activity, even fully integrated into the curriculum» [12]; p. 244

From this perspective, play qualifies as an educational tool that engages all aspects of the individual. Therefore, the experience of play deserves to be fully valued in the continuing professional development of primary school teachers and, more generally, in the field of education.

Disclosure of Interests.. The author declares that he has no conflicts of interest. The author is solely responsible for the content and writing of the article.

References

1. Lorenzoni, F.: Una scuola artigianale. Bambini. **3**(3), 33 (2016)
2. Francipane, M.: La scuola in gioco. Strategie ludomatetiche nella scuola materna ed elementare. IRRSAE Lombardia, Milano (1993)
3. Tisseron, S.: 3–6–9-12. Diventare grandi all'epoca degli schermi digitali. La Scuola, Bre-scia (2016)
4. Rossi, F.: Tecnologie digitali nei contesti educativi 0–6: tra esperienze in presenza e a distanza. In: Metastasio, R. (ed.) La media education nella prima infanzia (0–6). Percorsi, pratiche e prospettive. FrancoAngeli, Milano (2016)
5. Ministero dell'Istruzione e del Merito (MIM), Commissione nazionale per il Sistema integrato di educazione e di istruzione: Linee pedagogiche per il sistema integrato "0–6" p. 12. Roma (2021). https://www.mim.gov.it/-/linee-pedagogiche-per-il-sistema-integrato-zerosei. Accessed 13 Oct. 2025.
6. Seccia, R.: La famiglia e il contesto sociale. In: Cerini G., Spinosi M.: Le Linee Pedagogiche per Il Sistema Integrato 0–6. Documenti, Commenti, Normativa. Tecnodid, Napoli (2021).
7. Ministero dell'Istruzione e del Merito (MIM), Commissione per il sistema integrato: Orientamenti pedagogici sui LEAD: legami educativi a distanza. Un modo diverso per fare nido e scuola dell'infanzia p. 2. Roma (2020). https://www.istruzione.it/sistema-integrato-06/orientamenti.html. Accessed 14 Oct. 2025
8. Rivoltella, P.C.: Un'idea di scuola p. 1 (2018). https://piercesare.blogspot.com/2018/05/unidea-di-scuola.html. Accessed 14 Oct. 2025
9. Gazzetta ufficiale dell'Unione europea: Raccomandazione del Consiglio relativa ai sistemi di educazione e cura di alta qualità della prima infanzia. Bruxelles (2019), 2019/C 189/02, p. 8. https://eur-lex.europa.eu/legal-content/IT/TXT/PDF/?uri=CELEX:32019H0605(01). Accessed 14 Oct. 2025.
10. Bondioli, A.: Gioco e educazione. FrancoAngeli, Milano (1996)

11. Ministero dell'Istruzione, dell'Università e della Ricerca (MIUR): Indicazioni nazionali per il curricolo della scuola dell'infanzia e del primo ciclo d'istruzione. Roma, p. 19 (2012). https://www.mim.gov.it/documents/20182/51310/DM+254_2012.pdf. Accessed 14 Oct. 2025.
12. Salati, E.M.: Fondamenti di didattica. I.S.U.-Università Cattolica, Milano (2004)
13. Chiappetta Cajola, L.: Didattica del gioco e integrazione. Progettare con l'ICF. Carocci, Roma (2012)
14. Marangi, M.: Addomesticare gli schermi. Il digitale a misura dell'infanzia 0–6. Scholé, Brescia (2023).
15. Rivoltella, P.C.: *S*MART FUTURE. Didattica, media digitali e inclusione. FrancoAngeli, Milano (2014)
16. Cambi, F.: Osservazioni sulla media Education: a cominciare dalla scuola dell'infanzia? In: Di, Bari C., Mariani, A. Media Education 0–6. Le tecnologie digitali nella prima infanzia tra critica e creatività. Anicia, Roma (2018).
17. Iglesias Forneiro, M.L.: Valutare la sezione come spazio e contesto di apprendimento. Bambini, n° 7/settembre, p. 21 (1997).
18. Messina, L., De Rossi, M.: Tecnologie, formazione e didattica. Carocci, Roma (2015)
19. Page M., McKenzie, J.E., Bossuyt, P.M. et al.: The PRISMA 2020 statement: an updated guideline for reporting systematic reviews. BMJ 372:n71 (2021) https://doi.org/10.1136/bmj.n71. Accessed 14 Oct. 2025
20. Maraolo, A.E.: Una bussola per le revisioni sistematiche: la versione italiana della nuova edizione del PRISMA statement. Medici oggi, Anno XXV, Aprile (2021). [My translation].
21. Ghirotto, L.: La systematic review nella ricerca qualitativa. Metodi e strategie. Carocci, Roma (2020)
22. Butler, A., Hall, H., Copnell, B.: A guide to writing a qualitative systematic review protocol to enhance evidence-based practice. Worldviews Evid.-Based Nurs. **13**(3), 214–249 (2016). https://doi.org/10.1111/wvn.12134
23. Cipriani, R.: Il gioco tra play e game. In: Macchietti, S.S. (ed.) Il bambino, il gioco, il giocattolo. FISM, Roma (1989)
24. Unità Italiana di Eurydice - Agenzia Nazionale per lo Sviluppo dell'Autonomia Scolastica: L'educazione prescolare: una panoramica europea. Bollettino di Informazione Internazionale. Settembre, p. 2 (2007). https://www.indire.it/lucabas/lkmw_file/eurydice/TESTO_PARTE_I.pdf. Access 14 Oct. 2025
25. Ceruti, M., Bellusci, F.: Abitare la complessità. La sfida di un destino comune. Mimesis, Milano, Udine (2020)
26. Commissione Europea: La prima relazione sullo stato del decennio digitale chiede un'azione collettiva per plasmare la transizione digitale. (2024). https://digital-strategy.ec.europa.eu/it/news/first-report-state-digital-decade-calls-collective-action-shape-digital-transition. Access 14 Oct. 2025.
27. Falcinelli, F.: La "scuola digitale", a che punto siamo? In: Rivoltella, P.C. (ed.) *S*MART FUTURE. Didattica, media digitali e inclusione. FrancoAngeli, Milano (2014)
28. Pellegrini, M., Marsili, F.: Una valutazione dei software per condurre revisioni sistematiche: analisi delle caratteristiche e sondaggio a esperti. Form@re - Open Journal per la formazione in rete, vol. 21, n. 2, p. 125 (2021),. ISSN 1825–7321, https://doi.org/10.36253/form-11343. Access 14 Oct. 2025.
29. Villani, L.: PRISMA il Diagramma di flusso. In: https://luigivillani.it/prisma-il-diagramma-di-flusso/ p. 1 (2024). Access 14 Oct. 2025
30. Vigini, G.: Glossario di biblioteconomia e scienza dell'informazione. Bibliografica, Milano (1985)
31. Todres, L., Galvin, K.T. & Holloway, I.: The humanization of healthcare: A value framework for qualitative research. Int. J. Qual. Stud. Health Well Being 4:2, 68–77 (2009) DOI: https://doi.org/10.1080/17482620802646204.

32. Morcellini, M.: Il digitale fa bene ai bambini? Meltemi, Milano (2023)
33. Di Bari, C., Mariani, A.: Media Education 0–6. Le tecnologie digitali nella prima infanzia tra critica e creatività. Anicia, Roma (2018)
34. Postman, N.: Ecologia dei media. Armando, Roma (1981)
35. Gee, J.P.: Come un videogioco. Insegnare e apprendere nella scuola digitale. Raffaello Cortina, Milano (2013)
36. Mertala, P., Salomaa, S.: Kasvatuskeskeinen näkökulma varhaisvuosien mediakasvatukseen. In: Pekkala, L., Salomaa, S. & Spišák, S.: Monimuotoinen mediakasvatus. Kansallisen audiovisuaalisen instituutin julkaisuja. 1 pp. 154–155 (2016). http://www.mediataitokoulu.fi/monimuotoinen_mediakasvatus.pdf. Access 14 Oct. 2025
37. Arnab, S., et al.: The development approach of a pedagogically-driven serious game to support relationship and sex education (RSE) within a classroom setting. Comput. Educ. **69**, 15–30 (2013). https://doi.org/10.1016/j.compedu.2013.06.013
38. Tárraga-Sánchez, M.d.l.Á., Ballesteros-García, M.d.M., Migallón, H.: Teacher-developed computer games for classroom and online reinforcement learning for early childhood. Education Sciences. **13**(108), 1–29 (2023). https://doi.org/10.3390/educsci13020108
39. Aunio, P., Mononen, R.: The effects of educational computer game on low-performing children's early numeracy skills – an intervention study in a preschool setting. Eur. J. Spec. Needs Educ. **33**(5), 677–691 (2018) https://helda.helsinki.fi/items/494542b4-c55b-45a1-968d-8cb477d4110c
40. Delprino, F., Piva, C., Tommasi, G., Gelsomini, M., Izzo, N., Matera, M.: ABBOT: A Smart Toy Motivating Children to Become Outdoor Explorers. In: Proceedings of AVI Conference, Castiglione della Pescaia, Italy (2018). https://doi.org/10.1145/3206505.3206512
41. Herodotou, C.: Mobile games and science learning: A comparative study of 4 and 5 years old playing the game angry birds. Br. J. Educ. Technol. **49**(1), 6–16 (2018). https://doi.org/10.1111/bjet.12546
42. Pila, S., Aladé, F., Sheehan, K.J., Lauricella, A.R., Wartella, E.A.: Learning to Code via Tablet Applications: An Evaluation of Daisy the Dinosaur and Kodable as Learning Tools for Young Children (2018). in Internet. https://www.sciencedirect.com/science/article/pii/S0360131518302422. Access 14 Oct. 2025.
43. Vinter, A., Bard, P., Poulin-Charronnat, B.: A comparison of the impact of digital games eliciting explicit and implicit learning processes in preschoolers. International Journal of Child-Computer Interaction. 34, 100534 (2022). https://www.sciencedirect.com/science/article/abs/pii/S2212868922000538?via%3Dihub. Access 14 Oct. 2025.
44. da Silva, G.C.: game learning analytics can unpack Escribo play effects in preschool early reading and writing. Computers and Education Open. **3** (100066, 2022). https://doi.org/10.1016/j.caeo.2021.100066
45. Pynnönen, L., Hietajarvi, L., Kumpulainen, K., Lipponen, L.: Overcoming illiteracy through game-based learning in refugee camps and urban slums. Computers and Education Open. **3** (2022)
46. Wang, C.M., Lee, B.T., Lo, T.Y.: The Design of a Novel Digital Puzzle Gaming System for Young Children's Learning by Interactive Multi-Sensing and Tangible User Interfacing Techniques. Sustainability Learning in Education of Sustainability. **15**, 3036 (2023)
47. Papadakis, S., Kalogiannakis, M., Zaranis, N.: Educational apps from the Android Google Play for Greek preschoolers: A systematic review. In: Tárraga-Sánchez, M.D.L.Á., Ballesteros-García, M.D.M., Migallón, H.: Teacher-Developed Computer Games for Classroom and Online Reinforcement Learning for Early Childhood, vol. 13, pp. 4 (2023). in Education Sciences
48. Sood, M.R., Toornstra, A., Sereno, M.I., Boland, M., Filaretti, D., Sood, A.: A Digital App to Aid Detection, Monitoring, and Management of Dyslexia in Young Children (DIMMAND): Protocol for a Digital Health and Education Solution. JMIR Research Protocols. **7**, 2 (2018)

49. Neumann, M.M., Herodotou, C.: Evaluating YouTube videos for young children. Educ. Inf. Technol., 1–33 (2020). https://doi.org/10.1007/s10639-020-10183-7. http://hdl.handle.net/10072/393648
50. Damsma, P.: Hearing a Circle: uno studio esplorativo sulla sonificazione accessibile per bambini piccoli con cecità e ipovisione, p. 2 (2023). in Internet. https://advance.sagepub.com/doi/full/10.31124/advance.24563305.v1. Access 14 Oct. 2025.
51. Nesti, R.: App education nella prima infanzia, in Di Bari, C., Mariani, A., (a cura di), Media Education 0–6, Media Education 0–6. Le Tecnologie Digitali Nella Prima Infanzia Tra Critica e creatività, Anicia, Roma (2018).
52. Mattsson, P., Laike, T.: Young children's learning about lighting and turn-off behaviour in preschool environments. Energy & Buildings. **268**, 112193 (2022) https://www.sciencedirect.com/science/article/pii/S0378778822003644?via%3Dihub
53. Wang, C.M., Lee, B.T., Lo, T.Y.: The Design of a Novel Digital Puzzle Gaming System for Young Children's Learning by Interactive Multi-Sensing and Tangible User Interfacing Techniques. Sustainability. **15**, 3036 (2023). https://doi.org/10.3390/su15043036
54. Lehrl, S., Linberg, A., Niklas, F., Kuger, S.: The Home Learning Environment in the Digital Age–Associations Between Self-Reported "Analog" and "Digital" Home Learning Environment and Children's Socio-Emotional and Academic Outcomes. Frontiers in Psychology. 12, 592513, (2021). p. 2 marzo.
55. Susilowati, I.H., Nugraha, S., Hasiholan, B.P.: Screen Time for Preschool Children: Learning from Home during the COVID-19 Pandemic. Global Pediatric Health. vol. 8 marzo, (2021). p. 2.
56. Loos, S., Vittori, R.: 99 e + giochi cooperativi. Notes Edizioni, Torino (2011)
57. Masterman, E., Rogers, Y.: A framework for designing interactive multimedia to scaffold young children's understanding of historical chronology. Instructional Science. **30**(3), 221–241 (2002). https://doi.org/10.1023/A:1015133106888
58. Callaghan, M.N., Reich, S.M.: Mobile app features that scaffold pre-school learning: verbal feedback and leveling designs. Br. J. Educ. Technol. **52**(2), 787 (2021)
59. Lamrani, R., Abdelwahed, E.H.: Game-based learning and Gamification to improve skills in early years education. Computer Science and Information Systems. **17**(1), 339–356. https://doi.org/10.2298/CSIS190511043L
60. Aloizou, V., Linardatou, S., Boloudakis, M., Retalis, S.: Integrating a movement-based learning platform as core curriculum tool in kindergarten classrooms. Br. J. Educ. Technol. **00**, 1–27 (2024). https://doi.org/10.1111/bjet.13511
61. Yelland, N.J.: A pedagogy of multiliteracies: young children and multimodal learning with tablets. In: Lehrl, S., Linberg, A., Niklas, F. & Kuger, S.: The Home Learning Environment in the Digital Age-Associations Between Self-Reported "Analog" and "Digital" Home Learning Environment and Children's Socio-Emotional and Academic Outcomes. 12, pp. 592513 (2021). doi:https://doi.org/10.3389/fpsyg.2021.592513. Frontiers in Psychology
62. Dovigo, F.: Pedagogia del gioco. Idee e strumenti per la didattica. Carocci Editore, Roma (2025)

Theatre and Technology in Teacher Education: Innovative Teaching and Productive Hybridizations

Nadia Carlomagno[1(✉)], Valeria Vadalá[2], and Arianna Ricciardi[2]

[1] University Suor Orsola Benincasa of Naples, Naples, Italy
nadia.carlomagno@unisob.na.it
[2] University Pegaso, Naples, Italy
{valeria.vadala,arianna.ricciardi}@unipegaso.it

Abstract. The research explores the integration of theatrical practices and digital technologies in the training of future teachers, examining how bodily and emotional awareness can be enhanced through digital tools. Drawing on an approach based on Embodied Cognition theory and Art-Based Research, approximately 400 students from the University of Suor Orsola Benincasa in Naples participated in a hybrid workshop program alternating between in-person and online activities. The results show that technology can amplify bodily awareness, emotional connection, and listening skills, making the educational experience more meaningful. Theater, as a space for relational and embodied reflection, thus emerges as a powerful pedagogical mediator even in digital contexts.

Keywords: 4E Cognition Theory · Educational theater · Digital technologies · Teacher training

1 Introduction

Contemporary society is undergoing a profound transformation driven by the pervasive spread of digital technologies and artificial intelligence, giving rise to what is defined as the *onlife society* [1], in which the distinction between online and offline loses its significance. In this new hybrid habitat, which can be defined as the *infosphere* [1], human experience is continuously constructed through digital environments that shape the way we perceive reality, learn, and interact with others.

This occurs because technology assumes the characteristics of a *cognitive environment* where new communication systems can be structured, establishing relationships mediated by virtual environments and modifying modes of learning.

In this scenario, the training of future teachers cannot be limited to the acquisition of digital skills; it must promote a new way of *inhabiting* technology, not as mere users, but as embodied and aware subjects who interact with a complex ecosystem, developing critical reflection on new modes of learning processes and fostering interdisciplinary, multimodal, and creative approaches. Learning can no longer be configured as a linear

M. Adamoli et al. (Eds.): HELMeTO 2025, CCIS 2958, pp. 34–52, 2026.
https://doi.org/10.1007/978-3-032-31850-3_3

process but must be understood as a relational and situated experience, where bodily and emotional dimensions play a central role.

The pilot study presented here arises precisely from this awareness and aims to explore how theatrical practices can interact with digital technologies in the training of future teachers, fostering greater awareness of body perception, emotions, and the educational space [2]. The pilot study presented stems precisely from this awareness and aims to explore how theatrical practices can interact with digital technologies in the training of future teachers, in order to foster greater awareness of body perception, emotions, and the educational context [2]. Specifically, the research seeks to investigate whether, and in what ways, technology can enhance, or conversely, hinder the bodily, emotional and environmental awareness of future teachers.

From this perspective, theater emerges as a privileged relational space in the *here* and *now* (*Hit* et *Nunc*), where the experiential dimension is grounded in the authentic encounter of bodies and their capacity to co-generate meaning through shared action.

Theater is Living Perception, an "act of mutual presence" [3], a place where actor and spectator meet in a transformative process, beyond mere representation or theatrical fiction. In the onlife training process, bodily interaction becomes the epistemological core of the experience, situated in the contact and reciprocity of performative and emotional action, thus generating embodied learning.

In this scenario, the educational challenge lies in rethinking the training relationship as a dynamic, embodied, and interactive process in which the body and digital technologies can coexist within a new cognitive ecology.

2 Theoretical Framework

In this onlife society [1], where the dimensions of the real and the virtual constantly intertwine, the training of future teachers must rethink its epistemological and methodological categories, overcoming the traditional separation between physical presence and mediated presence, and repositioning the educational experience as an embodied and connected process, in which technology becomes an integral part of cognitive and relational construction.

The theoretical framework of this study develops from an interdisciplinary perspective that considers the boundary between different fields of knowledge as a privileged space [4]. In this meeting ground, educational research and the performing arts engage in dialogue, contaminating each other and generating new possibilities for knowledge and experimentation.

These are two research fields that may appear distant at first glance, but are in fact deeply interconnected and mutually fertile in promoting innovative training pathways [5]. A discussion on teacher education considers "learning as a center of multiplicative convergence to which the contributions of all those disciplines, whose expertise is perpetually intertwined with the specifically pedagogical, can be traced [...] in considering the subject in their entirety and development, as an active individual experiencing the surrounding reality, selecting, coding, and interpreting it [...]" [6].

It is precisely from these intersections that the possibility arises for educational and training experimentation aimed at investigating how theatrical practices, rooted in bodily and relational experience, can engage with digital tools in the training of future teachers, analyzing how bodily, emotional, and environmental perception can be enhanced or, conversely, hindered by digital instruments. The proposed experimentation is conceived as an attempt to reconstruct a new humanism within the context of current technological advancement. It seeks to counteract the progressive automation of training processes, reaffirming the centrality of bodily relationships, experience, and the creative dimension of learning.

This perspective is grounded in the multiple approach applied in educational research and the performing arts of 4E cognition theory, which understands cognitive processes as embodied, embedded/situated, extended, and enactive.

2.1 4E Cognition Theory

The 4E Cognition Theory encompasses a heterogeneous set of approaches that share a dynamic, interactive, and relational view of human knowledge and behavior. These perspectives converge on the idea that cognition should be understood by integrating neural and bodily activities that interact meaningfully and contextually with the environment. The mind is therefore not conceived as a purely internal or disembodied process, but as the result of a constitutive relationship between action, body, and context. The most representative schools of thought within the 4E Cognition paradigm define cognition as: *embodied*, because it depends on the body and its sensorimotor interactions; *situated* and *embedded*, as it develops within specific material, natural, and social contexts; *extended*, since it integrates tools, artifacts, and media as components of the cognitive process; and *enactive*, because it emerges from active interaction with the world and the construction of meaning.

2.2 Embodied Cognition

The *embodied cognition* approach [7, 8] assigns the body a constitutive role in cognitive processes, considering it a necessary and structural condition of thought, thereby rejecting the idea that the body is merely an instrument of the mind.

Cognitive neuroscience [9] has shown that sensorimotor experiences activate distributed neural networks connecting perception, action, and symbolic processing. Consequently, cognitive processes must be understood as integrated functions of a unified bodily and neural system, where perception, movement, and emotion constitute the core. From this perspective, knowledge is rooted in bodily experience and in the perceptual modalities through which the organism engages with the world.

2.3 Situated and Embedded Cognition

Situated cognition holds that cognitive processes are intrinsically influenced by physical and social contexts, which must be considered an integral part of any accurate characterization of cognition. The concept of context includes the physical, ecological, and socio-cultural environments in which an individual lives and acts.

From this perspective, concrete experience always takes place within a specific context, which gives meaning and direction to action. Learning, therefore, is never an isolated process but is rooted in the material and social environments that support it.

Dewey argued that authentic learning occurs when an individual engages in activities with practical and social relevance. Concrete experiences, therefore, are contextualized experiences, embedded in everyday life and collective practices [10].

This principle resonates with the perspective of *embedded cognition*, which views the environment not as a neutral backdrop but as an active part of the cognitive system. Objects, spaces, and social relationships directly contribute to the construction of meaning. Concrete experience can thus be interpreted as a form of *situated cognition*, in which knowledge emerges from the dynamic interactions between the individual and the material, cultural, and natural environment [11, 12].

2.4 Extended Mind

The *extended mind* thesis [13–15] asserts that the human mind is not confined within the skull but extends beyond the body, encompassing tools, artifacts, and environments that participate in everyday cognitive functioning.

Clark and Chalmers argue that the distinction between internal and external cognitive processes lacks a solid ontological basis. If an external process performs the same function that would normally be attributed to an internal process, it should be considered part of the cognitive system itself. The extended mind redefines the boundary between mind and world in functional terms, emphasizing the causal and integrated role that an external element plays within the overall cognitive system. In practice, experience is distributed between the subject and the world, as it occurs through the use of tools, artifacts, and technologies that expand the individual's cognitive capacities. This perspective helps to understand how experiential learning is made possible by the organism–environment integration, and how technologies and artifacts can amplify both the experience itself and the reflection that arises from it.

2.5 Enactivism

Enactivism represents the most radical perspective within 4E Cognition Theory. According to this theory, cognition does not consist of representing a preexisting world, but of bringing forth a meaningful world through active interaction between the organism and its environment. Knowledge is thus understood as a co-construction of meaning; to know is to "bring forth a world," where perception becomes a process of direct and dynamic engagement with the environment. The agent perceives insofar as they act: perception is itself a form of action. "The world is not a pre-given datum, but a domain of meaning continuously brought into existence through the embodied cognitive activity of the agent" [16]. According to this approach, knowledge is not the representation of a preexisting world, but the emergence of meaning through active interaction.

2.6 Body, Technology and Environment

Within the 4E Cognition paradigm, the body represents the convergence point of cognition, emotion, and action, where technology functions as a perceptual and relational extension, and the environment constitutes the vital and symbolic context in which knowledge manifests. Rethinking the role of the body in knowledge implies recognizing that learning is not an isolated mental process, but an act of presence that engages the entirety of the self in relation to the surrounding environment.

Every gesture and posture constitutes a form of relation to the world, a way of producing meaning [17]. Body, technology, and environment are therefore considered interdependent elements of a single knowledge system, structured through processes of perception, action, and reflection. Cognition is not limited to brain activity but manifests as a process of sensory, motor, emotional, and cultural integration.

In this integrated cognitive ecosystem, theater and performative practices become privileged spaces for embodied learning, capable of activating pedagogical practices in which experience translates into knowledge. The continuous dialogue between perception, action, and emotion gives rise to human experience, that is, the way we live, interpret, and make sense of the world.

In this perspective, theater assumes the role of a privileged pedagogical device, as an embodied practice that simultaneously engages cognitive, affective, and relational dimensions [3, 18]. It is through the body that the individual learns, inhabiting perceptual space and constructing meaning. The theatrical experience provides a learning context in which body, voice, gesture, and interaction become instruments of knowledge. Action becomes an intentional and constitutive act of the cognitive experience, consistent with the idea that "there is no perception of the world that does not refer to the acting body" [19]. The body is therefore not merely a didactic medium, but the subject itself of experience and knowledge, the "connective core, the interaction device between person and environment", in an adaptive and mimetic process in which skills and functions are exercised and developed [18].

From this perspective, technology is interpreted not as an alien or dehumanizing element, but as a perceptual and relational extension of the body, a true sensory prosthesis capable of intensifying and expanding the educational experience [20, 21].

The intersection of these three axes, embodiment, performativity, and technological mediation, defines a pedagogy of the *Connected Body*: theater and digital technologies in the training of future teachers, where education becomes both an aesthetic and cognitive experience. In this vision, learning means inhabiting the onlife world with sensory and reflective awareness, experiencing knowledge as a living and embodied relation [3, 10, 22, 23].

3 Theatre as Embodied Practice

Theater, more than any other artistic form, restores to the body its original function as a site of knowing. It is not merely an aesthetic language, but a mode of thought, a device that allows one to understand the world through direct and sensory experience. In an educational context, theater becomes a space for experimentation in which the body functions as a research tool, and relationships are configured as a field of shared knowledge. The theatrical act is founded on the encounter between presences, on the perceptual reciprocity between those who act and those who observe. It is a form of knowledge expressed through cohabiting the same space-time.

The learning that emerges from this process is not linear, but relational, in which the other becomes part of one's embodied thought. In theatrical work, the body is continually interrogated; it must unlearn habits, reactivate perception, and acknowledge its own vulnerability. The actor, like the educator, learns to inhabit the world through an exercise of presence. Every stage gesture is an act of awareness, a movement born from a quality of listening, listening to oneself, to the other, to the space, and to the rhythm that connects them.

From this perspective, theater training offers a model of education in presence, in which the body becomes a cognitive and affective medium [24]. The theatrical experience suspends the hierarchies between mind and body, between theory and practice. Knowledge is not constructed through concepts, but through embodied actions; one learns by doing, but above all, by feeling what one does. In the educational context, theater restores dignity to the sensory dimension of learning. The stage becomes a symbolic space in which knowledge manifests in the flesh, in the vibrations of the voice, and in shared breath.

In this horizon, education is configured as a performative process, in which every formative act is an event, an occurrence that engages the totality of the person, and the teacher becomes actor, playwright, and director of the lesson [18]. The theatrical action is not representation, but presence, a way of fully inhabiting the educational moment, experiencing it as both an aesthetic and transformative event [3]. The theatrical body is a conscious body, capable of inhabiting the tension between control and surrender. It is a body that does not merely execute, but responds, seeking a truth situated in experience. This type of learning cannot be transmitted, only lived. It is a form of tacit, implicit knowledge that settles in bodily memory and becomes pedagogical competence. Moreover, theater is the place where the body encounters the collective dimension of knowledge. Every scene is a communal act, constructed through constant dialogue among participants. This aspect is essential for the training of future teachers, as educating always entails operating within a relational context. The theatrical experience teaches that knowledge is a shared act, born from trust, listening, and cooperation. The stage thus transforms into an educational microcosm, a laboratory of sensitive democracy in which every voice contributes to the overall meaning of the action [25]. In this sense, theater fully aligns with the logic of *embodied cognition*, as it translates reflection into movement, ideas into gestures, and thought into lived experience. It is knowledge that does not separate, but unites body and mind, action and thought, emotion and language. Theater, therefore, does not teach so much how to act, as how to be present, how to dwell within the complexity of the educational experience with presence, awareness, and openness.

3.1 The Body Between Environment and Technology

Within the pedagogical landscape developed here, technology cannot be interpreted merely as a mediating tool, but as a cognitive environment that transforms the ways of perceiving, acting, and knowing. It integrates into educational processes as a sensory and relational prosthesis, redefining forms of presence and amplifying experiential possibilities. Far from posing a threat to the bodily dimension of learning, technology can become an extension of sensitivity, a lens that sharpens listening and expands the perceptual field [21, 26, 27].

When integrated from an *embodied* perspective, technology participates in a perception ecology in which body, environment, and device dynamically intertwine. It does not replace physical presence, but multiplies it, generating new forms of attention and awareness. Gesture, sound, and light become elements of a complex perceptual composition, in which the human being finds themselves immersed in a field of mediated, but no less authentic, relationships.

Perception, in this sense, is not a purely sensory act but a relational and intentional process: a way of engaging with the world and reorganizing its meaning through embodied experience [28]. Jakob von Uexküll's concept of *Umwelt* provides a valuable interpretive key for understanding this relationship. Every organism lives within its own perceptual world, a bubble of meanings constructed according to its sensory, motor, and emotional capacities. The environment, therefore, is not a neutral container, but a co-constructed horizon, continuously redefined by the interaction with the body that inhabits it [29].

In the educational domain, this means that each student, teacher, and group constructs their own "world of meaning" through the ways in which they perceive, act, and relate. Technology, when embedded in this context, can amplify and diversify these perceptual worlds, offering new thresholds of contact between internal and external, between corporeality and environment. The body is not diminished by digital tools but transformed into a broader sensory field, where perception extends beyond physical limits. The educational experience can thus be understood as a process of relational individuation, in which technology acts not as a barrier but as a threshold for crossing [30]. This vision requires a pedagogy capable of recognizing the complexity of mediated experience, not a merely instrumental use of technology, but a perceptual education that teaches how to "feel through" it. Teacher training must therefore promote a listening capacity able to navigate between real and virtual, between presence and distance, developing an intermedial sensitivity that integrates body, mind, and environment. In this direction, technology can be interpreted as an aesthetic space, a place where knowing transforms into experience, where perception is amplified and relationships become subtler.

From an educational perspective, the natural environment is also not a backdrop or stage setting, but a dialogic actor in the formative process. Outdoor experience fosters sensory reactivation, breaking the perceptual closure typical of school spaces and restoring the body's capacity to orient, breathe, and interact with the living matter of the world. The external environment thus becomes a matrix of meaning: light, sound, temperature, odors, and surfaces participate in the construction of cognitive experience, activating situated and bodily thinking. Outdoor education, in this view, takes the form of a perceptual and relational practice, in which the body reclaims its role as a knowledge tool. Walking, touching, listening, and breathing become cognitive acts that redefine the relationship with knowledge and with others [31].

The relationship between technology and environment is not contradictory, but complementary. Both are extensions of perception, different modalities through which the human being extends their presence. If the natural environment amplifies bodily sensitivity through direct contact, technology broadens its reach through mediation; in both cases, education can guide this extension toward forms of awareness and attentive engagement. In this sense, educational ecology [11] does not oppose the digital to the natural, but integrates them into a system of interactions in which body, environment, and media are co-constructed [32, 33].

When conceived as part of this perceptual ecology, technology contributes to the creation of a pluralistic environment of meaning, in which presence is expanded and perception becomes a field of learning. It acts both as a filter and as a mirror, a threshold through which experience can be reflected upon and intensified.

4 Methodology: Art-Based Research and CReAP+T Model

The methodological framework of the research is rooted in *Art-Based Research* (ABR), an epistemological approach that places artistic practices at the center of the knowledge process.

Originating within the social sciences and education, ABR considers art not as a mere representational tool, but as a form of inquiry and knowledge construction [34]. It is based on the idea that aesthetic languages, visual, performative, narrative, or bodily, allow for the exploration of the complexity of human experience, generating meanings that emerge from action, perception, and imagination.

From this perspective, artistic research becomes a way of thinking through doing, a mode of investigating reality through gesture, sound, movement, and relationship. ABR transcends the distinction between scientific and aesthetic knowledge, recognizing that understanding educational phenomena is also produced through emotion, sensitivity, and bodily engagement. Art thus acts as an embodied epistemic device, capable of making inner processes visible and translating participants' lived experiences into a tangible form. Applied to the educational context, this perspective acknowledges the pedagogical value of aesthetic experience [10]: to learn means to participate in a transformative event in which thought takes shape and experience becomes shared knowledge. ABR allows for the analysis of this dynamic through qualitative tools that combine observation, narration, and artistic reflection, offering a flexible and relational methodological framework.

Within this framework, the research was developed through the CReAP+T approach (Corporeality, Creativity, Relation, Emotion and Empathy, Action, Performativity, and Technology/Training) [35]. The model was conceived as a response to the limits of transmissive pedagogy, made evident during the pandemic transition, and proposes a systemic, non-linear, and transdisciplinary paradigm rooted in theatrical performative practices. CReAP+T integrates disciplinary and pedagogical knowledge, reconfiguring the educational process as a scenic and relational action. Its objective is to promote embodied, transformative, and creative learning, based on the integration of body, emotion, and thought, and capable of developing essential non-cognitive competencies for the training of contemporary teachers and educators.

The acronym CReAP+T summarizes its foundational pillars:

- *Corporeality*, understood as awareness of the body in action and as the primary site of knowledge;
- *Creativity*, as the capacity to generate divergent and flexible connections;
- *Relation*, understood as co-evolutionary dialogue between subjects and environments;

- *Emotion*, as a cognitive engine that guides attention and memory;
- *Empathy*, understood as the ability to recognize, understand, and share one's own and others' emotional states;
- *Action*, as a principle of experiential and transformative learning;
- *Performativity*, as the aesthetic and scenic quality of the educational act;
- *+Technology/Training*, as a sensory and cognitive extension of the body, capable of amplifying presence and perception.

The method operates through three fundamental pillars, which constitute the grammar of its educational action:

1. *The Protected Setting*

This is the preliminary condition in which the educational space is constructed as a safe and welcoming place, free from judgment and open to vulnerability. In this environment, mistakes are recognized as opportunities for discovery, and diversity becomes a resource. The setting creates conditions for trust, suspension of control, and openness to experience, laying the foundation for genuinely participatory learning.

2. *Bodily Training*

Derived from actor training, this represents the sensory and performative core of the method. Through exercises in breathing, attention, movement, and voice, the training activates a dimension of conscious presence and perceptual awakening. It is a process of alignment between body, mind, and space, in which educators and students learn to "feel themselves" and to "feel" the other. Bodily training thus becomes an embodied epistemic act that prepares participants for creative and relational action.

3. *The Autopoietic Feedback Loop*

This is the dynamic moment of co-created learning. It is not a unidirectional feedback, but a process of mutual transformation that emerges within the interactive flow of the relationship. The teacher, like the actor, constructs their educational action in response to the bodily and emotional signals of the group. In this perspective, the lesson is not a predefined sequence, but a performative event generated in the present, through the continuous adaptation between teaching and learning.

4. *Attention to Presence*

This does not refer to mere physical attendance or simple spatial placement in the classroom, but rather to an active, intentional and mindful presence, which involves attention, openness to listening, bodily, emotional, and cognitive engagement, as well as the ability to fully inhabit the educational moment.

The integration of these three elements realizes a performative pedagogy founded on presence and listening, in which knowledge is constructed through gesture, voice, and relationship. The integration of these three elements creates a performative pedagogy based on the body in action and in relation, where knowledge is not transmitted but embodied and experienced, emphasizing presence, listening, gesture, voice, and relational engagement. The body, understood as *bios scenico* [25], is the driving center of the formative process: not a tool, but the subject of knowledge.

The technological dimension, indicated by the "+ T", further expands the experiential field of the method. Digital technologies are conceived as sensory and relational environments capable of generating new forms of proximity and interaction. In this perspective, technology does not separate but intensifies presence, becoming a perceptual threshold through which body, voice, and space are renegotiated [30].

4.1 Research Design and Participants

The research design adopted is configured as a pilot study with a predominantly qualitative approach. The exploratory investigation aims to observe how theatrical practices, rooted in corporeality and sensory experience, can interact with technological environments and support the development of bodily, emotional, and relational awareness in students. The research is situated within the framework of studies based on performative practices and embodied learning processes, focusing not on the product of learning but on the experiential process through which it is generated, transformed, and manifested in the educational relationship.

The study involved approximately three hundred students enrolled in the degree programs in Primary Education and Educational Sciences at the Suor Orsola Benincasa University of Naples, who, during the 2024/2025 academic year, participated in the mandatory workshops on *Performative Didactic Dramaturgy*, based on the experimental application of the CReAP+T method. The entire program consisted of two three-hour sessions per group, alternating between in-person activities and interactions mediated by technology. The laboratory design was constructed to operationalize the three core components of the CReAP+T approach, the protected setting, bodily training, and autopoietic feedback loop, which guided both the educational design and data collection.

4.2 The Protected Setting

Each session began with the construction of the relational and symbolic space of the workshop. The physical environment, whether indoors or outdoors, was prepared as a space of suspended judgment and welcoming of diversity, promoting reciprocal listening and sensory exploration.

Bodily Training

The central component of each session consisted of sensory and performative training aimed at awakening presence and bodily awareness. Exercises, derived from theater pedagogy, included practices of breathing, mindful walking, voice listening, and spatial perception. The activity took place in a hybrid mode: part of the group operated in the classroom, while another part, connected in real time via earphones through Google Meet, moved freely in the open spaces of the university, particularly the garden, following the teacher's voice as a sonic guide.

This mode allowed participants to experience two different perceptual conditions:

- *In-person*, based on direct relationships and bodily contact;
- *Mediated*, where technology functioned as a perceptual magnifying lens, enhancing internal listening and concentration.

The alternation between the two experiences allowed for the exploration of whether and how technology intensified or hindered the quality of the sensory and relational experience.

The Autopoietic Feedback Loop

The concluding phase of each session was dedicated to a moment of shared reflection and feedback. Teachers and students participated in an autopoietic dialogical process, in which the experience was re-elaborated through words, gestures, drawings, or brief performative actions. Feedback was not intended as evaluation, but as an act of collective awareness, allowing the group to regenerate meaning from the lived experience.

Attention to Presence

In each session, students were required to maintain active presence, fostering bodily and emotional engagement through theatrical *training* activities and the *feedback* provided by the instructor. This created a dynamic, relational and transformative condition in which the individual genuinely participates in the learning process and the construction of meaning.

4.3 Data Collection Tools

Data collection was conducted through a multi-method approach consistent with the qualitative and performative nature of the study. The instruments were designed to capture the complexity of the observed educational phenomenon, with particular attention to participants' experiential, relational, and perceptual dimensions. In line with the principles of Art-Based Research, assessment did not aim to measure isolated variables, but to reconstruct meanings emerging from experience, through the triangulation of observation, narration, and self-perception. Three main tools were used for data collection:

Participant Observations

The workshop sessions were monitored through a participant observation protocol conducted by the teachers and researchers involved. The aim was to systematically document group dynamics, modes of interaction, levels of participation, and behavioral variations related to different settings (in-person and technology-mediated).

Direct observation allowed for the capture of aspects that are difficult to verbalize, constituting the subtle fabric of non-verbal communication and bodily presence.

Reflective Journals

At the end of each session, participants completed an individual reflective journal, structured through guiding questions designed to encourage personal elaboration of the experience. Sample questions included:

- How was this lesson for you? Describe what struck you the most and how you experienced it.
- Which exercises did you perform? Was there one that challenged you or that you particularly enjoyed? Why?
- What role did technology play in today's lesson? How did it influence your experience?
- Did you notice any differences in your perception of your body or emotions compared to the in-person training? In what way?

The reflective journals constituted the primary source of qualitative narrative data, allowing access to the subjective dimension of bodily experience and self-perception in relation to the environment. Text analysis was conducted using a thematic interpretive approach, aiming to identify core meanings related to presence, listening, bodily resonance, and technological mediation.

Pre/Post-Experience Questionnaires

To complement the qualitative evidence with descriptive quantitative elements, pre- and post-experience questionnaires were administered, specifically designed for the laboratory context. The questionnaires included both closed- and open-ended questions aimed at investigating:

- Modes of participation (Did you participate in the training in-person or online?);
- Perceived emotional state (How do you feel now? Options included happy, calm, motivated, relaxed, anxious, fearful, stressed, etc.);
- Subjective representation of the experience (Which word do you associate with the emotion or mood you selected?).

Comparing the data collected before and after the experience allowed for the identification of changes in participants' levels of well-being, concentration, and relational availability, providing empirical feedback on the transformative processes observed qualitatively. Overall, the triangulation of observations, journals, and questionnaires allowed for the construction of a multi-level map of the formative experience, capturing both the subjective and affective dimension as well as the relational and environmental one.

An analytical coding procedure was also established, aimed at organizing and making interpretable the diverse and complex qualitative data, in order to ensure greater methodological transparency and rigor in the interpretation of the results. Specifically:

- *Preliminary review of materials:* The field diaries, observations, and responses to the questionnaires (pre- and post-workshop experience) were analyzed to ensure a careful overall understanding of the students' lived experiences;
- *Identification of the most significant activities:* In relation to the research objectives, participants' bodily expressions, emotions, and reflections considered most meaningful were analyzed;
- *Grouping into thematic areas:* To highlight recurring patterns and dynamics within the workshop experience;
- *Interpretation of results:* The emerging themes were interpreted in light of the research objectives and the CReAP+T experimental approach, allowing an understanding of how the integration of theatre and digital technologies can be significant in the training of future teachers.

5 Results

The data analysis highlighted the formative and experiential effects of the *Performative Didactic Dramaturgy* workshop, exploring how bodily and theatrical practices, integrated with the use of technology, influenced participants' emotional, perceptual, and relational dimensions.

The results are presented from a dual perspective: on one hand, a quantitative reading, which shows variations in emotional states and perceived well-being as measured through the pre (Fig. 1) and post (Fig. 2) experience questionnaires; on the other hand, a qualitative perspective, which delves into the subjective experiences emerging from reflective journals and participant observations. This dual articulation allows for capturing both the general trends of the formative experience and the narrative depth of the individual and collective transformations generated by the workshop.

1. Quantitative Findings

Analysis of the pre/post questionnaires shows a clear improvement in emotional indicators and perceived well-being. In both sessions, there was a significant decrease in states of anxiety and stress, accompanied by a corresponding increase in positive emotions (happiness, calmness, relaxation, and motivation).

pre- training first session	**post- training first session**
339 in-persone 51 online	339 in-person 51 online
• **21 HAPPY 6,00 %**	• **78 HAPPY 20,00%**
• 20 nervous 5,7%	• 14 nervous 3,6%
• <u>38 students (calm)10,9%</u>	• <u>64 students (calm) 16,4%</u>
• **46 anxious 13,2%**	• **8 anxious 2,1%**
• 6 demotivated 1,7%	• 0 demotivated 0,00%
• 5 joyful 1,4%	• 24 joyful 2,6%
• **<u>28 Students (relaxed) 8,00%</u>**	• **<u>95 Students (relaxed) 24,4%</u>**
• **63 stressed 18,1%**	• **6 stressed 1,5%**

Fig. 1.

2. Qualitative Insights from Reflective Journals

Thematic analysis of the reflective journals was conducted on a selected sample of participants, prioritizing the accounts of those who participated in technology-mediated training. This choice was made to deepen the perceptual and relational dimension activated by the conscious use of digital devices, exploring how sound mediation and remote connection influenced the quality of bodily and sensory experience. Although this subgroup is numerically smaller compared to the total number of participants, their narratives proved particularly rich and meaningful, offering a privileged perspective for

pre- training *Second session*	post-training *Second session*
358 in-person 39 online	358 in-person 39 online
• 30 nervous 7,6%	• 8 nervous 2,1%
• 49 students (calm) 12,3%	• 75 students (calm) 19,3%
• 25 anxious 6,3%	• 10 anxious 2,6%
• 19 motivated 4,8%	• 26 motivated 6,7%
• 19 demotivated 4,8%	• 5 demotivated 1,3%
• 11 joyful 2,8%	• 16 joyful 4,1%
• 11 Students (relaxed) 2,8%	• 92 Students (relaxed) 23,7%
• 63 stressed 15,9%	• 7 stressed 1,8%

Fig. 2.

understanding the processes of presence, concentration, and introspection activated in the hybrid context of the workshop. The thematic analysis revealed four main cores of meaning that structure participants' experiences:

a) Presence and Bodily Awareness

Most students described the training as a moment of reconnection with themselves and with the environment, an experience that activated attention, listening, and bodily sensitivity. Many participants spoke of the "body as a compass" for the experience, rediscovered in its capacity to orient emotions and thoughts.

"It was like putting the outside world on pause to truly listen to my body and my emotions, without filters or distractions."

This rediscovery was accompanied by a sense of authenticity and freedom: the body, freed from perceptual and social constraints, became a space for knowledge and presence.

b) Emotional and Transformative Dimension

The training was perceived as an intensely emotional experience, capable of triggering reflection, vulnerability, and catharsis. Several students reported moments of emotional release, describing the workshop as a space for personal acceptance and discovery:

"I recognized my own need to express emotions and to accept my vulnerabilities."

The experience generated a transformative metacognitive process: students gained greater awareness of the connection between emotion, body, and learning, acknowledging the importance of non-verbal language in educational relationships.

c) The Role of Technology: Threshold and Perceptual Lens

Technology was perceived as a means to amplify perception, rather than as an obstacle. Sound mediation through headphones and the connection via Google Meet created an immersive isolation that intensified listening and concentration.

"Technology made an individual experience possible within a collective context, intimate yet shared."

"Through the headphones, I could hear the teacher's voice, but also the rain, the wind, the sound of the trees."

"Technology protected me; I felt freer without fear of judgment."

"With the headphones, it seemed the voice was speaking only to me; I was more focused and less distracted."

This combination of intimacy and connection generated a new form of presence: a hybrid experience in which technology acted as a sensory threshold rather than a distance. Bodily perception was, in many cases, more intense than in traditional training, with increased concentration and reduced exposure anxiety.

d) The Environment as an Educational Space

The university's natural context, particularly the garden, played a decisive role. Students described the outdoor dimension as regenerative and resonant, able to break the rigidity of the classroom and restore fluidity to the educational relationship.

"Being in a place different from the classroom helped me free my mind and feel part of the context."

"The natural environment made the exercise much more intense and meaningful... even university spaces normally marginal became an active part of the experience."

The environment was perceived as a co-agent of the experience: rain, wind, and natural sounds contributed to the creation of a full sensory experience, in which body, space, and technology intertwined harmoniously.

6 Discussion

The quantitative results from the pre- and post-experience questionnaires show the positive impact of the theatrical training on students' emotional dimension.

In both sessions, there was a significant decrease in anxiety and stress levels, accompanied by a corresponding increase in positive emotions, happiness, calmness, and relaxation, with an even more pronounced trend in the second session.

This pattern suggests that progressive familiarity with the performative pathway strengthened participants' ability to concentrate and engage in bodily listening, allowing them to inhabit the relationship between body, emotion, and environment with greater awareness. This effect can be attributed to a process of affective and cognitive regulation triggered by the aesthetic and sensory experience of the training, consistent with the perspective of *embodied cognition* [28] and transformative learning [36].

Alongside the quantitative data, the qualitative analysis of the reflective journals captures the experiential depth of this process. A crucial element concerns the subgroup of students who participated in technology-mediated training, numerically small but qualitatively highly significant. Despite the limited sample size, the journals collected in this condition provide extremely promising evidence, both in terms of descriptive richness and the density of reflections. The accounts indicate that technology, integrated into the performative setting, did not reduce the intensity of the experience; on the contrary, it amplified its perceptual and emotional component.

Many students describe the sensation of being in a "perceptual bubble," an intimate listening condition in which the body is perceived with greater clarity and freedom.

The testimonies confirm that technology, when used with pedagogical awareness and intentionality, can act as a sensory magnifying lens, fostering concentration and didactic trust. The concept of *Umwelt* finds concrete validation here: each participant constructed a personal perceptual space, an experiential microcosm that, while individual, remained in dialogue with the collective group.

The mediated experience, therefore, did not fragment the educational relationship but reconfigured it into new forms of intimacy, presence, and attentive listening.

Another key element emerging from the journals concerns the role of the physical environment as co-author of the formative experience. The university garden, rain, wind, and natural sounds were perceived not as neutral backgrounds but as active sensory agents capable of stimulating attention, relaxation, and awareness.

This dimension confirms that learning does not occur in isolation, but in constant interaction between body, space, and context. The combination of theater, technology, and environment produced a formative condition in which the boundaries between presence and distance, inside and outside, individual and collective dissolve, creating a truly embodied, relational, and situated experience.

From a methodological perspective, the overall results validate the operational coherence of the CReAP+T model, showing how its structure, protected setting, bodily training, and autopoietic feedback loop, can activate processes of reflection, emotional regulation, and transformative learning.

The experience suggests that the technological dimension of the model (+T) does not represent an accessory extension but a constitutive element that broadens the perceptual and relational scope of training, dynamically integrating corporeality and digital mediation.

7 Conclusion and Future Directions

This research confirms that theater and technology do not represent antagonistic dimensions, but complementary poles within the same educational horizon, grounded in conscious and relational corporeality. The laboratory experience has shown that when technology is intentionally integrated into a performative setting, it does not weaken the quality of bodily experience; on the contrary, it amplifies perceptual and emotional resonance, acting as a catalyst for attention, listening, and presence.

Theater, as an embodied practice, continues to represent a privileged pathway for the holistic development of the person, capable of activating processes of awareness, empathy, and transformation. In interaction with the technological dimension, it now finds a new possibility for extension and adaptation to contemporary educational contexts, which are increasingly hybrid, distributed, and interconnected.

The synergy between theatrical practices and digital media restores to education its aesthetic and experiential nature: a form of knowledge constructed through the body, relational interaction, and sensory engagement with the environment.

From this perspective, the body is no longer merely a conduit for learning but becomes its epistemic site, the point where thought, emotion, and action intersect to generate meaning. The experience with technology, far from diminishing presence, can become a threshold for perceptual intensification, fostering new modes of attention and introspection.

Theater, in turn, offers digital media a relational grammar, teaching how to inhabit space, manage time, and build trust even through a screen. The integration of these two dimensions fosters the creation of inclusive and multimodal learning environments, in which each participant can find their own mode of expression and engagement.

The body, voice, and gaze transform into instruments of connection, while technology becomes a means to democratize the educational experience, capable of modulating distances, expanding access, and valuing differences.

In this sense, the pedagogical relationship assumes a more fluid and dialogic form, oriented not toward the transmission of knowledge but toward the co-construction of embodied meanings. However, the short duration of the program, consisting of only two sessions per group, represents a potential limitation of the study, as a limited number of sessions may restrict the depth of the experimentation, the gradual development of bodily and emotional skills, and the opportunity to observe more significant developments and transformations in the participants.

For the future, we intend to expand the research to new contexts and disciplines, examining whether and to what extent digitally mediated bodily awareness can generate lasting effects on daily educational practice and on the management of relational complexity in classrooms.

1 Nadia Carlomagno is the author of the paper. She is the main researcher of the project; she wrote the Sect. 1 "Introduction", the Sect. 2 "Theoretical Framework", the Sect. 2.1 "4E Cognition Theory", the Sect. 2.2 "Embodied Cognition", the Sect. 2.3 "Situated and Embedded Cognition", the Sect. 2.4 "Extended Mind", the Sect. 2.5 "Enactivism", the Sect. 2.6 "Body, technology and environment", the Sect. 3. "Theatre as Embodied Practice", the Sect. 3.1 "The Body Between Environment and Technology" and the Sect. 4. "Methodology: Art-Based Research and CReAP+T Model"; 2 Valeria Vadalá is the co-author of the paper, she wrote the Sect. 6 "Discussion" and the Sect. 7. "Conclusion and Future Directions"; 3 Arianna Ricciardi is the co-author of the paper, she wrote the Sect. 4.1 "Research Design and Participants", the Sect. 4.2 "The Protected Setting", the Sect. 4.3 "Data Collection Tools" and the Sect. 5 "Results".

Disclosure of Interests. The authors have no competing interests to declare that are relevant to the content of this article.

References

1. Floridi, L.: The Onlife Manifesto: Being Human in a Hyperconnected Era. Springer Nature (2015)
2. Carlomagno, N.: I linguaggi non lineari della narrazione e della comunicazione nella scena e nella didattica. Scholé-Morcelliana, Brescia (2023)
3. Grotowski, J.: Vers un théâtre pauvre. L'Âge d'Homme, Losanna (1965)
4. Frauenfelder, E.: Perché una relazione tra pedagogia e biologia? Sezione RTH Brain Education Cognition, Napoli (2018)
5. Carlomagno, N.: Le potenzialità didattiche delle arti sceniche. Education Sciences and Society. (2020)
6. Frauenfelder, E., Santoianni, F.: a cura di. Le scienze bioeducative. Prospettive di ricerca (p. 39). Napoli, Liguori (2002)
7. Lakoff, G., Johnson, M.: Metaphors we Live by. University of Chicago Press, Chicago (1982)
8. Caruana, F., Borghi, A.: Il cervello in azione. Il Mulino, Bologna (2016)
9. Gallese, V., Fadiga, L., Fogassi, L., Rizzolatti, G.: Action recognition in the premotor cortex. Brain. **119**(Pt 2) (1996)
10. Dewey, J.: Experience and Education. Kappa Delta Pi, Indianapolis (1938)
11. Bateson, G.: Mente e natura. Adelphi, Milano (1972)
12. Ingold, T.: Being Alive. Routledge, London–New York (2011)
13. Clark, A., Chalmers, D.J.: The extended mind. Analysis. **58** (1998)
14. Wilson, R.A.: Boundaries of the Mind: the Individual in the Fragile Sciences: Cognition. Cambridge University Press, Cambridge (UK) (2004)
15. Menary, R. (ed.): The Extended Mind. MIT Press, Cambridge (MA) (2010)
16. Varela, F.J., Thompson, E., Rosch, E.: The Embodied Mind, Revised Edition: Cognitive Science and Human Experience. MIT Press, Cambridge (MA) (2017)
17. La Berthoz, A.: simplexité. Odile Jacob, Paris (2009)
18. Carlomagno, N.: Pratiche performative teatrali nella formazione di competenze didattiche. Nuova Secondaria, 40(10). La Scuola: Brescia (2022)
19. Berthoz, A., Petit, J.L.: Phénoménologie et physiologie de l'action. Odile Jacob, Paris (2006)
20. McLuhan, M.: Gli strumenti del comunicare. Il Saggiatore, Milano (2023)
21. Laurillard, D.: Insegnamento come scienza della progettazione. Costruire modelli pedagogici per apprendere con le tecnologie. FrancoAngeli, Milano (2014)
22. Montessori, M.: Il metodo della pedagogia scientifica applicato all'educazione infantile nelle Case dei Bambini. Maglione e Strini, Roma (1909)
23. Gallese, V., Morelli, U.: Cosa significa essere umani? Corpo, cervello e relazione per vivere nel presente. Raffaello Cortina Editore, Milano (2024)
24. Brook, P.: The Empty Space. Penguin Books, London (1968)
25. Barba, E., Savarese, N.: L'arte segreta dell'attore. Dizionario di antropologia teatrale (ried. 1995). Bulzoni, Roma (2011)
26. Rivoltella, P.C., et al.: Fare didattica con gli EAS. Episodi di apprendimento situato. La Scuola, Brescia (2013)
27. Carlomagno, N., Cordella, F.M., Minghelli, V., Rivoltella, P.C.: Performative didactics in a technological environment. REM. **13**(1), 2037–0830 (2021)
28. Merleau-Ponty, M.: Phénoménologie de la perception. Gallimard, Paris (1945)
29. Von Uexküll, J.: Mondes animaux et monde humain. (P. Müller, Trans.). Denoël, Paris (1965)
30. Simondon, G.: L'individuazione psichica e collettiva. Roma, DeriveApprodi (2001)
31. Waite, S. (ed.): Children Learning outside the Classroom. Routledge, London (2017)
32. Berthoz, A.: La semplessità (tr. it.). Codice, Torino (2011)
33. Sibilio, M.: L'interazione didattica. Scholé-Morcelliana, Brescia (2020)

34. Leavy, P.: Method Meets Art: Arts-Based Research Practice. Guilford Press, New York (2020)
35. Carlomagno, N., Minghelli, V.: Interpersonal distance in the CReAP+T method in distance learning. In: Casalino, G., et al. (eds.) Methodologies and Technologies for Online Higher Education Learning. HELMeTO 2021, pp. 199–214. Springer, Cham (2022)
36. Mezirow, J.: Transformative Dimensions of Adult Learning. Jossey-Bass, San Francisco (1991)

The Value of Blended MOOCs: A Return on Investment Perspective

Simona Ferrari[1(✉)] and Annarita Merigo[2]

[1] Cremit, Catholic University of the Sacred Heart, Milan, Italy
simona.ferrari@unicatt.it
[2] Ilab, Catholic University of the Sacred Heart, Milan, Italy
annarita.merigo1@unicatt.it

Abstract. This article examines the sustainability of Massive Open Online Courses (MOOCs) developed by CREMIT (Research Centre on Media Education, Innovation and Technology), in collaboration with ILAB (Innovation for Digital Didactics) of the Università Cattolica del Sacro Cuore, adopting a Return on Investment (ROI) perspective that integrates economic, institutional, and pedagogical dimensions. Since 2014, CREMIT has produced 39 MOOCs within the University's Third Mission, addressing diverse professional audiences. Recognizing the high organizational and financial costs associated with MOOC development, particularly in the post-Covid context, the authors propose a lifecycle-based analysis structured around three stages: Development, Management, and Improvement. Drawing on monitoring data, learning analytics, and participant feedback, the study identifies criteria for determining when a MOOC reaches the end of its lifecycle, including content obsolescence, updating costs, participant numbers, and engagement indicators. The paper conceptualizes ROI not as direct monetization, but as a combination of reputational impact, communication value, educational marketing potential, user loyalty, democratization of knowledge, and community building. To maximize both economic and pedagogical returns, the authors propose the "blended MOOC" as a strategic model integrating online courses within face-to-face or hybrid educational pathways. Empirical evidence from five blended formats demonstrates their effectiveness in enhancing teaching processes, fostering active learning, and extending educational impact. The study ultimately argues that MOOCs, when supported by a structured lifecycle and ROI framework, represent a strategic investment for higher education institutions, capable of bridging teaching, research, and public engagement while promoting sustainable and inclusive knowledge dissemination.

Keywords: MOOCs sustainability · MOOCs lifecycle · Blended MOOCs · ROI strategy

1 Introduction and Objectives

Since 2014, CREMIT (Research Centre on Media Education, Innovation and Technology), in collaboration with ILAB (Innovation for Digital Didactics) of the Università Cattolica del Sacro Cuore, has been producing and delivering MOOCs as part of the University's Third Mission. Overall, it has delivered 39 MOOCs dealing with the topic of

M. Adamoli et al. (Eds.): HELMeTO 2025, CCIS 2958, pp. 53–68, 2026.
https://doi.org/10.1007/978-3-032-31850-3_4

digital education, aimed at teachers, educators, psychologists, communications workers, pastoral workers, journalists, healthcare workers, and university students.

The creation of a MOOC (Massive Open Online Course) requires a significant organizational effort and has a considerable economic impact. The costs include both the use of advanced digital technologies and the employment of human resources in the various stages of its life cycle.

This aspect, combined with the characteristics of post-Covid MOOCs—focused on brevity, reusability of teaching materials, and the need for constant updating—led CREMIT to reflect on the sustainability of the production process and the design of a return on investment (ROI) program. The aim was to preserve free access to courses, maintain a high quality standard, and avoid reducing them to mere showcase tools for educational marketing.

This contribution outlines the adopted ROI strategy. In particular, it aims to:

1. provide a snapshot of the state of the art of MOOCs delivered so far and their resilience, through monitoring data analysis, in order to understand when a MOOC can be considered completed in its life cycle;
2. understand how design choices impact the cost of a MOOC by highlighting elements that shape ROI;
3. identify blended-instruction as a possible strategy of ROI.

2 MOOCs Lifecycle

To structure an effective return on investment proposal, it is necessary to start from the life cycle of a MOOC. The set of phases that a MOOC goes through, from its conception to its closure, serves as a guide not only for project management from an educational/pedagogical perspective—helping to plan, monitor, and verify the achievement of the established objectives—but also for the strategic planning of costs and partnerships. The three main phases that make up the life cycle of a MOOC, following the model proposed by Sanchez-Gordon & Luján-Mora [1], are: Development, Management, Improvement (Fig. 1). We begin here with a revision of this model considering CREMIT's MOOCs.

2.1 MOOCs Lifecycle Developed by CREMIT-Università Cattolica

Stage 1: Development. In the first stage, Development, the activities include the phases of course conceptualization and design, with the definition of objectives and the educational model, the structuring of the project team, and the planning of the communication strategy. The production phase (Construction) includes the development of original learning materials, video lectures, and learning objects, as well as the selection of complementary resources, such as OER. A coordinated graphic/visual intervention completes the production period, which ends with the upload on the platform. The software testing phase proposed in the Sanchez-Gordon & Luján-Mora model does not apply in this case, as it is the responsibility of the platform managers.

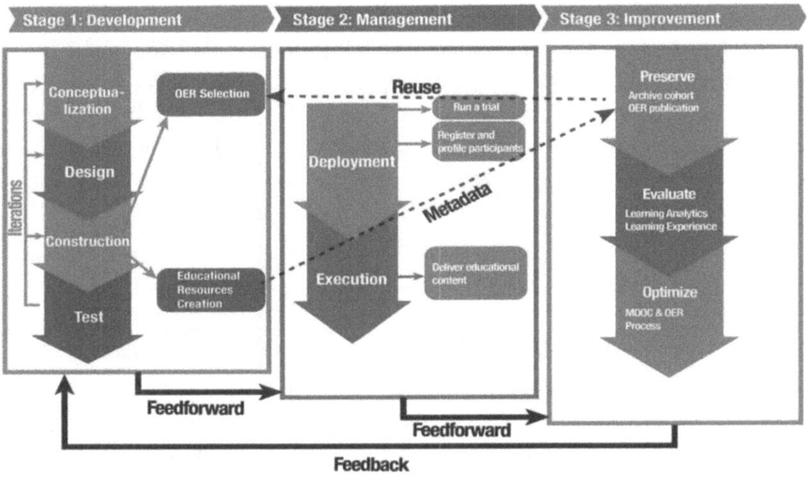

Fig. 1. MOOC lifecycle. Source: Sanchez-Gordon, S., Luján-Mora, S.: Lifecycle for MOOC Development and Management (2018).

In this first internship, CREMIT pays particular attention to the pedagogical model, which has undergone significant changes, especially in the transition from pre to post-Covid. In fact, in the pre-Covid period the pedagogical model guiding CREMIT MOOCs was rooted in four key principles: the social dimension of learning [2], the knowledge-building approach [3, 4], relational pedagogy [5] and a third space pedagogy strategy [6]. In the construction, CREMIT decided to base each module, which could be browsed either sequentially or hyper-textually, on created new educational resources following these elements:

- a quotation card aiming at attracting learners and activating their thinking;
- the specific learning objectives;
- two online video-lectures enriched by keywords and a final conceptual map;
- 2 or 3 in depth cultural and pedagogical materials that explain and enrich keywords;
- one e-tivity for enabling active and participative online learning [7];
- 2 or 3 bibliographic references;
- 2 or 3 existing OER selected and adapted for the module;
- a final test based on closed questions. Learners could complete the quiz once and then revise the given answers.

Each MOOC consisted of 8 content modules and an initial socialization and learning contract module, as a warm-up and ice-breaking phase. Learners were involved in different activities aiming at building an online community, welcoming them and verifying their access to the course [7, 8].

The final certificate of completion was automatically released through the platform to show the learning outcomes of the course and to give students' employers or institutions a visual proof of the attended path [9].

The four principles have been adapted to the post-Covid education scenario: a shift toward micro-learning (brevity and speed), ubiquitous learning (independent of spatial constraints, balancing synchronous and asynchronous elements), learner-centered approaches (catering to individual interests and needs), and the development of dynamic literacies [10]. Comparing pre and post-Covid model, we observe changes in time structures, an increase in self-paced learning, reduced feedback mechanisms, and fewer dedicated communication spaces (Table 1).

Table 1. Pre-Covid and post-Covid MOOCs. Design elements.

	Pre-Covid (2014–2021)	Post-Covid (2021–2025)*
Platform	Open Education by Blackboard	EduOpen
Orientation	FAQ	FAQ + minitutorial
Materials	Videolessons + materials + e-tivity	Videolessons + materials + e-tivity
Timing	Timed: weekly release	Open
Duration	8 modules	5–6 modules
Training hours	25	25
Tutoring	Asynchronous + synchronous	Light tutoring, asynchronous
Communication	Alerts, e-mail, 6 threads in forum	1 thread in forum
Assessment	End of module test	End of module test
Certification	Certificate	Certificate
Monitoring	Initial and final questionnaire	Final questionnaire

aLast updated date: August 14, 2025.

The first stage, Development, has a significant impact on costs. Consider all the reflection and research that goes into defining the pedagogical model and designing and producing the materials (see § 3.1).

Stage 2: Management. In the second stage of the lifecycle, the MOOC is deployed and executed. When the MOOC is made available (Deployment), it is accessible in an "introductory" mode, with a cover page displaying its main information and offering the possibility of enrollment. This phase lasts 2 weeks and allows for final checks of the content (Run a trial) by a small team (teachers, SMEs, tutors, instructional designers).

This is followed by the Execution phase. A new MOOC is always tutored (Pilot). The presence of a tutor has always been a distinctive feature of CREMIT MOOCs and plays a significant role in the pedagogical model [11]. E-tutor act as an observer of the online interaction among learners, as a filter with the staff in case of doubts, and as the community's animator. After the Pilot edition, the MOOC can be offered again either in a tutored or self-paced mode, with a light tutored action to support the social dimension of learning and to assist students in self-regulated learning processes [12]. With regard to cost impact, in stage 2 an important factor is the tutor (see § 3.1), not only for the role of facilitator and communicator with participants, but also for two additional required tasks: the development of the communication plan and FAQs, and the ongoing monitoring of the course (Monitoring), including forum message analysis (total number of messages, number of tutor messages), in order to identify possible redesign elements to be discussed in stage 3.

Stage 3: Improvement. This stage includes the evaluation and optimization of the MOOC for subsequent editions (some materials are updated and new educational resources are made available). At this stage, MOOCs are systematically analysed through evaluation quantitative and qualitative analyses (Evaluate): participants feedback through initial and final questionnaires, learning analytics (access, completion levels, forum message analysis, retention), focus groups and interviews (learning experience). This activity aims to provide specific feedbacks on the MOOC in order to determine the choice between two options: to relaunch the MOOC with a subsequent and updated edition (Optimize), or to hand it over to an additional working team (Community). The latter constitutes the final stage of the MOOC lifecycle but, at the same time, becomes a space for active discussion and exchange aimed at revitalizing the course according to the training needs of the moment [10]. The Community is supported by archiving tools (Preserve), which can ensure digital consultation of the contents.

From a cost perspective, the economic resources required in stage 3 are more limited compared to the other phases (see § 3.1), as they relate only to evaluation and optimization activities. The Community is excluded from this calculation.

The complete lifecycle of CREMIT MOOCs, in light of the Sanchez-Gordon & Luján-Mora model referenced at the beginning, is revised as follows (Fig. 2). The stage undergoing substantial modifications is the third, which is why we devote further analysis to it in the next paragraph.

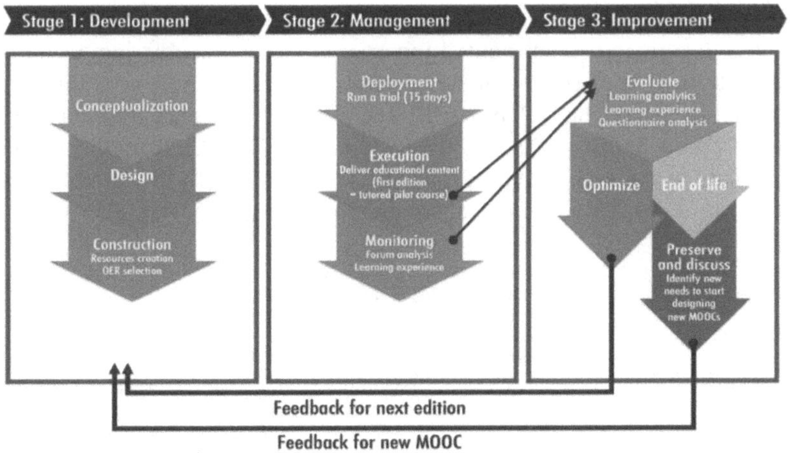

Fig. 2. CREMIT MOOCs complete lifecycle.

2.2 When Does a MOOC End its Life Cycle?

When can a MOOC be considered exhausted, that is, has its life cycle ended? After how many editions and based on what criteria? The ex-post evaluation included in stage 3 (Evaluate) examines three elements in particular: 1. Content consistency and cost of updating; 2. Number of participants; 3. Final monitoring and learning analytics data.

1. **Content consistency and cost of updating.** The first element leads to reflection on the timing and forms of knowledge updating, on digital-related content, and on how the approach to knowledge is changing [13, 14]. MOOCs, in turn, represent a training channel with a high risk of rapid obsolescence. In general, the work on the economic quantification of a MOOC has led us to estimate that the simple integration of learning resources or the need to update content should not exceed 10–15% (a limited economic investment – see § 3.1). This percentage makes a new edition of the MOOC sustainable. Otherwise, the MOOC should be archived.
2. **Number of participants.** MOOCs are mass courses; therefore, the number of participants should be a criterion to decide whether to maintain or archive it. Identifying the "break-even point" in relation to participant numbers is not simple, as it depends on several factors. First of all, MOOCs offered in Italian rather than English restrict the proposal to a specific target audience and cannot be compared with international MOOC data. Language is a necessary requirement in Italy, especially when addressing educational staff. The availability of technical solutions that reduce the costs of developing multilingual MOOCs may represent an opportunity to reach a wider audience. Moreover, at least two types of MOOCs exist: some are related to generalist topics and are therefore suited to attracting a large number of participants, while others focus on specialist themes with smaller expected groups. It would not be appropriate to apply the same numerical parameter, given the importance of using MOOCs to also support specialized training.

Finally, the pre-Covid and post-Covid shift must be considered. The literature shows how MOOCs experienced a substantial increase in user numbers, due to the need to prevent the interruption of education [15]. In Italy and Europe, however, this cannot be used as a criterion, given the lack of legal value of MOOC-issued certificates.

Table 2 presents the survey conducted on CREMIT MOOCs from this perspective. Between generalist and specialist proposals, the ratio is generally 2 to 1, and the decline from pre-Covid to post-Covid stands at around 50%.

Table 2. MOOC Scenario

Time	Tema	No. MOOCs	No. Participants	Mean	% Certificates	% Final Q
Pre-Covid (2014–21)	Broad course	16	18.401	1150	62,5	46,4
	Focused course	6	2.586	431	59,3	41,9
Post-Covid (2021–25)*	Broad course	11	5.726	520	31,4	45,5
	Focused course	6	1.461	243	61,2	81

aLast updated date: August 14, 2025.

To understand the data, it is necessary to observe the trend of participants in each MOOC over the course of the various editions (Figs. 3, 4).

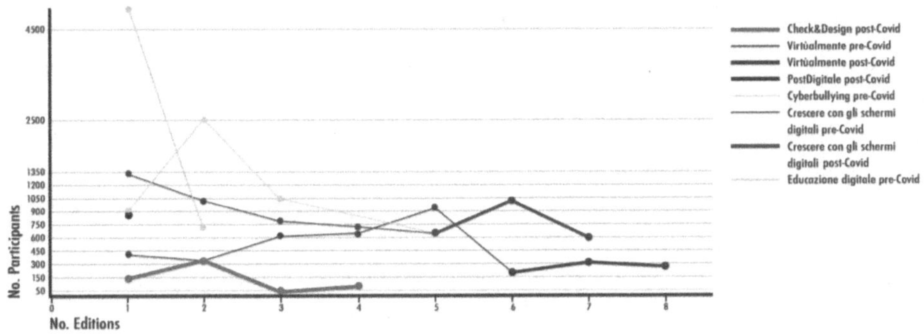

Fig. 3. Broad courses. Trend in the number of participants in the pre- and post-Covid periods.

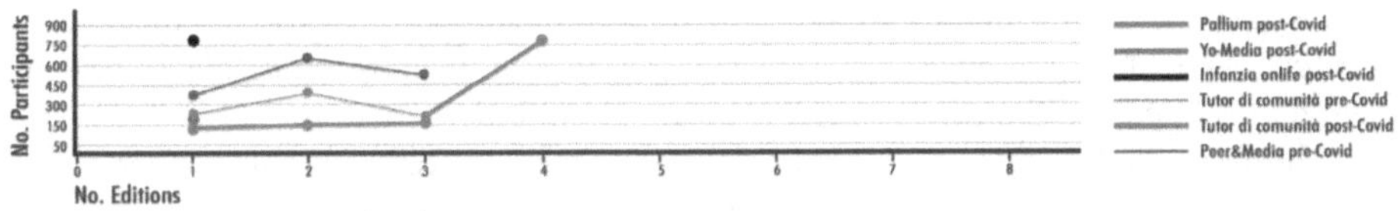

Fig. 4. Focused courses. Trend in the number of participants in the pre- and post-Covid periods.

The decrease in participants observed in the post-Covid period also led, as a consequence, to a decline in certificates issued in generalist-themed MOOCs (Table 2). However, in this regard, the analysis conducted during the ex-post evaluation phase highlighted a particular type of user, mainly interested in the content, who enrolls in multiple editions of the same MOOC but downloads the certificate only once (5.5% of the users of the MOOC "3-6-9-12. Growing up with digital screens" enrolled in three editions; 6.9% of the users of the MOOC "Virtùalmente" enrolled in three editions).

The return of students is an interesting element to CREMIT: in the post-Covid period, up to 8 MOOCs were registered, a sign of the presence of users interested in general culture topics, both generalists and specialists, who independently built a training pathway (Table 3).

Table 3. Retention in post-Covid MOOCs

No. partecipants	Enrolled in 2 MOOCs	Enrolled in 3 MOOCs	Enrolled in 4 MOOCs	Enrolled in 5 MOOCs	Enrolled in 6 MOOCs	Enrolled in 7 MOOCs	Enrolled in 8 MOOCs
7.187	650 9%	143 2%	65 0,9%	32 0,44%	9 0,13%	4 0,06%	3 0,04%

2.3 Final Monitoring and Learning Analytics Data.

The third indicator that guides the choice between re-edition or archiving a MOOC is provided by the collection of monitoring data, combined with learning analytics and initial and final questionnaires. Tracking data indicates that the model was effective in both pre- and post-Covid design:

- completion rate: as we can see in Table 2, a very high rate compared to the 5–10% documented in the literature [16];
- satisfaction: in pre-Covid 49% of the users were completely satisfied, and 36.5% were very satisfied (using a 6-point scale, from 1 = not at all satisfied to 6 = completely) – in post-covid 52% (completely satisfied) and 30% (very satisfied);
- student involvement: in pre-Covid more than 95% viewed all the proposed content; about a quarter (24.91%) are 'communicative' participants and 31% felt involved in a learning community – in post-Covid 79% of participants engaged with all the MOOC content, 47% of respondents rated forum discussions at level 6 on a satisfaction scale, while 44% reported feeling part of a learning community;
- Retention (post-Covid data): out of the total number of participants in post-Covid MOOCs (7,187), 650 enrolled in at least 2 MOOCs, 143 in 3 MOOCs, 65 in 4 MOOCs.
- Social dimension: the qualitative analysis of forums shows that even in self-paced MOOCs, participants are driven to share and engage in discussion with one another – even without the encouragement and moderation of a tutor. The data highlight how MOOCs can serve as incubators for a potential community – aimed at exchanging information, fostering dialogue and personal re-elaboration of the topics addressed, and sharing resources [10].

3 ROI's Proposal

In light of the MOOC lifecycle outlined above, to enhance and capitalize experiences conducted by CREMIT since 2014, it's necessary a ROI's strategy. It should be emphasized that this does not refer to ROI as direct monetization, as literature reports [17, 18], but rather to an indirect economic approach, which also involves extra-financial, institutional, and pedagogical aspects. To do this, it is necessary to review the MOOC lifecycle, assessing the economic impact of the three stages, and identify several ROI channels fitting with openness and cost-free.

3.1 Investment: Cost Items and Sources of Financing

Table 4 reports an overall cost estimate for a MOOC divided into the Development, Management and Improvement stages described in § 2.1.

Table 4. MOOCs lifecycle: cost items

Stage 1. Development	Total Investment (€)	Stage 2. Management	Total Investment (€)	Stage 3. Improvement	Total Investment (€)
Conceptualization + Design + Construction Materials Creation Multimedia Production Platform Graphic Design Coordinated Communication and Promotion Copyright on External resources	from 20,000 to 25,000	**Deployment + Execution + Monitoring** Tutoring Technical Support Ongoing monitoring	from 8,000 to 12,000	**Evaluate** Learning analytics Learning experience Questionnaire analysis **Optimize** Optimization and integration of materials for editions subsequent to the first	2,000 2,000 4,000

The possible sources of funding that CREMIT has drawn on since the first MOOCs in 2014 fall into four categories:

- Public funding (e.g., European call for proposals, Interreg). The MOOC is the outcome of a funded project that fully covers the costs of the pilot version;
- Private funding (e.g., Banking Foundations, Institutions, other Educational Bodies). The MOOC is the result of co-design/collaboration with a private entity that fully or partially covers the costs of the pilot version and/or subsequent editions;
- Internal funding. Costs are covered by the University, within the framework of its Third Mission, using revenues generated by other products or services;
- Mixed funding. Funding is obtained by combining two or more of the approaches described above.

3.2 Economic ROI - Institutional

A first type of ROI can be economic and/or institutional. Since MOOCs themselves are free of charge, this value can be related to three indicators: reputation, communication output, and educational marketing.

Reputation. The return in terms of reputation concerns the social, cultural, and economic impact that the University can exert on the territory and on society as a whole. Within the framework of the Third Mission – under which free MOOCs fall – reputation refers not only to the quality of research and teaching (the First and Second Missions), but also to the recognition of the University as an active agent in creating value for the common good [19, 20].

Communication output. Understood as the result of internal and external communication activities that disseminate the University's research and reflection in a format different from the traditional academic one (research article), represented here by the MOOC. This becomes a tool that generates positive impacts both in terms of reputation and of strengthening the academic brand, fostering trust in the institution, greater stakeholder engagement, and the activation of prestigious partnerships, also with a view to developing new projects and learning pathways [21, 22].

Educational marketing. The third indicator raises the possibility that MOOC users may be interested in accessing non-free services (e.g., personal counseling) or that, having appreciated the quality of the learning materials, they may wish to explore the topics covered in the MOOCs more deeply through university courses [18].

3.3 Pedagogical ROI

The second type of return on investment is pedagogical. In this case, the focus is on assessing the lasting educational benefits that may result from investing in a MOOC. Pedagogical return is a concept that emphasizes educational quality as a driver of individual and collective development; it is not always immediately visible but becomes evident over time in better student preparation, critical thinking skills, and the sharing of values that Università Cattolica has preserved over time (the value of the person, freedom of thought, and so forth). Within this framework, we have identified three types of returns that MOOCs are able to foster: retention and loyalty, new forms of democratization of knowledge, and community dimension.

Retention and loyalty. There is a certain level of retention among users of Università Cattolica's MOOCs, as shown by monitoring data (see § 2, Table 3) [10]. This demonstrates the ability of these courses to foster user loyalty, creating a sense of belonging, guiding learners toward other complementary courses, and encouraging future engagement in higher-level learning pathways. Building culture and skills is a constant and dynamic process that evolves over time and fosters deeper learning. If loyalty indicates recognized quality, the return reflects the desire to understand, explore, and discover new opportunities.

Democratization of knowledge. One of the first defining features of MOOCs is that they are open. These are courses that promote free access to knowledge regardless of learners' cultural background, social condition, economic means, available time, or access to traditional learning spaces. Online platforms make this openness possible and, at the same time, enable hybrid teaching models that differ in part from traditional approaches, such as blended learning – a phenomenon that expanded rapidly after Covid

[23, 24]. Revisiting the notion of communication output from above, in pedagogical terms, we realize that MOOCs make it possible to disseminate some of the outcomes achieved by academia not in a "social," lightweight manner, but within a structured pathway that allows even non-specialists to grasp their significance and explore them further.

Community dimension. A significant pedagogical return lies in the shared learning experience of MOOCs within a community-based rather than individual dimension. This means discovering the value of others, starting from the sharing of curiosity and interest in the topic addressed by the course. Referring to findings that identified potential elements for a community of practice among MOOC participants [25, 26], if such dynamics occur it means that MOOCs have succeeded in creating the conditions for a group of people to share, in the long term, knowledge and professional expertise through dialogue and exchange. A community of practice does not end with the conclusion of a course; rather, it generates relational capital and continuity that make learning more durable and profound.

3.4 Blended MOOC: Where Economic and Pedagogical ROI Meet

A possible strategy to maximize ROI in the approaches presented so far may consist in the use of MOOCs within blended training pathways. This approach goes beyond the conventional mode of MOOC delivery, making room for training activities that include face-to-face sessions and reinforce educational impact.

Already analyzed by several authors [27–29], the blended MOOC highlights the flexibility of these courses, their didactic integrability in numerous scenarios, their educational value, and the opportunity offered to teachers and educators to experiment with different contexts of online pedagogy and learning methodologies.

When applied to the MOOC life cycle, this training scenario can activate elements of economic ROI, making it possible to:

- justify a new edition of the MOOC even when the number of participants might otherwise lead to its end;
- support the production or re-edition of a specialized MOOC intended as a form of cultural promotion;
- recover additional financial resources for content updates exceeding the 10–15% threshold we calculated.

The blended MOOC experimentation carried out by CREMIT at Università Cattolica made it possible to activate 5 different formats (Table 5).

Table 5. CREMIT Blended MOOCs

MOOC Type	Case	Teaching Scenario
Pre MOOC	Master's level II "Il digitale a misura dello Zero-Sei. Attivare percorsi educativi integrati, creativi e partecipativi" Third Mission Projects	Before the training course
In between MOOC	University courses	Within the course, as a further study, with a classroom start and finish
Flipped MOOC	Third Mission Projects	Preparing for seminars or workshops
Post MOOC	Third Mission Projects	After the training course
Parallel MOOC	European Project	Two parallel courses, enjoyed by teachers and students, on the same topics

To assess the pedagogical effectiveness of the five blended MOOCs, we conducted explanatory research with eight in-depth interviews with: the scientific director of the Level II Master's program, the coordinator of the Level II Master's program, and university professors.

The interviews were administered after the June/July 2025 and were recorded. After a few questions describing the course and how the MOOC was used (Pre / In between / Flipped / Post / Parallel), 3 open ended questions were provided: How did the MOOC affect the teaching process? How did The MOOC affect the learning process? How was the student's use of the MOOC certified?

The results, according to the training staff's perceptions, are summarized in Table 6 and demonstrate the differences in the learning objectives of the five formats:

- *pre MOOC* fulfills the role of anticipating and problem-posing;
- *in between MOOC* allows content to be expanded beyond the classroom. The content can thus be shaped, reworked and produced; it represents a job aids to foster implementation into educational practice useful for student on campus and off campus;
- *flipped MOOC* active learning strategies in class time;
- *post MOOC* allows student to explore in greater depth according to student's interests and schedule;
- *parallel MOOC* allows teachers and students to work on a topic by comparing points of view.

Table 6. In-depth interviews results

MOOC Type	Teacher's evaluation
Pre MOOC	Recovery of knowledge; familiarising users with language relating to content; familiarising with the central issues; raising issues for discussion with a wider group of professionals.
In between MOOC	Enrich the university course with examples, practical materials, and discussion of ideas from forums; enable non-attending students to explore topics; enable future education professionals to experience methods of professional development; create opportunities to reflect on self-regulation.
Flipped MOOC	Guidance for professionals' work; returning to the classroom and designing materials and work tools; activating forms of participatory design; accompanying experimentation and documentation.
Post MOOC	In depth exploration and information; reflections.
Parallel MOOC	Intergenerational perspective; provide guided and supported work; offer a second level of in-depth analysis.

4 Conclusions and Perspectives

This paper aimed to contribute to the debate on the challenges and opportunities for MOOC as a form of sustainability education.

Producing MOOCs is both costly and time-consuming; however, according to the authors, they represent a strategic instrument for supporting the university's cultural role by seeking to balance economic sustainability and pedagogical value. From this perspective, the study proposes an enhancement of the MOOC model through the introduction of lifecycle analysis and return on investment (ROI) considerations.

The analyses of lifecycle open to guarantee MOOCs' long-term viability and to think to a MOOC as new forms of preserve knowledge. The sustainability of MOOCs is complex but represents a central issue in university system, nowadays. It's important to present a plan to support designing, production, implementation and monitoring of MOOC.

The analyses of ROI highlights how MOOC prompt reflections from cost to value, questioning the return on investment from a pedagogical perspective.

MOOCs are an investment for University, but elements described in this article are important for the creation of a MOOC analysis system to be proposed at institutional level, enabling the University to highlight the value of this type of training and to support the promotion of a MOOC culture among both administrators and teachers.

The pedagogical perspective allowed to see the MOOC as a challenge for traditional education and a way to discover new format for blended learning. The 5 blended situations characterizing the model developed by CREMIT can be used as a design scenario to foster this type of course into higher education. The model has shown resilience: despite the decline in enrollment, satisfaction, retention and engagement remain high, confirming its effectiveness, especially when combined with forms of blended instruction.

In conclusion, this paper seeks to demonstrate how MOOCs can serve as a strategic tool for:

- critically interrogating and responding to ongoing transformations in academic culture and to the contemporary challenges confronting higher education institutions [30];
- bridging the traditional core missions of universities—teaching and research—with the Third Mission, understood as a set of activities aimed at the valorization, transfer, and public dissemination of scientific knowledge;
- facilitating the communication of knowledge beyond conventional academic formats and institutional spaces, through approaches that promote dialogue with diverse stakeholders and generate tangible impacts on local communities and wider social contexts;
- contributing to the democratization of education, a foundational principle that has characterized MOOCs since their emergence.

Contributions.. According to CRediT system: Simona Ferrari: Conceptualization, Methodology, Investigation, Project administration, Supervision, Writing – Original Draft, Writing – Review & Editing. Annarita Merigo: Data curation, Resources, Visualization, Writing – Original Draft, Writing – Review & Editing.

Disclosure of Interests.. The authors declare that they have no known competing financial interests or personal relationships that could have appeared to influence the work reported in this paper.

References

1. Sanchez-Gordon, S., Luján-Mora, S.: Lifecycle for MOOC development and management. In: Emerging Trends, Techniques, and Tools for Massive Open Online Course (MOOC) Management, pp. 24–48. IGI Global, Information Science Reference, Hershey PA, USA (2018).
2. Ferrari, S., Rivoltella, P.C., Rizzi, C., Scott, F.: Designing MOOCs in higher Education. Outcomes of an experimentation at the Catholic University of Milan. REM. **7**(1), 1–10 (2015)
3. Laurillard, D.: Rethinking University Teaching: a Conversational Framework for the Effective Use of Learning Technologies, 2nd edn. Routledge Falmer, London (2002)
4. Gibbs, G., Jenkins, A.: Teaching Large Classes in Higher Education: how to Maintain Quality with Reduced Resources. Routledge, London (1992)
5. Gravett, K., Taylor, A.C., Fairchild, N.: Pedagogies of mattering: re-conceptualising relational pedagogies in higher education. Teach. High. Educ., 1–16 (2021)
6. Ferrari, S., Triacca, S., Braga, G.: Design for learning in the third space: opportunities and challenges. REM, 1–10 (2021)
7. Salmon, G.: E-Tivities: the Key to Active Online Learning. Routledge, London (2013)
8. Salmon, G.: E-Moderating: the Key to Online Teaching and Learning. Routledge, London (2011)
9. Bowen, K., Thomas, A.: Badges: a Common Currency for Learning. Change: The Magazine of Higher Learning. **46**(1), 21–25 (2014)

10. Ferrari, S., Merigo, A.: Rethinking online community beyond self-paced MOOCs. In: Hamonic, E., Sharrock, R. (eds.) Digital Education: Shaping Sustainable Lifelong Learning for All in the Era of AI. EMOOCS 2025. Lecture Notes in Computer Science, vol 15733, pp. 86–97. Springer, Cham (2025). https://doi.org/10.1007/978-3-032-00056-9_8
11. Ferrari, S., Triacca, S.: The strategic role of the E-tutor in new learning contexts. In: Agrati, L.S., et al. Bridges and Mediation in Higher Distance Education. HELMeTO 2020. Communications in Computer and Information Science, vol 1344, pp. 300–314. Springer, Cham. (2021).
12. Wong, J., Baars, M., Davis, D., Van Der Zee, T., Houben, G.J., Paas, F.: Supporting self-regulated learning in online learning environments and MOOCs: a systematic review. International Journal of Human–Computer Interaction. **35**(4–5), 356–373 (2019)
13. Cope, B., Kalantzis, M.: Ubiquitous Learning. University of Illinois Press (2009)
14. Russell, D.L.: Skimming and scanning reading techniques: speed reading and retaining important points to save time. Independently published (2023).
15. Chavoshi, A., Shahi, S.J.: Comparative analysis of the essential factors for the adoption of massive Open online courses in higher Education of a developing country: pre and post COVID-19. Weizenbaum Journal of the Digital Society. **4**(4) (2024)
16. Goopio, J., Cheung, C.: The MOOC dropout phenomenon and retention strategies. J. Teach. Travel Tour. **21**(2), 177–197 (2021)
17. Baker, R., Passmore, D.: Value and pricing of MOOCs. Education Sciences. **6**(14) (2016)
18. Liyanagunawardena, T., Lundqvist, K., Williams, S.: Massive Open online courses and economic sustainability. European Journal of Open Distance and E-Learning. **18**, 95–112 (2015)
19. Compagnucci, L., Spigarelli, F.: The Third Mission of the University: a Systematic Literature Review on Potentials and Constraints, Technological Forecasting and Social Change, vol. 161. Elsevier (2020).
20. Spulber, D.: Universities' third Mission is from teaching and doing research to dissemination of academic results and activities in society. Geopolitical, Social Security and Freedom Journal. **7**(2), 36–74 (2025)
21. Wymer, W., Casidy, R.: The influence of university brand strength on student satisfaction, loyalty, and word-of-mouth. Acad. Manag. Proc. **2015**, 12920 (2015)
22. Stukalina, Y.: Strategic brand positioning in a modern academia. In: ISMC 2019 - 15th International Strategic Management Conference, pp. 20–29 (2019)
23. Nascimbeni, F.: Open Education. OER, MOOC e pratiche didattiche aperte verso l'inclusione digitale educativa, Franco Angeli, Milano (2020).
24. Moura, V.F., Souza, C.A., Oliveira Neto, J.D., Viana, A.B.N.: MOOCS' Potential for Democratizing Education: An Analysis from the Perspective of Access to Technology. In: Themistocleous, M., Morabito, V. (eds.) Information Systems. EMCIS 2017 Lecture Notes in Business Information Processing, vol. 299. Springer, Cham (2017)
25. Wenger, E.: Communities of practice: the key to knowledge strategy. In: Knowledge and Communities pp. 3–20. Routledge, London (2009).
26. Wenger-Trayner, E., Wenger-Trayner, B.: Learning to Make a Difference: Value Creation in Social Learning Spaces. Cambridge University Press, New York (2020)
27. Ebner, M., Schön, S., Braun, C.: More than a MOOC—seven learning and teaching scenarios to use MOOCs in Higher Education and Beyond. In: Emerging technologies and pedagogies in the curriculum, pp. 75–87. Springer, Singapore (2020)
28. Pérez-Sanagustín, M., Hilliger, I., Alario-Hoyos, C., Delgado-Kloos, C.: H-MOOC framework: reusing MOOCs for hybrid education. Journal of Computing in Higher Education 29(1) (2017). Springer Science+Business Media, New York

29. Eradze, M., León Urrutia, M., Reda, V., Kerr, R.: Blended learning with MOOCs. From investment effort to success: a systematic literature review on empirical evidence. In: Digital Education: at the MOOC Crossroads where the Interests of Academia and Business Converge (EMOOCs Proceedings). Springer (2019)
30. Fleming, P.: Dark Academia. How Universities Die. Pluto Press, London (2021)

The A.C.A. MOOC Model: Integrating MOOCs into Blended University Teaching

Chiara Panciroli, Salvatore Messina(✉), Anita Macauda, Marika Mascitti, and Paola Rigoni

Alma Mater Studiorum - University of Bologna, Bologna, Italy
{chiara.panciroli,salvatore.messina10,anita.macauda, marika.mascitti,paola.rigoni2}@unibo.it

Abstract. Massive Open Online Courses (MOOCs) represent a major innovation in higher education, yet they are often perceived as supplementary and cognitively demanding tools, detached from formal learning pathways (Laurillard, 2013; De La Roca et al., 2018). This study presents a proposal for a pedagogical model for the structured integration of MOOCs within a blended university framework, grounded in dialogical, situated, and reflective approaches. The model is structured into three types of MOOC (Anticipatory, Consolidating, and Amplifying), each aligned with a distinct phase of learning. Therefore, based on their integration and combination, it develops into a cyclical instructional design seamlessly connecting the MOOCs to the in-class activities. Once the course is designed, targeted asynchronous materials can support the content in harmony with face-to-face teaching, enabling class time to focus more on deeper exploration and interactive activities. Within this framework, learning is conceived as a student-centered and adaptive process, while the teacher assumes the role of a "shadow facilitator," ensuring continuity between digital and physical spaces.

Keywords: MOOCs · blended learning · instructional design

1 Introduction: The Edvance Project

Edvance is a platform that serves as a Digital Education Hub (DEH), offering online education through next-generation MOOCs. The platform provides fully online, free, and open courses designed and delivered by faculty members from major Italian universities, with a strong focus on the development of advanced digital skills. The initiative was launched and funded under Italy's National Recovery and Resilience Plan (PNRR), Mission 4 "Education and Research", with the goal of expanding access to high-quality digital education for students, teachers, and professionals nationwide.

1.1 A New Model for Advanced Online Education

In recent decades, instructional design has undergone a profound transformation, shifting from an instruction-centred approach to one focused on learning. Originally developed

M. Adamoli et al. (Eds.): HELMeTO 2025, CCIS 2958, pp. 69–84, 2026.
https://doi.org/10.1007/978-3-032-31850-3_5

within a behaviourist and linear framework [1, 2], instructional design has progressively evolved towards a learning design perspective grounded in personal meaning-making, reflexivity, and learner experience. Contemporary pedagogy is now conceived as an open system in which objectives, activities, tools, and contexts interact dynamically and interdependently to generate authentic, participatory, and customisable learning experiences [3, 4].

This evolution has been driven, on the one hand, by the development of cognitive load theory [5], which has guided design practices towards strategies that minimise extraneous cognitive effort while enhancing the mental processes essential for schema construction; and, on the other, by a reflective and adaptive view of educational design that centres on the relationship between teaching and learning, between experience and reflection [6]. In this sense, design is no longer a prescriptive sequence of contents, but rather a dynamic ecosystem of mediations and interactions in which the teacher acts as a designer of learning environments and a facilitator of cognitive and socio-relational processes. It is precisely within this ecosystem that the Edvance project operates. Through its virtual library, it seeks to promote the access and use of high-quality MOOCs developed by a consortium of universities, and to foster their effective use in blended learning environments.

The Edvance platform offers fully online, open-access MOOC courses enriched with micro-credentials and open badges for the formal recognition of acquired competences. As one of Italy's three national Digital Education Hubs, the Edvance network brings together 17 academic institutions (including 14 universities and 4 HEI), along with numerous public and private partners. The courses address key areas of the digital transition, from Artificial Intelligence and Data Literacy to Digital Sustainability and the development of transversal and transdisciplinary competences, responding to the evolving needs of both the labour market and society.

Edvance promotes a modular and flexible approach to digital education, enabling students and professionals to build personalised learning pathways and strengthen targeted skills that can be integrated into formal academic or professional certifications. The project prioritises the production of high-quality MOOCs and the integration of online and face-to-face learning (blended learning), thereby contributing to the redefinition of national standards for digital education. By leveraging Artificial Intelligence tools and incorporating methodologies drawn from the humanities and creative disciplines, Edvance enhances the interactivity, inclusiveness, and pedagogical effectiveness of digital education, reducing dropout rates and providing new resources for both academic programmes and continuous professional development.

This open education approach ensures that learning resources are accessible, shareable, and reusable, fostering an ecosystem of collective knowledge that promotes innovation and collaboration across institutions.

1.2 Faculty Development and the Line of Action

Among the Work Packages of the Edvance project, one line of action is specifically dedicated to faculty development. Coordinated by the University of Bologna, in collaboration with the Polytechnic University of Milan, the University of Turin, and Ca′ Foscari University of Venice, this Work Package focuses on empowering university teachers with the pedagogical and digital competences required to integrate MOOCs effectively into their course design and teaching practice. The main objective of this WP is to support academic staff in embedding MOOC-based learning within blended and online teaching models, thereby fostering innovation in course planning and delivery. Training activities are designed to provide faculty with theoretical frameworks, methodological guidance, and practical tools for incorporating high-quality MOOCs into their curricula in a coherent and inclusive way. Furthermore, it promotes the dissemination of best practices in the design and implementation of MOOCs, ensuring alignment with national and international standards for digital education. An extensive review of international literature served as the starting point for this work, providing the theoretical and methodological foundations for the adoption of MOOCs within blended learning across partner universities. Building on this foundation, the University of Bologna has developed a process for the open and circular integration of the MOOC tool within course design. This process defines an iterative and participatory approach, enabling faculty to align MOOCs with disciplinary goals, pedagogical strategies, and student learning trajectories, while ensuring ongoing reflection and adaptation throughout the teaching-learning cycle.

2 MOOC's Integration in Blended Learning

Higher education has shifted from treating MOOCs as an opportunistic innovation to considering their integration as a matter of strategic academic redesign [7]. This evolution has been marked by a growing consensus: to fully harness the pedagogical potential of MOOCs, they must be embedded into the core architecture of teaching and learning, not merely appended as supplementary content [7–9]. The transformation entails moving beyond a utilitarian view of MOOCs as digital tools, toward treating them as structural elements capable of reconfiguring course design, learning processes, and institutional strategies [10]. At the center of this reflection lie several structural and didactic models that have attempted to classify the multiple ways in which MOOCs can be embedded in higher education. A pioneering model that paved the way for this development is the Hybrid MOOC model (H-MOOC) [11], which organizes integration strategies along two axes: the degree of institutional support and the level of curricular alignment. The model identifies four reference types: MOOCs as service, replacement, added value, and driver. These categories reveal the spectrum of hybridization practices, from minimal involvement (MOOCs used as voluntary resources) to full pedagogical redesign (MOOCs as central to curriculum delivery). Particularly significant is the "driver" model, in which MOOCs do not merely supplement instruction but become the structuring spine of a course, fully aligned with learning objectives, assessments, and institutional scaffolding.

This structural logic is also echoed in the concept of blended MOOCs (bMOOCs), a format that deliberately intertwines online MOOC content with in-person components. The success of bMOOCs hinges not only on the technological infrastructure but on the quality of interaction design, namely, the capacity to create a dialogic, participatory environment where students actively construct meaning through engagement with content, peers, and instructors [12]. When MOOCs are integrated with intentional interaction strategies, they significantly enhance student satisfaction, autonomy, and learning depth.

Another promising approach is the Interactive-MOOC (I-MOOC) Instructional Design model [13], which introduces a five-phase instructional cycle (analysis, design, development, realization, and evaluation), structured around the cultivation of creativity, personalization, and learning autonomy. The model foregrounds the imagineering learning experience, in which learners progress from cognitive stimulation to associative development and autonomous reflection. This framework highlights the potential of MOOCs not just to deliver content, but to shape innovative, learner-centered environments that promote critical thinking and creative output.

While these models illustrate the pedagogical potential of MOOCs, their effectiveness ultimately depends on how they are contextualized within specific educational ecosystems. In practice, the implementation of such frameworks is deeply influenced by local cultural, institutional, and linguistic factors. International experiences show that global MOOC initiatives often struggle to account for local specificities, thereby limiting their pedagogical impact [14]. An hybrid model developed in China offers an instructive response to this challenge: by combining global MOOC content with face-to-face sessions led by local instructors, it recontextualizes international materials within national curricula and classroom practices, thereby reinforcing cultural relevance and local engagement [15].

Meanwhile, in the United Kingdom [16], de Lima Guede applied a phenomenographic approach to study how lecturers were incorporating MOOCs into their teaching. Her analysis revealed that most instructors made internal course adjustments, such as aligning assessment with MOOC activities or integrating MOOC forums into class debates, even though these changes were rarely visible in formal curricula or course syllabi. This study offers a nuanced understanding of both the strengths and limitations associated with the integration of MOOCs into higher education, based on a phenomenographic analysis of university lecturers' and administrators' perceptions. Among the most widely recognized benefits is the enhancement of academic offerings: MOOCs were perceived as a valuable source of up-to-date, globally relevant content that enriched local curricula and contributed to aligning them with international standards. This curricular enhancement was seen not only as an academic advantage but also to increase institutional competitiveness.

Another key strength highlighted by participants concerns faculty development. By engaging with MOOC content, instructors accessed new knowledge, digital tools, and innovative teaching strategies, reinforcing a culture of lifelong learning and pedagogical renewal. MOOCs were also appreciated for the flexibility they offer students, allowing them to learn at their own pace, revisit course materials, and explore topics beyond the formal syllabus. This flexibility, in turn, was associated with greater personalization of the learning experience. From an institutional perspective, MOOCs were seen as a cost-effective solution to expand course offerings without requiring additional teaching staff. In some cases, MOOCs also provided students with internationally recognized certifications, thereby increasing the perceived value of their academic paths. Furthermore, the integration of MOOCs was associated with broader technological advancement, contributing to the university's digital transformation and the modernization of teaching practices. Despite these positive outcomes, the study also identified several critical issues. Chief among them was the challenge of maintaining student engagement and motivation in online environments, particularly in the absence of structured support. Participants also expressed concerns about the varying quality of MOOC content and its alignment with the learning objectives and academic level of local programs. In many cases, inconsistencies in content and pedagogy limited the effectiveness of integration.

These findings reflect a broader trend in higher education, which is undergoing a fundamental transformation driven by digitalization and changing expectations among students, institutions, and employers. As universities increasingly recognize the strategic role of technology in supporting learning, research, and professional development, the capacity to design flexible and inclusive digital learning environments has become a key institutional priority. The rapid shifts triggered by the COVID-19 pandemic have further underscored the urgency of this transition, highlighting the need for students to develop the digital competences essential for effective online learning and interaction [17]. This analysis lays the groundwork for the theoretical foundation of the instructional model developed at the University of Bologna. Rooted in these international frameworks and enriched by local experimentation, the Bologna model seeks to translate structural and didactic principles into a coherent and adaptable strategy for course design in digitally enhanced learning environments. The next section will explore these theoretical underpinnings in detail.

3 Theoretical Background: CLAS, Conversational Framework, and EAS

Recent literature has shown that the combination of digital technologies, collaborative learning, and reflective approaches can lead to transformative pedagogical models capable of integrating asynchronous and synchronous, individual and cooperative, digital and face-to-face learning moments [18, 19]. This perspective reframes blended learning not as a mere fusion of different modalities, but as an enabling, empowering, and transformative educational ecosystem: enabling, as it expands the temporal and spatial dimensions of learning; empowering, as it fosters interaction and knowledge construction; and transformative, as it generates reflective and immersive experiences that promote the development of transversal and metacognitive competences.

The evolution towards flexible and integrated educational models, however, requires a solid theoretical grounding capable of connecting the diverse epistemological perspectives of contemporary learning. Within this framework, EAS, CLAS, and the Conversational Framework (CF) offer three complementary perspectives for a modular, adaptive, and reflective learning design, particularly suited to the integration of MOOCs within blended learning pathways.

EAS – Situated Learning Episodes [20], originates from a pedagogical reinterpretation of mobile learning [21] understood not as the mere instrumental use of mobile technologies but as a cultural paradigm that redefines the boundaries of formal learning by extending them to informal and everyday contexts. The EAS model is grounded in a constructivist and situated perspective, in which learning is conceived as the active construction of meaning through experience, reflection, and technological mediation. At its core, the model assumes that teaching must be designed as a reflective and intentional process, capable of connecting the experiential dimension of learning with didactic design and metacognitive awareness. The EAS is structured according to a three-phase sequence: preparation, experience, and reflection, which translates Kolb's [40] experiential learning cycle and the principles of learning by doing into a coherent didactic framework.

The preparation phase introduces the problem or authentic situation to be addressed, stimulating curiosity and activating prior knowledge. In this stage, the teacher acts as the director of the learning process, designing materials, tools, and digital environments that serve as mediators. The experience phase represents the operational core of the episode: students act, experiment, and collaborate in solving the assigned task, using digital tools, open resources, and hands-on, laboratory-based methods. It is a highly social phase, centered on collaborative learning and the co-construction of meaning. The reflection phase allows learners to consolidate what they have learned, fostering awareness of both processes and outcomes. Through metareflective activities, discussion, self-assessment, and feedback, students transform their experience into formalized knowledge. This reflective cyclicity gives the EAS model a dynamic and modular structure, allowing the integration of asynchronous and synchronous, analog and digital, individual and collaborative moments. Modularity does not imply fragmentation; rather, it represents a form of flexible coherence, enabling the design of personalized and adaptive learning paths according to learners' needs and contextual conditions. From an epistemological perspective, the EAS model is grounded in three core principles: Situation, understood as an authentic context that gives meaning and direction to learning; Mediation, realized through the intentional use of tools, languages, and technologies to build cognitive bridges between experiences and concepts; Reflectivity, which ensures the transformation of experience into conscious and transferable knowledge. The role of technological mediation is crucial in this framework: mobile technologies, MOOCs, digital environments, and collaborative platforms function as devices of cognitive and social extension, capable of broadening learning contexts and supporting processes of documentation and reinterpretation.

CLAS – Contexts, Languages, Environments, Strategies [21] represents a model of integrated teaching grounded in an ecosystemic conception of knowledge and learning. Inspired by the theories of living systems [22–24], the model conceptualizes the educational process as an open, dynamic, and autopoietic system, in which the constitutive elements (contexts, languages, environments, and strategies) interact in a circular and recursive manner, mutually regenerating one another. The reference to contexts underscores the need to overcome the traditional distinction between formal and non-formal learning, promoting interconnection between educational institutions (schools, universities) and the cultural agencies of the local community (museums, theatres, archives, libraries, foundations, community spaces). Within this framework, the context becomes an educational device, an environment of meaning that contributes to the construction of significance and the continuity of formative processes. The focus on languages highlights the need to value multimodality and the transcoding of educational messages. Learning becomes more meaningful when it integrates verbal, visual, auditory, and bodily languages within a process of meaning-making that activates prior knowledge, fosters problematization, and stimulates conceptual and affective connections [25–27]. Environments, both physical and digital, represent the third pillar of the model and are conceived as spaces of mediation and interaction. The classroom, the laboratory, the e-learning platform, the MOOC, the repository, or the online collaborative environment become devices that support inquiry, discovery, and the creative re-elaboration of knowledge. Environments, both physical and digital, constitute the third pillar of the model and are conceived as spaces for mediation and interaction. The classroom, the laboratory, the e-learning platform, the MOOC, the repository, and the online collaborative environment become devices that foster inquiry, discovery, and the creative reworking of knowledge [28]. Strategies concern the intentional organization of teaching and learning processes. The CLAS model promotes the integration of diverse methodologies, from heuristic or dialogic lessons to cooperative learning, flipped learning, and project-based learning, within a framework of systemic coherence among learning objectives, operational activities, and assessment criteria. Finally, Laurillard's Conversational Framework (CF) [29, 30] offers a dialogical and cyclical perspective on technology-mediated learning. Laurillard conceives teaching as a design science, that is, an activity of designing educational conversations that interweave action, reflection, feedback, and re-elaboration. The framework distinguishes six types of learning, acquisition, inquiry, practice, production, discussion, and collaboration, which represent the various levels of interaction between teacher, learner, and digital environment. This articulation makes the model particularly suitable for designing hybrid learning experiences, in which technology supports the shared construction of knowledge and metacognitive reflection.

The Conversational Framework integrates seamlessly into digital learning environments, where dialogue can take synchronous or asynchronous, individual or collaborative forms through forums, sharing tools, automated feedback, and interactive activities. The scientific value of the Conversational Framework lies in its ability to make explicit mechanisms that sustain learning in terms of iteration, feedback, and reflection. In this sense, the model contributes to rebalancing the relationship between content, activity, and interaction, moving beyond a transmissive view of digital teaching and emphasizing the learner's active and dialogic participation [29, 30]. The Conversational Framework (CF) therefore provides both a theory of learning and an operational framework for instructional design. In the context of MOOCs and blended university teaching, the CF proves particularly useful for: ensuring a balance between content and interactive activities; structuring timely and multi-level feedback (teacher–student, peer–peer, self-assessment); promoting active and reflective forms of learning; supporting inclusion and dialogic participation even within large and diverse learning communities. From this perspective, the CF becomes not only a theoretical model, but also a quality criterion for contemporary instructional design: a tool for designing open, connected, and dialogic learning environments in which knowledge is constructed through a network of meaningful conversations, both digital and human.

In summary, the three models converge in outlining a vision of instructional design as an open, dynamic, and relational system. The integration of EAS, CLAS, and CF provides a robust theoretical framework for understanding how MOOCs can be incorporated into blended university courses not as supplementary tools, but as structural components of reflective, collaborative, and competence-oriented learning environments. Specifically, the ecology of knowledge and the three models converge toward a conception of MOOCs not as add-ons but as structural mediators of instructional design:

- with EAS, MOOCs provide asynchronous micro-experiences for preparation (activation, interactive micro-videos, resource analysis), enrich the experience (authentic tasks, simulations, cooperative activities), and support reflection (debriefing, concept mapping, multimodal artefacts) through distributed feedback;
- with CLAS, MOOCs function as environment and language: they extend educational contexts (across institutions; formal and non-formal), enrich mediating tools (texts, videos, simulations, authoring instruments), support active strategies (flipped, PBL, cooperative), and document evidence for assessment;
- with the CF, MOOCs become conversational spaces connecting students, teachers, peers, content, and technologies, making interactions traceable and integrating both intrinsic feedback (self-assessment, adaptive quizzes, practical activities) and extrinsic feedback (rubrics, comments, dialogic feed-back).

4 The A.C.A. MOOC Model: Anticipatory, Consolidating and Amplifying MOOCs

The proposed model integrates MOOCs into the teaching and learning process, where learning is seen as a dynamic and iterative process characterized by continuous interactions between online and in-presence activities. MOOCs are in fact not conceived as isolated online experiences, but as integral and complementary components of a blended educational ecosystem that leverages the availability of Open Educational Resources designed and constructed by an academic consortium and community of practice. In the proposed model, the integration of these resources follows a modular and adaptive approach, allowing instructors to select and combine one or more types of MOOCs depending on the intended learning outcomes, the characteristics of the learners, and the structure of the course. In this sense, the model identifies three typologies of MOOCs: Anticipatory, Consolidating, and Amplifying, each corresponding to a specific pedagogical function within the broader learning process, to support preparation, knowledge construction, or reflective extension, in a continuous and intentional learning ecology, thoughtfully designed between the teacher, the learner and the content [29, 30]. The ultimate goal of the model is therefore to transform MOOCs from massive repositories of content [31] into meaningful, socially constructed learning environments embedded in local pedagogical practices [32, 33]. An illustration of how the model can be implemented at the beginning of each learning unit is provided in Fig. 1, which depicts the guided decision-making process through which instructors determine whether and how to integrate one of the three types of MOOCs, based on a set of pedagogical and contextual choices.

4.1 Anticipatory MOOC

The anticipatory MOOC represents the preparatory phase of the learning cycle, and it's implemented before entering the class. It is meant to activate the learners' prior knowledge, introduce the conceptual framework of the topic and foster curiosity and engagement, before the in-person session. This phase draws from the idea of "advance organizers" [34, 35], according to which presenting new concepts before learning helps the learners scaffold the structure and the integration of new information. By providing contextual explanations, visual summaries and diagnostic quizzes, anticipatory MOOCs allow students to form preliminary cognitive schemes, reducing the extraneous cognitive load [5] when entering more complex tasks, during the in-person session. Additionally, the content of anticipatory MOOCs should be organized into short, focused sequences that employ different types of media (videos, animations, interactive quizzes with immediate feedback), to support the dual-channel processing [36] and allow learners to regulate their understanding at their pace and focus, thereby facilitating deeper encoding of information. Ensuring the multimodal communication of the academic content, the diverse learning preferences and linguistic backgrounds of the university students are accommodated, contributing to inclusivity and accessibility not only in the MOOC itself but also of the whole academic community. Finally, the anticipatory MOOCs perform an important motivational function. Especially when they include real-world case studies, authentic scenarios and social elements (such as forums and polls to share prior experiences or assumptions related to the topic), employing MOOCs before entering the class can promote situational interest [37] and expectancy beliefs [38] that sustain engagement across the learning journey.

4.2 Consolidating MOOC

The "Consolidating" MOOC is designed to stabilize, deepen, and extend the learning outcomes developed with the support of the teacher. It typically follows an in-person session devoted to problem-setting, during which the teacher introduces the central task, clarifies complex or ambiguous concepts, and creates the conditions for collaborative exploration and peer interaction. This face-to-face phase corresponds to the operationalization stage of the EAS approach [20], where students are actively engaged in authentic, context-rich activities such as simulations, case analyses, and project-based exercises, that enable them to apply theoretical concepts in meaningful ways. Consolidating MOOC then extends this process into the online environment, allowing learners to further elaborate and experiment with the knowledge constructed in class, reinforcing understanding and promoting continuity between learning episodes. In this sense, the consolidating MOOC represents a bridge between in-class learning and autonomous reflection, allowing learners to engage in individual or collaborative tasks in the digital environment. The idea on which it is built draws from the constructivist and experiential theories [39–41], emphasizing learning by doing and learning with others. In fact, in the digital learning platform the MOOC becomes a laboratory of practice, where learners can apply and test the knowledge they have constructed so far through digital case studies, interactive simulations, or project-based assignments. The distinctive feature of the consolidating MOOC is to align with the in-class activities, which should be oriented towards collaborative learning strategies and tasks. This phase reflects in facts the principles of cognitive apprenticeship [42], when the teacher explicates the mental processes behind a task resolution, and problem-based learning [43], leveraging the metacognitive power of modeling, scaffolding and progressive autonomy. Through the consolidating MOOC, the online and face-to-face environments are not meant to be sequential but reciprocally designed to amplify learning through dialogic and situated processes. From a pedagogical perspective, the consolidating MOOC thus functions as a space of guided autonomy that enables learners to consolidate knowledge through repetition, variation and application, all of which are key processes for long-term retention [44]. Moreover, many consolidating MOOCs integrate discussion forums and peer-feedback activities, which extend the dialogical dimension of the classroom into the online space, where learners can confront multiple perspectives, share interpretations, and collaboratively refine their understanding.

4.3 Amplifying MOOC

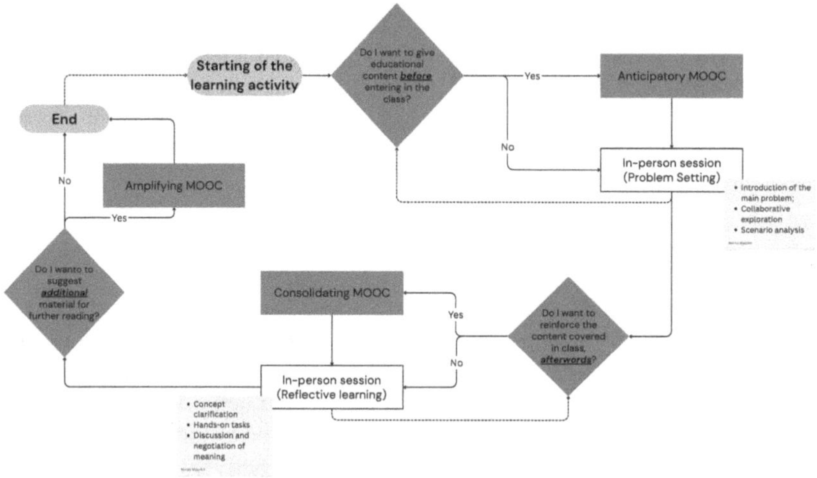

Fig. 1. Illustration of the A.C.A. MOOC model with the guided decision-making process

In the last stage of the learning cycle, after the last in-person session of a specific learning unit, the teacher can decide to implement an "Amplifying MOOC", that aims to expand learners' understanding beyond the immediate course objectives, fostering metacognition, transfer and lifelong learning or activities that require synthesis, evaluation and dissemination of knowledge, like performance-based tasks, reflective journals, and peer assessment exercises, through which students can connect their learning to broader contexts, disciplines, and professional practices. The pedagogical and theoretical foundation behind this phase is connectivism [32, 33], that emphasizes networked learning and knowledge distributed across digital nodes, but also the participatory culture [45], in which students in the digital age are seen not only as consumers but also as producers on content, contributing to open educational ecosystems and reinforcing learner agency [46]. In the lens of these paradigms, structured peer assessment through shared rubrics helps students internalize evaluative criteria and develop a higher understanding of quality and rigor, while ensuring that assessment, learning activities and intended outcomes remain coherent. At the same time, other activities like portfolio or showcase of created artifacts support students' transfer of learning and professional identity formation [47]. Finally, the amplifying MOOC transforms learning into an open, dialogical and self-regulated process that reinforces autonomy, encourages the exploration of adjacent knowledge domains and nurtures reflective practices, bringing the understanding to a higher level of learning and academic maturity.

5 An Example of a University Lesson in Three Phases with Integrated MOOCs

Although these courses fully fall within the MOOC (Massive Open Online Courses) category, they display operational characteristics typically associated with NOOCs (Nano Open Online Courses): short, targeted nano-courses designed for focused learning. In the literature, the term NOOC refers to very brief and highly focused online learning pathways, conceived according to the principles of microlearning. Each course is centered on specific micro-learning objectives addressing a single topic or competence and is structured into concise instructional units. The MOOC model adopted by the Digital Education Hub (DEH) closely aligns with this nano-format in several key respects:

- *Duration.* The Edvance's MOOCs correspond to modules worth 1 ECTS credit (approximately 25 h of total student workload). This limited duration promotes a more manageable and flexible learning experience, effectively addressing one of the main limitations of traditional MOOCs: their excessive length and consistently low completion rates.
- *Learning objectives.* The learning goals are clear and narrowly defined, aligned with the needs of a specific and targeted audience. Unlike generalist MOOCs designed for broad and heterogeneous global audiences, the DEH MOOCs are conceived to support university students, for instance by bridging learning gaps in foundational knowledge or enriching transdisciplinary pathways, as well as professionals seeking to update or expand their expertise in advanced digital competences.
- *Didactic traceability.* Through the use of a dedicated platform (Edvance) and a national micro-credentialing system, each learner leaves a verifiable record of their learning pathway. The completion of a MOOC is certified by open badges and micro-credentials issued by partner universities. This mechanism not only enhances learner motivation by formally recognizing the achievement of learning outcomes, but also enables the monitoring and evaluation of the pedagogical effectiveness of each module.

Within the DEH ecosystem, several MOOCs are fully embedded in university programs, serving as anticipatory, consolidating, or amplifying modules and contributing to the formal acquisition of academic credits. This approach redefines MOOCs as components of a structured blended framework, supported by shared quality standards and AI-based tools that enhance pedagogical traceability and ensure that learning outcomes are measurable, comparable, and transferable across institutions. Building on the model described above, this section presents a concrete example inspired by the practices developed within the Digital Education Hub (DEH). As outlined, the DEH's pedagogical framework integrates several complementary approaches, namely the Episodes of Situated Learning [20], the Conversational Framework [29], and the CLAS framework [21], in order to enhance the blended and situated dimensions of learning. From this perspective, a possible structure for a university lesson is presented, employing the three different modes of MOOC use (anticipatory, consolidating, and amplifying), each positioned at a distinct stage of the teaching and learning process. The examples that follow should not be interpreted as a fixed or prescriptive sequence, but rather as flexible and adaptable configurations of use. These demonstrate how the different types of MOOCs, when intertwined with the situated logic of the EAS framework, can foster the design of learning pathways that activate prior knowledge, promote collaborative elaboration, and stimulate metacognitive reflection. Such integration opens significant opportunities for the innovation of university teaching, where digital technology is no longer conceived merely as a functional tool but as a pedagogical and cognitive mediation device. The intentional use of MOOCs as anticipatory, consolidating, and amplifying components allows for the extension of time, space, and continuity in learning, strengthening the interplay between individual and collective processes and reinforcing students' agency and reflective engagement. The following section illustrates how, within a hypothetical teaching unit, these three phases can be implemented within a blended learning cycle that alternates between online activities (via MOOCs) and in-person sessions, thereby maximizing both interactivity and metacognitive reflection.

Phase *1:* providing an Anticipatory MOOC, before the in-person session. This phase can be implemented through a short asynchronous MOOC delivered in the days preceding the start of the course or a specific teaching module. For example, in a university course on the "Ethics of Artificial Intelligence", students might be assigned an introductory MOOC available on the Edvance platform prior to the beginning of the lessons. This online module, drawing on the existing Edvance resources, includes micro-video lectures (short 5–10 min clips) presenting the core concepts such as what constitutes an ethical algorithm, and the main principles and dilemmas of AI ethics, along with brief self-assessment quizzes and possibly a guided discussion forum hosted on the course platform. Students are asked to engage with the materials and complete a small anticipatory task: for instance, posting a short reflection in the MOOC forum on the ethical scenario presented, or formulating questions they would like to explore during the in-class session. This phase introduces key concepts, sparks curiosity, and sets the stage for collaborative work in class.

Phase *2:* providing a Consolidating MOOC after the in-person session. This modality serves to re-elaborate and deepen the concepts addressed during in-class sessions, offering students a second opportunity for reflection and formalization. The MOOC provides synthetic materials accompanied by guided exercises and self-assessment activities. Students are invited to reformulate the issues discussed in class by applying them to a new context, such as analyzing a case of algorithmic discrimination in automated recruitment systems. Working individually or in groups, they develop a digital artefact for further exploration (e.g. a concept map or a concise policy brief) that articulates the identified fairness criteria and proposes ethical guidelines for responsible AI use. These artefacts, collaboratively produced within digital environments (e.g., shared editors or concept-mapping tools), become publicly shared outputs within the course platform, where they are discussed and refined through peer review activities. In this phase, the instructor takes on the role of facilitator and cognitive mediator, overseeing the process, providing formative feedback, and suggesting theoretical references to strengthen the connection between practical experience and ethical principles. In this sense, the consolidating MOOC functions as a space for situated re-elaboration, fostering the transition from action to conceptual understanding within a blended and reflective learning framework.

Phase *3:* providing an Amplifying MOOC as the last step of the learning unit. This final phase unfolds through the MOOC platform, which acts as a digital environment for extending and deepening classroom learning. The instructor uploads all the materials used during the final debriefing session, including the artefacts produced by student groups (e.g. infographics, concept maps, and policy briefs) making them accessible to the entire class. Students are then invited to take part in a structured peer review activity: each participant analyzes another group's artefact and provides reasoned and constructive feedback, following an evaluation rubric prepared by the instructor. The peer review tasks are supported by guiding questions designed to foster critical reflection (e.g., Which argumentative strategies do you find most effective? What aspects of your own work could you improve after reading others' contributions?). In parallel, the instructor proposes a short metacognitive questionnaire that encourages reflection on both individual and collective learning processes (e.g., What is the main insight you have gained during this module? How has the discussion changed your perspective?). To conclude the phase, the instructor produces a brief synthesis video or an aggregated concept map, visualizing the interconnections among students' contributions, highlighting key outcomes, and addressing any misconceptions that may have emerged. Additional resources for further study are provided to encourage self-directed learning and ensure continuity of engagement beyond the course. Hence the term amplifying: the post-lesson MOOC does not simply close the learning process but rather extends and enriches it, enabling students to situate their learning within a broader conceptual and disciplinary framework and to develop a reflective awareness of their own cognitive and collaborative processes.

6 Conclusions

While this model offers a coherent and flexible framework for integrating MOOCs into blended learning and teaching, some limitations must be acknowledged. The approach requires considerable time and design effort from instructors, as well as additional engagement from students beyond scheduled classroom hours. In particular, the use of anticipatory MOOCs prior to the official start of a course may raise logistical challenges, as it presupposes learners' early participation and digital readiness. Additionally, to ensure the effective integration and sustainability of this blended model, universities must be equipped with a robust Learning Management System capable of hosting and sharing OERs, MOOCs, and student-generated materials. Such infrastructures are essential to promote meaningful exchange, institutional collaboration, and seamless interplay between online and in-person learning resources, ultimately fostering a dynamic and open digital learning ecosystem. Nevertheless, the pedagogical benefits of this model are substantial. Through online debriefing sessions, the public sharing of artifacts, and peer discussion, the restructuring function of the blended approach is fully realized: students compare their solutions, integrate diverse perspectives, and collaboratively consolidate the knowledge con-structed during previous phases. Pedagogically, the amplifying

MOOC represents a transformative learning moment, in which the laboratory experience is reinterpreted, formalized, and internalized as critical awareness. From a technological standpoint, the platform enables monitoring of cognitive and participatory processes through the tracking of learner interactions such as forum discussions, peer reviews, and reflective quizzes, thus providing valuable data for formative assessment. Finally, the issuance of a micro-credential or open badge upon completion of the full sequence (anticipatory MOOC, in-class activities, and amplifying MOOC) certifies the entire learning cycle, acknowledging not only disciplinary competences but also transversal skills such as collaboration, reflexivity, and critical thinking.

Disclosure of Interests. The authors have no competing interests to declare that are relevant to the content of this article.

References

1. Skinner, B.F.: Reinforcement today. Am. Psychol. **13**(3), 94 (1958)
2. Gagné, R.M.: Problem solving. In: Categories of Human Learning, pp. 293–317. Academic (1964)
3. De La Roca, M., Morales, M., Teixeira, A.M., Sagastume, F., Rizzardini, R.H., Barchino, R.: MOOCs as a disruptive innovation to develop digital competence teaching: a micromasters program edX experience. Eur. J. Open Distance E-learn. **21**(2) (2018)
4. Calvo, S., Lyon, F., Morales, A., Wade, J.: Educating at scale for sustainable development and social enterprise growth: the impact of online learning and a massive open online course (MOOC). Sustainability. **12**(8), 3247 (2020)
5. Sweller, J., Van Merrienboer, J.J., Paas, F.G.: Cognitive architecture and instructional design. Educ. Psychol. Rev. **10**(3), 251–296 (1998)
6. Laurillard, D., et al.: A constructionist learning environment for teachers to model learning designs. J. Comput. Assist. Learn. **29**(1), 15–30 (2013)
7. Sancassani, S., Baldoni, V., Brambilla, F.: La ricerca del giusto mezzo. Strategie di equilibro tra aula e digitale. Ediz. MyLab (2023)
8. Martiniello, L., Borrelli, L., Toto, G.A.: Design of a MOOC for Teaching and Research: the Innovative Experience of the MERGO Project. TeleXbe (2021)
9. Dede, C.: Immersive interfaces for engagement and learning. Science. **323**(5910), 66–69 (2009)
10. Pham, A.T.: Blended MOOCs in higher education: Analyzing student interaction and satisfaction. Contemporary. Educ. Technol. **17**(1), ep550 (2025)
11. Williams, R.T.: An overview of MOOCs and blended learning: integrating MOOC technologies into traditional classes. IETE J. Educ. **65**(2), 84–91 (2024)
12. Pérez-Sanagustín, M., Hilliger, I., Alario-Hoyos, C., Delgado Kloos, C., Rayyan, S.: Describing MOOC-based hybrid initiatives: the H-MOOC framework. Proc. Eur. MOOC Stakeholder Summit. **2016**, 159–172 (2016)
13. Pham, A.T., Abdullah, M.R.: Validating and prioritizing key indicators for blended MOOC implementation in English language learning using the fuzzy Delphi method. MethodsX, 103668 (2025)
14. Nittayathammakul, V., Rattanasak, S., Wannapiroon, P., Nilsook, P., Arora, R., Thararattanasuwan, K.: Imagineering MOOC instructional design model to enhance creative thinking and creative health media innovation. Int. J. Emerg. Technol. Learn. (IJET). **18**(19), 84–102 (2023)

15. Le, H.V., Ho, T.T.: Balancing act: exploring the integration of coursera MOOCs in Vietnamese higher education through a phenomenographic lens. Interact. Learn. Environ., 1–25 (2025)
16. Liu, C., Zou, D., Chen, X., Xie, H., Chan, W.H.: A bibliometric review on latent topics and trends of the empirical MOOC literature (2008–2019). Asia Pac. Educ. Rev. **22**(3), 515–534 (2021)
17. de Lima Guedes, K.K., Davis, H.C., Schulz, J.: Integrating MOOCs into traditional higher education modules: a MOOC-based blend framework. Res. Learn. Technol. **30** (2022)
18. Barber, W.: Collaborative learning in co-created digital space: the fully online learning. In: Handbook of Research on Barriers for Teaching 21st-Century Competencies and the Impact of Digitalization, 197 (2021)
19. Graham, C.R.: Blended learning systems. In: The Handbook of Blended Learning: Global Perspectives, Local Designs, 1, pp. 3–21 (2006)
20. Vázquez-Cano, E.: Artificial intelligence and education: a pedagogical challenge for the 21st century. Educ. Process Int. J. (EDUPIJ). **10**(3), 7–12 (2021)
21. Rivoltella, P. C., et al.: Fare didattica con gli EAS. Episodi di Apprendimento Situato. pp. 1–236). La scuola (2013).
22. Panciroli, C.: Verso un modello di didattica ecosistemica. Open Teach. **19**, 19–32 (2021)
23. Maturana, H., Varela, F.: Autopoiesis, and Cognition. Reidel Publishing Company (1980)
24. Capra, F.: Creativity and Leadership in Learning Communities, a Lecture at Mill Valley School District (1997)
25. Bateson, G.: Steps to an Ecology of Mind. Jason Aronson (1977)
26. Kress, G.: Multimodality: a Social Semiotic Approach to Contemporary Communication. Routledge (2009)
27. Calvani, A.: Principi di comunicazione visiva e multimediale Fare didattica con le immagini. Stampa (2011)
28. Panciroli, C., Macauda, A., Corazza, L.: Costruire relazioni di conoscenza attraverso artefatti digitali. Media e tecnologie per la didattica, 37–49 (2020).
29. Rivoltella, P. C., Rossi, P.G.: Il corpo e la macchina. Tecnologia, cultura, educazione (pp. 5–185). Scholé (2019).
30. Laurillard, D.: Rethinking University Teaching: a Conversational Framework for the Effective Use of Learning Technologies. Taylor and Francis (2002)
31. Laurillard, D.: Teaching as a Design Science: Building Pedagogical Patterns for Learning and Technology. Taylor and Francis (2012)
32. Jordan, K.: Initial trends in enrolment and completion of massive open online courses. Int. Rev. Res. Open Distrib. Learn. **15**, 133–160 (2014)
33. Siemens, G.: Connectivism a learning theory for the digital age. Int. J. Instr. Technol. Distance Learn. **2**, 3–10 (2005)
34. Downs, S.: Connectivism and Connective Knowledge. Essays of Meaning and Learning Networks. National Research Council, Canada (2012)
35. Ausubel, D.P.: Educational Psychology: a Cognitive View. Holt, Rinehart and Winston, New York (1968)
36. Ausubel, D.P.: The use of advance organizers in the learning and retention of meaningful verbal material. J. Educ. Psychol. **51**, 267–272 (1960)
37. Mayer, R.E.: Multimedia Learning. Cambridge University Press (2009)
38. Hidi, S., Ann Renninger, K.: The four-phase model of interest development. Educ. Psychol. **41**, 111–127 (2006)
39. Eccles, J.S., Wigfield, A.: Motivational beliefs, values, and goals. Annu. Rev. Psychol. **53**, 109–132 (2002)
40. Vygotsky, L.S.: Mind in Society. Development of Higher Psychological Processes. Harvard University Press (1978)

41. Kolb, D.A.: Experiential Learning Experience as the Source of Learning and Development. Prentice Hall, Englewood Cliffs, NJ (1984)
42. Dewey, J.: Experience and Education. Macmillan Company, New York (1938)
43. Collins, A., Brown, J., Holum, A.: Cognitive apprenticeship: making thinking visible. Am. Educ. Prof. J. Am. Fed. Teachers. **15** (1991)
44. Hmelo-Silver, C.E.: Problem-based learning: what and how do students learn? Educ. Psychol. Rev. **16**, 235–266 (2004)
45. Cepeda, N.J., Pashler, H., Vul, E., Wixted, J.T., Rohrer, D.: Distributed practice in verbal recall tasks: a review and quantitative synthesis. Psychol. Bull. **132**, 354–380 (2006)
46. Jenkins, H., Purushotma, R., Weigel, M., Clinton, K., Robison, A.J.: Confronting the Challenges of Participatory Culture: Media Education for the 21st Century. Confronting the Challenges of Participatory Culture (2009).
47. Wiley, D., Hilton, J.: Defining OER-enabled pedagogy. Int. Rev. Res. Open Distrib. Learn. **19**, 133–147 (2018)
48. Barnett, S.M., Ceci, S.J.: When and where do we apply what we learn? A taxonomy for far transfer. Psychol. Bull. **128**, 612–637 (2002)

Situated Psychological Agents and Virtual Role-Play for Soft Skills Training in Pre-service Teachers

Elena Dell'Aquila[1(✉)], Michela Ponticorvo[2], Di Fuccio Raffaele[1], Grazia De Angelis[1], Niccolò Maria Iannello[1], Nicola Luciano Pannofino[1], and Pierpaolo Limone[1]

[1] Pegaso University, Centro Direzionale Isola F2, 80143 Naples, Italy
elena.dellaquila@unipegaso.it
[2] University of Naples Federico II, Via Porta di Massa, 1, 80133 Naples, Italy

Abstract. This paper presents an approach to soft skills development in pre-service teacher education using Situated Psychological Agents (SPA) and virtual role-play environments. Grounded in embodied and situated cognition, the SPA framework conceptualizes avatars as expressive, psychologically grounded agents that support the enactment of emotionally and socially meaningful interactions. Within this model, two serious games, Enact and Accord, have been designed to foster core relational competencies such as communication, conflict management, and emotional regulation. These games immerse learners in scenarios where they must act, reflect, and adapt in response to realistic interpersonal dynamics. The agent's behavior, shaped by psychological theory (i.e. Rahim's taxonomy of conflict management styles; assertive communication frameworks) and expressed through multimodal cues (e.g., tone of voice, posture, gaze), supports learners in experimenting with different strategies while receiving contextualized feedback. Enact is structured as an assessment tool that maps user choices onto Rahim's model of conflict-handling styles, while Accord provides a formative space for practicing and refining relational skills. Together, they illustrate how SPA-based environments can support reflective, situated, and scalable soft-skills training in teacher education.

Keywords: Embodiment · Situated Psychological Agents · Educational Games · Virtual Role-Play · Avatar-Based Learning · Soft Skills Training · Pre-service Teachers

1 Introduction

In contemporary teacher education, the development of soft skills, such as communication, emotional regulation, conflict management, and perspective-taking, is increasingly recognized as fundamental to effective classroom practice. In line with current pedagogical standards and educational policy frameworks, pre-service teachers are increasingly expected to manage complex relational situations, decode subtle social cues, and respond

M. Adamoli et al. (Eds.): HELMeTO 2025, CCIS 2958, pp. 85–96, 2026.
https://doi.org/10.1007/978-3-032-31850-3_6

with clarity and empathy. These skills are essential for fostering inclusive, responsive classroom environments and for building constructive teacher-student relationships [1, 2].

However, traditional lecture-based instruction provides few structured opportunities to rehearse these skills before entering real classrooms. While microteaching and internships offer some experiential exposure, they are often limited by context, quality, or timing.

To address this gap, serious games have emerged as promising tools for simulating authentic interpersonal challenges within safe, guided environments. When grounded in sound pedagogical principles, such games allow learners to practice decision-making, experience the emotional consequences of their actions, and receive feedback that supports both self-awareness and strategy refinement [3].

This paper introduces Accord, a serious game designed within the Situated Psychological Agents (SPA) framework [4], which integrates psychological modelling, pedagogical mean, and interactive technology. Accord enables learners to engage with emotionally expressive digital agents in scenarios that mirror common school-based interactions (managing conflict with students) while exploring alternative ways to communicate and resolve tension.

Accord builds on the earlier development of Enact, a SPA-based game originally designed to evaluate conflict management styles through interactive role-play. While Enact was conceived primarily for assessment purposes, particularly as a dynamic equivalent to Rahim's conflict management questionnaire (Form B), Accord extends this approach into the domain of formative learning. Its focus lies not in identifying conflict styles, but in supporting the development of relational competence through guided practice, reflection, and feedback.

The theoretical grounding of this approach draws from multiple traditions. First, embodied cognition emphasizes that learning arises through bodily action, perception, and affective engagement, not just symbolic processing [5–7]. Second, situated learning theory holds that knowledge is constructed through participation in socially organized activities, where roles, tools, and norms mediate meaning-making [8]. Finally, Activity Theory conceptualizes learning as an expansive, tool-mediated process embedded in social systems [9]. The SPA model translates these principles into interactive environments where avatars act as expressive, psychologically plausible mediators of learning.

The aim of this paper is twofold: to articulate how SPA principles are operationalized in Accord through agent architecture, interaction design, and feedback mechanisms; and to present a methodology for its integration into teacher education programs. Through this lens, we explore how soft skills, often seen as tacit or intuitive, can be made visible, trainable, and transferable within technology-enhanced learning environments.

2 Theoretical Framework: The SPA Model

The Situated Psychological Agents (SPA) model [4] offers a conceptual and methodological framework for designing educational simulations that reflect the emotional and cognitive complexity of real human interaction. Rooted in educational psychology, activity theory, and artificial intelligence, SPA environments are conceived as experiential learning spaces where relational competences can be rehearsed, observed, and refined.

At the core of the SPA approach lies the idea that learning is situated: it unfolds through participation in socially and emotionally meaningful contexts. Drawing from Activity Theory [9], the model views digital agents as mediating tools that structure action, interpretation, and reflection. These agents are not just animated avatars, but psychologically modelled entities that simulate plausible social behavior, making them capable of triggering authentic emotional responses and pedagogically relevant dilemmas.

The framework also builds on socio-constructivist and social-cognitive theories of learning [10], emphasizing the integration of cognitive, emotional, and behavioral dimensions. In this perspective, soft skills such as communication or conflict management are not transmitted through instruction, but enacted through role-based interaction, self-regulation, and reflective feedback.

To enable this process, SPA environments adopt design principles from game studies and artificial intelligence. Scenarios are structured to provide dynamic and emotionally responsive exchanges, where each learner's action influences the evolving trajectory of the interaction. Artificial agents express states such as empathy, irritation, or openness, modeled on validated psychological theories, thereby supporting experiential learning through cause-effect dynamics.

In summary, SPA is not only a theoretical lens but a design methodology that operationalizes psychological concepts within digital environments. It provides a foundation for tools like Accord, where the aim is to translate theories of human behavior into interactive learning experiences that support pre-service teachers in developing relational competence in realistic and context-sensitive ways.

2.1 Architecture of Situated Psychological Agents

The architecture of Situated Psychological Agents (SPA) environments is not a simple layering of functionalities, but rather an interconnected system where psychological modelling, interactional expressivity, pedagogical purpose, and technological infrastructure converge into a coherent learning ecology. At its core lies the assumption that relational competence like any meaningful human skill, emerges not from isolated inputs, but from the continuous interplay of cognition, emotion, and context. The SPA model builds precisely on this interplay, offering learners a space in which to inhabit and reflect upon complex interpersonal situations through the mediation of intelligent, emotionally responsive agents.

These agents are far from being static characters or generic interlocutors. Drawing on validated psychological constructs, such as Rahim's taxonomy [11] of conflict management styles or assertive communication frameworks, they are designed to exhibit behaviours that resonate with learners as plausible and socially grounded. Their internal architecture enables them to react in ways that are contingent not only on user input, but also on emotional and motivational dynamics that evolve throughout the interaction. This psychological realism is what transforms a digital simulation into an emotionally engaging learning experience. Importantly, it allows learners to read not only the content of what is said, but also the quality of how it is conveyed, an essential shift for those in professions, like teaching, where relational nuance matters.

Interaction, in this context, becomes a rich multimodal exchange. SPA agents communicate not only through verbal channels but also through gaze, posture, tone, and timing.

These expressive cues are not ornamental. They represent observable behavioural patterns, verbal, non-verbal, and paralinguistic indicators, defined within a communicative model grounded in the dimensions of assertiveness, passivity, and aggressiveness [12]. These cues shape the rhythm and emotional texture of the dialogue, requiring the learner to interpret, adjust, and reflect in real time. This model allows for the structured observation of interactional styles, making it possible to link specific behaviours (e.g., interruptions, tone shifts, gaze avoidance) to broader communication strategies. As such, the cues are integral to relational meaning-making and pedagogical feedback.

The simulation becomes affectively charged, prompting empathic responses and engaging the learner's social cognition in real-time. It is through this embodied exchange that abstract theories, on empathy, regulation, or collaboration, are translated into lived micro-experiences.

The social intelligence of these agents is deeply rooted in theoretical models of communication. SPA environments embed communicative exchanges within broader institutional and cultural frames. Agents act in ways that implicitly convey norms of authority, emotional display, or politeness, depending on the scenario. In the case of teacher education, this may mean simulating a student's reluctance, or assertiveness, or ambivalence in a delicate conversation. These culturally-situated cues teach learners not only how to communicate, but how to position themselves within specific social roles, expectations, and power relations. In this way, SPA environments go beyond skill training to foster situated competence, the capacity to respond appropriately to context-specific interpersonal challenges.

The educational design of SPA systems is explicitly oriented toward the development of soft skills, particularly those aligned with the ACCORD competence framework, including effective communication, conflict management, and emotional awareness. But rather than framing learning through success/failure dichotomies or gamified scoring, the system privileges relational effectiveness and reflective processing. Feedback, whether emergent through agent reaction or structured during debriefing, encourages learners to connect their choices with psychological outcomes and to consider alternative courses of action [2]. Learning here unfolds through iteration, experience, reflection, adaptation, much in line with experiential learning models.

Underlying this entire architecture is a robust technological framework informed by the Simulation Technology approach (SimTech) [2], which refers to the use of formal models to simulate social phenomena and psychological theories, which enables the simulation of emotionally and socially dynamic micro-worlds. Rather than implementing generic interaction mechanics, SimTech enables the dynamic representation of complex constructs, such as negotiation processes, leadership styles, or conflict resolution strategies, within computational environments. These simulations allow learners not only to observe but to inhabit and experiment with theoretical models through interactive and emotionally responsive experiences.

The system registers not only what is said, but how interactions unfold over time, adapting the feedback accordingly. This dynamic infrastructure supports automated feedback, user tracking, and remote deployment, making SPA systems scalable and adaptable to different learning contexts.

What emerges from this architecture is not simply a tool for training communication, but a space in which psychological theory is enacted, pedagogical goals are embodied, and learners are invited to engage relationally, emotionally, and reflectively. Thus, SPA environments do not merely illustrate soft skills, they make them available as practices to be inhabited, experienced, and transformed.

2.2 The Role of Embodied Agents

Within the SPA framework, the concept of the embodied agent plays a pivotal role in shaping the learning experience. As highlighted, these are not generic avatars but expressive and psychologically-informed entities designed to simulate plausible social interactions. What sets them apart is not just their ability to mimic human communication, but their capacity to embody cognitive, emotional, and behavioral patterns that resonate with learners on an experiential level.

Rather than being passive recipients or scripted interlocutors, SPA agents function as dynamic mediators of relational experience. Their reactions are shaped by theoretical models, such as conflict management styles or assertive communication, but are enacted in ways that invite interpretation, adjustment, and reflection. In this sense, agents serve both as mirrors and as catalysts. They reflect the learner's communicative stance through immediate, affective cues, like shifts in tone, posture, or facial expression, and at the same time provoke new forms of awareness by responding in ways that demand emotional regulation and strategic recalibration.

Therefore, this process is not merely reactive, it is situated and embodied. When a learner engages with a simulated disagreement, the agent's response is multimodally rich: a glance, a change in the tone and vocal rhythm, all of which carry socio-emotional weight. These signals activate the learner's social cognition, prompting empathic resonance, hesitation, or revaluation, much like what occurs in real-world encounters. It is precisely this affective immediacy that distinguishes SPA environments from text-based simulations or traditional training protocol, as here, learning is not described, it is felt and negotiated.

Equally important is the way in which these agents are embedded within cultural and institutional scripts. The behaviour of an agent is not culturally neutral; it reflects the implicit rules and expectations that govern professional interactions within specific settings. For teacher education, this might involve the subtle enactment of authority dynamics between educators and students, or the emotional undercurrents present in collegial disagreement. By operating within these normative frames, agents enable learners to rehearse not only "how" to communicate, but also "when," "to whom," and "under what expectations." In doing so, they contribute to the development of what we might call situated competence, the ability to act appropriately within a given relational and institutional ecology.

Beyond the experiential, the design of these agents reflects a deeper ambition: to connect psychological theory with pedagogical intentionality through the medium of interaction. Each agent is, in effect, a micro-theory in motion, operationalizing constructs such as emotional contagion, perspective-taking, or conflict resolution in ways that are not abstract but actionable. For pre-service teachers, this means that learning occurs not in the form of theoretical exposition but as embodied trial and reflection. The SPA environment becomes, in this sense, a living laboratory where the social dynamics of teaching can be rehearsed, reinterpreted, and internalized.

This perspective challenges the instrumental view of educational technology as a means of content delivery. Instead, SPA links technology with the co-construction of meaning, a space where relational skills are not transmitted but cultivated through iterative cycles of doing, feeling, and understanding. What emerges is a form of training that is not only cognitively robust, but also emotionally grounded and professionally relevant.

3 Game Design and Implementation: Accord and Enact

Both Enact and Accord are designed as single-player serious games, where individual learners navigate simulated social situations through embodied interaction with psychologically grounded agents. While Enact and Accord operate within the same SPA-based framework, sharing psychological modelling, multimodal agent expressivity, and dynamic feedback mechanisms, their respective purposes reflect a progressive evolution from measurement to formation. Rather than representing two separate paths, Accord emerges as a pedagogical extension of the foundations established by Enact, translating an evaluative tool into a formative environment.

Enact was originally developed to offer a game-based operationalisation of the Rahim Organizational Conflict Inventory [11], with the aim of assessing how individuals manage conflict in asymmetric relationships such as those between teachers and students. Its scenarios and agent reactions are carefully structured to reflect the logic of the questionnaire, allowing researchers to observe conflict-handling styles, integrating, avoiding, dominating, compromising, or obliging, within simulated school-based interactions. The key objective of Enact is thus not to train, but to capture behaviourally rich data that can validate and expand the psychometric application of Rahim's model in educational contexts. Within Enact the user is tasked with resolving a conflict scenario filled with emotional stakes and requiring interpersonal negotiation. Each situation presents rich contextual information, including emotional cues and clearly defined role dynamics, immersing learners in challenges that mirror everyday relational situations. While serving as a tool for behavioral assessment, Enact goes beyond traditional surveys by eliciting authentic dialogue choices and tracking users' preferred conflict-resolution strategies in real time. This experiential format reflects the Rahim model of conflict-handling styles and supports the system's primary objective: assessing how participants navigate interpersonal tension, prioritize values, and attempt to reach a resolution. Through this mechanism, Enact transforms classic psychometric models into interactive, ecologically valid simulations (Fig. 1).

Accord builds directly upon this foundation but reorients the simulation toward a formative aim. While it inherits the psychological backbone of Enact, it introduces new mechanisms designed to support learners in developing relational competences, not

Fig. 1. Screenshot from Enact: conflict scenario simulation.

merely revealing them. Assertive communication [13], conflict negotiation strategies [11], and emotional regulation [10] are presented not as diagnostic constructs, but as skills to be explored, experimented with, and refined through guided interaction. The game scaffolds decision-making, offers adaptive feedback, and encourages reflection, thus enabling users to recognise not only which styles they tend to adopt, but also how effective those styles are in context and what alternatives might be more constructive. Users can replay scenarios, test different approaches, and receive formative feedback on how their behaviour shapes interactional outcomes.

This transition, from Enact focussing on style recognition to Accord emphasising on relational transformation, shows how SPA environments can evolve from psychological measurement instruments into educational tools.

Ultimately, Enact and Accord represent complementary phases in the design of SPA-based learning: Enact helps us understand how individuals approach conflict; Accord helps them become more aware, adaptable, and effective in managing it. At the end of each scenario, the Accord game provides learners with a debriefing interface that visualizes the conflict resolution styles they have enacted. This debriefing phase maps the player's dialogue choices onto Rahim's model of conflict-handling styles. This contextualized feedback enables learners to see how their communicative decisions correspond to psychological constructs (e.g., Avoiding, Integrating, Compromising, Obliging), promoting metacognitive awareness and invites learners to reflect on the effectiveness and situational appropriateness of their strategies. This kind of visual feedback reinforces the idea that relational competence is about understanding how different styles function in dynamic interpersonal contexts (Fig. 2).

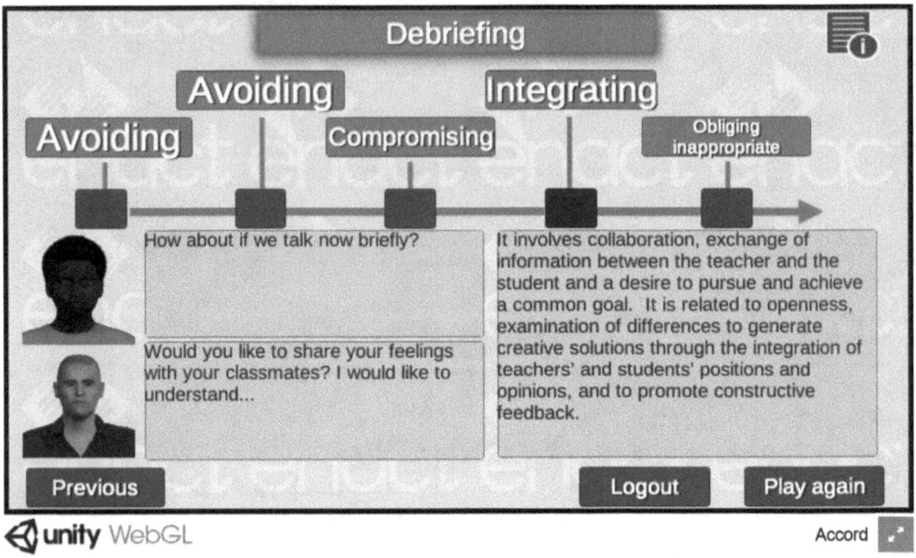

Fig. 2. Screenshot from Accord: user interface with feedback options and dialogue paths.

4 Methodological Framework

The evaluation of Accord is designed as a mixed-method study, situated within pre-service teacher education programs that focus on building relational competence, conflict management, and emotional awareness. The core aim of the methodology is to explore how SPA-based environments foster the development of soft skills and to gain insight into how learners engage psychologically with embodied role-play experiences.

The study adopts a pre/post intervention design at evaluating both the effectiveness and experiential quality of SPA-based learning in supporting the development of soft skills, with both quantitative and qualitative data collection. Participants will be pre-service teachers enrolled in graduate-level courses in education and pedagogy, specifically modules on classroom management and inclusive education. The intervention is embedded into the curriculum, ensuring ecological validity by replicating real-life educational constraints and objectives.

Each participant engages individually with the Accord game over a structured session, followed by facilitated debriefing with tutors or instructional designers. The same participants are evaluated before and after the session using psychological instruments, gameplay analytics, and structured reflections. This within-subject design allows the study to detect individual changes across cognitive, emotional, and behavioral dimensions

The methodology integrates three complementary sources:

- Self-report instruments: to evaluate baseline conflict styles, the ROCI-II Form B is used [11], alongside instruments such as the Teachers' Sense of Efficacy Scale (TSES) [14]; and Emotion Regulation Questionnaire (ERQ) [15].
- Behavioral data: automatically logged during gameplay sessions, includes dialogue choices, reaction times, emotional state selections, and feedback interactions. These data are coded in relation to the underlying psychological models (e.g., conflict style dynamics), enabling quantitative modeling of decision-making under emotional tension.
- Reflective materials: reflections and tutor observations capturing learner insights and emotional awareness and encourage metacognitive insight and skill awareness. Learners are encouraged to complete brief reflective journals post-game session, where they express perceived challenges, emotional responses, and lessons learned. Tutors provide observational notes on non-verbal indicators, emotional reactions, and depth of reflection, supporting a multimodal account of learning. This reflective layer helps trace metacognitive engagement, offering data on self-awareness, role identification, and the potential integration into real practice.

The quantitative data will be analyzed through paired-sample comparisons (pre/post), while qualitative materials will be thematically analyzed [16] to trace changes in self-perception, relational awareness, and transfer of behaviour. This dual lens will help to clarify how learners internalize the simulation, how they interpret their avatar's choices, and how they generalize insights into broader teaching practice.

To strengthen the validity of the findings, a triangulation strategy will be adopted by comparing behavioral data from gameplay, self-report questionnaires, and qualitative reflections. This approach will help identify consistent patterns or notable discrepancies in how participants experience and respond to the training process.

5 Expected Outcomes and Discussion

As highlighted throughout this work, rather than simulating abstract dynamics, Accord engages learners in realistic, emotionally charged scenarios where they must respond, adapt, and reflect. This experiential process enhances not only procedural knowledge but also metacognitive insight: participants become more aware of how their communicative choices affect relational outcomes, and how different styles of interaction (e.g., collaborative, avoidant, assertive) operate in context. Prior studies have emphasized how this kind of embodied role-play promotes engagement, empathy, and perspective-taking [4, 17] crucial dimensions for relational competence.

The expected outcomes include an improvement in teachers' communicative skills, especially in high-stress or emotionally demanding classroom situations. Through practice and guided feedback, learners are expected to develop a greater awareness of conflict management strategies and a more flexible use of different interpersonal styles, understanding that effective communication depends on context and intention.

Yet, participants are likely to show better emotional self-regulation when faced with disagreement or misunderstanding, becoming more aware of both personal emotional landscape and the relational signals emerging from their interlocutors. Finally, enhance reflective capacity through feedback mechanisms integrated into gameplay that encourage learners to analyze their own actions and responses, promoting authentic self-awareness and growth.

While direct observation of behavioural transfer to real classrooms lies beyond the current scope, the study aims to capture learners' perceived readiness to apply these strategies in future practice. As pre-service teachers' sense of efficacy is positively correlated with their communication skills, teacher education programs should complement content knowledge with communication competence and self-efficacy through targeted training activities [18]. Self-report instruments, such as ROCI II for conflict management and teacher self-efficacy and emotional regulation scales will help assess attitudinal changes, while qualitative reflections will provide insight into how participants internalize and generalize the experience.

The use of real-time affective feedback, embedded in agent behaviour, is also expected to sustain users' motivation and deepen relational awareness. These dynamics, consistent with current findings in embodied and emotionally adaptive learning, would position Accord as a reflective simulator of interpersonal meaning-making, capable of bridging abstract theory and everyday educational practice [19, 20].

Ultimately, Accord is designed to fill a gap in teacher education by offering a structured yet flexible environment in which learners can safely explore complex relational scenarios, receive targeted feedback, and experiment with alternative strategies. By combining psychological realism, pedagogical intent, and experiential interactivity, the game contributes to an emerging model of soft-skill formation that is both measurable and meaningful.

6 Conclusions

This study proposes a psychologically grounded and pedagogically structured approach to soft skills training in teacher education through the development and implementation of the SPA-based game Accord. Anchored in the principles of embodied and situated learning, the model demonstrates how digital role-play environments can simulate complex relational dynamics in ways that are both experientially meaningful and educationally impactful.

By integrating psychological theory, pedagogical aim, and structured feedback, Accord offers pre-service teachers a safe space to rehearse and reflect on communicative and emotional strategies, bridging the gap between abstract knowledge and real-world classroom demands.

The expected outcomes, such as improved communication confidence, better conflict management styles, enhanced emotional regulation, and stronger reflective capacity, highlight the potential of such tools to support professional growth in a domain often overlooked in traditional teacher training.

Rather than replacing human interaction, SPA environments complement it by offering learners a space where they can slow down, experiment with alternative strategies, and observe their relational patterns, making it possible to build experience and awareness before confronting real interpersonal situations.

This supports the formation of a relational mindset, attentive, flexible, and self-aware, which is essential for inclusive and responsive teaching.

In continuity with Activity theory, this approach shows how digital tools, when conceived as mediators of goal-directed, socially situated action, can foster meaningful engagement and reshape learning participation in professional contexts. While further empirical validation will be needed to assess long-term impact and classroom transfer, Accord offers a promising direction for the integration of game-based simulations in professional development.

Moreover, future work may extend this model to other contexts, such as in-service training or intercultural education, and explore the use of adaptive feedback and AI-driven analytics to personalize learning trajectories. Indeed, while promising, the present study is not without limitations. Simulated environments, though carefully designed, cannot fully capture the complexity and unpredictability of real-world social interactions. Future developments could integrate live activities or classroom-based observations to enhance ecological validity.

Moroever, relying on self-report instruments introduces potential biases linked to self-perception and social desirability. To address this, future research will continue to combine multiple data sources, behavioral, reflective, and observational, offering a more balanced understanding of learner engagement and growth.

There are also considerations around access and usability: SPA-based environments require a certain level of digital competence and technological resources. Efforts to improve accessibility, such as mobile optimization, will be crucial to ensure a broaden adoption.

Despite these challenges, this work contributes to building a scalable, adaptive, and learner-centered approach to soft skills training. Expanding the model across domains, exploring its long-term impact, and leveraging AI for personalization will further strengthen its potential in shaping meaningful and future-ready educational experiences.

In sum, this research contributes to rethinking soft skills not as intangible or peripheral, but as learnable, observable, and trainable competences, central to the identity and effectiveness of contemporary educators.

This reconceptualization is especially significant when applied across the various stages of teacher education. Each educational cycle (i.e. early childhood, primary, or secondary) faces distinct relational, emotional, and communicative demands. For example, teachers working with young children often deal with challenges related to emotional containment and non-verbal attunement, while secondary educators must frequently face more complex negotiations and peer-group dynamics. The flexibility of SPA-based environments enables the design of context-sensitive scenarios that reflect these differentiated needs. By adapting simulations to reflect the specific social and emotional ecosystems of each school level, the model supports the development of soft skills in a situated, relevant, and developmentally appropriate way. In doing so, it aligns teacher training with the real-world interpersonal challenges that educators face in their everyday professional lives, regardless of age group or subject area.

Disclosure of Interests: The authors have no competing interests to declare that are relevant to the content of this article.

References

1. Vallone, F., Dell'Aquila, E., Dolce, P., Marocco, D., Zurlo, M.C.: Teachers' multicultural personality traits as predictors of intercultural conflict management styles: evidence from five European countries. Int. J. Intercult. Relat. **87**, 51–64 (2022). https://doi.org/10.1016/j.ijintrel.2022.01.006
2. Hamka, A., Pranata, S.: Teachers and Leaders in Vocational Education and Training: by OECD. OECD Reviews of Vocational Education and Training, OECD Publishing, Paris (2021)
3. Dell'Aquila, E., Marocco, D., Ponticorvo, M., Di Ferdinando, A., Schembri, M., Miglino, O.: Educational games for soft-skills training in digital environments. In: Advances in Game-Based Learning. Springer (2017). https://doi.org/10.1007/978-3-319-06311-9
4. Ponticorvo, M., Dell'Aquila, E., Marocco, D., Miglino, O.: Situated psychological agents: a methodology for educational games. Appl. Sci. **9**(22), 4887 (2019). https://doi.org/10.3390/app9224887
5. Fugate, J.M., Macrine, S.L., Cipriano, C.: The role of embodied cognition for transforming learning. Int. J. Sch. Educ. Psychol. **7**(4), 274–288 (2019). https://doi.org/10.1080/21683603.2018.1443856
6. Shapiro, L., Stolz, S.A.: Embodied cognition and its significance for education. Theory Res. Educ. **17**(1), 19–39 (2019). https://doi.org/10.1177/1477878518822149
7. Glenberg, A.M., Witt, J.K., Metcalfe, J.: From the revolution to embodiment: 25 years of cognitive psychology. Perspect. Psychol. Sci. **8**(5), 573–585 (2013). https://doi.org/10.1177/1745691613488669
8. Lave, J., Wenger, E.: Situated Learning: Legitimate Peripheral Participation. Cambridge University Press (1991)
9. Engeström, Y.: Expansive Learning at Work: toward an Activity-Theoretical Reconceptualization. Cambridge University Press (2009)
10. Bandura, A.: Self-Efficacy: the Exercise of Control, (11). Freeman (1997)
11. Rahim, M.A.: A measure of styles of handling interpersonal conflict. Acad. Manag. J. **26**(2), 368–376 (1983). https://doi.org/10.5465/256541
12. Dryden, W., Constantinou, D.: Assertiveness Step by Step, Sheldon (2004)
13. Alberti, R., Emmons, M.: Your Perfect Right: Assertiveness and Equality in your Life and Relationships. New Harbinger Publication (2017)
14. Tschannen-Moran, M., Hoy, A.W.: Teacher efficacy: capturing an elusive construct. Teach. Teach. Educ. **17**(7), 783–805 (2001). https://doi.org/10.1016/S0742-051X(01)00036-1
15. Gross, J.J., John, O.P.: Individual differences in two emotion regulation processes: implications for affect, relationships, and Well-being. J. Pers. Soc. Psychol. **85**(2), 348–362 (2003). https://doi.org/10.1037/0022-3514.85.2.348
16. Braun, V., Clarke, V.: Using thematic analysis in psychology. Qual. Res. Psychol. **3**(2), 77–101 (2006). https://doi.org/10.1191/1478088706qp063oa
17. Huifen, G., Yan, M., Aizhu, W., Zhu, X., Lijiao, D., Wenxiang, F.: Who can benefit from immersive virtual reality in education? Effectiveness of IVR in teaching using meta-analysis. In: 2021 Tenth International Conference of Educational Innovation through Technology, pp. 320–325 (2021)
18. Saka, M., Surmeli, H.: Examination of relationship between preservice science teachers' sense of efficacy and communication skills. Procedia Soc. Behav. Sci. **2**(2), 4722–4727 (2010). https://doi.org/10.1016/j.sbspro.2010.03.747
19. Williams, B., Brown, T., Benson, R.: Feedback in the digital environment. In: Feedback in Higher and Professional Education, pp. 125–139. Routledge (2012)
20. Narciss, S.: Designing and evaluating tutoring feedback strategies for digital learning. Digit. Educ. Rev. (23), 7–26 (2013)

Digital Pathways to Inclusion: A Framework for Refugee and Migrant Students in Italian Higher Education

Lidia Scifo[1] and Giovanni Fulantelli[1,2(✉)]

[1] LUMSA University, Palermo, Italy
lidia.scifo@lumsa.it, giovanni.fulantelli@cnr.it
[2] Institute for Educational Technologies, National Research Council of Italy, Palermo, Italy

Abstract. Higher education institutions are increasingly required to address two interconnected challenges: the growing diversity of student populations and the rapid digital transformation of teaching, learning, and governance. In Italy, these challenges are particularly relevant for refugee and migrant-background students, who often face barriers related to access, recognition of prior qualifications, language support, financial sustainability, and participation in academic life. This paper proposes an evidence-informed framework for inclusive higher education in the era of artificial intelligence and digital innovation. The study adopts an integrative review methodology combining academic literature, institutional reports, policy documents, and Italian case studies, including initiatives such as UNICORE, the Manifesto of the Inclusive University, and CIMEA recognition practices. The analysis identifies nine strategic domains for inclusive universities: access, recognition of qualifications, economic support, language and academic support, digital inclusion, wellbeing, inclusive pedagogy, governance, and employability. Findings show that inclusion remains uneven across universities, often limited to project-based initiatives rather than fully institutionalised strategies. Educational technologies, including online learning environments, AI-supported multilingual tools, digital credentialing systems, and learning analytics, can enhance inclusion when embedded within ethical and human-centred institutional strategies. Based on these results, the paper introduces the **Inclusive Digital Readiness Model** and a set of **Guidelines for an Inclusive University** to support strategic development in the Italian higher education context. The findings align with UNESCO, UNHCR, and European Commission frameworks while translating them into an operational perspective tailored to Italy. The paper concludes by outlining policy and research implications for embedding inclusion into governance, teaching, and digital transformation agendas across higher education.

Keywords: higher education · refugees · migrants · inclusion · artificial intelligence · educational technology · Italy

M. Adamoli et al. (Eds.): HELMeTO 2025, CCIS 2958, pp. 97–116, 2026.
https://doi.org/10.1007/978-3-032-31850-3_7

1 Introduction

Higher education institutions across Europe are increasingly required to address two interconnected challenges: the growing diversity of student populations and the rapid digital transformation of teaching, learning, and governance. Within this evolving landscape, the inclusion of refugee and migrant-background students has become one of the most urgent equity issues facing contemporary universities. According to the United Nations High Commissioner for Refugees [1], more than 120 million people are forcibly displaced worldwide, and only around 9% of young refugees worldwide access higher education, a figure that remains far below global participation rates and below the 15by30 target, which aims to reach 15% participation by 2030 [2]. Refugee participation in higher education thus represents one of the most critical equity challenges of our time, linking humanitarian protection to long-term development and social cohesion [3–5].

Italy offers a particularly significant case within this scenario. Owing to its geographical position and migration history, the country functions both as an entry point and as a place of long-term settlement for refugees and asylum seekers arriving in Europe [6]. In recent years, Italian universities have progressively developed initiatives aimed at widening participation for students with refugee status or migrant backgrounds.

Among the most relevant examples is UNICORE (University Corridors for Refugees), launched in 2019 through collaboration between UNHCR, the Italian Ministry of University and Research, the Ministry of Foreign Affairs, and a growing network of universities and civil associations. The programme enables refugee students residing in 13 developing countries to access master's degree programmes in Italy through facilitated admission procedures, scholarships, and mentoring pathways [7]. By 2025, more than 300 students had participated, and 45 universities had joined [8]. A second important initiative is the Manifesto of the Inclusive University (*Manifesto dell'Università Inclusiva*), a voluntary commitment promoted by UNHCR Italy since 2019. Signatory institutions pledge to remove administrative, linguistic, and financial barriers affecting students with international protection and to adopt inclusive governance practices [9]. Other national actors reinforce these efforts. In particular, CIMEA, Italy's ENIC-NARIC centre, supports the recognition of prior qualifications through instruments such as the European Qualifications Passport for Refugees [10]. Together, these initiatives have contributed to the emergence of a multilevel ecosystem of support for refugee learners in Italian higher education.

However, evidence suggests that institutional responses remain uneven. In their mapping of 98 Italian universities, De Maria and colleagues [11] identified a wide range of initiatives, including admission support, hospitality programmes, and social inclusion activities, but often characterised by localised actions rather than comprehensive institution-wide strategies. Important barriers therefore persist, including difficulties in navigating admissions, delays in documentation and recognition procedures, financial precarity, linguistic challenges, psychosocial stress, and limited access to reliable information [12–18].

These challenges increasingly intersect with digital transformation. Universities now rely extensively on online admissions systems, virtual learning environments, digital credentialing procedures, and hybrid teaching models [19–21]. While such developments may enhance flexibility, accessibility, and continuity, they may also reproduce inequalities related to connectivity, device availability, digital literacy, language, and access to culturally responsive online pedagogy [22, 23]. Inclusion in higher education must therefore be understood not only as physical access to campus, but also as meaningful participation in digitally mediated academic life.

From a theoretical perspective, this shift reflects a broader movement from integration to inclusion. Integration often assumes that students adapt to pre-existing institutional norms, whereas inclusion implies that institutions transform their cultures, policies, pedagogies, and infrastructures in response to learner diversity [24, 25]. Applied to higher education, this perspective requires universities to rethink governance systems, teaching practices, student support services, and digital environments as interconnected dimensions of equity.

Despite growing attention to these issues, no comprehensive framework currently exists to systematise the main dimensions of inclusion for refugee and migrant-background students in Italian higher education while explicitly incorporating digital transformation and emerging AI-related opportunities and risks. This paper addresses that gap through an integrative review methodology combined with qualitative document analysis. It aims to identify recurring barriers and enabling factors, examine how educational technologies and AI may support inclusive participation, and synthesise the findings into the **Inclusive Digital Readiness Model** and a set of **Guidelines for an Inclusive University.**

2 Background and Related Work

2.1 From Integration to Inclusion

The conceptual distinction between integration and inclusion is central to understanding how universities can support refugee and migrant-background students. Historically, policies addressing migration and education in Europe, Italy included, have often used the term integration to indicate processes through which newcomers adapt to the host society's existing norms, values, and institutions [26]. Within higher education, this approach implicitly assumes that refugee and migrant-background students must conform to pre-established academic standards and procedures, positioning them as guests who must learn to fit into an unaltered institutional culture [27].

By contrast, *inclusion* represents a paradigmatic shift. As Booth and Ainscow [24] define it in their influential *Index for Inclusion*, inclusion is a continuous process of identifying and removing barriers to participation and learning for all students. It entails transforming institutional cultures, policies, and practices rather than merely accommodating difference. The 2020 *UNESCO Global Education Monitoring Report* reinforces this perspective, framing inclusion as the responsibility of education systems to adapt to the diversity of learners, rather than expecting learners to adapt to the system [27].

In higher education, inclusion thus involves redesigning structures, curricula, and pedagogies to promote equitable participation. It requires universities to move beyond episodic support measures, such as scholarships or mentoring programs, toward systemic strategies that ensure sustainability and accountability [28]. The shift from integration to inclusion also implies a cultural transformation within higher education institutions:

universities are increasingly called to recognise diversity not as a challenge to manage, but as a source of enrichment, innovation, and academic vitality for the whole community [29, 30].

2.2 The Inclusive University as an Evolving Model

The concept of the *inclusive university* extends the principles of inclusive education, originally developed in the context of disability and special needs, to encompass all forms of diversity, including linguistic, cultural, socioeconomic, and migratory differences. An inclusive university is not defined merely by the presence of diverse students, but by the institution's capacity to create enabling environments that support their participation, belonging, and academic success [31]. At least four interrelated dimensions characterise the inclusive university model:

1. **Inclusive policies and governance.** Institutional commitment must be embedded in strategic plans, budgets, and leadership structures. The *Manifesto of the Inclusive University* in Italy exemplifies this dimension, as signatory universities formalise annual action plans encompassing access, recognition, financial support, and student wellbeing [8].
2. **Inclusive teaching and learning.** Pedagogical innovation plays a decisive role. Teaching approaches based on the Universal Design for Learning (UDL) framework promote flexibility in learning objectives, materials, and assessment, enabling students to engage according to their individual strengths and circumstances [32].
3. **Support and participation.** Beyond classroom practices, inclusion depends on networks of support, tutoring, counselling, peer mentoring, and cultural mediation, that foster student agency and wellbeing [33, 34].
4. **Data and accountability.** Inclusive universities collect and analyse data disaggregated by student characteristics (without stigmatization) to monitor participation and outcomes, informing evidence-based policies [35, 36].

In the Italian context, the inclusive university remains a developing concept. While several institutions have adopted elements of inclusivity, systematic implementation often depends on local leadership and project-based funding [37]. The challenge is thus to move from *good practices* to *institutionalised practices*, sustained by governance mechanisms and measurable indicators.

2.3 Digital Inclusion as a Core Component of Institutional Inclusion

Digital technologies are not neutral tools; they shape educational experiences, participation opportunities, and power relations within universities. As several scholars have argued, digitalisation in higher education both reflects and may reinforce existing inequalities if not critically designed and governed. For refugee and migrant-background students, digital infrastructures can therefore either expand opportunities or reproduce barriers, depending on how they are implemented and integrated into institutional practices [38–44].

In the Italian higher education context, digital inclusion can be understood through two interconnected dimensions: technological accessibility and pedagogical inclusivity. Technological accessibility refers to students' ability to access and effectively use digital systems such as admissions platforms, learning management systems (LMS), online libraries, and student service portals. For refugees and asylum seekers, who may experience unstable connectivity, limited digital literacy, or lack of devices, universities should ensure alternative access modes, technical support, and device loan schemes [45]. Pedagogical inclusivity concerns the design of digitally mediated learning environments that recognise linguistic and cultural diversity. Online and blended learning can mitigate geographical constraints and increase flexibility, but only when accompanied by culturally responsive teaching, multilingual resources, and sustained human support networks [46, 47].

More specifically, digital technologies may support inclusion through at least three complementary pathways. First, digital administrative infrastructures, such as online application systems, e-document recognition procedures, digital credentialing tools (e.g., EQPR e-certificates), multilingual information portals, and open data repositories, can simplify admission and recognition processes, increasing transparency and reducing bureaucratic bottlenecks. This is particularly relevant for students whose educational trajectories have been disrupted or whose documentation is incomplete [48, 49].

Second, digital learning environments enable flexibility through blended and online courses, language-learning platforms, virtual classrooms, and remote tutoring systems. These tools can accommodate diverse linguistic, geographical, and life circumstances, allowing students to begin academic preparation even before physically arriving in the host country [23, 50–53]. In Italy, examples include preparatory pathways associated with the UNICORE programme, where online environments have supported linguistic and academic readiness before enrolment.

Third, AI-based educational technologies, including adaptive learning systems, automated translation, accessibility tools, and learning analytics, may provide more personalised forms of support for students with varying linguistic and cultural backgrounds [40, 54, 55]. At the same time, their adoption raises important concerns regarding data privacy, algorithmic bias, over-reliance on automation and the potential deskilling of human support roles, and the digital divide [56–58]. For this reason, technological innovation should reinforce rather than replace the relational dimensions of teaching, mentoring, and student support [59–61].

Digital technologies can also serve as bridging mechanisms between recognition, access, and learning. For instance, CIMEA's digital platforms for credential evaluation and EQPR's electronic passports simplify qualification recognition and reduce bureaucratic barriers. Similarly, online preparatory courses for UNICORE candidates delivered through virtual classrooms have facilitated linguistic and academic readiness before arrival in Italy.

3 Methodology

3.1 Research Design and Research Questions

This study adopts an integrative review methodology [62, 63] combined with Qualitative Document Analysis [64, 65]. This design was selected because the topic under investigation, the inclusion of refugee and migrant-background students in higher education, and the role of digital technologies in supporting such inclusion, is interdisciplinary, practice-oriented, and documented across heterogeneous forms of evidence.

Unlike traditional systematic reviews, which often prioritise narrowly defined empirical studies, integrative reviews allow the inclusion and synthesis of multiple source types, including peer-reviewed research, conceptual contributions, institutional reports, policy frameworks, and documented practices. This is particularly appropriate in emerging fields where relevant knowledge is distributed across academic and non-academic contexts.

Qualitative Document Analysis complements the review by enabling a systematic interpretive reading of texts, with attention to meanings, priorities, recurring themes, and implicit assumptions embedded in policy and institutional materials. Together, these approaches support the development of an evidence-informed framework with practical relevance for higher education institutions.

Given the heterogeneous nature of the corpus, formal risk-of-bias procedures typical of clinical systematic reviews were not applicable. Instead, sources were appraised according to criteria of methodological transparency, institutional credibility, relevance to the research questions, transferability of findings and clarity of documented practices or recommendations. Greater interpretive weight was assigned to sources demonstrating stronger transparency, empirical grounding, or institutional authority.

The study was guided by the following research questions:

1. What barriers and enabling factors affect the access, participation, and success of refugee and migrant-background students in Italian higher education?
2. Which institutional practices and policies, including those supported by educational technologies, effectively promote inclusion?
3. How can these findings be synthesised into a coherent model for strategic institutional development?

3.2 Scope of the Review, Source Identification and Data Extraction

The review focused on sources addressing the inclusion of refugee, asylum seeker, and migrant-background students in higher education, with particular attention to the Italian context and to digital inclusion issues. Materials published between 2010 and 2025 were prioritised in order to capture developments linked to post-2015 European migration dynamics, the expansion of digital higher education, and recent advances in artificial intelligence. Sources were identified through iterative searches in major academic databases, including Scopus, ERIC, and Google Scholar, complemented by targeted consultation of institutional repositories and official websites such as: UNHCR, UNESCO, European Commission, Council of Europe, CIMEA, CRUI and Italian universities involved in inclusion initiatives.

Search combinations included terms related to refugees, migration, higher education, inclusion, student success, digital inclusion, educational technology, AI, UNICORE, and qualification recognition. Rather than pursuing statistical exhaustiveness, the search process aimed to achieve conceptual saturation across the main dimensions of the topic.

Documents were included when they met at least one of the following criteria:

- addressed access, participation, retention, or success of refugee or migrant-background students in higher education;
- examined university policies or institutional strategies relevant to inclusion;
- discussed digital learning, educational technology, or AI applications connected to inclusive participation;
- documented Italian initiatives or European experiences relevant to the Italian system;
- provided empirical findings, conceptual insights, or policy recommendations of clear relevance.

Sources were excluded when they:

- focused exclusively on primary, secondary, or non-higher education settings;
- addressed migration without educational relevance;
- consisted of opinion pieces lacking substantive evidence or analytical value;
- duplicated already represented content.

A structured review matrix was used to organise information extracted from selected sources. For each document, the following aspects were recorded where available: author(s) / organisation; year of publication; country or institutional context; target population; type of intervention or policy; role of technology (if relevant); barriers identified; enabling factors; outcomes or recommendations. This procedure supported transparency and comparability across heterogeneous sources.

3.3 Analytical Procedure

The corpus was analysed through thematic qualitative synthesis. Coding followed a combined deductive–inductive logic.

Deductive coding was initially informed by the conceptual framework of the study, particularly the dimensions of policy and governance; pedagogy and student support; digital inclusion; ethics and AI; access and participation.

Inductive coding was subsequently used to identify recurring patterns emerging directly from the corpus.

During the coding process, particular attention was devoted to the intersection between inclusion and digital innovation, with the aim of identifying how educational technologies may concretely support more equitable participation in higher education. Several recurring examples of technology-enhanced inclusion emerged across the analysed sources. These included the use of online preparatory language courses designed to support refugee and migrant-background students before enrolment, digital platforms facilitating the evaluation and recognition of prior qualifications, and remote tutoring or peer-mentoring systems delivered through learning management systems. The review also highlighted the growing relevance of AI-based translation and accessibility tools, which may help foster multilingual learning environments and reduce participation barriers for students with diverse linguistic backgrounds.

Specifically, through iterative comparison, codes were progressively clustered into nine broader analytical domains.

4 Results

The integrative review and qualitative document analysis revealed that the inclusion of refugee and migrant-background students in higher education depends on the interaction of structural, pedagogical, social, organisational, and technological factors. Findings indicate that inclusion depends on coordinated actions across multiple institutional domains.

The findings also indicate that educational technologies increasingly intersect with inclusion strategies. In some cases, they function as catalysts for access, flexibility, and personalised support; in others, they risk generating new inequalities when poorly designed or weakly governed. The evidence suggests that digital innovation contributes to inclusion only when embedded within coherent institutional strategies and human-centred pedagogical approaches.

4.1 Recurring Barriers to Inclusion

A first major finding concerns the persistence of barriers affecting students from refugee and migrant backgrounds throughout their university trajectories.

At the point of entry, common obstacles include difficulties in navigating admission procedures, limited access to reliable information, language barriers, and uncertainty regarding the recognition of previous qualifications. Visa constraints, residence documentation issues, and fragmented communication between institutions may further delay or prevent enrolment. Economic precarity and unstable housing conditions also reduce the feasibility of university participation, particularly for students with forced migration experiences.

During academic participation, students may encounter culturally unresponsive teaching practices, weak peer integration, limited access to tailored support services, and difficulties in balancing study with employment or family responsibilities. Several sources also emphasise psychosocial stress, uncertainty regarding legal status, and reduced sense of belonging.

Digital barriers were equally recurrent. While universities increasingly rely on online systems for enrolment, communication, and learning, not all students possess equal levels of device access, connectivity, digital confidence, or familiarity with institutional platforms. This suggests that digital transformation may unintentionally amplify exclusion when not accompanied by inclusive design and targeted support.

4.2 Enabling Practices and Strategic Responses

Alongside these barriers, the review identified a growing number of enabling practices implemented by universities, public agencies, and international organisations.

These practices indicate that inclusive higher education becomes more achievable when institutions move beyond reactive responses toward systemic planning.

Examples include dedicated admission channels for refugee students, conditional enrolment procedures, flexible recognition pathways, scholarships and fee waivers, targeted language support, mentoring schemes, counselling services, and staff development in intercultural competence.

Italian initiatives such as UNICORE and the Manifesto of the Inclusive University emerged as particularly significant reference points. They demonstrate how multi-stakeholder partnerships may widen access while supporting academic and social integration. However, their implementation across institutions remains uneven, often depending on local commitment rather than coordinated national frameworks.

Digital technologies also emerged as important enablers. Online learning environments can support flexibility and continuity for students with disrupted educational trajectories. AI-supported multilingual tools may facilitate communication and access to information. Digital credentialing systems and micro-credentials can streamline recognition procedures, while learning analytics may help institutions identify disengagement risks and offer timely support.

Yet technology alone does not guarantee inclusion. Ethical governance, data protection, and human oversight remain essential.

4.3 The Nine Strategic Domains of Inclusive Universities

Through thematic synthesis, findings were organised into nine recurring domains representing the core dimensions of institutional inclusion:

1. Access and Admission
2. Recognition of Qualifications
3. Financial and Housing Support
4. Language and Academic Support
5. Digital Inclusion and Educational Technologies
6. Wellbeing and Psychosocial Support
7. Inclusive Teaching and Assessment
8. Governance and Monitoring
9. Employability and Transitions

These domains suggest that inclusion should be interpreted as an ecosystem rather than a standalone service. Universities performing well in one area while neglecting others may still generate exclusionary experiences.

The study also highlighted examples of technology-enhanced practices within these domains. These included multilingual admission portals, digital document repositories, scholarship management systems, online tutoring platforms, accessible learning management systems compliant with recognised accessibility standards, tele-counselling services, AI-supported translation tools, data dashboards for monitoring student progression, and e-portfolio systems supporting employability pathways.

For each domain, evidence was summarised into principles and recommended actions, which together informed the development of two outputs:

1. The **Inclusive Digital Readiness Model**, describing progressive stages of institutional inclusion in digitally mediated universities;
2. **Guidelines for an Inclusive University**, translating recurring findings into strategic recommendations.

4.4 The Inclusive Digital Readiness Model

To operationalise these findings, the study proposes the Inclusive Digital Readiness Model, a conceptual framework describing how universities may progressively evolve from fragmented and reactive responses toward systemic and transformative approaches to inclusion in digitally mediated higher education (Fig. 1). The model interprets inclusion as an institutional capacity that develops over time through the alignment of governance, pedagogy, support systems, and digital infrastructures.

The four levels should not be understood as rigid or strictly linear stages. Universities may display characteristics associated with different levels simultaneously across organisational domains. For example, an institution may have advanced digital services while still relying on project-based inclusion practices, or strong student support systems without fully embedding inclusion into strategic governance. For this reason, the model functions primarily as a strategic lens for analysing institutional readiness and identifying priorities for further development.

- **Level 1 – Emerging**: isolated, reactive, or compliance-driven measures with limited coordination. Inclusion depends largely on individual commitment or temporary initiatives.
- **Level 2 – Developing**: pilot projects, growing awareness, and partial coordination across selected services or departments.
- **Level 3 – Established**: structured services, reliable support systems, inclusive teaching practices, and coherent digital infrastructures integrated into routine operations.
- **Level 4 – Transformative**: inclusion embedded across governance, curriculum design, staff development, quality assurance, and digital strategy, with continuous improvement informed by data and stakeholder participation.

In this perspective, progression across levels reflects not only the expansion of services, but a deeper cultural and organisational shift: from compensatory support for specific groups toward a university model in which diversity is recognised as a driver of innovation, quality, and academic excellence. The model is not intended as a prescriptive framework, but as a flexible analytical tool supporting institutional reflection and context-sensitive implementation.

4.5 Guidelines for an Inclusive University

While the Inclusive Digital Readiness Model describes progressive stages of institutional maturity, the Guidelines for an Inclusive University identify the strategic actions through which such progression may occur. Derived from the thematic synthesis, the guidelines translate recurring evidence into practical directions for universities seeking to strengthen inclusion in a coherent and sustainable manner. Rather than functioning as isolated

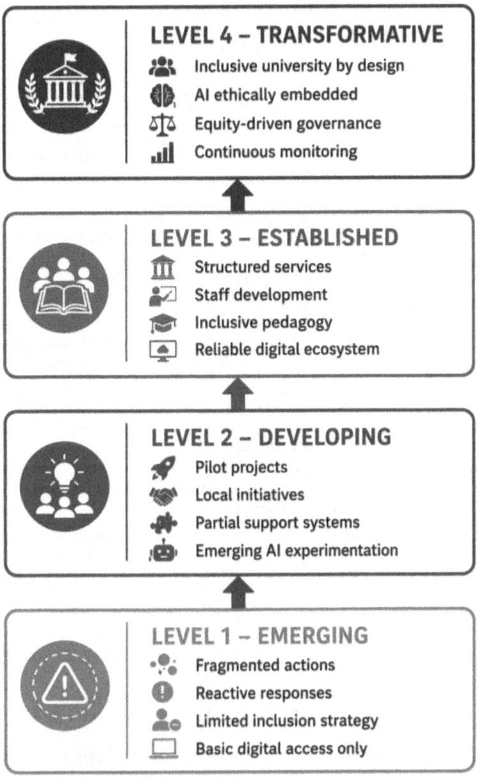

Fig. 1 The Inclusive Digital Readiness Model conceptualises institutional maturity across four progressive levels, from fragmented responses to transformative inclusion. Progress is evaluated through ten cross-cutting strategic domains combining student support, governance, pedagogy, digital transformation, and ethical AI adoption.

interventions, they should be understood as mutually reinforcing components of an institutional ecosystem. Guidelines are summarized in Table 1.

Taken together, these guidelines suggest that inclusion should not be treated as the responsibility of individual champions or temporary projects, but as a shared institutional commitment embedded in governance, pedagogy, student support, and digital transformation strategies. Their implementation may vary according to institutional size, mission, and available resources, but their combined logic points toward a more equitable and future-oriented university model.

Table 1. Guidelines for an Inclusive University.

Strategic Domain	Guideline	Examples of Digital Enablers
1. Access and Admission	Ensure transparent, flexible, and multilingual admission procedures adapted to diverse documentation conditions.	Multilingual portals, online orientation, AI-supported helpdesks

(*continued*)

Table 1. *(continued)*

Strategic Domain	Guideline	Examples of Digital Enablers
2. Recognition of Qualifications	Facilitate rapid and fair recognition of prior formal, non-formal, and informal learning.	Digital credential repositories, e-certificates, interoperable databases
3. Economic and Housing Support	Reduce material barriers through scholarships, fee waivers, and housing pathways.	Student service platforms, dashboards for equity monitoring
4. Language and Academic Support	Provide sustained linguistic, academic, and mentoring support throughout students' trajectories.	Online tutoring systems, blended language courses, AI translation tools
5. Digital Inclusion	Guarantee access to devices, connectivity, digital literacy, and accessible online environments.	Inclusive LMS platforms, accessibility plugins, device loan systems
6. Wellbeing and Belonging	Promote psychosocial support, peer networks, and a sense of belonging on campus and online.	Tele-counselling, peer community platforms, wellbeing apps
7. Inclusive Teaching and Assessment	Embed flexibility, intercultural responsiveness, and Universal Design for Learning into curricula.	Learning analytics, adaptive feedback tools, accessible assessment systems
8. Governance and Leadership	Institutionalise inclusion through leadership structures, staff development, and data-informed planning.	Institutional dashboards, reporting systems, integrated data platforms
9. Employability and Transitions	Support transitions into further study, internships, and employment opportunities.	E-portfolios, career platforms, digital job-matching services

5 Discussion

5.1 Interpreting Inclusion through a Systemic and Digital Lens

The findings confirm that inclusion in higher education is a systemic process rather than a discrete set of support measures. Italian universities have demonstrated strong engagement through initiatives such as University Corridors for Refugees (UNICORE) and the Manifesto of the Inclusive University, but the persistence of uneven practices highlights the need for coherent institutional strategies that integrate policy, pedagogy, and technology.

In this perspective, the proposed Guidelines for an Inclusive University go beyond summarizing good practices by framing inclusion as a process of institutional learning, mediated by digital technologies. Digital infrastructures have become central enablers of accessibility, flexibility, and transparency in contemporary higher education [66–70]. However, their effectiveness depends on meaningful pedagogical integration, institutional readiness, and ethical governance [56, 71, 72].

By situating educational technologies within the inclusive university model, the study extends the conceptualisation of inclusion from the physical to the digital campus, aligning with contemporary understandings of learning ecologies that span formal and informal, onsite and online environments [73–75]. This multidimensional view resonates with UNESCO's assertion that inclusive education must adapt to the diversity of learners across all modalities of participation [27].

5.2 Alignment with International and European Frameworks

The **guidelines** are consistent with the principles articulated in major international frameworks promoted by UNESCO, UNHCR, and the European Commission, which frame inclusive higher education as both a matter of equity and a strategic investment in democratic and sustainable societies, while offering a more operational translation specifically tailored to the Italian higher education context.

UNESCO has consistently emphasised that inclusion requires systemic adaptation to learner diversity rather than selective compensatory interventions [27]. Similarly, UNHCR initiatives such as the 15by30 strategy and the Global Compact on Refugees highlight the importance of safe and equitable pathways to tertiary education [2, 76]. In the European context, recent policy agendas have linked widening participation with digital transformation, accessibility, and social cohesion [77].

The present study extends these principles by translating them into an operational model specifically adapted to the Italian university context. In doing so, the Italian case demonstrates how global and regional frameworks can be localised through coordinated institutional actions, transforming international commitments into measurable practices.

5.3 Digital Infrastructures, Educational Technologies and AI as Mediators of Inclusion

The integration of digital and AI-based technologies emerges as both an opportunity and a challenge. On the one hand, technological infrastructures enable new modalities of inclusion, such as online preparatory courses for refugees abroad, remote mentoring, adaptive language learning tools, and digital credentialing. These innovations can significantly lower barriers of distance, cost, and bureaucracy [45, 78–80].

On the other hand, technological adoption without critical reflection risks generating digital exclusion. Refugee and migrant-background students may lack stable internet access, devices, or digital literacy, which can compound existing vulnerabilities [53, 81]. Moreover, AI systems used for translation or learning analytics can unintentionally reproduce bias if not carefully designed and monitored [53, 56, 82, 83].

Therefore, the ethical dimension of digital inclusion becomes central. Following Popenici and Kerr, Chan, Poravska-Pomsta [84, 85], the pedagogical use of AI should reinforce, not replace, human relationships in teaching and support. For Italian universities, this means adopting a human-centred digitalisation strategy, ensuring that technological choices are guided by inclusivity, accessibility, and respect for students' agency and privacy.

5.4 From Project-Based Initiatives to Institutional Governance

A recurrent finding of the review concerns the fragmented nature of inclusion initiatives in Italy. Many universities host dedicated offices or projects, but few integrate inclusion into long-term governance structures or quality assurance mechanisms. Sustainable progress requires moving from project logic to institutional logic. Inclusion should be embedded into governance systems, budgeting processes, staff development plans, quality assurance mechanisms, and digital transformation agendas.

The proposed Inclusive Digital Readiness Model is intended to support this transition by providing a theoretical benchmark for continuous reflection and evidence-based decision-making.

Based on the Inclusive Digital Readiness Model and on the Guidelines for an Inclusive University, it is possible to envisage digital tools that connect with institutional data systems and reporting cycles (e.g., for the Manifesto of the Inclusive University or national quality assurance processes), enabling universities to embed inclusion into their strategic planning and resource allocation. This approach aligns with the concept of inclusive governance, which frames inclusion as a shared institutional responsibility rather than the domain of individual champions or temporary projects [77].

Finally, the use of a shared framework may also encourage horizontal learning across institutions, enabling universities to compare progress, exchange practices, and strengthen national coordination in this area.

5.5 Contributions to Research and Future Directions

From a research perspective, the study offers three main contributions. First, it introduces the concept of inclusive university as a digitally mediated system, bridging the literatures on higher education inclusion, migration studies, educational digital infrastructures, and AI in education. Second, it proposes guidelines and a practically oriented model that translate dispersed evidence into actionable domains and maturity indicators. Third, it highlights the Italian case as a relevant laboratory for understanding how institutional autonomy, national initiatives, and European policy frameworks interact.

Future research should empirically validate the proposed model through pilot implementations in universities, comparative studies across European systems, and participatory inquiry involving students themselves. Mixed-method approaches combining institutional data, student narratives, and learning analytics may be particularly valuable in examining how inclusive practices influence access, persistence, wellbeing, and academic success.

6 Conclusions

This study examined the evolving landscape of inclusion for refugee and migrant-background students in Italian higher education, situating the issue at the intersection of institutional policy, pedagogical innovation, and digital transformation. The findings confirm that inclusive universities are not created through admission policies alone. Rather, they emerge when institutions redesign governance structures, teaching practices, student support services, and digital infrastructures around the diversity of their learners.

The paper offers three main contributions. First, it advances a systemic conceptualization of inclusion integrating social, cultural, and digital dimensions, understanding inclusion not as a static condition but as a continuous institutional process that connects social justice goals with organisational change and requires the redesign of governance, pedagogy, and technological infrastructures. Second, it translates broad international and European principles promoted by UNESCO, UNHCR, and the European Commission into an operational framework tailored to the Italian higher education context, articulated through strategies that emphasise access, recognition of qualifications, linguistic and academic support, digital participation, wellbeing, inclusive teaching, governance, and employability. Third, it introduces the Inclusive Digital Readiness Model and related guidelines as tools for strategic improvement

For Italian higher education, these findings suggest that inclusion should be integrated more explicitly into funding priorities, strategic planning, quality assurance systems, staff development, and digital transformation agendas. At a time when universities are simultaneously expanding their digital reach and confronting deep social inequalities, the challenge of inclusion cannot be addressed by technological solutions alone, but requires institutional reflexivity, ethical digital governance, and a commitment to viewing diversity as a constitutive element of academic excellence. In this perspective, investments in AI and educational technologies should be guided by accessibility, equity-oriented design, and social responsibility. Italian initiatives such as UNICORE, EQPR, and the Manifesto of the Inclusive University demonstrate that meaningful and inclusive innovation is possible when universities act as communities of practice through coordinated partnerships that bridge global frameworks with local realities.

This study has some limitations. As an integrative review based on available literature and public documentation, it may not capture informal, unpublished, or emerging practices developed within individual universities. In addition, the focus on the Italian higher education context limits the direct generalisability of the findings, although the inclusion of European policy references offers broader relevance. Finally, because digital inclusion and educational technologies evolve rapidly, the framework and guidelines proposed here should be periodically updated and further validated through pilot applications in universities and comparative studies across different national contexts.

Future research should empirically validate the proposed framework through pilot implementations, comparative European case studies, participatory inquiry involving students, and longitudinal monitoring of institutional change. As digital environments and AI systems continue to evolve, inclusion frameworks will also require periodic revision and contextual adaptation.

Ultimately, refugee and migrant-background students should not be regarded as peripheral beneficiaries of support, but as central participants in the future of European universities. In this perspective, digital pathways to inclusion are also pathways to a renewed idea of higher education, one that combines technological advancement with democratic values, academic excellence, and shared knowledge creation.

Authors' Contributions. The authors contributed equally to all phases of the study, including conceptualization, methodology, analysis, writing, and revision of the manuscript.

Disclosure of Interests. The authors have no competing interests to declare that are relevant to the content of this article.

References

1. UNHCR: UNHCR Education Report 2025: The Unbreakable Promise: Resilience and Resolve in Refugee Education (2025). https://www.un-ilibrary.org/content/books/9789211545456
2. UNHCR: 15by30 Roadmap: Expanding Higher Education, Skills and Self-Reliance for Refugees (2019). https://www.unhcr.org/media/15by30-roadmap-expanding-higher-education-skills-and-self-reliance-refugees
3. Naylor, R., Terry, L., Rizzo, A., Nguyen, N., Mifsud, N.: Structural inequality in refugee participation in higher education. J. Refug. Stud. **34**(2), 2142–2158 (2021)
4. Dryden-Peterson, S.: Right where we Belong: how Refugee Teachers and Students Are Changing the Future of Education. Harvard University Press, Cambridge (2022)
5. Erdoğan, Z.: Assessing the criteria for equality of the right: refugees' higher education from the perspective of human rights. Milli Eğitim Dergisi. **52**(237), 577–602 (2023)
6. Fulantelli, G., Pipitone, V.: Rethinking education in a context of forced migration. Ital. J. Educ. Technol. **25**(1), 6–17 (2017)
7. UNHCR: UNICORE. University Corridors for Refugees (2026). https://universitycorridors.unhcr.it/universities/
8. UNHCR Italia: Rifugiati: arrivato in Italia un nuovo gruppo di studenti rifugiati del progetto UNICORE dei corridoi universitari (2025). https://www.unhcr.org/it/
9. UNHCR: Manifesto on an Inclusive University (2019). https://www.unhcr.org/it/media/manifesto-inclusive-university-unhcr-pdf
10. Council of Europe: European Qualifications Passport for Refugees (EQPR): Implementation Report 2022. Council of Europe Publishing, Strasbourg (2022)
11. De Maria, F., De Vincenzi, C., Ferrara, B.: Italian universities' actions targeting refugees, asylum seekers, and migrants: an initial mapping. Form@re. **23**(1), 198–212 (2023)
12. Rizzolatti, I.: Access to higher education: a comparative law analysis of the institutional and societal barriers refugees must overcome. UIC Law Rev. **56**, 737–768 (2022)
13. Tarozzi, M., Vittori, L.: The reception process of refugee students at the University of Bologna: Funneled procedural facilitations as a reception model. LLL. **22**(45), 245–261 (2024)
14. Bertozzi, R.: University students with migrant background in Italy: which factors affect opportunities? Ital. J. Sociol. Educ. **10**(1), 23–42 (2018)
15. Giudici, D.: Who feels safe? Uncertain futures and enduring aspirations in Italy. Geopolitics. **31**(2), 618–638 (2026)
16. Gola Boutros, M., Pimentel, D., Esteves, A.: Refugees' access to higher education in Italy: an opportunity lost for the 'lost generation'. In: The Palgrave Handbook of Youth Mobility and Educational Migration, pp. 119–129. Springer International Publishing, Cham (2022)
17. Stewart, J., El Chaar, D., McCluskey, K., Borgardt, K.: Refugee student integration: a focus on settlement, education, and psychosocial support. J. Contemp. Issues Educ. **14**(1) (2019)
18. Elala, S.S.: Educational pathways in Italy: Emanuel's perspective. Reflective essay for the special issue "community sponsorship and complementary pathways: global movements for resettling refugees driven by local actors". J. Int. Migr. Integr. **26**(4), 2241–2248 (2025)
19. Rof, A., Bikfalvi, A., Marques, P.: Pandemic-accelerated digital transformation of a born digital higher education institution. Educ. Technol. Soc. **25**(1), 124–141 (2022)
20. Deroncele-Acosta, A., Palacios-Núñez, M.L., Toribio-López, A.: Digital transformation and technological innovation on higher education post-COVID-19. Sustainability. **15**(3), 2466 (2023)
21. Nieto-Taborda, M.L., Luppicini, R.: Accelerated digital transformation of higher education in the wake of COVID-19: a systematic literature review. Int. J. Changes Educ. **2**(2), 123–138 (2025)

22. Halkic, B., Arnold, P.: Refugees and online education: student perspectives on need and support in the context of (online) higher education. Learn. Media Technol. **44**(3), 345–364 (2019)
23. Reinhardt, F., Zlatkin-Troitschanskaia, O., Happ, R., Nell-Müller, S.: Online technology for promoting the inclusion of refugees into higher education: a systematic review of current approaches and developments. In: Research Handbook on International Migration and Digital Technology, pp. 182–194 (2021)
24. Booth, T., Ainscow, M.: Index for Inclusion: Developing Learning and Participation in Schools. Centre for Studies on Inclusive Education, Bristol (2002)
25. Favaro, G., Luatti, L.: Il tempo dell'integrazione. I centri interculturali in Italia. Franco Angeli, Milano (2008)
26. Shakya, Y.B., et al.: Aspirations for higher education among newcomer refugee youth in Toronto: expectations, challenges, and strategies. Refuge. **27**, 65–78 (2010)
27. UNESCO: Global Education Monitoring Report 2020: Inclusion and Education – all Means all. UNESCO Publishing, Paris (2020) https://unesdoc.unesco.org/ark:/48223/pf0000373724
28. Ager, A., Strang, A.: Understanding integration: a conceptual framework. J. Refug. Stud. **21**(2), 166–191 (2008)
29. Stoeber, H., Morrisroe, A.: Higher Education Diversity Strategies for Migrant and Refugee Inclusion: the Uni(di)Versity Atlas on Inclusion. European University Association, Brussels (2021)
30. Abamosa, J.Y.: Social inclusion of refugees into higher education: policies and practices of universities in Norway. Educ. Rev. **75**(6), 1181–1201 (2023)
31. Pascarella, E.T., Terenzini, P.T.: How College Affects Students: a Third Decade of Research, vol. 2. Jossey-Bass, San Francisco (2005)
32. CAST: Universal Design for Learning Guidelines, Version 2.2. CAST (2018) http://udlgui delines.cast.org
33. Juvonen, J., Lessard, L.M., Rastogi, R., Schacter, H.L., Smith, D.S.: Promoting social inclusion in educational settings: challenges and opportunities. Educ. Psychol. **54**(4), 250–270 (2019)
34. Deardorff, D.K., Iuliano, R.: More than Welcome: Intercultural Integration of Migrants in and through Higher Education. UNESCO Publishing, Paris (2026)
35. Claeys-Kulik, A.L., Jørgensen, T.E., Stöber, H.: Diversity, Equity and Inclusion in European Higher Education Institutions: Results from the INVITED Project. European University Association, Brussels (2019)
36. European Commission, et al.: Equity and Inclusion in Higher Education: Mapping Policy Approaches and Gaps in Evaluation. Publications Office of the European Union, Luxembourg (2025) https://data.europa.eu/doi/10.2766/2151058
37. Dal Zotto, E., Marchetti, C.: Lights in the night from asylum: innovative integration practices and signs of a new citizenship in Italy. Quad. Sociol. **96**(LXVIII), 79–100 (2024)
38. Selwyn, N., Facer, K.: The sociology of education and digital technology: past, present and future. Oxf. Rev. Educ. **40**(4), 482–496 (2014)
39. Castañeda, L., Selwyn, N.: More than tools? Making sense of the ongoing digitizations of higher education. Int. J. Educ. Technol. High. Educ. **15**(1), 22 (2018)
40. Facer, K., Selwyn, N.: Digital Technology and the Futures of Education: Towards 'Non-Stupid' Optimism. Futures of Education Initiative, UNESCO, Paris (2021)
41. Decuypere, M., Grimaldi, E., Landri, P.: Introduction: critical studies of digital education platforms. Crit. Stud. Educ. **62**(1), 1–16 (2021)
42. Traxler, J.: Decolonising Digital Language Learning in Palestine (2023)
43. Jones, A., et al.: Supporting immigrant language learning on smartphones: a field trial. Stud. Educ. Adults. **49**(2), 228–252 (2017)

44. Bradley, L., Guichon, N., Kukulska-Hulme, A.: Migrants' and refugees' digital literacies in life and language learning. ReCALL. **37**(2), 147–156 (2025)
45. Bozkurt, A., et al.: A global outlook to the interruption of education due to COVID-19 pandemic: navigating in a time of uncertainty and crisis. Asian J. Distance Educ. **15**(1), 1–126 (2021)
46. Durak, G., Çankaya, S., Oncu, S., Rienties, B.: Exploring equity, diversity, and inclusion in blended learning: trends and insights. Open Praxis. **17**(4), 749–767 (2025)
47. Lomellini, A., Lowenthal, P.R., Snelson, C., Trespalacios, J.H.: Accessible and inclusive online learning in higher education: a review of the literature. J. Comput. High. Educ. **37**(3), 1306–1329 (2025)
48. Moussa, A., Wollny, C., Switzer, C.: Bridging the gap: leveraging online higher education for displaced persons. In: Technology for Societal Transformation: Exploring the Intersection of Information Technology and Societal Development, pp. 251–268. Springer Nature, Singapore (2025)
49. Ocheredko, O., Siemon, D.: Beyond access: rethinking refugee integration through information systems. In: ICIS 2025 Proceedings (2025)
50. Kukulska-Hulme, A.: Mobile incidental learning to support the inclusion of recent immigrants. Ubiquit. Learn. Int. J. (2015)
51. Moser-Mercer, B., Hayba, E., Goldsmith, J.: Higher education spaces and protracted displacement: how learner-centered pedagogies and human-centered design can unleash refugee innovation. In: UNESCO Chair Conference on Technologies for Development, pp. 41–52. Springer International Publishing, Cham (2016)
52. Fulantelli, G., Pipitone, V., Taibi, D., Todaro, G., Arrigo, M., La Guardia, D.: Le tecnologie digitali per rispondere ai bisogni formativi dei migranti forzati. In: Convegno Nazionale Didamatica, pp. 313–322 (2018)
53. Fulantelli, G., Taibi, D., Todaro, G., Pipitone, V., La Guardia, D., Arrigo, M.: A mobile learning platform to guarantee education continuity for unaccompanied foreign minors and refugees. In: Bastiaens, J.T. (ed.) Proceedings of EdMedia + Innovate Learning, pp. 1636–1640. Association for the Advancement of Computing in Education (AACE), Amsterdam (2019)
54. Zawacki-Richter, O., Marín, V.I., Bond, M., Gouverneur, F.: Systematic review of research on artificial intelligence applications in higher education: where are the educators? Int. J. Educ. Technol. High. Educ. **16**, 39 (2019). https://doi.org/10.1186/s41239-019-0171-0
55. Vo, T.K.A.: Transforming language learning with AI: adaptive systems, engagement, and global impact. Eng. Proc. **107**(1), 7 (2025). https://doi.org/10.3390/engproc2025107007
56. Williamson, B., Eynon, R.: Historical threads, missing links, and future directions in AI in education. Learn. Media Technol. **45**(3), 223–235 (2020). https://doi.org/10.1080/17439884.2020.1798995
57. Holmes, W., Miao, F.: Guidance for Generative AI in Education and Research. UNESCO Publishing, Paris (2023)
58. García-López, I.M., Trujillo-Liñán, L.: Ethical and regulatory challenges of generative AI in education: a systematic review. Front. Educ. **10**, 1565938 (2025)
59. Klimova, B., Chen, J.H.: The impact of AI on enhancing students' intercultural communication competence at the university level: a review study. Lang. Teach. Res. Q. **43**, 102–120 (2024)
60. Sajja, R., Sermet, Y., Cikmaz, M., Cwiertny, D., Demir, I.: Artificial intelligence-enabled intelligent assistant for personalized and adaptive learning in higher education. Information. **15**(10), 596 (2024)
61. Charkhian, D.: Exploring the Potential of AI for Improving Inclusivity in University Portals. Master's thesis, Drexel University (2025)

62. Broome, M.E.: Integrative literature reviews for the development of concepts. In: Rodgers, B.L., Knafl, K.A. (eds.) Concept Development in Nursing: Foundations, Techniques and Applications, pp. 231–250. W.B. Saunders Company, Philadelphia (2000)
63. Toronto, C.E., Remington, R. (eds.): A Step-by-Step Guide to Conducting an Integrative Review, 1st edn. Springer International Publishing, Cham (2020). https://doi.org/10.1007/978-3-030-37504-1
64. Altheide, D., Coyle, M., DeVriese, K., Schneider, C.: Emergent qualitative document analysis. In: Hesse-Biber, S.N., Leavy, P. (eds.) Handbook of Emergent Methods, pp. 127–151. Guilford Press, New York (2008)
65. Bowen, G.A.: Document analysis as a qualitative research method. Qual. Res. J. **9**(2), 27–40 (2009)
66. Gaebel, M., Zhang, T., Stoeber, H., Morrisroe, A.: Digitally Enhanced Learning and Teaching in European Higher Education Institutions. European University Association, Brussels (2021)
67. Staring, F., Brown, M., Bacsich, P., Ifenthaler, D.: Digital higher education: Emerging quality standards, practices and supports. OECD Education Working Papers, No. 281, 1–97 (2022)
68. OECD: OECD Digital Education Outlook 2023. OECD Publishing, Paris (2023)
69. Amiel, T.: Digital infrastructures for education: Openness and the common good. UNESCO IdeasLAB Blog (2024). https://www.unesco.org/en/articles/digital-infrastructures-education-openness-and-common-good
70. Rajasekaran, S., Adam, T., Tilmes, K.: Digital Pathways for Education, No. 42386. World Bank Group, Washington, DC (2024)
71. Selwyn, N.: Education and Technology: Key Issues and Debates. Bloomsbury Publishing, London (2021)
72. Amiel, T.: Open education and platformization: critical perspectives for a new social contract in education. Prospects. **54**, 341–350 (2024). https://doi.org/10.1007/s11125-023-09660-x
73. Peters, M., Romero, M.: Lifelong learning ecologies in online higher education: Students' engagement in the continuum between formal and informal learning. Br. J. Educ. Technol. **50**(4), 1729–1743 (2019)
74. Sangrà, A., Raffaghelli, J.E., Veletsianos, G.: Lifelong learning ecologies: linking formal and informal contexts of learning in the digital era. Br. J. Educ. Technol. **50**(4), 1615–1618 (2019)
75. Bozkurt, A., Stracke, C.M.: The shift toward openness in education and the implications for learning ecosystems and ecologies. In: Distributed Learning Ecosystems: Concepts, Resources, and Repositories, pp. 31–46. Springer Fachmedien, Wiesbaden (2023)
76. UNHCR: Global Compact on Refugees. United Nations High Commissioner for Refugees, Geneva (2018) https://www.unhcr.org/about-unhcr/overview/global-compact-refugees
77. European Commission: Towards Equity and Inclusion in Higher Education in Europe. Eurydice Report. European Commission, Brussels (2022)
78. Scardigno, F.: The cultural integration of young refugees: an experience within the Italian academic context. Ital. J. Sociol. Educ. **11**(3), 283–303 (2019)
79. Celik, E., Norton, L.S., Sarrica, M.: The academic integration of international students at an Italian university: exploring communication channels, feeling of belonging and social support. Psychol. Hub. **40**(1), 7–14 (2023)
80. Gamba, E.: A multi-level governance of resilience: civil society, universities and local governments for the support of refugee students in Italy. Peace Hum. Rights Gov. **9**(1), 49–76 (2025)
81. Drolia, M., Papadakis, S., Sifaki, E., Kalogiannakis, M.: Mobile learning applications for refugees: a systematic literature review. Educ. Sci. **12**(2), 96 (2022). https://doi.org/10.3390/educsci12020096
82. Baker, R.S., Hawn, A.: Algorithmic bias in education. Int. J. Artif. Intell. Educ. **32**(4), 1052–1092 (2022)

83. Lee, J., Hicke, Y., Yu, R., Brooks, C., Kizilcec, R.F.: The life cycle of large language models: A review of biases in education. arXiv preprint https://arxiv.org/abs/2407.11203 (2024)
84. Popenici, S.A.D., Kerr, S.: Exploring the impact of artificial intelligence on teaching and learning in higher education. Res. Pract. Technol. Enhanc. Learn. **12**(1), 1–13 (2017). https://doi.org/10.1186/s41039-017-0062-8
85. Porayska-Pomsta, K., Holmes, W., Nemorin, S.: The ethics of AI in education. In: Handbook of Artificial Intelligence in Education, pp. 571–604. Edward Elgar Publishing, Cheltenham (2023)

Inclusion, Accessibility and Human Rights

Virtual Museums as Inclusive Third Spaces in Online Higher Education

Alessia Sozio[1], Monica Di Domenico[2], Maria Carbone[3], and Tonia De Giuseppe[4](✉)

[1] Pegaso Telematic University, Naples, Italy
alessia.sozio@unipegaso.it
[2] University of Salerno, via Giovanni Paolo II, 132, –84084 Fisciano, (SA), Italy
[3] Pegaso Telematic University, Naples, Italy
[4] Giustino Fortunato University, Viale Raffaele Delcogliano, 12, 82100 Benevento, Italy
t.degiuseppe@unifortunato.eu

Abstract. This paper reports preliminary evidence from an exploratory study on the integration of virtual museums (VMs) into online university courses, conceived as "third spaces" for learning capable of connecting curricular and cultural dimensions. Drawing on an existing dataset ($N \approx 43$), the analysis explores perceived outcomes in terms of inclusion, participation, and reflective learning. The theoretical framework combines Universal Design for Learning (UDL), the Community of Inquiry perspective for e-learning, and museum learning scholarship. The study adopts an exploratory descriptive design based on questionnaire data and a descriptive thematic reading of short open-ended comments. Initial results indicate a favorable disposition toward VMs and suggest preliminary perceived benefits for engagement and critical reflection. Implications for instructional design, limitations, and directions for future research are discussed.

Keywords: Virtual museum · inclusion · third space

1 Introduction

Higher education is undergoing a transformation—accelerated by the COVID-19 pandemic—that calls for a revision of instructional models (Means et al., 2013). Contemporary pedagogical debate highlights the need to move beyond traditional schooling models by promoting learning environments that are more flexible, personalized, and connected to the outside world (Aiello et al., 2017; Sibilio, 2020). European and national strategies - the Digital Education Action Plan 2021–2027, the National Digital School Plan, and the PNRR - recognize digitalization as a key lever for inclusion and resilience (European Commission, 2020; MIUR, 2015; PNRR, 2021). In this landscape, online higher education requires approaches capable of sustaining meaningful participation, inclusion, and reflexivity, consistent with the literature on distance and blended learning (Means et al., 2013; Laurillard, 2012; Garrison, Anderson, & Archer, 2000). Against this backdrop, Schweibenz defines the virtual museum as "a logically related collection of

M. Adamoli et al. (Eds.): HELMeTO 2025, CCIS 2958, pp. 119–128, 2026.
https://doi.org/10.1007/978-3-032-31850-3_8

digital objects composed in a variety of media [...] its objects and the related information can be disseminated all over the world" (Schweibenz, 1998). This definition underlines how designing and building inclusive virtual museums presents significant opportunities to promote prosocial behaviors among visitors, a "third space" between formal and informal knowledge (Bhabha, 1994; Gutiérrez, 2008).

2 Theoretical Framework and Related Work

Inclusive design, as proposed by Universal Design for Learning (UDL), frames inclusion as a design problem rather than the remediation of individual deficits. UDL encourages multiple means of engagement, representation, and action/expression in order to reduce barriers to access and participation (CAST, 2024). In online higher education, the Community of Inquiry (CoI) model complements this perspective by describing how meaningful learning emerges from the interplay of teaching, social, and cognitive presence (Garrison et al., 2000). In parallel, research on museum learning—also in its virtual forms—emphasizes the situated and constructive nature of experience, where learners build meaning through dialogue, interpretation, and contextual cues (Hein, 1998; Falk & Dierking, 2000; Parry, 2007). Finally, traditions of reflective learning highlight how structured reflection consolidates understanding and supports deeper learning processes (Mezirow, 1991). Within this framework, constructive alignment provides a reference for coherently linking learning objectives, activities, and assessment (Biggs & Tang, 2011), while collaborative learning research offers principles for designing high-quality interactions (Johnson, Johnson, & Smith, 2014). Within this theoretical framework we conceptualize the virtual museum as a deliberately designed third space - an educational arrangement where academic objectives meet cultural participation and where learners can negotiate meanings across personal and disciplinary registers (Bhabha, 1994; Gutiérrez, 2008). In this perspective, the virtual museum is not a repository of digitized artefacts but a participatory cultural environment that can be pedagogically orchestrated to sustain attention, emotion, and dialogue, and to enable horizontal, co-creative learning roles (Hein, 1998; Parry, 2007; ICOM, 2022; Jenkins, 2006a, 2006b). This interpretation also resonates with the concept of open heritage, which emphasises the accessibility, participatory use, and educational recontextualisation of cultural heritage through digital technologies (Di Tore et al., 2022a). This is consistent with "new museology", which understands the museum as a dynamic space where visitors co-construct meanings rather than passively receive them (Hein, 1998). By overcoming constraints of space and place, virtual museums can extend these participatory dynamics into online courses, supporting collaborative inquiry and interaction beyond traditional modes of classroom communication (Parry, 2007). When supported by interactive and immersive technologies, these environments may also contribute to broader learning ecologies in which perception, action, and meaning-making are closely interconnected (Di Tore et al., 2022b; Gomez Paloma 2022). Based on the UDL approach, multiple means of representation can be realized through multimodal curation (e.g., images, captions, timelines, audio descriptions); multiple means of engagement through relevance, choice, and affective hooks; and multiple means of action/expression through flexible outputs (e.g., short written reflections, audio notes, infographics) (CAST, 2024; Schweibenz,

1998). These levers reduce entry barriers, support self-regulation, and legitimize diverse communicative repertoires. Thanks to a CoI approach, teaching presence is enacted through curated prompts and scaffolds, social presence through dialogic activities and peer acknowledgement, and cognitive presence through guided meaning-making around exhibits (Garrison et al., 2000). Reflective prompts and short cycles of interpretation further connect the experience to perspective transformation and deep learning (Mezirow, 1991). Taken together, these designable elements—choice, multimodality, and dialogic prompts—offer a coherent rationale for why a virtual museum sequence may function as an inclusive third space in online higher education. As a complementary lens, we position ecological and inclusion-oriented approaches (Bronfenbrenner, 1979; Booth & Ainscow, 2011) and Flipped Inclusion (Corona & De Giuseppe, 2020; (Bateson, 1972; Bergmann, 2012)) as supportive to the above framework, insofar as they emphasize participation, cultural transformation, and the structuring of collaborative dynamics.

3 Methodology

From these premises arise our research questions:
RQ1. What perceptions and expectations do students express toward VMs integrated into online courses (interest, usefulness, inclusion)?
RQ2. In what ways do VMs function as a "third space" that facilitates participation, peer exchange, and meaning-making?
RQ3. What evidence of reflective learning emerges in student products and diaries/posts?

We adopted an essential mixed-methods approach (Creswell & Plano Clark, 2007): on the one hand, descriptive statistics of the scales and a measure of familiarity with virtual museums; on the other, qualitative extracts from open-ended responses analyzed thematically (Braun & Clarke, 2006). The questionnaire was administered in two waves: before the activity (T0, the course setting) and during the exhibition experience (T1). The analysis focused on descriptive statistics for the questionnaire items and on the descriptive categorisation of short open-ended responses. The findings are therefore interpreted as exploratory evidence of participants' perceptions and perceived affordances of virtual museums, rather than as evidence of change or causal effects.

4 Context and Dataset

The study is situated within the context of online higher education and examines the educational use of virtual museums as digitally mediated environments for participation, cultural engagement, and inclusive learning. Within this framework, the virtual museum is approached not simply as a repository of digitized content, but as a potentially meaningful educational space in which learners may encounter cultural heritage through forms of access and interaction that differ from those typically associated with conventional academic settings. This contextual framing is central to the paper, as it allows the virtual museum to be interpreted as a possible third space at the intersection of formal learning, cultural mediation, and participatory experience. The dataset comprises approximately 43 participants with heterogeneous profiles and varying degrees of prior familiarity with virtual museums Fig. 1. Although limited in scale and not statistically representative, the sample offers a sufficiently differentiated basis for exploring how learners perceive this type of environment and which educational affordances they associate with it. From an analytical perspective, the dataset is used here as an exploratory empirical basis for identifying recurrent perceptions linked to accessibility, collaboration, engagement, and meaningful learning. Accordingly, the evidence is not intended to support broad generalizations, but rather to provide a grounded first insight into how virtual museums may be experienced and interpreted within online university teaching.

5 Results

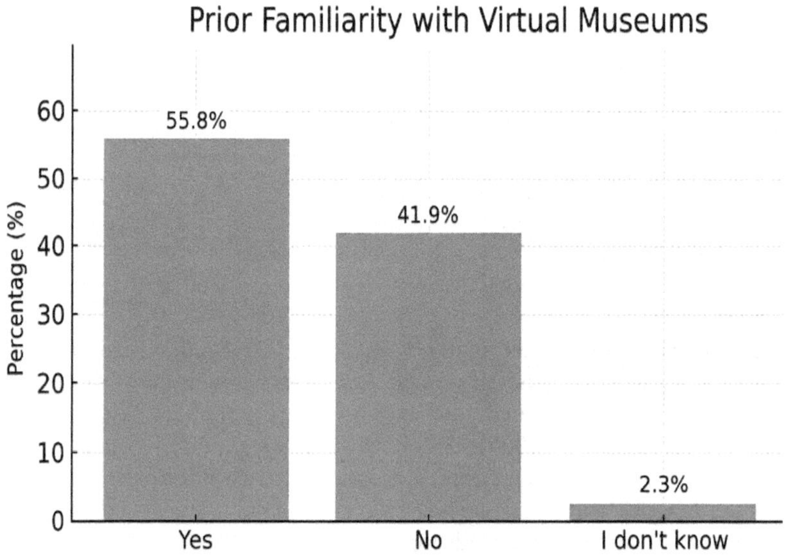

Fig. 1. Familiarity with virtual museums (percentages)

The findings delineate a consistently positive pattern in participants' perceptions of virtual museums as educational environments. Familiarity with virtual museums appears to be present to a meaningful extent within the sample, and these environments are generally regarded as relevant, accessible, and pedagogically worthwhile in the context of higher education. More significantly, the overall distribution of responses suggests that participants do not perceive the virtual museum merely as a digitized repository of cultural content, but as a potentially active learning environment capable of supporting inclusion, interaction, and reflective engagement (Campitiello et al. 2022). From this perspective, the empirical evidence is broadly consistent with the theoretical framing advanced in the paper, according to which the virtual museum may function as a third space situated at the intersection of formal education, cultural mediation, and participatory experience. The most immediate evidence concerns the inclusive dimension of the

Table 1. Descriptive statistics for questionnaire items (M = mean, SD = standard deviation, N = sample size)

Scale	N	M	SD
B1. I believe a virtual museum can be a meeting space for people with different backgrounds	42	3.76	1.03
B3. In a virtual museum I feel free to express personal opinions and interpretations	42	3.57	1.15
B4. In case of online conflicts, I can find shared and respectful solutions	42	3.60	0.91
B5. Virtual environments can reduce physical and cognitive barriers to cultural access	42	4.19	0.86
B6. Taking part in a virtual museum makes me feel part of a learning community	42	3.62	0.85
C1. I try to understand the emotions and viewpoints of others in digital settings	42	3.83	0.99
C2. I feel responsible for contributing to a respectful, collaborative climate online	42	4.24	0.82
C3. I like working in groups or co-creating content (e.g., digital exhibitions, forums, labs)	42	4.07	0.92
C4. I am willing to help others overcome technological or communicative difficulties	42	4.29	0.81
D1. Participating in VM activities makes me feel more motivated and curious	42	3.86	0.98
D2. Digital immersive experiences increase my sense of belonging to the group	42	3.45	1.13
D3. I feel appreciated and recognized when sharing ideas in virtual environments	42	3.36	1.27
D4. Visiting or interacting with a VM improves my mood and self-esteem	42	3.24	1.23
D5. I believe the VM can promote collective well- being and solidarity	42	3.64	1.06
E1. I have a general understanding of how AI works and its applications	43	3.74	0.93
E2. I think AI can support personalized learning	43	4.07	0.91
E3. I consider training for responsible AI use to be important	43	4.58	0.70
E4. I often support or encourage other participants during online activities	42	3.48	0.92
F1. I try to connect what I learn with my personal experiences	43	4.40	0.79
F2. I study to deeply understand concepts, not just to pass	43	4.40	0.85
F3. I am more interested in understanding ideas than memorizing details	43	4.33	0.94
F4. I enjoy discussing what I learn with other people	43	4.35	0.78

(*continued*)

Table 1. (*continued*)

Scale	N	M	SD
F5. I try to see how new knowledge connects with other knowledge	43	4.33	0.89
F6. I study only to pass the exam or finish the task	43	1.91	1.00
F7. I memorize what is necessary without worrying about understanding it	43	1.49	0.86
F8. I focus only on what will be assessed	43	1.77	1.00
F9. I avoid putting in more effort than necessary	43	1.67	0.87

experience. Participants report particularly favourable evaluations of the extent to which virtual museums may reduce physical and cognitive barriers to access (B5: M = 4.19), alongside positive perceptions of their capacity to create opportunities for encounter among individuals with different backgrounds (B1: M = 3.76) (Table 1). These results are noteworthy because they suggest that inclusion is perceived not only in infrastructural or technological terms, but also as a relational and cultural condition. In other words, the virtual museum is valued not simply for extending access, but for enabling forms of participation that may support shared presence, interpretive plurality, and broader cultural involvement. Such a reading strengthens the argument that digital environments can support inclusive learning when they are designed and experienced as spaces of mediation rather than as static channels of content delivery. A similarly coherent pattern emerges in relation to collaborative and socio-affective dimensions. Participants express a strong sense of responsibility for maintaining a respectful and constructive online climate (C2: M = 4.24), a marked willingness to support peers facing communicative or technological difficulties (C4: M = 4.29), and a broadly positive orientation toward collaboration and co-creation (C3: M = 4.07). Taken together, these responses indicate that the virtual museum may create conditions favourable to prosocial engagement and peer-supported participation—an aspect of particular importance in online learning contexts, where social presence is often fragile and where participation frequently depends on careful pedagogical orchestration. Although the indicators related to belonging and interpersonal recognition are comparatively more moderate (e.g., D2: M = 3.45; D3: M = 3.36), they remain positive overall. This suggests that the experience may contribute to a meaningful sense of community, even if the intensity of such effects is likely contingent upon the quality of facilitation, task design, and opportunities for interaction embedded in the educational setting. The most robust pattern is found in the area of meaningful and reflective learning. Participants report high levels of agreement with items associated with deep engagement, including connecting learning to personal experience (F1: M = 4.40), studying in order to understand rather than simply to complete a task (F2: M = 4.40), discussing ideas with others (F4: M = 4.35), and integrating new knowledge with what is already known (F5: M = 4.33). By contrast, indicators associated with more superficial approaches to learning remain consistently low, such as studying only to pass (F6: M = 1.91), memorizing without seeking under-standing (F7: M = 1.49), or focusing exclusively on assessed content (F8: M = 1.77). This contrast is especially significant because it indicates that participants tend to associate the virtual museum experience with an interpretive and dialogic mode of learning, rather than with a narrowly instrumental orientation. The experience appears, at least at the perceptual level, to encourage a form of engagement in which cultural content is not simply consumed, but actively connected to prior knowledge, discussion, and personal reflection. The qualitative comments further reinforce this interpretation. Participants repeatedly refer to the experience as one that can "break down barriers," "encourage active participation," and support "knowledge and ongoing updating," there-by highlighting recurring themes of accessibility, agency, and meaning-making. While these qualitative data (Table 2) remain limited in depth and should not be over interpreted, they nevertheless contribute to the internal consistency of the findings by revealing convergence between the descriptive trends and participants' own ac-counts. Overall, the results support a cautious but coherent conclusion: when embedded within a pedagogically structured activity, the virtual museum is perceived as a flexible and inclusive environment capable of sustaining participation, fostering reflective learning (Mezirow, 1991), and strengthening the relationship between learners, cultural heritage, and the online educational community (Johnson, Adams Becker, Estrada, & Freeman, 2011).

Table 2. Qualitative themes and extracts from open-ended responses

Inclusion/Otherness	"Breaks down barriers."
Inclusion/Otherness	"It can help overcome barriers that would otherwise prevent full enjoyment and understanding."
Inclusion/Otherness	"It can foster inclusion and collective well-being by making culture accessible to all, overcoming physical, economic, and geographical barriers. It offers educational and artistic experiences that stimulate participation, dialogue, and personal growth, thus contributing to a more equitable and aware society."
Meaning-making	"It encourages active participation"
Meaning-making	"It certainly stimulates curiosity and active participation."
Meaning-making	"As a process of knowledge and ongoing updating."

6 Discussion

Our findings position the virtual museum as a designed third space is consistent with inclusion and engagement aims. Because the study is exploratory, based on self-reported data, and conducted without a control condition, the results should be interpreted as participants' perceptions of the educational affordances of virtual museums rather than as evidence of change or causal effects. Quantitatively, learners reported sustained effort and interest alongside a sense of belonging. Qualitatively, they described moving from description to interpretation through guided prompts, affective resonance, and peer-mediated reflection. Taken together, these strands clarify the mechanisms through which the sequence operates. Two practical design levers emerge. First, advance organizers and wayfinding cues help manage cognitive load while maintaining openness to interpretation. Second, dialogic accountability (clear prompts, time-boxing, and response norms) converts solitary impressions into shared understanding without stifling originality. Assessment should value process traces (linking evidence, responsiveness to peers) alongside product quality to avoid performative reflection. These results generalize to comparable online contexts where instructors can curate accessible exhibits and structure short, assessable outputs. Future evaluations should test causal claims (e.g., quasi-experimental comparisons) and examine durability of outcomes through delayed post-measures. Despite the promising pattern of results, the present study has several limitations that should be acknowledged. First, the sample size is relatively small and drawn from a single course context, which limits the generaliability of the findings. Second, outcomes rely primarily on self-reported perceptions measured through Likert-type items; therefore, responses may be influenced by social desirability and individual interpretation of the items rather than objective learning outcomes. Third, although the questionnaire was administered in two waves (T0 before the activity at school and T1 during the exhibition experience), the study does not include a control condition or an alternative activity. Consequently, observed differences between T0 and T1 cannot be interpreted as causal effects attributable to the virtual museum experience. In addition, the different administration contexts (classroom vs. exhibition setting) may have shaped students' responses through novelty effects or situational engagement. Fourth, the qualitative component is based on short comments, which provides valuable signals but limits depth and interpretive richness. Future work should strengthen the research design by including comparison groups (e.g., a non-museum digital learning activity), administering both waves in comparable conditions when feasible, and extending measurement beyond perceptions to include performance indicators (e.g., task artefacts assessed with rubrics, learning analytics, or delayed post-tests). A richer qualitative strand (e.g., interviews or focus groups) would also help clarify mechanisms—such as belonging, agency, and meaning-making—through which virtual museums may function as inclusive third spaces in online higher education.

7 Conclusion

Although preliminary and not generalizable, these results align with the state of the art on the role of immersive technologies and cultural platforms in supporting motivation, perceived presence (Chiesa et al., 2020; Lee et al., 2020; Marty, 2008), deep processing, and dialogic engagement - provided that experiences are designed as tasks of inquiry and co-creation rather than mere guided tours. In this contribution, we have examined the inclusive virtual museum as a post-digital learning environment in which cultural mediation practices, bodies, data, and algorithms co-construct learning experiences. Empirically, the questionnaire data indicate an overall favourable perception of virtual museums: more than half of the respondents reported prior familiarity with digital museum visits, while item-level means were generally positive for accessibility, collaboration, peer support, and meaningful learning. Items concerning belonging, interpersonal recognition, mood, and self-esteem received comparatively more moderate evaluations. Comparisons between T0 and T1 suggest a generally more favourable perception during the museum experience on selected indicators, although this cannot be attributed causally in the absence of a control condition. From this perspective, the inclusive virtual museum can function as a formative third space capable (Bhabha, 1994) of fostering prosocial attitudes and meaningful learning when designed with navigation-by-design patterns, multimodal accessibility, and participatory curatorship. The integration of VMs into online university courses - supported by UDL principles and reflective, collaborative practices - shows potential for promoting inclusion and participation. The approach outlined here offers a viable pathway for instructors and institutions seeking to leverage digital cultural heritage as a pedagogical resource.

Disclosure of Interests. The authors have no competing interests to declare that are relevant to the content of this article.

References

Aiello, P., et al.: A study on Italian teachers sentiments, attitudes and concerns towards inclusive education. **20**, 10 (2017). https://www.iris.unisa.it/handle/11386/4682089

Bateson, G.: Steps to an Ecology of Mind. Chandler, San Francisco, CA (1972)

Bergmann, J.: Flip your Classroom: Reach every Student in every Class every Day. International Society for Technology in Education (2012)

Bhabha, H.K.: The Location of Culture. Routledge (1994)

Biggs, J., Tang, C.: Train-the-trainers: implementing outcomes-based teaching and learning in Malaysian higher education. Malays. J. Learn. Instr. **8**, 1–19 (2011)

Booth, T., Ainscow, M.: Index for inclusion: developing learning and participation in schools. CSIE. (2011)

Braun, V., Clarke, V.: Using thematic analysis in psychology. Qual. Res. Psychol. **3**(2), 77–101 (2006)

Bronfenbrenner, U.: The Ecology of Human Development: Experiments by Nature and design. Harvard University Press (1979)

Campitiello, L., De Giuseppe, T., Todino, M.: Musei e accessibilità. FrancoAngeli. (2022)

CAST. UDL Guidelines 3.0. Wakefield, MA: CAST. udlguidelines.cast.org+2udlguidelines.cast.org+2 (2024).

Champion, E., Rahaman, H.: Cultural heritage infrastructures and virtual museums. In: Champion, E. (ed.) Cultural Heritage Infrastructures in Digital Humanities, pp. 1–20 (2020)

Chiesa, M., et al.: La realtà virtuale a scuola: le parole dei ragazzi. Je-LKS/Atti. (2020)

Creswell, J.W., Clark, V .P.: Mixed methods research. Thousand Oaks, CA (2007)

Corona, F., De Giuseppe, T.: Flipped Inclusion. Modelli e strategie per una didattica inclusiva, FrancoAngeli (2020)

Creswell, J. W., & Plano Clark, V. L.: Designing and Conducting Mixed Methods Research, 3rd (ed.). SAGE (2018)

Dewey, J.: Esperienza e educazione, tr. it., Firenze: La Nuova Italia (1961 b) (1981)

De Giuseppe, T.: Individui e società: Sentimenti dissonanti ed esclusioni emarginanti. In: De Giuseppe, T., Corona, F. (eds.) La disabilità in parossistica ciclicità di esclusione e inclusione Pedagogia + Didattica, vol. 1, pp. 3–13. Erickson (2015)

De Giuseppe, T., Corona, F.: La flipped inclusion tra paradigmi esistenziali e mission d'inclusività sistemica. Res. Trends Hum. Educ. Philos. **7**, 79–90 (2020)

Di Tore, P. A., Messina, C., Recupero, A.: Open Heritage. LED Edizioni (2022a)

Di Tore, P.A., Sibilio, M., Mangione, G.R., Corona, F.: Embodied education and immersive technologies: toward new learning ecologies. Ital. J. Educ. Technol. **30**(3), 261–278 (2022b)

European Commission: Digital Education Action Plan 2021–2027. Publications Office of the European Union, Resetting education and training for the digital age (2020)

Falk, J.H., Dierking, L.D.: Learning from Museums: Visitor Experiences and the Making of Meaning. Md, AltaMira Press, Lanham (2000)

Garrison, D.R., Anderson, T., Archer, W.: Critical inquiry in a text-based environment: computer conferencing in higher education. Internet High. Educ. **2**(2–3), 87–105 (2000)

Gómez Paloma, F.: The neuroeducational approach. Pensa MultiMedia (2022)
Gutiérrez, K.: Developing a sociocritical literacy in the third space. Read. Res. Q. **43**(2), 148–164 (2008)
Hein, G.E.: Learning in the Museum. Routledge (1998)
International Council of Museums (ICOM): ICOM Museum Definition (Versione Approvata 24 Agosto 2022). ICOM, Paris (2022)
Jenkins, H.: Convergence Culture: where Old and New Media Collide. NYU Press, New York (2006a)
Jenkins, H.: Confronting the Challenges of Participatory Culture: Media Education for the 21st Century (2006b)
Laurillard, D.: Teaching as a Design Science. Routledge (2012)
Lee, I., Ali, S., Zhang, B., DiPaola, D., Breazeal, C.: Developing: Middle School Students' AI Literacy (2021). https://doi.org/10.1145/3408877.3432513
Means, B., Toyama, Y., Murphy, R., Baki, M.: The effectiveness of online and blended learning: a meta-analysis of the empirical literature. Teach. Coll. Rec. **115**(3), 1–47 (2013)
Mezirow, J.: Transformative Dimensions of Adult Learning, vol. 350, pp. 94104–91310. Jossey-bass, San Francisco, CA (1991)
Parry, R.: Recoding the museum: Digital heritage and the technologies of change. Routledge (2007)
Rivoltella, P.C.: Media education. Idea, metodo, ricerca, pp. 5–263. ELS La Scuola (2017)
Schweibenz, W.: The "Virtual Museum": new perspectives for museums to present objects and information using the internet as a knowledge base and communication system. In: Zimmermann, H.H., Schramm, V. (eds.) Knowledge Management und Kommunikationssysteme: Workflow Management, Multimedia, Knowledge Transfer. Proceedings des 6. Internationalen Symposiums für Informationswissenschaft (ISI '98), Prague, 3–7 November 1998, pp. 185–200. UVK, Konstanz (1998)

Designing Equitable Adaptive Assessment: Psychometrics, Bayesian Reasoning, and Dynamic Models of Learning in Online Higher Education

Irene Gianeselli[1](✉), Dario Ianes[1], Benedetta Zagni[2], Silvia Dell'Anna[1], Alessandro Oronzo Caffò[3], and Andrea Bosco[3]

[1] Free University of Bozen-Bolzano, Faculty of Education, Viale Ratisbona 16, I-39042 Brixen-Bressanone (BZ), Italy
{irene.gianeselli,dario.ianes,silvia.dellanna}@unibz.it

[2] Edizioni Centro Studi Erickson, Via del Pioppeto 24, 38121 Trento (TN), Italy
benedetta.zagni@erickson.it

[3] Department of Education, Psychology, Communication Sciences, University of Bari "Aldo Moro", Palazzo Chiaia-Napolitano, Via Scipione Crisanzio 42, 70122 Bari (BA), Italy
{alessandro.caffo,andrea.bosco}@uniba.it

Abstract. This paper proposes a conceptual framework for reinterpreting advanced psychometric models as formative and inclusive tools for online assessment in higher education. Current digital assessment practices often emphasize summative purposes, reinforcing structural inequalities and privileging students with stronger prior preparation. The proposed framework repositions assessment as a dynamic, learner-centred, and equity-oriented process that supports reflection and growth. Grounded in constructivist and inclusive principles, it integrates four complementary methodological components: Item Response Theory (IRT) and Computerized Adaptive Testing (CAT), Bayesian reasoning, Markov chain modelling, and learning analytics with social network analysis (SNA). Each component is reconceptualized as a pedagogical resource: adaptive testing calibrates item difficulty to learner ability; Bayesian updating expresses progress as probabilistic evidence; Markov models trace cognitive flexibility through mastery transitions; and network analytics reveal the role of relational, social components of learning. A simulated proof-of-concept with 500 virtual learners illustrates how these models can operate coherently within an adaptive psychometric design implemented in R. Results hypothetically shows that cognitive mastery and social connectedness co-evolve, generating distinct inclusion profiles that inform formative and relational interventions. While conceptual, the study highlights the potential of psychometric–pedagogical integration to promote transparency, agency, and equity in digital learning, and outlines directions for empirical validation and ethical implementation.

Keywords: Inclusive Assessment · Psychometrics · Online Higher Education

M. Adamoli et al. (Eds.): HELMeTO 2025, CCIS 2958, pp. 129–146, 2026.
https://doi.org/10.1007/978-3-032-31850-3_9

1 Introduction

Assessment constitutes a core dimension of educational practice, simultaneously serving both formative and summative functions.

In online education, this dual role is particularly salient: formative assessment provides ongoing feedback to guide instruction and support learning, whereas summative assessment certifies achievement at specific points in time [1]. The effectiveness of online assessment thus depends on balancing these complementary functions within environments that are data-rich yet pedagogically fragile [2].

Current practices, however, often privilege summative purposes, positioning assessment primarily as a gatekeeping mechanism that classifies learners against uniform benchmarks. Such approaches risk exacerbating inequalities by privileging students already advantaged in terms of prior knowledge and digital literacy, while marginalizing those whose learning trajectories are more diverse or non-linear [3, 4].

Prior to conceptualizing the adaptive assessment model proposed in this study, a longitudinal scientometric analysis was conducted on 4,877 publications indexed in Scopus and Web of Science between 1971 and 2023, with the aim of examining the structural evolution of research on educational assessment. The analysis revealed a dual disciplinary configuration in which a methodological pole (psychometrics, Item Response Theory, Rasch modelling, validity, reliability) co-evolves with a pedagogical pole (curriculum, teaching, learning), both connected through the central domain of educational measurement. Thematic cluster analyses identified three major areas: a consolidated methodological core centred on psychometric modelling and statistical validation; a broad educational measurement nucleus integrating evaluative constructs with demographic and contextual descriptors; and an applied pedagogical cluster focused on students, curriculum, and teaching practices.

This "dual spine" structure highlights both the stability and the heterogeneity of the field, showing how assessment functions as a translational bridge between technical innovation and pedagogical practice. Importantly, although scientific production peaked around 2014 before gradually declining, the conceptual core of the field has remained remarkably stable. This persistence motivated the present study's attempt to translate established psychometric rigor into an inclusive, formative, and equity-oriented adaptive assessment framework.

In other terms, within the present framework, these findings provide a historical and theoretical grounding for reinterpreting advanced measurement models as tools capable of sustaining formative, transparent, and pedagogically meaningful assessment.

A growing body of literature has therefore emphasized the need for assessment systems that are transparent, formative, and inclusive, capable of fostering engagement, cognitive flexibility, and responsiveness to feedback [5, 6].

The present paper contributes to this discourse by advancing a conceptual framework in which psychometric techniques—Item Response Theory (IRT), Computerized Adaptive Testing (CAT), Bayesian reasoning, learning analytics, and Markov chain modelling—are reinterpreted as pedagogical tools. Rather than being restricted to measurement, these methods are positioned as resources for formative feedback and instructional adaptation.

Grounded in a constructivist and inclusive perspective [7–9], the framework conceptualizes assessment as a dynamic and developmental process that not only documents learning but actively enhances it. In line with the principles of Universal Design for Learning (UDL), it emphasizes flexibility, multiple means of engagement, and accessible feedback, thereby promoting learner autonomy and educational equity.

Assessment is thus reframed as a formative and instructional practice that sustains learning itself [10]. By integrating advanced psychometric techniques, the framework bridges formative and summative purposes, positioning assessment as an inclusive pedagogical act [11].

Finally, this contribution does not aim at empirical validation but rather illustrates, through a simulated and prototypical scenario, how the proposed adaptive psychometric design could operate in practice. The simulation serves as a proof-of-concept, exemplifying the potential of integrating psychometric precision with inclusive pedagogical intent in online higher education contexts. Simulation was chosen also to test the internal coherence of the model before empirical validation.

2 Conceptual Framework

This research advances the idea that psychometric tools, traditionally applied for standardized measurement, can be reinterpreted within a pedagogical design aimed at supporting formative feedback, learning, and reflection for both learners and educators. The proposed framework is grounded in a constructivist and inclusive vision, which treats psychological and pedagogical constructs as dynamic processes co-constructed in digital learning environments.

Within this perspective, three interrelated constructs guide the model.

Learner engagement, defined as the behavioural, emotional, and cognitive involvement of students in learning activities [12], is operationalized through both direct responses and behavioural traces such as persistence in online tasks and frequency of contributions.

Cognitive flexibility, understood as the ability to reorganize knowledge and strategies when facing complex problems, is examined through patterns of transition between mastery states rather than through static achievement scores [13].

Feedback responsiveness, the learner's capacity to interpret and apply evaluative information, is captured by measuring changes between pre- and post-intervention assessments and by estimating the probability that feedback has produced measurable gains [14].

Each construct is linked to a corresponding methodological approach that translates it into analysable data.

Item Response Theory (IRT) [15] models the probability of a correct response as a function of learner ability and item parameters, while Computerized Adaptive Testing (CAT) applies these principles in real time by updating ability estimates after each response and selecting subsequent items that maximize information [16, 17].

Bayesian reasoning reframes assessment outcomes as posterior probabilities of mastery, moving beyond binary pass–fail judgments and allowing the estimation of instructional impact through probabilistic effect sizes [18].

Markov chain models [19, 20] provide a formal representation of sequential learning processes, estimating the likelihood of transitions between states such as low, medium, and high mastery, and enabling the observation of cognitive flexibility as a temporal trajectory [21].

At a collective level, learning analytics integrated with social network analysis (SNA) [22] combine performance and interactional data to identify central and peripheral actors in collaborative learning spaces, thereby linking achievement with social inclusion.

Embedding these methodological techniques within a pedagogical framework reconceptualizes assessment as dynamic, formative, and explicitly inclusive.

Engagement, flexibility, and responsiveness are no longer treated as static indicators but as developmental trajectories that evolve through interaction with feedback and context. This shift generates data that are not only psychometrically robust but also pedagogically feasible, ensuring that assessment practices align with the broader mission of contemporary online education: to promote equity by reducing barriers, recognizing learner differences, and fostering meaningful and equitable participation [23].

3 Method

This process should sustain a virtuous cycle of formative and reflexive thinking about teaching and learning, in which educators gain greater awareness of their evaluative practices and develop critical reflection leading to pedagogical growth. Assessment thus becomes not only a tool for learners' development but also a catalyst for instructors' professional learning [5].

When teachers learn to use assessment not merely to measure outcomes but to orient and adapt their instructional practice, the feedback loop closes. Evaluation informs pedagogy, pedagogy refines evaluation, and the formative cycle is effectively activated.

This section first outlines the pedagogical rationale guiding the methodological choices and then details the technical implementation of the simulated analytical procedures.

3.1 Research Design

The study adopts a mixed-methods design [24] integrating psychometric modelling, Bayesian reasoning, and learning analytics. Such an approach reflects the intrinsic heterogeneity of online higher education, which produces multiple layers of data, responses to structured items, traces of interaction within digital platforms, and self-assessments capturing reflective dimensions of learning.

None of these sources, if considered in isolation, can adequately represent the complexity of students' learning trajectories. By combining these methodological perspectives, the framework aims to capture both individual performance and collective processes, ensuring that assessment functions as a pedagogical and inclusive mechanism rather than as a device that reproduces inequality.

3.2 Participants and Context

To illustrate the framework's potential operation, we envision a prototypical online course enrolling approximately 500 students, consistent with IRT standards for stable item calibration and parameter estimation. The cohort is deliberately heterogeneous, including participants with strong prior preparation, others with limited academic background, and some with specific learning difficulties.

Variations in digital literacy and socio-cultural background add further layers of diversity. Such heterogeneity mirrors the authentic conditions of online education and underscores the need for adaptive assessment approaches that move beyond uniform benchmarks.

Adaptive testing, probabilistic reasoning, and analysis of social participation are therefore mobilized as tools that make diversity visible and valuable, transforming it from a source of bias into an opportunity for personalized feedback and inclusion.

3.3 Data Sources

The conceptual design integrates four complementary data streams, each contributing to the calibration and interpretability of the proposed psychometric framework.

Item-level responses to curriculum-embedded quizzes within the learning management system (LMS) serve as the primary source for estimating individual ability parameters through Item Response Theory and for implementing Computerized Adaptive Testing procedures. Structured pre- and post-test scores act as longitudinal benchmarks, supporting Bayesian modelling of posterior mastery probabilities and the estimation of instructional effect sizes. Sequential response data from self-assessment surveys are modelled using Markov chain techniques to capture state transitions across levels of mastery, hesitation, or disengagement, operationalizing cognitive flexibility as a dynamic process rather than a static outcome.

Learning analytics logs provide high-frequency traces of cognitive performance and interactional behaviour within collaborative forums; combined with social network analysis, they enable the examination of achievement in relation to inclusion and participation patterns The aggregation of these heterogeneous sources yields a multidimensional dataset that enables both micro-level inferences about individual trajectories and macro-level analyses of collective dynamics, ensuring that assessment remains simultaneously rigorous, adaptive, and pedagogically meaningful.

3.4 Analytical Procedures

Item Response Theory (IRT) and Computerized Adaptive Testing (CAT) are applied to the LMS quizzes. Items are pre-calibrated according to their difficulty, discrimination, and guessing parameters. When a student initiates the test, the algorithm begins with a provisional ability estimate; after each response, this estimate is updated, and the next item is selected to maximize information about the learner's ability level.

For example, a student answering two medium-difficulty items correctly will receive a more challenging one, whereas another who responds incorrectly will encounter a simpler one. The process continues until the standard error of the estimate falls below a predefined threshold or until the maximum number of items is reached. Each student thus faces a tailored sequence of items, ensuring that assessment is both precise and equitable.

Bayesian reasoning is applied to structured pre- and post-tests. Instead of relying on mean differences and *p*-values, posterior distributions are estimated for each learning outcome [25, 26]. For instance, a student may have a 90% probability of mastering a concept after the course, compared to 50% before instruction.

Effect sizes are then calculated to determine whether improvements can be considered educationally meaningful [27].

This probabilistic feedback benefits both learners (who see their progress as a continuum rather than a pass/fail result) and instructors, who gain evidence about which instructional components were most effective. The feedback loop thus enables teachers to recalibrate their strategies in an inclusive direction, giving particular attention to learners whose probability of mastery remains low despite instruction.

Markov chain models are applied to discrete states of mastery based on responses from surveys and tests [21]. Responses are coded, as usual, as correct/incorrect or completion/non-completion of learning steps. Transition matrices are then estimated to observe whether learners remain stable, oscillate, or shift abruptly between states. For example, one learner may progress steadily from low to medium mastery, while another alternates between medium and high without consolidation. These trajectories are not interpreted as deficiencies but as diagnostic signals of different cognitive styles and feedback responsiveness. Learners receive reflective feedback on how they approach tasks (whether consistently, hesitantly, or strategically) transforming assessment into a form of orientation and self-awareness, rather than a static judgment.

Learning analytics and social network analysis (SNA) are jointly applied to test scores and forum logs [28]. By integrating performance indicators with measures of social centrality, the analysis identifies students who not only perform well but also occupy influential positions within the online learning community. Conversely, learners who score poorly and remain peripheral in interaction networks can be detected early as potentially at risk of exclusion. Different patterns may emerge. High-performing but socially isolated students, the *Solitary High Achievers*, highly socially active yet academically struggling ones, the *Social Butterflies*. Students with poor academic success and low social integration, the *Struggling Outsiders*. And finally, the academically successful and socially integrated students, the *Integrated Leaders*.

Rather than stigmatizing any group, the model provides instructors with effective insights to design balanced peer configurations, where strong, socially connected learners support others, and isolated or struggling participants are integrated more effectively. Assessment thereby becomes a driver of collaborative and universal pedagogy.

4 Simulative Scenario

To illustrate how the proposed framework could operate in practice, a simulated application was developed within a prototypical online course in Educational Psychology enrolling approximately 500 virtual students.

The objective of this proof-of-concept exercise was to evaluate the feasibility and interpretability of integrating psychometric and probabilistic models to generate formative, inclusive, and pedagogically meaningful feedback.

The simulation focused on the integration of four key methodological components (Item Response Theory, Bayesian updating, Markov modelling, and Social Network Analysis) to explore how an adaptive psychometric design could operate in practice.

The simulation was implemented in R (version 4.5.1, 2025) using standard packages (*dplyr*, *purrr*, *tibble*, *ggplot2*, *reshape2*, *expm*, *igraph*, and *ggraph*). It was entirely based on synthetic data generated *ex novo* within a controlled environment to examine the model's internal coherence, relational structure, and formative potential. The virtual item bank comprised 300 four-option multiple-choice items parameterized under a 3PL IRT model, with discrimination parameters $a \approx 0.7$–2.0, difficulty $b \in [-2, 2]$, and guessing $c \approx 0.05$–0.15. Each response was dichotomously scored ($1 =$ correct, $0 =$ incorrect). This fully simulated design, inspired by previous work on adaptive psychometric environments [20, 21, 35], extends prior approaches to encompass both cognitive and social dimensions of learning. It does not aim at empirical validation but at illustrating the internal logic and educational implications of the proposed adaptive framework.

4.1 Simulation Design: IRT and Bayesian Inference

A virtual item bank of 300 multiple-choice questions aligned with the course learning outcomes was pre-calibrated using a three-parameter logistic (3PL) Item Response Theory model [29].

For each item, three parameters were estimated: discrimination (a_i), which reflects how sharply the item differentiates between learners of different ability levels; difficulty (b_i), indicating the point on the latent ability continuum where the probability of a correct response is 0.5 (after adjusting for guessing); and guessing (c_i), representing the lower asymptote of the item characteristic curve, or the probability of answering correctly by chance.

The probability that a learner with latent ability θ answers item i correctly is given by the standard logistic function:

$$P_i(\theta) = c_i + (1 - c_i)\frac{1}{1 + e^{-a_i(\theta - b_i)}}$$

This model, originally formulated by Birnbaum [29], represents the item characteristic curve (ICC), where a_i determines the steepness of the slope (discrimination), b_i the location along the ability continuum ($b_i \in [-2, +2]$), and c_i the lower asymptote reflecting the probability of guessing.

Each of the 500 virtual learners received an initial latent ability $\theta_i \sim \mathcal{N}(0, 1)$.

During the adaptive testing phase, the Computerized Adaptive Testing (CAT) engine selected items that maximized the Fisher information function around the current estimate $\hat{\theta}_i^{(t)}$.

On average, each adaptive testing session required 10.3 items (SD ≈ 1.2) to achieve the precision threshold (SE ≤ 0.35), drawn from a total pool of 300 pre-calibrated items.

This efficiency illustrates the adaptive selectivity of the CAT algorithm, which minimizes testing load while maintaining psychometric accuracy.

After each response, the estimate was updated using Maximum Likelihood Estimation until the standard error of measurement dropped below 0.35 or the session reached a cap of 25 items.

Posterior mastery probabilities were subsequently computed through Bayesian updating:

$$P(M_i \mid R) = \frac{P(R \mid M_i)P(M_i)}{P(R)}$$

This equation, derived from Bayes' theorem [30], formalizes the process of updating beliefs about a learner's mastery considering new evidence. The term $P(M_i)$ represents the *prior probability* that learner i has mastered a given concept before observing any response; $P(R \mid M_i)$ is the likelihood of producing the observed response given mastery; and $P(R)$ serves as a normalization constant ensuring that posterior probabilities sum to one.

In adaptive assessment, this rule allows evidence from each learner's response to iteratively refine their estimated proficiency.

Rather than treating performance as dichotomous (correct/incorrect), Bayesian inference produces a continuum of belief about mastery, offering probabilistic feedback that is inherently formative. This perspective aligns with recent arguments that emphasize the epistemic transparency of Bayesian reasoning over traditional significance testing based on p-values [31], and with contemporary pedagogical uses of Bayesian models to interpret learning as an updating process of prior knowledge [32].

In the simulated scenario, the average probability of mastery increased from 0.27 at baseline (pre) to 0.47 after the adaptive phase (post), illustrating how probabilistic feedback can serve as a continuous and interpretable indicator of learning progress (see Fig. 1).

4.2 Cognitive Transitions: A Markovian Model

To trace the temporal evolution of learning, self-assessment data were gathered after ten learning units. For ease of interpretation and visualization, the ten checkpoints were grouped into three broader phases: an early phase (Units 1–3), a middle phase (Units 4–7), and a late phase (Units 8–10). These aggregated phases were subsequently mapped (see Fig. 1).

Transitions across these states were modelled using a first-order Markov chain, defined by the transition matrix P, where each element P_{ij} represents the conditional probability of moving from state i to state j between two consecutive time points. The empirical transition matrix derived from the simulated self-assessment data was (L → M → H):

$$P = \begin{bmatrix} 0.78 & 0.21 & 0.01 \\ 0.11 & 0.63 & 0.26 \\ 0.00 & 0.21 & 0.79 \end{bmatrix}$$

The obtained transition probabilities reflect a moderately progressive learning process.

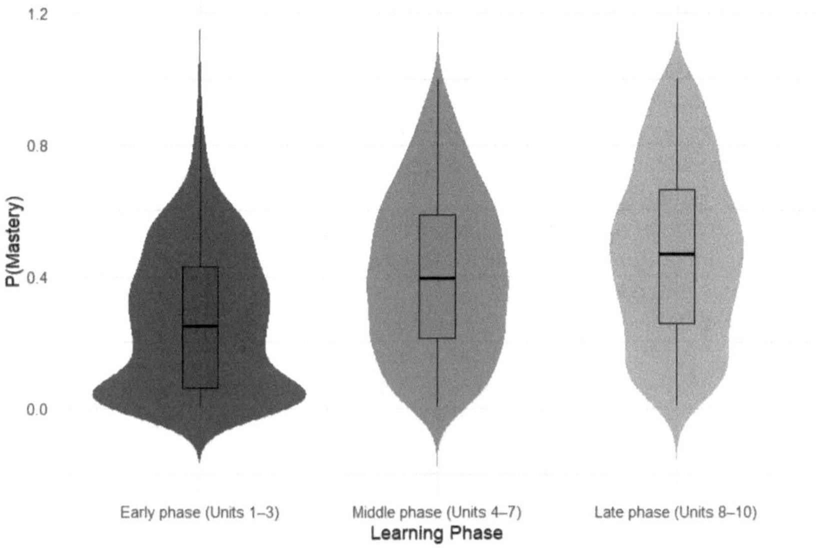

Fig. 1. Distribution of learners' self-assessment–based mastery probabilities across the early, middle, and late learning phases. Each violin depicts the density of posterior estimates obtained via Bayesian updating following adaptive testing. The upward shift from early to late phases reflects the temporal evolution of learning across the ten self-assessment checkpoints.

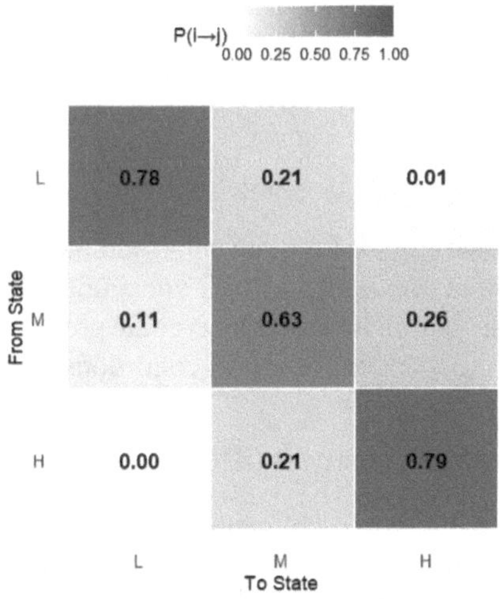

Fig. 2. Heatmap representation of the transition probabilities between mastery states (Low, Medium, High) across consecutive assessment phases. Darker cells correspond to higher transition likelihoods. The predominance of upper-diagonal values (e.g., L → M, M → H) reflects progressive learning patterns and limited regression.

In other terms, learners starting in *Low mastery* have a 21% probability of improving to *Medium*, while 1% progress directly to *High*.

The *Medium* group shows greater upward mobility (26% → High) alongside a 63% persistence rate, indicating gradual but stable improvement.

Backward transitions remain limited (e.g., 11% from *Medium* to *Low*), suggesting that adaptive feedback effectively supports consistent forward movement while minimizing regression.

Following previous research [21, 22], the Markovian framework can also be used to quantify cognitive flexibility—that is, the learner's ability to shift between mastery states in response to feedback.

Frequent transitions ($L \leftrightarrow M \leftrightarrow H$) indicate adaptive responsiveness, whereas high self-loops (e.g., P_{LL}, P_{MM}) reveal potential stagnation zones.

Visualizing these probabilities through a heatmap enables instructors to identify where scaffolding is most needed and where adaptive feedback produces the most meaningful gains (see Fig. 2).

4.3 Long-Term Dynamics

By iteratively multiplying P, the distribution of learners across mastery states at time t can be expressed as $\pi_t = \pi_0 P^t$, where π_0 denotes the initial state distribution [20, 21, 33]. As $t \to \infty$, the sequence π_t converges toward a stationary distribution:

$$\pi = \lim_{t \to \infty} \pi_0 P^t$$

representing the long-term equilibrium of the system, in which successive applications of P no longer alter the proportions of learners across states.

In our simulation the results was:

$$\pi = [0.18, 0.36, 0.46]$$

This configuration predicts that, in the long run, approximately 18% of learners remain in *Low mastery*, 36% stabilize in *Medium*, and 46% consolidate *High mastery* (see Fig. 3). In stochastic terms, this distribution indicates an ergodic process, a system that converges toward stable proportions independent of initial conditions.

4.4 Simulated Social Network Analysis (SNA)

To incorporate the social dimension of inclusion into the adaptive psychometric design, a simulated social network analysis (SNA) was implemented.

Whereas the previous components modelled cognitive, probabilistic, and temporal aspects of learning process, the present simulation represents assessment as a relational process emerging from patterns of participation and their interaction.

In this context, the objective was to reproduce, within a synthetic environment, the structural inequalities that typically characterize online learning networks and to examine how these topological configurations correlate with learners' probabilistic mastery.

The virtual network of $N = 500$ learners was generated according to the Barabási–Albert preferential attachment model [34], which assumes that each new node connects

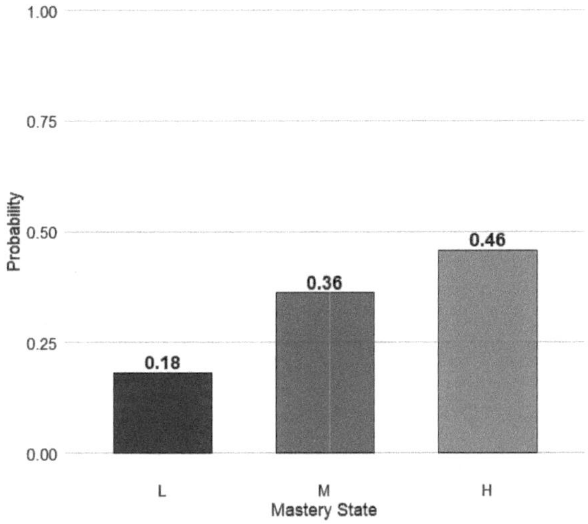

Fig. 3. Long-term equilibrium of the Markov chain obtained after iterative propagation of the empirical transition matrix. The system stabilizes with approximately 18% of learners in Low mastery, 36% in Medium, and 46% in High, representing an ergodic process that converges toward stable proportions independent of initial conditions, with the non-trivial implication that the training path stabilizes the performance of individuals with most high-level performance scores.

to existing ones with probability proportional to their current degree. Formally, the probability that learner *i* receives a new connection is expressed as

$$\Pr(\mathrm{i}) = \frac{\mathrm{k_i}}{\sum_{\mathrm{j}} \mathrm{k_j}}$$

where k_i denotes the number of existing connections of node *i*. This generative rule yields a scale-free topology with a power-law degree distribution

$$P(k) \propto k^{-\gamma}, \quad 2 < \gamma < 3$$

closely mirroring empirical observations of online learning environments in which few highly active participants act as "hubs" and many others remain on the periphery [28, 35]. Such network heterogeneity is pedagogically significant because it reflects differential opportunities for visibility, feedback, and cognitive engagement within digital classrooms.

For each learner *i*, three variables were simulated. The posterior mastery probability M_i was sampled from a Beta distribution, $M_i \sim \mathrm{Beta}(2, 3)$, consistent with the asymmetric patterns observed after the Bayesian adaptive phase.

The normalized degree centrality $C_i = \frac{k_i}{N-1}$ represented individual participation within the network. To reflect the co-evolution of social and cognitive dimensions, mastery was modelled as a weighted function of both an independent baseline U_i and the centrality score, according to

$$M_i = \lambda Z(C_i) + (1 - \lambda) Z(U_i), \quad \lambda = 0.4$$

where $Z(\cdot)$ denotes standardization to zero mean and unit variance. The values were then mapped to the interval [0, 1] through the cumulative normal transformation $M_i' = \Phi(M_i)$ ensuring comparability with the probabilistic scale of mastery adopted throughout the framework. Each learner's participation index was computed as

$$P_i = 0.7M_i' + 0.3C_i + \varepsilon_i, \quad \varepsilon_i \sim \mathcal{N}\left(0, 0.05^2\right)$$

representing an integrated measure of cognitive and social engagement.The resulting network displayed the expected scale-free structure with mean degree $k \approx 6$. Pearson correlation between mastery and centrality was estimated as

$$\rho_{MC} = \text{corr}\left(M_i', C_i\right) = 0.45$$

indicating a moderate positive relationship between learners' connectedness and their probabilistic mastery. In other terms, even moderate coupling suggests that participation has measurable formative effects. To explore structural gradients of inclusion, degree centrality was partitioned into quintiles, defining three network zones: *Peripheral*, *Intermediate*, and *Central*.

The mean mastery probabilities across these strata were $M_{\text{Peripheral}} = 0.40$, $M_{\text{Intermediate}} = 0.47$, $M_{\text{Central}} = 0.64$, with corresponding standard deviations of 0.20, 0.22, and 0.22 respectively.

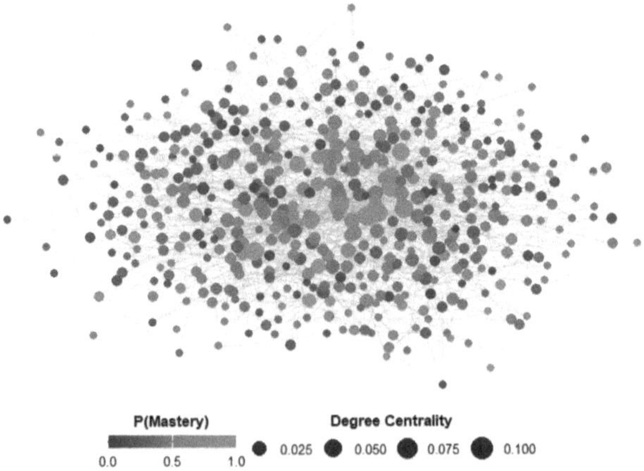

Fig. 4. Simulated scale-free learning network of $N = 500$ learners generated with the Barabási–Albert model. Node size represents degree centrality, and colour encodes posterior mastery probability (grey → low, red → medium, blue → high). A clear gradient emerges from peripheral low-mastery nodes to central high-mastery hubs, suggesting that social connectedness and cognitive mastery co-evolve within the adaptive psychometric framework.

Graphical representation of the simulated network (see Fig. 4) depicts the expected scale-free configuration generated by the Barabási–Albert model, with node size proportional to degree centrality and colour encoding posterior mastery probability. A dense, bluish nucleus of highly connected learners emerges at the centre, surrounded by a broad periphery of smaller, reddish nodes with lower mastery levels. This visual gradient reflects the moderate positive association between social connectedness and cognitive mastery ($\rho = 0.45$), showing how participation and learning co-evolve within the simulated environment.

Central high-mastery hubs (large blue nodes in the core) represent integrated learners who combine strong social connectivity with high probabilistic mastery.

Peripheral low-mastery learners (small grey-red nodes along the edges) illustrate participants who remain marginal both socially and cognitively, forming potential exclusion zones.

High-performing but socially peripheral learners appear as isolated blue nodes on the outer boundary: they achieve strong mastery despite limited interaction, suggesting autonomous but disconnected trajectories.

Socially active yet lower-mastery participants are visible as larger red nodes near the intermediate belt of the network: they engage actively but still require cognitive consolidation.

5 Discussion

The simulation presented in this study illustrates the feasibility and conceptual coherence of integrating psychometric, probabilistic, and network-based approaches within a unified pedagogical framework for online assessment. Beyond methodological demonstration, the results substantiate the central proposition that psychometric tools can serve formative, inclusive, and reflexive educational purposes [5, 6]. The adaptive processes modelled through Item Response Theory, Bayesian updating, and Markov chains collectively highlight assessment as a dynamic system that both measures and promotes learning, rather than a static mechanism of classification.

Complementing these cognitive and temporal dynamics, the simulated Social Network Analysis (SNA) situates assessment within its relational context, suggesting that the probabilistic evolution of mastery unfolds through structures of participation.

5.1 Pedagogical Implications

Adaptive testing and probabilistic reasoning substantially enhance the transparency and interpretability of feedback in online environments. Expressing progress as a probability of mastery rather than a binary score supports learners' self-regulation and motivation while providing instructors with evidence about which instructional components are most effective [17–19, 25–27]. This probabilistic approach aligns with constructivist conceptions of learning as a continuous process of updating and refining knowledge structures [7–9].

The Markov-based analysis of cognitive transitions [19–21] adds a temporal and process-oriented layer, allowing instructors to visualize patterns of responsiveness and cognitive flexibility over time. Fluctuations in learning states are not interpreted as instability but as evidence of active engagement with complexity, a hallmark of deep learning [13, 14]. Similarly, the integration of social network analysis [22, 28] extends assessment beyond cognition, linking performance with participation. The observed association between network centrality and upward mastery transitions underscores the formative value of peer interaction and collaborative engagement.

More specifically, the simulated network revealed four distinct inclusion profiles (central high-mastery hubs, peripheral low-mastery learners, high-performing but socially isolated participants, and socially active yet lower-mastery students) each suggesting differentiated pedagogical needs. Recognizing these profiles allows educators to design adaptive interventions that align feedback and collaboration patterns with learners' network positions, transforming assessment data into actionable social-pedagogical insight.

From a theoretical standpoint, the framework contributes to bridging the historical divide between psychometrics and pedagogy [4]. The "dual spine" structure identified in the scientometric mapping (comprising a methodological and a pedagogical pole) is here operationalized as an integrated ecosystem. IRT and Bayesian reasoning, traditionally confined to measurement, are reinterpreted as mechanisms for formative reflection and adaptive instruction. In this sense, the framework expands the epistemological reach of measurement science and situates it within the discourse of learning design [10, 11].

5.2 Equity and Inclusion

A central implication concerns educational equity. Traditional summative assessments tend to amplify pre-existing disparities by privileging students with stronger prior knowledge or digital literacy [2, 3]. In contrast, adaptive and probabilistic assessment redistributes opportunities for success by tailoring item difficulty, offering iterative feedback, and valuing process over outcome [5, 6, 23]. Learners at risk of exclusion (such as those positioned at the network periphery) can be identified early and supported through targeted pedagogical interventions.

The simulated SNA conceptually illustrates how structural inequality emerges in digital participation patterns, with peripheral nodes showing lower mastery probabilities ($M = 0.40$) and central hubs higher ones ($M = 0.64$). Such gradients confirm that social connectedness operates as both a cognitive resource and a potential source of inequity if left unaddressed.

The integration of social metrics enables the detection of both cognitive and participatory exclusion, positioning assessment as an ethical and relational practice. This formative use of data reframes analytics from instruments of control into mechanisms of care and empowerment [23]. To sustain this vision, fairness-by-design must guide every stage of adaptive psychometric implementation, ensuring equity of representation in item banks and datasets, transparent decision rules for feedback generation, and accessible communication of results for learners with diverse cognitive, linguistic, or sensory profiles [36–38].

Ethical assurance arises when human judgment and computational inference operate in dialogue. Data-driven systems should be periodically audited using diverse learner cohorts, while educators retain interpretive responsibility for contextualizing results. Fairness, in this perspective, is not a compliance parameter but a pedagogical stance that turns assessment into a practice of justice. For instance, adaptive dashboards could highlight learners whose probability of mastery stagnates while their participation declines, prompting timely, personalized feedback.

Moreover, the framework highlights the need to consider neurodiversity among both learners and educators, recognizing that attentional styles, cognitive profiles, and processing differences shape how assessment is experienced and enacted [9]. Inclusivity thus becomes not only a matter of access but of epistemic pluralism, valuing diverse ways of knowing and demonstrating understanding.

6 Conclusion

While the simulation validates the internal logic of the framework, several limitations must be acknowledged. The current design assumes stable item parameters and homogeneous testing conditions, whereas real educational environments are affected by behavioural, affective, and contextual variability. Furthermore, the framework's application requires computational infrastructure and psychometric expertise that may not be universally available across institutions [15–18]. In other terms, while the conceptual proposal is coherent and timely, a critical examination of its internal consistency and practical transferability to authentic educational settings remains essential.

Future empirical studies should therefore test this conceptual design in authentic LMS contexts, examining data ethics, item fairness, and the pedagogical interpretability of probabilistic feedback. Mixed-method evaluations combining quantitative modelling and qualitative inquiry will be essential to assess both technical performance and educational meaning [24, 26, 27].

Ultimately, the proposed framework invites a step beyond inclusion.

Indeed, particular attention should be given to validating the network-adaptive dimension introduced in this study, empirically assessing whether relational profiles and centrality–mastery correlations observed in simulation replicate within real online cohorts. Such evidence would confirm the feasibility of integrating social topology into psychometric feedback loops and advance the development of genuinely inclusive adaptive assessment systems.

Inclusion ensures access and participation; moving beyond it means using assessment to cultivate agency, dialogue, and mutual recognition. By reframing assessment as a developmental and empowering process, psychometric tools are repositioned as catalysts for pedagogical awareness, fostering reflective, transparent, and equitable digital ecosystems [37, 38]. Assessment thus becomes not an endpoint but a shared process of meaning-making and collective growth toward equity, a transformation at once methodological and ethical.

7 Statements and Declarations

Funding. The authors did not receive support from any organization for the submitted work.

Competing Interests. The authors declare that they have no competing interests.

Data Availability. This study is based exclusively on simulated data generated within a controlled computational environment to test the internal coherence of the proposed adaptive assessment framework. No empirical data, personal data, or identifiable information were used. The R scripts used to generate the synthetic datasets and perform all analyses are available from the corresponding author upon reasonable request.

References

1. Gikandi, J.W., Morrow, D., Davis, N.E.: Online formative assessment in higher education: A review of the literature. Comput. Educ. **57**(4), 2333–2351 (2011). https://doi.org/10.1016/j.compedu.2011.06.004
2. Perera-Diltz, D.M., Moe, J.L.: Formative and summative assessment in online education. Couns. Human Serv. Fac. Publ. **37** (2014) https://digitalcommons.odu.edu/chs_pubs/37
3. Shepard, L.A.: The role of assessment in a learning culture. Educ. Res. **29**(7), 4–14 (2000). https://doi.org/10.3102/0013189X029007004
4. Stiggins, R.J.: From formative assessment to assessment for learning: A path to success in standards-based schools. Phi Delta Kappan. **87**, 324–328 (2005)
5. Black, P., Wiliam, D.: Assessment and classroom learning. Assess. Educ. **5**(1), 7–74 (1998). https://doi.org/10.1080/0969595980050102
6. Wiliam, D.: Embedded Formative Assessment. Solution Tree Press, Bloomington (2011)
7. Amor, A.M., et al.: International perspectives and trends in research on inclusive education: A systematic review. Int. J. Incl. Educ. **23**(12), 1277–1295 (2019). https://doi.org/10.1080/13603116.2018.1445304
8. UNESCO: Inclusive education: The way of the future. In: Conclusions and recommendations of the 48th session of the International Conference on Education (ICE). UNESCO, Paris (2008)
9. Shaeffer, S.: Inclusive education: a prerequisite for equity and social justice. Asia Pac. Educ. Rev. **20**, 181–192 (2019). https://doi.org/10.1007/s12564-019-09598-w
10. Banks, J., González, T., Mueller, C., Pacheco, M., Scott, L.A., Trainor, A.A.: Reflexive quality criteria: questions and indicators for purpose-driven special education qualitative research. Except. Child. **89**(4), 449–466 (2023). https://doi.org/10.1177/00144029231168106
11. Linn, R.L.: The standards for educational and psychological testing: guidance in test development. In: Downing, S.M., Haladyna, T.M. (eds.) Handbook of Test Development, pp. 41–52. Routledge, New York (2011)
12. Fredricks, J.A., Blumenfeld, P.C., Paris, A.H.: School engagement: potential of the concept, state of the evidence. Rev. Educ. Res. **74**(1), 59–109 (2004). https://doi.org/10.3102/00346543074001059
13. Spiro, R.J., Jehng, J.-C.: Cognitive flexibility and hypertext: theory and technology for the nonlinear and multidimensional traversal of complex subject matter. In: Nix, D., Spiro, R.J. (eds.) Cognition, Education, and Multimedia: Exploring Ideas in High Technology, pp. 163–205. Lawrence Erlbaum, Hillsdale (1990)
14. Shute, V.J.: Focus on formative feedback. Rev. Educ. Res. **78**(1), 153–189 (2008). https://doi.org/10.3102/0034654307313795
15. Embretson, S.E., Reise, S.P.: Item Response Theory for Psychologists. Lawrence Erlbaum, Mahwah (2000)
16. Wainer, H. (ed.): Computerized Adaptive Testing: A Primer, 2nd edn. Lawrence Erlbaum, Mahwah (2000)
17. van der Linden, W.J., Glas, C.A.W. (eds.): Computer Adaptive Testing: Theory and Practice. Kluwer, Dordrecht (2000)

18. Gelman, A., Carlin, J.B., Stern, H.S., Dunson, D.B., Vehtari, A., Rubin, D.B.: Bayesian data analysis, 3rd edn. Chapman & Hall/CRC, Boca Raton (2013). https://doi.org/10.1201/b16018
19. Stewart, W.J.: Numerical methods for computing stationary distributions of finite irreducible Markov chains. In: Grassmann, W.K. (ed.) Computational Probability, pp. 81–111. Springer, Boston (2000)
20. Bosco, A.: Content-based and data-driven integration. Markov chain models for the inspection of response dynamics in psychological testing. In: Pollice, A., Mariani, P. (eds.) Methodological and Applied Statistics and Demography I. SIS 2024 Italian Statistical Society Series on Advances in Statistics. Springer, Cham (2025). https://doi.org/10.1007/978-3-031-64346-0_14
21. Bosco, A.: Markov chain models for inspecting response dynamics in psychological testing. arXiv (2024) https://doi.org/10.48550/arXiv.2403.17982
22. Wasserman, S., Faust, K.: Social Network Analysis: Methods and Applications. Cambridge University Press, Cambridge (1994). doi:https://doi.org/10.1017/CBO9780511815478
23. Ramirez-Montoya, M.S., Weber, J.C., Cox, G., Tenorio-Sepulveda, G.C.: Inclusive digital education on open platforms: A case study of the complexity of the future of education. Comput. Sch., 1–18 (2024)
24. Fetters, M.D., Curry, L.A., Creswell, J.W.: Achieving integration in mixed methods designs: principles and practices. Health Serv. Res. **48**(6 Pt 2), 2134–2156 (2013). https://doi.org/10.1111/1475-6773.12117
25. Pastore, M.: I limiti dell'approccio NHST e l'alternativa Bayesiana. G. Ital. Psicol. **36**, 925–938 (2009). https://doi.org/10.1421/30944
26. Wasserstein, R.L., Schirm, A.L., Lazar, N.A.: Moving to a world beyond "$p < 0.05$". Am. Stat. **73**(sup1), 1–19 (2019). https://doi.org/10.1080/00031305.2019.1583913
27. Cohen, J.: Statistical Power Analysis for the Behavioral Sciences. Academic, New York (1969). https://doi.org/10.4324/9780203771587
28. Pearson, N.S., Major, J.C., Godwin, A., Kirn, A.: using social network analysis to study the social structures of inclusion. In: Proceedings of the ASEE Annual Conference Exposition, Salt Lake City, ASEE (2018)
29. Birnbaum, A.: Some latent trait models and their use in inferring an examinee's ability. In: Lord, F.M., Novick, M.R. (eds.) Statistical Theories of Mental Test Scores, pp. 395–479. Addison-Wesley, Reading, MA (1968)
30. Bayes, T.: An essay towards solving a problem in the doctrine of chances. Philos. Trans. R. Soc. Lond. **53**, 370–418 (1763)
31. Wagenmakers, E.-J., et al.: Bayesian inference for psychology. Part I: theoretical advantages and practical ramifications. Psychon. Bull. Rev. **25**(1), 35–57 (2018). https://doi.org/10.3758/s13423-017-1343-3
32. Pastore, M., Calcagnì, A.: Measuring distribution similarities between samples: A distribution-free overlapping index. Front. Psychol. **10**,1089. (2019). https://doi.org/10.3389/fpsyg.2019.01089
33. Norris, J.R.: Markov Chains. Cambridge University Press, Cambridge (1997)
34. Barabási, A.-L., Albert, R.: Emergence of scaling in random networks. Science **286**(5439), 509–512 (1999). https://doi.org/10.1126/science.286.5439.509
35. Paranamana, P., Luna, N., Mullett, M.: Belief evolution in society over time: dynamics based on random and homophily-based networks, and applications. In: Yang, Z., von Briesen, E. (eds) Proceedings of the 2024 International Conference of the Computational Social Science Society of the Americas. CSSSA 2024. Springer Proceedings in Complexity. Springer, Cham (2025). https://doi.org/10.1007/978-3-031-89692-7_1
36. Li, Z., Wang, Y., Ge, C., Chen, X.: Evolutionary dynamics of information diffusion with sending–receiving interactions. Appl. Math. Model. **151**, 116457 (2026). https://doi.org/10.1016/j.apm.2025.116457

37. Frinco, M., Sironi, E.M., Frinco, R.: Informazioni psicometriche dei test. Perché sono indispensabili per la clinica e la didattica. Psicol. Clin. Svilupp. **28**(1), 3–7 (2024)
38. Xalxo, P.V., Kindo, J., Kachhap, P.: Online education ecosystem—exploring the challenges and opportunities. Eur. J. Educ. **60**(2), e70085 (2025)

Examining the Efficacy of UDL-Oriented Intelligent Tutoring Systems in Learning Processes: A Multidimensional Approach to Digital Inclusion

Emanuele Marsico[1,2](✉), Umberto Barbieri[1], Alfonso Filippone[1,2,3], Raffaele Di Fuccio[1], and Maria Concetta Carruba[1]

[1] Department of Psychology and Education, Pegaso Telematic University, Isola F2 Business Center, 80132 Naples, Italy
{emanuele.marsico,umberto.barbieri,alfonso.filippone, raffaele.difuccio,mariaconcetta.carruba}@unipegaso.it

[2] Department of Humanities. Arts, Cultural Heritage, Education, University of Foggia, Antonio Gramsci Avenue, 89, 71122 Foggia, Italy

[3] Department of Agriculture, Food, natural resources and Engineering, University of Foggia, Foggia, Italy

Abstract. This study investigates the effectiveness of an Universal Design for Learning (UDL)-oriented Intelligent Tutoring Systems (ITS) compared to a generic chatbot in educational context, with a particular focus on the moderating role of digital competencies. A case-control experimental design was employed with 99 participants from the TFA support VIII cycle at the University of Foggia (control group: n = 55; experimental group: n = 44). The UDL-based ITS incorporated three core modules - Student, Domain, and Teaching - utilizing Mixture of Agents methodology with advanced language models (GPT-4, Mixtral 8x7b, Meta Llama 3 8B) to provide personalized, adaptive learning experiences. Primary outcomes examined global affectivity (Self-Assessment Manikin), perceived academic self-efficacy, and usability (System Usability Scale, Chatbot Usability Scale). Digital competencies were assessed using the MyDigiSkills questionnaire. Results revealed complex interaction patterns between digital competencies and intervention effectiveness. Information Literacy emerged as a robust predictor across all usability dimensions (standardized coefficients: 0.215–0.450), with a significant negative interaction effect between group membership and Information Literacy. ($B = -2.251$, $p = .003$), suggesting compensatory effects particularly benefiting users with lower digital competencies. Problem-solving skills significantly predicted conversation quality ($B = 2.019$, $p = .010$). Both systems exceeded good usability thresholds, though no significant differences were found in self-efficacy between groups ($U = 1274.500$, $p = .650$). Multivariate analysis revealed significant dimensional effects in affective measures ($F(1.624, 157.571) = 9.266$, $p < .001$, $\eta^2 p = 0.087$) with substantial temporal stability (rs range: 0.458–0.604). These findings indicate that UDL-oriented ITS provide differential benefits based on users' digital literacy levels, supporting adaptive scaffolding strategies for inclusive educational technology design.

M. Adamoli et al. (Eds.): HELMeTO 2025, CCIS 2958, pp. 147–164, 2026.
https://doi.org/10.1007/978-3-032-31850-3_10

Keywords: Universal Design for Learning · Intelligent Tutoring Systems · Digital Competencies · Educational Technology · Self-Efficacy · Usability

1 Introduction

The integration of chatbots in educational contexts represents a significant advancement at the intersection of technology and pedagogy, with the potential to radically transform traditional teaching and learning paradigms. Educational chatbots, powered by artificial intelligence (AI) and natural language processing (NLP), have evolved from simple automated response systems to sophisticated tools capable of delivering highly personalized and adaptive learning experiences [17–20].

The present study is situated within the theoretical framework of Universal Design for Learning (UDL) applied in educational contexts. Specifically focusing on comparative analysis between a UDL-oriented Intelligent Tutoring System (ITS) and a generic chatbot.

This research aims to investigate the effectiveness of Intelligent Tutoring Systems (ITS) designed according to Universal Design for Learning (UDL) principles compared to generic chatbots in educational settings. Universal Design for Learning represents a pedagogical framework that seeks to eliminate educational barriers and promote individualized learning through three fundamental principles: providing multiple means of representation, engagement, and action/expression. UDL-oriented ITS integrate these principles to offer personalized and adaptive learning experiences that account for student diversity.

The central research question focuses on examining whether the use of a UDL-oriented ITS is associated with higher levels of self-efficacy and global affectivity, in addition to improved usability compared to a generic chatbot trained exclusively on instructional material content. Self-efficacy, defined as individuals' beliefs in their capabilities to organize and execute actions necessary to manage prospective situations, represents a fundamental construct in educational psychology. Numerous studies have demonstrated that elevated self-efficacy levels correlate positively with academic performance, motivation, and adoption of self-regulated learning strategies.

The primary objective of this research is to analyze the effects of both tool types on global affectivity and self-efficacy domains. Global affectivity in educational contexts refers to the complex array of emotions, attitudes, and feelings that students develop toward learning, which significantly influence their engagement and academic success. Secondary objectives include examining usability differences between the two tool types and analyzing the role of prior digital competencies in relation to perceived tool usability, self-efficacy levels, and global affectivity.

The experimental design involves a direct comparison between two conditions: an experimental group that will interact with the UDL-oriented ITS and a control group that will utilize a generic chatbot. This configuration will enable isolation of specific effects of the UDL approach within intelligent tutoring systems contexts. Usability assessment proves particularly crucial, considering that previous research has demonstrated how perceived ease of use and perceived usefulness significantly influence acceptance and effectiveness of AI-based educational technologies.

The inclusion of prior digital competencies as a moderating variable addresses the need to understand how individual differences in digital literacy may influence interaction with advanced intelligent tutoring systems. Recent studies have highlighted how students' digital competencies can significantly moderate the effects of educational technologies on learning outcomes and user satisfaction.

This experimental procedure is situated within the broader context of research on next-generation intelligent tutoring systems, which are evolving toward increasingly personalized and inclusive approaches. The integration of UDL principles into ITS represents a significant innovation that could revolutionize personalized education approaches, offering more equitable and effective educational solutions for students with diverse learning styles and needs.

1.1 Evolution of Chatbots in Educational Contexts: Principal Advantages and Challenges

Educational chatbots have evolved from rudimentary AI systems with limited, context-insensitive responses to advanced tools leveraging Large Language Models (LLMs), which enable dynamic, context-aware interactions and significantly improved natural language understanding and generation. For example, the EduChat platform integrates LLM-based chatbots to facilitate structured small-group discussions, promoting balanced participation and collaborative knowledge building. In specialized domains such as chemistry and physics, chatbots show promise in supporting complex tasks: Pernaa et al. (2024) found that AI chatbots can personalize learning in chemistry teacher training, though current limitations include difficulty handling multimodal chemical information, while Riabko and Vakaliuk (2024) demonstrated that customized chatbots can offer physics students guidance comparable to human tutors. In medical education, chatbots like ChatGPT may enhance student-patient interactions and provide tailored learning experiences, yet raise important ethical, transparency, and critical thinking concerns [17–11–32].

Educational chatbots offer substantial advantages including personalized learning that adapts content and pacing to individual needs, promoting inclusivity and engagement, continuous 24-h support that provides immediate feedback and bridges traditional instructional gaps, virtual facilitation of group discussions that enhances collaborative learning, and accelerated research capabilities through information retrieval and analysis [20–17–11]. However, significant challenges accompany these benefits: ethical and privacy concerns regarding data security and algorithmic bias require rigorous guidelines, the risk of academic dishonesty necessitates stringent integrity policies, current technological limitations affect comprehension of complex, contextualized content, excessive dependence may reduce human interaction and impede social skill development, and rapid technological evolution demands continuous educator training and curricular adaptations that strain institutional resources [32–5–26].

2 Theoretical Framework

2.1 Theoretical Models Supporting Chatbot Implementation in Educational Contexts

Educational chatbot implementation is theoretically grounded in several models that explain their effectiveness. The Unified Theory of Acceptance and Use of Technology (UTAUT2) by Venkatesh et al. (2012) provides a comprehensive framework examining user acceptance through constructs including performance expectancy, effort expectancy, social influence, and facilitating conditions; Antony and Ramnath (2023) successfully applied UTAUT2 to analyze student perceptions of educational chatbots, demonstrating its utility in predicting behavioral intention. Constructivist learning theory supports chatbot implementation by emphasizing learners' active role in knowledge construction, with chatbots serving as virtual tutors that provide scaffolding and personalized feedback essential for meaningful learning. Additionally, cognitive load theory explains chatbot benefits through their capacity to reduce extraneous cognitive load—minimizing time and effort spent searching for information—thereby enabling students to focus more effectively on essential instructional material and improving educational outcomes [18–31].

Educational chatbots demonstrate complex, multifaceted effects on learning processes. Deng and Yu's (2023) meta-analysis revealed medium-to-high effects on overall learning outcomes, with significant improvements in explicit reasoning ($d = 1.190$), learning performance ($d = 1.033$), and knowledge retention ($d = 0.691$). Chatbots function as virtual tutors providing personalized feedback, research assistants for information synthesis, and practice partners for skill development, exemplified by the MERLIN project's demonstrated improvements in student motivation and knowledge acquisition. However, evidence on engagement remains mixed: while Antony and Ramnath (2023) found students value chatbots for personalized assistance and simplified interactions, Deng and Yu (2023) detected no significant effects on engagement or critical thinking, though interest in learning showed modest improvement ($d = 0.842$). Significant challenges include information accuracy and reliability concerns, risks of excessive dependence that may diminish critical thinking, privacy and data security issues [8–31], and potential exacerbation of educational inequalities through unequal access. While chatbots can enhance reasoning abilities, performance, and retention, their engagement effects appear context-dependent, requiring further investigation and careful attention to ethical considerations [18–1].

2.2 UDL Between Self-efficacy and Global Affectivity

This study centers on Universal Design for Learning (UDL) methodology, an inclusive educational approach providing all students with success opportunities regardless of abilities or learning styles [21–23], founded on the premise that instruction should be designed for flexibility and accessibility across diverse learners [9]. UDL operates through three fundamental principles: multiple means of representation (presenting content through various modalities), multiple means of action and expression (enabling diverse knowledge externalization approaches), and multiple means of engagement (capturing student interest based on motivational diversity) [25]. UDL guarantees equal learning opportunities even for students with special educational needs [12]. This pedagogical approach relies on psychological variables crucial to effective learning, particularly learning motivation and self-efficacy, defined as individual perception of task-completion capabilities, which proves essential in UDL-structured pathways for anxiety reduction and enhanced learning comfort [24]. The authors focused on self-efficacy as the principal psychological construct indicating effective learning processes, though recognizing limitations without learning outcome evaluation, thus incorporating global affectivity assessment to capture interfering variables and immediate learning condition impacts [3]. Secondary objectives include analyzing perceived usability of both tools and examining how prior digital competencies relate to tool usability, self-efficacy levels, and global affectivity [19].

2.3 Digital Competencies and Usability

This project examines the relationship between students' digital competencies and study support tools through bidirectional factors: user capabilities for optimal tool utilization and system adaptability itself. While user capabilities are only partially identifiable through self-efficacy scales (which evaluate learning rather than tool use), system adaptability is reliably assessed through usability scales. Students confident in their digital capabilities may perceive systems as more usable and less frustrating, leading to higher scale scores despite objectively unchanged ITS usability, whereas students with low digital self-efficacy may feel overwhelmed by technical complexities, negatively affecting their evaluations. Both tools feature intuitive user interfaces that reduce potential biases related to the ITS's more complex structural rationale compared to generic chatbots. Although predominantly technical, the UDL approach remains critically important and may provide thc key analytical turning point. It is hypothesized that UDL-oriented ITS ensures greater accessibility for users with limited digital literacy, enabling functional integration between learning process implementation and improved educational material usability, resulting in a more inclusive system than generic chatbots.

3 Materials and Methods

3.1 Methodology

Objectives. The investigation is structured around one primary objective and two secondary objectives, organized according to a hierarchy of empirical relevance. The primary objective consists of systematic analysis of the differential effects of two tool types—UDL-oriented ITS and generic chatbot—on the domains of global affectivity and self-efficacy. The secondary objectives comprise: (a) comparative examination of usability between the two tool types and (b) analysis of the role of prior digital competencies in relation to perceived tool usability, self-efficacy levels, and global affectivity.

Research Hypotheses. The central research question is articulated in the following formulation: is the use of a UDL-oriented ITS associated with higher levels of self-efficacy, global affectivity, and improved usability compared to a generic chatbot trained exclusively on proposed instructional material content? This question was operationalized through the following hypothetical structure:

- H_0 (Null Hypothesis): The ITS and generic chatbot exhibit equivalent impact on the dependent variables under examination.
- H_1 (Alternative Hypothesis): The ITS is associated with significantly higher levels of self-efficacy, global affectivity, and improved usability compared to the generic chatbot.

Experimental Design. The study adopted a case-control experimental design with pre-test and post-test using independent samples. The experimental protocol was structured in five sequential phases:

1. Preliminary phase (10 min): introduction to the experiment and initial questionnaire administration.
2. Preliminary questionnaire (15 min): demographic data collection, informed consent, randomized group assignment, and Self-Assessment Manikin administration for global affectivity evaluation.
3. Instructional phase: delivery of a lesson on social stories, followed by a structured 15-min break.
4. Interaction phase (30 min): study period supported by the assigned tool (ITS or generic chatbot).
5. Assessment phase (15 min): administration of evaluation scales (SAM, SUS, BUS-11, Perceived Academic Self-Efficacy Scale).
6. Concluding phase (20 min): completion of digital competencies questionnaire (MyDigiSkills).

The latent variables subject to measurement are articulated into two macro-categories:

Psychological variables: Perceived Academic Self-Efficacy and Global Affectivity

User Experience variables: Generic Usability and Chatbot-specific Usability

This methodological structure was designed to ensure rigorous analysis of the differential effects of both tools while controlling for potential confounding variables through randomization and baseline measurement of variables of interest.

3.2 Definition and Architecture of the ITS

An Intelligent Tutoring System (ITS) can be defined as an advanced computer system whose purpose is to provide personalized instruction and feedback to students without direct intervention from a human teacher; it is configured as an educational support tool that adopts an articulated architecture, typically comprised of three main components—the Student Module, the Domain Module, and the Teaching Module—each of which has been developed to adhere to Universal Design for Learning (UDL) principles, thereby ensuring multiple means of representation, expression, and engagement to optimize instructional intervention effectiveness (Fig. 1).

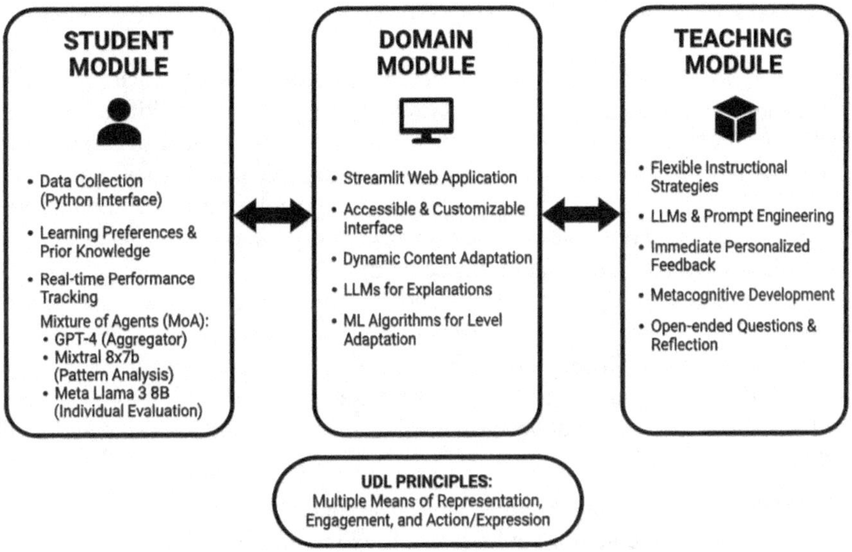

Fig. 1. Architecture of the UDL-oriented ITS

Student Module. The Student Module of the Intelligent Tutoring System (ITS) represents a fundamental component in structuring the personalized approach to education; it is founded upon a complex structure of data collection and management that aims to dynamically adapt the educational process to each learner's specific needs, in strict accordance with Universal Design for Learning (UDL) principles. The application of these principles is designed to promote inclusive pedagogy that ensures diverse content representation modalities, diversified forms of expression, and active student engagement, enabling them to interact with instructional material in ways that respond to their specific preferences and individual needs [27].

The integration of the Mixture of Agents (MoA) method distinguishes itself by transcending mere classification of student learning needs, orienting instead toward development of a personalized and dynamic educational model that conforms to flexibility and accessibility criteria inherent in UDL guidelines [30]; this model proves particularly effective in providing learning experiences that adapt in real-time to the learner's evolving needs.

The system collects data through a Python-developed interface designed to acquire information regarding learning preferences, prior knowledge, and specific variables related to course content. These data are subsequently processed and structured for employment within the system; during learning sessions, additional real-time information is collected, such as response accuracy, response times, question frequency, and assistance requests, which proves essential for dynamically and personally adapting the educational pathway. This information is recorded and tracked to ensure optimal precision in student profile analysis, thereby enabling the system to formulate educational recommendations that are consistent with UDL principles and responsive to individual learner needs.

The core of the ITS approach resides in the capacity to optimize the learning pathway by leveraging advanced language models (LLMs) operating jointly within the Mixture of Agents (MoA) method [14–30]. In this context, diverse agents collaborate to accurately assess the learner's profile and propose targeted pedagogical strategies; among these agents, GPT-4 serves as an aggregator of evaluations and collected information, Mixtral 8x7b processes classifications based on recurring learning patterns [16], and Meta Llama 3 8B provides independent evaluation based on individual student characteristics [28]. The integration and synergy among these agents enable the system to adapt not only to diverse learning needs but also to ensure constant alignment with UDL principles, thereby improving the quality and effectiveness of the instructional experience; it is thus evident that adopting a multi-agent educational strategy proves crucial for addressing challenges related to educational need diversification, promoting inclusive and flexible education.

Domain Module. The Domain Module, within the context of our study, does not employ multiple means of representation but leverages the Streamlit framework to create a web application accessible to all, characterized by an interface customizable according to each student's idiosyncrasies. The domain module receives input data produced by the Student Module and consequently adapts content presentation to respond precisely to learner needs. In this regard, the approach employs three principal technologies, Streamlit, for customizable web interface development; advanced language models (LLMs), utilized to generate detailed explanations; and machine learning (ML) algorithms, designed to adapt content to the student's competency level.

An essential aspect of this module is its adherence to UDL principles, pursued through diverse strategies. The web application is designed to be accessible from a variety of devices and to support assistive technologies, thereby ensuring personalized accessibility; content is dynamically adapted through data from the Student Module, enabling real-time material presentation aligned with learner capabilities and preferences; finally, the interface is customizable such that each student can modify the appearance and arrangement of information according to their individual needs.

This configuration enables addressing educational challenges with an approach that not only improves the learning experience but also ensures greater inclusivity and flexibility, in accordance with UDL principles; in this manner, the domain module does not merely transmit information but becomes a dynamic support tool capable of adapting to each student's specific characteristics, thereby optimizing the learning process.

Teaching Module. The Teaching Module is configured for educational strategy implementation; it adheres to UDL guidelines through adoption of flexible instructional strategies designed to offer diversified learning pathways capable of responding to each learner's individual needs. Educational pathway personalization is achieved through utilization of advanced language models (LLMs) and Prompt Engineering techniques, which enable provision of immediate and constructive feedback modeled according to learner responses and needs. Additionally, the module encourages metacognitive development, learning self-awareness, through employment of open-ended questions and suggestions, thereby stimulating students to reflect critically on their own learning process.

From a technological perspective, the Teaching Module utilizes language models (LLMs) to facilitate natural interactions and provide feedback, and Prompt Engineering to personalize LLM responses and adapt instructional strategies based on the learner's educational pathway progression. This advanced technological approach ensures high-quality instructional support that proves not only pertinent to student needs but also capable of dynamically adapting to them.

3.3 Generic Chatbot Description

The control chatbot was designed to provide support on storytelling-related content without adhering to UDL guidelines. Unlike the ITS, the control chatbot offers standardized and non-personalized interactions, serving as a benchmark for evaluating. the impact of UDL guideline adherence on educational support effectiveness. The chatbot comprises three principal components: a user interface that enables interaction through textual messages, a processing engine that utilizes advanced language models (LLMs) to generate responses based on user inputs, and a knowledge base containing static storytelling information.

The chatbot's technological architecture includes utilization of Large Language Models (LLMs), GPT-4, to comprehend and generate natural text; however, unlike the UDL ITS, Prompt Engineering is not employed to optimize responses, and machine learning (ML) methods integration for dynamic educational experience adaptation is absent. This standardized structure, while less flexible than that adopted for the ITS, offers a fundamental comparison point for evaluating differences in effectiveness and usability between personalized and non-personalized approaches.

Therefore, the UDL-based ITS design aims to provide an inclusive and personalized learning experience aligned with Universal Design for Learning principles. Conversely, the control chatbot serves as a benchmark for evaluating the impact of UDL guideline adherence on usability and learning support effectiveness, providing a useful comparison term for understanding benefits associated with integrating an advanced and adaptive educational architecture versus a more rigid and standardized approach.

3.4 Scales Employed

Self-Assessment Manikin. The Self-Assessment Manikin (SAM) is a non-verbal instrument evaluating emotional responses to stimuli, based on Russell's emotion model with three 9-item subscales: Valence (pleasantness, represented by facial expressions from happy to sad), Arousal (activation level from calm to excited, depicted through stylized figures), and Dominance (perceived control, shown through figures ranging from small/helpless to large/powerful) [7].

Perceived Academic Self-efficacy Scale. This scale analyzes students' beliefs about their capabilities to regulate study motivation, maintain focus, organize academic activities, and find effective learning support. It represents a reduced 9-item version of the original 19-item instrument, utilizing a 5-point Likert scale [4].

System Usability Scale. The System Usability Scale (SUS) evaluates product or system usability through 10 items on a 5-point Likert scale. It is widely employed due to its universality, comprehensive subjective experience evaluation, and cost-effectiveness [10].

Chatbot Usability Scale. The Chatbot Usability Scale (BUS-11) measures chatbot ease of use and effectiveness through user evaluations across five dimensions: ease of use, reliability, satisfaction, efficiency, and comprehension capability. This scale provides quantitative data to improve user-chatbot interaction by identifying experience strengths and weaknesses [6].

MyDigiSkills Questionnaire. This 82-item self-assessment questionnaire evaluates digital competency across DigiComp.2.2's five areas, providing immediate feedback on competency levels. Created by ALL DIGITAL under Creative Commons license based on the European Commission's DigCompSAT project, with the Italian version curated by Repubblica Digitale as part of national digital inclusion initiatives.

3.5 Sample Characterization and Participant Profile

The study involved 99 participants from the TFA support VIII cycle at the University of Foggia, asymmetrically distributed between control (n = 55) and experimental groups (n = 44). Participants were predominantly female (87.27% control, 84.09% experimental) with mean ages of 41.24 years (SD ± 8.96) and 44.55 years (SD ± 11.12) respectively, and high educational attainment exceeding 88% graduates in both groups (89.09% control, 88.64% experimental). Teaching experience varied heterogeneously: the control group showed bimodal distribution between novice teachers (32.73% no experience) and intermediate professionals (30.91% with 3–6 years), while the experimental group polarized toward advanced experience (36.36% with >7 years).

Digital competencies revealed sophisticated technological profiles with near-universal daily technology use (Internet: 96.36% control, 100% experimental; PC: 80.00% control, 84.09% experimental). Information and Data Literacy predominantly showed advanced (61.82% control, 56.82% experimental) and intermediate levels (34.55% control, 43.18% experimental), with similar patterns in Communication and Collaboration. Digital Content Creation concentrated at intermediate levels (60.00% control, 61.36% experimental) with limited advanced competencies (29.09% control, 27.27% experimental). Notably, over half of participants lacked prior chatbot experience (58.18% control, 54.55% experimental), significant for intervention interpretation. Study habits favored autonomous learning (87.27% control, 75.00% experimental) with moderate time commitment (2–5 h weekly: 47.27% control, 45.45% experimental).

3.6 Verification of Group Equivalence and Analysis of Statistical Assumptions

Statistical inference validity relied on careful assumption analysis and group equivalence verification. Systematic examination of distributional properties revealed complex patterns guiding methodological choices.

Distributional Properties and Statistical Assumptions. Shapiro-Wilk tests revealed significant normality violations in key measures, particularly Self-Assessment Manikin dimensions. Pleasure and Arousal showed baseline violations in both groups (PP: control $W = 0.953$, $p = .030$; experimental $W = 0.939$, $p = .022$; A: control $W = 0.945$, $p = .014$; experimental $W = 0.936$, $p = .017$), intensifying at post-test. System Usability Scale violated normality only in controls ($W = 0.934$, $p = .005$) while maintaining normal distribution experimentally ($W = 0.960$, $p = .134$), whereas Chatbot Usability Scale showed deviations across all subscales. Levene's test revealed heteroscedasticity in participant age ($F(1, 97) = 5.054$, $p = .027$), self-efficacy scores ($F(1, 97) = 4.087$, $p = .046$), and perceived chatbot accessibility ($F(1, 97) = 5.826$, $p = .018$).

Experimental Group Equivalence. Non-parametric analysis revealed substantial group equivalence. Demographic composition showed no significant disparities in gender distribution ($\chi^2(1) = 0.204$, $p = .652$, Cramer's $V = 0.045$) or education level ($\chi^2(2) = 0.116$, $p = .944$, Cramer's $V = 0.034$). Teaching experience distribution was balanced ($\chi^2(3) = 5.430$, $p = .143$, Cramer's $V = 0.234$). Digital competencies showed comparable distributions across Information Literacy ($\chi^2(2) = 2.178$, $p = .337$, Cramer's $V = 0.148$), Communication & Collaboration ($\chi^2(2) = 0.459$, $p = .795$, Cramer's $V = 0.068$), and Digital Content Creation ($\chi^2(2) = 0.041$, $p = .980$, Cramer's $V = 0.020$), with no significant differences in AI/chatbot experience.

3.7 Methodological Implications

These patterns necessitated non-parametric approaches or robust statistical methods due to widespread normality violations, with appropriate corrections for identified heteroscedasticity. Substantial group equivalence in socio-demographic characteristics and digital competencies strengthens internal validity while minimizing systematic confounders. Non-homogeneous age distribution suggests considering this variable as a covariate, while digital competency balance eliminates the need for specific statistical controls.

4 Results

The investigation of intervention effects focused on three principal domains: affective dimensions, perceived self-efficacy, and system usability. For each domain, appropriate analyses were conducted considering both data nature and statistical assumption violations encountered.

4.1 Affective Dimensions

Analysis of affective components, measured through the Self-Assessment Manikin (SAM), revealed complex patterns of emotional response. Given the violation of the sphericity assumption (Mauchly's $W = 0.769$, $\chi^2(2) = 25.240$, $p < .001$), the Greenhouse-Geisser correction ($\varepsilon = 0.812$) was implemented in the repeated measures analysis of variance. Results evidenced a significant main effect of Dimension (F(1.624,

157.571) = 9.266, $p < .001$, $\eta^2p = 0.087$), modulated by a marginally significant interaction with the experimental group ($F(1.624, 157.571) = 2.549$, $p = .092$, $\eta^2p = 0.026$). The analysis revealed no significant effects for the Time × Dimension interaction nor for the three-way interaction, suggesting temporal stability of emotional responses across groups.

Post-hoc comparisons provided greater granularity in understanding differences between affective dimensions. The PP dimension showed significant differences both with respect to A (mean difference = −0.619, SE = 0.157, $t = -3.946$, $p < .001$, $d = -0.292$) and PC (mean difference = −0.916, SE = 0.237, $t = -3.868$, $p < .001$, $d = -0.432$), while the comparison between A and PC did not reach statistical significance (mean difference = −0.297, SE = 0.246, $t = -1.204$, $p = .695$, $d = -0.140$).

4.2 Perceived Self-Efficacy

Examination of self-efficacy required a non-parametric approach, given the violation of normality assumptions evidenced by the Shapiro-Wilk test in both control group ($W = 0.939$, $p = .008$) and experimental group ($W = 0.905$, $p = .002$). Analysis using the Mann-Whitney test revealed no significant differences between groups ($U = 1274.500$, $p = .650$, $r = 0.053$), with comparable medians between control group (M = 31.800, SD = 6.792) and experimental group (M = 31.295, SD = 4.887).

4.3 Usability Assessment

Usability analysis integrated two complementary perspectives through the System Usability Scale (SUS) and the Chatbot Usability Scale (BUS-11). SUS scores exceeded the good usability threshold (68) in both groups, with the control group recording a mean of 77.318 (SD ± 16.686) and the experimental group 73.182 (SD ± 14.621). Analysis revealed no statistically significant differences between groups ($U = 1430.000$, $p = .122$, $r = 0.182$).

Detailed analysis of BUS-11 dimensions revealed differentiated but consistent response patterns. Conversation Quality showed the highest scores in both groups (Control: M = 14.509, SD = 3.090; Experimental: M = 14.750, SD ± 2.829), followed by Functionality Quality (Control: M = 11.873, SD ± 2.887; Experimental: M = 11.341, SD ± 2.332) and Perceived Accessibility (Control: M = 7.345, SD ± 2.145; Experimental: M = 6.818, SD ± 1.603). Privacy, Security, and Response Time dimensions showed similar patterns between groups, without statistically significant differences.

4.4 Construct Relationships

Correlational analyses revealed that Information Literacy consistently correlated with system usability (SUS: $rs = 0.371$, $p < .001$) and BUS-11 subscales ($rs = 0.320$–0.404, $p < .001$). Digital problem-solving correlated positively with perceived functionality quality ($rs = 0.353$, $p < .001$) and negatively with arousal ($rs = -0.233$, $p = .020$). Affective measures showed strong temporal stability ($rs = 0.458$–0.604, $p < .001$), whereas self-efficacy remained largely independent from other dimensions, indicating construct specificity.

4.5 Predictive Patterns in BUS-11 Subscale Analysis

Hierarchical regression models examined how digital competencies and group membership predicted BUS-11 dimensions.

Predictive Model Analysis. For perceived accessibility, the final model explained $R^2 = 0.321$ ($F(7,91) = 6.159$, $p < .001$), with significant effects of Information Literacy ($B = 1.622$, $SE = 0.459$, $p < .001$) and experimental group ($B = 6.756$, $SE = 1.855$, $p < .001$), qualified by a group × Information Literacy interaction ($B = -2.251$, $SE = 0.734$, $p = .003$). Functional quality was predicted by Information Literacy ($B = 2.043$, $SE = 0.638$, $p = .002$) and problem-solving competencies ($B = 1.384$, $SE = 0.682$, $p = .045$) in a model with $R^2 = 0.306$ ($F(7,91) = 5.740$, $p < .001$), which also showed a significant group × Information Literacy interaction ($B = -2.346$, $SE = 1.020$, $p = .024$). Conversation quality ($R^2 = 0.288$, $F(7,91) = 5.259$, $p < .001$) was strongly influenced by problem-solving competencies ($B = 2.019$, $SE = 0.771$, $p = .010$), Information Literacy ($B = 1.885$, $SE = 0.722$, $p = .011$), and experimental group membership ($B = 8.455$, $SE = 2.917$, $p = .005$).

4.6 Model Robustness and Validity

Diagnostics confirmed model robustness: Condition Index <30, Q-Q plots supported normality, Cook's Distance <1, and standardized residuals within ±3 SD. Sequential models showed significant variance increases for accessibility ($\Delta R^2 = 0.132$, $p < .001$) and functional quality ($\Delta R^2 = 0.086$, $p = .013$), with a marginal but coherent increase for conversation quality ($\Delta R^2 = 0.062$, $p = .054$).

4.7 Pattern Convergence and Implications

Three key patterns emerged: Information Literacy was a consistent predictor across usability dimensions (B range: 1.622–2.043) with systematic group interactions; problem-solving competencies significantly influenced conversation quality ($B = 2.019$, $p = .010$); and negative interactions between group and Information Literacy indicated a compensatory ITS effect, especially benefiting users with lower digital competencies in accessibility and functional quality.

4.8 Empirical Evidence and Theoretical Contributions

Multivariate analysis of affective dimensions demonstrated a significant Dimension effect ($F(1.624,157.571) = 9.266$, $p < .001$, $\eta^2 p = 0.087$) and temporal stability (rs = 0.458–0.604, $p < .001$), supporting the view that ITS emotional impact is mediated by stable individual traits. Self-efficacy showed no group differences ($U = 1274.500$, $p = .650$), indicating maintained integrity in technologically mediated learning. Usability analyses confirmed scores above good usability thresholds with positive correlations to digital competencies, while BUS-11 subscale interactions suggested nuanced moderation mechanisms.

4.9 Integrated Overview of the Results

Three overarching patterns emerge from the data analysis. First, while UDL-oriented design failed to produce direct superiority in psychological outcomes (self-efficacy) or affective response, it demonstrated significant interaction effects indicating adaptive capacity for users with varying digital literacy levels. Second, both systems achieved usability benchmarks conventionally associated with technology acceptance, yet differential benefits manifested exclusively through competency-intervention interactions rather than aggregate system comparison. Third, affective and self-efficacy outcomes revealed substantial temporal stability and trait-mediated patterns, suggesting these dimensions may be less responsive to architectural design variations than usability-related dimensions, which demonstrated sensitivity to user-system alignment mechanisms. These findings support a reconceptualization of educational technology effectiveness from direct system comparisons toward adaptive scaffolding frameworks that calibrate technological complexity to individual user capabilities.

5 Discussion

This study examined an Intelligent Tutoring System (ITS) based on Universal Design for Learning (UDL) framework effectiveness, investigating digital competencies as user experience moderators. Analysis revealed complex interactions between individual user characteristics and technological intervention effectiveness.

The UDL-designed ITS achieved high flexibility in adapting to students' study strategies through content access modalities and enhanced engagement. Key applicability elements include multimodal study trajectories, immediate personalized feedback, and enhanced reflective and metacognitive capacities, alongside transversal competency development in critical thinking and problem solving [15].

Results indicate the necessity for differentiated ITS design explicitly considering users' digital competency levels. Information Literacy's differential intervention effectiveness suggests opportunities for dynamic calibration mechanisms adapting support to individual characteristics. Findings support adaptive scaffolding strategies, particularly for users with lower digital competencies, with functionality optimization requiring competency profile consideration, emphasizing accessibility for high-competency users and incremental support for less experienced users.

Affective measures demonstrated substantial temporal stability ($rs = 0.458$–0.604, $p < .001$), suggesting that emotional responses to educational technologies reflect stable dispositional characteristics rather than transient reactions. This stability pattern, combined with the significant main effect of affective dimensions ($F(1.624, 157.571) = 9.266$, $p < .001$, $\eta^2p = 0.087$), indicates that affective experiences within UDL-oriented systems are psychologically coherent and consistent over time. Critically, the non-significant Time × Dimension and three-way interactions confirm that emotional consistency persists across both groups, supporting the theory that UDL design principles, by providing multiple means of engagement and representation, establish stable affective conditions regardless of users' initial technological exposure. The independence of self-efficacy from affective measures (construct specificity: self-efficacy showed no interaction with temporal dynamics) further clarifies that UDL effectiveness operates through distinct psychological mechanisms: affective regulation via design flexibility and self-efficacy maintenance through preserved perception of competence. These findings suggest that UDL-oriented ITS create emotionally stable learning environments that facilitate adaptive engagement for diverse digital competencies, advancing the theoretical understanding of how inclusive design translates into consistent psychological experiences.

5.1 Design and Implementation Implications

Results have substantial implications for UDL-based ITS design. Information Literacy emerged as a consistent perceived usability predictor, with standardized coefficients ranging from 0.215 to 0.450 across dimensions, necessitating design that explicitly considers varying digital competency levels through differential support mechanisms.

The interaction pattern between digital competencies and intervention effectiveness proved particularly relevant: users with lower Information Literacy levels showed differential benefits from the UDL-oriented approach, suggesting the system provides effective support for those potentially encountering educational technology access barriers, with direct implications for adaptive support system implementation.

Conversation quality emerged as crucial, strongly influenced by problem-solving competencies ($B = 2.019$, $p = .010$), suggesting the importance of calibrating dialogic interaction based on users' capacity to address complex problems through progressive scaffolding strategies dynamically adapting to competency levels.

6 Conclusions

6.1 Limitations and Future Perspectives

Despite promising results, it is necessary to consider some methodological limitations that suggest directions for future research. The specificity of the sample within the educational context. and the cross-sectional nature of the study limit results generalizability. Future research could benefit from a longitudinal approach that permits examination of temporal evolution of user-system interaction and potential development of digital competencies through prolonged ITS use.

The utilization of self-assessment measures for digital competencies, although validated, could be integrated in the future with objective behavioral metrics.

Furthermore, implementation of mixed methods, combining quantitative data with in-depth qualitative analyses, could provide richer understanding of mechanisms through which digital competencies influence intervention effectiveness.

Finally, the absence of learning outcome analysis does not allow establishment of the real impact of UDL-oriented ITS on learning processes but only permits indirect inference of dynamics based on perceived academic self-efficacy levels.

In this regard, it is deemed necessary to continue this research line by considering solid measures relating to learning outcomes in future projects. Moreover, it would be necessary to expand affectivity evaluation by also considering its long-term fluctuations and including analysis of anxiety state impact. Finally, starting from self-efficacy as primary construct, we aim to expand experimentation by including other complex constructs such as learning motivation in the reference model.

These findings highlight the necessity of incorporating adaptive support features that respond dynamically to users' needs. Mechanisms such as real-time scaffolding, tailored feedback, and accessible interface design can enhance the learning experience, particularly for those with limited digital skills. From a design perspective, it is essential that ITS platforms not only optimize instructional delivery but also promote equitable access by accommodating the varying levels of digital literacy among learners. In doing so, ITS, grounded in UDL principles, can contribute meaningfully to the creation of more inclusive and effective digital learning ecosystems. Integrating Universal Design for Learning principles into ITSs does more than improve technical usability, it makes these systems genuinely inclusive learning companions. By adapting in real time to diverse student needs, they help break down barriers and open up equitable learning opportunities for all, leaving no one behind.

Disclosure of Interests The authors have no competing interests to declare that are relevant to the content of this article.

References

1. Alfirević, N., Garbin Praničević, D., Mabić, M.: Custom-trained large language models as open educational resources: an exploratory research of a business management educational Chatbot in Croatia and Bosnia and Herzegovina. Sustainability. **16**(12), 4929 (2024)
2. Antony, S., Ramnath, R.: A phenomenological exploration of Students' perceptions of AI Chatbots in higher education. IAFOR J. Educ. Technol. Educ. **11**(2), 7–38 (2023)
3. Bartimote-Aufflick, K., Bridgeman, A., Walker, R., Sharma, M., Smith, L.: The study, evaluation, and improvement of university student self-efficacy. Stud. High. Educ. **41**(11), 1918–1942 (2016)
4. Biasci, V., Vincenzo, C.D., Patrizi, N.: Relazioni tra autoregolazione dell'apprendimento, motivazioni e successo accademico degli studenti. Identificazione di fattori predittivi del rischio di drop-out. Ital. Journal Educ. Res., 181–198 (2017)
5. Birenbaum, M.: The Chatbots' challenge to education: disruption or destruction? Educ. Sci. **13**, 711 (2023)
6. Borsci, S., Prati, E., Malizia, A., Schmettow, M., Chamberlain, A., Federici, S.: Ciao AI: the Italian adaptation and validation of the Chatbot usability scale. Pers. Ubiquit. Comput. **27**, 2161–2170 (2023)
7. Bradley, M.M., Lang, P.J.: Measuring emotion: the self-assessment manikin and the semantic differential. J. Behav. Ther. Exp. Psychiatry. **25**(1), 49–59 (1994)
8. Bravo, F.A., Cruz-Bohorquez, J.M.: Engineering education in the age of AI: analysis of the impact of Chatbots on learning in engineering. Educ. Sci. **14**(5), 484 (2024)
9. Bray, A., et al.: What next for universal Design for Learning? A systematic literature review of technology in UDL implementations at second level. Br. J. Educ. Technol. **55**(1), 113–138 (2024)
10. Brooke, J.: SUS: a retrospective. J. Usability Stud. Arch. **8**, 29–40 (2013)
11. Cai, Z., Park, S., Nixon, N., Doroudi, S.: Advancing Knowledge Together: Integrating Large Language Model-based Conversational AI in Small Group Collaborative Learning. In: Extended Abstracts of the CHI Conference on Human Factors in Computing Systems (CHI EA '24) (2024)

12. Dempsey, A.M., Nolan, Y.M., Lone, M., Hunt, E.: Examining motivation of first-year undergraduate anatomy students through the lens of universal Design for Learning (UDL): a single institution study. Med. Sci. Educ. **33**(4), 945–953 (2023)
13. Deng, X., Yu, Z.: A meta-analysis and systematic review of the effect of Chatbot technology use in sustainable education. Sustainability **15**(4), 2940 (2023)
14. Ho, N., Schmid, L., Yun, S.-Y.: Large language models are reasoning teachers (2022). https://doi.org/10.48550/ARXIV.2212.10071
15. Hooshyar, D., Ahmad, R.B., Yousefi, M., Fathi, M., Horng, S.J., Lim, H.: SITS: a solution-based intelligent tutoring system for students' acquisition of problem-solving skills in computer programming. Innov. Educ. Teach. Int. **55**(3), 325–335 (2018)
16. Jiang, A. Q.et al.: Mixtral of experts. arXiv (2024). https://doi.org/10.48550/arXiv.2401.04088. https://arxiv.org/abs/2401.04088
17. Lieb, A., Goel, T.: Student Interaction with NewtBot: An LLM-as-tutor Chatbot for Secondary Physics Education. In: Extended Abstracts of the CHI Conference on Human Factors in Computing Systems (CHI EA '24) (2024)
18. Neo, M., et al.: Enhancing Students' online learning experiences with artificial intelligence (AI): the MERLIN project. Int. J. Technol. **13**(5), 1023–1034 (2022)
19. Owenz, M., Cruz, L.: Addressing student test anxiety through universal design for learning alternative assessments. Coll. Teach., 1–11 (2023)
20. Pernaa, J., Ikävalko, T., Takala, A., Vuorio, E., Pesonen, R., Haatainen, O.: Artificial intelligence Chatbots in chemical information seeking: narrative educational insights via a SWOT analysis. Informatics. **11**(2), 20 (2024)
21. Rao, K., Ok, M.W., Bryant, B.R.: A review of research on universal design educational models. Remedial Spec. Educ. **35**(3), 153–166 (2014)
22. Riabko, A.V., Vakaliuk, T.A.: Physics on autopilot: exploring the use of an AI assistant for independent problem-solving practice. Educ. Technol. Q. **2**(1), 56–75 (2024)
23. Rusconi, L., Squillaci, M.: Effects of a universal design for learning (udl) training course on the development teachers' competences: a systematic review. Educ. Sci. **13**(5), 466 (2023)
24. Sala-Bars, I., Mumbardó-Adam, C., Adam-Alcocer, A.L.: Moving towards preservice teachers' implementation of universal design for learning: the central role of self-efficacy. Teachers Teach., 1–19 (2024)
25. Seok, S., DaCosta, B., Hodges, R.: A systematic review of empirically based universal design for learning: implementation and effectiveness of universal design in education for students with and without disabilities at the postsecondary level. Open J. Soc. Sci. **6**(05), 171 (2018)
26. Tarisayi, K.S.: Strategic leadership for responsible artificial intelligence adoption in higher education. In: CTE Workshop Proceedings, vol. 11, pp. 4–14 (2024)
27. Taylor, D.L., Yeung, M., Bashet, A.Z.: Personalized and Adaptive Learning, pp. 17–34 (2021). https://doi.org/10.1007/978-3-030-58948-6_2
28. Touvron, H., et al.: LLaMA: open and efficient foundation language models. arXiv (2023). https://doi.org/10.48550/arXiv.2302.13971. https://arxiv.org/abs/2302.13971
29. Venkatesh, V., Thong, J.Y.L., Xu, X.: Consumer acceptance and use of information technology: extending the unified theory of acceptance and use of technology. MIS Q. **36**(1), 157–178 (2012)
30. Wang, J., Wang, J., Athiwaratkun, B., Zhang, C., Zou, J.: Mixture-of-agents enhances large language model capabilities . arXiv (2014). https://doi.org/10.48550/arXiv.2406.04692. https://arxiv.org/abs/2406.04692
31. Xu, X., Chen, Y., Miao, J.: Opportunities, challenges, and future directions of large language models, including ChatGPT in medical education: a systematic scoping review. J. Educ. Eval. Health Prof. **21**, 6 (2024)

32. Zarei, M.: ChatGPT, a friend or a foe in medical education: a review of strengths, challenges, and opportunities. Shiraz E-Med. J. **25**(6), e145840 (2024)
33. Zarouk, M.Y.S.A., Khaldi, M.: Towards an intelligent tutoring system developing metacognition: cyclical model. In: In 2015 10th International Conference on Intelligent Systems: Theories and Applications (SITA), pp. 1–6. IEEE (2015)

Unplugged Activities to Foster Active and Meaningful Learning of Computer Science for Primary School Children

Rachele Passi[1](✉), Ileana Bodini[1], Andrea Loreggia[1], Valerio Villa[1], Silvia Ceccacci[2], and Agnese I. Telloni[2]

[1] Università di Brescia, Brescia, Italy
{r.passi,ileana.bodini,andrea.loreggia,valerio.villa}@unibs.it
[2] Università di Macerata, Macerata, Italy
{silvia.ceccacci,agnese.telloni}@unimc.it

Abstract. This study investigates the design, implementation, and evaluation of an unplugged educational pathway grounded in Universal Design for Learning principles, aimed at fostering computational thinking and introductory artificial intelligence literacy among primary school children. Conducted in an informal, summer-camp setting, the pathway translated abstract concepts from computer science and artificial intelligence into playful and socially situated activities aimed at fostering engagement, representation, and action and expression. Using a multiple case study design, qualitative and quantitative data were collected. Results highlight progressive gains in computational thinking skills alongside high levels of engagement and reflective awareness. Beyond child-centered outcomes, this study provides design principles that are transferable to pre-service teacher education. The findings contribute to the ongoing discussion on integrating Universal Design for Learning and artificial intelligence in higher education contexts, highlighting pathways for innovation, equity, and diversity in teacher training and curriculum design.

Keywords: Universal Design for Learning (UDL) · Computational Thinking (CT) · Artificial Intelligence (AI) · Primary Education · Teacher Training · Inclusive Learning · Unplugged Activities · Multimodal Learning

1 Introduction

In an era dominated by digital technologies, it is essential that schools adopt educational strategies that are both deliberate and culturally informed. Such strategies should foster meaningful learning while supporting the teacher's evolving role as a cultural mediator, guiding students in understanding fundamental computer science (CS) concepts and, in particular the principles, application and limitations of artificial intelligence (AI). In this sense, the teacher acts as

M. Adamoli et al. (Eds.): HELMeTO 2025, CCIS 2958, pp. 165–186, 2026.
https://doi.org/10.1007/978-3-032-31850-3_11

an interpreter between technological culture and learners' everyday experience, creating bridges between abstract computational ideas and meaningful contexts for students' understanding [1–3]. Teaching CS and AI thus goes beyond technical skills, emphasizing critical thinking, problem-solving, communication, and modeling.

Primary education occupies a pivotal role in this process. Both the literature and national curriculum guidelines consistently emphasize the imperative of integrating coding, unplugged activities, and constructivist pedagogical approaches to render CS and AI engaging and accessible from the earliest years [4]. At this developmental stage, children acquire fundamental cognitive structures that underpin logical reasoning, problem solving, and creativity [5,6]. The early introduction of concepts related to computation and AI—such as pattern recognition, decision-making, and automation—serves to strengthen these capacities, as children's natural curiosity and cognitive flexibility allow them to grasp complex ideas most effectively through developmentally appropriate, exploratory, and hands-on learning experiences [7,8].

Evidence indicates that excessive screen exposure during early development may adversely affect attention, sleep, and social development [9,10], whereas concrete, motor-based experiences have been demonstrated to enhance executive functions, working memory, and problem-solving skills in children [11,12].

Building on the considerations outlined above, this study aims to explore the design and implementation of unplugged activities for primary school children within an informal educational context, specifically summer camps for ages 6–11. In this frame, the teacher is conceived as a researcher and reflective practitioner who plans educational actions, designs tasks, enacts the pathways by adapting activities to classroom dynamics, observes the outcomes, and reflects on them to potentially redesign the activities [13,14]. The study aims not only to understand how teacher-led activities can foster logical, narrative, and critical competences, contributing to innovative educational practices that present CS as a discipline of thought, but also to serve as a laboratory for exploring foundational AI concepts, relying on inclusive Universal Design for Learning (UDL) principles in authentic learning contexts.

The research pursued two complementary objectives. First, it aimed to design an educational path based on unplugged activities devoted to informal contexts and promoting engagement, autonomy, persistence, socio-emotional dimensions, and early AI-literacy. Second, it aims to examine and significantly assess children's cognitive processes, problem-solving strategies, and algorithmic reasoning—more broadly, skills related to computational thinking (CT) and AI understanding—which constitutes a gap in the literature [15]. These objectives are also aligned with exploring how inclusive, flexible, and student-centered approaches (UDL) can enhance learning outcomes in AI-related contexts, providing insights relevant for both primary education and teacher training programs.

Summarizing, the chosen theoretical lenses should allow to shed light on both the development of computational and AI-related competences and the pedagogical conditions that facilitate meaningful and inclusive learning experiences.

In this perspective, the project also resonates with possible promising avenues for applying UDL to the design of activities in AI. Although implemented in primary education, these unplugged pathways can serve as a model for teacher training programs or, more generally, laboratory for exploring inclusive, flexible, and student-centered teaching approaches

2 Theoretical and Analytical Framework

CT refers to the cognitive processes involved in formulating problems and designing their solutions so that they can be executed by an information-processing agent, either human or machine [16]. It encompasses a set of interrelated skills and dispositions—such as abstraction, decomposition, algorithmic thinking, pattern recognition, and evaluation—that enable learners to approach complex problems systematically and creatively [17,18]. As an essential component of digital literacy, CT is increasingly recognized as a transversal competence applicable across disciplines, supporting reasoning, creativity, and problem-solving in authentic contexts [7,19].

Although many studies have examined the evaluation of CT, assessing these skills remains challenging due to the abstract nature of concepts and the multiplicity of correct approaches [15]. Literature highlights the lack of a universally accepted scale and the diversity of tools used, such as rubrics for CT sub-skills, web-based automated assessment tools (e.g., Dr. Scratch[1]), qualitative interviews, in-class observations, and task-based assessments [15,20–23].

To address the challenges of assessing CT, our study adopted a multimodal assessment strategy, combining observation, analysis of artifacts, and self-reflection to capture both objective performance and subjective experience. Psychometric approaches, including factor analysis, were employed to design composite scores, ensuring that dimensions such as abstraction, problem-solving, algorithmic thinking, and process awareness validly reflect the underlying cognitive constructs [24–26].

In designing unplugged activities, we relied on UDL framework as a valuable foundation to promote accessibility and inclusivity in education. UDL is grounded on three core principles that guide the design of educational activities [27,28]:

(a) Providing multiple means of engagement (MME), involves strategies that stimulate interest, motivation, and persistence. In CS classrooms, this might involve offering coding or unplugged activities at different challenge levels, opportunities for collaborative problem-solving, or tasks connected to students' prior experiences with technology, games, or everyday phenomena.
(b) Providing multiple means of representation (MMR), concerns presenting computational concepts through multiple communication channels—symbolic, visual, and hands-on formats—so that learners with diverse perceptual, linguistic, or cognitive profiles can access and meaningfully contribute to the

[1] https://www.drscratch.org/.

activity. For example, algorithms can be explored through flowcharts, physical role-play, or block-based coding interfaces.

(c) Providing multiple means of action and expression (MMAE), entails allowing students to express their understanding in multiple ways—through written pseudocode, oral explanations, diagrams, tangible manipulatives (e.g., cards, tokens), or digital tools—so that each learner can demonstrate CT skills according to their strengths and preferences.

The design of activities are further informed by semiotic mediation, situated cognition, and cognitive diversity, which together frame the learning processes underlying CT. Semiotic mediation emphasizes the role of signs, symbols and tools as mediators of cognitive activity, highlighting how learners construct meaning through interaction with cultural artifacts [29], while situated cognition emphasizes that knowledge is inherently tied to the contexts in which it is acquired and applied, underlining the importance of social, material and task-related conditions for meaningful learning [30,31]. Cognitive diversity complements these epostemiological perspectives by acknowledging that learners bring varied prior knowledge, strategies and ways of thinking, which shape how they engage with and interpret concepts [32]; this is also aligned with theories of multiple intelligences and successful intelligence, as proposed by Gardner and Sternberg [33,34].

By weaving these theoretical frameworks together, it becomes possible to interpret learning as a dynamic process in which signs, artifacts, social interactions, and individual differences collectively influence how learners represent, reason, and problem-solve. UDL principles intersect with this model by showing how the learning environment can promote accessibility, engagement, and agency: learners exercise choice and autonomy (UDL 7.1), sustain effort and persistence (UDL 8), and develop emotional and social awareness (UDL 9).

In this integrated view, semiotic mediation, situated cognition, and cognitive diversity are not separate considerations but are interwoven with UDL-informed practice, providing a coherent interpretation of how cognitive, emotional, social, and contextual dimensions interact to support meaningful engagement with CT concepts.

3 Context and Research Methodology

The activities were implemented in a municipal summer camp in Lombardy, Italy, primarily in Verolanuova (BS) and surrounding rural communities.

The first author, a computer engineer, acted as both initiator and sole instructor, integrating technical expertise in CS and AI with a pedagogical perspective. Drawing on this technical background, core computational principles were identified and translated into hands-on, interactive activities. Engineering training facilitated the abstraction and decomposition of complex concepts, enabling the development of simplified yet faithful models that guided each activity and structured the progression of skills across sessions. Technical knowledge was thus transformed into pedagogically meaningful experiences, employing games, narratives and tangible artifacts—such as drawings, tokens, and pseudocode—that children could manipulate and interpret.

A total of 45 children participated in the study, organized into three groups of 15, each attending the camp in a different week. Participants' ages ranged from 6 to 11 years, with a mean age of 9.0 years (standard deviation [SD] = 1.5), allowing for systematic observation of age-related differences in social dynamics and collaborative behaviors within mixed-age settings.

With regard to prior experience in CT participants did not undergo a formal pre-assessment using standardized instruments. However, preliminary information was collected through parental inquiries during the enrollment phase and informal observations conducted during the initial familiarization activities with the chldren. Based on the sources, it emerged that all children aged 11 years (six children in the total sample) had previously taken part in school-based educational robotics courses, which included activities with Micro:bit and ELECFREAKS Wonder Robot kits, programming with Scratch, and work with LEGO® Spike robotics kits—educational platforms widely used to foster foundational CT skills in K-12 learners [36–41]. Otherwise, younger participants had only limited or introductory exposure to CT concepts, mainly through general school activities or informal use of digital tools. Thus, aside from the 11-year-old subgroup, the baseline level of CT competence was relatively homogeneous across the sample.

Most participants came from a relatively homogeneous socio-cultural background: due to geographic and school proximity, they were often classmates or children already familiar with each other through extracurricular activities such as sports and local associations. Linguistic and cultural diversity was limited. Families were mostly characterized by a middle socio-economic profile, with both parents generally employed in dependent work (e.g., mother as an office worker, father as a manual laborer). Family composition showed two prevalent patterns: single-child households, occasionally within contexts of parental separation, and larger families with three or more children. Children were well supported, with attentive and caring parents. Differences in attitudes toward digital technology were also observed: some families —particularly larger families or those with older parents— tended to limit access to devices, while others allowed more extensive use, sometimes exposing children, especially boys, to early or excessive interaction with digital tools, perceived as instruments of social assertion or "adultization".

Activity selection, teaching methodologies, and assessment procedures were systematically guided by ideative, educational, and evaluative criteria:

- Ideative criteria: alignment with educational objectives (CT, problem-solving, collaboration), adaptability to resources and progressive skill development [35,42];
- Educational criteria: application of active, inclusive methodologies, including cooperative and experiential learning, inquiry-based approaches, narrative and gamified strategies, peer teaching and structured reflection [2,43–48];
- Evaluative criteria: integration of systematic observation conducted by the instructor during the sessions, self- and peer-assessment, learning journals and rubrics maintained by children, authentic artifacts and portfolios to monitor learning and provide formative feedback [49–53].

During the design and implementation phase, these criteria were operationalized. Baselines were established during the first session of each week, and longitudinal observations recorded participants' strategies, interactions, and performance, enabling within-subject analyses over time. Data were collected using multiple complementary sources:

- Teacher's direct observations of students' behavior, strategies, and interactions (systematic observation) including field notes, verbatim records of students' statements, and other in-class annotations [54];
- Students' self-assessment forms and personal diaries, completed at the end of each session (metacognitive and reflective evidence of learning processes);
- Artifacts and work produced by students, including concept maps, drawings, tokens, and other authentic productions (portfolio and semiotic assessment, namely the interpretation of students' meaning-making processes through their visual and symbolic representations).

This study adopts a qualitative, design-based research (DBR) approach [55, 56], aiming to explore how primary school children engage with computational concepts in informal, extracurricular contexts. By integrating theory and practice, the study investigates learning processes and representations of CT and AI through iterative design, implementation, and evaluation of unplugged activities. This dual focus allows for a rich understanding of both cognitive and pedagogical dimensions of learning.

Data were analyzed using inductive thematic analysis, guided by multiple interpretive lenses. UDL informed the interpretation of accessibility, engagement, and agency. Semiotic mediation provided insight into how artifacts act as semiotic mediators of the CS concepts and how signs produced by the children evolve supporting meaning-making. Situated cognition highlighted the role of context and social interactions in learning, and cognitive diversity emphasized how varied prior knowledge, strategies, and perspectives shaped students' engagement and interpretation of content. By integrating these lenses with DBR principles, the methodology should support a deep understanding of the cognitive, metacognitive and affective dimensions of learning in informal contexts.

Ethical considerations were carefully addressed: parental consent and child assent were secured before participation. Participants' confidentiality was maintained, and all data were anonymized. Children's well-being and comfort were prioritized throughout the activities.

4 The Educational Path

Table 1 provides an overview of the activities that were designed, implemented, and evaluated throughout the study, elucidating how each was grounded in existing literature and educational frameworks, while incorporating targeted adaptations for the intended age group and original contributions developed by the first author.

These pathways exemplify the breadth of CT concepts explored—from algorithms and problem-solving to AI, communication protocols, and network

Table 1. Genesis of the Unplugged Educational Pathways

No.	Activity	Inspirational Sources	Original Contributions and Adaptations
1	Pretending to Be an Algorithm	Classic algorithm exercises from CS education literature [7]	1. Adjusted for group size, age range 6–11 2. Venn diagrams were introduced as a visual aid to concretize logical operators, supporting the transition from perceptual to symbolic reasoning 3. The game "Guess Who?" was reinterpreted as a logical modeling exercise, making the process of classification both accessible and playful (Fig. 1)
2	The Robot Makes a Mistake: Who Is Right?	Error detection and debugging tasks in unplugged CS activities [57, 58]	1. Adapted classic error-detection exercises for children aged 6–11, using concrete, age-appropriate scenarios (e.g., the"three switches and a lightbulb" riddle). 2. Emphasized collaborative hypothesis testing, peer discussion, and reflective reasoning to foster critical awareness of AI fallibility and independent verification skills.
3	Create a Story with AI... Then Revise It!	AI-assisted story generation exercises [59]	1. Adapted AI-assisted story generation for children aged 6–11 2. Used drawing-based scaffolding to bridge concrete modification and creative text production 3. Encouraged students to recognize AI-generated text as a starting point for personal, reflective authorship 4. Supported development of early editorial awareness and critical engagement with digital content
4	Who Decides? AI or Us?	Ethical AI case studies [60]	1. Adapted ethical AI case studies for primary school children (ages 6–11) 2. Simplified dilemmas and scenarios to make ethical reflection age-appropriate 3. Encouraged discussion on human oversight vs. AI autonomy 4. Promoted critical thinking and awareness of ethical implications in everyday AI use
5	AI in the Real World	Popular science AI examples [59]	1. Adapted real-world AI examples for primary school children (ages 6–11) 2. Encouraged exploration of AI in everyday life through brainstorming and pair work 3. Used observation diaries and plenary discussions to support reflection and metacognitive awareness 4. Helped children distinguish beneficial features from intrusive or unwanted AI behaviors 5. Fostered early critical thinking about algorithmic technologies and their impact on personal and collective decisions
6	Public-Key Cryptography	CS security exercises [61]	1. Adapted cryptography exercises for primary school children (ages 6–11) 2. Used visual and hands-on materials to illustrate encryption and decryption 3. Supported concrete understanding of abstract security concepts
7	Guess the Hidden Image	CNN-based image recognition examples [57]	1. Screenless adaptation of CNN-based image recognition tasks 2. Used cards and physical grids to simulate image features and convolutional processing 3. Enabled children to grasp AI pattern recognition without digital devices
8	The Communication Networks Game	Networking exercises in CS pedagogy [57]	1. Simplified networking exercises for young learners 2. Used cooperative gameplay to illustrate network topologies and information flow
9	The Path of Instructions	Classic instruction-following and sequencing exercises [58]	1. Adapted classic sequencing and instruction-following exercises for mixed-age groups as a treasure hunt 2. Adjusted task complexity to scaffold logical reasoning and procedural thinking 3. Promoted understanding of cause-effect relationships and stepwise execution

Fig. 1. "Pretending to Be an Algorithm": introduction and familiarization with the game "Guess Who"

security— while showing a pedagogical approach guided by UDL principles. Role-playing, visual schematics, hands-on manipulations, collaborative discussions, and reflective exercises were intentionally included in each activity to provide varied entry points to abstract concepts, aligned with MME, MMR and MMEA.

In the following, we focus on one of the implemented activities, "The Communication Networks Game". Students are invited to embody nodes within a digital network, interacting through tangible artifacts that act as semiotic mediators (Fig. 2):

- Beads represent data packets, with different colors and sizes encoding source, destination, and payload information. They allow learners to visualize, manipulate, and track the flow of information.
- Strings connect the nodes physically, serving as indices of network links. Their layout makes network topology and possible alternative paths immediately perceptible, supporting understanding of redundancy and fault tolerance.
- Color-coded identity cards indicate node identities and roles, functioning as symbolic markers that help learners internalize addressing rules, authentication, and role assignment.

By engaging physically, visually, and socially with these artifacts, students gain multiple entry points to engagement, representation, and action/expression, allowing cognitive, social, and affective dimensions of learning to unfold simultaneously. In tune with the theory of semiotic mediation, the activity transforms

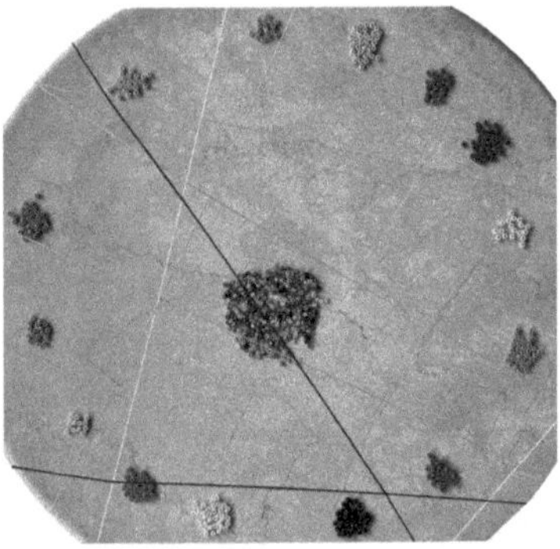

Fig. 2. Initial setup of "The Communication Networks Game": large beads around the table represent network nodes, smaller and alphabet beads in the center encode messages and destinations, and strings simulate connections between nodes, illustrating network topology, data flow, and fault tolerance in a tangible, hands-on activity.

abstract network concepts—routing, redundancy, fault tolerance, and acknowledgment protocols—into tangible, actionable experiences, scaffolding understanding from concrete interactions to higher-level reasoning.

The following UDL principles guided the design:

- Engagement (UDL 7): children act as network nodes in a cooperative, game-like scenario, negotiating alternative routes and managing simulated faults, which promotes motivation and social collaboration;
- Representation (UDL 8): messages are materialized through beads and strings, headers and trailers are visually distinct, and node identities are color-coded, providing multiple, concrete representations of abstract network concepts;
- Action & Expression (UDL 9): participants physically transmit packets, solve routing problems, respond with ACKs[2], and reflect collectively on strategies and outcomes, fostering autonomy, problem-solving, and metacognitive awareness.

5 Presentation of Data

5.1 Qualitative Analysis

This study focuses on a multiple case study design to explore how the unplugged activities described above can support primary school children's learning of CS concepts in informal contexts. This methodology allows in-depth examination of individual cases while enabling cross-case comparison to identify common themes

[2] ACKs, or acknowledgments are messages sent by the recipient to confirm the successful receipt of a packet, simulating reliability mechanisms in real network protocols.

and patterns [62–64], capturing diverse experiences and perspectives [65]. Qualitative data were primarily derived from children's diaries, reflective journals, and observational notes collected by the instructor during the sessions. Children's reflections were categorized to trace progression from concrete observations to abstract reasoning and to capture the development of metacognitive awareness. This approach aligns with prior research emphasizing the challenges of evaluating CT skills, including multiple correct solutions, diverse strategies, and the absence of a universally accepted scale [15,20,21,23].

The qualitative dimension also captured students' subjective experiences of perceived difficulty and their engagement with problem-solving, offering insights that purely quantitative metrics might overlook. To exemplify these findings, several excerpts from students' diaries documenting their experiences with "The Communication Networks Game" illustrate how the UDL-informed design provided multiple entry points for engagement, representation, and action/expression, thereby supporting both conceptual understanding and collaborative problem-solving in concrete CS tasks.

For instance, one student reflected:

> "When my wire was cut by my friend impersonating the network administrator, I had to think of another way to send the message. I looked at the wires and found a new friend to pass it through. It felt like fixing a broken road." *(Student A, 9 years old)*

This highlights embodied understanding of fault tolerance and the activation of cooperative problem-solving (UDL 7 – Engagement; UDL 9 – Action & Expression).

Another student noted:

> "I liked when the admin broke the connections, because then we had to talk to find new roads. It was like a real team of computers helping each other." *(Student B, 10 years old)*

This excerpt illustrates the social and collaborative dimension of learning, where encountering difficulties becomes a catalyst for negotiation and teamwork (UDL 7 – Engagement).

Reflections also revealed the development of metacognitive awareness and procedural understanding:

> "At the beginning, I was just passing beads. Then I understood I was making rules. We invented how to answer, and it worked better." *(Student C, 9 years old)*

This statement evidences the shift from simple execution to reflective construction of shared protocols (UDL 9 – Action & Expression).

The introduction of ACKs further reinforced the connection between action and conceptual understanding:

> "When I got the message back with my color, I felt sure it arrived. It was like the computer saying 'ok'. Now I know what ACK means." *(Student D, 8 years old)*

Here, the student demonstrates the internalization of reliable communication principles, linking symbolic cues to functional outcomes (UDL 8 – Representation; UDL 9 – Action & Expression).

Finally, students' reflections revealed progression toward abstraction:

> "Now I understand that computers don't really 'see' the message, they just read datas like we did with the beads." *(Student E, 10 years old)*

This exemplifies the transition from concrete, sensory experiences to symbolic reasoning, consistent with the semiotic mediation framework and the principles of CT/UDL.

5.2 Quantitative Analysis

Quantitative data were summarized using composite scores for each participant across seven dimensions, chosen to capture both objective performance and subjective experience. For each dimension, a score was computed by integrating multiple sources of evidence, including systematic observations, authentic student productions, reflective notes, and peer- and self-assessments. These scores were then normalized to ensure comparability across participants and dimensions.

The seven dimensions were divided into objective and subjective categories. Objective dimensions, largely derived from the literature, included Abstraction, Problem-Solving Skill, Algorithmic Thinking, Comprehension, and Transfer, reflecting cognitive processing, strategic reasoning, procedural structuring, and the ability to apply learned concepts in new contexts [16,66]. Subjective dimensions, informed both by existing studies and by the specific aims of this research, included Perceived Difficulty and Process Awareness, capturing participants' perceived challenges and their ability to verbalize reasoning and strategies [18].

To analyze changes over time, composite scores from baselines (first sessions) and final sessions were compared using the Wilcoxon signed-rank test, while Linear Mixed Models were applied to examine trends across all sessions, including a random effect for participants to account for individual differences.

Figure 3 presents all evaluation dimensions in a single multi-session trend graph, displaying normalized scores across the nine summer camp sessions. This visualization allows immediate comparison of the development of each dimension over time, highlighting both overall trends and individual variations (Table 2).

Objective cognitive skills, such as Problem Solving Skill and Algorithmic Thinking, showed gradual and cumulative growth. Subjective dimensions, including Process Awareness and Perceived Difficulty, exhibited non-linear patterns: Perceived Difficulty initially decreased and then increased during more complex activities (sessions 6 and 7), while process awareness displayed a temporary dip before rising in the final sessions. Transfer was operationalized as the number of contexts in which students successfully applied learned concepts, showing gradual improvement over time.

Table 2. Summary of Evaluation Dimensions with Quantitative and Qualitative Insights

Dimension	Measurement / Scale	Observed Trend and Notes
Problem Solving	Instructor-coded rubric, 0–4	1. Gradual improvement across sessions 2. Students identified alternative solutions when disruptions occurred (e.g., re-routing messages when wires were "cut") 3. Cooperative problem-solving enhanced engagement and practical understanding (UDL 7 – Engagement)
Algorithmic Thinking	Instructor-coded rubric, 0–4	1. Increased ability to plan sequences of actions and anticipate outcomes 2. Reflections indicated understanding of rules and protocols, e.g., students realizing they were "making rules" for message passing 3. Applied strategic reasoning in dynamic scenarios (UDL 9 – Action & Expression)
Abstraction	Instructor-coded rubric, 0–4	1. Shift from concrete bead-passing to symbolic reasoning about data flow 2. Students connected tangible actions to digital concepts (e.g., messages and ACKs) 3. Demonstrates the ability to generalize from physical to conceptual representations (UDL 8 – Representation)
Comprehension	Instructor-coded rubric, 0–4	1. Improved understanding of network topology, redundancy, and fault tolerance 2. Students articulated how data moves and how alternative paths work 3. Evidenced internalization of operational principles through reflections
Transfer	Observation of application in new contexts, count 0–n	1. Gradual increase in contexts where students applied learned strategies 2. Students demonstrated flexibility, e.g., applying the same routing logic to different "network disruptions"
Process Awareness	Researcher-coded (diaries, discussions, observations), 0–5	1. Initially variable, with temporary dips mid-sessions 2. Reflections show students becoming aware of their own reasoning, e.g., noticing how they invented new rules 3. Verbalization and collaborative discussion increased metacognitive awareness (UDL 9 – Action & Expression)
Perceived Difficulty	Self-report Likert scale 1–5	1. Initially low as students gained confidence 2. Increased during more complex activities (sessions 6–7, Table 1) 3. Student comments reveal engagement with challenging tasks without frustration, fostering resilience (UDL 7 – Engagement)

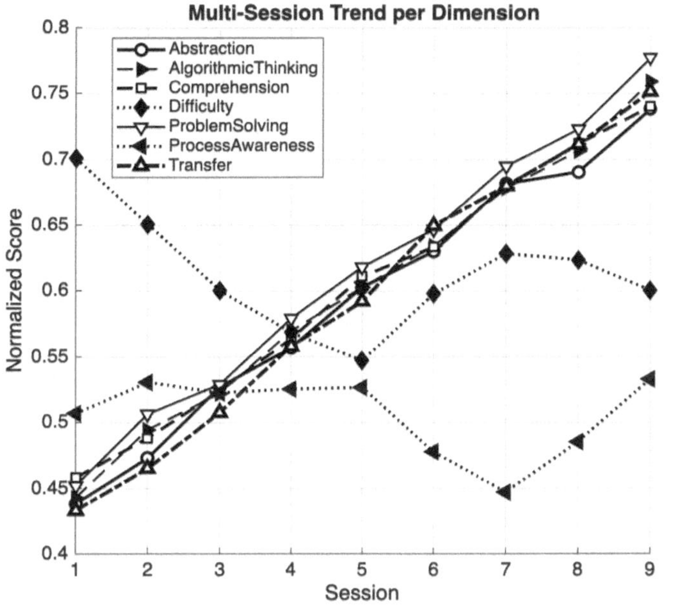

Fig. 3. Normalized trajectories of all evaluation dimensions across the nine summer camp sessions. The figure illustrates longitudinal trends over time, enabling comparison of dimension-specific patterns and highlighting both overall progression and inter-individual variability.

By systematically monitoring and analyzing data over time, educators can identify the most effective strategies and make targeted adjustments to optimize learning outcomes. Such longitudinal assessment also allows detection of patterns not immediately observable during classroom interactions, providing insights to support proactive interventions. This approach is particularly valuable for recognizing and addressing challenges faced by students with social or family difficulties, ensuring that learning environments remain inclusive and responsive to individual needs.

Evaluation Dimensions, Measurement Tools, Scales, and Scoring Criteria

Problem Solving, Algorithmic Thinking, Abstraction, Comprehension
Measurement Tool: Instructor-coded rubric
Scale / Range: Ordinal 0–4
Scoring Criteria:

- 0: none / incorrect
- 1: minimal / random / incomplete
- 2: partial / simple correct
- 3: planned / complex with minor errors / good abstraction / mostly correct

- 4: systematic / optimized / advanced abstraction / fully coherent and accurate

Process Awareness

Measurement Tool: Researcher-coded (diary entries, interviews, group discussions, instructor observation of verbalization)
Scale / Range: Ordinal 0–5
Scoring Criteria: 0: none, 2: low, 3: moderate, 4: high, 5: very high

Perceived Difficulty

Measurement Tool: Child self-report
Scale / Range: Likert 1–5
Scoring Criteria: 1: very easy, 2: easy, 3: moderate, 4: difficult, 5: very difficult

Transfer

Measurement Tool: Observation of spontaneous application in new contexts
Scale / Range: Count (0–n)
Scoring Criteria: Number of contexts in which the concept was correctly applied

For completeness, the full evaluation rubric used to assess each student across all dimensions is provided in Appendix A.

6 Discussion and Conclusions

The present study first aimed to design an educational pathway grounded in unplugged activities within informal learning contexts, fostering engagement, autonomy, persistence, and socio-emotional growth. Secondly, it sought to investigate and meaningfully assess children's cognitive processes, problem-solving strategies, and algorithmic reasoning—key facets of CT for which a universally recognized evaluation framework is still lacking in the literature.

The summer camp activities, designed and analysed according to this twofold objective, demonstrated that complex CT and AI concepts can be rendered both accessible and engaging for primary school learners aged 6–11. By translating abstract concepts into tangible, playful, and socially interactive experiences, students were able to experiment with, reason about, and reflect on computational processes in meaningful ways. As highlighted in prior research [66,70], employing diverse models and representations allows learners to approach computational content from multiple perspectives. In this study, drawings, physical manipulatives, embodied actions and AI-generated narratives enabled students to select representations that best matched their learning preferences, enhancing both engagement and conceptual understanding. The integration of quantitative and qualitative analyses suggested that students progressed in CT skills while remaining actively involved, curious and motivated to explore, understand and engage deeply in the learning process. Through systematic, longitudinal assessment, quantitative measures highlighted gains in problem-solving, abstraction, and algorithmic reasoning. This continuous monitoring also uncovered subtle learning patterns, offering educators actionable insights to refine strategies, support proactive interventions, and provide hands-on experiences that illustrate AI principles, fostering inclusive learning for all students, particularly those encountering social or familiar difficulties. Complementary qualitative evidence captured students' experiences, collaborative behaviors, and initial exposure to AI concepts, enriching the interpretation of learning outcomes. Collectively, these findings indicate that UDL-informed, multimodal, and socially and AI-situated activities effectively foster both cognitive growth and learner involvement, supporting the hypothesis that unplugged designs can scaffold CT and foundational AI understanding in inclusive learning contexts.

Students' reflections (A–E), discussed in Sect. 5.1, provide qualitative evidence of how UDL-aligned activities supported different dimensions of learning. Student A demonstrated an embodied understanding of fault tolerance and engaged in cooperative problem-solving, describing how alternative strategies emerged when disruptions occurred. This reflection highlights active engagement and flexible strategy use during the activity (UDL 7, 9).

Student B emphasized the role of negotiation and teamwork when facing challenges, reporting how peer interaction supported task completion and sustained engagement (UDL 7). The account illustrates the presence of collaborative reasoning processes during the activity.

Student C described a shift from executing predefined actions to collaboratively constructing communication rules. This transition indicates increased awareness of the underlying procedures and the emergence of metacognitive processes related to planning and rule formation (UDL 9).

Student D connected concrete signals used during the activity to a broader conceptual understanding of how information is transmitted and acknowledged. This reflection shows how tangible experiences supported abstraction and the construction of symbolic representations (UDL 8, 9).

Finally, Student E reported progress toward higher levels of abstraction by linking concrete manipulations to symbolic data processing. The reflection evidences the ability to generalize learned principles beyond the immediate task context, indicating emerging transfer and analytical reasoning skills (UDL 8).

These findings extend prior research on unplugged and inclusive computational learning [67–70] by showing how UDL principles can guide the design of activities that simultaneously promote engagement, representation, and action/expression. Artifacts such as Venn diagrams, classification tables, AI-generated narratives, beads, strings, color-coded identity cards and everyday scenarios acted as cognitive mediators [71], facilitating reflection and awareness and aligning with Vygotskij's historical-cultural perspective [72].

As noted earlier in this paper, an additional contribution of the study pertains to assessment. Existing literature highlights the absence of universally accepted frameworks for evaluating CT and AI understanding and the considerable heterogeneity of tools employed, including rubrics for sub-skills, online coding platforms, interviews, classroom observations, and task-based assessments [66,73]. In response, this study developed a customized evaluation scale that integrates quantitative performance metrics with qualitative indicators of engagement, thereby providing a context-sensitive model applicable to analogous learning environments.

Such an approach has the potential to capture a more comprehensive picture of learners' progress, fostering a deeper understanding of both cognitive and affective dimensions of learning, and the early development of AI literacy, supporting more targeted and reflective instructional practices.

The study has certain limitations: it was a pilot experience with a relatively homogeneous group of students and a limited number of cases, so findings should be interpreted cautiously regarding generalizability. Nevertheless, the design principles appear transferable to other contexts, particularly for teacher preparation. Teacher training can leverage these activities in experiential and reflective professional development pathways, engaging pre- and in-service educators in observation, simulation, and reflection on how CT and AI concepts can be scaffolded, differentiated, and made meaningful for diverse learners.

Future applications may integrate unplugged, digital, and AI-supported activities to construct scalable, inclusive, and interdisciplinary learning pathways that bridge primary and higher education. Such developments could foster continuity across educational levels and equip teachers with the competence to design learning environments that are not only accessible and motivating, but also intellectually stimulating, ethically grounded, and responsive to the cognitive, emotional, and social diversity of learners.

Moreover, future research could adopt a longitudinal perspective, following students over time to explore the medium-term impacts of unplugged pathways on computational thinking, AI literacy, and engagement with technology. Such studies would provide insights into skill retention, conceptual transfer, and the lasting effects of UDL-informed, multimodal instruction, informing curriculum design, teacher training, and educational policy.

Combining short-term interventions with longitudinal follow-ups, these approaches can support the development of evidence-based, inclusive learning pathways that foster foundational computational and AI skills across developmental stages.

Disclosure of Interest. The authors declare that they have no competing interests.

A Evaluation Rubric

In this appendix, we provide the detailed evaluation rubric used for assessing Problem Solving, Algorithmic Thinking, Abstraction, Comprehension, and additional dimensions such as Transfer, Process Awareness, and Perceived Difficulty. This table can be used by instructors to assign scores and annotate observations for each student.

Building on established frameworks for CT and assessment in CS education [16,18,66], and informed by UDL principles [67], this study adopted a purpose-built evaluation rubric to document and analyze students' performance and learning processes across the proposed unplugged activities (Table 3).

Table 3. Evaluation Rubric for Student Assessment

Student:				
Age:				
Activity:				
Dimension / Criterion	**Scale / Range**	**Score**	**UDL Alignment**	**Notes / Observations**
Problem Solving	0–4		UDL 7, 9	Number and quality of alternative solutions proposed, ability to adapt strategies when unexpected events occur, engagement in cooperative problem-solving.
Algorithmic Thinking	0–4		UDL 9	Ability to plan sequences of actions, anticipate outcomes, and apply rules/protocols. Reflects understanding of structured problem-solving and procedural logic.
Abstraction	0–4		UDL 8	Degree to which the student can move from concrete, hands-on actions to symbolic or conceptual representations, recognizing patterns or general principles.
Comprehension	0–4		UDL 8	Understanding of activity structure, underlying concepts (e.g., network topology, AI principles), and procedural rules. Ability to explain rationale behind actions.
Transfer	0–n		UDL 8, 9	Number of distinct contexts or situations in which the student successfully applies a learned concept, strategy, or skill. Demonstrates the ability to generalize knowledge and adapt it beyond the original activity. Higher counts indicate deeper understanding and flexibility.
Process Awareness	0–5		UDL 9	Reflective insight into own thinking, reasoning, and problem-solving processes. Includes ability to verbalize strategies, recognize errors, and modify approaches during activity.
Perceived Difficulty	1–5		UDL 7	Student's self-reported level of challenge experienced during the activity. Captures perceived ease or difficulty, providing insight into engagement, motivation, and resilience. 1 = very easy, 5 = very difficult.

References

1. Vygotsky, L.S.: Mind in Society: The Development of Higher Psychological Processes. Harvard University Press, Cambridge, MA (1978)
2. Bruner, J.S.: The Culture of Education. Harvard University Press, Cambridge, MA (1996)

3. Santagata, R., Zannoni, C., Stigler, J.W.: Learning from lesson analysis: a study of preservice teachers' ability to reflect on the process of teaching and learning. J. Teach. Educ. **58**(1), 77–94 (2007). https://doi.org/10.1177/0022487106295729
4. Commission, E.: Digital Education Action Plan (2021–2027): Resetting Education and Training for the Digital Age. Publications Office of the European Union, Luxembourg (2022)
5. Bruner, J.S.: The Process of Education. Harvard University Press, Cambridge, MA (1960)
6. Piaget, J.: Science of Education and the Psychology of the Child. Viking Press, New York (1970)
7. Bers, M.U.: Coding as a Playground: Programming and Computational Thinking in the Early Childhood Classroom. Routledge, New York (2018)
8. Resnick, M.: Lifelong Kindergarten: Cultivating Creativity through Projects, Passion, Peers, and Play. MIT Press, Cambridge, MA (2017)
9. American Academy of Pediatrics: Media and young minds. Pediatrics **138**(5), e20162591 (2016). https://doi.org/10.1542/peds.2016-2591
10. Twenge, J.M., Campbell, W.K.: Associations between screen time and lower psychological well-being among children and adolescents: evidence from a population-based study. Preventive Med. Rep. **12**, 271–283 (2018). https://doi.org/10.1016/j.pmedr.2018.10.003
11. Diamond, A.: Executive functions. Annu. Rev. Psychol. **64**, 135–168 (2013). https://doi.org/10.1146/annurev-psych-113011-143750
12. Gopnik, A.: The Gardener and the Carpenter: What the New Science of Child Development Tells Us About the Relationship Between Parents and Children. Farrar, Straus and Giroux, New York (2016)
13. Jaworski, B.: Grappling with complexity: co-learning in inquiry communities in mathematics teaching development. In: Hoines, M.J., Fuglestad, A.B. (eds.) Proceedings of PME 28, vol. 1, pp. 17–36. , Bergen, Norway (2004)
14. Cusi, A., Malara, N.A.: The intertwining of theory and practice: Influences on ways of teaching and teachers' education. In: English, L., Kirshner, D. (eds.) Handbook of International Research in Mathematics Education, 3rd edn., pp. 504–522. Taylor & Francis (2016)
15. Yeni, S.: Exploring computational thinking assessment in introductory programming courses. ResearchGate (2017)
16. Wing, J.M.: Computational thinking. Commun. ACM **49**(3), 33–35 (2006). https://doi.org/10.1145/1118178.1118215
17. Grover, S., Pea, R.: Computational thinking in K-12: a review of the state of the field. Educ. Res. **42**(1), 38–43 (2013). https://doi.org/10.3102/0013189X12463051
18. Shute, V.J., Sun, C., Asbell-Clarke, J.: Demystifying computational thinking. Educ. Res. Rev. **22**, 142–158 (2017). https://doi.org/10.1016/j.edurev.2017.09.003
19. Brennan, K., Resnick, M.: New frameworks for studying and assessing the development of computational thinking. In: Proceedings of the Annual Meeting of the American Educational Research Association (2012)
20. Armoni, M., Gordon, M., Harel, D.: Teaching scenario-based programming: an additional paradigm for the high school computer science curriculum. Comput. Sci. Eng. **17**(6), 64–71 (2015). https://doi.org/10.1109/MCSE.2015.110
21. Field, D.: Computational thinking: A digital age skill. International Society for Technology in Education (2009)

22. Repenning, A., Ioannidou, A., Webb, D.: Computational thinking and the development of a new assessment instrument. In: Proceedings of the 41st ACM Technical Symposium on Computer Science Education, pp. 265–269. ACM (2010). https://doi.org/10.1145/1734263.1734360
23. Werner, L., Denner, J., Campe, S., Kawamoto, D.C.: The fairy performance assessment: measuring computational thinking in middle school. In: Proceedings of the 43rd ACM Technical Symposium on Computer Science Education, pp. 215–220. ACM (2012). https://doi.org/10.1145/2157136.2157224
24. Jöreskog, K.G., Sörbom, D.: LISREL 8: Structural equation modeling with the SIMPLIS command language. Lawrence Erlbaum Associates, Hillsdale, NJ (1993)
25. Nunnally, J.C.: Psychometric theory, 2nd edn. McGraw-Hill, New York (1978)
26. DeVellis, R.F.: Scale development: Theory and applications. Sage, Newbury Park, CA (1991)
27. CAST: Universal Design for Learning Guidelines version 2.2. CAST, Wakefield, MA (2018). http://udlguidelines.cast.org
28. Rose, D.H., Meyer, A.: Teaching Every Student in the Digital Age: Universal Design for Learning. ASCD, Alexandria, VA (2002)
29. Bartolini Bussi, M.G., Mariotti, M.A.: Semiotic mediation in the mathematics classroom: artifacts and signs after a Vygotskian perspective. ZDM - Int. J. Math. Educat. **41**(3), 289–301 (2009). https://doi.org/10.1007/s11858-009-0189-1
30. Brown, J.S., Collins, A., Duguid, P.: Situated cognition and the culture of learning. Educ. Res. **18**(1), 32–42 (1989). https://doi.org/10.3102/0013189X018001032
31. Lave, J., Wenger, E.: Situated Learning: Legitimate Peripheral Participation. Cambridge University Press, Cambridge (1991)
32. Hong, J.C., Lin, H.Y.: Effects of learning style on students' performance in computer-assisted instruction. Comput. Educat. **34**(2), 161–173 (2000). https://doi.org/10.1016/S0360-1315(99)00055-3
33. Gardner, H.: Frames of Mind: The Theory of Multiple Intelligences. Basic Books, New York (1983)
34. Sternberg, R.J.: Beyond IQ: A Triarchic Theory of Human Intelligence. Cambridge University Press, Cambridge (1985)
35. Montessori, M.: The Discovery of the Child. Ballantine Books, New York (1967)
36. Ching, Y.-H., et al.: Educational robotics for developing computational thinking: a systematic review of empirical research. Front. Educat. (2023). https://doi.org/10.3389/feduc.2023.10078047
37. Chalmers, C.: Robotics and computational thinking in primary school. Int. Child-Comput. Int¿ **17**, 93–100 (2018). https://doi.org/10.1016/j.ijcci.2018.05.002
38. Paraskevopoulou-Kollia, E.-A.: Computational thinking in primary and pre-school children: a systematic review of the literature. Educat. Sci. (2025)
39. Microsoft MakeCode: Educational programming platform. https://www.microsoft.com/makecode(Accessed2026)
40. ELECFREAKS: Micro:bit 32-in-1 Wonder Robot Building Kit. https://www.elecfreaks.com (Accessed 2026)
41. LEGO Education: LEGO® Spike Prime Set. https://education.lego.com/en-us/products/lego-education-spike-prime-set/45678(Accessed2026)
42. Lillard, A.S.: Montessori: The Science Behind the Genius. Oxford University Press, New York (2013)
43. Dewey, J.: Experience and Education. Macmillan, New York (1938)
44. Kolb, D.A.: Experiential Learning: Experience as the Source of Learning and Development. Prentice Hall, Englewood Cliffs, NJ (1984)

45. Hmelo-Silver, C.E.: Problem-based learning: what and how do students learn? Educ. Psychol. Rev. **16**, 235–266 (2004). https://doi.org/10.1023/B:EDPR.0000034022.16470.f3
46. Topping, K.J.: Trends in peer learning. Educ. Psychol. **25**(6), 631–645 (2005). https://doi.org/10.1080/01443410500345172
47. Deterding, S., Dixon, D., Khaled, R., Nacke, L.: From game design elements to gamefulness: defining "gamification". In: Proceedings of the 15th International Academic MindTrek Conference, pp. 9–15. ACM (2011). https://doi.org/10.1145/2181037.2181040
48. Flavell, J.H.: Metacognition and cognitive monitoring: a new area of cognitive-developmental inquiry. Am. Psychol. **34**, 906–911 (1979). https://doi.org/10.1037/0003-066X.34.10.906
49. Black, P., Wiliam, D.: Assessment and classroom learning. Assessment Educat.: Princip. Policy Pract. **5**(1), 7–74 (1998). https://doi.org/10.1080/0969595980050102
50. Wiggins, G.P.: Assessing Student Performance: Exploring the Purpose and Limits of Testing. Jossey-Bass, San Francisco (1993)
51. Moskal, B.M.: Scoring rubrics: what, when and how? Practical assessment. Res. Evaluat.7(3) (2000). https://doi.org/10.7275/96j3-xz08
52. Nicol, D., Macfarlane-Dick, D.: Formative assessment and self-regulated learning: a model and seven principles of good feedback practice. Stud. High. Educ. **31**(2), 199–218 (2006). https://doi.org/10.1080/03075070600572090
53. Barrett, H.C.: Multiple intelligences in the classroom. Educ. Leadersh. **65**(2), 15–20 (2007)
54. Ndihokubwayo, K., Uwamahoro, J., Ndayambaje, I.: Implementation of the competence-based learning in Rwandan physics classrooms: first assessment based on the reformed teaching observation protocol. Phys. Educ. **57**(4), 045027 (2022). https://doi.org/10.1088/1361-6552/ac69a2
55. Design-Based Research Collective: Design-based research: an emerging paradigm for educational inquiry. Educ. Res. **32**(1), 5–8 (2003). https://doi.org/10.3102/0013189X032001005
56. Barab, S.A., Squire, K.D.: Design-based research: putting a stake in the ground. J. Learn. Sci. **13**(1), 1–14 (2004). https://doi.org/10.1207/s15327809jls1301_1
57. CS Unplugged: CS Unplugged Activities. https://classic.csunplugged.org/activities/(Accessed2026)
58. Bell, T., Witten, I., Fellows, M.: Computer science unplugged: off-line activities and games for all ages. ACM Inroads **5**(4), 80–86 (2014). https://doi.org/10.1145/2682630.2682633
59. Rolka, K., Papadopoulos, T.: AI in primary education: promoting computational thinking and ethical awareness. J. Educat. Technol. Soc. **24**(3), 45–60 (2021)
60. Gresalfi, M., Horn, I.S.: Designing learning activities for young children to explore algorithmic thinking. Comput. Educat. **142**, 103644 (2019). https://doi.org/10.1016/j.compedu.2019.103644
61. Curzon, P., McOwan, P., Dorling, M.: Teaching Computing Unplugged: Strategies and Activities. Springer, Cham (2014)
62. Baxter, P., Jack, S.: Qualitative case study methodology: study design and implementation for novice researchers. Qualit. Report **13**(4), 544–559 (2008)
63. Thomas, G.: How to Do Your Case Study: A Guide for Students and Researchers. SAGE Publications, London (2011)

64. Adams, R., Smith, J., Lee, K.: Multiple case study designs in educational research: a practical overview. Educ. Res. Rev. **35**, 100432 (2022). https://doi.org/10.1016/j.edurev.2022.100432
65. Kyngäs, H.: The qualitative research process in the context of nursing. Springer Nature, Cham (2020)
66. Weintrop, D., et al.: Defining computational thinking for mathematics and science education. J. Sci. Educ. Technol. **25**(1), 127–147 (2016). https://doi.org/10.1007/s10956-015-9581-5
67. Meyer, A., Rose, D.H., Gordon, D.: Universal Design for Learning: Theory and Practice. CAST Professional Publishing, Wakefield, MA (2014)
68. Al-Azawei, A., Serenelli, F., Lundqvist, K.: Universal design for learning (UDL): a content analysis of peer-reviewed journal papers from 2012 to 2015. J. Scholarship Teac. Learn. **17**(3), 31–56 (2017). https://doi.org/10.14434/josotl.v17i3.24286
69. diSessa, A.A.: Computational dintellectual history. Comput. Sci. Educ. **28**(2), 65–83 (2018). https://doi.org/10.1080/08993408.2018.1456819
70. Brackmann, C.P., Román-González, M., Robles, G., Moreno-León, J., Casali, A., Barone, D.: Development of computational thinking skills through unplugged activities in primary school. In: Proceedings of the 12th Workshop on Primary and Secondary Computing Education (WiPSCE '17), pp. 65–72. ACM (2017). https://doi.org/10.1145/3137065.3137069
71. Rabardel, P.: Les hommes et les technologies: approche cognitive des instruments contemporains. Armand Colin, Paris (1995)
72. Vygotskij, L.S.: Thought and Language. MIT Press, Cambridge, MA (1934)
73. Román-González, M., Pérez-González, J.C., Jiménez-Fernández, C.: Which cognitive abilities underlie computational thinking? Criterion validity of the computational thinking test. Comput. Hum. Behav. **72**, 678–691 (2017). https://doi.org/10.1016/j.chb.2016.08.047
74. Chen, P., et al.: Fostering computational thinking through unplugged activities. STEM Educat. J. **10**(1), 1–16 (2023)
75. Sun, L., et al.: Comparative experiment of the effects of unplugged and plugged-in programming on computational thinking skills in early primary students. Comput. Educat. **178**, 104407 (2024). https://doi.org/10.1016/j.compedu.2024.104407
76. Bell, T., Lodi, M.: Constructing computational thinking without using computers. Construct. Found. **14**(3), 342–351 (2019)
77. Zeng, Y., et al.: Teaching programming and computational thinking in early childhood education: a case study of an unplugged programming and CT curriculum. Front. Psychol. **14**, 10577223 (2023). https://doi.org/10.3389/fpsyg.2023.10577223
78. Dağ, F., et al.: The effect of an unplugged coding course on primary school students' development of computational thinking skills. J. Comput. Assist. Learn. **39**(4), 1023–1035 (2023). https://doi.org/10.1111/jcal.12789
79. World Health Organization: Guidelines on physical activity, sedentary behaviour and sleep for children under 5 years of age. WHO, Geneva (2019). https://www.who.int/publications/i/item/9789241550536
80. Bocconi, S., et al.: Developing computational thinking in compulsory education: Implications for policy and practice. European Commission - Joint Research Centre, Luxembourg (2022)
81. CAST: Universal Design for Learning Guidelines version 2.0. CAST, Wakefield, MA (2011)

82. Blikstein, P.: Digital fabrication and 'making' in education. In: Walter-Herrmann, J., Büching, C. (eds.) FabLabs: Of Machines. Makers and Inventors. Transcript Verlag, Bielefeld (2013)
83. Viera, C., Eastham, N., Taub, R.: Computer science education in informal learning environments: a review of the evidence. IJCSIS **2**(2), 40–53 (2018)

A Three-Dimensional Framework for AI-Enhanced Inclusion in Higher Education: Integrating Functional, Experiential, and Equity Dimensions

Sobia Yasmeen[1(✉)] and Valeria Di Martino[2]

[1] Università degli Studi di Bari Aldo Moro, 70121 Bari, Italy
s.yasmeen1@phd.uniba.it
[2] Università degli Studi di Palermo, 90133 Palermo, PA, Italy
valeria.dimartino@unipa.it

Abstract. The rapid advancement of artificial intelligence (AI) presents transformative opportunities for fostering inclusive learning in international higher education. This conceptual study examines the intersection of AI technologies and inclusive pedagogy, exploring how AI-driven tools can address the diverse needs of learners across linguistic, cultural, cognitive, and physical dimensions. Drawing on interdisciplinary literature from educational technology, accessibility studies, and global policy frameworks, the paper proposes a three-dimensional conceptual framework positioning AI simultaneously as a pedagogical tool, a learning environment, and a system-level catalyst for equity. The framework consists of three interdependent dimensions: (1) Functional Dimension – employing AI to enable adaptive learning, assistive technologies, and collaborative learning; (2) Experiential Dimension – using AI to create immersive, interactive, and culturally responsive digital learning spaces; and (3) Equity Dimension – promoting inclusion by addressing systemic challenges such as algorithmic bias, the digital divide, and ethical concerns. By integrating these dimensions in a circular model, the framework positions inclusion as a core design principle rather than a secondary outcome, providing a comprehensive and contextually adaptable approach to AI-enhanced higher education. To enable empirical validation, the study operationalizes the framework through evaluation indicators across functional, experiential, equity, and integrated cross-dimensional outcomes. The proposed framework offers both theoretical and practical guidance for institutional leaders, educators, and policymakers seeking to leverage AI for equitable learning environments.

Keywords: AI-Supported Strategies · Inclusive Learning Environments · International Higher Education · Conceptual Analysis

1 Introduction

The fast-growing capabilities of artificial intelligence (AI) technologies are transforming the environment of global higher education institutions, and they have revolutionary potential with regards to inclusiveness, accessibility, and innovations that empower

M. Adamoli et al. (Eds.): HELMeTO 2025, CCIS 2958, pp. 187–204, 2026.
https://doi.org/10.1007/978-3-032-31850-3_12

learners [1]. With the rising heterogeneity of student populations that include diverse linguistic, cultural, cognitive, and physical abilities, the need for equalized and adaptable learning environments has never been greater as learning institutions address new students with their unique backgrounds and needs [2, 3]. Although AI is commonly linked with automation, data analysis, and teaching efficiency, its educational potential to promote inclusive learning settings has not been studied extensively in the scientific literature [4, 5].

Recent research points out the opportunities of AI-based systems for content-adapted delivery, multilingual support, assistive technologies, and individualized teaching based on real-time feedback from learners [1, 6]. These functions are especially valuable in cross-border higher education where language skills, cultural adjustment, and the prior learning experience can be serious factors impacting learning outcomes. However, issues related to algorithmic bias, digital inequality, and ethical governance explain why AI in inclusive education environments should be researched and used critically and contextually [7, 8].

The current paper aims at bridging the theoretical and practical gap by performing a conceptual analysis of AI-assisted inclusive learning strategies in higher education delivery at the global level. Based on the interdisciplinary literature on educational technology [9, 10], inclusive pedagogy [11, 12], and higher education policy [13, 14], the research seeks to build a framework for understanding how to embrace AI as a pedagogical tool, learning environment, and systemic conduit of educational equity. By doing so, it adds to the growing discussion on the means and ways in which AI may be implemented in a responsible and efficient way that would make learning more inclusive, accessible, and successful for every learner [1, 15].

2 Literature Review

According to recent studies, the role of AI in transforming the higher education environment can be significant [16, 17]. Ajani et al. [1] observe the dual potential of AI as both a facilitator and a disruptor of higher education. In their review, they identify AI's capacity to increase learning efficiency by automating processes, enabling predictive analytics, and facilitating intelligent content delivery. However, they also highlight institutional readiness issues that hinder effective AI implementation, especially in low-resource environments. Deri et al. [17] extend this discussion through a global review of AI applications in higher education institutions. Their findings suggest that artificial intelligence should emerge from the integration of technology with pedagogical design rather than existing as an independent solution. This requires interdisciplinary coordination among educators, technologists, and policymakers.

The intersection of inclusive education and AI has become a subject of significant academic interest. Galdames-Calderón and colleagues [2] provide a convincing account of AI applications incorporating accessibility features for students with diverse linguistic, cognitive, and physical needs. Their research highlights AI's potential to enable differentiated instruction and multimodal learning experiences particularly valuable for international and non-traditional learners. In a scoping review, Pagliara et al. [4] identify the proliferation of AI-powered assistive technologies including speech-to-text applications, real-time translation services, and adaptive support tools that enable learners with disabilities to participate fully in academic environments. However, they caution against assuming universal applicability of these tools without careful consideration of contextual factors.

Alhammadi and colleagues [3] propose a holistic conceptual framework for AI implementation in higher education institutions that aligns institutional policy, stakeholder education, and ethical safeguards. Their model incorporates Universal Design for Learning (UDL) principles that focus on anticipating and designing for differentiated learning needs. Similarly, Okunlaya et al. [18] propose integrating AI-facilitated library services within digital transformation models as an optimal approach to enhance inclusivity by aligning AI tools with student engagement and learning outcomes. According to Mariyono and Nur [19], collaboration emerges as a key outcome of AI-assisted environments. They argue that AI fosters socially engaged learning through personalized feedback, real-time analytics, and adaptive learning environments. These features prove especially valuable in cultivating a sense of belonging among marginalized student groups.

Ethical concerns remain central to discussions of AI integration in inclusive education. Several scholars [7, 20] emphasize the risks of algorithmic bias, data privacy violations, and lack of transparency in AI-driven decisions. These issues prove especially critical in international higher education settings where diverse student populations may be disproportionately affected. Addressing these risks requires the adoption of ethical frameworks, inclusive algorithm training datasets, and critical audits of AI tools. Institutions must ensure that AI systems are designed and implemented in alignment with human-centered principles, fairness, and the European Union's General Data Protection Regulation (GDPR). Ul Hassan et al. [8] demonstrate that in the absence of adequate infrastructure and digital literacy, AI innovations can widen rather than bridge existing divides. They advocate for cross-national collaboration to address the digital divide through equitable policy development and capacity-building initiatives.

Effective deployment of AI in inclusive learning settings hinges on the readiness of faculty and institutional infrastructure. Studies [5, 21] indicate that the success of AI-supported strategies depends largely on how well educators are trained to integrate these tools into pedagogy. Faculty members must be equipped with AI literacy, inclusive instructional design knowledge, and ethical awareness. Furthermore, institutions should invest in ongoing professional development, resource support, and a shared culture of innovation. Without adequate educator preparation, even the most advanced AI tools risk becoming underutilized or misapplied. They suggest that in higher education, AI-related competencies may be included in the standards of professional education. The literature reviewed depicts that AI-based approaches can provide potentially fruitful avenues towards achieving inclusive learning environments within the global higher education. The opportunities are connected with the possibility of AI customizing the learning process, improving access and real-time feedback. Nevertheless, ethical issues, infrastructural inequalities and educator training are also an issue. An integrated policy-pedagogical-technological approach is a necessity to guarantee the positive implications of AI on the inclusive and equitable global education systems.

2.1 AI-Supported Strategies

Artificial Intelligence (AI)-aided strategies have emerged as highly sought-after change agents within higher education institutions, transforming teaching, learning, and administrative processes. These approaches encompass a wide range of applications, including intelligent tutoring systems, adaptive learning platforms, automated assessment tools, AI-based feedback mechanisms, and predictive analytics for student performance monitoring. Ajani et al. [1] characterize these AI-supported strategies as vital innovations capable of responding to the increasing complexity and diversity of higher education. They argue that these strategies enable institutions to optimize instructional content and enhance learner engagement through automation and personalization. Notably, AI enables real-time responses to student needs based on learning patterns while suggesting appropriate interventions.

Universal Design for Learning (UDL) serves as a foundational approach for fostering inclusivity in diverse educational environments. The integration of AI within UDL frameworks enables adaptive learning by responding to individual learner profiles. As proposed by Alhammadi et al. [3], AI can dynamically adjust content delivery, offer multilingual support, and provide real-time feedback, thereby aligning with UDL's emphasis on multiple means of engagement, representation, and expression. Mariyono and Nur [19] characterize AI-supported strategies as inherently collaborative and innovative. Their research demonstrates that AI technologies, including enhanced discussion forums, collaborative bots, and peer-pairing algorithms, enable active learning and intercultural interaction particularly valuable in international higher education settings. They argue that AI transcends mere automation by facilitating social and cognitive interactions in online educational contexts.

A wide range of AI-driven tools including speech-to-text applications, multilingual chatbots, real-time translation services, and virtual tutors have emerged as enablers of inclusion in higher education. These tools prove especially valuable for students with disabilities, non-native language speakers, and those from underrepresented backgrounds [4, 6]. When integrated with institutional learning management systems, they offer personalized and accessible educational experiences that consolidate multiple support functions. Research indicates that AI-coupled strategies enhance access to academic support, facilitate cultural transitions, and provide personalized interfaces with institutional systems. Beyond their educational functions, these tools contribute to student wellbeing and retention.

Nevertheless, the adoption of AI-backed strategies requires careful consideration. Chaka [7] and Dzogovic et al. [5] caution against potential pitfalls including algorithmic bias, opacity in AI decision-making, and over-reliance on technology. They advocate for ethical frameworks and human-centered design principles in AI tool development and deployment. Sabri and colleagues [21] emphasize the necessity of faculty training and preparation. Their research demonstrates that while AI-mediated strategies hold significant potential, their effectiveness depends on educators' capacity to integrate these tools meaningfully into pedagogical practice. Institutions should therefore invest in ongoing professional development and cultivate AI literacy among faculty. AI-driven approaches are transforming teaching and learning quality by enabling personalized, accessible, and adaptive education. These approaches show considerable promise for enhancing inclusivity, connectivity, and engagement in diverse international learning contexts. However, successful implementation requires careful attention to ethical concerns, faculty and student readiness, and equitable technology access. The literature supports a holistic approach that aligns AI tools with pedagogical objectives and inclusive principles to realize their full potential in higher education.

2.2 Inclusive Learning Environments

Inclusive learning environments refer to learning environments that are designed with careful thoughts to provide similar access, participation and achievement to all learners despite the differences in their backgrounds insofar as culture, language, cognition, and physical abilities are concerned (UNESCO, 2020). The concept of inclusivity in the international higher education has grown as a response to the global diversity, mobility and the growing number of students with marginalized or under-represented backgrounds.

As Galdames [15] highlights, inclusive learning environments prove critical in global higher education where students vary significantly in language proficiency, cultural background, and prior learning experiences. Inclusion extends beyond physical access to encompass meaningful engagement through culturally responsive instruction and technology-enhanced support. Pagliara et al. [4] emphasize the role of AI and digital tools in enabling flexible pedagogical approaches, multimodal learning resources, and customized content delivery that facilitate access for learners facing constraints in traditional classrooms. Universal Design for Learning (UDL) principles, as noted by Alhammadi et al. [3], support diverse learners' engagement, representation, and expression capabilities, while AI can further enhance inclusiveness by adapting content and assessments to individual learner profiles.

Mariyono and Nur [19] underscore the social dimension of inclusion, demonstrating that collaborative and AI-mediated peer engagement fosters belonging among international students through group projects and cross-cultural interactions. However, Sabri et al. [21] caution that technological interventions alone prove insufficient without accompanying faculty awareness and training in culturally relevant pedagogy and scaffolded assessments. Persistent challenges including systemic inequalities, digital divides, language barriers, and algorithmic bias remain significant concerns. Ul Hassan et al. [8] recommend institutional policies explicitly targeting accessibility, inclusive curricula, and comprehensive student support systems.

Wang et al. [6] further demonstrate that inclusive environments enhance student satisfaction, engagement, and persistence through culturally competent communication, comprehensive assessment practices, and AI-supported academic advising. Overall, inclusive learning requires dynamic, adaptable ecosystems that combine AI-enhanced pedagogy, sustained faculty development, and systemic policy reforms to sustain equitable and culturally responsive higher education settings.

2.3 Critical Synthesis and Research Gaps

While the reviewed literature demonstrates AI's transformative potential in inclusive education, several critical gaps and contradictions emerge that warrant careful examination. First, there exists a fundamental tension between technological optimism and pedagogical reality. Studies such as those by Ajani et al. [1] and Deri et al. [17] emphasize AI's efficiency gains and automation capabilities, yet scholars like Chaka [7] and Sabri et al. [21] highlight substantial implementation barriers including faculty resistance, insufficient training infrastructure, and institutional inertia. This paradox suggests that technological capability does not automatically translate into educational impact, and that the pathway from AI potential to realized inclusion remains inadequately theorized.

Beyond this conceptual tension, a significant methodological gap characterizes the existing body of work. The majority of studies are either purely conceptual or report on small-scale pilot implementations [2, 4, 15], lacking the longitudinal empirical validation necessary to understand how AI-supported inclusion scales across diverse institutional contexts. Particularly notable is the absence of large-scale, cross-national comparative studies that could illuminate how AI integration functions differently across varied resource environments, regulatory frameworks, and pedagogical cultures. Furthermore, research focused on low- and middle-income countries remains remarkably scarce, despite these contexts facing the most acute inclusion challenges and potentially benefiting most from well-designed AI interventions [8].

While ethical considerations receive consistent mention throughout the literature, they remain undertheorized in relation to inclusive pedagogy specifically. Authors such as Chaka [7] and Dzogovic et al. [5] identify critical risks including algorithmic bias, data privacy violations, and opacity in AI decision-making processes. However, few scholars propose actionable frameworks for embedding ethical safeguards directly within pedagogical design rather than treating ethics as a separate compliance concern. The disconnect between AI ethics discourse conducted primarily in computer science and philosophy and the practical realities of inclusive education represents a significant theoretical gap requiring interdisciplinary bridge-building.

A related limitation concerns the fragmentation of existing frameworks, which tend to treat AI as either a pedagogical tool or a learning environment while rarely integrating system-level policy dimensions with classroom-level pedagogical practice in a coherent manner. This compartmentalization limits the potential for holistic institutional adoption. Most studies focus on one dimension of AI integration while neglecting the dynamic interplay between technological functionality, learner experience, and institutional equity structures. The present study directly addresses these identified gaps by proposing an integrated three-dimensional framework that unifies functional, experiential, and equity perspectives while maintaining critical awareness of implementation challenges, contextual constraints, and ethical imperatives. By doing so, it moves beyond isolated discussions of AI tools or environments to position AI as a multifaceted systemic intervention requiring coordinated technological, pedagogical, and policy-level responses.

3 Methodology

This study employs a conceptual analysis approach to explore AI-assisted strategies in promoting inclusive learning experiences within international higher education contexts. Conceptual analysis represents an established qualitative research method designed to analyze, explicate, and interconnect core concepts across theory and practice [22]. This approach proves especially appropriate for emerging interdisciplinary fields such as AI in higher education, where rapidly evolving technologies intersect with pedagogical and institutional structures.

3.1 Integrative Literature Review

The study adopts a non-empirical, exploratory design aimed at synthesizing existing literature, theoretical frameworks, and policy guidelines. The primary objective is to develop a conceptual framework illustrating how AI technologies can function simultaneously as pedagogical tools, learning environments, and system-level interventions that ensure inclusive educational practices. This framework-building approach aligns with established methodologies for advancing theoretical understanding in nascent research domains where empirical evidence remains fragmented.

This study utilizes an integrative review approach, defined as a form of research that reviews, critiques, and synthesizes representative literature on a topic in an integrated way such that new frameworks and perspectives are generated [24, 25]. This methodological approach proves particularly suited to emerging interdisciplinary topics requiring conceptual development rather than definitive empirical answers. Unlike systematic reviews, which answer specific research questions through exhaustive search protocols and quality appraisal checklists, integrative reviews address broader conceptual questions by combining diverse sources including theoretical papers, empirical studies, and policy documents. They explicitly emphasize synthesis and theory-building over evidence aggregation, acknowledging the interpretive role of researchers in framework construction.

3.2 Literature Search Process

A purposeful literature search was conducted between November 2024 and January 2025, consulting multiple primary databases and focusing on studies published in 2022, 2023, 2024, and 2025. Scopus and Web of Science provided access to peer-reviewed articles with demonstrated citation impact and rigorous peer review processes. ERIC (Education Resources Information Center) offered education-specific research with explicit pedagogical focus. Google Scholar enabled identification of grey literature, conference papers, and emerging scholarship not yet indexed in traditional databases. Institutional repositories provided access to policy documents, white papers, and institutional frameworks related to AI ethics and inclusive education governance. Rather than employing Boolean search strings designed for systematic reproducibility, this study utilized conceptual searching appropriate for integrative reviews. Initial broad search terms combined variations of "artificial intelligence", "higher education", and inclusion-related concepts including "accessibility", "diversity", "equity", and "international students".

From initial results, the search strategy followed conceptual threads emerging organically from the literature itself. For example, early sources discussing adaptive learning directed attention toward Universal Design for Learning frameworks. References to algorithmic bias guided exploration of AI ethics literature. Mentions of assistive technology prompted investigation of disability studies perspectives. This iterative, theory-driven approach allowed the search strategy to evolve responsively as the conceptual landscape became clearer.

3.3 Selection Criteria and Corpus Development

Approximately fifty sources were initially identified through database searching and reviewed for potential relevance. From this initial corpus, twenty-one sources were selected for in-depth analysis and direct citation in framework development. Selection criteria were applied flexibly rather than as rigid inclusion rules, consistent with integrative review protocols. Theoretical relevance to the intersection of AI technologies and inclusive education proved paramount. The review deliberately sought diversity of perspectives, balancing technologically optimistic viewpoints with critical approaches highlighting implementation challenges and limitations. Disciplinary breadth was intentionally cultivated, incorporating insights from computer science, education, disability studies, and policy analysis to ensure multifaceted understanding. Publication quality and scholarly impact, indicated by journal reputation, citation metrics, or institutional authority, informed but did not solely determine selection. Sources were included if they addressed AI implementation in higher education contexts, engaged substantively with issues of inclusivity, accessibility, or learner diversity, or proposed conceptual models, frameworks, or strategies relevant to inclusive AI deployment. Sources were excluded if they focused exclusively on K-12 education, presented purely technical AI research without educational application, or lacked substantive engagement with inclusion dimensions.

3.4 Analytical Procedures

Each selected source underwent systematic analysis to extract information relevant to framework construction. Analysis identified core concepts and theoretical contributions that could inform the emergent model. AI applications and specific technologies discussed were documented to understand practical manifestations of theoretical ideas. Inclusion dimensions addressed by each source—whether linguistic, cognitive, physical, or cultural—were noted to ensure comprehensive framework coverage. Identified challenges, gaps, or ethical concerns raised by authors were catalogued to inform critical dimensions of the framework. Implications for pedagogy, institutional practice, or policy emerging from each work were synthesized to connect theory with implementation pathways. The extracted data underwent thematic analysis employing constant comparative methods to identify patterns, relationships, and organizing principles.

Through iterative coding and comparison, three overarching dimensions emerged as fundamental to understanding AI's role in inclusive education: the Functional Dimension encompassing AI as a pedagogical tool, the Experiential Dimension capturing AI's role in creating immersive learning environments, and the Equity Dimension addressing AI as a system-level catalyst for institutional change. These dimensions structure the proposed conceptual framework and represent an interpretive synthesis of the reviewed literature grounded in rigorous analytical procedures.

This study acknowledges explicitly that as an integrative review, it does not claim exhaustive coverage of all potentially relevant literature. The conceptual framework presented represents one possible synthesis informed by the reviewed sources, theoretical assumptions detailed in Sect. 3.4, and the authors' combined expertise in educational technology and inclusive pedagogy. Alternative frameworks emphasizing different dimensions or relationships remain possible and would contribute valuably to ongoing scholarly dialogue. The strength of integrative reviews lies not in comprehensiveness but in conceptual coherence and generation of novel theoretical perspectives that advance understanding in emerging fields.

To ensure credibility of the conceptual synthesis, the analysis employed triangulation across disciplines, incorporating diverse perspectives from educational theory, computer science, disability studies, and inclusive education scholarship. Peer-reviewed and policy-relevant sources were prioritized to maintain scholarly rigor and practical relevance. Throughout the analytical process, reflexivity was practiced by critically assessing biases inherent in technological optimism and examining limitations of universal framework applicability across varied global contexts. Multiple iterations of framework development and refinement occurred through ongoing dialogue between co-authors, ensuring that emerging interpretations were challenged and strengthened through collaborative critique.

4 A Three-Dimensional Framework for AI-Driven Inclusion

4.1 Conceptual Framework Development

Inclusive education in higher education has traditionally relied on pedagogical adjustments, accessibility accommodations, and culturally responsive teaching practices. However, AI introduces novel dimensions of responsiveness through real-time data analysis, adaptive content delivery, and intelligent learning environments. Previous studies [7, 15] have identified how AI technologies intersect with educational systems, yet fewer have systematically examined implications for inclusivity across diverse international settings. Drawing on interdisciplinary research from educational technology, accessibility studies, and global policy frameworks—including Universal Design for Learning (UDL) principles and UNESCO inclusive education policies [23]—this study conceptualizes AI not merely as a technological tool but as an active component in inclusive learning design requiring careful pedagogical integration and ethical governance.

This study proposes a three-dimensional conceptual framework positioning AI simultaneously as (1) a pedagogical tool, (2) a learning environment, and (3) a system-level catalyst for equity and inclusion. These dimensions encapsulate AI's multifaceted contributions in an integrated, cyclical model (Fig. 1).

1. **AI as a Pedagogical Tool (Functional Dimension).** AI-powered adaptive learning platforms adjust learning material difficulty in real time based on individual learner

performance, thereby accommodating different learning paces and capabilities. Virtual tutors and intelligent chatbots provide personalized feedback, scaffold complex content, and offer multilingual support, enhancing comprehension for international learners with varied linguistic backgrounds.
2. **Dimension 2: AI as a Learning Environment (Experiential Dimension).** AI-enabled immersive technologies including virtual reality (VR) and augmented reality (AR) create experiential learning opportunities accessible regardless of students' physical capabilities or geographic locations. International students benefit from participation through AI-powered assistive technologies such as screen readers, speech recognition systems, and predictive text interfaces that reduce barriers to engagement.
3. **Dimension 3: AI as a System-Level Catalyst (Equity Dimension).** At the institutional scale, AI-driven analytics facilitate evidence-based policy development through systematic analysis of student engagement patterns and identification of vulnerable or underserved populations. This data-informed approach enables proactive interventions and cultivates institutional cultures of continuous improvement oriented toward equity and inclusion.

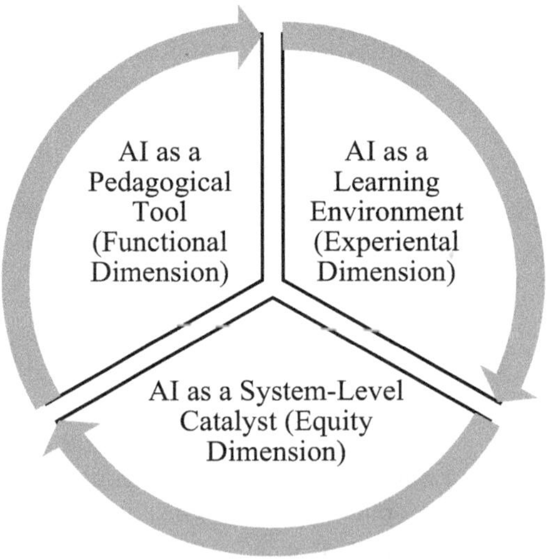

Fig. 1. Conceptual model positioning AI in circular form

The conceptual model presented positions AI adoption within a holistic ecosystem requiring alignment across pedagogical design, institutional policies, and ethical safeguards. By integrating adaptive technologies, faculty capacity building, and strategic deployment of analytics to inform inclusive decision-making, universities can better serve diverse student populations. As the framework emphasizes, inclusion cannot be achieved through technology alone but requires synthesis of inclusive pedagogy, sustained policy commitment, and ethical leadership. This integrated perspective reinforces AI's transformative potential in shaping accessible and equitable higher education ecosystems. Together, these three dimensions create a comprehensive framework positioning inclusion as a central design principle rather than a supplementary consideration in AI adoption within higher education.

4.2 Framework Evaluation Indicators

Building on the conceptual framework outlined above, this section operationalizes the theoretical dimensions into measurable indicators. To facilitate future empirical validation and enable institutions to assess how they operationalize this framework in their specific contexts, evaluate the quality and inclusiveness of their AI adoption, and monitor their AI integration practices, the proposed indicators correspond to each framework dimension and allow systematic evaluation of both implementation processes and inclusion outcomes. Specifically, the selected indicators aim to capture both the technical competencies and the critical, ethical awareness necessary for responsible AI integration in higher education.

The evaluation framework comprises four interrelated categories of indicators. The first three categories align directly with the conceptual framework's dimensions (Functional, Experiential, and Equity), offering guidance for developing measurement systems that can assess specific aspects of AI integration within each domain. The fourth category captures cross-dimensional outcomes that emerge from the synergistic interaction of all three dimensions, reflecting the circular, interconnected nature of the framework (Fig. 1).

- **Functional Dimension Indicators.** Institutions should track adoption rates of AI-powered adaptive learning tools across courses and disciplines, indicating breadth of technological integration. Accessibility coverage measures proportions of course materials available in multiple formats including text, audio, and visual representations accommodating diverse learning needs. Multilingual support capacity can be quantified by enumerating languages supported across institutional AI systems, directly addressing linguistic inclusion for international students. Response time metrics for AI chatbot query resolution provide insight into efficiency and effectiveness of AI-mediated student support. Personalization accuracy examines correlations between AI-recommended resources and subsequent student performance improvements, validating whether adaptive systems genuinely enhance learning outcomes.
- **Experiential Dimension Indicators.** Engagement metrics including time-on-task and interaction frequency within AI-enhanced learning environments reveal whether students actively participate or merely passively access materials. Accessibility compliance measures percentages of digital learning environments meeting WCAG 2.1 AA international standards, ensuring legal and ethical obligations are fulfilled. Immersive learning access tracks numbers of students with disabilities or those learning remotely who successfully participate in VR and AR experiences, demonstrating whether advanced technologies expand rather than restrict access. Cultural responsiveness can be assessed through student satisfaction surveys disaggregated by nationality and ethnicity, measuring whether content resonates across diverse backgrounds.

Collaborative participation indicators examine percentages of students from underrepresented groups actively engaging in AI-facilitated group work, revealing whether these tools foster or hinder social inclusion.

- **Equity Dimension Indicators.** Completion rate equity calculates disparity ratios in course completion between international and domestic students, or between students with and without disabilities, rendering invisible inequalities visible. Support access equity examines utilization rates of AI-powered academic support services across demographic groups ensuring resources reach those most in need. Resource allocation transparency measures percentages of institutional AI budgets directed specifically toward inclusion-focused tools rather than efficiency or cost-saving applications. Bias audit outcomes document numbers of algorithmic biases identified and remediated annually through systematic review processes. Policy integration assesses proportions of institutional policies explicitly incorporating AI ethics and inclusion principles, indicating systemic commitment beyond rhetoric.
- **Integrated Cross-Dimensional Indicators.** Sense of belonging surveys capture student perceptions of institutional inclusion climate, with scores disaggregated by relevant characteristics to identify differential experiences. Academic performance equity tracks reductions in achievement gaps between traditionally marginalized students and majority populations over time. Retention and persistence rates for international students and students with disabilities indicate whether AI-enhanced inclusion translates into sustained enrollment and degree completion. Faculty confidence measures through self-reported competence in using AI tools for inclusive pedagogy reveal whether professional development initiatives prove effective. Student satisfaction captured through Net Promoter Scores for AI-enhanced learning experiences provides direct user feedback on quality and value of technological integration.

These indicators collectively provide foundations for rigorous mixed-methods evaluation combining quantitative metrics with qualitative testimonials from students and faculty. Institutions implementing the framework should establish baseline measures before AI integration, conduct ongoing assessment throughout implementation, and track longitudinal trends to identify areas of success and those requiring adjustment. The indicators are intentionally designed for adaptability across institutional contexts while maintaining focus on advancing equity and inclusion through thoughtful AI integration.

5 Discussion

The integration of AI technologies into inclusive higher education presents both transformative opportunities and significant challenges requiring careful consideration. While the three-dimensional framework proposed in this study offers a comprehensive approach to conceptualizing AI's role in fostering inclusion, successful implementation depends critically on institutional preparedness, policy coherence, and sustained faculty development. Ethical risks including the potential for AI systems to reinforce existing biases or inadvertently marginalize already vulnerable student populations must be addressed through inclusive design principles and continuous critical assessment [24]. The literature emphasizes that AI implementation strategies cannot rely solely on technological solutions but must be grounded in pedagogical redesign, institutional culture transformation, and careful attention to learners' social-emotional needs. Inclusive AI adoption extends beyond providing access to tools; it requires creating meaningful access through empowering learner agency and ensuring equitable participation.

The proposed framework illustrates how AI can transcend efficiency-driven applications to enable equity-centered innovation in higher education. However, realizing this potential requires institutional preparedness, policy alignment across organizational levels, and continuous faculty training programs. Ethical risks such as algorithmic bias, decision-making opacity, and inequitable technology access must be systematically mitigated through responsible AI design practices, transparent governance policies, and ongoing auditing procedures. Inclusion emerges not from technology deployment alone but from synergistic integration of pedagogy, institutional culture, and ethical leadership committed to equity as a core institutional value.

5.1 Framework Application: Toward Contextualized Implementation

The practical application of the proposed framework may be exemplified through its integration within a European higher education institution characterized by a heterogeneous student body. In such contexts, the Functional Dimension may manifest through the deployment of AI-powered Learning Management Systems (LMS) equipped with multilingual transcription services, adaptive assessment tools, and real-time performance analytics. These systems enable differentiated instruction and immediate pedagogical interventions based on learner needs.

In parallel, the Experiential Dimension is operationalized via immersive digital platforms such as intelligent tutoring systems and sentiment-aware discussion forums. These tools not only facilitate personalized learning but also foster social engagement by identifying patterns of disengagement and triggering timely instructor support.

At the institutional level, the Equity Dimension entails the systematic use of disaggregated data to detect participation disparities among subgroups, such as international students or learners with disabilities. Evidence-informed interventions, including policy revisions and inclusive support services, are then implemented to ensure equity in learning outcomes. For instance, algorithmic audits may be commissioned to assess the fairness of recommendation systems, particularly in steering students toward differentiated academic pathways.

This operational model underscores the interdependence of the three dimensions and illustrates how inclusive AI integration requires alignment between technological infrastructure, pedagogical practice, and governance mechanisms. Rather than serving as a blueprint, the framework offers a flexible schema adaptable to institutional diversity and capable of informing both localized implementation and cross-national comparisons.

5.2 Framework Limitations and Contextual Constraints

While the proposed framework offers a theoretically robust model for AI-enhanced inclusion, its applicability is subject to several structural and contextual constraints. First, it presumes the availability of baseline technological infrastructure, a condition not uniformly met across global educational contexts. In low- and middle-income countries, challenges such as limited broadband access, insufficient hardware, and unreliable power supply often preclude the effective use of even basic AI tools [8]. Without substantial infrastructural investment, the framework risks reinforcing the very exclusions it seeks to mitigate.

Second, linguistic and cultural bias remains an unresolved limitation of current AI systems. Natural Language Processing (NLP) tools, for instance, frequently underperform when applied to underrepresented languages or non-Western accents [4], compromising their inclusivity. Moreover, educational traditions that emphasize oral knowledge transmission or collective learning may conflict with individual-centered AI platforms, revealing an epistemological misalignment between technological design and local pedagogical paradigms.

Additionally, institutional resistance plays a non-negligible role in shaping implementation outcomes. Entrenched academic norms, lack of faculty training, and skepticism toward algorithmic decision-making have been identified as critical barriers to AI adoption in pedagogical contexts [7, 21]. These barriers may result in selective or superficial adoption, undermining the systemic ambition of the framework.

Disciplinary variation also introduces challenges. While fields such as STEM may benefit from automation and predictive analytics, others—particularly in the performing arts or craft-based vocations—rely on embodied knowledge not easily captured by algorithmic logic [19]. The assumption of universal applicability must thus be tempered by recognition of disciplinary diversity.

Ethical considerations further complicate implementation. The collection and processing of learner data, although central to the framework's Equity Dimension, may generate tensions in contexts where data privacy norms diverge or where historical abuses of surveillance technologies have eroded trust [14]. Responsible implementation therefore requires culturally sensitive data governance strategies aligned with both institutional and legal standards such as the GDPR.

These constraints do not invalidate the framework but highlight the need for contextual calibration. Future research should prioritize the development of localized adaptation protocols, particularly for under-resourced institutions, and explore co-design approaches with affected communities to ensure culturally and ethically responsive implementation.

6 Conclusion and Future Directions

This conceptual study has proposed a three-dimensional framework for understanding AI's role in fostering inclusive learning environments within international higher education. By conceptualizing AI simultaneously as a pedagogical tool (Functional Dimension), a learning environment (Experiential Dimension), and a system-level catalyst (Equity Dimension), the framework positions inclusion as a core design principle rather than a supplementary consideration in educational technology adoption. The integrative literature review and subsequent conceptual analysis reveal that while AI technologies hold significant potential for addressing diverse learner needs—including linguistic, cultural, cognitive, and physical dimensions—their successful implementation requires careful alignment of technological capabilities with pedagogical objectives, institutional policies, and ethical safeguards. The framework emphasizes that meaningful inclusion cannot emerge from technological deployment alone but demands synergistic integration across all three dimensions, supported by sustained faculty development, transparent governance mechanisms, and continuous critical assessment of equity outcomes.

The proposed evaluation indicators operationalize the framework's theoretical dimensions, offering institutions concrete metrics for assessing their AI integration practices across functional effectiveness, experiential quality, and equity impact. These indicators facilitate systematic monitoring of both implementation processes and inclusion outcomes, enabling evidence-based refinement of institutional approaches. This study advances scholarly discourse by bridging fragmented discussions of AI in education through unifying functional, experiential, and equity perspectives within a coherent conceptual model. It explicitly addresses the disconnect between technological optimism and pedagogical reality by foregrounding implementation challenges alongside opportunities, extends AI ethics discourse beyond compliance frameworks by embedding ethical considerations directly within pedagogical design principles, and moves beyond linear tool-adoption models toward holistic institutional transformation through its circular, interdependent structure that reflects the systemic nature of inclusive education.

The framework offers actionable guidance for multiple stakeholder groups with differentiated practical implications. Educators can leverage the functional dimension to personalize learning pathways, reduce accessibility barriers, and support multilingual, multicultural classrooms through AI-powered adaptive tools that respond to individual learner profiles and provide real-time scaffolding. Institutional leaders may utilize the framework to inform strategic decisions regarding curriculum design, resource allocation, and student support infrastructure, particularly through systematic analysis of engagement data and equity metrics that reveal participation disparities and enable proactive interventions. Policymakers can draw upon the equity dimension to develop governance frameworks that promote inclusion, accessibility, and fairness while mitigating risks associated with algorithmic bias and digital divides across diverse global contexts, ensuring that AI deployment aligns with human-centered principles and regulatory requirements such as GDPR.

Within the European higher education context specifically, the framework aligns with regional policy priorities including the European Accessibility Act, Digital Education Action Plan, and data protection regulations, offering a policy-aware approach to AI integration that respects both ethical imperatives and legal constraints. Institutions can operationalize the model by integrating AI-enhanced adaptive learning within existing Learning Management Systems, deploying assistive technologies for students with disabilities and international learners, and implementing ethical AI analytics to identify and address participation disparities through evidence-informed interventions. Cross-institutional collaboration through mechanisms such as Erasmus+ and European University Alliances can facilitate knowledge sharing and infrastructure development, enabling scalable inclusive AI strategies across both well-resourced and underrepresented educational settings while building regional capacity for responsible AI adoption.

As acknowledged throughout this paper, several important limitations constrain the framework's immediate applicability and warrant explicit attention. The framework presumes baseline technological infrastructure not universally available across global contexts, particularly in low- and middle-income countries where digital divides, limited broadband access, insufficient hardware, and unreliable power supply often preclude effective use of even basic AI tools. Linguistic and cultural biases embedded within current AI systems, especially in Natural Language Processing tools, may undermine inclusivity for underrepresented languages and non-Western pedagogical traditions, revealing epistemological misalignments between individual-centered AI platform design and collective learning paradigms valued in some cultural contexts. Institutional resistance manifested through entrenched academic norms, lack of faculty training, and skepticism toward algorithmic decision-making represents a critical barrier that may result in selective or superficial adoption, undermining the framework's systemic ambition. Disciplinary variation introduces additional complexity, as fields relying on embodied knowledge or craft-based expertise may not benefit equally from automation and predictive analytics designed primarily for STEM contexts. Ethical tensions surrounding data collection and processing, particularly in contexts where historical surveillance abuses have eroded trust or where privacy norms diverge significantly from Western frameworks, require culturally sensitive data governance strategies that balance the equity benefits of learner analytics against legitimate privacy concerns.

These constraints do not invalidate the framework but underscore the necessity for contextual calibration and adaptive implementation strategies that respond to local conditions, resources, and values. Future research should prioritize empirical validation of the framework through mixed-methods studies across diverse institutional contexts, with particular attention to under-resourced settings where inclusion challenges are most acute and where the risks of technology-driven exclusion are greatest. Longitudinal investigations are needed to assess how AI-enhanced inclusion scales over time and whether initial gains in accessibility translate into sustained improvements in student engagement, persistence, and achievement across varied pedagogical cultures, regulatory environments, and resource constraints. Comparative cross-national studies could illuminate contextual factors that enable or impede successful implementation, revealing how the interplay of infrastructure readiness, policy support, cultural values, and institutional capacity shapes outcomes in different settings and informing the development of localized adaptation protocols that preserve the framework's conceptual integrity while allowing operational flexibility. Additionally, participatory co-design approaches involving affected student communities, particularly those from marginalized backgrounds, would strengthen the framework's cultural responsiveness and ethical grounding by centering lived experiences of exclusion and ensuring that AI tools genuinely serve rather than inadvertently harm vulnerable populations. Such research would also benefit from attention to disciplinary differences, exploring how the framework might be adapted for fields where algorithmic logic poorly captures essential learning processes, and examining whether different dimensions merit differential emphasis depending on disciplinary epistemologies and pedagogical traditions.

As AI continues to reshape higher education at an accelerating pace, the imperative remains to deploy these technologies with intentionality, ethical purpose, and unwavering commitment to equity rather than merely efficiency or cost reduction. The framework presented here aspires to guide that process—not as a prescriptive blueprint imposing uniform solutions across heterogeneous contexts, but as a flexible conceptual tool adaptable to institutional diversity and capable of fostering genuinely inclusive learning ecosystems where all students, regardless of linguistic background, cultural identity, cognitive profile, or physical ability, can access, engage with, and succeed in higher education. By maintaining critical awareness of both opportunities and risks, by centering equity alongside functionality, and by recognizing that inclusive AI integration requires sustained effort across pedagogical, institutional, and policy levels, the international higher education community can work toward realizing AI's transformative potential in service of justice and human flourishing rather than merely technological advancement.

Disclosure of Interests. The authors have no competing interests to declare that are relevant to the content of this article.

Attributions. The contribution represents the result of a collaborative effort by the authors; specifically, Sobia Yasmeen is the author of §§ 1, 2, 2.1, 2.2, 3, 3.2, 3.3, 4.1, 5; Valeria Di Martino is the author of §§ 2.3, 3.1, 3.4, 4.2, 5.1, 5.2, 6.

References

1. Ajani, O.A., Akintolu, M., Afolabi, S.O.: The emergence of artificial intelligence in higher education: prospects and challenges of AI. Int. J. Res. Bus. Soc. Sci. **13**(8), 1–14 (2024). https://doi.org/10.20525/ijrbs.v13i8.3507
2. Galdames-Calderón, M., Stavnskær Pedersen, A., Rodriguez-Gomez, D.: Systematic review: Revisiting challenge-based learning teaching practices in higher education. Educ. Sci. **14**(9), 1008 (2024). https://doi.org/10.3390/educsci14091008
3. Alhammadi, Y., Alhazmi, A.K.: Towards effective AI adoption in higher education: a comprehensive conceptual model. J. Sci. Technol. **30**(3), 45–60 (2025). https://doi.org/10.20428/jst.v30i3.2758
4. Pagliara, S.M., et al.: The integration of artificial intelligence in inclusive education: a scoping review. Inform. **15**(12), 774 (2024). https://doi.org/10.3390/info15120774
5. Dzogovic, S., Zdravkovska-Adamova, B., Serpil, H.: From theory to practice: a holistic study of the application of artificial intelligence methods and techniques in higher education and science. Hum. Res. Rehabil. **14**(2), 1–16 (2024). https://doi.org/10.16993/hrr.106
6. Wang, H., et al.: Scientific discovery in the age of artificial intelligence. Nature. **620**(7972), 47–60 (2023). https://doi.org/10.1038/s41586-023-06221-2
7. Chaka, C.: Fourth industrial revolution—a review of applications, prospects, and challenges for artificial intelligence, robotics and blockchain in higher education. Res. Pract. Technol. Enhanc. Learn. **18**, 002 (2023). https://doi.org/10.1186/s41039-023-00180-2
8. Ul Hassan, M., Murtaza, A., Rashid, K.: Redefining higher education institutions (HEIs) in the era of globalisation and global crises: a proposal for future sustainability. Eur. J. Educ. **60**(1), e12822 (2025). https://doi.org/10.1111/ejed.12822
9. Roy, A.: Technology in teaching and learning. Int. J. Innov. Educ. Res. **7**(4), 414–422 (2019). https://doi.org/10.31686/ijier.Vol7.Iss4.1433

10. Tuma, F.: The use of educational technology for interactive teaching in lectures. Ann. Med. Surg. **62**, 231–235 (2021). https://doi.org/10.1016/j.amsu.2021.11.019
11. Garg, S., Sharma, S.: Impact of artificial intelligence in special need education to promote inclusive pedagogy. Int. J. Inf. Educ. Technol. **10**(7), 523–527 (2020). https://doi.org/10.18178/ijiet.2020.10.7.1414
12. Belenkova, L.Y., Skudnyakova, Y.V., Bosov, D.V.: Digital pedagogy in the system of inclusive higher education. Interacción y Perspectiva: Rev. Trab. Soc. **12**(1), 27–42 (2022). https://doi.org/10.15359/ri.12-1.2
13. Chan, C.K.Y.: A comprehensive AI policy education framework for university teaching and learning. Int. J. Educ. Technol. High. Educ. **20**(1), 38 (2023). https://doi.org/10.1186/s41239-023-00388-4
14. Slimi, Z., Carballido, B.V.: Navigating the ethical challenges of artificial intelligence in higher education: an analysis of seven global AI ethics policies. Tem J. **12**(2), 1–15 (2023). https://doi.org/10.18421/TEM122-09
15. Galdames, I.S.: Integration of artificial intelligence in higher education: relevance for inclusion and learning. SciComm. Rep. **4**(1), 1–12 (2024). https://doi.org/10.28991/scirep-2024-03-01-01
16. Singh, R.J.: Transforming higher education: the power of artificial intelligence. Int. J. Multidiscip. Res. Arts Sci. Technol. **1**(3), 13–18 (2023). https://doi.org/10.5281/zenodo.8190171
17. Deri, M.N., Singh, A., Zaazie, P., Anandene, D.: Leveraging artificial intelligence in higher educational institutions: a comprehensive overview. Rev. Educ. Derecho. **30**, 1–20 (2024). https://doi.org/10.23854/edurec.30
18. Okunlaya, R.O., Syed Abdullah, N., Alias, R.A.: Artificial intelligence (AI) library services innovative conceptual framework for the digital transformation of university education. Lib. Hi Tech. **40**(6), 1869–1892 (2022). https://doi.org/10.1108/LHT-02-2022-0041
19. Mariyono, D., Nur Alif Hd, A.: AI's role in transforming learning environments: a review of collaborative approaches and innovations. Qual. Educ. All. **2**(1), 265–288 (2025). https://doi.org/10.21552/qea/2025/1/14
20. Ul Hassan, M., et al.: Deconstructing the one-size-fits-all model: a systematic review of personalized acute care strategies. Rev. J. Neurol. Med. Sci. Rev. **3**(2), 1–15 (2025). https://doi.org/10.5281/zenodo.8190172
21. Sabri, H. et al.: Performance of three artificial intelligence (AI)-based large language models in standardized testing; implications for AI-assisted dental education. J. Periodontal Res. **60**(2), 121–133 (2025). https://doi.org/10.1111/jre.13239
22. Jabareen, Y.: Building a conceptual framework: philosophy, definitions, and procedure. Int J Qual Methods. **8**(4), 49–62 (2009). https://doi.org/10.1177/160940690900800406
23. Hardy, I., Woodcock, S.: Inclusive education policies: discourses of difference, diversity and deficit. Int. J. Incl. Educ. **19**(2), 141–164 (2015). https://doi.org/10.1080/13603116.2014.915305
24. Torraco, R.J.: Writing integrative literature reviews: guidelines and examples. Hum. Resour. Dev. Rev. **4**(3), 356–367 (2005). https://doi.org/10.1177/1534484305278283
25. Whittemore, R., Knafl, K.: The integrative review: updated methodology. J. Adv. Nurs. **52**(5), 546–553 (2005). https://doi.org/10.1111/j.1365-2648.2005.03621.x

Engagement in Teacher Education: an Exploratory Study of Simplexity and the Six Thinking Hats

Naomi La Manna[1(✉)], Alessio Di Paolo[2], and Maurizio Sibilio[2]

[1] University of Macerata, Macerata, (MC) 62100, Italy
n.lamanna@unimc.it
[2] University of Salerno, Fisciano (SA), 84084, Italy
{adipaolo,msibilio}@unisa.it

Abstract. This study examines the potential of integrating the simplexity paradigm [1–2–3] with De Bono's Six Thinking Hats method (1985) [4] in teacher education. Based on the premise that contemporary learning environments are shaped by complex cognitive, emotional, and social dynamics, the research aims to identify pedagogical strategies capable of fostering authentic and sustainable engagement in hybrid training contexts. The exploratory study involved 365 student teachers enrolled in the specialization program for support teaching at the University of Salerno, divided into a control group (in-person lessons) and an experimental group (online lessons). Participants attended a 30-h course on simplex didactics and the Six Hats method, during which they experienced their integrated application through metacognitive and cooperative activities designed to encourage reflection on teaching practice and the management of educational complexity. Data were collected using the adapted Italian version of the Engagement Questionnaire [5] and analyzed through t-tests. Results revealed significant differences in the emotional dimension of engagement, with higher involvement among in-person participants compared to those online. Findings suggest that the synergy between simplexity and lateral thinking may effectively enhance behavioral and cognitive engagement even in virtual environments, while the emotional component requires further investigation to identify influencing factors. Nevertheless, this integrated perspective appears promising for promoting higher engagement levels in online learning contexts as well.

Keywords: engagement · didactic simplex · teaching · lateral thinking · inclusion

1 Introduction*

In contemporary teacher education, increasingly complex cognitive, emotional, and social dynamics demand pedagogical approaches capable of addressing non-linearity and interconnection in learning processes. Within this framework, the Simplexity paradigm [1–2–3] and De Bono's Six Thinking Hats method (1985) [4] offer a dual contribution: on

M. Adamoli et al. (Eds.): HELMeTO 2025, CCIS 2958, pp. 205–220, 2026.
https://doi.org/10.1007/978-3-032-31850-3_13

one hand, a theoretical lens that helps make complexity manageable through principles and properties such as modularity, flexibility, and probabilistic anticipation; on the other, an operational structure that intentionally diversifies thinking processes—informative, emotional-intuitive, creative, critical, prospective, and metacognitive—to support more reflective and adaptive teaching decisions. The integration of these two approaches thus responds to the need to foster authentic and sustainable engagement, particularly in hybrid and online contexts, where the management of educational action requires constant regulation across behavioral, cognitive, and emotional dimensions. Recent literature defines engagement as a multidimensional and interdependent construct encompassing behavioral, emotional, and cognitive components, whose activation emerges from the dynamic interaction between individuals, environments, and instructional strategies. Within this perspective, Simplexity can guide the design of flexible and inclusive learning pathways, while the Six Thinking Hats method serves as a metacognitive device that enables teachers to balance and regulate different "thinking postures" required in professional practice. It is therefore hypothesized that the synergy between these two models may influence the various dimensions of engagement—enhancing the quality of action (behavioral), strategic investment in learning tasks (cognitive), and, at the same time, supporting the emotional dimension through reflective and cooperative practices. The present study explores this hypothesis within a 30-h training program involving 365 pre-service support teachers at the University of Salerno, organized into a control group (face-to-face) and an experimental group (online). The intervention included theoretical and practical activities designed to experience the integration of Simplex Didactics and the Six Thinking Hats method through metacognitive and cooperative tasks. Engagement was measured using the Italian adapted version of the Engagement Questionnaire [5] and analyzed through independent samples t-tests. Preliminary results suggest that the proposed integration effectively enhances behavioral and cognitive engagement even in virtual environments, whereas the emotional dimension remains more sensitive to the immediacy and relational proximity typical of in-person instruction. These findings provide theoretical and practical insights for rethinking teacher education through reflective, creative, and adaptive frameworks, while also opening new avenues for investigating the role of socio-emotional dynamics in hybrid learning environments.

2 Engagement: a Multidimensional Construct

From the review of the reference literature [6], it emerges that the term engagement should be understood as a multidimensional construct, consisting of intrinsically related and interdependent components [7, 8]. According with Fredricks et al.[8], it is configured as a meta-construct within which behavioral, emotional, and *cognitive vectors* [9, 10] operate, which, if considered synergistically, allow the school experience to be described in a holistic and comprehensive way [11]. The proposed integration between Simplexity [12] and the Six Thinking Hats [4] would offer not only an interpretative framework to understand how engagement emerges from the dynamic interaction of multiple action schemes adopted by educational actors, but also as a tool that would allow the teacher to manage the complexity of the learning context. However, many scholars have attempted to identify a theoretical framework that would allow engagement to be interpreted unanimously within the scientific community. As emerged to a review of studies conducted over the past ten years [6], it has emerged that the theoretical framework most used by researchers considers this construct as consisting of three specific dimensions: *behavioral*, *emotional*, and *cognitive* [5–7–8]. In literature, the behavioral dimension is articulated into three main areas: *positive conduct*, which refers to compliance with rules and the absence of deviant behaviors [13, 14]; *commitment to educational activities*, which includes persistence, attention, concentration, and active participation [15, 16]; and *participation in school and administrative activities* [13, 14]. The emotional component of engagement concerns the student's affective reactions during the school experience, such as interest, happiness, boredom, sadness, and anxiety [16, 17]. This dimension highlights the role of reciprocal regulation of emotions within the learning system, considering the emergence of affective states as the result of the interaction among subjects, environment, and teaching strategies. This perspective allows the overcoming of the dichotomy between situational and personal interests, highlighting the importance of the co-*construction of the sense* of belonging and motivation within the educational system [8]. The cognitive dimension focuses on psychological investment in learning, including flexibility in problem solving, preference for challenging tasks, and the adoption of self-regulation strategies [17, 18]. These cognitive processes are interpreted as dynamic and adaptive schemes that allow students to self-organize and respond flexibly to the complexity of the learning context, promoting the transfer and generalization of skills. Considering engagement as a multidimensional construct, the hypothesis is that Simplexity and the Six Thinking Hats method could affect, due to their intrinsic characteristics, both from a cognitive and behavioral and emotional point of view, thus assuming a central role as an operational tool for teachers for the dynamic and modular management of educational complexity. For example, the use of the white and blue hats to consciously apply principles such as modularity, adaptability, and co-regulation could promote higher levels of engagement in its dimensions, flexibly calibrating teaching strategies to students' needs in inclusive and complex contexts [8]. These properties are typical of creative thinking, related to the theory of six thinking of De Bono, focused on an idea that a color can represent a modality to express a specific way to do, related with a personal cognitive property. In this sense, the association between color and action shows a particular way to analyze the word and their personal decipherment of phenomena.

3 Six Thinking Hats and Simplexity: a Possible Integration

3.1 Simplexity: Principles and Properties

Within contemporary pedagogical research, the paradigm of Simplexity [19] has progressively consolidated its relevance as a theoretical and methodological framework capable of addressing the increasing complexity of educational systems. Originating in neurophysiology, Simplexity describes how living organisms, through evolutionary adaptation, develop biological mechanisms that transform complex situations into manageable actions, ensuring both efficiency and flexibility. Transposed into the educational domain, this paradigm offers a systemic–creative perspective that enables teachers to interpret and manage the intricate cognitive, emotional, and relational dynamics that characterize learning environments [3–20–21]. As Van Geert and Steenbeek [22] observe, educational contexts can be considered complex adaptive systems in which continuous interaction among multiple variables requires reflective, non-linear, and adaptive responses. Berthoz [23] identifies within Simplexity a set of six properties—modularity, speed of response, reliability, flexibility, memory, and generalization—and six principles of action—inhibition and rejection, specialization and selection, probabilistic anticipation, deviation, cooperation and redundancy, and sense. These elements constitute an integrated framework that connects biological adaptability with cognitive and metacognitive processes. When applied to teaching, they allow educators to design learning pathways that are dynamic, inclusive, and open to innovation. For instance, modularity enables teachers to deconstruct complex tasks into smaller, manageable components, later reintegrated into coherent didactic plans [12]. Speed of response becomes central in managing classroom dynamics, particularly in moments of student disengagement, while reliability ensures consistency and accuracy through differentiated strategies responsive to learners' individual needs. Equally essential is flexibility, which allows teachers to modify approaches based on contextual variables and the evolving needs of the class. Memory supports the consolidation of experiential knowledge, allowing educators to draw on previous practices, whereas generalization facilitates the transfer of learned strategies to new situations, an ability particularly relevant in inclusive education. In addition, the rules of action reinforce these properties through cognitive and affective regulation: inhibition and rejection promote creative detours by suppressing automatic responses [2], while specialization and selection guide attention toward essential information, enhancing instructional focus. The rule of probabilistic anticipation allows teachers to foresee potential reactions and adapt in real time, and cooperation and redundancy strengthen cognitive reliability through collaborative and iterative practices. Finally, the rule of sense highlights the importance of meaning-making as a motivational and reflective dimension of teaching [3–23]. In this view, the Simplexity framework supports the transition from intuitive to reflective professional practice [24, 25]. Teachers are encouraged to become aware of the implicit mechanisms guiding their pedagogical choices and to transform them into intentional, evidence-informed actions. Reflection before, during, and after teaching thus emerges as a metacognitive process that enables adaptation, creativity, and resilience within increasingly heterogeneous and dynamic learning environments. Consequently, Simplexity not only provides a theoretical model for interpreting educational complexity but also constitutes a practical compass for developing flexible, inclusive, and context-sensitive teacher education.

3.2 Six Thinkings Hats Method

According to Moseley et al. [26], the act of thinking involves the activation of a variety of mental processes used to solve problems, make decisions, plan, evaluate ideas, and organize information in meaningful ways [27]. Within this framework, Edward de Bono [28, 29] defines thinking as a purposeful mental process through which individuals gather, elaborate, and apply information to generate original solutions and construct meaning from experience. Thinking, therefore, is not a purely rational activity, but an intentional act of interpretation and creation that integrates logic, emotion, and creativity. De Bono distinguishes between two main forms of thinking: vertical and lateral thinking. Vertical thinking corresponds to a traditional, logical, and analytical mode of reasoning that proceeds linearly through a sequence of steps toward a defined solution. It is based on rules, reasoning, and established knowledge frameworks [28, 29]. Lateral thinking, in contrast, represents a creative and divergent approach that enables individuals to examine problems from new perspectives, challenge habitual cognitive patterns, and explore unconventional pathways [30]. As De Bono [28] observes, it is "a way of using the mind… a mental habit, a mental attitude" (pag.11) that promotes transformation and innovation through a deliberate shift of perspective. By encouraging the restructuring of information and the development of new associations, lateral thinking nurtures creativity and adaptability, two skills increasingly necessary in educational practice [29–31–32]. In the educational field, creative and lateral thinking are considered higher-order cognitive abilities that play a crucial role in fostering meaningful learning, critical reflection, and innovative teaching [33–34–35]. Creative thinking enables students to move beyond the reproduction of knowledge, engaging them in active problem-solving and idea generation. At the same time, it represents a forma mentis for teachers, supporting flexibility, metacognitive awareness, and the ability to design inclusive learning environments [36, 37]. In this regard, De Bono's Six Thinking Hats method [4] stands out as one of the most widely recognized models for fostering creative and reflective thinking. Initially designed for professional and organizational contexts, it has since been adapted for educational purposes as a structured framework for cognitive diversification. The method introduces six metaphorical "hats," each representing a specific thinking mode: the white hat corresponds to the objective and informative dimension, guiding the collection and analysis of relevant data; the red hat gives legitimacy to emotions and intuitions, acknowledging their central role in value-based decision-making; the yellow that promotes a constructive and optimistic approach oriented toward identifying opportunities and positive outcomes; the black hat embodies critical and logical analysis, essential for identifying weaknesses, risks, and potential problems; the green hat represents creativity and innovation, stimulating the generation of new ideas and perspectives; finally, the blue hat symbolizes control and metacognition, ensuring coherence, regulation, and organization throughout the thinking process [4]. This multimodal structure allows learners and teachers alike to engage with problems from multiple viewpoints, encouraging balance between creativity and criticality, intuition and reasoning. In the context of today's protean and complex educational environments [38], where teachers must respond to the diverse needs of students [39, 40], the Six Hats method offers a valuable pedagogical tool for promoting inclusive and participatory learning. By integrating emotional, cognitive, and relational dimensions of thought, it enables educators to design didactic interventions that are flexible, reflective, and capable of fostering authentic engagement.

Ultimately, the pedagogical relevance of lateral thinking and the Six Hats model lies in their ability to break the rigidity of traditional, linear teaching models. They encourage teachers to adopt an adaptive mindset that recognizes complexity as an opportunity for innovation rather than as an obstacle. In doing so, De Bono's approach aligns with contemporary perspectives on educational simplexity [3–21], which emphasize the need for reflective, non-linear, and creative strategies to navigate the intricate dynamics of learning processes. In this sense, lateral thinking becomes not only a cognitive tool but also an epistemological stance that underpins a renewed vision of teacher professionalism, one that integrates logic and creativity, emotion and reason, structure and openness in a coherent pedagogical synthesis.

3.3 Simplex Chromatisms: A Possible Integration

From what has been written so far, interesting insights emerge that contribute to constructing the research hypothesis of the present project, which refers to the possible educational applications of a hypothetical approach integrating Simplexity and the Six Thinking Hats. In both perspectives, indeed, the search for different, adaptive, and alternative solutions to usual situations represents the expression of freedom of choice within the wide repertoire of possible solutions, in order not to get lost in complexity [23–41]. Both approaches also suggest non-linear ways of thinking and the ability to anticipate, adapt, and solve problems in a dynamic and innovative way. For this reason, teachers could develop an educational approach that not only responds to students' individual needs but also stimulates their active participation, promoting an inclusive, engaging, and dynamic learning environment [27]. Metacognition (referring to the awareness of one's own thinking process), in this sense, is an essential competence for teachers, who must be able to reorient their approach, wearing all the "hats", according to students' needs and the unpredictable dynamics that emerge in the classroom [27]. Each principle and each property, therefore, would require a different hat to be consciously implemented, as hypothesized in Tables 1–2.

Table 1. Properties of simplexity and Six Thinking Hats [27].

Properties of Simplexity	Six Thinking Hats
Specialization and modularity	White hat
Rapidity	Yellow hat – Black hat
Reliability	Blue hat
Flexibility, vicariance, and adaptation to change	Green hat – Red hat
Memory	White hat
Generalization	White hat

First of all, it is useful to highlight how the separation of functions and modularity, as well as memory and generalization, would be placed under the sign of the white hat, which represents the neutral and informative approach: in this case, the teacher would assume the role of organizer of knowledge, capable of presenting clear and structured information, but also of fostering transversal connections between concepts, thus promoting a deep and flexible understanding of action. Rapidity, a quality often required by the rhythm of teaching, would be interpreted through a double perspective: that of the yellow hat, which would emphasize its effectiveness and responsiveness, and that of the black hat, which would invite maintaining attention to the quality and risks of actions. In this sense, the teacher should therefore be able to balance operational readiness and critical rigor. Reliability would find expression in the blue hat, a symbol of ordered thinking, planning, and coherence. Being reliable means ensuring a predictable and structured environment in which students can feel safe and guided. Finally, properties such as flexibility, vicariousness, and the ability to adapt to change would be linked to the interaction between the green hat, which embodies innovation, and the red hat, which expresses empathy and attention to the emotional climate of the classroom. In an ever-evolving educational context, the teacher should be ready to reinvent strategies and respond sensitively to the changing needs of students, integrating creativity and intuition into their daily practice.

Table 2: Rules of simplexity and Six Thinking Hats [27].

Rules of Simplexity	Six Thinking Hats
Inhibition and the rule of rejection	Red hat – White hat
Specialization and selection	White hat
Cooperation and redundancy	Blue hat
Probabilistic anticipation	Yellow hat – Black hat
Detour	Green hat
Meaning	Red hat

According to the principles of simplex teaching [2], the teacher is also called to inhibit and select: knowing how to say no to misleading or irrelevant stimuli, as required by the principle of rejection, is a competence that could be supported by the interaction between the red hat, which would capture the emotional dimension of the educational relationship, and the white hat, which would guide logical and conscious evaluation. Cooperation and redundancy, often invisible but fundamental in building a stable and safe learning community, would emerge with the blue hat, highlighting the need for a regulatory thinking that *harmonizes educational interactions* [27]. Probabilistic anticipation, that is, the ability to foresee reactions and learning developments based on subtle clues, could be supported by the positive vision of the Yellow Hat and the critical sense of the black hat: the effective teacher is the one who knows how to anticipate the needs of the class and prevent difficulties. From this perspective, deviation also becomes a resource that would be expressed through the Green Hat: stepping outside established patterns turns into didactic innovation, the ability to propose alternative and stimulating learning paths. Finally, in the Red Hat one could find the deep meaning of educational action, which has its roots in relationship and intentionality: it reminds us that teaching is not only about transmitting knowledge, but also about connecting with the emotions, motivations, and personal stories of students [27]. For this reason, it is believed that De Bono's Six Hats metaphor [4] offers, through the imaginative act of wearing a hat, the opportunity to reflect on and analyze one's own teaching action. Moreover, proposing this metaphor as an exercise within training groups could offer the possibility to reflect on one's own teaching practice to make it more engaging and, therefore, more capable of responding to the educational needs of each student [27].

4 Method

4.1 Objective

The present study aims to investigate whether there are differences in engagement levels between the control group, which attended face-to-face lessons, and the experimental group, which participated online. The objective is to examine whether a teaching approach that integrates the principles and properties of Simplexity with the use of De Bono's Six Thinking Hats can foster active participation across different types of learning environments.

4.2 Sample and Procedure

The exploratory study involved a total of 365 pre-service teachers enrolled in specialization courses for support teaching at the University of Salerno. The analyzed sample, aged between 25 and 61 years, represents an adult population engaged in a continuing education pathway aimed at teacher professionalization. Sixty percent of the participants reported having prior experience as support teachers. Participants were divided into two groups: a control group consisting of 188 trainees who attended face-to-face lessons, and an experimental group consisting of 177 trainees who attended the same training activities online. The two groups were considered homogeneous, as participants were randomly assigned to teaching classes by the university institution responsible for organizing the course. Consequently, the research team did not exert any form of manipulation in assigning trainees to their respective classes, thus ensuring conditions of initial equivalence between the groups. Both groups participated in a 30-h training program focused on Simplex Didactics and De Bono's Six Thinking Hats method, structured into 20 h of theoretical instruction and 10 h of practical activities. This training program enabled participants to experience the integrated application of both methodologies through individual and collaborative work. The methodological framework was based on a metacognitive and cooperative approach, aimed at encouraging participants to critically reflect on their teaching practices and to explore how adaptive and creative strategies can foster student engagement. In particular, the practical activities involved dividing participants into small groups of no more than 10 individuals. Each group was required to design a classroom scenario that included a student with a disability. Subsequently, with the support of the metaphors of the Six Thinking Hats, participants were asked to design teaching actions that consciously applied the principles and properties of simplexity. Specifically, the activities addressed: general didactics (e.g., using the property of rapidity to respond effectively to a decrease in students' attention); subject-specific didactics (e.g., applying the principle of inhibition and rejection to structure a lesson on a specific content area); and special didactics (e.g., applying the property of memory to design an inclusive lesson for a classroom context involving a student with a disability). The overall aim of the program was to support the development of teachers' creative thinking and to promote a non-linear approach to teaching. Data collection was conducted before and after the training intervention in order to compare participants' engagement levels across the two different learning settings (face-to-face and online).

4.3 Search Tool

To evaluate the effectiveness of the intervention, the Engagement Questionnaire developed by [5] and subsequently adapted into Italian [42] was used. The questionnaire examines three main dimensions of engagement-behavioral, emotional, and cognitive-through a total of 54 items. Specifically:

- Behavioral engagement (17 items) assesses attention and active participation in learning activities;
- Emotional engagement (17 items) measures interest, motivation, and affective involvement in learning processes;
- Cognitive engagement (20 items) evaluates commitment to understanding, problem-solving, and metacognitive reflection.

The psychometric analysis of the Italian version of the questionnaire revealed satisfactory levels of internal consistency for each dimension (Table 3). The behavioral dimension showed a Cronbach's alpha coefficient of 0.826; the emotional dimension reported an alpha value of 0.771; and the cognitive dimension presented a Cronbach's alpha of 0.863 [42]. Considering the scale as a whole, the analysis yielded a very high reliability index (Cronbach's alpha = 0.925), confirming the strong internal consistency of the instrument [42].

Quantitative data were analyzed using independent samples t-tests, with software Jamovi, to examine the presence of statistically significant differences in the three engagement dimensions between the face-to-face and online groups.

Table 3: Reliability of the Engagement Questionnaire [5] adapted into Italian [42].

Behavioral engagement	Cronbach's $\alpha = 0.826$
Emotional engagement	Cronbach's $\alpha = 0.771$
Cognitive engagement	Cronbach's $\alpha = 0.863$
Overall scale reliability	Cronbach's $\alpha = 0.925$

5 Results and Discussion

The item-level analysis made it possible to examine more analytically the differences between the group that attended face-to-face training and the group that participated online, highlighting a complex and non uniform pattern across the three dimensions of engagement. Overall, the majority of items did not show statistically significant differences between the two groups, suggesting a substantial comparability of learning experiences across the two training contexts for several aspects of engagement.

Behavioral engagement (Items A1–A17) (Table 4): with regard to the behavioral dimension, most items related to rule compliance (A1, A2), effort in task completion (A3, A4, A5), and attention management (A6, A7, A9, A10) did not reveal statistically significant differences. This finding suggests that behaviors such as punctuality, persistence when facing challenging tasks, participation in learning activities, and the application of acquired knowledge tend to manifest similarly in the two settings, likely due to the guided and intentional structure of the proposed training activities.

However, some item-specific differences emerged. In particular, items A8 ("When I am in class, I listen attentively") and A11 ("When I do not understand something in class, I ask the teacher to clarify it") showed statistically significant differences, with higher values reported by participants attending face-to-face lessons. These results suggest that specific behaviors related to active listening and requesting clarification may be facilitated by physical proximity and direct interaction with the instructor. Nevertheless, these findings should be interpreted with caution, especially in light of the violation of the homogeneity of variance assumption in some cases, which advises against overestimating the magnitude of the observed differences.

The remaining behavioral items, including those related to interaction with the teacher (A16) and perceived mastery of content (A17), did not reach statistical significance, reinforcing the view that, overall, behavioral engagement is not strongly differentiated by the instructional modality.

Emotional engagement (Items B18–B34) (Table 5): a partially different pattern emerged for the emotional dimension. Although several items related to sense of belonging (B19), general interest in learning (B18), and peer support dynamics (B30, B31) did not show significant differences, some items displayed noteworthy variations.

Specifically, statistically significant differences were observed for items B20 ("When I am distracted during the lesson, I feel worried or annoyed"), B22 ("When working in a group, I feel annoyed if I am distracted"), B24 ("I am interested in simplexity exercises"), B29 ("I am all ears when my teacher teaches something new"), and B34 ("I volunteer to express doubts or questions"). These items suggest that emotional engagement, particularly in terms of affective reactivity, situational interest, and relational involvement, may be more sensitive to the characteristics of face-to-face learning contexts. At the same time, the absence of significant differences across many emotional engagement items indicates that the affective experience of learning is not uniformly compromised in online settings, but rather modulated by specific interactive and relational conditions. Accordingly, it would not be appropriate to interpret these results as evidence of a general reduction in emotional engagement in distance learning, but rather as the emergence of selective differences related to particular aspects of the educational experience.

Cognitive engagement (Items C35–C54) (Table 6): the cognitive dimension presents a picture of substantial homogeneity. None of the analyzed items showed statistically significant differences between the two groups. Items related to perseverance in studying (C35, C48), self-regulation (C36, C43, C53), information integration (C37, C51, C52), and strategic use of knowledge (C40, C41, C44) suggest that cognitive and metacognitive investment processes are comparable across the two instructional settings.

This pattern appears consistent with the hypothesis that structured, reflective, and simplexity-oriented teaching activities may support cognitive processes in a similar manner even within digital environments. At the same time, the lack of statistically significant differences calls for caution and discourages overly optimistic interpretations, acknowledging that the study design does not allow these outcomes to be attributed exclusively to the adopted methodological approach.

Taken together, the item-level analyses outline an articulated engagement profile, in which differences between face-to-face and online instruction appear to be limited to specific aspects, primarily associated with the emotional dimension and certain interactive behaviors (Table 7). The predominance of non-significant items, especially within the behavioral and cognitive dimensions, suggests a substantial equivalence of training experiences across the two contexts, at least with respect to effort, participation, and cognitive investment.

Table 4. Items behavioral dimension

Independent sample tests				
		Statistics	WG	p
A1	t of Student	0.5757	363	0.283
A2	t of Student	-0.0644	363	0.526
A3	t of Student	-0.2847	363	0.612
A4	t of Student	-0.8234	363	0.795
A5	t of Student	0.0320	363	0.487
A6	t of Student	-1.9752	363	0.975
A7	t of Student	-2.7374	363	0.997
A8	t of Student	2.3878	363	0.009
A9	t of Student	-1.5768	363	0.942
A10	t of Student	0.7072	363	0.240
A11	t of Student	3.6118a	363	<,001
A12	t of Student	0.4393a	363	0.330
A13	t of Student	1.0567a	363	0.146
A14	t of Student	-1.9567	363	0.974
A15	t of Student	0.1199a	363	0.452
A16	t of Student	1.4083a	363	0.080
A17	t of Student	0.9897	363	0.161

Nota. H_a $\mu0 > \mu1$

a Levene's test is significant ($p < .05$), suggesting a violation of the assumption of equal variances

Table 5. Items emotional dimension

Independent sample tests				
		Statistics	WG	p
B18	t of Student	-0.4510	363	0.674
B19	t of Student	0.2336	363	0.408
B20	t of Student	3.8065a	363	<,001
B21	t of Student	-0.5503	363	0.709
B22	t of Student	1.8158	363	0.035
B23	t of Student	1.0677	363	0.143
B24	t of Student	1.8128	363	0.035
B25	t of Student	-1.1649	363	0.878
B26	t of Student	-0.2742	363	0.608
B27	t of Student	1.5470	363	0.061
B28	t of Student	0.0404	363	0.484
B29	t of Student	2.2437	363	0.013
B30	t of Student	0.7820	363	0.217
B31	t of Student	1.0023	363	0.158
B32	t of Student	-0.2893	363	0.614
B33	t of Student	0.6659	363	0.253
B34	t of Student	1.9077	363	0.029

Nota. H_a $\mu 0 > \mu 1$

a Levene's test is significant ($p < .05$), suggesting a violation of the assumption of equal variances

Table 6. Cognitive size of items

Independent sample tests				
		Statistics	GDL	p
C35	t of Student	−0.0220a	363	0.509
C36	t of Student	0.2629	363	0.396
C37	t of Student	−0.6021	363	0.726
C38	t of Student	−0.4964	363	0.690
C39	t of Student	−0.9304	363	0.824
C40	t of Student	−0.7609	363	0.776
C41	t of Student	−0.8542	363	0.803
C42	t of Student	0.9519	363	0.171

(*continued*)

Table 6. *(continued)*

Independent sample tests				
		Statistics	GDL	p
C43	t of Student	0.8199	363	0.206
C45	t of Student	−1.5156	363	0.935
C44	t of Student	1.0918a	363	0.138
C46	t of Student	−1.2306a	363	0.890
C47	t of Student	1.4087	363	0.080
C48	t of Student	0.7371	363	0.231
C49	t of Student	0.6745	363	0.250
C50	t of Student	0.1585	363	0.437
C51	t of Student	1.4102	363	0.080
C52	t of Student	1.1802	363	0.119
C53	t of Student	0.9778	363	0.164
C54	t of Student	−1.4211	363	0.922

No. H_a $\mu 0 > \mu 1$

a Levene's test is significant ($p < .05$), suggesting a violation of the assumption of equal variances

Table 7. Comparison between face-to-face and online instruction across engagement dimensions

Engagement dimension	*t*	df	*p*	Interpretation
Behavioral	−0.017	363	0.507	No significant difference between face-to-face and online groups
Emotional	2.257	363	0.012	Higher emotional engagement in face-to-face instruction
Cognitive	0.173	363	0.431	Comparable levels of cognitive engagement across instructional modalities

Note. Independent samples t-tests were conducted to compare engagement levels between face-to-face and online groups (H_a: $\mu_0 > \mu_1$). For the cognitive dimension, Levene's test was significant ($p < .05$), indicating a potential violation of the homogeneity of variance assumption; therefore, results should be interpreted with caution.

6 Conclusions

The present study offered a theoretical empirical exploration of the possible interconnections between the simplex didactics paradigm and De Bono's Six Thinking Hats method within initial teacher education, using engagement, across its behavioral, cognitive, and emotional dimensions, as a key interpretative lens. The aim was not to establish causal relationships between the adopted training approach and the observed levels of engagement, but rather to examine whether the differences identified between face-to-face and online learning contexts were consistent with the hypothesis of a potential contribution of the proposed integration. At the scale level, the findings indicate that no statistically significant differences emerged between face-to-face and online participants with respect to behavioral and cognitive engagement. This evidence appears consistent with the assumption that an intentionally designed instructional approach, grounded in modularity, reflexivity, and metacognitive regulation, may support comparable levels of active participation and cognitive investment even within digital environments. From this perspective, simplex didactics and the Six Thinking Hats seem to provide a methodological framework capable of supporting the organization of teaching action and the management of educational complexity, regardless of the mode of delivery.

Item-level analyses, however, offer a more nuanced picture. While the majority of behavioral and cognitive items did not show significant differences between groups, some item-specific variations emerged, particularly in relation to interactive behaviors such as attentive listening and requesting clarification from the instructor. These findings suggest that certain participatory practices may be facilitated by physical proximity and direct interaction, even though they do not translate into systematic differences at the dimensional level. In contrast, the emotional dimension of engagement appeared more sensitive to instructional modality. Statistically significant differences observed at both the scale and item levels indicate that affective involvement, especially in terms of emotional reactivity, situational interest, and relational engagement, tended to be higher in face-to-face contexts. Nevertheless, these differences cannot be attributed exclusively to the instructional setting, as additional factors such as familiarity with digital environments, screen-related fatigue, or individual characteristics of participants may also have contributed to the observed outcomes. Overall, the data suggest that the integration of simplex didactics and the Six Thinking Hats is compatible with satisfactory levels of engagement, particularly in the behavioral and cognitive dimensions, even within online learning environments. At the same time, emotional engagement emerges as the most sensitive dimension, closely linked to the relational and interactive conditions of the learning context. These findings should be interpreted in light of the exploratory nature of the study and its methodological limitations, notably the exclusive reliance on standardized quantitative instruments, which constrains the ability to fully capture the complexity of socio-emotional learning processes.

In light of these considerations, future research may further examine these preliminary findings through more articulated methodological designs, integrating qualitative, longitudinal, and observational approaches to explore more deeply how reflective and creative devices inspired by simplexity and lateral thinking intersect with emotional and relational dynamics in hybrid training contexts. From this standpoint, the proposed theoretical integration should not be regarded as a definitive model, but rather as an open interpretative framework capable of informing further reflection and experimentation in the field of teacher education.

Competing Interests. The authors declare that they have no known competing financial interests or personal relationships that could have appeared to influence the work reported in this paper.

References

1. Berthoz, A.: La simplexité. Odile Jacob, Paris (2009). EAN13: 9782738196798
2. Sibilio, M.: La didattica semplessa. Liguori, Napoli (2013). https://doi.org/10.4000/essais.401
3. Sibilio, M.: La semplessità: proprietà e principi per agire il cambiamento. Morcelliana, Brescia (2023) EAN 9788828404538
4. De Bono, E.: Edward de Bono's Six Thinking Hats (2005)
5. Abbasi, M., Ghamoushi, M., Mohammadi Zenouzagh, Z.: EFL learners' engagement in online learning context: development and validation of potential measurement inventory. Univ. Access Inf. Soc. **23**(3), 1467–1481 (2024). https://doi.org/10.1007/s10209-023-00993-0
6. La Manna, N., Zappalà, E., Sibilio, M.: Engagement, edugame and learning: a systematic literature review. J. Inclusive Method. Technol. Learn. Teach. **4**(3), ISSN 2785–5104 (2024)
7. Hookham, G., Nesbitt, K.: A systematic review of the definition and measurement of engagement in serious games. In: Proceedings of the australasian computer science week multiconference, pp. 1–10 (2019). https://doi.org/10.1145/3290688.3290747
8. Fredricks, J.A., Blumenfeld, P.C., Paris, A.H.: School engagement: potential of the concept, state of the evidence. Rev. Educ. Res. **74**(1), 59–109 (2004). https://doi.org/10.3102/00346543074001059
9. Guthrie, J.T., Anderson, E., Alao, S., Rinehart, J.: Influences of concept-oriented reading instruction on strategy use and conceptual learning from text. Elem. Sch. J. **99**(4), 343–366 (1999). https://doi.org/10.1086/461929
10. Guthrie, J.T., Wigfield, A.: Engagement and motivation in reading, New York (2000)
11. Trowler, V.: Student engagement literature review. High. Educ. Acad. **11**(1), 1–15 (2010)
12. Berthoz, A.: Simplexity: Simplifying Principles for a complex World. Yale University Press, New Haven–London / Éditions Odile Jacob, Paris (2012)
13. Finn, J. D.: School Engagement & Students at Risk (1993)
14. Finn, J.D., Pannozzo, G.M., Voelkl, K.E.: Disruptive and inattentive-withdrawn behavior and achievement among fourth graders. Elem. Sch. J. **95**(5), 421–434 (1995). https://doi.org/10.1086/461853
15. Birch, S.H., Ladd, G.W.: The teacher-child relationship and children's early school adjustment. J. Sch. Psychol. **35**(1), 61–79 (1997). https://doi.org/10.1016/S0022-4405(96)00029-5
16. Skinner, E.A., Belmont, M.J.: Motivation in the classroom: Reciprocal effects of teacher behavior and student engagement across the school year. J. Educ. Psychol. **85**(4), 571 (1993)
17. Connell, J. P., & Wellborn, J. G.: Competence, Autonomy, and Relatedness: A Motivational Analysis of Self-System Processes (1991)
18. Corno, L., Mandinach, E.B.: The role of cognitive engagement in classroom learning and motivation. Educ. Psychol. **18**(2), 88–108 (1983). https://doi.org/10.1080/00461528309529266
19. Berthoz, A.: La semplessità. Codice, Torino (2011) ISBN: 978-88-7578-187-3
20. Pace, E.M., Viola, I., Di Nocera, A.M., Aiello, P.: Riflessività e ricerca nella "formazione ibrida" dei futuri docenti di sostegno. Lifelong Lifewide Learn. **17**(39), 23–33 (2021)

21. Sibilio, M.: La didattica semplessa: Una traiettoria non lineare della ricerca educativa. Rev. Synth. **136**, 477–493 (2015). https://doi.org/10.1007/s11873-015-0284-4
22. Van Geert, P., Steenbeek, H.: The good, the bad and the ugly? The dynamic interplay between educational practice, policy and research. Complicity Int. J. Complexity Educ. **11**(2) (2014)
23. Berthoz, A.: Sketching a theory of simplexity. Hors Collect., 25–35 (2019)
24. Schon, D.: Learning, reflection and change (2004). Accessed 11 Apr 1983
25. Shulman, L.S., Shulman, J.H.: How and what teachers learn: A shifting perspective. J. Curric. Stud. **36**(2), 257–271 (2004). https://doi.org/10.1080/0022027032000148298
26. Moseley, G.L.: Distorted body image in complex regional pain syndrome. Neurology. **65**(5), 773–773 (2005). https://doi.org/10.1212/01.wnl.0000174515.07205.11
27. Di Paolo, A., La Manna, N., Sibilio, M.: Perception of teaching action: Chromatisms of simplexity. Ital. J. Health Educ. Sport Inclusive Didact. **9**(1) (2025)
28. De Bono, E.: Lateral thinking: A textbook of creativity. MICA Management Resources, London (1970)
29. De Bono, E.: Creatività e pensiero laterale. BUR, Milano (2015)
30. Jesson, J.: Developing creativity in the primary school. McGraw-Hill Education, London (2012)
31. Goleman, D., Boyatzis, R.: Emotional intelligence has 12 elements. Which do you need to work on? Harv. Bus. Rev. **84**(2), 1–5 (2017) https://hbr.org/2017/02/emotional-intelligence-has-12-elements-which-do-you-need-to-work-on
32. Guilford, J.P.: Creativity: Yesterday, today and tomorrow. J. Creat. Behav. **1**(1), 3–14 (1967). https://doi.org/10.1002/j.2162-6057.1967.tb00002.x
33. Ahmed, K.A., Sharif, N., Ahmad, N.: Factors influencing students' career choices: empirical evidence from business students. J. SE Asian Res., 1–15 (2017). https://doi.org/10.5171/2017.718849
34. Astuti, M., Arifin, Z., Mutohhari, F., Nurtanto, M.: Competency of digital technology: the maturity levels of teachers and students in vocational education in Indonesia. J. Educ. Technol. **5**(2), 254–262 (2021). https://doi.org/10.23887/jet.v5i3.35108
35. Rosca, I.G., Todoroi, D.: Creativity in conscience society. Amfiteatru Econ. **13**(30), 599–619 (2011)
36. Waks, S.: Lateral thinking and technology education. J. Sci. Educ. Technol. **6**(4), 245–255 (1997)
37. Zollo, I., Kourkoutas, E.E., Sibilio, M.: Creatività, pensiero divergente e pensiero laterale per una didattica semplessa. Educ. Reflect. Pract. **1**, 5–17 (2015). https://doi.org/10.3280/ERP 2015-001001
38. Morrison, K.: School leadership and complexity theory. Routledge, London (2012). https://doi.org/10.4324/9780203603512
39. Pavone, M.R.: Scuola e bisogni educativi speciali. Mondadori Università, Milano (2015)
40. Cottini, L.: Didattica speciale e inclusione scolastica. Carocci, Roma (2017) ISBN: 9788843088188
41. De Bono, E.: Creatività e pensiero laterale. Rizzoli, Milano (1998)
42. La Manna, N., Zappalà, E., Sibilio, M. Fostering Students' Engagement and learning through Simplex Didactics Approach1. https://doi.org/10.30958/aje.X-Y-Z

AI against Hate: Smart Tools and Education for Safer Online Spaces

Maryna Manchenko(✉)

CESIE ETS, via Roma, 94, 90134 Palermo, Italy
maryna.manchenko@cesie.org

Abstract. This study presents the objectives, methodology, and preliminary outcomes of Hatedemics (2024–2026), a CERV project aimed at countering online hate speech and disinformation through the Hatedemics AI-powered digital platform and a participatory educational approach [1]. With 13 partners across five EU countries (Italy, Malta, Poland, and Spain, as well as Estonia and France), Hatedemics unites techno-logical innovation with human-rights and fact-checking based educational approach to foster digital literacy and civic engagement, particularly among young people and educators.

This contribution focuses on the project's implications for Higher Education and how its methodologies and tools (such as AI-driven Hatedemics platform and the participatory toolkit) can enhance teaching, training, and counter-narrative strategies across the EU.

Through stakeholder focus groups, co-creation workshops, and expert interviews in the four pilot countries (Italy, Spain, Poland and Malta), the project has identified key pedagogical challenges that the platform and an educational toolkit can address. The project embeds legal, ethical, and gender-sensitive assessments, complying with the EU AI Act [2], and is focused on cross-sector cooperation between NGOs/CSOs, universities, media, and public institutions, as recommended by the Council of Europe's Recommendation CM/Rec (2022)16 [3]. Subsequent paragraphs, however, are indented.

In summary, Hatedemics demonstrates how ethically designed AI technologies can be integrated into pedagogical process in order to empower educators and students to critically address online hate and disinformation, and into research process by mapping out the connections and main narratives of the channels on fringe social media platforms such as Telegram.

Keywords: Hate Speech · Disinformation · Education

1 Introduction

Disinformation and hate speech are tightly interleaved since the former is often used to foster the latter (Heller, 2021). Leveraging the amplifying opportunities offered by the participatory nature of SMPs (Marwick and Lewis, 2017), disinformation can be used to trigger underlying social prejudices and activate digital online movements that can, in turn, explode into online hate and harassment (Heller, 2021). Disinformation and hate

M. Adamoli et al. (Eds.): HELMeTO 2025, CCIS 2958, pp. 221–233, 2026.
https://doi.org/10.1007/978-3-032-31850-3_14

speech have in particular proliferated during the Covid-19 pandemic "jeopardising the health of millions of people worldwide, undermining confidence in vaccines and science, and dividing communities and countries'‘(Secretary-General of the United Nations, 2021). For instance, conspiracy theories attributing the spread of the virus to Jews, Muslims, Christians, or minority groups have fuelled discriminatory speech against such individuals, in some instances resulting in online hatred against them in response to Covid-19 (Önnerfors, 2021). Also, in this case, the observed diffusion of hate speech and disinformation were significantly correlated.

Hate speech and disinformation share some common features. They normalise violence and exploit fear and prejudices, and, at the same time, they exploit viral transmission and the lack of source transparency of social media (Young et al., 2018). However, EU projects tend to address hate and disinformation as separate phenomena without exploring the possible synergic activities derived from studying them under a unified framework.

While there is a number of government- and platform-led interventions, as well as regulatory and content moderation-related mechanisms, the phenomenon and the spread of online hate and disinformation proves that there is a necessity for balanced approaches that combine tech innovation with educational actions (Gagliardone et al., 2015).

The Hatedemics project (2024–2026), co-funded under the Citizens, Equality, Rights and Values programme (CERV), was conceptualised as a response to challenges by uniting an AI-driven approach and tools (Hatedemics platform) with participatory education approaches (educational toolkit). The project's consortium is composed of 13 partners from Italy, Malta, Poland, Spain, Estonia, and France and aims to strengthen the preventive and reactive measures against hate speech and disinformation online and empower NGOs/CSOs, factcheckers, public authorities and youngsters as activists to effectively prevent and combat polarisation, the spread of racist, xenophobic and intolerant speech, as well as conspiracy theories.

This paper examines the conceptual foundations, methodology and preliminary results of the Hatedemics project, with particular attention to its implications for higher education. It also examines how the project's outputs, specifically the Hatedemics platform and the educational toolkit, can be integrated into educational process to promote critical thinking and media literacy.

2 Project Overview and Partnership

Hatedemics is a two-year project supported by the European Commission under the CERV programme. The Hatedemics consortium consists of 13 partners, among which research centres, NGOs, factchecking organisations, and public institutions from Italy, Malta, Poland, Spain, Estonia, and France. The involvement of both NGOs and factchecking organisations is a part of the project's approach to strengthen the preventive and reactive measures against hate speech and disinformation online.

The project aims to empower NGOs/CSOs, factcheckers, public authorities and youngsters as activists to effectively prevent and combat polarisation, the spread of racist, xenophobic and intolerant speech, as well as conspiracy theories. Its primary objective is to address online hate and fake news, with a specific emphasis on tackling the often overlooked and interrelated issues that intersect between hate speech and disinformation.

The project's goal is to raise awareness and improve skills and critical thinking by advancing AI-based technologies that monitor, detect and record hate speech and disinformation on social media, create dialogue-based counter-narratives that support professionals and activists and facilitate advanced reporting activities by implementing an effective human-in-the-loop approach, whereby automated suggestions are always validated by human operators, who always have the final say on the posted content, and automatically assess behavioural changes determined by the counter-narrative intervention. The combination of these technologies allows for more focused and timely online interventions (i.e. advanced targeted search followed by relevant textual suggestions), resulting in a more efficient and effective professional and volunteer effort. This approach is based on maintaining fairness and balance and ensuring adherence to legal and ethical standards.

The project hence focuses on the development of the Hatedemics Platform, as well as design and deployment of interactive training and educational paths, informed by a commitment to EU values and rights in order to raise awareness and foster the active participation of EU-27 citizens.

In the educational contexts, Hatedemics provides educators with a possibility to integrate digital literacy training and counter-narrative creation into their curricula by providing innovative, tested and open-access tools. Hatedemics unites technological innovation with human-rights and factchecking based educational approach to foster digital literacy and civic engagement, particularly among young people and educators in both formal and non-formal educational settings.

3 Methodology

3.1 Research Design

The Hatedemics project adopts a mixed-method methodological framework designed to ensure that the platform and educational toolkit respond to real challenges and needs across cultural and linguistic contexts.

In the first stage of the project the consortium focused on data collection with a specific focus on qualitative methods. Within the framework of the project, qualitative research played a fundamental role in understanding the complexities, diversity of perspectives, and nuances of the human experience.

Hence, focus groups and semi-structured interviews were chosen as essential techniques for collecting meaningful, profound, and contextualised data on social phenomena. They were identified due to the necessity to delve into individual experiences and perceptions, contextualise social phenomena and shared approaches, identify underlying factors and mechanisms of the spread of online hate speech, as well as disinformation policies, practices and technological infrastructure, and, subsequently, generate knowledge focused on action and amplify the voices of marginalized groups and the experiences of vulnerable minorities. Partners conducted two focus groups in each of the four pilot countries (Italy, Spain, Poland and Malta) – one online and one offline.

Focus groups were conducted in order to collect in-depth qualitative data on experiences, challenges, and perceptions related to hate speech, misinformation, and conspiracy theories. Each pilot leader invited from 4 to 8 participants representing NGOs/CSOs, journalists, fact-checkers and educators. A semi-structured discussion guide assured coherence across sessions that lasted from 1,5 to 2 h (both online and offline).

Semi-structured expert interviews complemented the data collection process and allowed for a deeper exploration of the participants' professional experiences and challenges they shared. Interviews lasted between 60 to 90 min and were held in-person or online. Each of the pilot leaders conducted at least 3 in-depth interviews with educators, policy makers, academics etc.

During the next stage, the partners held co-creation workshops in the four pilot countries. They were conducted as participatory, online sessions aimed at creating a fruitful discussion to explore and co-design educational applications for the Hatedemics platform. The workshops aimed at assessing the pedagogical potential of the Hatedemics platform within diverse educational contexts, and generating practical pedagogical applications to inform the development of an educational toolkit addressing hate speech and disinformation. Each workshop brought together 10–15 participants from different professional backgrounds – educators in both formal and non-formal education, media literacy experts, representatives of NGOs/CSOs etc. The sessions that were held online, lasted over 2 h and used a collaborative Figma board that served as a digital workspace for brainstorming, exchange of ideas, and feedback.

This preparatory phase ensured the usability of both of the main project products – the Hatedemics platform and the educational toolkit - across cultural and linguistic contexts and gathered innovative educational solutions (for e.g., joint learning path-ways for students and parents to analyse disinformation and hate speech narratives using the platform collaboratively).

Hence the platform and the toolkit address both the needs of educators working with young people, as well as those of NGO/CSO operators, media professionals, public authorities, and young activists, as it allows them to monitor and analyse online content (by mapping Telegram channels), identify potential threats, and generate context-sensitive counter speech.

3.2 Participants

At the present stage (1, 5 years after the beginning of the project) the project engaged approximately 180 participants across its focus groups, interviews, co-creation workshops and first stage of pilot activities, divided into main stakeholder categories:

- NGOs/CSOs representatives;
- journalists;
- factcheckers;
- educators;
- policy makers;
- researchers and academics;
- young activists.

The project also actively engages wider public via social media, projects website, policy webinars, conferences and in the future – through a social media campaign that will use the video footage and interviews conducted during the second stage of the piloting and workshops.

3.3 Data Analysis and Ethical Considerations

Qualitative data were analysed separately by each pilot leader. They then prepared national reports that later were analysed and used by the work package leader in the preparation of the general report. They analysed the videos, recordings and transcripts of the interviews and focus-groups to identify recurrent themes, challenges, suggestions of good practices and other groups of content that derived from the discussions and interviews.

The data and preliminary results, that derive from the first stage of piloting, focused on participants' perceptions of hate speech persistency and patterns, both online and offline, challenges in media literacy education, and expectations toward AI-based interventions such as Hatedemics platform.

The project embeds legal, ethical, and gender-sensitive assessments, complying with the EU AI Act (European Commission, 2024), and is focused on cross-sector cooperation between NGOs/CSOs, universities, media, and public institutions, as recommended by the Council of Europe's Recommendation CM/Rec (2022)16 (Council of Europe, 2022).

All research activities complied with the EU General Data Protection Regulation (GDPR) and were reviewed by the lead of the ethics-focused work package. Informed consent was obtained from all participants of all research activities.

4 Research Activities in Italy: Main Findings and Outcomes

The research conducted within the framework of the Hatedemics project in Italy, consisted of two focus groups (one online, one offline), five in-depth interviews and a co-creation workshop, that took place online, via Zoom platform. The findings from these activities hence informed the future stages of the project, particularly the approaches to the development of the Hatedemics platform and conceptualisation and creation of the participatory educational toolkit.

The co-creation workshop focused on the planning of the educational activities, that will be discussed in the chap. 6. This chapter will discuss only the preliminary results, deriving from both focus groups and interviews.

4.1 Focus Groups

The focus groups in Italy were organised from July to September of 2024. Due to vacation period and the beginning of the academic year in Italy, as well as experts' conflicting schedules they were separated in time by about 2 months.

The offline or face-to- face focus group was held in in Palermo in the beginning of July with the participation of four experts: representatives of academia and civil society organisation, working on the project related to the topics of the research and/or directly with the target. The online focus group was held online via Zoom in the first part of September 2024. 4 participants took part: academics, OSINT analysts, journalists and experts on the topics. All of the research activities were recorded and transcribed in Italian to ensure the accuracy of the interpretation of data. Following transcription, they were analysed in order to identify the answers to the key questions, group key patterns, themes, and insights that aligned with the research objectives.

The results of these focus groups shows the following tendencies.

The participants defined hate speech as expression that incites violence or call for discrimination against certain groups of people (often those already marginalised and/or vulnerable). Many stated that it can be a powerful tool for spreading harmful narratives, propaganda and conspiracy theories.

Many of the respondents work in fields where they have direct exposure to hate speech (journalism, education, human rights and civil society activism). They not only encounter hate speech in their daily work and have to deal with its consequences (specifically when working on social issues, such as migration, equality and diversity, and/or with vulnerable groups), but many of them at certain points also became the targets of hate speech themselves.

A number of participants stated that online disinformation on social and political issues creates challenges for them in their everyday work. It affect people with whom they work, make their day-to-day activities (in education, journalism, youth works etc.), much more difficult. The same is true for conspiracy theories, especially those regarding people with migrant background, religious groups, women etc.

When asked about the groups, most affected by these phenomena, the participants named people with migrant background, refugees, women, and representatives of the LGBTQIA+ community, as well as representatives of religious minorities. Majority of the participants stated that there are certain groups who are more susceptive and vulnerable to the effects of hate speech, disinformation and conspiracy theories, hence more likely to disseminate and spread these narratives. One of the distinctive factors identified by the participants were elderly people who might have lower media literacy skills and youngsters, who are more vulnerable to extremist ideologies and propaganda.

The participants discussed the Italian legal framework on hate speech and disinformation, particularly online, and expressed their dissatisfaction with the current state of things compared to the legal frameworks of other EU states. They paid specific attention to the failure of the DDL Zan bill that was aimed at protecting groups targeted by hate, based on gender, gender identity, sexual orientation and disability, and the lack of an alternative.

The participants identified educational programs and media literacy campaigns as the activities that bring the most results in raising awareness on hate speech and disinformation, especially in schools and among young people, and enhancing critical thinking and fact-checking skills. When asked about the potential providers of such programmes and campaigns, the participants named NGOs/CSOs (by themselves of in collaboration with various educational institutions) and local governments.

In terms of specific educational approaches and methodologies, the participants named activities, aimed at recognising hate speech and disinformation; programs focused on non-violent communication and media literacy; open discussions in classrooms and communities to raise awareness; various reporting mechanisms and collaboration with social media platforms to remove harmful content. They also stated that co-creation and multi-stakeholder approaches are essential for the success of these initiatives.

The participants also stated that, while working on prevention strategies, it is important to find a balance between combating hate speech and disinformation and protecting free speech. At the same time, according to some of the participants, right-wing parties are more likely to focus on defending free speech over taking measures against hate speech, while civil society and left-wing parties more often focus on advocacy for stronger regulations of social media platforms and against hate speech.

When asked about AI-based tools for detecting hate speech on social media, the participants were aware of certain ones, but stated that not all of them are effective. Among common limitations they named lack of context awareness and nuance, ineffectiveness of removal based on key words, false positives/negatives, and lacking "sense of humour" or a possibility to understand sarcasm and jokes. Some of the participants work with AI/based OSINT tools that they use primarily for monitoring. They confirmed that human oversight is necessary and essential for data collection as they have a number of limits, discussed above. Among useful data that can be collected by these tools, are: frequency with which the key words are used, geographical mapping, day-to day overview and other statistical data useful for research.

Among potential functionalities and applications of the Hatedemics platform, participants named recognising hate speech in different languages and cultural contexts, at the same time distinguishing between hate speech and legitimate content. They also expressed interest in a plug-in that would be able to verify information on web pages and link to the proofs, or, otherwise, signalise that the proof is missing hence the information cannot be considered reliable. Amng the potential users, the respondents named educators, NGO operators, schools, other educational institutions and governmental agencies.

When shown the platform prototype, the participants from both focus groups expressed interest in its potential use. They stated that it can have a number of applications both in education and in combating hate speech and disinformation on online platforms. They appreciated the approach to the creation of counter narratives, specifically for working with the youth, and many of them said that it can be integrated into media literacy programs focused on hate speech, disinformation, and responsible online communication. At the same time, they expressed some concerns, specifically about the time of response (how fast the platform will work, how fast the answers will be generated and how the proposed results will vary) and its possible limitation in non-English-speaking environments.

Participants proposed several improvements for the next iteration of the platform, such as making it faster and more responsive, as well as working on localisation and adaptation it to different linguistic and cultural contexts. This, in their opinion, can make it extremely useful not only for educational purposes, but also for debunking and verifying information in real time.

4.2 Interviews

The interviews in Italy took place from July to September 2024. The researchers paid attention to the interviewees' profiles in order to involve as wide range of experts as possible.

A total of 5 in-depth expert interviews were conducted. All of the interviews were held via Zoom. All of the research activities were recorded and transcribed in Italian to ensure the accuracy of the interpretation of data. Following transcription, they were analysed in order to identify the answers to the key questions, group key patterns, themes, and insights that aligned with the research objectives.

The results of these interviews shows the following tendencies.

Participants defined as expressions that incite hatred or violence towards people or groups of people based on their identity factors. All of them are engaged in educational, research and/or advocacy work focused on hate speech and disinformation with youth as the target of their work activities.

All of the interviewees stressed the role of media literacy in empowering youth to combat hate speech and disinformation, the importance of foster critical thinking and resistance against manipulations. One of them stated that it's much more complex than just "giving them smartphones and thinking that they know how to use them better, because they don't".

All of the interviewees agree that conspiracy theories can escalate the levels of hate and disinformation both on- and offline. As some of the examples, they named conspiracies like moon landing denial, Pizzagate and antisemitic conspiracies.

Among those targeted more often they named groups that are in vulnerable/disadvantaged positions in Italy, such as women (also in politics), LGBTQIA+ community, ethnic and/or religious minorities. Youth and marginalised groups were named as the most vulnerable to spread hateful or unverified narratives, specifically adolescents who heavily rely on social media, as well as socially and culturally disadvantaged groups. All of the participants stated the importance of media literacy to protect vulnerable populations, including older people and individuals without digital literacy competences from spreading these narratives.

Participants were all aware of European legislative measures against hate speech and disinformation, particularly the Council of Europe's frameworks, Digital Services Act and Code of Conduct. However, like focus groups' participants, they expressed frustration about the lack of national legislation in Italy that has crucial gaps regarding hate speech and disinformation.

When asked about effective tools and programmes, the interviewees named educational programs focused on media literacy ad critical thinking, online platforms, and especially - trainings for educators. In particular, they gave examples of international and EU projects under Erasmus+ and CERV programmes, such as COMMIT; debunking and pre-bunking activities; European Observatory of Online Hate (EOOH) and European media observatory that monitors disinformation (EDMO).

Majority of the interviewees expressed concerns about balancing freedom of speech with the need to report and remove hate speech, disinformation, misinformation, malinformation and conspiracy theories from online spaces. Many of them spoke the need for clearer algorithms, better legal framework and punitive measures, specifically for platforms and accounts that spread harmful narratives.

The interviewees confirmed that they use AI-based tools for monitoring hate speech and disinformation trends on social media platforms and expressed interest to use new tools in the future. At the same time, major part of the interviewees also spoke about their concerns about limitations and bias of such tools (reliance on human verification, etc.). Some of the respondents were sceptical while speaking about AI tools created with smaller budgets and in the framework of EU-funded projects, as, in their opinion, they can never be as functional as "for-profit" tools that are taught with big data and are constantly funded. Participants were interested in the use of AI in addressing hate speech, specifically in educational approaches, detection, and possibly even design of counter-speech campaigns. Hence, they appreciated the demonstration of the Hatedemics platform prototype.

Among the potential applications and functionalities of the platform, they named its ability to simulate hate speech conversations for educational purposes, that can be used for training of young people and professionals. They expressed that this functionality can be very useful for youth workers, educators, advocacy groups and policy makers.

5 The Hatedemics Platform

The Hatedemics platform represents the core of the Hatedemics project. It's an AI-driven digital platform that allows the researcher to detect and analyse data from scraped Telegram channels, and provides multilingual counter speech suggestions based on fact-checked and human rights-oriented content in English, Italian, Spanish, Polish and Maltese.

Informed by the results of the preliminary research, that was discussed above, it's main functionalities include:

- a possibility for content monitoring and mapping of public Telegram channels to identify patterns of hate speech, disinformation, and conspiracy theories, key words used, as well as the connections between he channels that disseminate these narratives;
- multilingual counter-speech generation that allows students to have an experience of a simulated conversation with a person that spreads have speech, disinformation and conspiracy theories, and learn to respond to them in English, Italian, Maltese, Polish, and Spanish, with adaptation to local cultural and linguistic context;
- educational interface that provides a number of educational activities focused on hate speech and disinformation.

Conceptualised on the basis of the data collected during the research stage, and annotated by native speakers from project countries, it has can be used both by researchers and educators, as it provides valuable data and serves not only for educational purposes but also as a research tool for studying online hate speech, disinformation and conspiracy theories in Europe.

6 Educational Toolkit

The Hatedemics educational toolkit was conceptualised and developed by partners as a pedagogical complement to the Hatedemics AI-driven platform, turning the technological innovation approach into easy-to-use classroom-friendly materials. It is a practical and pedagogical resource designed to empower educators, youth workers, civil society actors, and public institutions to respond to hate speech and disinformation. The toolkit builds upon the conducted research and co-creation workshops, during which the participants had a chance to propose certain activities that they themselves found effective and discuss them in small groups.

The toolkit's aim is to strengthen educators' and young people's capacities against the spread of hate speech, disinformation and conspiratorial content. Designed for educators, teachers, trainers, NGOs, and local authorities, it provides both definitions and theoretical part, and easy-to-use activities that can help young people recognise and respond to hate and manipulations online.

The first part of the toolkit introduces the key concepts of hate speech, disinformation, and their intersectionality. These sections clarify terminology and clarify the role of stereotypes and scapegoating in the spread on harmful narratives, manipulations and propaganda. The inclusion of logical fallacies and cognitive biases offers educators and other potential users more information on the potential of critical thinking and media literacy for prevention and counteraction.

The second part focuses on practical responses. It is focused on the importance of education, thoughtful reaction and solidarity while dealing with these phenomena online. The toolkit offers strategies that allow to respond to harmful content through calm and respectful counter- and alternative narratives that promote empathy and inclusion. The approach is human-centric, urging users to engage with respect, remain calm and focus on messages rather than emotions or individuals. The main idea is that reacting to hate speech is not simply an act of confrontation, but is an action focused on care and civic responsibility in order to help to create safer, more respectful digital spaces. The toolkit merges these approaches with broader aims of media and information literacy in order to train young people to be thoughtful creators and users of media, capable of thinking critically, identifying manipulation, verifying information and verifying sources. It proposes various methods used by professional fact-checkers, for e.g. lateral reading (to learn to question authorship, intent and credibility), in order to further strengthen learners' ability to deconstruct narratives and evaluate evidence.

The third section contains a series of educational activities developed through co-creation workshops. Some of these activities are "Spot the Hate Speech!" and "Spot the Counter Narrative". These exercised are aimed to focus on understanding and combine learning with critical analysis to encourage discussion and thoughtful empathetic approach. Each activity is supported by detailed instructions, debriefing questions, and safety guidelines as both educators and students are dealing with difficult subjects can be triggering.

In a nutshell, the Hatedemics Educational Toolkit is a bridge between technology and practice, and a practical guide, complimenting the Hatedemics platform. It translates data and analysis into educational activities and provides teachers, activists and young citizens with practical tools to strengthen resilience against manipulation and focus on a culture of dialogue, inclusion and respect.

7 Implications for Higher Education

The findings and tools, developed within the framework of the Hatedemics project and based on the preliminary results deriving from its activities, have significant implications for education, specifically higher education. As the project overall is focused on raising awareness about the phenomena of hate speech, disinformation and conspiracy theories, one of its goals is to address the existing educational programmes, both in formal and non-formal education. While addressing these phenomena, it is crucial to address the way universities and educational institutions in general prepare future educators and journalists to navigate digital spaces.

Both the Hatedemics platform and educational toolkit provide useful tools and guidelines that allow educators to integrate AI-driven instruments and human-rights-based educational approaches within academic programmes.

The Hatedemics platform can be used not only as a research tool to analyse online hate speech and disinformation, but also as an interactive educational resource that allows students to simulate conversations, create counter-narratives and learn how to reply to harmful narratives in a calm and respectful way. At the same time, by analysing the data collected from public channels on Telegram, students and educators can get a better understanding of how digital ecosystems shape opinions and how harmful narrative spread through fringe platforms.

For educators in higher education institutions, these resources offer a possibility to integrate new approaches into traditional teaching practices. Instead of approaching hate speech and disinformation mainly as topics of discussion, the Hatedemics tools give students a possibility to become active investigators, counter-narrative creators and communicators. In a number of disciplines, such as media and communication, political science, psychology, sociology and education, the Hatedemics platform can be used as a tool for participatory assignments. Students can analyse online narratives, identify manipulation techniques, critically assess them and design counter-narratives.

The Hatedemics educational toolkit, with its emphasis on empathy and human-centred approach, can be used in higher education and contribute to the development of critical thinking and media literacy skills as well. The activities and exercises that are proposed in the toolkit (for e.g. "Recognising hate speech", "Analysing logical fallacies", and constructing alternative narratives), can be integrated into a number of courses, such as media ethics, intercultural communication, teacher education.

In terms of approaches, adopted by the Hatedemics project, that can be successfully integrated into the higher education, there is also a possibility to adopt co-creation as pedagogical practice. This approach can redefine teacher–student relationship, improve engagement and enrich curriculums. This participatory approach also resonates with the concept of transformative higher education, which emphasise student partnership, diversity, and social impact. The project's co-creational workshops, focus groups and interviews revealed that when students act as co-creators rather than passive recipients, of knowledge their engagement and interest in a subject increase significantly.

The tools developed in the framework of the project have applications for teacher professional development as well. It allows educators to enhance their confidence in addressing sensitive topics, integrating AI tools into their classrooms and co-create parts of their curricula together with their students.

8 Conclusion

The Hatedemics project's preliminary findings confirm that the phenomena of hate speech and disinformation are not isolated but interconnected and mutually reinforcing. They rely on emotional manipulation and fear and thrive in situations where digital literacy skills are lacking. The Hatedemics platform and educational toolkit address these issues in complementary ways – the one by enabling monitoring and counter narrative simulations through AI, the other by providing educators and learners with the activities and guidance focused on enhancing their knowledge and skills on the topic. This dual technological and pedagogical approach derives from the project's human-centred methodology.

From an educational perspective, Hatedemics allows for integrating media literacy, critical thinking, and awareness into formal and non-formal learning. Higher education institutions have a crucial role in mainstreaming these competences within curricula across various disciplines - from media studies and education to political and computer science. The project's approaches align with the broader vision of universities as spaces not only for learning, but also for cultivating active and responsible citizenship.

In a nutshell, the Hatedemics project and its developments show that combating online hate speech and disinformation requires more than detection. It requires education, dialogue, and empathy. By turning technology into an opportunity for learning, the project contributes to building digital spaces where knowledge, respect, and responsibility can prevail over manipulation and hate.

Disclosure of Interests. The author has no competing interests to declare that are relevant to the content of this article.

References

1. Council of Europe: Recommendation CM/Rec(2022)16 on combating hate speech (2022). https://www.coe.int/en/web/combating-hate-speech/recommendation-on-combating-hate-speech
2. European Commission: Proposal for a Regulation Laying Down Harmonised Rules on Artificial Intelligence (AI Act) (2024). https://eur-lex.europa.eu/eli/reg/2024/1689/oj/eng
3. European Commission: EU Code of Conduct+ on Countering Illegal Hate Speech Online (2025). https://commission.europa.eu/strategy-and-policy/policies/justice-and-fundamental-rights/combatting-discrimination/racism-and-xenophobia/eu-code-conduct-countering-illegal-hate-speech-online_en
4. Farkas, J., Neumayer, C.: Post-Truth, Fake News and Democracy: Mapping the Politics of Falsehood. Routledge (2021)
5. Gagliardone, I., Gal, D., Alves, T., Martinez, G.: Countering Online Hate Speech. UNESCO (2015)

6. Heller, B.: Enlisting useful idiots: the ties between online harassment and disinformation. Colo. Tech. Law J. **19**, 19 (2021)
7. Marwick, A., Lewis, R.: Media Manipulation and Disinformation Online. Data & Society Research Institute, New York (2017)
8. Önnerfors, A.: Conspiracy Theories and COVID-19: the Mechanisms behind a Rapidly Growing Societal Challenge (2021)
9. Secretary-General of the United Nations: At UN / Press Freedom Covid-19 (2021). https://media.un.org/avlibrary/en/asset/d261/d2615719
10. Young, D.G., Jamieson, K.H., Poulsen, S., Goldring, A.: fact-checking effectiveness as a function of format and tone: evaluating FactCheck.org and FlackCheck.org. Journalism Mass Commun. Q. 95(1), 49–75 (2018)

Countering Online Hate in Higher Education: Monitoring, Critical Digital Literacy, and Pedagogical Innovation

Federico Faloppa[1], Andrea Borruso[2], Nannerel Fiano[3], Giovanni Fulantelli[2](✉), Andrea Nelson Mauro[2], Stefano Pasta[4], and Davide Taibi[2]

[1] University of Reading, Reading, UK
f.faloppa@reading.ac.uk
[2] National Research Council of Italy, Institute for Educational Technology, Palermo, Italy
{andrea.borruso,giovanni.fulantelli,andrea.nelson.mauro, davide.taibi}@cnr.it
[3] Università degli Studi di Milano, Milan, Italy
nannerel.fiano@unimi.it
[4] Catholic University of the Sacred Heart, Milan, Italy
stefano.pasta@unicatt.it

Abstract. Digital platforms have become key environments for the emergence, amplification, and normalization of online hate speech, with major implications for democratic participation, social cohesion, and the protection of fundamental rights. Higher Education institutions are increasingly called upon to address these challenges by integrating socio-technical inquiry, critical digital literacies, and pedagogical practices that foster responsible and inclusive digital citizenship. This paper proposes a multi-layered perspective on the prevention and interpretation of online hate speech based on three complementary case studies: (1) large-scale monitoring of online hate through the *Mappa dell'Intolleranza* (*Map of Intolerance*) project; (2) the use of critical digital literacy methods and open-source data pipelines within university curricula; and (3) a university e-tivity for recognizing and interpreting hostile content on TikTok within an Information Literacy course. By putting these experiences into dialogue, the paper argues that effective responses to online hate require the convergence of empirical observation, interpretative competencies, and pedagogical innovation. The study contributes to current debates on the role of universities in promoting democratic, ethical, and rights-based digital environments.

Keywords: hate speech · higher education · digital literacy · media education · online platforms

1 Introduction

The widespread diffusion of digital platforms has profoundly transformed communicative practices and the processes through which opinions, emotions, and conflicts circulate in the public sphere. As highlighted by numerous studies on algorithmic cultures, the

M. Adamoli et al. (Eds.): HELMeTO 2025, CCIS 2958, pp. 234–245, 2026.
https://doi.org/10.1007/978-3-032-31850-3_15

growing centrality of platforms concerns not only technical mediation but also directly shapes forms of participation, cognitive dynamics, and collective representations that guide public debate [1–3]. Within this ecosystem, phenomena such as polarization, algorithmic personalization, virality, and discursive fragmentation provide fertile ground for the emergence and amplification of various forms of hostility, including online hate speech, which is recognized as one of the major social and educational challenges of our time [4, 5].

Yet hate speech remains a concept marked by definitional ambiguity. It is increasingly understood as a continuum of practices ranging from stereotypes and symbolic exclusion to explicit incitement to violence [6]. Legal, sociological, linguistic, and pedagogical traditions emphasize different aspects of the phenomenon, making it difficult to identify a single exhaustive definition. Contemporary scholarship increasingly describes hate speech as a continuum ranging from stereotypes, symbolic exclusion, and coded hostility to explicit threats and incitement to violence [7].

Online hate speech has become one of the defining tensions of contemporary platform societies. While digital media have expanded opportunities for participation, expression, and community-building, they have also intensified visibility, virality, and the rapid circulation of discriminatory narratives. Hate phenomena today are shaped not only by individual prejudice but also by algorithmic amplification, platform incentives, and polarized communicative cultures. Moreover, hostility in digital environments is not limited to overt insults. It often circulates through irony, memes, dog whistles, dehumanizing metaphors, recurring stereotypes, and coordinated communicative practices that are more difficult to detect through conventional moderation systems [7].

Recent literature confirms the multidimensional complexity of online hate. Santerini [8] and Brena [9] emphasize the cultural and cognitive roots of hostile behaviors, while empirical and interdisciplinary research on platforms shows how hate is influenced by factors such as stereotypes, group dynamics, disinformation, and echo-chamber processes [10]. This complexity is further compounded by the definitional ambiguity of the concept of hate speech itself: according to Pasta [11], it is an "ambiguous but useful" category, as also confirmed by the author's studies on automated detection systems [3], which highlight the difficulties in distinguishing between hostility, conflict, polarization, and genuinely discriminatory content.

Platform studies show that hate phenomena are deeply intertwined with digital infrastructures. Recommendation systems, engagement metrics, and moderation policies shape visibility and amplification [2, 12]. Automated detection systems also present limits, especially when dealing with irony, coded language, and contextual meanings [3]. In the social web various forms of hate speech and flame wars (flaming) are experienced, amplified, and sometimes countered. These flame wars are marked by the violent polarization of viewpoints, where personal attacks overshadow the content of debates, diverting attention from the issue at hand [13].

The effects of online hate are equally multidimensional. Beyond harms suffered by direct targets, repeated exposure to hostile discourse may discourage participation, normalize intolerance, and reduce the quality of democratic debate in digital public spheres [7].

In response to this complexity, there is a growing need to develop integrated approaches that combine the socio-technical dimension of digital media, the protection of fundamental rights, the promotion of critical and participatory competencies, and the design of inclusive and reflective educational spaces. For this reason, effective responses cannot rely on legal sanctions alone, but require coordinated interventions involving education, platform governance, critical literacy, and broader cultural change. Media literacy frameworks, critical digital pedagogy, and data epistemologies therefore provide an integrated theoretical foundation for educational responses to online hate.

Higher Education occupies a strategic position in this context, as young adults and university students increasingly rely on digital platforms for information, learning, identity construction, and civic participation. Universities not only educate citizens and professionals capable of understanding the media ecosystem, but also act as cultural and democratic actors with a responsibility to promote more equitable, inclusive, and rights-based digital environments.

As emphasized by Mihailidis and Thevenin [14] and UNESCO [15], media and information literacy is now an essential civic competence, indispensable for democratic participation.

The three case studies presented in this paper provide a concrete and multi-perspective illustration of how Higher Education can respond to the challenges posed by hate speech through complementary, situated, and multidisciplinary approaches. Each case study focuses on a different level of intervention: socio-technical and policy analysis; the development of literacy and critical tools; and innovative pedagogical practices and teaching activities.

The first case concerns the Mappa dell'Intolleranza project, which combines legal, sociological, and computational expertise to analyze large-scale manifestations of hate on X/Twitter, integrating data analysis methods, geolocation, and advanced NLP techniques based on large language models [16]. The project highlights emerging trends such as the intersectionality of hate, the relationship between stereotypes and virality, the role of major urban centers, and the importance of understanding the cultural dimension of the phenomenon beyond a purely normative perspective [17–19].

The second case study focuses on the need to develop Critical Digital Literacy skills, in line with critical digital pedagogy approaches [20, 21] and studies on data epistemologies [22]. It is closed related to recent interdisciplinary inquiries into the evolving relationship between media trust, journalistic authority, and AI-driven content curation within platform-based media ecosystems, which highlight the urgent need to reframe algorithmic systems not only as technical infrastructures but as cultural and epistemic forces [23]. Through the use of open-source tools and data pipelines, students learn to investigate the informational architecture of platforms and to recognize phenomena such as representational bias, misinformation, polarization, and forms of hate speech.

The third case presents a university e-tivity aimed at identifying and interpreting hostile content on TikTok in the context of the Israel–Palestine war. By applying the interpretative framework Online Hate Spectrum [24], students learn to distinguish different levels of hostility, moving beyond simplified dichotomies (hate/no hate). The activity integrates individual analysis and collaborative discussion, fostering critical sensitivity and socio-media awareness

2 The *Mappa dell'Intolleranza* Project

2.1 Project: Background, Latest Edition, and Research Developments

The *Mappa dell'Intolleranza* (*Map of Intolerance*) project, originally conceived by Vox -Italian Observatory on Rights [25], in collaboration with the University of Milan (department of Italian and Supranational Public Law), the University of Bari "Aldo Moro", the Catholic University of Milan (department of Sociology, ITSTIME), and the University of Rome La Sapienza, aims to map online hate on social media, particularly on X (formerly Twitter). Now in its ninth edition, the project seeks to provide a tool for understanding the dynamics of online hate, to foster theoretical reflection on hate speech and the phenomenology of hatred, and to develop effective prevention initiatives through applied research.

The eighth and most recent edition of the project analysed the spread of online hate speech through the extraction and geolocation of posts on X containing sensitive keywords. This edition was supported by the first three institutions listed above, which originally gave rise to the project, and involved new partners and research teams, including two additional units from the University of Milan, the Giovanni Degli Antoni Department of Computer Science and the Human Hall research centre, as well as The Fool, a leading Italian company in the field of digital intelligence.

As in previous editions, posts were classified into six categories: misogyny, antisemitism, Islamophobia, xenophobia, ableism, and homo-transphobia [26]. This edition also employed large language models (LLMs) to identify the impact of negative stereotypes on the formation and dissemination of hate speech. In addition to examining how hate manifests itself across different Italian cities and affects the six target categories, the analysis also explored the viral potential of discriminatory discourse on social media.

2.2 Project Results

Regarding the scale of hate-related phenomena, data collected between January and November 2024 show a significant increase in antisemitism, together with a rise in xenophobia and Islamophobia. Women account for 50% of those targeted by hate speech. In the case of misogyny, 20.81% of discriminatory content is produced by women themselves, suggesting forms of self-objectification. This new edition of the Map also made it possible to examine the role of intersectionality, which is becoming increasingly relevant in anti-discrimination policy studies.

From a geolocation perspective, the analysis confirms a higher incidence of hate speech in large cities: Milan stands out for misogyny and xenophobia, while Rome stands out for antisemitism and homo-transphobia.

For the first time, the project also focuses on the relationship between hate speech and stereotypes. The latest edition of the Map of Intolerance sheds light on both the definitions of hate speech and stereotypical language, as well as on the legal and cultural tools that can be deployed in response, thereby encouraging reflection on the Council of Europe Recommendation CM/Rec(2022)16.

2.3 Emerging Trends and Future Challenges: Legal, Educational, and Socio-Technical Implications

The latest edition of the Map of Intolerance highlights several significant trends that contribute to a deeper understanding of the evolving nature of online hate speech. Firstly, the findings confirm the central role of echo chambers within social media environments. Platform dynamics often expose users to homogeneous viewpoints and emotionally reinforcing content, thereby intensifying polarization and facilitating the circulation of hostile narratives among like-minded communities. In such contexts, hate speech can become normalized, amplified, and socially legitimized. Secondly, the analysis underscores the impact of negative stereotypes and, more broadly, of entrenched cultural configurations, on the production and dissemination of hate speech. Prejudices linked to gender, ethnicity, religion, disability, or sexual orientation continue to provide symbolic frameworks through which discriminatory discourse is articulated and reproduced online. This suggests that hate speech should not be interpreted solely as an individual communicative act, but also as an expression of wider cultural and social structures.

A further relevant trend concerns the growing verticalization of online hate. Rather than taking the form of generic hostility, hate speech increasingly targets specific groups through specialized narratives, symbols, and communicative codes. This process makes discriminatory discourse more adaptable, recognizable within particular online communities, and potentially more difficult to identify through conventional moderation systems.

These findings point to the need for a multidimensional response. Greater attention should be devoted to the relationship between stereotypes and hate speech, especially in order to understand how cultural representations feed discriminatory communication. In addition, intersectional discrimination must be taken into account, as multiple identity factors may overlap in shaping vulnerability and exposure to online hostility.

The results of the Map provide further insights from a legal perspective: the results suggest the need to reflect on new tools capable of addressing hate speech beyond the limits of existing laws and regulatory frameworks. In rapidly evolving digital environments, traditional legal categories often struggle to respond effectively to emerging forms of platform-mediated harm.

Educational strategies are equally crucial. Counter-narratives, critical media literacy, and responsible uses of social networks should be promoted in order to prevent increasingly radical forms of hate. In this regard, the project has already generated practical educational outcomes, including work-experience activities aimed at teaching young people how to use social media responsibly and critically.

Finally, the mapping also calls for renewed reflection on the relationship between the protection of individual rights and technological innovation, particularly in light of the growing use of Artificial Intelligence in content moderation, recommendation systems, and automated decision-making. Balancing innovation, freedom of expression, and the protection of vulnerable groups will remain one of the key challenges for future research and policy.

2.4 Academic Impact and Public Engagement of the Project

With regard to the academic context, the Map of Intolerance project has also generated significant value as a tool for teaching, research, and public engagement. The project was presented at the University of Milan to audiences including students, academic staff, and representatives of civil society, thereby fostering dialogue between the university and the wider community on the social, legal, and cultural implications of online hate speech. In this sense, the initiative functioned not only as a research project, but also as a platform for knowledge transfer and civic awareness.

Within the university environment, students had the opportunity to engage with the project during lectures and seminars focused on the protection of fundamental rights, digital citizenship, and the challenges posed by platform societies. By discussing empirical data, methodological approaches, and regulatory issues emerging from the project, students were able to connect theoretical concepts with contemporary social phenomena.

The project also served as a valuable resource for students undertaking dissertations and thesis work related to constitutional rights, anti-discrimination policies, media regulation, and online hate speech. Access to the project's framework and findings enabled students to develop research grounded in real-world data and current public debates, strengthening both their analytical skills and their awareness of the relationship between law, technology, and society.

3 Critical Digital Literacy in Higher Education through the TASKs Project: Methods, Tools and Educational Perspectives

3.1 From the TASKs Research Experience to Critical Digital Literacy

In the current platformized media ecosystem, where algorithms shape visibility, attention, and information flows, critical digital literacy can no longer be understood solely as the ability to evaluate sources or recognize misinformation. It increasingly requires the capacity to understand how digital infrastructures operate, how data are generated and organized, and how platforms influence public discourse through metrics, recommendation systems, and interaction architectures. These competencies are particularly relevant in higher education, especially in programs related to media studies, journalism, communication, digital humanities, and teacher education. From a pedagogical perspective, project-based learning, inquiry-based learning, and experiential approaches are particularly suitable for developing such competencies, as they engage students with authentic socio-technical problems.

Within this perspective, the experience developed through the TASKs project (*Trust, Authority, Sense and Knowledge*) offers a valuable case study. TASKs investigated media trust and journalistic authority in contemporary digital environments through an integrated approach combining production, content, and audience dimensions. Alongside interviews and survey research, the project developed a digital methods infrastructure capable of collecting and analysing large-scale data from online platforms and news environments.

One of the most significant outcomes of TASKs was the design of a modular system for the systematic monitoring of content from multiple sources, including YouTube,

Instagram, TikTok, and RSS feeds. The main objective was to collect, normalize, document, and archive structured data for longitudinal and comparative analysis. The system was based on reproducible *ETL* (*Extract, Transform, Load*) pipelines and relied on open-source tools such as Miller, jq, DuckDB, GDAL/OGR, Bash scripting, and Python-based utilities. This architecture enabled the automated harvesting of public data, the cleaning and harmonization of heterogeneous formats, and the production of datasets ready for qualitative, quantitative, or computational analysis.

3.2 Tools and Learning Applications

The TASKs infrastructure generated a substantial empirical archive, including approximately 520,000 records across multiple platforms, such as YouTube videos and comments, TikTok metadata and comments, Instagram posts, and RSS news articles. These materials can be repurposed in higher education for a wide range of teaching activities.

Beyond its scientific relevance, this infrastructure also proved to have strong educational potential. Students can directly observe how data are never "naturally given," but rather produced through a chain of methodological decisions, including source selection, API constraints, metadata availability, filtering criteria, deduplication rules, timestamping, and normalization choices. In this sense, working with digital pipelines helps students understand the epistemological dimension of data and the non-neutrality of digital methods.

Such datasets can support multiple forms of learning and inquiry. They enable students to conduct content analysis on topics, narratives, stereotypes, and communicative styles across platforms. They also allow exploration of engagement metrics, such as likes, shares, comments, and views, in order to reflect on platform logics and visibility economies. At a methodological level, students can experiment with introductory computational approaches, including sentiment analysis, topic modelling, named entity recognition, and cross-platform comparison. At the same time, these activities create opportunities to critically discuss the ethical implications of data extraction, privacy boundaries, platform governance, and methodological transparency.

In courses focused on media literacy or online hate speech, these tools are particularly valuable because they allow students to investigate how hostile narratives circulate, how stereotypes are embedded in platform discourse, and how recommendation systems may reinforce polarization. Rather than learning about these phenomena only in abstract terms, students can examine real communicative traces and understand the socio-technical conditions that shape them.

3.3 Open-Source Pedagogy, Challenges and Future Developments

A central feature of the TASKs experience lies in the use of open-source software and documented workflows. This promotes transparency, reproducibility, and skill transferability. Students are not positioned as passive users of proprietary dashboards or closed platforms, but as active learners capable of understanding and modifying research processes.

This pedagogical dimension is particularly important in higher education. Many students consume digital media daily while remaining unaware of the infrastructures that structure their online experience. Introducing open-source methods into the curriculum helps bridge this gap by making invisible systems visible. It also supports interdisciplinary dialogue, allowing students from social sciences and humanities backgrounds to engage with technical tools without reducing learning to purely instrumental skills. This is especially important for students in humanities and social science programs, who increasingly need technical and infrastructural literacy to critically interpret contemporary media systems.

Naturally, integrating such methods into university teaching also presents challenges. Technical barriers, uneven digital skills, time constraints, and platform instability must be taken into account. The TASKs project itself documented issues related to API limits, changes in platform accessibility, and the fragility of some unofficial access methods. These limitations, however, can themselves become part of the learning process, helping students reflect critically on dependency, governance, and the politics of platform access.

Future educational developments may include real-time dashboards, automated alerts, containerized learning environments, and simplified interfaces for non-technical students. More broadly, the TASKs experience demonstrates that critical digital literacy in higher education should include not only interpretation of media content, but also practical understanding of the infrastructures through which digital knowledge is produced, circulated, and contested.

4 Detection Practices of Hate Speech: A University e-tivity–Case Study

4.1 Hate Speech as an Ambiguous but Useful Category

The definitional complexity of hate speech has long been recognized in interdisciplinary scholarship [27]. Legal, sociological, linguistic, and educational approaches often emphasize different dimensions of the phenomenon, making it difficult to adopt a single, universally accepted definition. In this sense, hate speech may be considered an "ambiguous but useful" category [11]: ambiguous because its boundaries are context-dependent and historically variable, yet useful because it identifies communicative practices that target individuals or groups on the basis of identity markers and that may undermine dignity, inclusion, and democratic coexistence. This ambiguity also emerges in research employing algorithmic automation for hate speech detection [3].

This ambiguity becomes even more evident in digital environments, where hostility is frequently expressed through irony, memes, sarcasm, coded language, visual remixing, and coordinated practices of harassment rather than through explicit insults alone. Contemporary online racism often takes banalised, normalised, and apparently ordinary forms, embedded in everyday digital interaction rather than limited to overt extremist discourse [28]. The persistence of insufficient moderation systems and opaque accountability mechanisms on many platforms further complicates efforts to contain harmful narratives.

A relevant normative framework for addressing this complexity is offered by Recommendation CM/Rec(2022)16 of the Committee of Ministers of the Council of Europe (132nd session). Rather than proposing a rigid binary distinction between lawful and unlawful speech, the Recommendation conceptualises hate speech as a graduated phenomenon requiring differentiated responses.

It identifies three levels of severity (sometimes informally referred to as categories, although levels better captures their progressive nature). The first level concerns the most serious forms of hate speech that may amount to criminal offences, such as incitement to violence, serious threats, or expressions prohibited under national and international law. The second level includes harmful expressions that may not reach the criminal threshold but may justify civil, administrative, or regulatory interventions, including institutional sanctions or platform moderation. The third level concerns speech that falls outside criminal or administrative liability, yet "can nevertheless cause or amplify prejudice, intolerance and hatred, raise concerns in terms of tolerance, civility, inclusion and respect for the rights of others, and threaten social cohesion and democratic stability" [6].

This third level, which we might refer to as the 'citizenship' level, is especially relevant for educational contexts, since it indicates that not all harmful discourse should be approached primarily through punishment; many cases instead call for pedagogical, dialogical, and preventive responses [29].

4.2 From the Spectrum of Online Hate Indicators to a TikTok e-tivity

This perspective is coherent with the educational rationale of the university e-tivity presented here, conducted during the academic years 2023–2024 and 2024–2025 within the Information Literacy course of the Master's Degree in Media Education at the Catholic University of the Sacred Heart (Milan).

Students were not asked merely to classify content as hateful or non-hateful. Instead, they were invited to analyse videos, captions, comments, hashtags, visual rhetoric, and interaction dynamics through a multidimensional lens inspired by the *Spectrum of Online Hate Indicators*, an interpretive framework developed through research conducted by the Mediavox Observatory at the Catholic University [24]. This model proposes seven indicators that characterise online hate in increasing intensity: public visibility; targeting of a group or symbolic representative; explicit hate expression; absence of any intention to persuade or "redeem" the target; intention to harm; potential to trigger violent responses; and explicit incitement to hatred or violence. The authors emphasise that these indicators should not be interpreted as a rigid linear sequence, but as a heuristic spectrum through which different combinations of signals may reveal different degrees and forms of hostility.

Students were asked to carry out a research and recognition task focused on identifying cases online hate speech on TikTok, within the broader polarised discursive landscape of the current conflict in Palestine (diverse groups targeted). This context was selected because it combined geopolitical relevance, emotional polarisation, identity-based narratives, and strong algorithmic circulation.

Across the two editions of the activity, students collected and analysed 408 TikTok videos. The cases were examined using interpretive categories of hate speech studied during the course [28]. This process enabled students to critically engage with key phenomena such as the role of fast thinking in heuristics [2], the emergence of new authorship standards on social media, the banalisation of content in flame wars, the rhetoric linked to anonymity, the impact of the spiral of silence on social platforms, digital illiteracy, the cultural role of memes, the post-truth framework, and the concept of margin effect [10].

They examined how hostility may emerge gradually through accumulative cues such as stereotyping, scapegoating, dehumanisation, delegitimisation, exclusionary humour, conspiracy narratives, and repeated symbolic aggression. A single TikTok post may appear ambiguous in isolation, yet become clearly discriminatory when interpreted within a wider thread of comments, recurring hashtags, or platform-specific meme cultures.

4.3 Educational Outcomes

Particular pedagogical relevance emerged from borderline cases, where satire, political criticism, provocative language, or irony overlapped with identity-based hostility.

These ambiguous cases proved especially useful because they required contextual reasoning, collaborative interpretation, and ethical reflection. Students had to justify their judgments, compare perspectives, and recognise that hate speech detection cannot rely exclusively on lexical markers or automated tools. This finding aligns with the limitations identified in computational research, where algorithms often perform better in detecting explicit incitement or violent rhetoric than in recognising contextual, ironic, or coded hostility.

The most controversial examples were later discussed collectively in class. This second phase was crucial, transforming the e-tivity from a classificatory exercise into a reflective pedagogical practice. Students developed greater awareness of the social consequences of digital communication, the fragility of online coexistence, and the importance of counter-speech, empathy, and civic responsibility.

This perspective is coherent with the educational rationale of the university e-tivity presented here, conducted during the academic years 2023–2024 and 2024–2025 within the Information Literacy course of the Master's Degree in Media Education at the Catholic University of the Sacred Heart (Milan).

5 Conclusions

This paper has argued that Higher Education can play a strategic role in understanding and countering online hate when research, teaching, and civic responsibility are approached in an integrated manner. The three case studies demonstrate complementary dimensions of intervention.

Large-scale monitoring initiatives such as the Mappa dell'Intolleranza provide valuable evidence on trends, targets, territorial dynamics, stereotypes, and evolving forms of hostility. Critical digital literacy pathways help students understand how platforms, algorithms, and data infrastructures shape visibility, participation, and discrimination. Situated pedagogical practices such as e-tivities enable learners to engage directly with authentic media content, transforming abstract concepts into reflective judgment and ethical awareness.

Taken together, these dimensions outline a replicable model for universities seeking to respond to online hate through evidence-based and educationally grounded strategies. Rather than treating hate speech solely as a legal or technical issue, the paper suggests framing it also as a pedagogical and democratic challenge. This is particularly urgent in contexts where repeated exposure to hostile discourse may normalize intolerance and reduce critical sensitivity toward discrimination.

Future developments may include comparative cross-national studies, longitudinal assessments of student learning outcomes, and the design of interdisciplinary curricula connecting media education, data studies, and human rights education. In increasingly platformized societies, universities remain crucial spaces for cultivating critical publics capable of recognizing, interpreting, and challenging digital hatred. Their role is therefore not only educational, but also civic and democratic.

Author Contributions. Federico Faloppa contributed to the theoretical framing of hate speech and the introductory sections; Andrea Borruso, Giovanni Fulantelli, Andrea Nelson Mauro, and Davide Taibi contributed to the section on critical digital literacy and the TASKs project; Nannerel Fiano contributed to the section on the *Mappa dell'Intolleranza* project and related legal perspectives; Stefano Pasta contributed to the section on the university e-tivity and educational practices for detecting online hate speech. All authors contributed to the overall conception of the paper, discussion of results, and final revision of the manuscript.

Disclosure of Interests. The authors have no competing interests to declare that are relevant to the content of this article.

References

1. Dunn, P.: Moderazione automatizzata e discriminazione algoritmica: il caso dell'hate speech. Rivista Italiana di Informatica e Diritto. **4**(1) (2022)
2. Seyfert, R., Roberge, J.: Algorithmic Cultures: Essays on Meaning, Performance and New Technologies, pp. 1–25 (2016)
3. Pasta, S.: Hate speech research: algorithmic and qualitative evaluations. A case study of anti-gypsy hate on twitter. Res. Educ. Media. **15**(1), 130–139 (2023)
4. Jo Cox Commission on hatred, intolerance, xenophobia and racism: Final report, The Pyra-mid of hatred in Italy (2017)
5. Commission on fact-finding investigation: Final document approved on the nature, causes, and recent developments of hate speech, with attention to the evolution of European legis-lation (2022)
6. Council of Europe: Combating Hate Speech. Cedex, Luxembourg (2022)
7. Faloppa, F.: L'hate speech, questo sconosciuto. In: Speciale Hate Speech, Lingua Italiana Treccani (2020)
8. Santerini, M.: La mente ostile. Forme dell'odio contemporaneo. Raffaello Cortina, Milano (2021)
9. Brena, S.: Parole in Tempesta. Dizionario della contemporaneità. Il Saggiatore, Milano (2024)
10. Bail, C.: Terrified: how Anti-Muslim Fringe Organizations Became Mainstream. Princeton University Press, Princeton (2016)
11. Pasta, S.: Lo "spettro dell'odio online": una proposta di classificazione tra valutazioni algoritmiche e qualitative. In: Crescenza, G. (ed.) Educare in tempi di odio e violenza. Sfide pedagogiche e istituzionali, pp. 113–126. Progedit, Bari (2024)

12. Gillespie, T.: Custodians of the Internet: Platforms, Content Moderation, and the Hidden Decisions that Shape Social Media. Yale University Press, New Haven (2018)
13. Pasta, S.: Social network conversations with young authors of online hate speech against migrants. In: Monnier, A., Boursier, A., Seoane, A. (eds.) Cyberhate in the Context of Migrations, pp. 187–214. Palgrave Macmillan, London (2022)
14. Mihailidis, P., Thevenin, B.: Media literacy as a core competency for engaged citizenship in participatory democracy. Am. Behav. Sci. **57**(11), 1611–1622 (2013)
15. UNESCO: Media and Information Literacy Curriculum for Educators and Learners. UNESCO Publishing, Paris (2021)
16. Ceravolo, P., Mohammadi, F., Tamborini, M.A.: Active learning method- ology in LLMs fine-tuning. In: Shiaeles, S., Kolokotronis, N., Bellini, E. (eds.) Proc. 2024 IEEE Int. Conf. On Cyber Security and Resilience (CSR) – Workshops, pp. 743–749. IEEE (2024). ISBN 979-8-3503-7536-7.). https://doi.org/10.1109/csr61664.2024.10679450E
17. D'Amico, M.: Parole che separano. Cortina, Milano (2023)
18. D'Amico, M., Siccardi, C. (eds.): La Costituzione non odia. Giappichelli, Torino (2021)
19. Di Furia, M., Centrone, B., Rizzi, A., Traetta, L.: Interpretare e contrastare i discorsi d'odio: una prospettiva intersezionale. QTimes (2024)
20. Selwyn, N.: Education and Technology: Key Issues and Debates. Bloomsbury, London (2021)
21. Stommel, J.: Critical Digital Pedagogy: a Definition. Hybrid Pedagogy (2014)
22. Kitchin, R.: The Data Revolution: Big Data, Open Data. Data Infrastructures and Their Consequences. Sage, London (2014)
23. Fulantelli, G., Taibi, D., Splendore, S., Fisichella, M.: 1st workshop on detecting trust, authority, sense and knowledge in online news media production. In: Proc. of the 18th ACM International Conference on Web Search and Data Mining (WSDM '25), pp. 1114–1115. ACM, New York (2025)
24. Forzinetti, E., Della Vedova, M., Pasta, S., Santerini. M., Indicators for characterising online hate speech and its automatic detection. Cornell University, Ithaca (2024). http://arxiv.org/abs/2402.08462
25. Vox Diritti. https://www.voxdiritti.it. Accessed 19 Aug 2025
26. Mohammadi, M., Ceravolo, P., Maghool, S., Tamborini, M., D'Amico, M.E.: EHLD: a General Data Framework for Harmful Language Detection and Evaluation. Digital Library Perspectives (2026)
27. Schweppe, J., Perry, B.: A continuum of hate: delimiting the field of hate studies. Crime Law Soc. Chang. **77**, 503–528 (2022)
28. Pasta, S.: Razzismi 2.0. Analisi socio-educativa dell'odio online. Scholé, Brescia (2018)
29. Pasta, S.: Cittadinanza onlife e odio 2.0: Media Literacy con gruppi eletti a bersaglio nel web sociale. In: Rondonotti, M. (ed.) Tecnologie, comunità, inclusione sociale, pp. 153–178. eCampus University Press, Novedrate (CO) (2024)

Students' Perspectives on the Ideal and Real University Professor: An International Comparative Survey

Antonella Nuzzaci(✉)

University of Messina, Messina, ME 98122, Italy
antonella.nuzzaci@unime.it

Abstract. In the last two decades, the Bologna Process and subsequent European reforms have increasingly emphasized the quality of university teaching along-side research. However, while research evaluation is firmly established, teaching quality has often remained underexplored. The QUALITI Project (Erasmus+ KA2), coordinated by the University of L'Aquila with partners from Spain, Romania, Lithuania and Poland, aimed to address this gap by developing indicators and methodologies for assessing and improving didactic quality in Higher Education Institutions (HEIs). This paper presents the results of an international survey involving 7,724 students across 133 European universities, designed to outline the profile of the "ideal" university professor as compared to the "real" one encountered in their learning experience. A mixed-methods design was employed, combining quantitative scales with open-ended questions, to capture students' perceptions regarding knowledge, communication, relational skills, pedagogical practices, and use of innovative methodologies. Findings show convergence on key traits: profound disciplinary competence, clarity of instruction, trustful relationships with students, use of appropriate teaching resources, and alignment between assessment and course objectives. Nonetheless, gaps persist between the ideal and real dimensions, particularly concerning flexibility, student engagement, and innovative teaching approaches. The study provides a comprehensive framework for understanding students' expectations of effective academic teaching, with implications for the professional development of university lecturers and institutional policies aimed at promoting high-quality teaching in European Higher Education.

Keywords: Higher Education · Teaching Quality · Student Perceptions · University Professor Profile · QUALITI Project · Didactics · Pedagogical Innovation

1 Introduction

In the last twenty years, following the Bologna Declaration (1999) and the subsequent European Higher Education reforms, the debate on the quality of teaching has progressively intensified [1, 2]. The Bologna Process, originally focused on harmonizing university structures and promoting student mobility, has increasingly been associated

M. Adamoli et al. (Eds.): HELMeTO 2025, CCIS 2958, pp. 246–269, 2026.
https://doi.org/10.1007/978-3-032-31850-3_16

with the need to strengthen mechanisms of quality assurance not only in research but also in teaching and learning. However, despite numerous initiatives, the evaluation of teaching quality continues to lag the consolidated practices used for assessing research outputs, thereby reinforcing the perception of teaching as an undervalued dimension of academic life. Several comparative studies confirm that students consistently attribute great importance to both didactic and relational dimensions of teaching, even when institutional evaluation systems tend to overlook them [3–5].

Several European reports [6–8] stress that international rankings privilege research productivity as a proxy for institutional excellence, while pedagogical effectiveness remains largely invisible [9, 10]. This imbalance has critical implications: it discourages investment in teaching, undermines the professional development of lecturers, and contributes to the perception of Higher Education Institutions (HEIs) as research-driven rather than learning-centered communities. Empirical studies further confirm that there is little or no correlation between research quality and teaching quality [11–13]. A recent cross-sectional study in Lebanon further corroborates this weak link between research productivity and student-perceived teaching quality [14]. This evidence is further reinforced by later analyses highlighting how the relationship between research performance and teaching effectiveness is context-dependent and often weak [15]. Excessive emphasis on research, as Arum & Roksa [16] demonstrate, risks marginalizing didactic planning and reducing attention to the pedagogical dimension of academic work.

At the same time, universities face the challenge of increasingly heterogeneous student populations, including adult learners, international students, refugees, and individuals with special educational needs. In this scenario, effective teaching requires diversified methods, inclusive approaches, and structured pedagogical skills. Yet, the pedagogical preparation of university professors remains uneven across Europe and often less systematically addressed than in primary or secondary education. The European Parliament [17] and the High-Level Group on the Modernisation of Higher Education

[18] have underlined the urgency of enhancing the didactic repertoire of lecturers, stressing the need for professional development initiatives that integrate methodological, technological, and relational competencies.

Four main issues emerge as central in the current debate:

- the absence of robust, comparable, and reliable indicators for assessing the quality of teaching and learning;
- the need for institutional policies that explicitly support teaching excellence and innovation;
- the recognition of pedagogical training as an essential component of academic professionalism;
- the necessity of creating high-quality, student-centered learning environments, particularly for disadvantaged or underrepresented groups.

The response to these challenges has been multifaceted but fragmented. While some universities have introduced teaching centers, staff development programs, and student evaluation mechanisms, practices remain highly variable across countries and institutions. What is still missing is a systematic framework capable of providing evidence-based and comparable data on teaching quality across Europe.

It is precisely in this context that the Erasmus+ QUALITI Project (Didactic QUALity Assessment for Innovation of Teaching and Learning Improvement) was conceived [19]. Coordinated by the University of L'Aquila with partners from Spain, Romania, Lithuania, Poland, and Italy, QUALITI sought to design and test innovative instruments for evaluating teaching quality, strengthen the pedagogical training of lecturers, and foster a culture of continuous improvement in teaching and learning practices. Among its activities, an international survey involving more than 7,700 students was conducted to investigate the characteristics of the "ideal" and "real" university professor. The survey results, which form the core of this contribution, provide valuable insights into students' expectations, experiences, and perceptions of academic teaching, and offer concrete directions for improving the quality of Higher Education in Europe.

2 Theoretical Framework

The conceptual background of this study builds on a wide body of literature addressing the complexity of defining and evaluating teaching quality in Higher Education.

A first strand of research emphasizes the multidimensional nature of teaching, encompassing disciplinary expertise, methodological competencies, relational sensitivity, and professional ethics [20, 21]. Teaching quality is thus not reducible to knowledge transmission, but involves designing learning environments that foster deep learning, critical thinking, and student engagement. Classic reviews of teaching effectiveness underline that such attributes are consistently associated with positive student learning outcomes [3, 4].

A second perspective concerns the relationship between research and teaching. While traditional academic culture often assumes a positive correlation, empirical studies show limited or inconsistent associations [11, 15]. This suggests that research excellence does not automatically translate into teaching excellence, highlighting the need for specific pedagogical training.

A third dimension relates to student-centered learning, increasingly recognized as a key principle in European policy documents [22, 23]. The focus here is on inclusivity, learner autonomy, and active methodologies, which require lecturers to shift from being transmitters of content to facilitators of learning. Theories of constructive alignment

[24] and approaches to student engagement [25] provide reference frameworks for rethinking teaching practices. Moreover, structural models confirm that enhancing instructors' digital teaching skills not only improves teaching quality directly but also boosts student motivation and engagement — highlighting the strategic role of digital competence in modern Higher Education [26]. More recent conceptual models have expanded these approaches, proposing comprehensive frameworks for student engagement in higher education [27].

Finally, scholars stress the importance of professional development for university teachers, pointing to the necessity of structured and continuous pedagogical support [28–31]. Initiatives such as teaching centers, peer review of teaching, and didactic innovation projects are seen as essential to foster sustainable quality improvements. Systematic reviews confirm that pedagogical innovation is a growing priority in higher education, though unevenly implemented across institutions [32]. Furthermore, recent European reports emphasize the importance of peer learning and institutional support for teaching innovation [7].

In summary, the theoretical framework guiding this study integrates:

1. Didactic and pedagogical models [20, 21, 28];
2. Policy frameworks and European standards (ESG, Bologna Process, EUA reports);
3. Research on student engagement and perceptions [25, 33–35];
4. Debates on academic professionalism and the balance between research and teaching [11, 15].

3 The QUALITI Project

The Erasmus+ KA2 Project QUALITI – Didactic QUALity Assessment for Innovation of Teaching and Learning Improvement was launched in 2019 as a Strategic Partnership for Higher Education (KA203) [36–39]. The initiative was coordinated by the University of L'Aquila (Italy) and involved partner institutions from five European countries: Universitat de Barcelona (Spain), Valahia University of Târgoviște (Romania), Vilnius University and Siuolaikiniu Didaktiku Centras (Lithuania), SSW Collegium Balticum (Poland), and ilmiolavoro srl (Italy).

The project emerged in response to the persistent imbalance between the evaluation of research and teaching within Higher Education Institutions (HEIs). While national and international systems rely heavily on research-based metrics, indicators capable of capturing the quality of teaching remain underdeveloped, fragmented, and often indirect. The QUALITI Project sought to address this gap by:

- Designing and testing direct indicators for evaluating the quality of university teaching, aligned with the Standards and Guidelines for Quality Assurance in the European Higher Education Area [22];
- Defining the pedagogical profile of the university lecturer, with emphasis on student-centered approaches and didactic competencies;
- Developing training and support tools for the continuous professional development of lecturers, including methodological and didactic guidelines;
- Promoting innovation in teaching and learning, with attention to active methodologies, interdisciplinary strategies, and the integration of digital tools [26, 40].

The project adopted a holistic approach that operated on three interrelated levels:

- Institutional level – building systems for measuring and evaluating teaching quality;
- Planning level – establishing quality benchmarks to guide the design and improvement of teaching practices;
- Individual level – enhancing the methodological and pedagogical skills of lecturers to implement student-centered learning.

To ensure the reliability of its proposals, the project developed and piloted three Intellectual Outputs (IOs):

- Teaching Quality Indicators Framework (TQIF): a system of direct, valid, and comparable indicators for assessing teaching quality;

- University Teacher Profile (IO2): a reference framework describing the cultural, professional, and didactic attributes of effective lecturers;
- OER – Methodological Fieldbook (IO3): a set of open-access resources providing guidance for pedagogical training and innovation.

The impact of the project was multidimensional. At institutional level, it reinforced awareness of the importance of teaching quality within academic policies. For professors, it supported the acquisition of new pedagogical skills and enhanced engagement with teaching. For students, it contributed to more meaningful learning experiences and higher perceived quality of education.

Within this framework, a large-scale international survey was designed to explore students' perceptions of the ideal and real university professor. The following sections present the methodological design of the survey and the analysis of results.

4 Methodology

The research design of the QUALITI Project was grounded in a mixed-methods approach, combining quantitative and qualitative techniques in order to capture the complexity of teaching and learning processes in Higher Education. Methodological triangulation [41] was employed to strengthen the reliability, validity, and interpretative depth of the findings, ensuring that different perspectives converged on the same constructs.

4.1 Research Design

The methodological strategy integrated three complementary levels:

1. *Theoretical research:*
   - A review of the international literature on teaching quality and student perceptions;
   - A meta-analysis of existing studies to identify patterns and critical gaps;
   - The development of conceptual frameworks and direct descriptors for teaching evaluation.
2. *Exploratory research:*
   - A large-scale survey of students in five European countries (Italy, Spain, Romania, Lithuania, Poland), aimed at reconstructing the profile of the "ideal" professor as compared to the "real" one encountered in practice;
   - Complementary surveys with lecturers to capture their perceptions of teaching-learning processes;
   - Semi-structured interviews with experienced professors and focus groups with external stakeholders, in order to enrich the analysis of expectations and professional competences.
3. *Experimental research:*
   - Training sessions and pilot testing focused on lecturers' methodological skills (design, evaluation, communication, relational management, use of digital technologies);

– Implementation of professional development activities within the partner institutions.

4.2 Survey Instrument

The student survey represented the central component of the research. The instrument included:

- *19 items* in a 4-point Likert scale (1 = totally disagree; 4 = totally agree), measuring qualities and competencies of the ideal university professor (disciplinary knowledge, clarity, communication, relational trust, pedagogical innovation, assessment practices);
- *4 open-ended questions*, asking students to describe the characteristics they appreciated most in the professor of their last attended course;
- *8 socio-demographic questions*, covering gender, age, country, nationality, degree course, and field of study.

The questionnaire was made available in six languages (national and English versions), adapted to partner contexts, and distributed online. Two administration phases were conducted to mitigate the effects of the COVID-19 pandemic.

4.3 Validity and Reliability

Particular attention was given to the validation of the student questionnaire. Content validity was ensured through a systematic review process involving external experts in pedagogy and evaluation, who assessed the correspondence between items and the intended constructs. In addition, preliminary pilot administrations were conducted in all partner countries, allowing the refinement of wording, cultural adaptation, and testing of cross-linguistic equivalence. Construct validity was verified through exploratory and confirmatory factor analyses, which confirmed the unidimensional coherence of the scale. Internal consistency reached very high levels (Cronbach's Alpha = .948 for 7,724 valid cases), indicating that the 19 items captured complementary but non-redundant aspects of teaching quality. Intercoder reliability for the qualitative coding of open responses exceeded 90%, further confirming the robustness of the interpretative process.

Statistical Analyses. The quantitative data were processed using both descriptive and inferential statistics. Descriptive analysis provided a detailed overview of students' perceptions of the "ideal" professor across the main dimensions (disciplinary knowledge, clarity, communication, relational trust, innovation, assessment practices). Correlation matrices and heatmaps were used to examine the interrelations among variables. Subsequently, inferential analyses were conducted to explore the role of contextual and demographic factors. ANOVA tests revealed significant differences in perceptions across countries, disciplines, gender, and age groups ($p < .001$), highlighting the contextual variability of teaching quality perceptions. Post-hoc comparisons were performed to identify which specific groups differed significantly from one another. In addition, regression models were used to test the predictive power of certain variables (e.g., trust, clarity, flexibility) on overall student satisfaction and perceived teaching quality.

Qualitative Analyses. The open-ended responses were subjected to thematic content analysis. Codes were developed inductively and then aggregated into broader categories reflecting competencies and relational traits (e.g., "supportive," "innovative," "clear communicator"). This analysis added interpretative richness to the quantitative findings, providing illustrative evidence of the ways in which students describe the characteristics of both ideal and real professors.

Overall, the methodological approach guaranteed not only the collection of reliable and comparable data across different cultural contexts, but also the possibility of triangulating numerical results with students' narratives. This ensured a deeper understanding of the expectations and experiences of the student body with regard to teaching quality in European Higher Education.

5 Survey Instrument and the Ideal University Teacher Scale (IUTS)

The Ideal University Teacher Scale (IUTS) was specifically developed within the QUALITI Project to capture students' perceptions of the ideal and real professor. Its construction drawing on both the international literature on teaching quality [3–5] and on prior survey instruments measuring didactic and relational competencies.

5.1 Structure of the Instrument

The questionnaire was structured to collect two complementary types of data:

- Quantitative data, obtained through a 19-item Likert-type scale (1 = totally disagree; 4 = totally agree), addressing key dimensions of effective teaching, such as disciplinary knowledge, clarity of presentation, flexibility, communication, relational trust, use of technology, active methodologics, and alignment between objectives and assessment;
- Qualitative data, derived from 4 open-ended questions, asking students to describe the qualities they most appreciated in the professor of their last course;
- Contextual data, collected through 8 socio-demographic variables (gender, age, nationality, country of study, subject area, degree cycle, and year of enrollment).

The survey was available in six languages (Italian, Spanish, Romanian, Lithuanian, Polish, English) and adapted to the cultural contexts of participating universities. Students could choose their preferred language when completing the online questionnaire.

5.2 Validation and Reliability

The IUTS was subjected to a multi-step validation process:

- Content validation: expert reviewers (evaluation specialists and university professors) checked the correspondence between items and targeted constructs;
- Pilot testing: preliminary administration and statistical analysis refined the wording of items and ensured cross-cultural equivalence

– Factor analysis: exploratory and confirmatory analyses confirmed the unidimensional coherence of the scale.

The instrument demonstrated excellent psychometric properties, with Cronbach's Alpha = .948 across 7,724 valid cases. This indicates that the items captured coherent but non-redundant aspects of teaching quality (Table 1).

Table 1. Scale Statistics

Indicator	Value
Mean (scale total)	61.49
Variance	120.79
Standard deviation	10.99
Number of items	19

These results confirm the internal consistency and discriminatory power of the instrument. Correlation analysis among the 19 IUTS items confirmed strong positive relationships between disciplinary knowledge, clarity, and assessment alignment (r > .70), while relational dimensions (trust, communication) also showed robust correlations with student engagement (r ≈ .65). The integration of technology and the use of active methodologies presented slightly lower but significant correlations (r ≈ .45–.55), suggesting that these are perceived as complementary rather than central attributes. Overall, the heatmap highlights the multidimensional but coherent nature of the IUTS scale (Fig. 1).

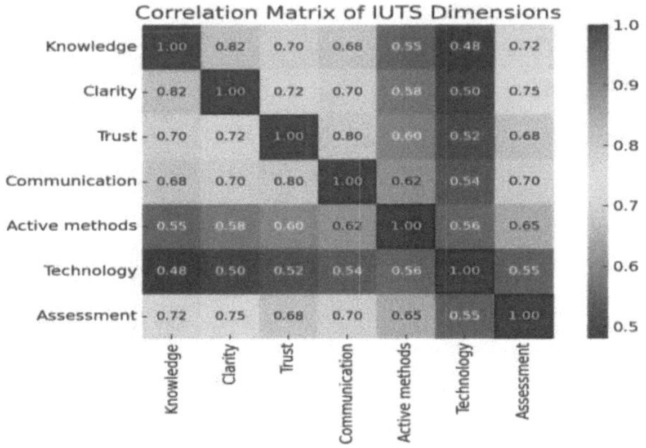

Fig. 1. The heatmap of the correlations

The heatmap of the correlations between the main dimensions of the IUTS scale shows how the highest correlations emerge between Knowledge, Clarity, Trust and Communication (r ≈ .70–.82), Active methods and the use of Technologies show moderate correlations (r ≈ .48–.56), indicating that they are perceived as useful but less central, and assessment is strongly connected to Clarity and Knowledge (r ≈ .72–.75), confirming the importance of consistency between objectives and assessment.

The heatmap shows the correlations among the seven core dimensions of the Ideal University Teacher Scale. Strong associations are visible between disciplinary knowledge, clarity, trust, and communication (r > .70), suggesting that students perceive these traits as a coherent cluster of fundamental teaching qualities. Active methodologies and technology integration present moderate but significant correlations (r ≈ .45–.55), reflecting their complementary rather than central role. Assessment is strongly linked to knowledge and clarity (r > .70), underlining the importance of alignment between objectives and evaluation.

5.3 Treatment of Open Questions

Responses to the four open-ended questions were analyzed through content analysis. Codes were assigned to recurrent words, adjectives, and descriptors (e.g., "knowledgeable", "supportive", "clear", "innovative"), and then aggregated into broader categories of competencies and traits. Inter-coder agreement reached 98%, ensuring reliability of interpretation.

The combination of quantitative and qualitative dimensions allowed the IUTS to function both as a measurement tool and as a framework for constructing the cultural and professional profile of the "ideal" university professor.

6 Sample Characteristics

The survey was administered to a large and diverse student population, involving 7,724 valid respondents across 133 European universities in Italy, Spain, Romania, Lithuania, and Poland. This broad coverage allowed the study to capture perceptions across a variety of cultural and institutional contexts.

6.1 Gender Distribution

The sample was predominantly female, reflecting broader enrollment trends in European Higher Education (Fig. 2) (Table 2):

Table 2. Gender distribution of respondents

Gender	Frequency	Percentage
Female	5,485	71.0%
Male	2,194	28.4%
Other	45	0.6%
Total	**7,724**	**100%**

Respondents were mainly young adults enrolled in first-cycle programs, though the age range was broad (17–70 years) (Fig. 3) (Table 3):

The mean age of participants was 25.1 years

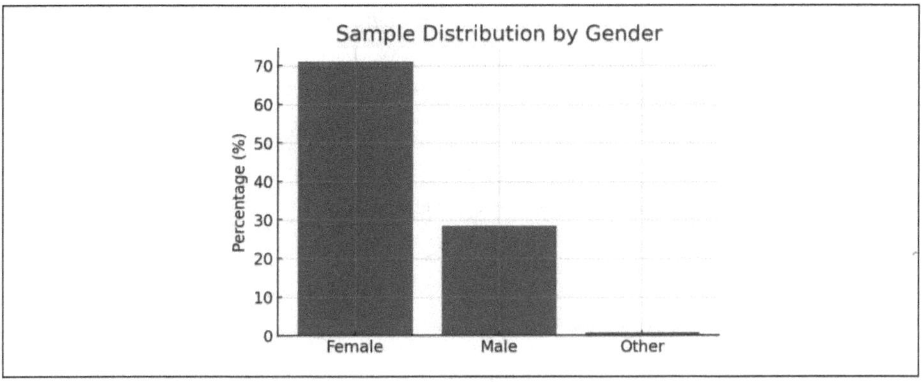

Fig. 2. Sample Distribution by Gender

Table 3. Age distribution of respondents

Age group	Percentage
17–25	93.9%
26–35	5.2%
> 35	0.9%

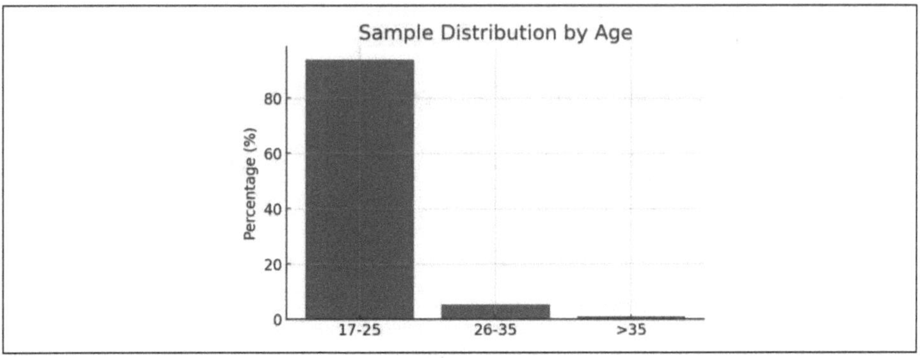

Fig. 3. Sample Distribution by Age

6.2 Higher Education Qualification

Students were distributed across the three Bologna cycles, with a prevalence of first-cycle enrolments (Table 4):

Table 4. Distribution by degree cycle

Degree cycle	Percentage
Bachelor's degree (first cycle)	69.8%
Single-cycle/Master's degree	26.8%
PhD / Specialization (third cycle)	3.4%

6.3 Nationalities and Countries

The survey reached students of 114 different nationalities, reflecting the international diversity of European Higher Education. The majority were enrolled in the partner countries, but additional European contexts were also represented.

6.4 Disciplinary Areas

Participants came from a wide range of subject areas. The most represented faculties were Education (24.5%), Social Sciences, Humanities, and STEM disciplines, with smaller proportions from fields such as Tourism Sciences (0.6%).

The demographic composition of the sample ensures both representativeness and variability, allowing for comparative analyses across gender, age, field of study, and nationality. This provides a robust foundation for interpreting student perceptions of the "ideal" and "real" professor in the following sections.

7 Descriptive Analysis: The Ideal Professor (Part I)

Students were asked to evaluate the qualities of the ideal university professor across multiple dimensions. The responses show a clear convergence on fundamental academic and relational competencies.

7.1 Disciplinary Knowledge and Clarity

A vast majority of students highlighted the importance of professors demonstrating in-depth knowledge of their subject area (94.1% agreement) and clearly explaining the syllabus at the beginning of each course (91.3%) (Table 5).

Table 5. Importance of disciplinary knowledge and syllabus clarity

Item	% Agree/Strongly Agree
Shows an in-depth understanding of the subject taught	94.1%
Clearly illustrates the course syllabus (objectives, etc.)	91.3%

7.2 Communication and Atmosphere

Students emphasized the professor's ability to communicate freely and spontaneously (86.9%) and to create a respectful, trust-based relationship (84.8%). These relational aspects were considered essential for fostering a positive learning climate (Table 6).

Table 6. Relational qualities of the ideal professor

Item	% Agree/Strongly Agree
Communicates openly and creates an informal atmosphere	86.9%
Builds trust with students	84.8%

7.3 Commitment and Student Engagement

When asked about the importance of professors encouraging student commitment to study, 73.2% agreed. Although lower than other items, this reflects the dual perception: while students recognize its value, they often associate responsibility for effort more with themselves than with the lecturer (Table 7).

Table 7. Importance of encouraging student commitment

Item	% Agree/Strongly Agree
Discusses the need for students' hard work	73.2%

7.4 Integration of Technology and Teaching Resources

Students attributed high importance to the integration of digital technologies in teaching (84.8% agreement). They also emphasized the need for professors to provide adequate and varied teaching materials tailored to learning objectives (84.2%) (Table 8).

Table 8. Use of technology and teaching materials

Item	% Agree/Strongly Agree
Incorporates digital technology into lessons	84.8%
Uses appropriate teaching materials and bibliographic resources	84.2%

While students valued participation, classroom discussion, and teamwork, the levels of agreement were slightly lower compared to other dimensions. Around 83.7% considered classroom participation essential, while only 70–73% agreed on the importance of teamwork and interactive methodologies. This suggests that students recognize their value but perceive them as less frequently applied in practice (Table 9).

Table 9. Importance of active methodologies

Item	% Agree/Strongly Agree
Stimulates participation and exchange of views	83.7%
Promotes teamwork and collaborative strategies	70.8%
Employs interactive methodologies	73.4%

Clear instructions for classroom activities and access to learning materials were also considered crucial. Approximately 80.7% of respondents agreed that professors should provide explicit instructions, while 85.5% valued the provision of supporting materials (books, articles, tutorials) (Table 10).

Table 10. Clarity of instructions and support

Item	% Agree/Strongly Agree
Provides clear instructions and sufficient time for activities	80.7%
Provides the necessary materials to support learning	85.5%

These findings suggest that students do not only value assessment fairness and transparency (87.0% agreed on the need for alignment between objectives and evaluation), but also perceive a strong connection between their university training and their future professional careers (76.0% emphasized this link). This highlights how the role of the professor is increasingly seen as bridging academic and professional spheres. Taken together, the results allow us to outline the profile of the ideal professor: a teacher competent in the discipline (94.1%), clear in exposition (91.3%), capable of establishing relationships based on trust and open communication (84.8%), able to integrate technologies (84.8%) and varied teaching materials (84.2%), oriented towards active participation (83.7%) and fair evaluation, and attentive to the connection between theory, practice, reality and professionalization (Table 11).

Table 11. Assessment and professional orientation

Item	% Agree/Strongly Agree
Uses assessment strategies aligned with learning objectives	87.0%
Provides training linked to professional competences	76.0%

In summary, students outline the ideal professor as a teacher competent in the discipline and clear in exposition, capable of establishing relationships based on trust, able to integrate technologies and teaching materials, oriented towards active participation and fair evaluation, attentive to the connection between theory, practice, reality and professionalization.

8 Ideal vs. Real University Professor

A central aim of the survey was to compare students' perceptions of the "ideal" professor with the qualities observed in their "real" professors, i.e. those met in the most recent university module attended.

8.1 Areas of Convergence

Some traits showed strong alignment between the ideal and real dimensions:

- *Disciplinary expertise*: most students confirmed that their professors demonstrated solid knowledge of the subject.
- *Provision of materials and resources*: professors generally offered adequate support through bibliographic resources and teaching materials.
- *Assessment practices*: students reported consistency between learning objectives and evaluation methods in many cases.

8.2 Areas of Divergence

However, several important discrepancies emerged:

8.1.1 *Flexibility:* while 77.8% of students considered adaptability of the syllabus to classroom needs essential, this was reported as rarely implemented in practice.
8.1.2 *Relational dimension*: although 84.8% valued trust and open communication, many students felt that real professors did not always succeed in fostering a welcoming and informal atmosphere.
8.1.3 *Active methodologies:* teamwork, interactive strategies, and problem-based learning were rated highly desirable (70–83%), but only sporadically experienced. Traditional lecture formats continued to dominate.
8.1.4 *Use of digital technologies:* although students expect integration of technological tools (84.8%), their actual use was described as limited and uneven across courses and countries.

8.3 Perceived Gaps

The gap between ideal and real teaching was particularly evident in three domains (Fig. 4):

1. *Pedagogical innovation* (active and student-centered methodologies);
2. *Relational competencies* (trust, dialogue, accessibility);
3. *Adaptability and inclusiveness* (addressing diverse needs of students, including disadvantaged groups).

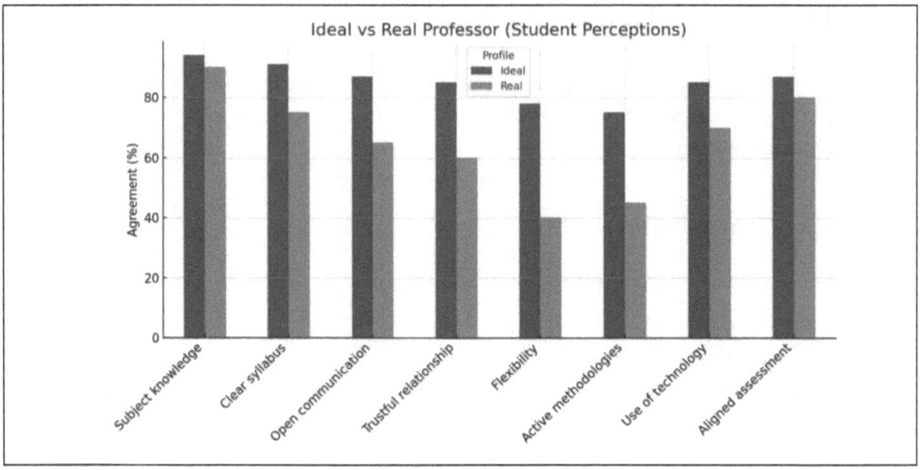

Fig. 4. Ideal *vs* Real Professor

Table 12. Ideal *vs.* Real professor: main discrepancies

Dimension	Ideal (% agree)	Real (perceived)	Gap
Subject knowledge	94%	High	Low
Clear syllabus	91%	Medium	Moderate
Open communication	87%	Lower	High
Builds trust	85%	Lower	High
Flexibility in syllabus	78%	Low	High
Active methodologies	71–83%	Low	High
Use of technology	85%	Moderate	Moderate
Assessment aligned to goals	87%	Medium/High	Low/Moderate

8.4 Interpretation

The discrepancies summarized in Table 12 confirm that, although students generally recognize the solidity of disciplinary knowledge and assessment practices, other aspects—such as flexibility, open communication, and active methodologies—remain weak in practice. In other words, while the 'ideal' professor is envisioned as a pedagogical innovator and relational guide, the 'real' professor is still perceived as more traditional, knowledge-centered, and less flexible.

9 Comparative Analysis: Country, Gender, Age, and Discipline

To further explore variations in perceptions, a set of ANOVA tests was conducted on the IUTS Index and on individual items of the scale. Results confirmed that student characteristics and academic contexts significantly influence expectations of the "ideal professor."

9.1 Country Effect

The variable "country" showed the strongest and most consistent differences ($F = 211.2$, $p < .001$). Students from some countries emphasized relational aspects (trust, communication), while others prioritized structure and clarity of teaching (Table 13) (Fig. 5).

Table 13. Country differences (selected items)

Item	Significant differences observed
In-depth subject knowledge	Higher in Spain, Italy
Flexibility of syllabus	Higher in Lithuania, Poland
Trustful relationship with students	Higher in Romania, Spain
Use of digital technologies	Higher in Lithuania

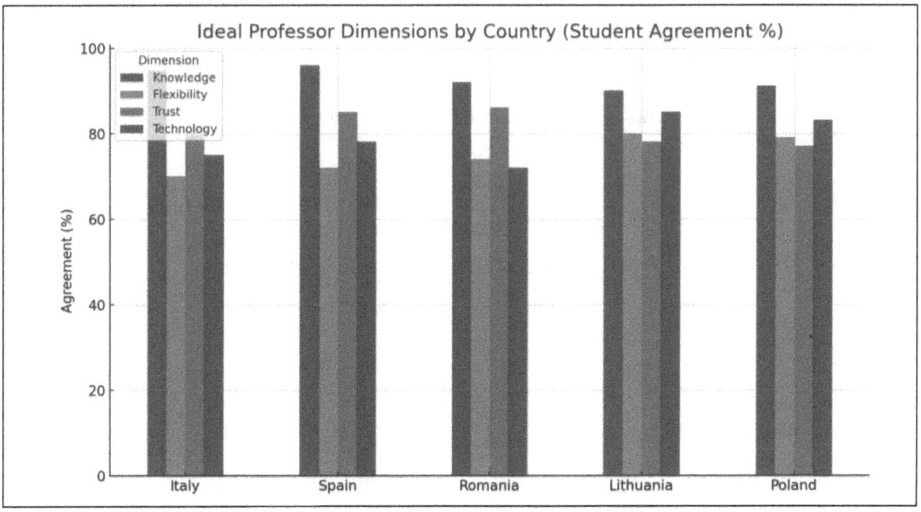

Fig. 5. Ideal Professor Dimensions by Country

The country comparison chart shows the main differences in students' perceptions of the ideal teacher:

- Italy and Spain emphasize disciplinary knowledge.
- Romania and Spain give more weight to trust and relationship.
- Lithuania and Poland stand out for the flexibility of the syllabus and the use of digital technologies.

9.2 Gender Differences

Gender was significant for several items, though with smaller effect sizes. Female students tended to place greater emphasis on clarity, communication, and relational trust, while male students scored slightly higher on the importance of digital technologies (Table 14).

Table 14. Gender differences (selected items)

Item	Higher agreement in…
Builds trust with students	Female students
Clear syllabus explanation	Female students
Integration of technology	Male students

9.3 Age Differences

Age showed a significant effect on the IUTS Index ($F = 2.09$, $p < .001$), though Fisher's F indicated moderate variance. Younger students (17–25) valued relational and communicative aspects more, while older students (>30) stressed practical orientation and professional competences (Table 15).

Table 15. Age differences (selected trends)

Age group	Priority dimension
17–25	Trust, open communication
26–35	Digital technologies, problem-based learning
>35	Professional skills, theory–practice links

9.4 Disciplinary Areas

Differences also emerged across fields of study. Students in Education and Social Sciences emphasized relational trust, flexibility, and communication, while those in STEM disciplines prioritized disciplinary knowledge, clarity, and structured assessment (Table 16).

Table 16. Disciplinary differences

Area of study	Priority dimension(s)
Education	Trust, dialogue, inclusiveness
Social Sciences	Flexibility, student-centered methodologies
STEM	Clarity, structured evaluation, knowledge
Humanities	Interdisciplinary approaches, reflection

These patterns suggest that expectations of the 'ideal professor' are not homogeneous across Europe but deeply shaped by contextual and demographic variables. National context appears to be the most decisive factor, reflecting different academic cultures and traditions. Gender and age highlight generational differences in the way students perceive teaching priorities, while disciplinary fields orient students' preferences toward either academic rigor or pedagogical innovation. This confirms that teaching quality cannot be interpreted as a universal model, but as a context-sensitive construct.

10 Discussion: The Profile of the Ideal University Professor

The survey results allow us to delineate a composite portrait of the "ideal professor" as envisioned by students across five European countries. This profile integrates disciplinary competence, relational sensitivity, and pedagogical innovation.

10.1 Core Competencies

Students consistently emphasized the importance of:

- *Profound disciplinary knowledge* – mastery of content is considered the foundation of credibility and authority.
- *Clarity and structure* – transparent presentation of objectives, contents, and assessment methods fosters trust and motivation.
- *Alignment between objectives and evaluation* – fairness in assessment emerged as a central requirement of quality teaching.

10.2 Relational and Communicative Skills

Equally central were relational qualities:

- *Open and respectful communication* – fostering dialogue and a comfortable classroom atmosphere.
- *Trust-based relationships* – professors are expected to show empathy, availability, and genuine concern for students' learning.
- *Encouragement of commitment* – while students recognize their own responsibility, they expect professors to inspire engagement and effort.

10.3 Pedagogical Innovation

Students valued methodologies that go beyond traditional lectures, such as:

- *Integration of digital tools* – perceived as essential for contemporary learning environments.
- *Active learning strategies* – teamwork, problem-solving, and interactive approaches, even though these are not yet widely practiced.
- *Connection between theory and practice* – supporting the transfer of knowledge into professional competences.

10.4 Divergences and Gaps

The contrast between the ideal and the real professor highlights critical gaps:

- Limited flexibility in adapting curricula to student needs;
- Insufficient use of interactive and student-centered methodologies;
- Uneven integration of technologies;
- Variability across countries, disciplines, and demographic groups.

These discrepancies should not be interpreted as isolated shortcomings of individual instructors, but rather as indicators of systemic tensions within contemporary higher education. The persistence of traditional teaching models alongside rising expectations for pedagogical innovation highlights the need for institutional frameworks that actively support methodological renewal, professional development, and student-centered design.

10.5 Implications

The findings suggest that the "ideal" university professor is not only a transmitter of knowledge but also a pedagogical designer, relational mentor, and innovator. This requires universities to:

- Recognize and reward teaching quality alongside research performance;
- Provide systematic training in pedagogical and methodological skills;
- Foster inclusive and student-centered learning environments;
- Support innovation through institutional policies and incentives.

By clarifying students' expectations, the study contributes to the broader debate on how to redefine academic professionalism in line with the challenges of the European Higher Education Area [42, 44].

11 Conclusions and Policy Implications

This study, conducted within the Erasmus+ QUALITI Project, has provided empirical evidence on how students in five European countries conceive the profile of the ideal professor and how this compares to the "real" professors they encounter. With more than 7,700 respondents, the research offers a robust and nuanced picture of the current state of teaching quality in European Higher Education.

11.1 Main Findings

- The ideal professor is perceived as a knowledgeable expert, a clear communicator, a relational mentor, and a pedagogical innovator.
- While disciplinary competence and clarity are widely recognized in real professors, gaps remain in terms of student-centered methods, flexibility, and use of technologies.
- Contextual differences (country, discipline, gender, age) significantly shape expectations, showing that teaching quality cannot be understood as a universal model but rather as a dynamic and contextualized construct.

While the sample size is robust and geographically diverse, its demographic composition reflects a predominance of female students and first-cycle enrolments. This distribution mirrors broader participation trends in European higher education, yet it may partially influence the perception patterns observed. Future studies should aim to include more balanced demographic segments and longitudinal perspectives in order to further validate and generalize these findings.

11.2 Implications for Universities

The results suggest that universities need to:

1. Rebalance the research–teaching nexus, granting greater institutional recognition to didactic excellence;
2. Introduce systematic training and support for lecturers in pedagogy, communication, and innovative methodologies;
3. Foster inclusive learning environments, addressing the diversity of student populations;
4. Promote evidence-based policies, grounded in reliable indicators and international comparability;
5. Encourage innovation and interdisciplinarity, aligning teaching with the skills demanded by contemporary labor markets.

11.3 Conclusions and Future Directions

The contribution presented has allowed for an in-depth reflection on the theme of teaching quality in higher education, providing significant empirical evidence of the gap between the "ideal" and the "real" profile of the university professor. The results of the study highlight how, alongside consolidated disciplinary competences, students increasingly attribute importance to relational and methodological-didactic dimensions, which are considered essential for meaningful learning experiences. It is precisely in this tension between expectations and reality that the most pressing challenge for European universities lies.

Several implications emerge. On the one hand, there is the need to rethink the role of the professor, no longer as a mere transmitter of knowledge but as a facilitator of active, inclusive, and professionally oriented learning processes. On the other, there is the urgency to strengthen systems of pedagogical training and professional development for university teachers, which remain too fragmented and uneven across the countries of the European Higher Education Area. This means envisioning structured initial and on-going training pathways capable of integrating innovative methodologies, critical use of technologies, and attention to the diversity of student populations.

Another key element concerns institutional policies: the risk of an excessive focus on research to the detriment of teaching is well documented, and the data presented here confirm its effects. Universities and national systems must formally recognize the value of teaching through evaluation and career criteria that also reward teaching quality. This requires a cultural shift that cannot be delegated solely to individual professors but must be translated into systemic actions supported at the European level (EHEA, EUA, European Commission).

At the same time, the results show that the voice of students is a valuable yet still underutilized resource. The possibility of involving them systematically in the processes of evaluation and co-design of teaching appears to be a promising path for making quality improvement more effective and authentic. The centrality of student engagement, as highlighted by recent studies, constitutes a decisive factor for educational success.

Finally, it should be emphasized that the construction of the "ideal" university professor cannot be understood as a static and uniform model, but rather as a dynamic and contextual horizon, which varies according to countries, institutional settings, disciplines, and student profiles. This invites us to move beyond the idea of a single recipe for quality and instead to develop flexible and adaptable frameworks, such as those proposed by the QUALITI Project, which offer concrete tools while remaining open to contextualization.

In perspective, universities are therefore called upon to face a crucial task: bridging the gap between the ideal and the real, by valorizing best practices, promoting innovation and interdisciplinarity, and above all, reinforcing a culture of teaching that fully acknowledges the role of professors as architects of quality learning environments. Only in this way will it be possible to provide effective responses to the challenges of the knowledge society, ensuring for Europe not only excellence in research but also university teaching that meets students' expectations and the demands of the future.

Further research should explore longitudinally how student expectations evolve, particularly in post-pandemic contexts where digital and blended learning have become structural components of Higher Education [38, 42–44]. Comparative analyses across additional countries would also enrich the generalizability of findings.

Acknowledgments. This study was funded by the European Community. We thank all partners involved in the Qualiti Project, as well as the rectors of Italian and foreign universities who made the execution and success of the project possible.

Disclosure of Interests. The author declares no competing interests relevant to the content of this article.

References

1. Paris Communiqué: European Higher Education Area: EHEA Ministerial Conference. EHEA, Paris (2018). https://ehea.info/media.ehea.info/file/2018_Paris/77/1/EHEAParis2018_Communique_final_952771.pdf

2. EHEA: Yerevan Communiqué. EHEA Ministerial Conference, Yerevan (2015). https://ehea.info/media.ehea.info/file/2015_Yerevan/70/7/YerevanCommuniqueFinal_613707.pdf
3. Feldman, K.A.: Effective college teaching from the students' and faculty's view: matched or mismatched priorities? Res. High. Educ. **28**(4), 291–344 (1988). https://doi.org/10.1007/BF01006402
4. Douna, P., Kyridis, A., Zagkos, C., Ziontaki, Z., Pandis, P.: The ideal university teacher according to the views of Greek students. Int. J. High. Educ. **4**(2), 145–158 (2015). https://doi.org/10.5430/ijhe.v4n2p145
5. Weinberg, B.A., Hashimoto, M., Fleisher, B.M.: Evaluating teaching in higher education. J. Econ. Educ. **38**(3), 197–210 (2007). https://doi.org/10.3200/JECE.40.3.227-261
6. Biggs, J., Tang, C.: Teaching for Quality Learning at University, 4th edn. McGraw-Hill, Maidenhead (2011)
7. European Commission: Education, Audiovisual and Culture Executive Agency (EACEA) / Eurydice: The European Higher Education Area in 2018: Bologna Process Implementation Report. EACEA, Bruxelles (2018)
8. Hazelkorn, E.: Rankings and the Reshaping of Higher Education: the Battle for World-Class Excellence, 2nd edn. Palgrave Macmillan, London (2015). https://doi.org/10.1057/9781137446671
9. European University Association (EUA): Trends 2018: Learning and Teaching in the European Higher Education Area. European University Association, Brussels (2018) https://eua.eu/resources/publications/757:trends-2018-learning-and-teaching-in-the-european-higher-education-area.html
10. European Students' Union: Fighting for students' rights since 1982 (2022). https://esu-online.org/wp-content/uploads/2022/12/ESU-2022-review.pdf.
11. Hattie, J., Marsh, H.W.: The relationship between research and teaching: A meta-analysis. Rev. Educ. Res. **66**(4), 507–542 (1996). https://doi.org/10.2307/1170652
12. Bauer, K.W., Bennett, J.S.: Alumni perceptions used to assess undergraduate research experience. J. High. Educ. **74**(2), 210–230 (2003). https://doi.org/10.1080/00221546.2003.11777197
13. Gibbs, G.: Using Assessment to Support Student Learning. Leeds Met Press, Leeds (2010)
14. Sacre, H., Akel, M., Haddad, C., Hallit, R., Akoury, H., Hallit, S.: The effect of research on the perceived quality of teaching: A cross-sectional study among university students in Lebanon. BMC Med. Educ. **23**(1), 31 (2023). https://doi.org/10.1186/s12909-023-03998-8
15. Brew, A.: Imperatives and challenges in integrating teaching and research. High. Educ. Res. Dev. **29**(2), 139–150 (2010). https://doi.org/10.1080/07294360903552451
16. Arum, R., Roksa, J.: Academically adrift: Limited learning on college campuses. University of Chicago Press, Chicago (2011)
17. European Parliament: Internationalisation of higher education (Study IP/B/CULT/IC/2014-002). Directorate-General for Internal Policies, Brussels (2015)
18. European Commission: High Level Group on the Modernisation of Higher Education: Report on Improving the Quality of Teaching and Learning in Europe's Higher Education Institutions, Brussels (2014)
19. Nuzzaci, A.: QUALITI PROJECT. Teaching in higher education between process Indicators, didactic profile of the university professor and methodological skills. Intellectual Outputs, Pensa MultiMedia S.R.L. Lecce (2023)
20. Kember, D., Gow, L.: Orientations to teaching and their effect on the quality of student learning. J. High. Educ. **65**(1), 58–74 (1994). https://doi.org/10.1080/00221546.1994.11778474
21. Biggs, J.B., Tang, C.: Teaching for Quality Learning at University, 4th edn. Open University Press, Maidenhead (2011)

22. European Association for Quality Assurance in Higher Education (ENQA): Standards and Guidelines for Quality Assurance in the European Higher Education Area (ESG). ENQA, Brussels (2015)
23. European Commission: Report to the European Commission on Improving the Quality of Teaching and Learning in Europe's Higher Education Institutions. Publications Office of the European Union, Luxembourg (2013)
24. Biggs, J.: Teaching for Quality Learning at University, 2nd edn. Open University Press (2003)
25. Kuh, G.D.: What student engagement data tell us about college readiness. Peer Rev. **11**(2), 4–8 (2009) https://api.semanticscholar.org/CorpusID:154899214
26. Zhang, J., Wu, Y.: Impact of university teachers' digital teaching skills on teaching quality in higher education. Cogent Educ. **12**(1), 2436706 (2025). https://doi.org/10.1080/2331186X.2024.2436706
27. Kandiko Howson, C., Buckley, A.: Quantifying learning: measuring student outcomes in higher education in England. Politics Gov. **8**(2), 6–14 (2020). https://doi.org/10.17645/pag.v8i2.2564
28. Gibbs, G.: Dimensions of Quality. Higher Education Academy, York (2010)
29. Trigwell, K.: Relations between teachers' emotions in teaching and their approaches to teaching in higher education. Instr. Sci. **40**(3), 607–621 (2012). https://doi.org/10.1007/s11251-011-9192-3
30. Sackdanouvong, K.: Quality of teaching in higher education: A systematic literature review. Lao Soc. Sci. J. **1**(2), 37–51 (2024). https://doi.org/10.71026/lss.2024.02005
31. Dransfield, M., Wood, M., Su, F.: Following the yellow brick road? Developing inspir-ing learning and teaching in the pursuit of teaching excellence in higher education. J. Furth. High. Educ. **46**(7), 972–987 (2022). https://doi.org/10.1080/0309877X.2022.2029833
32. Major, J. et al.: Pedagogical innovation in higher education: defining what we mean. Int. J. Innov. Teach. Learn. High. Educ. **1**(3), 1–18 (2020). https://doi.org/10.4018/IJITLHE.2020070101
33. Chickering, A.W., Gamson, Z.F.: Seven principles for good practice in undergraduate education. AAHE Bull. **39**(7), 3–7 (1987)
34. Yakup, Ö., Boyacı, A.: The role of student engagement in student out-comes in higher education: implications from a developing country. Int. J. Educ. Res. **110**(5), 101880 (2021). https://doi.org/10.1016/j.ijer.2021.101880
35. Kahu, E.R., Nelson, K.: Student engagement in the educational inter-face: understanding the mechanisms of student success. Higher Educ. Res. Dev. **37**(1), 58–71 (2018). https://doi.org/10.1080/07294360.2017.1344197
36. Nuzzaci, A.: Teaching Quality Indicators Framework – TQIF (IO1). Pensa Multimedia s.r.l., Lecce (2023)
37. Nuzzaci, A.: University Teacher Profile Learning/Teaching Focused – TPLTF (IO2). Pensa Multimedia s.r.l., Lecce (2023)
38. Nuzzaci, A.: Methodological-Didatics Guidelines for the "Learning/Teaching Focused Teacher" – OER (IO3). QUALITI - Didactic QUALity Assessment for Innovation of Teaching and Learning Improvement. Pensa MultiMedia S.R.L., Lecce (2023)
39. Nuzzaci, A., Ercole, L., Marcozzi, I., Spetia, L.: QUALITI project: didactic quality assessment for innovation of teaching and improvement of learning. Scuola Democratica. **3**, 545–555 (2021)
40. Jovičić Vuković, A., Stanojević, D., Maksić, S.: The quality of online higher education teaching during the COVID-19 pandemic: evidence from Serbia. Acta Educationis Generalis. **14**(3), 83–92 (2024). https://doi.org/10.2478/atd-2024-0020
41. Creswell, J. W., Plano Clark, V. L.: Designing and Conducting Mixed Methods Research. SAGE Publication, Los Angeles (2007).

42. Lundberg, A., Stigmar, M.: University teachers' shifting views of successful learning environments in the future. Scand. J. Educ. Res. **67**(6), 964–979 (2023). https://doi.org/10.1080/00313831.2022.2115127
43. European University Association (EUA): Quality Assurance Fit for the Future (2023). https://www.eua.eu/publications/reports/quality-assurance-fit-for-the-future.html eua.eu+11
44. Jarni, N., Gurr, D.: A futures perspective on learning and teaching in higher education: an essay on best and next practices. Trends High. Educ. **3**(3), 793–811 (2024). https://doi.org/10.3390/higheredu3030045

Formative Assessment and Innovative Feedback

Teacher-Aligned Grading of Open-Ended Questions Using Shot-Based and Rubric-Based LLM Evaluation

Valentina Scorza(✉), Giacomo Cassano, and Nicoletta Di Blas

Politecnico di Milano, Piazza Leonardo da Vinci 32, Milano 20133, Italy
{valentina.scorza,giacomo.cassano,nicoletta.diblas}@polimi.it
https://www.polimi.it

Abstract. Open-ended questions play a crucial role in education, assessing not only students' knowledge but also their critical thinking and conceptual understanding. However, grading such responses is time-consuming and difficult to scale in large classes. While previous research has explored using large language models (LLMs) for automated grading, these approaches typically produce generic scores that do not reflect a teacher's individual evaluation style, whether implicit or explicit via predefined rubrics. In this work, we focus on bringing the teacher's perspective to the center of AI assessment, proposing two complementary approaches. The Shot-Based Approach leverages examples of teacher-graded responses to guide the model, capturing the instructor's implicit grading style. In contrast, the Rubric-Based Approach relies on explicit evaluation criteria, assigning scores to the key elements specified by the teacher and integrating them into a final grade through a structured formula. Both approaches were tested with GPT-4o and GPT-4o Mini on real datasets of student responses and teacher evaluations from university courses. Results highlight complementary strengths: GPT-4o Mini excels at identifying key concepts, while GPT-4o is more reliable in performing rubric-based calculations. LLMs can enforce rubric consistency and detect deviations from grading criteria, yet struggle with highly creative or very poor responses. Pedagogically, AI can improve efficiency, consistency, and fairness, but human oversight remains essential, making LLMs powerful assistants rather than replacements for educators.

Keywords: Open-Ended Questions · Automated Grading · Large Language Models (LLMs) · Shot-Based Learning · Rubric-Based Evaluation · Educational Technology

1 Introduction

Open-ended questions play a crucial role in education, assessing more than factual recall by requiring students to demonstrate critical thinking, problem-solving, and reasoning [1]. Unlike multiple-choice questions, they encourage deeper engagement and higher-order cognitive skills [6,15]. However, grading

M. Adamoli et al. (Eds.): HELMeTO 2025, CCIS 2958, pp. 273–292, 2026.
https://doi.org/10.1007/978-3-032-31850-3_17

these student responses is time-consuming, labor-intensive, and difficult to scale in large classes [12].

Automated evaluation systems have been proposed to support grading, but they often produce generic scores that fail to reflect the teacher's individual perspective. Effective assessment requires attention not only to correctness but also to reasoning quality, argument structure, conceptual understanding and other elements that vary across subjects, question types, and learning objectives. By placing the teacher at the center of AI assessment, the system ensures that evaluation is coherent with the subject matter (e.g., emphasizing grammatical accuracy, content relevance, or conceptual depth according to the discipline) and aligned with the instructor's teaching style. Without this alignment, automated grading risks inconsistency and may neglect dimensions that are essential for instructors or specific to the subject matter, leading to evaluations that lack validity.

This study investigates how GPT-4o and GPT-4o Mini evaluate student responses, questioning whether these models can truly assist, reliably support, or even emulate the teacher in grading, and exploring how far AI has advanced in replicating human judgment. We propose a teacher-centered approach using two complementary methods. The Shot-Based Approach leverages exemplar responses with teacher-assigned grades and feedback to guide the scoring of student answers, aiming to capture implicit grading patterns expressed through examples. The Rubric-Based Approach uses evaluation criteria and a scoring formula provided by the instructor, assigning partial scores for each component specified in the rubric and combining them into a final grade, thus modeling explicit and rule-based evaluation practices.

By centering the teacher's perspective, this work explores how AI can enhance the fairness, consistency, and pedagogical value of assessment while aligning with the discipline and the instructor's unique grading style, going beyond overall accuracy by analyzing grading stability, score dispersion, and score distributions. Through a systematic comparison of GPT-4o and GPT-4o Mini across both approaches, this study highlights the strengths and limitations of current language models in supporting or replicating human evaluators, clarifying when AI can effectively assist grading and when human oversight remains essential.

1.1 Research Questions

This study addresses the following research questions.

Shot-Based Approach

- **RQ1:** In the Shot-Based setting, how do GPT-4o and GPT-4o Mini compare, and how does grading performance vary across datasets, question types, and numbers of teacher-provided examples?
- **RQ2:** How does the Shot-Based Approach behave across the scoring scale in terms of grading stability and score dispersion for different teacher-assigned score ranges?

Rubric-Based Approach

- **RQ3:** In the Rubric-Based setting, how do different model configurations compare in approximating teacher grades?
- **RQ4:** To what extent do Rubric-Based configurations reproduce teacher scoring behavior across the grading scale in terms of score dispersion and distribution?

2 State of the Art

2.1 Background

The automated evaluation of open-ended student responses has evolved significantly over the past decades, driven by advances in natural language processing and machine learning. Early approaches relied on rule-based methods, including string matching, pattern recognition, and syntactic analysis [2,10]. While effective for exact matches, these methods struggled to handle variations in phrasing or meaning. Statistical techniques, such as Latent Semantic Analysis (LSA) [9,14], Latent Dirichlet Allocation (LDA), and TF-IDF, improved semantic understanding but remained limited in capturing contextual and sentence-level meaning.

The introduction of word embeddings, including Word2Vec, GloVe, and FastText [5], enhanced semantic recognition by modeling word usage across large corpora and capturing synonymy and contextual similarity. However, these embeddings still faced challenges with sentence-level semantics, word order, and polysemy. Recurrent neural networks (RNNs) and Long Short-Term Memory networks (LSTMs) [16,17] addressed sequential dependencies and improved contextual modeling, yet they proved inefficient for long sequences and complex sentence structures. Contextual embeddings, such as Sentence-BERT (SBERT) [13], further enabled meaningful sentence-level comparisons, although they continue to lack interpretability and robust reasoning capabilities.

Large language models (LLMs), including GPT, mark a significant advancement [8], capturing nuanced language patterns and enabling flexible, semantically aware assessment across diverse domains.

2.2 Related Works

The advent of Large Language Models (LLMs) has brought a broad technological revolution, including new possibilities for automated assessment of open-ended questions. These models enable evaluations based on semantics, coherence, and reasoning rather than surface similarity. Advanced large language models can interpret paraphrasing, implicit reasoning, and varied expression, enabling dynamic and context-aware assessments that were previously unattainable with traditional approaches.

Several studies have examined the capabilities and limitations of LLM-based evaluation. Chang and Ginter [3] evaluated ChatGPT for grading in Finnish, highlighting language-specific challenges and the importance of prompt clarity. Lee et al. [11] combined LLMs, in-context learning, and chain-of-thought reasoning for middle school Earth Science questions, showing improved alignment with human graders through human-in-the-loop approaches, while noting scalability limitations. Impey et al. [7] applied GPT-4 to grading MOOC assignments across disciplines, reporting strong performance in science subjects but limitations for open-ended humanities questions, particularly in handling complex and subjective reasoning.

Despite recent advances, most studies focus on generic model performance and standard alignment metrics, largely overlooking the teacher's role in assessment. Important gaps remain, including limited alignment with specific evaluation styles and insufficient attention to grading rubrics, which are crucial for consistent and interpretable automated assessment.

This work addresses these gaps by examining the strengths and limitations of recent LLMs in assessing open-ended questions and exploring ways to improve their adaptability and reliability in automated grading.

3 Implementation

This study evaluates open-ended student responses using two complementary approaches, both implemented with the LangChain framework [4] and guided by prompt engineering techniques. LangChain is an open-source framework for building applications with large language models, providing tools to manage memory, structure inputs and outputs, and chain prompts for complex interactions. Prompt engineering involves designing precise instructions that guide the model to produce relevant, consistent, and clear outputs.

The first method, the Shot-Based Approach, leverages one-shot or few-shot examples of responses previously graded by the instructor. By learning from these examples, the model captures the teacher's implicit grading style, reflecting how the instructor evaluates responses based on implicit judgment patterns and holistic assessment cues rather than formal criteria. The second approach, Rubric-Based Approach, relies on explicit grading criteria provided by the instructor. The model analyzes each response to determine the presence of the key elements specified in the rubric and assigns partial scores accordingly, which are then combined into a final grade using a teacher-defined formula. This approach promotes systematic and consistent evaluation, aligned with both the instructor's standards as well as the subject's specific requirements.

Both approaches are implemented using GPT-4o and GPT-4o Mini as the underlying language models to perform the evaluation of student responses.

Together, these methods show how AI can support educators by capturing implicit criteria and applying explicit ones, aligning with human grading complexity and assessment requirements.

3.1 Shot-Based Approach

The proposed Shot-Based Approach is an example-driven grading framework designed to emulate the instructor's evaluation style. Each example consists of a student response, the corresponding numerical grade, and the qualitative feedback provided by the instructor.

The system is evaluated under four configurations, defined by the number of examples included in the prompt: $k1$, $k3$, $k5$, and $k7$. Table 1 summarizes the composition of each configuration in terms of the examples provided to the model.

In the one-shot configuration ($k1$), the model is provided only with an ideal student answer, selected by the instructor, which serves as a reference for evaluation. In the few-shot configurations ($k3$, $k5$, $k7$), this ideal answer is progressively augmented with additional examples. These examples are added in pairs, up to a maximum of six additional instances, resulting in a total of 3, 5, or 7 examples, respectively.

The additional examples are selected to cover a balanced range of grades, allowing the model to capture grading nuances across different levels of student performance.

For each evaluation, the model receives as input the question, the student response to be graded, the ideal student answer, the selected supplementary examples, and the formatting instructions for the output. These elements are structured into a single prompt that instructs the model to generate both (i) a numerical score on a 0–5 scale and (ii) detailed, constructive feedback justifying the assigned score.

This design encourages the model to align both scoring and feedback with patterns observed in instructor-provided examples, thereby promoting consistency and pedagogical relevance in automated assessment.

An example of the prompt template used in the Shot-Based Approach is reported in Appendix A.

Table 1. Shot-Based Configurations and Examples Included in the Prompt

Configuration	Examples included
$k1$	Ideal student answer only
$k3$	Ideal student answer + 2 graded examples
$k5$	Ideal student answer + 4 graded examples
$k7$	Ideal student answer + 6 graded examples

3.2 Rubric-Based Approach

The Rubric-Based evaluation method is implemented through a two-phase prompt-chaining architecture, in which multiple prompts are executed sequentially and the output of one phase is used as input for the subsequent phase.

This design enables the model to decompose the evaluation task into simpler, well-defined steps.

In the first phase, the model is prompted with three inputs: the student's response, an instructor-provided rubric and the formatting instructions for the output. The prompt instructs the model to assess the student response against each rubric criterion independently, producing a binary partial outcome (satisfied or not satisfied) for each criterion, together with explanatory feedback.

In the second phase, the partial outcomes generated in the first phase are aggregated using an instructor-defined scoring function. Each rubric criterion is represented as a binary variable, and the final score is computed by applying fixed penalties for unmet mandatory criteria (SITUATIONAL, TELLING, SELLING, SHIFT) and fixed bonuses for satisfied optional criteria (OPT1, OPT2). The computation starts from the maximum attainable score, applies the corresponding penalties and bonuses, and finally constrains the result to the valid scoring range. The weights were defined by the instructor to reflect the relative importance of mandatory and optional criteria.

Formally, let SIT, TEL, SEL, SHF, OPT1, and OPT2 $\in \{0,1\}$ denote the binary outcomes of the rubric criteria. The final score F is computed as:

$$F = \text{clamp}_{[0,10]}\Big(10 - 2.4 \cdot (1 - \text{SIT}) - 2.4 \cdot (1 - \text{TEL}) - 2.4 \cdot (1 - \text{SEL}) - 2.4 \cdot (1 - \text{SHF}) + 0.8 \cdot \text{OPT1} + 0.8 \cdot \text{OPT2}\Big) \tag{1}$$

where $\text{clamp}_{[0,10]}(x) = \max(0, \min(10, x))$.

Following the instructor's grading guidelines, the final scores produced by the Rubric-Based Approach were rounded to the nearest integer before comparison with teacher-assigned grades.

By separating the evaluation of individual rubric criteria from the numerical aggregation of partial outcomes, this architecture ensures a structured, transparent, and reproducible grading process. Moreover, the modular nature of the two-phase prompt chain allows the system to accommodate different instructor-defined rubrics and scoring schemes, thereby supporting consistent and interpretable automated assessment.

The prompt templates used in the Rubric-Based Approach, instantiated with different textual inputs, are reported in Appendix A.

GPT Configurations. The system is evaluated using GPT-4o and GPT-4o Mini across four different configurations. In the standard configurations, GPT-4o or GPT-4o Mini is used in both the first and second phases of evaluation, including the aggregation of partial rubric outcomes.

To verify the correctness of the final scores produced in the second phase, two additional configurations are introduced in which the aggregation step is performed mathematically using the instructor-defined scoring formula described in Eq. 1, without consulting the language model. These configurations are referred to as GPT-4o Calculated and GPT-4o Mini Calculated, respectively. This setup allows us to directly compare model-based aggregation with its exact mathematical counterpart.

Table 2 summarizes the four configurations considered in the study, indicating the model or method employed in each evaluation phase.

Table 2. Summary of GPT Evaluation Configurations Used in the Study

Configuration	Phase 1	Phase 2
GPT-4o	GPT-4o	GPT-4o
GPT-4o Calculated	GPT-4o	Mathematically calculated (Eq. 1)
GPT-4o Mini	GPT-4o Mini	GPT-4o Mini
GPT-4o Mini Calculated	GPT-4o Mini	Mathematically calculated (Eq. 1)

4 Method

4.1 Datasets

This study involved two professors from the Politecnico di Milano, each contributing datasets of student responses from exam assessments.

The first professor (Professor A) provided responses from two exams in the *Technologies for Information Systems* course, focusing on six open-ended questions related to communication. The first exam included 37 student responses and the second 43, with scores assigned on a 0–5 scale along with instructor feedback. This dataset was used with the Shot-Based Approach.

The second professor (Professor B) contributed 276 student responses to a single exam question from the *Leadership and Innovation* course. A detailed rubric and a formula for aggregating partial scores were provided to guide evaluation. The rubric ensured that student responses addressed the key concepts required by the instructor, while awarding additional points for other relevant optional concepts. Given the availability of clear evaluation criteria and a structured scoring method, this dataset was used for the Rubric-Based evaluation approach.

4.2 Evaluation Metrics

To evaluate the alignment between AI-generated scores and human assessments, we employed a combination of standard and custom metrics. Standard metrics, including Accuracy, Mean Absolute Error (MAE), Quadratic Weighted Kappa (QWK) and Frequency, were used to quantify general agreement and predictive performance. **Accuracy** measures the proportion of exact matches between AI and human scores, **MAE** captures the average magnitude of prediction errors regardless of direction, **QWK** evaluates agreement on ordinal scales while penalizing larger discrepancies more heavily than smaller ones and **Frequency** analyzes how often specific scores are assigned by AI and human evaluators across the dataset, helping to identify systematic tendencies such as overuse or underuse of certain grades. These measures provide a solid baseline for assessing consistency between automated and human grading.

However, standard metrics alone do not fully capture the complexity of the evaluation process. To enable a more fine-grained analysis, we introduced two custom metrics specifically designed to provide a deeper insight into the evaluation:

- **Relaxed Accuracy:** Extends the definition of accuracy by considering AI predictions correct if they fall within a predefined tolerance of the human-assigned grade. This accounts for the inherent subjectivity in open-ended responses and captures pedagogically acceptable near matches.
- **Score Dispersion Analysis:** Measures the variability of AI scores compared to human assessments through standard deviation. By quantifying deviations and distribution patterns, this metric highlights whether the AI evaluates consistently or exhibits irregularities that could undermine reliability.

By combining standard and custom metrics, we obtain both a general assessment of agreement and a deeper understanding of the nuances in the AI's grading behavior.

5 Results

5.1 Professor A (Shot-Based Approach)

RQ1: Model Comparison and Overall Grading Performance. Analyses conducted on both Dataset A and Dataset B revealed no statistically significant differences between GPT-4o and GPT-4o Mini across all key evaluation metrics (MAE, QWK, and accuracy). Paired t-tests returned p-values exceeding the 0.05 threshold in all comparisons, indicating that observed differences are not statistically meaningful. Given this equivalence, GPT-4o Mini was selected for subsequent analyses.

The few-shot evaluation system exhibited variable performance depending on question type and the number of examples provided (k-shots). Tables 3 and 4 summarize the strict and relaxed accuracies, as well as the MAE and QWK values for both Dataset A and Dataset B.

In Dataset A, Questions 2 and 6 consistently achieved the highest strict and relaxed accuracies, lowest MAEs, and strongest QWK values across all k-shot levels. Question 6 reached perfect relaxed accuracy at k=3 and k=5, while Question 2 maintained QWK values above 0.79 across all example counts. Conversely, Question 1 showed decreasing strict accuracy with additional examples and low QWKs (<0.11), indicating difficulty in generalizing to its structure. Question

5, although scoring poorly under strict accuracy (<0.11), demonstrated high relaxed accuracy (>0.8), suggesting that the model frequently produced predictions within an acceptable margin of error.

Dataset B confirmed these trends while revealing some question-specific differences. Question 1 improved with more examples, attaining strict accuracy of 0.58 and QWK of 0.86 at k=7. Question 3 achieved high relaxed accuracy (up to 0.88) and strong QWK (0.79). Question 4 remained challenging, with low strict and relaxed accuracies and QWK below 0.4, whereas Question 6 showed variable performance across all the metrics.

Overall, despite variability in strict performance across individual questions, relaxed accuracy remained consistently high (>0.7) for most questions. Performance generally improved with increasing numbers of examples, particularly for mid-range scores, whereas extreme scores, either very high or very low, remained more difficult for the model to predict accurately. These findings indicate that the system is effective at approximating teacher assessments within a reasonable margin of error, even when exact score alignment is limited.

Table 3. Strict and Relaxed Accuracy, GPT-4o Mini, Dataset A vs. Dataset B

	Dataset A				**Dataset B**			
Question	**k1**	**k3**	**k5**	**k7**	**k1**	**k3**	**k5**	**k7**
Strict Accuracy								
1	0.24	0.22	0.30	0.08	0.19	0.23	0.49	0.58
2	**0.73**	**0.76**	**0.70**	**0.76**	0.26	0.30	0.33	0.26
3	0.11	0.14	0.16	0.35	0.30	0.30	0.42	0.47
4	0.08	0.19	0.41	0.46	0.12	0.16	0.26	0.26
5	0.08	0.11	0.11	0.08	0.21	0.30	0.33	0.35
6	0.49	0.51	0.62	0.57	0.19	0.16	0.19	0.28
Mean	0.29	0.32	0.38	0.38	0.26	0.26	0.35	0.38
Relaxed Accuracy (Tolerance = 1)								
1	0.84	0.62	0.59	0.49	**0.74**	**0.77**	**0.84**	**0.86**
2	**0.92**	**0.89**	**0.95**	**0.95**	**0.77**	**0.79**	**0.84**	**0.74**
3	0.41	0.65	0.54	0.78	**0.81**	**0.88**	**0.84**	**0.86**
4	0.54	0.57	0.76	0.73	0.44	0.49	0.53	0.51
5	**0.81**	**0.81**	**0.86**	**0.86**	0.67	0.63	0.72	0.74
6	**0.95**	**1.00**	**1.00**	**0.97**	0.49	0.58	0.56	0.63
Mean	0.75	0.76	0.78	0.80	0.65	0.71	0.74	0.74

RQ2: Score Stability and Dispersion Across the Grading Scale. Beyond absolute grading performance, the Shot-Based Approach was analyzed in terms of grading stability and score dispersion across the scoring scale. Table 5 reports

Table 4. MAEs and QWKs for GPT-4o Mini (Datasets A and B)

	MAE				QWK			
Question	**k1**	**k3**	**k5**	**k7**	**k1**	**k3**	**k5**	**k7**
Dataset A								
1	0.95	1.24	1.22	1.49	0.11	0.10	0.10	0.08
2	0.38	0.35	0.35	0.32	0.79	0.84	0.83	0.80
3	1.68	1.30	1.35	0.95	0.27	0.54	0.50	0.70
4	1.43	1.32	0.95	0.95	0.49	0.56	0.73	0.71
5	1.11	1.08	1.03	1.05	0.09	0.07	0.08	0.11
6	0.57	0.49	0.38	0.46	0.55	0.61	0.71	0.63
Mean	1.02	0.96	0.88	0.87	0.38	0.45	0.49	0.51
Dataset B								
1	1.07	1.00	0.67	0.56	0.68	0.72	0.82	0.86
2	1.05	0.95	0.86	1.02	0.63	0.70	0.76	0.68
3	0.91	0.84	0.77	0.72	0.73	0.78	0.79	0.79
4	1.63	1.47	1.30	1.37	0.29	0.35	0.38	0.39
5	1.21	1.19	1.02	1.00	0.45	0.50	0.62	0.61
6	1.47	1.37	1.44	1.28	0.49	0.56	0.49	0.57
Mean	1.07	1.00	0.86	0.86	0.54	0.56	0.63	0.67

dispersion values for each teacher-assigned score and k-shot configuration for both datasets.

Across both Dataset A and Dataset B, increasing the number of examples generally reduced score dispersion for mid-range teacher scores (2–3), indicating improved stability and stronger alignment with human grading behavior. These score ranges exhibited lower variance and more consistent predictions as k increased.

In contrast, high scores (4–5) and low scores (0–1) demonstrated greater dispersion with increased k, likely due to the presence of ideal answers that elevated grading standards or the difficulty of consistently differentiating partially correct from incorrect responses.

Overall, the Shot-Based evaluation system shows potential in replicating human-like grading behavior, particularly for mid-range responses, while performance remains question-dependent and requires refinement for extreme scores and challenging question types.

5.2 Professor B (Rubric-Based Approach)

RQ3: Comparison of Rubric-Based Model Configurations. The rubric-based zero-shot evaluation was conducted on four configurations: GPT-4o, GPT-4o Calculated, GPT-4o Mini and GPT-4o Mini Calculated. Table 6 presents the accuracies and relaxed accuracies for the four configurations.

Table 5. Score Dispersion Analysis for GPT-4o Mini Model on Dataset A and Dataset B

	Dataset A				Dataset B			
Teacher Score	**k1**	**k3**	**k5**	**k7**	**k1**	**k3**	**k5**	**k7**
0	2.35	1.98	1.44	1.20	1.73	1.50	1.46	1.43
1	1.92	1.62	1.60	0.79	1.73	1.45	1.15	0.94
2	1.83	2.00	0.58	0.41	0.89	0.85	0.75	0.80
3	0.90	0.60	0.74	0.74	0.88	1.07	1.00	1.14
4	1.03	1.21	1.64	1.61	1.62	1.86	1.61	1.61
5	1.13	1.15	1.14	1.25	1.53	1.45	1.42	1.43

Table 6. Accuracies and Relaxed Accuracies for Different Configurations

	Accuracy	**Tolerance = 1**	**Tolerance = 2**
GPT-4o	0.21	0.36	0.60
GPT-4o Calculated	0.21	0.36	0.60
GPT-4o Mini	0.39	0.51	0.83
GPT-4o Mini Calculated	0.39	0.56	0.73

Strict accuracy indicates that GPT-4o achieves the lowest alignment with human grading (0.214), while GPT-4o Mini and GPT-4o Mini Calculated reach higher agreement (0.391 and 0.395, respectively). GPT-4o Calculated produces identical results to GPT-4o, confirming that GPT-4o performs formula-based computation correctly. In contrast, GPT-4o Mini Calculated diverges from GPT-4o Mini, reflecting errors in mathematical score calculation. Overall, absolute performance is lower than in the Shot-Based evaluation, but relaxed accuracy remains robust.

Relaxed accuracy increases for all configurations. With a tolerance of ± 1, GPT-4o Mini (0.507) and GPT-4o Mini Calculated (0.562) outperform GPT-4o (0.362). At ± 2 points, GPT-4o Mini reaches 0.826, exceeding GPT-4o (0.598) and GPT-4o Mini Calculated (0.728). The other metrics support these trends: the MAE is lower for GPT-4o Mini (1.536) versus GPT-4o (2.467), and the QWK is higher (0.739 vs. 0.514), confirming stronger alignment with human grading.

RQ4: Score Dispersion and Distribution Across the Grading Scale. The analysis of score dispersion (Table 7) highlights how the variability of GPT-4o Mini's evaluations differs across teacher-assigned scores. Low and high extremes, such as 0, 2, 8, 9, and 10, exhibit higher standard deviations (2.50, 3.16, 2.08, 2.88, and 1.89, respectively), indicating greater inconsistency in the model's grading at the margins. In contrast, mid-range scores, particularly 5 and 6, show lower dispersion (1.00 and 0.83), suggesting that the model is more stable and reliable when evaluating average-level responses. These patterns indicate that GPT-4o Mini struggles to consistently assess edge cases while performing more coherently in the central range of the scoring scale. Analogous results were obtained with the other configurations, further validating this trend.

Table 7. Analysis of GPT-4o Mini Score Dispersion by Teacher Scores

Teacher Score	0	2	4	5	6	7	8	9	10
Standard Deviation	2.50	3.16	2.18	1.00	0.83	1.73	2.08	2.88	1.89

Table 8 shows the distribution of scores. The teacher assigns a variety of values across the scale, including mid-range scores (2, 4, 6, 7, 9), whereas GPT-4o predictions are concentrated on specific scores (0, 3, 5, 8, 10), overestimating some low scores and underestimating high ones. GPT-4o Mini better approximates the teacher's distribution, while the GPT-4o Mini Calculated variant slightly shifts mid-range predictions but preserves extreme scores. Overall, GPT-4o Mini most closely replicates the teacher's scoring patterns.

Table 8. Frequencies of Scores for Different Configurations

Score	Teacher	GPT-4o	GPT-4o Mini	GPT-4o Mini Calculated
0	**23**	**33**	**23**	**23**
1	0	0	0	0
2	4	0	1	0
3	**0**	**61**	**0**	**51**
4	20	4	0	2
5	**1**	**73**	**49**	**59**
6	32	5	66	2
7	13	1	0	0
8	**45**	**69**	**75**	**55**
9	26	0	0	0
10	**112**	**30**	**62**	**84**

In summary, GPT-4o Mini exhibits the most reliable performance for automated rubric-based grading, despite lower overall absolute scores and some inaccuracies in formula-based computation.

6 Discussion

This study highlights important differences in how GPT-4o and GPT-4o Mini operate within Shot-Based and Rubric-Based grading frameworks. While both models demonstrate clear potential, their performance reveals trade-offs that help clarify the role of LLMs in educational assessment.

In the Shot-Based Approach, both models showed an ability to approximate teacher grading patterns by leveraging examples, thereby aligning more closely with human judgment. However, extreme responses, either very poor or highly creative, remained problematic, underscoring that exposure to examples alone does not capture the full nuance of human evaluation.

The Rubric-Based Approach provides additional insights. The rubric applied in this study assigns penalties of 2.4 points for each of four missing key concepts and awards 0.8 points for each of two optional concepts. This structure naturally leads to expected score clusters around 0, 3, 5, 8, and 10. GPT-4o's scores followed this expected distribution, reflecting its strength in precise, rule-based computation. However, GPT-4o sometimes failed to identify all relevant concepts, resulting in partial misalignments. GPT-4o Mini, in contrast, was more flexible in recognizing key elements and distributing partial credit, achieving closer alignment with teacher scores despite occasional miscalculations in the final totals.

Interestingly, teacher-assigned scores frequently included intermediate values such as 4, 6, 7, and 9, which are less consistent with the rubric's scoring scheme. This suggests that the teacher applied holistic or contextual judgment beyond the strict rubric, introducing subjectivity into the evaluation process. Such variability complicates alignment between AI-generated scores and human grading but also reveals a potential strength of LLMs: their capacity to highlight inconsistencies between rubric-based criteria and actual grading practices.

A qualitative inspection of individual responses (see Appendix B) confirms that many of these discrepancies arise when students express correct conceptual understanding implicitly, without using the explicit terminology required by the rubric.

Overall, the findings indicate that GPT-4o and GPT-4o Mini offer complementary strengths (precision versus flexibility) and can assist instructors by improving grading consistency, highlighting discrepancies, and providing preliminary assessments, while leaving the final judgment to human evaluators.

7 Limitations and Future Works

Despite promising results, this study has several limitations. First, the dataset is limited in size and scope, drawn from a specific academic context, which restricts the generalizability of findings across subjects, institutions, and diverse student populations. Second, the analysis focuses solely on the GPT-4o model family, leaving model-specific biases and differences in grading performance unexplored. Third, the evaluation relies on teacher-assigned scores as ground truth, which may introduce bias due to the inherent variability and subjectivity in human grading.

Future research should address these limitations by expanding the dataset to include more courses, institutions, and student populations, and by testing multiple LLMs to better understand model-specific strengths and weaknesses. Additionally, alternative evaluation strategies should be explored; for example, reversing the validation process (first generating AI-assigned scores and then having teachers review them) could provide a more objective benchmark for assessing AI grading reliability. These improvements would enhance alignment with human judgment, increase robustness, and ensure broader applicability in diverse educational settings.

8 Conclusions

This study investigated the effectiveness of GPT-4o and GPT-4o Mini in automating the grading of student responses using Shot-Based and Rubric-Based approaches. Both approaches exhibited limitations when assessing responses at the extremes, either very low-quality or highly creative and complex, underscoring the need for human supervision in such cases to ensure accurate evaluation.

The Shot-Based Approach demonstrated higher alignment with human grading compared to the Rubric-Based method, particularly when evaluated using relaxed accuracy criteria, which allow for a small margin of error relative to teacher-assigned scores. This indicates that few-shot learning enables the models to approximate teacher judgment more closely.

In contrast, the Rubric-Based Approach demonstrated strengths in enhancing grading consistency, particularly in cases where teacher evaluations diverged from strict rubric criteria. GPT-4o performed well in the precise computation of final scores but somtimes failed to identify all relevant concepts. Conversely, GPT-4o Mini exhibited greater flexibility in detecting key elements and assigning partial credit, which led to better overall alignment with human assessments despite occasional inaccuracies in the final score calculations.

Overall, the findings suggest that LLMs should not be considered a replacement for human graders but rather as valuable assistants. These models can improve grading consistency, generate preliminary assessments, and identify potential discrepancies, while human oversight remains crucial, particularly for responses that are highly creative, complex, or otherwise challenging to evaluate.

Disclosure of Interest. The authors have no competing interests to declare that are relevant to the content of this article.

A Appendix: Prompting Examples

This appendix reports examples of the prompt templates used in the Shot-Based and Rubric-Based approaches, illustrating how inputs are structured and how instructions are conveyed to the language model.

Shot-Based Approach

Prompt Template.

```
Evaluate the student's answer based on the question and the
    ideal answers provided, giving a score from 0 to 5.

Follow these rules:
Starting from the question and the ideal answer, extract the
    main points that the student should have addressed in
    their response.
If the student answer addresses all the main points, assign a
     score of 5.
If the student answer does not address any of the main points
    , assign a score of 0.
If the student answer addresses some but not all the main
    points, assign a score between 0 and 5 based on the
    relevance and completeness of the response.
Provide constructive, concise explanation of the reasons for
    the score assigned to help the student improve their
    answer.

Question:
{question}

Student answer:
{studentAnswer}

Ideal answer:
{idealAnswer}

Examples:
{examples}

Follow these instructions to generate the output:
{formattingInstructions}
```

Rubric-Based Approach

Phase 1—Partial Score Generation (Prompt). Given the rubric and a student response, the model is instructed to evaluate each criterion independently and to provide a binary outcome together with a brief justification.

```
Based on the provided student's answer, evaluate the
    following aspects.
Read carefully the student's answer and evaluate each aspect
    separately.
For each aspect, provide a detailed explanation of why the
    score was set to true or false, explicitly referring to
    the student's answer when necessary.
```

```
Rubric:
{rubric}

Student answer:
{studentAnswer}

Follow these instructions to generate the output:
{formattingInstructions}
```

Rubric Definition Used in Phase 1. The rubric provided to the model as textual input is reported below.

```
1) SITUATIONAL:
If the text explicitly or implicitly refers to Situational
   Leadership, set SITUATIONAL to true, otherwise false.

2) TELLING:
If the text explicitly states that Andrew's initial behavior
   is "telling" (the word "telling" must be used), set
   TELLING to true, otherwise false.

3) SELLING:
If the text explicitly states that Andrew's behavior shifts
   to "selling" (the word "selling" must be used), set
   SELLING to true, otherwise false.

4) SHIFT:
If the shift from telling to selling is attributed to the
   follower's level of readiness or confidence, set SHIFT to
    true, otherwise false.
Note: References to increased autonomy alone are not
   sufficient.

5) OPT1:
If the text reports a transition in readiness (e.g., from low
    competence/high commitment to some competence/low
   commitment), set OPT1 to true, otherwise false.

6) OPT2:
If the text mentions task and supportive behavior as
   dimensions of the model, or explicitly associates telling
   /selling with these dimensions, set OPT2 to true,
   otherwise false.
```

Phase 2—Score Aggregation. The binary outcomes produced in Phase 1 are aggregated using the instructor-defined scoring function described in Eq. 1. In standard configurations, the model is prompted to apply this formula; in configurations labeled *Calculated*, the same aggregation is performed deterministically to verify correctness.

```
Based on the identified concepts in the partial scores given
    in input,
calculate the final score according to the following rules:

Formula:
{formula}

Partial scores:
{partialScores}

Follow these instructions to generate the output:
{formattingInstructions}
```

Scoring Function Used in Phase 2. The scoring function provided to the model as textual input is reported below.

```
Starting final score: 10

Deductions:
- If SITUATIONAL = false, subtract 2.4
- If TELLING = false, subtract 2.4
- If SELLING = false, subtract 2.4
- If SHIFT = false, subtract 2.4

Additions:
- If OPT1 = true, add 0.8
- If OPT2 = true, add 0.8

Note: The final score cannot exceed 10 and cannot be lower
    than 0.
```

Worked Example (Illustrative). As an illustration, consider the following Phase 1 outputs:

- SITUATIONAL = true
- TELLING = true
- SELLING = false
- SHIFT = false
- OPT1 = true
- OPT2 = false

Applying the aggregation rule of Eq. 1 yields:

$$F = 10 - 2.4 \cdot (1-1) - 2.4 \cdot (1-1) - 2.4 \cdot (1-0) - 2.4 \cdot (1-0) + 0.8 \cdot 1 + 0.8 \cdot 0 \\ = 6.0,$$

resulting in a final score of $F = 6.0$.

B Appendix: Qualitative Analysis of Grading Discrepancies

This appendix provides a qualitative analysis of representative grading discrepancies observed under the Rubric-Based evaluation with **GPT-4o**. Rather than focusing on isolated cases, the analysis highlights recurring patterns that help contextualize the quantitative results reported in the main text.

Recurrent Patterns of Discrepancy

Across multiple student responses, discrepancies between teacher-assigned scores and Rubric-Based scores produced by GPT-4o show recurring patterns.

In most cases, students correctly identify the relevant leadership model and demonstrate a coherent understanding of the scenario, but this understanding is expressed implicitly. Key aspects of the rubric, such as the explicit use of terms like *telling* or *selling*, or a clear attribution of behavioral changes to the follower's level of readiness, are often missing. As a result, GPT-4o marks only a subset of mandatory criteria as satisfied, leading to lower Rubric-Based scores, whereas instructors tend to assign moderate scores based on a more holistic evaluation.

In a smaller number of cases, GPT-4o does not identify one or more rubric elements even when related concepts are mentioned, typically due to ambiguous or incomplete formulations in the student response. This produces additional penalties under the Rubric-Based scheme.

When student responses explicitly follow the rubric structure and terminology, GPT-4o and the instructor assign similar scores, indicating that rubric-based evaluation can closely approximate human grading when criteria are clearly and explicitly addressed.

Interpretation

Taken together, these qualitative observations indicate that similar numerical discrepancies may arise from different underlying response characteristics. Rather than reflecting a failure of the model to understand the task, most misalignments stem from the contrast between strict rubric enforcement and holistic human grading practices.

In this respect, GPT-4o exhibits a more rigid application of the rubric, requiring explicit and unambiguous satisfaction of each criterion. When key concepts are expressed implicitly or partially, GPT-4o tends to mark the corresponding rubric elements as unsatisfied, leading to lower automated scores. In contrast, GPT-4o Mini appears more permissive in recognizing partially expressed concepts, accepting a broader range of formulations as valid evidence of criterion satisfaction and therefore producing scores that are more closely aligned with teacher assessments in several cases.

These qualitative patterns complement the quantitative metrics by explaining why score dispersion is concentrated in specific ranges and by clarifying the conditions under which Rubric-Based grading aligns (or diverges) from human assessment.

References

1. Black, P., Wiliam, D.: Developing the theory of formative assessment. Educ. Assess. Eval. Account. **21**, 5–31 (2009). https://doi.org/10.1007/s11092-008-9068-5
2. Callear, D., Jerrams-Smith, J., Soh, V.: CAA of short non-MCQ answers. In: Proceedings of the 5th Computer Assisted Assessment Conference, pp. 1–14. Loughborough University, Loughborough (2001)
3. Chang, L-H., Ginter, F.: Automatic short answer grading for finnish with ChatGPT. In: Proceedings of the AAAI Conference on Artificial Intelligence, vol. 38., no. 21, pp. 23173–23181 (2024). https://doi.org/10.1609/aaai.v38i21.30363
4. Harrison Chase. LangChain. https://www.langchain.com. Accessed 2024 (2023)
5. Gomaa, W.H., Fahmy, A.A.: Ans2vec: a scoring system for short answers. In: Hassanien, A., Azar, A., Gaber, T., Bhatnagar, R., F. Tolba, M. (eds.) The International Conference on Advanced Machine Learning Technologies and Applications (AMLTA2019). AMLTA 2019. AISC, vol. 921, pp. 586–595. Springer, Cham (2020). https://doi.org/10.1007/978-3-030-14118-9_59
6. Hauer, K., et al.: Twelve tips for assessing medical knowledge with open-ended questions: designing constructed response examinations in medical education. Med. Teach. **42**, 880–885 (2020). https://doi.org/10.1080/0142159x.2019.1629404
7. Impey, C., et al.: Using large language models for automated grading of student writing about science. In: International Journal of Artificial Intelligence in Education (2025). https://doi.org/10.1007/s40593-024-00453-7
8. Kasneci, E., et al.: ChatGPT for good? On opportunities and challenges of large language models for education. Learn. Individual Differ. **103**, 102274 (2023). https://doi.org/10.1016/j.lindif.2023.102274
9. Landauer, T., Foltz, P., Laham, D.: An introduction to latent semantic analysis. Discourse Process. **25**, 259–284 (1998). https://doi.org/10.1080/01638539809545028
10. Leacock, C., Chodorow, M.: Crater: automated scoring of short-answer questions. Lang. Res. Evaluat. - LRE **37**, 389–405 (2003). https://doi.org/10.1023/A:1025779619903
11. Lee, G-G., et al.: Applying large language models and chain-of-thought for automatic scoring. Comput. Educat.: Artif. Intell. **6**, 100213 (2024). https://doi.org/10.1016/j.caeai.2024.100213
12. Magliano, J.P., Graesser, A.C.: Computer-based assessment of student-constructed responses. Behav. Res. Methods **44**, 608–621 (2012). https://doi.org/10.3758/s13428-012-0211-3
13. Ndukwe, I.G., et al.: Automatic grading system using sentence-BERT network. In: Artificial Intelligence in Education. In: Bittencourt, I.I., et al. (eds.) Artificial Intelligence in Education, pp. 224–227. Springer International Publishing, Cham (2020)
14. Ormerod, C., et al.: Automated short answer scoring using an ensemble of neural networks and latent semantic analysis classifiers. Int. J. Artif. Intell. Educat. **33**(3), 467–496 (2023). https://doi.org/10.1007/s40593-022-00294-2
15. Tan, S., et al.: Enabling open-ended questions in team-based learning using automated marking: impact on student achievement, learning and engagement. J. Comput. Assist. Learn. **38**, 1347–1359 (2022). https://doi.org/10.1111/jcal.12680
16. Xia, L., et al.: Attention-based bidirectional long short-term memory neural network for short answer scoring. In: Guan, M., Na, Z. (eds.) Machine Learning and Intelligent Communications, pp. 104–112. Springer International Publishing, Cham (2021)

17. Zhang, L., et al.: An automatic short-answer grading model for semi-open-ended questions. Interact. Learn. Environ. **30**(1), 177–190 (2022). https://doi.org/10.1080/10494820.2019.1648300

Evaluating Formative and Innovative Assessment in Engineering Physics: Student Perspectives on Potentials and Challenges

Maysa Anastacio Bernardo Flor da Rosa[1], Michel Corci Batista[1], Oscar Rodrigues dos Santos[1], Diego Fogaça Carvalho[2,3], and André Luís dos Santos Domingues[1,3](✉)

[1] Universidade Tecnológica Federal do Paraná, Cornélio Procópio, Campo Mourão, PR, Brazil
{maysarosa,michel,oscarsantos,anddomingues}@utfpr.edu.br
[2] Universidade Estadual do Vale do Acaraú, Sobral, CE, Brazil
[3] Universidade Anhanguera Uniderp, Campo Grande, MS, Brazil

Abstract. This study analyzes students' perception of the evaluation proposal applied in the Physics III course in the Electronic Engineering program at a federal university. The qualitative research identifies potentialities and challenges in the assessment process, highlighting the formative and innovative nature of the evaluation, which integrates diagnostic moments, monitoring, and ongoing feedback. Student protagonism in self-regulating learning, diversification of assessment instruments, and the importance of practices linking technical-scientific and socio-emotional competencies are highlighted. Results indicate that formative assessment, combined with active and flexible methodologies, contributes to active engagement and practical learning, especially in hybrid and remote contexts. The study improves engineering course teaching practices, fostering student autonomy and comprehensive development.

Keywords: Formative Assessment · Hybrid Learning · Electronic Engineering · Active Methodologies · Student Perception

1 Introduction

The assessment of learning in higher education has been the subject of numerous debates and studies, with a growing international consensus on the limitations of traditional models and the need for more holistic approaches, particularly due to the growing need to overcome the traditional approach focused exclusively on summative assessment and formal examinations [13, 27, 29]. The predominance of this traditional model limits understanding of the teaching-learning process, reducing it to a classificatory and disciplinary instrument that often demotivates students and hinders the internalization of concepts [10, 29]. However, incorporating Massive Open Online Courses (MOOCs) into blended learning approaches has proven effective in improving learning outcomes and fostering self-directed and lifelong learning strategies, particularly in technical and engineering courses [21].

M. Adamoli et al. (Eds.): HELMeTO 2025, CCIS 2958, pp. 293–307, 2026.
https://doi.org/10.1007/978-3-032-31850-3_18

Based on this understanding, several studies indicate that assessment should be considered a continuous, formative, and collaborative process, in which the student plays an active role, reflecting on their learning and assuming responsibility for their progress [29, 31, 32]. This perspective promotes the disarticulation of assessment as an "authoritarian arm of the teacher" into an instrument that fosters the integral development of the student, thereby strengthening autonomy and self-efficacy [13, 16].

In this sense, the Physics III course, offered in the Electronic Engineering program at a federal university located in the Central-West region of Paraná, constituted the ideal setting for implementing an assessment proposal that combines diagnostic, formative, and summative assessment, as indicated by the National Curricular Guidelines (DCN) for Engineering Education. This assessment seeks to measure knowledge and develop fundamental competencies for professional practice, such as problem-solving, effective communication, critical thinking, and collaborative skills [13, 16].

The proposal was organized to be integrated with the course activities, using digital platforms (*Google Classroom*) in synchronous and asynchronous formats, allowing flexibility and adaptability to the contemporary context of hybrid learning. This context has gained prominence, especially in recent years [30]. It continues to evolve through the integration of advanced technologies, such as virtual worlds and intelligent tutoring systems, to enhance engagement and personalized learning further [14]. During implementation, students actively negotiated the weights of assessment activities and monitored their performance, demonstrating the development of metacognition and accountability for learning [20].

Based on the responses collected at the end of the course, it was possible to assess students' perceptions of the assessment process, assigning them the role of regulators of their own learning and communicators of pedagogical needs to the teacher. According to Bardin [4], analyzing these responses allows us to identify emerging categories that reflect the positive and negative aspects highlighted by students, providing relevant data for improving pedagogical and assessment practices.

Therefore, this study aims to analyze students' perceptions of the assessment proposal applied in Physics III, identifying elements related to the process's strengths and challenges, with a view to providing practical contributions to Electronic Engineering education. This approach seeks to align assessment with students' real needs, establishing a formative assessment culture that fosters effective learning and skill development.

Furthermore, this study aims to analyze the main learning assessment processes used in Engineering teaching and to verify the potential of assessment instruments for developing group work. The aim is also to critically examine students' perceptions of the process, highlighting its positive and negative aspects, and discuss the contributions of this model to improving teaching practices. In this way, the work seeks to expand understanding of effective assessment models in technological higher education, promoting practices that value student autonomy and continuous learning improvement.

2 Theoretical Framework

Learning assessment has been the subject of discussion and study in the educational field, revealing distinct concepts and practices that directly impact student development. Traditionally, assessment was conceived as a mechanism for measuring and classifying performance, almost exclusively through tests and exams that reflect a predominantly summative and quantitative approach [10]. This approach limits assessment to the final judgment of student learning, without considering intermediate stages that could contribute to the continuous improvement of the educational process.

However, authors such as Régnier [28] and international scholars such as Black and Wiliam [5] and Hattie & Timperley [21] emphasize the importance of articulating diagnostic, formative, and summative assessments, which, when integrated, enhance the effects of evaluation as a learning regulation tool. Diagnostic assessment allows students' prior knowledge, difficulties, and needs to be identified early in the process, guiding appropriate teaching practices. Formative assessment plays a guiding and procedural role by providing ongoing feedback, fostering reflection, and encouraging students to self-manage their learning path. On the other hand, a summative assessment summarizes the results achieved, serving as a conclusive assessment of the content's achievement.

In the context of higher education, and specifically in engineering programs, the need to overcome classificatory and restrictive practices becomes even more urgent, as the training of these professionals demands the complex development of technical, interpersonal, and problem-solving skills. The literature shows that the predominance of summative assessment, characterized by the use of essay and multiple-choice tests, aligns with traditional teaching methodologies, typically expository, which reinforce memorization and the lack of critical articulation of knowledge [26]. This scenario motivates the review and innovation of assessment practices in engineering education to reflect current educational demands. This perspective is reinforced by reports from bodies such as the Accreditation Board for Engineering and Technology (ABET) and the European Network for Accreditation of Engineering Education (ENAEE), which advocate for competency-based assessments.

Among the alternatives being investigated and implemented are instruments that promote active student participation, such as group work, project development, oral presentations, self-assessment, and peer review. Studies by Gibbs & Simpson [17] and Boud and Falchikov [7] have extensively documented the benefits of such approaches for deep learning and self-regulation across higher education contexts, including engineering. These practices place students in the leading role in their assessment process, fostering autonomy, critical thinking, and shared responsibility for learning [31, 32]. Group work, in addition to promoting the exchange of knowledge and the development of socio-emotional skills, also allows for the integration of fundamental knowledge in Engineering, such as systems thinking and interdisciplinarity.

More specifically, producing scientific articles has been identified as a promising assessment strategy in technical disciplines, such as Physics, within Engineering programs. This strategy aligns with pedagogical recommendations from organizations like the American Society for Engineering Education (ASEE), which emphasize research and communication skills. Through this tool, students are encouraged to conduct research, organize information, write scientifically, and present results, thereby consolidating conceptual knowledge and expanding the communicative and methodological skills essential to their professional development [32]. A professor should supervise the preparation of articles to guide and foster critical reflection, rigorous research, and argumentative coherence in the work developed.

The theoretical framework supporting this assessment approach aligns with the integrated assessment perspective, which does not segment assessment moments or types, aiming to articulate diagnoses, feedback, and conclusive judgments within a continuous and participatory pedagogical dynamic. This concept is supported by the normative documents for engineering education, which emphasize the need to develop joint competencies associated with creating, communicating, and applying technical and scientific knowledge [9].

Furthermore, the literature indicates that, to be effective, assessment strategies must consider the context and real-world teaching conditions, adapting to in-person, remote, or hybrid learning modalities. In this regard, the use of MOOCs as components of blended learning has been explored to enhance learning outcomes and promote self-directed learning among students in fields such as Computer Science, reflecting innovative pedagogical practices [22]. In this sense, proposals that incorporate active methodologies, such as guided studies and projects, along with diversified assessments, have proven capable of engaging students and facilitating learning, especially in subjects with abstract and challenging content, such as Physics III, the focus of this research [11].

In summary, the set of studies analyzed highlights the need to introduce diverse, contextualized, and interactive assessment tools that broaden conceptual understanding, develop technical and social skills, and strengthen students' connection to their educational process. Advanced approaches involving virtual worlds and intelligent tutoring systems, for instance, have shown significant potential to foster motivation and improve performance by creating immersive, personalized learning experiences, thereby contributing to critical life skills and digital competencies [14]. This shift would entail overcoming the traditional paradigm centered on written exams and promoting assessments that foster meaningful learning, intellectual autonomy, and the comprehensive development of future engineers. The systematic design of such assessment systems, particularly within digital learning environments like Moodle, leveraging modern theories such as Constructive Alignment, is effective in promoting stable and reliable student outcomes in STEM disciplines, further supporting the move towards innovative evaluation practices [23].

3 Methodology

From a methodological perspective, this study employs a qualitative approach and has a descriptive objective. As for the procedures, it is a bibliographic and observational research study that uses the Participant Observation technique.

Initially, a bibliographic review was conducted to substantiate the theme and structure the research, aiming to identify the main learning assessment processes used in Engineering teaching, in accordance with Gil's [18] recommended methodological procedures.

The research was developed from the researcher's direct contact with the environment and participants, characterizing a qualitative approach that prioritizes the analysis of meanings, beliefs, and attitudes, aspects that cannot be reduced to quantification [25]. This participant observation enabled deeper immersion in the students' learning environment and assessment process, allowing the researcher to understand the nuances of their perceptions and interactions in real time, thereby enriching the descriptive power and ecological validity of the findings. Consistent with the study's aim to analyze students' perceptions of the assessment proposal in Physics III, identifying its strengths and challenges, this contact occurred in a hybrid environment, combining synchronous and asynchronous activities, via *the Google Classroom platform*, during the Physics III discipline of the Electronic Engineering course at a federal university in the Central-West region of Paraná, Brazil, specifically during the second academic semester of 2021. The Physics III discipline had a total enrollment of 64 students during this period. From this population, 48 students voluntarily participated in the research, providing responses that were subsequently analyzed. While this study adopts a qualitative lens to explore student perceptions, other research has demonstrated the robustness of well-designed digital assessment systems in hybrid contexts, effectively integrating diagnostic, formative, and summative components within platforms like Moodle to ensure consistent evaluation outcomes.

To guarantee ethical precepts, the research project was submitted for consideration by the Institution's Research Ethics Committee (CEP) in May 2021, accompanied by the necessary documentation: Institutional Authorization Form, Liability Term, Informed Consent Form (ICF), and Consent Form for the Use of Image, Sound, and Voice (TCUISV), intended for research participants. These documents contained detailed information on objectives, procedures, confidentiality, risks, benefits, inclusion and exclusion criteria, and contact details for any clarifications. After evaluation, the Institution's Research Ethics Committee authorized the research in accordance with Consolidated Opinion No. 4,915,287 58.

Data was collected through participant observation during the course assessment activities, the researcher's field diary, and student-generated documents, particularly the self-assessments completed as part of the assessment proposal. To ensure voluntary participation and data integrity, students were individually invited via email, which included a link to a *Google Forms survey containing* the Informed Consent Form. Students were allowed to withdraw at any time without penalty.

Data analysis was employed in Bardin's [4] content analysis to systematically interpret textual content and identify the multiple dimensions present in students' responses. This structured approach ensured a rigorous and objective examination of the qualitative data, enhancing the reliability of the thematic categorization and the validity of the interpretations by providing a transparent framework for identifying recurring patterns and underlying meanings in the student feedback. Data processing followed the classic steps of this method:

1. **Pre-analysis** – preparing the material and skim reading the responses for prior familiarization and definition of the thematic recording units.

2. **Exploration of the material** – inductive coding of the content, based on identifying relevant units of meaning, which were grouped into semantic categories, allowing the data set to be organized into thematic blocks.
3. **Processing of results** – inference and interpretation of the established categories, correlating them with specific research objectives, especially regarding students' perceptions of the assessment methods used and the emotions triggered during the process.

The analysis focused on deepening students' perceptions of the assessment process, highlighting their active participation in learning, self-regulation of their own academic development, and reflective evaluation of the course. From the students' perspective, this procedure revealed both the strengths and challenges of the assessment approach implemented in Physics III, expanding our understanding of the influence of assessment processes on learning. The synergy between direct participant observation and the systematic application of Bardin's [4] content analysis enabled a robust triangulation of data, ensuring a credible and comprehensive representation of student voices. This integrated approach strengthened the validity of our interpretations by enabling both an immersive understanding of the context and a structured analysis of textual data. These aspects will be presented and discussed in detail in the next section, Results and Discussion, which also includes the students' course evaluation from their perspective, allowing for a more comprehensive understanding of the relationship between the implemented assessment approach and participants' perceptions.

4 Results and Discussion

This section presents the main results of the qualitative analysis of student responses, organized into thematic categories and subcategories according to the coding process. The study followed the assumptions of Bardin's [4] Content Analysis, allowing us to identify students' perceptions of the assessment process implemented in the Physics III course of the Electronic Engineering program.

From the responses, initial codes that emerged with greater frequency and relevance were identified, as summarized below:

- **Evaluation Proposal:** Reports on the differentiated, calm, dynamic, and unconventional way the evaluation was applied, highlighting its importance for learning.
- **Methodology:** Reports related to the teacher's discipline delivery differed from the traditional method.
- **Professional Development:** Comments highlighting the importance of assessment activities for developing essential skills for professional training.
- **Didactics:** Reflections on the teacher's clarity, commitment, and concern for student learning.
- **Accumulation of tasks:** Difficulties reported by students due to the simultaneity of activities required by different subjects.
- **Limitations of ERE (Emergency Remote Teaching):** Negative aspects of technological difficulties, transmission quality, physical distance, and impacts on practical laboratory classes.

In a second step, the codes were grouped into categories and subcategories, resulting in three main categories and six subcategories:

- **Category 1 - Innovative Practices:** subdivided into 'Evaluation Proposal' and 'Methodology';
- **Category 2 - Challenges of Emergency Remote Teaching (ERE)**: subdivided into 'Accumulation of Tasks' and 'ERE Limitations';
- **Category 3 - Skills and Competencies:** subdivided into 'Professional Development'.

This organization enabled us to highlight the multiplicity of evaluative aspects students mobilized as they reflected on their experience in the course. Table 1 presents the frequency with which each initial code was identified in the approximate responses of 48 students, considering that some students did not respond or had insufficient responses for analysis.

Table 1. Frequency of Codes Presented in Student Responses.

Initial Code	Frequency	Percentage
Evaluation Proposal	33	68.7%
Methodologies	31	64.5%
Didactics	16	33.3%
Task Backlog	5	10.4%
Limitations of Emergency Remote Education (ERE)	16	33.3%
Professional Development	8	16.6%

Note. Data from the research, prepared by the authors.

4.1 Innovative Assessment Practices

The category 'Innovative Assessment Practices' emerged significantly in student responses, representing a central aspect of the assessment process for Physics III. As presented, the category is subdivided into three subcategories: Assessment Proposal, Methodology, and Didactics, which will be detailed below, referencing the frequencies revealed in Table 1.

The assessment approach was reported by 33 of the 48 participants, accounting for 68.7% of the coded references (Table 1), demonstrating its relevance to students. According to the reports, assessment was perceived as more than a measuring instrument, assuming a formative role that integrates diagnosis, monitoring, and ongoing feedback. This perspective guides students to understand their learning critically and independently.

It is noteworthy, for example, that assessment activities were not limited to traditional tests and were organized in diverse formats, including synchronous and asynchronous moments. One participant said, "*The assessment proposal was very positive, as it focused not only on tests but also on activities that help students understand and apply the content.*" This recognition of evaluative diversity highlights the transformation of the role of assessment beyond simply verifying learning, moving closer to the precepts of integrative and formative evaluation [9, 20].

The students' active participation in defining the weights for assessment activities reinforced the perception of a collaborative process. The elements of self-management and negotiation were fundamental to engagement, allowing students to regulate their learning processes while suggesting necessary adjustments to the teacher [20].

The methodologies adopted, with 31 mentions (64.5%, Table 1), were highlighted by the participants as one of the essential innovative elements in the development of the discipline. The methodological foundation was based on the flipped classroom format, which combined prior study of content through videos in a virtual environment with synchronous classes aimed at in-depth discussion of topics and resolving doubts [3, 10].

This model allowed for more efficient time management and continuous reflection on the content. One testimonial illustrates this benefit: "*The flipped classroom format helped me organize myself and complete the coursework without it piling up [...] I liked how the teacher taught the classes; it made me see a different approach to teaching, not just the traditional approach most teachers teach us in the classroom.*"

Another point emphasized concerns integrating synchronous and asynchronous moments to foster interaction and flexible learning. Students received videos in advance and completed exercises that supported subsequent discussions, promoting active and collaborative learning. According to the report, "*In my opinion, it was the videos on Thursday before the synchronous class, with the content, because it already gave students an idea of what would be discussed in the synchronous class.*" This organization aligns with studies that point to the flipped classroom as a methodology that enhances engagement and autonomy, both of which are fundamental for developing the skills required in higher education [13, 16].

It is worth noting that despite the potential of the methodology, challenges related to technical limitations and the remote teaching infrastructure itself were reported, such as connection weaknesses, which compromised the quality of teaching via digital platforms: "*A negative point about the discipline would be the use of the Meet platform for classes, which at times left the classes with low quality, not to mention some connection difficulties.*"

Didactics, mentioned by 16 participants (33.3%, Table 1), was identified as a determining factor for the course's success, despite the challenge of understanding complex content, especially in physics. Students highlighted the difficulty they often have in connecting theoretical concepts to their practical applications, which can lead to a lack of interest in the course. This perception aligns with previous studies [6, 15, 24, 33, 34].

To overcome these obstacles, the teaching method was guided by innovative resources, such as videos, podcasts, forums, and experimental activities, and by the professor's commitment to integrating theory and practice in a facilitative manner. A typical report highlights this assessment: "*Your non-traditional methods made me more interested in learning more, especially regarding theoretical issues.*"

Another statement reinforces the positive assessment of the teaching method adopted: "*Physics 3 was a completely different experience compared to my experience as a student; I had never studied this way before. One of the positive aspects was the method the teacher used, where we students took advantage of the synchronous moments to delve deeper into the material and ask questions.*"

These reports emphasize that clear communication, multiple interaction channels, and close teacher monitoring contributed to a more dynamic process, reducing difficulties and promoting greater engagement. Thus, applied didactics converged toward a break from the traditional paradigm, being essential to meeting the needs and expectations of students in remote and hybrid learning [3, 12].

Data from the three subcategories indicate that students perceive innovative practices in assessment, methodology, and teaching as interdependent and fundamental to the success of the teaching-learning process in Physics III. With significant mention rates, particularly in the assessment proposal (68.7%) and methodology (64.5%), the importance of an integrated and collaborative model that breaks with traditional practices and adapts to the contemporary conditions of technological higher education is evident.

The combination of the flipped classroom with a diversified proposal for formative assessment and interactive and flexible teaching methods provided an educational environment that promotes the development of technical-scientific and socio-emotional skills, which are fundamental for the training of engineers [13, 16].

Furthermore, the semantic analysis of the responses demonstrated the students' protagonism in regulating and understanding their learning process [20], bringing the assessment process closer to a space for negotiation and collective knowledge construction. Finally, these innovative practices indicate a promising path for the continuous improvement of Physics teaching, especially in hybrid and remote contexts, where the appropriate use of technologies and active methodologies is essential to ensure engagement and practical learning.

4.2 Challenges and Limitations in the Evaluation Process

The 'Challenges of Emergency Remote Learning (ERE)' category highlights the challenges faced by students and teachers amid abrupt changes in teaching during the pandemic. The forced migration from in-person to remote learning has brought to light various obstacles related to access, methodologies, and workload, directly impacting the learning and assessment process.

The challenges highlighted by participants are reflected in the data extracted from the responses, in which the codes 'Accumulation of tasks' and 'ERE limitations' appear with relevant frequency, respectively 10.4% and 33.3% in the responses, demonstrating the importance of these issues for students in remote teaching conditions.

During the period when the assessment proposal was implemented, the pandemic required a hybrid remote and in-person learning model, with classes and activities organized as Remote Pedagogical Activities, delivered in synchronous and asynchronous sessions within a virtual classroom. In this emergency setting, several demands accumulated, creating a feeling of overload among students.

This perception of task volume is directly linked to the complexity of the educational landscape, which, for many, has resulted in anxiety and difficulties managing time and academic demands. As reported by Agen & Ezquerra [1], students' emotions influence their interest and motivation to learn, and the current context has produced a debilitating effect, with high levels of anxiety that impair learning processes and performance [8].

Consequently, students experienced moments when the excessive accumulation of tasks made the process exhausting and confusing. This situation was reinforced by the reports obtained during the research, which consistently criticized the volume and organization of activities and assessments.

This context requires reflection and adjustments to pedagogical planning, with a view to balancing demands and considering the particularities of emergency remote teaching, so that the evaluation process is meaningful and better adapted to students' realities, taking into account their limitations and the home environment in which learning takes place.

The emergence of Emergency Remote Learning (ERE) was a rapid and necessary response to the social isolation imposed by the SARS-CoV-2 pandemic. This teaching modality, delivered via digital platforms, served as an emergency alternative to maintain class continuity and minimize educational losses.

However, this adaptation process occurred abruptly, and teachers, students, and educational systems had to unexpectedly adapt to the new format, which demanded the search for new techniques, strategies, and teaching practices that reconfigured the entire education system [2, 11, 19].

Among the limitations highlighted are difficulties with internet access and with adequate technological resources for remote activities. Unequal access to technology and connectivity has negatively impacted many students, exacerbating educational inequalities and imposing additional barriers to learning.

This reality highlighted the pressing need to implement and expand public policies to universalize internet access, so that remote learning can become effective and democratic, overcoming the limitations faced in many Brazilian homes.

Furthermore, the virtualization of practical classes, especially those that rely on laboratories and in-person experiences, posed a particular challenge for Emergency Remote Teaching, requiring creativity and innovation from teachers but not always ensuring the complete assimilation of practical content.

Participants' reports reinforce these aspects, demonstrating that, even with efforts to address these limitations, structural difficulties and the adverse conditions of social isolation continue to impact student performance and motivation.

Based on the analysis of data collected on the challenges faced in Emergency Remote Education, we concluded that adopting this model, although necessary to ensure educational continuity during the pandemic, highlighted a series of difficulties that significantly impacted teachers and students.

The overload resulting from task accumulation is a factor in emotional and academic exhaustion, underscoring the need to rethink how activities are organized to promote a balanced, less stressful learning experience.

On the other hand, limitations related to internet access, adequate equipment, and a home environment conducive to study highlight existing socioeconomic and structural inequalities, underscoring the need for public policies that ensure digital inclusion and support the success of remote learning.

These difficulties also highlight the importance of ongoing teacher training, enabling them to use technologies effectively and to adapt methodologies and assessments to the specificities of the remote context.

Thus, the results indicate that the future of educational policies and practices must be grounded in flexibility, inclusion, and sensitivity to each student's particular circumstances, seeking innovative solutions that guarantee an equitable and high-quality education, even in the face of crises and exceptional situations such as the one currently being experienced.

4.3 Skills and Competencies

The third category that emerged from the data analysis concerns the skills and competencies students developed during remote learning, especially in a highly complex subject like Physics III. This set of skills is not limited to mastery of technical content. It also extends to improving autonomy, time management, independence in using technologies, and developing critical thinking skills concerning teaching itself. Recent research, for instance, highlights how blended learning models integrating massive open online courses (MOOCs) can significantly enhance self-education skills and foster lifelong learning strategies among students in engineering and related fields [22].

16.6% of participants explicitly mentioned professional development as an essential component of their educational process. This demonstrates students' growing concern with learning technical content and acquiring skills valued in the job market, ultimately impacting their motivation and engagement with the subject.

In terms of professional development, many students highlighted that the assessment and the methodologies employed helped develop broader competencies beyond mastery of specific content. This development includes skills such as self-assessment, critical thinking, complex problem-solving, and adaptation to digital tools, which are essential competencies for their academic and professional development. Some reports exemplify this perception: "*The assessment proposal made me reflect on my competencies and encouraged me to seek alternatives to solve the problems presented. This certainly strengthens my professional capacity to act independently.*" Another student added: "*The ability to organize my time and the need to plan activities, imposed by the remote format, were fundamental to developing my autonomy. This will certainly contribute to my future career.*"

These statements indicate that students perceived the assessment beyond its classificatory function, valuing its diagnostic and formative functions, which aligns with the arguments of Fontes et al. [15] and Bacich & Moran [3] on the importance of assessment for the construction of knowledge and the integral development of the student.

It is also essential to highlight the increased critical awareness among students regarding the learning process. Remote learning, mediated by the constant use of digital platforms, encouraged the improvement of skills related to self-management, such as self-monitoring and continuous reflection on mistakes and successes in assessment processes.

This professional development movement also directly relates to the skills needed to deal with the challenges posed by Emergency Remote Learning (ERE), which requires students to be proactive and resilient in adapting to the new teaching format. As highlighted in subsection 4.2, the rapid changes required a mental and operational reorganization, which translated into significant learning beyond the content, positively influencing the professional profiles developed by students.

The ‘Skills and Competencies - Professional Development’ category highlighted the positive impact that appropriate assessment can have on students’ development, especially in challenging scenarios such as remote learning. The data indicate that over 16% of students valued this aspect, demonstrating the need to design assessments that not only measure content but also foster students’ comprehensive development and preparation for professional life.

Furthermore, the qualitative analysis shows that assessment can be a conducive space for developing students’ autonomy and critical thinking, fostering an active and reflective approach to learning. These results reinforce the importance of investing in innovative, context-specific assessment practices that align with 21st-century competencies and address the complexities of contemporary education.

Still, it is crucial to recognize the limitations and challenges imposed by the emergency context, such as difficulties accessing technological resources and the emotional impact of isolation, which, although not directly discussed in this category, interfere with students’ performance and overall development.

Finally, when establishing correlations between the identified categories (Innovative Practices 68.7%, Methodologies 64.5%, Limitations and Accumulation of Tasks related to ERE with 33.3% and 10.4% respectively, and Professional Development 16.6%), it is concluded that the development of professional skills and competencies is deeply intertwined in an evaluation process that dialogues with both methodological innovation and overcoming the challenges of remote teaching.

The findings concerning didactics and methodology resonate strongly with the principles of constructive alignment and student-centered learning championed by Régnier [28] and Sant’Anna [31], who advocate for assessment as a continuous, formative, and collaborative process. The observed shift from a traditional, teacher-centric approach to one where students actively negotiate assessment weights and monitor their performance directly reflects Hadji’s [20] emphasis on metacognition and self-regulation. This not only contrasts with the limitations of summative assessment paradigms [10, 26] but also provides empirical evidence supporting the National Curricular Guidelines for Engineering Education [9], which call for the development of a broader range of competencies beyond mere technical knowledge. The integration of diversified evaluation instruments and continuous feedback, particularly in a hybrid learning environment, underscores its potential as a robust tool for fostering both technical and socioemotional skills, moving beyond the ‘authoritarian arm’ of traditional assessment as conceptualized by Gee [16] and Filatro & Cavalcanti [13]. Therefore, the perceived effectiveness of these innovative practices is not merely anecdotal but signifies a pedagogical paradigm shift towards deeper, more meaningful learning and the holistic development of future engineers.

Thus, the interwoven nature of innovative assessment, adaptable methodologies, and responsive teaching, as perceived by students, not only addresses the immediate challenges of hybrid and remote learning but also fundamentally redefines the assessment landscape in engineering education. These findings underscore the critical role of participatory and integrated assessment models in cultivating autonomous, engaged, and competently developed professionals, aligning with contemporary calls for pedagogically sound, inclusive, and responsive assessment practices. This broader interpretative lens confirms that practical assessment is less about measuring outcomes and more about shaping the entire learning journey, thereby profoundly impacting the quality of teaching and the comprehensive training of future engineers.

5 Final Considerations

The study conducted an in-depth analysis of Physics III students' perceptions of the assessment methodology in a hybrid learning context, with adaptations to Emergency Remote Learning. The assessment model adopted, which combined diagnostic, formative, and summative assessments integrated into the course activities, demonstrated effectiveness in measuring knowledge and developing essential competencies such as problem-solving, effective communication, critical thinking, and collaboration. This alignment with the National Curriculum Guidelines reinforces the importance of assessments beyond traditional classification in actively supporting the comprehensive training of future engineers. Indeed, the literature consistently highlights the potential of systematically designed assessment frameworks, even in digital learning environments, to yield stable, valid evaluation results, underscoring the benefits of moving beyond traditional paradigms [23].

Innovative assessment practices demonstrated the possibility of transcending the paradigm of written and static tests, offering students diverse activities in synchronous and asynchronous formats that fostered engagement, autonomy, and protagonism in the learning process. This aligns with studies that showcase the potential of blended learning and the use of online platforms, such as MOOCs, to engage students and promote self-directed learning, demonstrating effectiveness across various institutions and disciplines [21]. Assessments were perceived as formative tools that enabled continuous diagnostics, feedback, and performance monitoring, stimulating students' metacognition and self-regulation throughout their academic journey. This approach helped students view assessment as a dynamic and integrative process, reinforcing constructive criticism and personal responsibility for learning.

Furthermore, the model encouraged students' active participation in collaborative activities, such as group work and projects, strengthening social and interpersonal skills crucial to engineering education, including systemic and interdisciplinary thinking. Developing these transversal skills and consolidating technical knowledge are essential to preparing students for the job market and the challenges of professional practice.

However, the research also revealed significant challenges related to the conditions of Emergency Remote Learning. The overload caused by the excessive accumulation of assignments and assessments was identified as a source of emotional and academic strain, generating anxiety and difficulties in time management and educational demands. These aspects compromised student motivation and performance, underscoring the need to rethink the organization and volume of assessment activities to promote a more balanced, healthy learning environment.

Likewise, structural limitations, such as poor internet access, inadequate equipment, and unfavorable home environments, have highlighted the socioeconomic inequalities that permeate the current educational context. This reality highlights the urgency of implementing public policies that promote digital inclusion and support the success of remote and hybrid learning, minimizing learning barriers.

Furthermore, the results indicate that ongoing teacher training is essential to use technology effectively, adapt methodologies and assessments to the specificities of remote learning, and increase flexibility and sensitivity to students' specific circumstances. Teacher preparation is key to improving educational practices and promoting equitable, high-quality education, even under adverse circumstances.

Therefore, the findings of this study support the idea that assessment in higher education technology should be pluralistic, contextualized, and interactive, encouraging active student participation and fostering meaningful and autonomous learning. Aligning assessment strategies with students' real needs and demands, while considering their social and academic context, is essential for developing inclusive and innovative education in engineering.

For future research, we suggest expanding the study to other disciplines and courses to assess the applicability and impact of innovative assessment models across contexts, including the integration of emerging technologies, such as virtual worlds and intelligent tutoring systems, to enhance learning motivation and outcomes. We also recommend continued research into the support students need to overcome the identified inequalities, deepening teacher training in the pedagogical use of digital technologies, and developing flexible assessments sensitive to students' diverse realities.

Disclosure of Interests. The authors have no competing interests to declare that are relevant to the content of this article.

References

1. Agen, S., Ezquerra, S.: Avaliação formativa e metodologias ativas: um desafio para o ensino superior. Revista de Educação Contemporânea. **10**(2), 112–125 (2021)
2. Arruda, M.R.: Estratégias de avaliação e desenvolvimento de competências no ensino remoto. Educação e Tecnologia na Prática. **12**(3), 45–56 (2020)
3. Bacich, L., Moran, J.: Metodologias ativas para uma educação inovadora. Penso, Porto Alegre (2018)
4. Bardin, L.: Análise de conteúdo. Tradução de Luís Antero Reto. Edições 70, São Paulo (2016)
5. Black, P., Wiliam, D.: Assessment and classroom learning. Assess. Educ.: Principles, Policy Pract. **5**(1), 7–74 (1998)
6. Borrachero Cortés, M., Dávila Acedo, C., Airado, M.C.A.: Reflexões sobre o ensino da Física: desafios e perspectivas. Revista Educación. **40**(2), 135–150 (2017)
7. Boud, D., Falchikov, N. (eds.): Rethinking Assessment in Higher Education: Learning for the Longer Term. Routledge, New York (2007)
8. Bzuneck, J.: Avaliação integrada no ensino superior: fundamentos e aplicações. Appris, Curitiba (2018)
9. Brasil.: Ministério da Educação: Diretrizes Curriculares Nacionais para os cursos de Engenharia. MEC, Brasília, DF (2018)
10. Buriasco, R.L.C. de: Algumas considerações sobre avaliação educacional. Estudos em Avaliação Educacional 22, 155–177 (2000)
11. Cassati, L.: Estratégias avaliativas no ensino de Engenharia: desafios e perspectivas. Revista Brasileira de Ensino de Engenharia. **42**(1), 45–56 (2020)
12. Conrad, J., Ceshini, L., Cunha, S.: A avaliação na educação híbrida: reflexões e práticas inovadoras. Revista de Ensino. **30**(1), 23–38 (2022)

13. Filatro, A., Cavalcanti, M.: Avaliação formativa e desenvolvimento profissional na educação em Engenharia. Revista de Educação em Engenharia. **9**(2), 101–115 (2018)
14. Filippone, A., Bariberi, U., Marsico, E., Nadim, M.A., Di Fuccio, R.: Enhancing learning motivation through virtual worlds and intelligent tutoring systems: a narrative review. In: Ardimento, P., et al. (eds.) Higher Education Learning Methodologies and Technologies Online. HELMeTO 2024. Communications in Computer and Information Science, vol. 2467. Springer, Cham (2025). https://doi.org/10.1007/978-3-031-94002-6_26
15. Fontes, T., et al.: Dificuldades e estratégias no ensino de Física em cursos de Engenharia. Revista Brasileira de Ensino de Ciências Exatas. **11**(4), 210–220 (2019)
16. Gee, J.P.: Discurso, análise do discurso e aprendizagem. Parábola Editorial, São Paulo (2005)
17. Gibbs, G., Simpson, C.: Conditions under which assessment supports Students' learning. Learn. Teach. High. Educ. **1**(1), 3–31 (2004)
18. Gil, A.C.: Métodos e técnicas de pesquisa social, 6th edn. Atlas, São Paulo (2010)
19. Haddad Ferreira, T., Barbosa, M.: Avaliação e desenvolvimento profissional no ensino remoto: desafios e perspectivas. Revista Educação Técnica. **15**(1), 70–85 (2020)
20. Hadji, C.: Avaliação da aprendizagem escolar, 2nd edn. Instituto Piaget, Lisboa (1994)
21. Hattie, J., Timperley, H.: The power of feedback. Rev. Educ. Res. **77**(1), 81–112 (2007)
22. Hulai, O., Kabak, V., Savaryn, P.: Blended learning with MOOCs: an example of use in the training of computer science students. In: Ardimento, P., et al. (eds.) Higher Education Learning Methodologies and Technologies Online. HELMeTO 2024. Communications in Computer and Information Science, vol. 2467. Springer, Cham (2025). https://doi.org/10.1007/978-3-031-94002-6_20
23. Hulai, O., Shemet, V., Moroz, I.: Design and Organization of Assessment Using the MOODLE. In: Ardimento, P., et al. (eds.) Higher Education Learning Methodologies and Technologies Online. HELMeTO 2024. Communications in Computer and Information Science, vol. 2467. Springer, Cham (2025). https://doi.org/10.1007/978-3-031-94002-6_23
24. Mellado Jiménez, M., et al.: Dificuldades na aprendizagem da Física: uma análise qualitativa. Revista de Ensino de Ciências. **12**(3), 78–85 (2014)
25. Minayo, M.C.S.: O desafio do conhecimento: pesquisa qualitativa em saúde, 0th edn. Hucitec, São Paulo (2002)
26. Moreira, M.A., Gravonski, I., Fraile, R.: A avaliação da aprendizagem na Engenharia: uma revisão crítica. Educação em Revista. **42**, 227–250 (2016)
27. Pinho, A.P., Mello, C.L.: Avaliação formativa e sua implementação em cursos de Engenharia. Revista Educação em Foco 5(2), 98–110 (202b
28. Régnier, G.: A avaliação pedagógica: aspectos históricos e conceituais. Cortez, São Paulo (2002)
29. Rosa, M.A.B.F., Batista, M.C., Santos, O.R.: Contribuciones de la autoevaluación a la formación de estudiantes de Física 3. TECNÉ, EPISTEME Y DIDAXIS: TED (REVISTA DE LA FACULTAD DE CIENCIA Y TECNOLOGÍA). **55**, 190–207 (2024)
30. Rosa, F., et al.: Ensino híbrido nas disciplinas de Engenharia: adaptações e experiências recentes. Revista Tecnologia e Educação. **15**(3), 87–98 (2023)
31. Sant'Anna, D.: A participação ativa dos estudantes no processo avaliativo: práticas e desafios. Revista Educação e Tecnologia. **7**(1), 55–68 (2014)
32. Santos, M.E.: Competências comunicativas e metodológicas na formação em Engenharia. Revista Brasileira de Educação Tecnológica. **8**(2), 120–134 (2016)
33. Solbes, J.L.: La enseñanza y aprendizaje de la Física: una revisión crítica. Revista Iberoamericana de Física. **23**(1), 33–39 (2011)
34. Vázquez, C., Manassero, M.: Dificultades en la comprensión de conceptos físicos: un estudio con estudiantes universitarios. J. Phys. Educ. **39**(4), 293–299 (2008)

Focus Groups and Reflective Practice: A Methodological Proposal for Expanding Teachers' Perceptions of Large-Scale Assessments for Pedagogical Development

Débora Cristina Aureliano Rossi Delalibera[1], Diego Fogaça Carvalho[1,2,3], Gislaine Bueno de Almeida[1], Osmar Pedrochi Junior[4], and André Luís dos Santos Domingues[3,5](✉)

[1] Universidade Pitágoras Unopar Anhanguera, Londrina, PR, Brazil
[2] Universidade Estadual do Vale do Acaraú, Sobral, CE, Brazil
[3] Universidade Anhanguera Uniderp, Campo Grande, MS, Brazil
anddomingues@utfpr.edu.br
[4] Universidade Federal do Maranhão, Imperatriz, MA, Brazil
osmar.pedrochi@ufma.br
[5] Universidade Tecnológica Federal do Paraná, Cornélio Procópio, PR, Brazil

Abstract. Large-scale assessments, such as the "*Prova Paraná*", have played a fundamental role in monitoring the quality of education within public school networks, aiming to diagnose students' skills and difficulties across various learning stages. These diagnostic assessments provide essential quantitative indicators that support decision-making, pedagogical planning, and educational policies aimed at continuously improving the educational process. However, effective use of these assessments goes beyond mere data collection, requiring educators to critically and contextually analyze results, thereby enhancing pedagogical development and improving teaching practices. This study proposes and methodologically substantiates the use of focus groups as a strategy to broaden teachers' understanding of large-scale assessment results, fostering critical and collective reflection on the data and its implications for school planning. The focus group methodology, recognized for promoting the exchange of experiences and perceptions among participants, is highlighted as a valuable tool for collective knowledge construction and for addressing challenges in interpreting and using assessment data. *This* proposal outlines expected outcomes, including strengthening teacher autonomy, promoting pedagogical strategies better aligned with students' real needs, and overcoming difficulties arising from insufficient quality feedback on assessment results. Therefore, this work emphasizes the importance of continuous formative practices to transform assessment data into concrete instruments for contextualized educational development.

Keywords: Focus Groups · Reflective Practice · Large-Scale Assessments · Teacher Professional Development

M. Adamoli et al. (Eds.): HELMeTO 2025, CCIS 2958, pp. 308–321, 2026.
https://doi.org/10.1007/978-3-032-31850-3_19

1 Introduction

Large-scale assessments, such as the "*Prova Paraná*", have played a fundamental role in monitoring educational quality in public school systems, seeking to diagnose students' strengths and weaknesses at different stages of learning [16]. These diagnostic assessments are necessary tools that provide essential quantitative indicators for decision-making, pedagogical planning, and educational policies to improve the educational process [16].

However, the discussion of large-scale assessments goes beyond mere data production, emphasizing the need to consider teachers' perceptions and actions alongside the results. Teachers' preparation for administering the "*Prova Paraná*", how they receive and share the results with students, and, most importantly, how they reflect on the relationship between this assessment and pedagogical practice are crucial aspects of the evaluation to develop a formative character and contribute to the improvement of teaching [3, 11].

Teacher reflection on pedagogical practice, based on authors such as Schön [17] and Alarcão [2], is a process that goes beyond merely technical knowledge and effectively occurs within educational action. This reflection is crucial for teachers to identify difficulties, problematize situations, and implement new strategies that meet students' needs [10]. From this perspective, focus and study groups foster dialogue, the exchange of experiences, and the collective development of solutions to school challenges, constituting important spaces for continuing teacher education [11].

Furthermore, the literature highlights the challenges posed by insufficient feedback on assessment data to schools and students, which can compromise the effective use of results for pedagogical improvement [16]. The lack of adequate access to guidelines and teaching materials, as well as the imposition of external goals and the consequent reduction in teacher autonomy, can hinder the educational process, compromising the quality of teaching and teachers' capacity for innovation [16, 17].

In this context, state initiatives such as the "*Formadores em Ação*" group of educators emphasize the importance of collaborative spaces for reflection on the "*Prova Paraná*" and its implications for teaching practice, encouraging the contextualization of assessment and the search for pedagogical strategies that address the gaps identified in the results [9]. Thus, analyzing teacher perceptions through focus groups becomes a valuable tool for understanding and problematizing the impacts of large-scale assessment, contributing to a more reflective education sensitive to local specificities [3, 11].

Therefore, it is essential to recognize that large-scale assessment, beyond its quantitative aspect, must be understood as an integral part of the educational process, involving reflection, dialogue, and the transformation of teaching practices. Strengthening pedagogical autonomy and promoting ongoing teacher education are key to ensuring that assessments, such as the "*Prova Paraná*", fulfill their formative role and improve the quality of public education. To this end, this paper proposes a structured methodological framework for integrating focus groups into teachers' continuous professional development, aiming to foster a more critical and formative engagement with large-scale assessment results.

2 Theoretical Framework

In contemporary education, assessment plays a fundamental role in pursuing teaching quality and improving pedagogical practices. This chapter presents the theoretical foundation guiding the research, exploring the multiple dimensions of the assessment process and its intrinsic relationship with the reflective teacher. Initially, the figure of the reflective teacher is discussed, whose practices are essential to constructing meaningful, contextually relevant teaching.

Next, the general concepts of assessment are addressed, emphasizing its diagnostic and formative role in the school environment. The focus then shifts to large-scale assessment, highlighting its role in public education policies and its growing influence in Brazil since the 1990s, particularly in the implementation of the National Basic Education Assessment System (SAEB) and the "*Prova Paraná*".

Finally, the subsection dedicated to the Paraná Assessment offers a specific analysis of the regional context of these assessment practices, providing an in-depth understanding of the challenges and implications arising from these external assessments in the reality of teachers and schools in Paraná.

2.1 Large-Scale Assessments: Context and Challenges

Large-scale assessments are essential tools for monitoring and improving public education quality, especially when diagnosing students' strengths and weaknesses. In Brazil [5], these external assessments gained traction in the 1990s with the creation of the National Basic Education Assessment System (SAEB) and, later, with the implementation of the "*Prova Brasil*" and other state assessments, such as the "*Prova Paraná*" [4, 6]. These instruments aim to provide detailed school performance indicators that inform public policies and pedagogical strategies.

External assessments play multiple roles in the education system, including diagnosing the teaching-learning process, providing accountability, and comparing networks, schools, and students [15]. According to Correa and Santos [6], "external assessments are used to develop public policies in the education system, seeking to equalize student retention in school with the quality of the teaching-learning process" (p. 30). However, the impacts of these assessments go beyond collecting quantitative data, as they directly influence teaching practices and school management.

Pressure for results can, for example, lead to narrowing the curriculum, eroding teacher autonomy, and adopting pedagogical practices focused exclusively on meeting external goals [6, 8]. This dynamic highlights essential challenges at the interface between large-scale assessment and pedagogical practice, highlighting the need for in-depth reflection on the formative use of results and teacher co-accountability.

Furthermore, analysis that focuses exclusively on quantitative data limits understanding of the implications and experiences of teachers regarding assessments, underscoring the importance of qualitative approaches that consider teachers' perceptions and experiences. As Lopes and Barbosa [14] point out, "the results of large-scale assessments [...] initiate an organized and systematic reflection on educational practice, enabling improvements and filling gaps in pedagogical activities" (p. 34), which can only be fully captured by research that prioritizes the qualitative dimension.

2.2 Focus Group: Concept and Methodological Potential

The focus group is a qualitative methodology that constitutes a rich technique for data collection in exploratory and interpretive research. According to Gatti [11], "the focus group allows for the development of theories in the field, because group interaction explores previously existing ideas, surprises, and introduces new categories and forms of understanding, which support new and useful inferences related to the problem under examination" (p. 13). This approach is based on the interaction among participants who share experiences and opinions on a specific topic, enabling diverse perspectives to emerge and the collective construction of meaning.

Among the advantages of focus groups for qualitative research, we highlight the potential to foster collective reflection and exchange ideas in an open and comfortable environment, thereby encouraging active participation [11]. This dynamic enriches understanding of the phenomenon under study by allowing the identification of multiple perspectives, divergences, and consensuses, fundamental to analytical depth.

In the educational context, focus groups have proven suitable for investigating pedagogical practices, teaching perceptions, and continuing education processes, as they foster dialogue and shared problematization of professional experiences [7]. Furthermore, according to Gatti [11], "the duration of the focus group meeting and the number of sessions depend on the problem and the style of the group, and, in general, one or two sessions provide the information necessary for a good analysis" (p. 28), which highlights the flexibility and efficiency of the method.

Thus, the choice of a focus group as the technique in this study allows us to capture teachers' individual opinions about the "*Prova Paraná*" and understand the collective interactions and reflections that permeate their teaching practices regarding external assessments. This contributes to a more in-depth, contextually grounded analysis of the impacts of large-scale assessments on the school environment.

3 Materials and Methods

This study is configured as a theoretical and propositional investigation, whose objective is to systematize and methodologically substantiate the use of focus groups as a tool to broaden teachers' perception of the results of large-scale assessments, with an emphasis on the development of reflective thinking and the formative use of these data.

The choice of the focus group as a central technique in the methodological proposal is based on its recognized capacity to promote collective interaction and the shared construction of knowledge, as highlighted by Gatti [11]: "the focus group allows the development of theories in the field, because in group interaction it greatly explores previous ideas, surprises, and introduces new categories and forms of understanding" (p. 13). Thus, the proposed methodology values group dynamics as a privileged space for critical reflection on the "*Prova Paraná*" results and their implications for pedagogical practices.

To analyze the data that would arise from the application of this proposed methodology, it is recommended to use Content Analysis [3], due to its ability to organize and rigorously interpret the discourses and emerging collective constructions, complemented by discourse analysis to capture the underlying meanings, values, and ideological representations present in teaching perceptions.

Thus, this methodological proposal aims to improve pedagogical practice through a systematic, collective, reflective process, using the focus group as a space to articulate large-scale assessment results with the development of contextualized educational strategies.

4 Discussion of the Proposed Methodological Model and its Potential Outcomes

This section details the proposed methodological model for implementing focus groups and discusses its potential implications for expanding teachers' understanding of large-scale assessment results, specifically the "*Prova Paraná*". The aim is to illustrate how collective reflection and dialogue, facilitated by focus groups, could help expand teachers' understanding of these external evaluations. This model emphasizes how teachers might interpret, engage with, and integrate assessment data into their pedagogical practices. Drawing on theoretical frameworks of discourse analysis, this section explores how such an approach could reveal implicit meanings, values, and beliefs underlying teachers' discourses, providing insight into their attitudes towards the formative potential of large-scale assessments. The discussion also explores the challenges and opportunities that teachers perceive regarding access to results, the quality of feedback, and the degree of autonomy in their professional contexts. Through this detailed exploration, it is argued that focus groups can serve as reflective spaces that foster critical thinking, collaborative problem-solving, and the development of practical strategies to address educational gaps identified in the assessment outcomes. This model highlights the value of collective reflection in promoting a more contextually relevant and meaningful use of assessment data, ultimately enhancing teaching quality and student learning in public schools.

4.1 Proposed Applications of Focus Groups in Large-Scale Assessment Analysis

This subsection further elaborates on the proposed methodological model by detailing how focus groups can be effectively applied to analyze teachers' perceptions of large-scale assessment results [18], such as the "*Prova Paraná*". The aim is to articulate how this qualitative approach, integrated into a systematic framework, can foster critical reflection and enhance pedagogical development.

Methodologically, the use of focus groups to explore teachers' perceptions is strongly supported by authors such as Gatti [11], who emphasize their capacity to foster an open discussion environment. In such settings, participants feel comfortable expressing diverse opinions and exploring various perspectives, leading to detailed and in-depth information. Gatti [11] posits that focus groups can facilitate the emergence of new inquiries and the development of field-specific theories through group interaction, which expands participants' categories and understandings of the topic at hand.

For analyzing data generated by these proposed focus group dynamics, established qualitative methodologies are recommended. Bardin [3] provides a robust framework for Content Analysis, enabling the systematic organization, coding, categorization, and interpretation of qualitative and quantitative results gathered during focus group sessions. This ensures rigor and clarity in inferring meanings from participants' discourses. Complementing this, Gondim [12] highlights that discourse analysis can reveal hidden meanings, values, and ideological representations related to the investigation topic, thereby broadening the understanding of teachers' perceptions regarding external evaluations.

The formative potential of assessment is a crucial consideration for the proposed model. It is essential that the results of large-scale tests, such as the "*Prova Paraná*", be used not only for diagnostic purposes but also as catalysts for reflection and the adaptation of pedagogical practice. Drawing on discussions of pedagogical practice in teacher training, the methodology proposes that teaching teams interpret results in detail to inform targeted interventions that address identified learning gaps. Tozetto and Gomes [19] reinforce this perspective, underscoring how reflective pedagogical practice contributes to continuous improvement in teaching. Similarly, Schön [17] emphasizes the importance of reflective professionals who continuously evaluate their practice to drive educational advancements.

Therefore, within this theoretical and methodological proposal, focus groups are positioned as valuable tools for structured discussions on large-scale assessments and their impact on schools and teachers. Their application is envisioned to support ongoing professional training and the transformative evolution of teaching practices in response to contemporary educational demands.

4.2 Ethical and Practical Considerations for Implementing Focus Groups

Conducting focus groups in qualitative research requires strict adherence to ethical principles to safeguard participants' rights, alongside meticulous methodological care to cultivate an open, welcoming environment that respects diverse viewpoints. A fundamental aspect of this is the unwavering guarantee of confidentiality for both records and participants' identities, as underscored by Gatti [11], which fosters freedom of expression.

Researchers are obligated to thoroughly explain the data collection process to participants, including formally requesting consent for recordings that will be transcribed and analyzed, while consistently reiterating the commitment to confidentiality. This procedure aligns with established ethical regulations, such as CNS resolution no. 466/2012 in Brazil, and practical recommendations from scholars like Lervolino and Pelocioni [13], who advise detailing group operations and securing consent for audio recordings while emphasizing material confidentiality.

For discussions to flow naturally and ideas to emerge spontaneously, the setting must be welcoming and relaxed, providing participants with a sense of security to articulate their opinions without apprehension of judgment or reprisal. Gatti [11] highlights the importance of an "environment open to discussion, where members feel comfortable expressing their opinions and taking any perspective they wish, actively participating". This atmosphere is crucial for generating rich content and fostering group synergy, both of which are essential to the quality of the insights obtained [1].

Furthermore, the focus group moderator plays a critical role, requiring expertise to lead sessions with clear explanations of the research's purpose, participants' roles, and interaction norms. It must be explicitly communicated that there are no "right" or "wrong" answers, and that all ideas and diverse opinions are equally valued [11].

This guidance helps mitigate anxiety and encourages spontaneous engagement. To ensure discussions remain organic and reveal genuine insights, Gatti [11] also advises against providing participants with overly detailed information about the research object beforehand, as this could lead to preconceived opinions that might interfere with the natural progression of the dialogue.

In essence, these ethical and practical considerations are paramount for conducting focus groups that uphold participants' rights and establish an environment conducive to open discussion, thereby ensuring the scientific integrity and societal relevance of the collected research data.

4.3 Proposals for Implementing Focus Groups in Educational Contexts

Based on the theoretical and methodological framework explored in this study, which highlights the potential of focus groups for reflective practice, we propose a structured approach for their implementation in educational contexts, such as schools, networks, or municipalities. These groups are conceptualized as collective spaces designed for analysis and discussion, where education professionals, particularly teachers and pedagogues, can critically reflect on the results of external assessments, discuss pedagogical practices, and collectively develop strategies to address identified learning gaps. This section outlines key considerations for organizing, conducting, and maximizing the impact of these proposed focus groups.

This structured approach is particularly vital given the persistent challenges identified earlier in effectively translating quantitative assessment data into actionable pedagogical insights and fostering teacher autonomy. While large-scale assessments provide invaluable diagnostic indicators, their full formative potential often remains untapped due to factors such as insufficient feedback quality and limited opportunities for collective reflection. The proposed framework aims to bridge this gap by offering a systematic methodology for educators to engage deeply with assessment results, moving beyond mere data consumption to active, critical interpretation and strategic planning. By doing so, it seeks to empower teachers not only as implementers but also as co-creators of educational improvements, fostering a culture of continuous professional development anchored in reflective practice.

Organization and Composition of Focus Groups. The organization of focus groups should prioritize forming collectives that share similar professional realities, particularly concerning the grades served and the daily challenges faced. Consistent with the literature on group dynamics, the participation of teachers working in similar grades is anticipated to foster more productive discussions, as they share everyday experiences and challenges, thereby facilitating exchange and the collective construction of knowledge. This composition is expected to expand the possibilities for interpreting and understanding assessment results, primarily supporting the redefinition of pedagogical practice.

While homogeneity in professional reality is key to fostering relatable discussions, optimal group size is also essential. Gatti [11] suggests that focus groups typically consist of 6 to 12 participants to ensure rich interaction without becoming unmanageable, a recommendation we adopt for these educational contexts. This size allows for diverse viewpoints to emerge while ensuring every participant has ample opportunity to contribute. Furthermore, including school pedagogues or coordinators in these groups, particularly when they also teach specific subjects or are intimately familiar with grade-level curricula, can add a valuable systemic perspective and facilitate integrating group insights into broader school planning. Their participation can bridge the gap between classroom-level challenges and institutional support structures, promoting a holistic approach to educational development.

Furthermore, the central theme of each group should be carefully aligned with the specific needs of the professionals and the municipality or educational network's reality. The analysis of the "*Prova Paraná*" and its implications is envisioned as a structuring axis for these discussions. Our theoretical exploration highlights a perceived need for an in-depth reflection process on the "*Prova Paraná*" results, indicating that some teachers and teaching teams may lack sufficient information about available materials, how to access and utilize them, and how to apply them in the classroom, as well as opportunities for discussions and reflections on pedagogical practice based on these results.

To operationalize these 'specific training steps,' it is recommended that initial sessions be dedicated not only to understanding the mechanics of accessing data platforms provided by the educational authority (e.g., the "Sistema de Avaliação da Educação Básica" - SAEB platform or Paraná's specific portals), but also to interpreting the statistical representations within the reports. This includes demystifying concepts such as item descriptors, performance scales, and comparative benchmarks. Training should cover how to navigate these digital resources, extract relevant data for specific grade levels or subjects, and critically interpret graphical and textual feedback. Workshops focused on these technical aspects, led by district-level specialists or experienced "*Formadores em Ação*", would precede or be integrated into the initial focus group meetings, ensuring that all participants possess a foundational understanding of the assessment data before engaging in deeper pedagogical reflection. This empowers teachers to independently analyze results, fostering a sense of ownership over the assessment process rather than viewing it as an external imposition.

Therefore, the proposed focus group methodology should incorporate specific training steps to access and use these materials effectively, thereby promoting greater teacher autonomy in managing information related to large-scale assessments.

Frequency and Duration of Sessions. Regarding meeting frequency, we suggest organizing activities in quarterly cycles. This periodicity is designed to allow for continuous reflection and evaluation of the impacts of actions implemented between meetings. Such a frequency is expected to promote sustained participant engagement without overburdening their existing school routines, enabling careful analysis and planning of ongoing pedagogical interventions.

The choice of quarterly cycles aligns with typical academic calendars and assessment timelines, enabling reflection on assessment results and their dissemination before significant pedagogical planning periods. For instance, a session following the release of

"*Prova Paraná*" results could focus on initial data interpretation and strategy formulation. Subsequent quarterly sessions could then be dedicated to monitoring the implementation of these strategies, discussing observed classroom impacts, and adjusting interventions as needed. This iterative cycle supports continuous improvement, moving beyond one-off training events to embed reflective practice within the ongoing rhythm of school life. Flexibility, however, remains paramount; in cases where urgent pedagogical challenges arise or specific data analyses require more immediate attention, supplementary shorter online check-ins could be integrated to maintain momentum without disrupting regular schedules.

Concerning duration, the academic literature on focus group methodology consistently recommends planned meetings that prioritize focus and effectiveness. Gatti [11] advises that meetings should ideally last between an hour and a half and no more than three hours, noting that one or two sessions generally yield sufficient information for a thorough analysis. This recommended time span aims to ensure participants maintain focus, allow for in-depth discussions, and prevent burnout and exhaustion among those involved.

For sessions approaching the three-hour mark, integrating short, structured breaks (e.g., 10–15 min) is advisable to maintain participant energy and focus. The optimal number of sessions (one or two) per cycle, as suggested by Gatti [11], should be determined by the complexity of the topic and the depth of discussion required. For introductory phases or when addressing multifaceted challenges, two sessions per cycle might be more appropriate: one for an initial data deep dive and problem identification, and a second for collaborative solution generation and action planning. Documentation of each session's key insights and decisions is crucial, ensuring continuity and enabling participants to revisit discussions and track progress.

Dynamics and Conduction of Sessions. Sessions should be led by specialized trainers who possess both a deep knowledge of the topic and strong facilitation skills. These moderators must be able to guide dialogue, mediate potential conflicts, encourage plural participation, and ensure that all voices are heard, while respecting differences and divergences. The mediator's role is crucial in creating a favorable environment where participants feel comfortable expressing their perceptions, challenges, and proposed strategies for applying external evaluation results.

To achieve this, moderators should employ a range of facilitation techniques, including active listening, strategic probing questions, and summarization of key points to ensure clarity and progression. They must be adept at managing group dynamics, gently redirecting off-topic discussions, encouraging quieter participants, and respectfully challenging assumptions without creating an adversarial environment. For example, open-ended questions like 'What specific patterns or discrepancies do you observe in these results compared to your classroom experience?' or 'How might these data inform a revised approach to teaching a particular skill?' can stimulate deeper analysis and shared problem-solving. This nuanced guidance helps to transform individual observations into collective insights and actionable strategies.

Emphasizing the importance of effective moderation, it is noteworthy that focus groups, rooted in an interactionist perspective, aim to reveal how an issue is constructed and transformed through group discussion. Therefore, the moderator plays a pivotal role in structuring interactions, ensuring that the debate is productive and that inferences can emerge from collective discourses, as highlighted by Gatti [11], who states that "The excerpts of the speeches show the meanings so that starting points for analysis can be obtained, therefore, the sequences of speeches are valuable for these interpretations" (p. 58).

Beyond verbal exchanges, the sessions can incorporate small group activities or 'think-pair-share' formats to ensure broader engagement before returning to full-group discussion. Recording sessions, primarily in audio, is crucial for capturing the richness of the dialogue. This process necessitates not only prior informed consent, as discussed in Sect. 4.2, but also careful consideration of transcription methods and anonymization protocols during analysis to protect participant confidentiality. Furthermore, where feasible, the presence of a co-moderator or research assistant can prove invaluable for diligent note-taking, managing technical aspects (e.g., screen sharing of assessment reports), and observing group non-verbal cues, allowing the primary moderator to fully focus on facilitating the discussion flow.

Furthermore, the proposed dynamic for these sessions includes the use of support materials and easily accessible reports and answer sheets provided by the State educational authority. This ensures that participants can directly engage with the data and thoroughly understand the descriptors of the assessed skills. This approach aligns with the recommendation that assessment answer sheets and reports should be readily available to the school community. Thus, the focus group is intended to help transform abstract data into a concrete, actionable tool for teaching practice.

Objectives and Expected Results. The focus groups, as proposed, should therefore not only enable a deeper understanding of assessment data but also foster critical reflection and the planning of pedagogical interventions consistent with identified real needs. In this sense, it is crucial to recognize that the results of external assessments, often utilized primarily for diagnostic and accountability purposes, possess a significant educational role. This role can be fully realized provided that pedagogical teams have detailed and reflective access to the data, allowing them to critically "reflect on them, seeking strategies to serve as tools for educational development."

Specifically, the short-term objectives include:

1. **Enhanced data literacy:** Teachers will demonstrate improved capacity to interpret raw assessment data, understand its statistical significance, and relate it to curriculum standards.
2. **Increased critical reflection:** Participants will engage in more nuanced analysis of assessment results, moving beyond surface-level interpretations to explore underlying causes and contextual factors that influence student performance.
3. **Collaborative strategy development:** Teaching teams will collaboratively generate concrete, localized pedagogical interventions and adjustments informed by the identified learning gaps.
4. **Shared understanding of formative potential:** Educators will recognize and articulate how large-scale assessment data can serve as a formative tool for continuous improvement, rather than solely for diagnostic or accountability purposes.

Ultimately, the implementation of these proposed focus groups represents an innovative strategy to overcome challenges associated with teachers' potential lack of access to information and limited opportunities to reflect on assessment data. The systematic organization of these meetings, combined with ongoing monitoring and training, is projected to promote significant improvements in pedagogical practice, fostering educational development that is robustly contextualized within local realities.

Looking beyond immediate outcomes, the long-term expected results of this methodological approach are transformative for the educational ecosystem:

1. **Sustainable pedagogical improvement:** teachers will consistently integrate data-driven insights into their daily planning, leading to more responsive and effective teaching practices that directly address student needs.
2. **Increased teacher autonomy and efficacy:** By empowering teachers with comprehensive data interpretation skills and collaborative spaces for strategy development, their sense of professional autonomy and self-efficacy in navigating external assessments will be significantly bolstered.
3. **Enhanced student learning outcomes:** Over time, the refined pedagogical strategies are expected to translate into measurable improvements in student achievement and reduced learning disparities.
4. **Strengthened school culture of reflection:** The institutionalization of these focus groups will foster a school-wide culture of continuous professional learning, critical inquiry, and collective problem-solving, moving the educational community towards greater adaptability and resilience. This systematic engagement facilitates a dynamic feedback loop where assessment data informs practice, and practice, in turn, informs the interpretation and use of future assessments, ensuring an ongoing cycle of educational development.

5 Final Considerations

This study embarked on a theoretical and propositional investigation, aiming to systematize and methodologically substantiate the integration of focus groups as a strategic tool for broadening teachers' perceptions of large-scale assessment results, particularly those from "*Prova Paraná*". Our central argument lies in the potential of focus groups to foster reflective thinking and the formative use of assessment data, moving beyond a purely diagnostic or accountability-driven approach.

This shift is not merely theoretical; it addresses a pressing need in public education, where large-scale assessments, while providing critical quantitative data, often fall short of empowering educators with the qualitative insights required for meaningful pedagogical transformation. By explicitly advocating the focus group methodology, this study provides a concrete mechanism for translating abstract numbers into contextualized discussions, shared professional dilemmas, and collaboratively forged solutions. This approach actively counters the potential for assessments to be perceived as external impositions, instead reframing them as integral components of a dynamic, teacher-led improvement cycle.

The framework proposed herein underscores the value of collective reflection and the construction of shared knowledge among educators. By providing a structured methodological framework, we emphasize how focus groups can facilitate a deeper, more contextually grounded understanding of assessment outcomes, empowering teachers to analyze data and translate insights into critically improved pedagogical practices. This approach is anchored in established literature on reflective practice and formative assessment, advocating for enhanced teacher autonomy and collaborative problem-solving within the educational context.

Recommendations for educational administrators and public policymakers include institutionalizing the systematic implementation of focus groups within schools and networks, explicitly linking these initiatives to continuous professional development. Ensuring teachers have easy and detailed access to assessment reports, templates, and comprehensive pedagogical support materials is paramount. Such integrated strategies - combining information access, dedicated spaces for collective reflection, and ongoing teacher training - represent a promising pathway. They enable large-scale assessment results to transcend their role as mere diagnostic instruments and become practical tools for sustained, contextualized educational development.

To effectively institutionalize this framework, administrators and policymakers must consider not only funding and logistical support but also fostering a culture of trust and psychological safety within schools. This includes providing dedicated time slots for these group meetings within teachers' work schedules, ensuring access to trained facilitators (who may be pedagogues or experienced teachers themselves), and establishing clear communication channels to disseminate insights from these groups into system-wide improvements. Furthermore, 'comprehensive pedagogical support materials' implies not just access to results, but also resources for interpreting data through a pedagogical lens, examples of effective interventions, and continuous training in reflective practices. Such strategic investments are essential to prevent these initiatives from becoming isolated events and instead integrate them as foundational elements of ongoing professional growth.

In essence, this work presents the focus group methodology as a robust theoretical and practical framework for enriching the qualitative dimension of large-scale assessment analysis. It serves as a vital mediator between quantitative data and teachers' lived experiences, reinforcing shared responsibility for leveraging assessment outcomes. The proposed approach is designed to expand pedagogical autonomy and cultivate meaningful interactions that underpin continuous improvements in teaching practices. Ultimately, this systematic proposal offers a crucial strategy for enhancing educational quality, driven by critical reflection, informed dialogue, and the collective construction of knowledge - fundamental elements for addressing the multifaceted challenges confronting contemporary public education.

The strength of this proposal lies in its pragmatic approach to transforming assessment data from a mere evaluation metric into a vibrant catalyst for pedagogical innovation. By bridging the gap between macro-level assessment policies and micro-level classroom realities, it offers a scalable and sustainable model for teacher professional development that respects the complexity of teaching and learning. This work, therefore, serves as a crucial blueprint for future research to empirically validate the impact of such focus group interventions on teacher efficacy, student outcomes, and the overall culture of educational institutions. Ultimately, the systematic implementation of this methodological framework holds immense potential to democratize assessment, making it a truly collaborative tool for continuous improvement in education.

Disclosure of Interests. The authors have no competing interests to declare that are relevant to the content of this article.

References

1. Abreu, N. R. de, Baldanza, R. F., Gondim, S. M. G.: Os grupos focais on-line: das reflexões conceituais à aplicação em ambiente virtual. JISTEM - Journal of Information Systems and Technology Management 6(1), 5–24 (2009)
2. Alarcão, I.: Formação reflexiva de professores: Estratégias de supervisão. Porto Editora, Porto (1996)
3. Bardin, L.: Análise de conteúdo. Edições 70, Lisboa (2011)
4. Bonamino, A.: A evolução do SAEB: Desafios para o futuro. Em Aberto. **29**(96), 113–126 (2016)
5. Brasil, Ministério da Educação: Diretrizes e políticas nacionais para avaliação. MEC, Brasília, DF (2012)
6. Correa, C. S., Santos, L. M.: O olhar dos professores sobre as avaliações externas e seus impactos nas práticas pedagógicas. Revista Educação Pública (2018). https://educacaopublica.cecierj.edu.br/artigos/18/21/o-olhar-dos-professores-sobre-as-avaliaes-externas-e-seus-impactos-nas-prticas-pedaggicas. Last Accessed 15 May 2024
7. Corrêa, A.M.C., de Oliveira, G., de Oliveira, A.C.: O grupo focal na pesquisa qualitativa: princípios e fundamentos. Revista Prisma. **2**(1), 34–47 (2021)
8. Delalibera, D.C.A.R., Carvalho, D.F.: Emissão de feedbacks pelos docentes no processo de ensino e aprendizagem no curso de graduação em Direito. Revista Inter-Ação. **49**(1), 104–120 (2024)
9. Formadores em Ação: Programa de formação continuada e reflexão sobre Prova Paraná. Secretaria de Educação do Paraná. (n.d.)
10. Freire, P.: A educação na cidade, 5th edn. Cortez, São Paulo (2001)
11. Gatti, B.A.: Grupo focal na pesquisa em Ciências Sociais e Humanas. Líber Livro, Brasília (2005)
12. Gondim, S.M.G.: Grupos focais como técnica de investigação qualitativa: Desafios metodológicos. Paidéia (Ribeirão Preto). **12**(27), 149–161 (2002)
13. Lervolino, S.A., Pelicioni, M.C.F.: A utilização do grupo focal como metodologia qualitativa na promoção da saúde. Revista Da Escola De Enfermagem Da USP. **35**(2), 115–121 (2001). https://doi.org/10.1590/S0080-62342001000200004
14. Lopes, L.P., de Barbosa, J, R.C.: A prática docente frente às avaliações em larga escala no Brasil. Revista JRG de Estudos Acadêmicos. **7**(16), e161312 (2024)
15. de Menegão, R., C.S.G.: Os impactos da avaliação em larga escala nos currículos escolares. Práxis Educativa. **11**(3), 641 (2016)
16. Paraná, Secretaria da Educação: Ementa formadores municípios (2024). https://professor.escoladigital.pr.gov.br/sites/professores/arquivos_restritos/files/documento/2024–06/formadores_acao_municipio_ementa_curso2024.pdf. Last Accessed 15 May 2024
17. Schön, D.A.: The Reflective Practitioner: how Professionals Think in Action. Basic Books, New York (2000)

18. de Souza, L.K.: Recomendações para a realização de grupos focais na pesquisa qualitativa. PSI UNISC. **4**(1), 52–66 (2020)
19. Tozetto, S.S., de Gomes, T.S.: A prática pedagógica na formação docente. Reflexão e Ação. **17**(2), 181–196 (2009)

AI as a Co-designer in Teacher Education: The Moderating Role of Professional Agency on Feedback Uptake

Viviana Vinci[1(✉)], Laura Sara Agrati[2], Pierangelo Berardi[1], and Arianna Beri[3]

[1] Foggia University, Foggia 71100, Italy
viviana.vinci@unifg.it
[2] Pegaso University, Naples 80100, Italy
[3] Bergamo University, Bergamo 24100, Italy

Abstract. The introduction of generative artificial intelligence (AI) into educational settings is reshaping the teacher's role within a hybrid, algorithmic ecosystem marked by a tension between familiarity and distrust [1–3]. Moving beyond a purely instrumental view, this study advances the concept of AI as a "co-designer" [4–6], a dialogic partner whose central operational mechanism is the provision of feedback. This research aims to develop and test an explanatory model of the factors that predict the perceived usefulness of AI in instructional design among pre-service teachers. The study employed a sequential explanatory mixed-methods design. The quantitative phase involved 191 pre-service teachers ($N = 191$) from the University of Foggia, who engaged in an AI co-design activity. A multiple regression model was tested, including Perceived Feedback Quality, Uptake, Dialogic Reflexivity, and Teacher Agency as predictors of perceived usefulness. Quantitative results ($R^2 = .219$) indicate that perceived feedback quality is the strongest and most statistically significant predictor of perceived usefulness ($\beta = .322$, $p < .001$). Dialogic Reflexivity did not emerge as a significant predictor. A moderation analysis revealed a crucial interaction ($p = .036$): the positive effect of uptake (the action of integrating AI suggestions) on usefulness was found to be significant only for teachers reporting a high level of agency. Preliminary qualitative analysis helped interpret these findings, highlighting a "pragmatic reflexivity" (focused on the product) and "agency as a critical filter" for negotiating algorithmic suggestions. We conclude that the value of AI as a co-designer is not automatic. It is determined primarily by the *pragmatic quality* of its output and, decisively, by the teacher's professional agency — the competence to critically govern this interaction.

Keywords: Teacher Agency · AI in Education · Co-design

M. Adamoli et al. (Eds.): HELMeTO 2025, CCIS 2958, pp. 322–336, 2026.
https://doi.org/10.1007/978-3-032-31850-3_20

1 The Algorithmic Ecosystem and the Role of the Teacher

The advent of generative artificial intelligence (AI) is shaping a new epistemological and pedagogical horizon. Its impact, though not yet fully codified, is already manifesting as a transformative force in the field of education [7]. A review of the literature reveals a complex dialectic within the teaching community [2].

On one hand, a prospective enthusiasm is emerging among pre-service teachers who, despite acknowledging their limited technical mastery, perceive favorably the potential of large language models for automating preparatory tasks and designing individualized learning paths [8]. On the other hand, a deep-rooted skepticism is consolidating among in-service teachers, driven by concrete and multidimensional fears. These concerns range from the problematic epistemic reliability of algorithmic outputs - whose validity is undermined by the recurrence of factual errors and "hallucinations" [9, 10] - to the crucial issue of ethical equity. The latter is jeopardized by the tendency of these systems to reproduce and amplify harmful sociocultural biases and stereotypes [11].

This critical reservation is finally exacerbated by a fundamental pedagogical concern: the fear that students may not yet possess the cognitive and metacognitive style required to critically evaluate algorithmically-generated information, thus transforming from conscious users into passive recipients [12].

The epistemological core of the current debate lies in moving beyond the conception of artificial intelligence as a mere 'tool' to be added to the teaching repertoire and instead recognizing it as a transformative agent: an actor that reshapes the very syntax of the educational ecosystem, which has now become intrinsically hybrid and algorithmic. This radical reconfiguration makes imperative the need for professional development pathways that equip teachers with the critical and operational competences to navigate this complexity, maximizing its benefits while governing its challenges [13, 14].

It is precisely within this new pedagogical architecture that our investigation situates its contribution, by advancing and analyzing the concept of AI as a "heuristic co-designer" [1]. Abandoning a purely functionalist view, AI is conceptualized here not as an executor of commands, but as a dialogic partner. The central mechanism through which this partnership is realized is the provision of feedback: an artifact designed to trigger metacognitive and reflective processes. The literature confirms the viability of this approach, highlighting how algorithmic feedback can generate personalized interactions and tailored support, with a significant impact, especially for the most vulnerable student populations [15–17].

Within the co-design model, AI-generated feedback constitutes the central mechanism through which the partnership between teacher and algorithm is concretely realized. If dialogue represents the process, feedback is its most significant output—an artifact capable of triggering a cycle of revision and improvement [18]. The literature on AI in education has extensively documented the potential of these tools in providing "rapid and personalized responses" and "immediate feedback," especially in complex learning contexts [19].

This potential extends across multiple application domains: from enhancing educational accessibility through specific accommodations [20] and serving as a conversational partner for language learning [21], to writing support, where dedicated tools provide suggestions that bolster the user's confidence in the creative process [22].

However, the effectiveness of such a mechanism cannot be taken for granted. The literature on formative assessment teaches that, to be effective, feedback must be of high quality: clear, specific, and action-oriented [23]. This quality is intrinsically linked to the user's perceived usefulness, a key construct in technology acceptance models [24]. It is the perception of receiving a valuable contribution that drives a professional to integrate a new tool into their practice.

This principle must be entirely recalibrated when facing a scenario where one of the interlocutors in the evaluative dialogue is an algorithm. The resulting question is as inevitable as it is complex: what factors predict the perceived usefulness of AI support in instructional design? What is the relationship between these factors?

To navigate the complexity of the interaction between teachers and artificial intelligence, our research proposes a conceptual architecture founded on the dynamic interplay of four key constructs: the quality of AI-generated feedback; uptake, understood as the concrete action of reception and integration by the user; dialogic reflexivity, meaning the metacognitive process triggered by the exchange; and finally, teacher agency, which serves as the fulcrum of the entire model.

Below, we delineate the theoretical foundations of each construct, showing how their integration is essential for understanding and guiding this new pedagogical scenario.

1.1 Feedback as a Process

The concept of feedback is central to participatory and formative assessment strategies.

The literature defines it as crucial information for improving performance, bridging the gap between the current result and the expected quality standard [25, 26]. To be truly formative, feedback must be comprehensible and anchored in previously shared criteria, thereby transforming into an internal generative process that enables the student to actively construct their own learning [27, 28].

However, the process is not monolithic. It is essential to distinguish between feedback production (giving) and its reception (receiving), two distinct yet interdependent phases [29]. This duality justifies the distinction of the first two pillars of our model: on one hand, feedback quality, which refers to the intrinsic characteristics of the algorithmic output, and on the other, uptake, which describes the concrete action of receiving, interpreting, and integrating that output by the user. This latter concept is closely linked to "feedback literacy" [30] - that is, the ability to make sense of received information and use it to improve one's own strategies.

1.2 Dialogic Reflexivity as a Knowledge Construction Mechanism

The mere presence of high-quality feedback and an act of reception is not sufficient.

Socio-constructivist research teaches us that deep learning emerges from dialogue and the shared construction of meaning [31, 32]. This leads us to the third construct of our model: dialogic reflexivity.

To define its operational mechanisms, it is effective to adapt the reflective thinking model proposed by Michelini [33], which articulates its development through three fundamental and interconnected conditions. In this transposition, the AI's output becomes the "material" with which the teacher initiates a reflective conversation [34] to restructure their own understanding. This output also acts as an emancipatory mirroring, a mirror that makes the teacher's pedagogical conceptions visible, allowing for their re-elaboration. Both processes are fulfilled within the community of thought, the dialogic context where reflection is enriched and becomes shared knowledge.

1.3 Teacher Agency

Finally, in a hybrid ecosystem, the interaction among the preceding constructs is mediated and governed by the human role. This brings us to the fourth and most critical pillar: teacher agency, a complex of competences and dispositions that define the teacher's capacity for intentional action [35].

Transcending a purely individualistic view, Biesta and Tedder [36] define agency as an ecological and relational phenomenon: action does not occur *in* one's environment, but *through* it. Goal achievement is always the result of the interaction between individual efforts, available resources (including AI output), and contextual factors. In this sense, teacher agency is the capacity to navigate this interaction, transforming a technological resource into a meaningful and conscious pedagogical action.

This leads us to a fundamental dialectical tension: on one hand, interaction with automated systems can diminish the sense of human control, generating potential resistance from professionals who see their decisional autonomy threatened [37]; on the other hand, as highlighted by Nucci et al. [38], the irreplaceable role of professional competence strongly emerges.

According to this perspective, agency is not resistance to technology, but the indispensable professional competence needed to leverage its output. It is the "agentic" teacher who, through a process of evaluation, revision, and critical adaptation, transforms a generic AI suggestion into a high-quality teaching practice. Agency, therefore, manifests in the ability to "actively approve, adapt, or resist" algorithmic suggestions [37].

2 Methods

This investigation is based on an exploratory sequential explanatory mixed-methods design (QUAN $\rightarrow$ qual). This approach, chosen for its ability to combine analytical breadth and depth, involves an initial quantitative phase aimed at mapping the perceptions and practices of a large sample, followed by a second qualitative phase designed to explore, explain, and interpret the emerging numerical results.

The study was conducted during 2025 and involved 205 pre-service teachers enrolled in the single-cycle Master's Degree program in Primary Education at the University of Foggia. The investigation took place within the Instructional Technology workshop, a structured context in which participants were asked to use AI as a co-design tool to develop a learning activity.

The inquiry was developed around one main research question - what factors influence the perceived usefulness of the AI tool in instructional design - and four specific hypotheses, consistent with the theoretical framework: it was hypothesized that the perceived quality of AI feedback would directly increase perceived usefulness (H1); that part of this effect would be mediated by uptake, defined as the effective revision of the received suggestions (H2); that the scope of AI support for design would produce a direct and mediated incremental effect (H3); and finally, that teacher agency would act as a moderator, amplifying the effect of uptake (H4).

The procedure required each participant to interact with the system in real-time to refine their design drafts. The resulting artifacts were then submitted to an AI-based digital environment to receive feedback, which acted as a stimulus to trigger further revisions and a critical reflection on the adopted pedagogical choices.

Of these, 191 provided informed consent for their data to be processed for research purposes, resulting in a participation rate of 93.2%.

The sample profile is characterized by a marked prevalence of the female gender (n = 186; 97.4%) compared to the male gender (n = 5; 2.6%). Regarding the highest educational qualification obtained, the majority of participants hold a high school diploma (n = 110; 57.6%). A significant segment of the sample has already completed a prior academic path, with 36 participants holding a bachelor's degree (18.8%), 34 a master's degree (17.8%), and 2 a PhD (1.0%). Seven participants (3.7%) did not specify this information.

In professional terms, almost the entire sample (n = 186; 97.4%) has no prior teaching experience, confirming the pre-service nature of the study group, while a small minority (n = 5; 2.6%) is already in-service.

A particularly significant finding, which defines the sample's specificity in relation to the research objectives, is the high rate of familiarity with generative AI tools. The vast majority of participants (n = 179; 93.7%) reported having already used these technologies, compared to a small percentage (n = 12; 6.3%) with no direct experience.

Among the 179 participants who have used AI, the purposes of use are heterogeneously distributed. The most represented category is use for individual study (n = 63; 35.2% of users), followed by use for personal and entertainment purposes (n = 53; 29.6%). It is of considerable interest that a relevant portion of the sample (n = 51; 28.5%) has already explored the potential of these tools for creating teaching activities, foreshadowing a proactive integration into their future professional practice. A smaller share (n = 12; 6.7%) indicated other purposes of use. This profile highlights a sample that is not only exposed to but already actively engaged in exploring the affordances offered by artificial intelligence, making it particularly suitable for an investigation into emerging perceptions and practices in this educational context.

2.1 Quantitative Methods

At the conclusion of the design process, an online questionnaire (CAWI - Computer-Assisted Web Interviewing) was administered to collect quantitative data. The variables were operationalized as follows: the dependent variable, perceived usefulness, was measured using a single item on a 1-to-10 Likert scale. Feedback quality was calculated as the mean of six 10-point Likert items assessing the perceived relevance, clarity, personalization, perceived usefulness, fairness, and formative nature of the feedback; the scale demonstrated excellent internal consistency ($\alpha = .94$). Uptake, a measure of the degree of design modification, and agency, professional autonomy (obtained by inverting the original scale), were mean-centered. Dialogic reflexivity was operationalized by counting how many of three categories with high metacognitive or strategic value ("Reflect critically," "Define learning objectives," "Build assessment tools") participants selected in the multiple-choice item (range 0–3); this score was also subsequently centered. Finally, dialogic intensity, calculated as the number of prompts exchanged with the AI and centered, was included as a control variable (Table 1).

Data were prepared for analysis in Excel. Missing values, being less than 5% for each variable, were handled using column mean imputation to preserve the final sample size of 191 cases. No outlier treatment was performed, as the variables were derived from closed-range scales. Continuous predictors were mean-centered to mitigate multicollinearity and facilitate the interpretation of interaction terms, in line with the recommendations of Aiken & West [39].

To answer the research questions and test the hypotheses, a hierarchical multiple regression analysis was conducted. Mediation analyses with bootstrapping procedures and moderation tests were also performed to explore the model's more complex relationships, such as the indirect effect of uptake and the conditional influence of agency.

2.2 Qualitative Methods

The second phase of the study, qualitative in nature, was designed with an explanatory purpose: to gain a deeper understanding and give meaning to the patterns that emerged from the quantitative analysis, particularly to comprehend the complex role of dialogic reflexivity and teacher agency. This phase focused on the textual data collected via the open-ended questions of the CAWI questionnaire, which included the participants' reflections on the revision process, their feedback integration strategies, and the transcripts of their dialogues with the artificial intelligence.

The methodological approach adopted for the analysis of this textual corpus was textual analysis. The entire analysis process was conducted within the RStudio statistical development environment.

The analytical process involved several steps. First, the textual data were imported and prepared using the readxl package for importing from the Excel file, and the dplyr and tidyr packages for dataset manipulation and cleaning. Subsequently, the entire textual corpus was decomposed into minimal units of analysis (single words and bigrams), using the functions of the tidytext package. Stop words (e.g., articles, prepositions, conjunctions) were removed from these units to isolate the most conceptually significant terms. The final objective of this phase is to provide a "thick" and contextualized understanding of the psychological and professional mechanisms underlying the interaction between pre-service teachers and artificial intelligence tools, explaining the "why" behind the quantitative results.

Table 1. Operationalization of constructs and description of measurement items.

Construct (Abbreviation)	Item Used (Exact Wording)	Scale/Measure Type	Operational Definition
Perceived Usefulness (PU)	*On a scale from 1 ("not at all useful") to 10 ("extremely useful"), how useful did you find the dialogue with AI during the activity design phase?*	Likert Scale (1–10)	Overall subjective assessment of the usefulness of AI support in the design process.
Uptake Level (UL)	*On a scale from 1 ("not at all") to 10 ("a great deal"), how much did you modify your initial idea as a result of the interaction with AI?*	Likert Scale (1–10)	Degree of integration/modification made to the design following the AI dialogue.
Dialogic Reflexivity (DR)	*Derived from the count (0–3) of selected options among: "Reflect critically," "Define learning objectives," "Build assessment tools."*	Count Index (0–3)	Number of reflective/strategic categories selected, indicating the breadth of support requested.
Teacher Agency (Agency)	*On a scale from 1 ("only my judgment") to 10 ("I followed the AI entirely"), how much did you rely on your own judgment versus the AI's suggestions?*	Reversed Likert Scale (1–10)	Degree of perceived decision-making autonomy by the teacher regarding AI suggestions.
Perceived Feedback Quality (QualFeed)	*Mean of the six items: [Relevant], [Clear], [Customizable], [Useful], [Fair], [Formative]*	Mean of Likert Items (1–10)	Composite score of the overall perceived quality of the responses provided by the AI.
Dialogic Intensity (Iteraz.)	*Count of non-empty "Question n posed to AI and response" + "Further questions" columns completed.*	Count (integer)	Total number of recorded question-answer exchanges (proxy for the quantity of interaction).

3 Data Analysis

Quantitative data analysis was conducted to address the research questions concerning the predictors of the perceived usefulness of artificial intelligence in instructional design and to test the formulated mediation and moderation hypotheses.

3.1 Descriptive Statistics and Correlations

As a preliminary step, the Pearson correlation matrix among the study's key variables was examined ($N = 191$). Perceived usefulness showed a positive and statistically significant correlation with perceived feedback quality ($r = .43$, $p < .001$), suggesting that positively rated feedback is associated with a higher perceived usefulness of the tool. Uptake also showed a positive and significant correlation with perceived usefulness ($r = .23$, $p = .002$), indicating that a greater degree of integrating AI suggestions is associated with higher perceived usefulness.

Conversely, agency showed a significant negative correlation with perceived usefulness ($r = -.22$, $p < .01$) and with uptake ($r = -.28$, $p < .001$), suggesting that participants with higher perceived autonomy tend to rate AI as less useful and to integrate its suggestions less. Dialogic reflexivity, operationalized as a 0–3 count of metacognitive/strategic categories, did not show significant correlations with either perceived usefulness ($r = .03$) or uptake ($r = .11$).

3.2 Multiple Regression Model

Subsequently, a multiple linear regression model was tested to predict perceived usefulness using dialogic reflexivity, uptake, teacher agency, the interaction term between dialogic reflexivity and agency, feedback quality, and dialogic intensity as predictors.

The overall model was found to be statistically significant ($F(6, 184) = 8.58$, $p < .001$) and accounted for approximately 21.9% of the variance in perceived usefulness ($R^2 = .219$, Adjusted $R^2 = .193$).

Within the model, two predictors emerged as significant:

- Perceived feedback quality was the strongest predictor ($\beta = 0.322$, $t = 5.54$, $p < .001$), fully confirming hypothesis H1. Feedback rated as higher quality is associated with a significantly higher perceived usefulness.
- Uptake showed a positive, albeit more modest, effect ($\beta = 0.083$, $t = 2.13$, $p = .035$). Integrating AI suggestions contributes positively to perceived usefulness, partially supporting the idea that concrete action is relevant.

Contrary to expectations, dialogic reflexivity ($\beta = -0.057$, $p = .56$), teacher agency ($\beta = -0.069$, $p = .17$), the interaction between reflexivity and agency ($\beta = 0.012$, $p = .83$), and dialogic intensity ($\beta = 0.018$, $p = .73$) were not found to be significant predictors of perceived usefulness in this multivariate model. Consequently, hypothesis H3 (direct or indirect effect of DR) and hypothesis H4 (moderation by Agency on the effect of DR) were not supported by this analysis.

3.3 Mediation and Moderation Analysis

To further explore the relationships, mediation (PROCESS Model 4, 5000 bootstraps) and moderation analyses were conducted.

First, to test hypothesis H2, a mediation analysis examined whether Uptake (UL) mediated the relationship between Perceived Feedback Quality (QualFeed) and Perceived Usefulness (PU), while controlling for dialogic reflexivity and agency. The analysis did not show a significant indirect effect (Effect = 0.038, 95% CI [−0.003, 0.081]).

This finding does not support hypothesis H2, indicating that the action of integrating feedback is not a statistically significant pathway through which feedback quality influences perceived usefulness in this model.

Exploratively, a second mediation model was tested to see if uptake could mediate the (already non-significant) effect of dialogic reflexivity on perceived usefulness. Consistent with the regression and correlation analyses, this test also showed no significant indirect effect (Effect = 0.009, 95% CI [−0.025, 0.046]), confirming that reflexivity (as measured) does not act upon perceived usefulness via uptake.

Regarding hypothesis H4, the moderation analysis of agency on the effect of uptake revealed a significant interaction (B = 0.035, $p = .036$). The simple slopes analysis showed that the positive effect of uptake on perceived usefulness is significant and relevant only for participants with high levels of agency (+1 SD), whereas it is negligible for those with low agency (−1 SD). This supports a modified version of hypothesis H4: autonomy does not have a direct effect nor does it moderate reflexivity's negligible effect, but rather amplifies the positive impact of concrete action (uptake) on perceived usefulness.

3.4 Qualitative Analysis

To elaborate on and explain the quantitative results - particularly the lack of a direct effect of reflexivity and the complex role of agency - a thematic analysis was conducted on the participants' open-ended responses, supported by a computational text analysis within the RStudio environment.

The lexical frequency analysis showed that the terms most frequently used by participants are not abstract concepts, but words grounded in practice (lit. "anchored in practice"), such as 'activity', 'assessment', 'children', and 'classroom' (Fig. 1).

The bigram analysis further corroborated this finding, revealing that the most common word pairs were 'final product' and 'teaching activity' (Fig. 2).

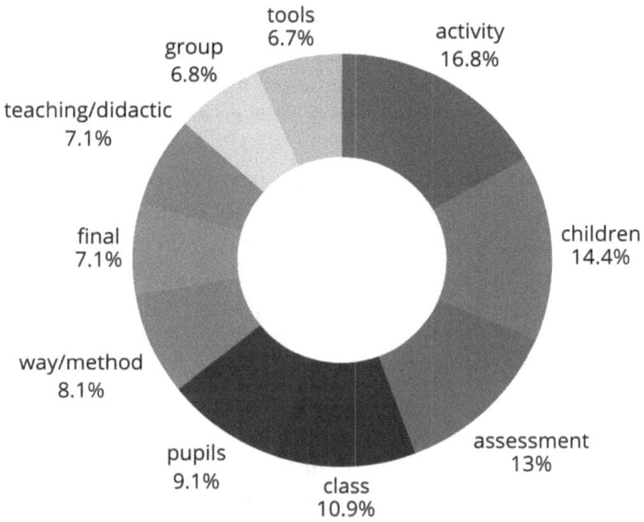

Fig. 1. Frequency of the 10 most common monograms (single words) used by participants in the open-ended response corpus.

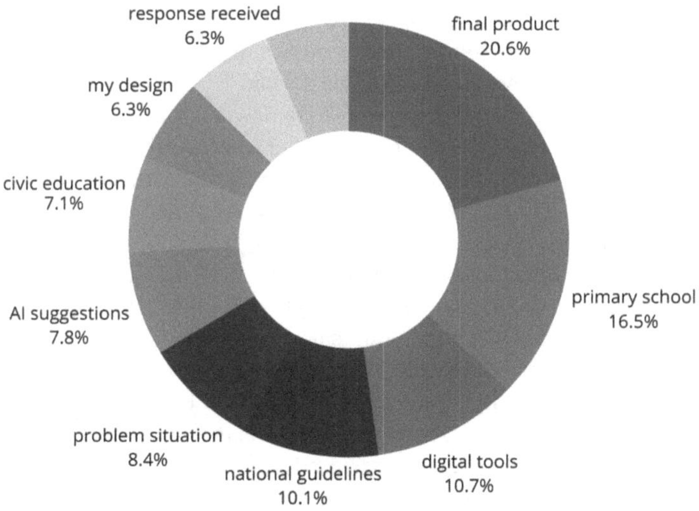

Fig. 2. Frequency of the 10 most common bigrams (word pairs) in the open-ended response corpus, indicating primary conceptual associations.

4 Discussion of Results

The quantitative results indicate that the perceived usefulness of AI in instructional design is primarily driven by the quality of the feedback received. The action of integrating this feedback (uptake) contributes positively, but its impact is significantly greater for teachers who perceive high professional autonomy (agency). Dialogic reflexivity, at least as measured quantitatively in this study, does not emerge as either a direct or indirect predictor. These findings will be discussed in light of the theoretical framework and the implications for educational practice, anticipating the importance of the qualitative analysis for exploring the mechanisms that did not emerge from the aggregate metrics in greater depth.

From the lexical exploration and thematic analysis of the open-ended responses, three key themes emerged that offer an interpretive key for the quantitative results. The first theme, termed "Pragmatic Reflexivity," indicates that the reflection stimulated by AI does not appear to be primarily abstract or metacognitive in nature, but rather instrumental and focused on solving specific design problems and on the operational improvement of the final product. This could help explain why the quantitative measure of dialogic reflexivity (based on more strategic categories) was not significantly correlated with perceived usefulness.

The second theme, "Agency as a Critical Filter," suggests that teacher autonomy manifests not as a stable trait, but as a dynamic process of negotiation, selection, and critical adaptation of AI-provided suggestions, filtered through the teacher's experience and knowledge of the specific classroom context. This theme helps to interpret the negative correlation between agency and perceived usefulness/uptake at the bivariate level, and the moderating role of agency that emerged in the regression analysis.

Finally, the third theme concerns the impact of the interaction on "Professional Awareness": many participants described how the dialogue with AI, despite its limitations, strengthened their perception of competence and their identity as instructional designers capable of governing the technological tool.

These themes provide a useful interpretive framework for understanding the complexity of the interaction between pre-service teachers and artificial intelligence, moving beyond a simple reading of the statistical coefficients. They underscore the importance of considering not only *if* AI is used, but *how* it is integrated into the reflective and decision-making practices of education professionals

This study aimed to develop an explanatory model of the perceived usefulness of artificial intelligence in instructional design, integrating cognitive, behavioral, and professional dimensions. The results clearly indicate that the value attributed to these tools by pre-service teachers is primarily anchored in the quality of the algorithmic output. The perception of clear, pertinent, and relevant feedback emerged as by far the most stable and significant predictor, suggesting that, beyond the enthusiasm for AI's dialogic potential, teachers evaluate its effectiveness based on a pragmatic criterion: its ability to provide a tangible, high-level contribution to their work.

The concrete action of integrating such feedback (uptake) proved to be a necessary second step, although its direct effect is more modest. However, the most sophisticated finding of this research lies in the role of the teacher's critical agency. Professional autonomy does not act as a direct predictor, but as a catalyst that amplifies the effectiveness of uptake. This finding challenges a simplistic view of agency as mere resistance to technology; on the contrary, it frames it as the professional competence that allows one to discern, adapt, and leverage AI suggestions, transforming a mechanical action into a conscious design practice.

In contrast, dialogic reflexivity, despite being a fundamental process, operates at a deeper qualitative level, one that aggregate metrics alone struggle to capture, as indicated by the non-significant result in our quantitative model.

These results lead us to outline specific future perspectives. In terms of research, it is indispensable to deepen the qualitative analysis to explore the discursive strategies and adaptation practices that characterize high-agency teachers. In terms of training, the need emerges to design interventions that go beyond technical training. It is necessary to promote a "pedagogy of the prompt", aimed at teaching teachers how to elicit high-quality feedback, and, in parallel, pathways for the development of critical agency, so that they are able to manage such feedback effectively and autonomously. Only through this dual track will it be possible to transform the dialogue with the algorithm from a simple interaction into a truly transformative partnership.

5 Conclusion and Future Perspectives

The results of this study, while offering a robust explanatory model for the perceived usefulness of AI, open new and important avenues of inquiry that unfold along three main axes: further in-depth qualitative analysis, the extension of the research design to include experimental approaches, and the development of new measurement instruments.

While this study offers significant insights, it is important to consider its exploratory nature when interpreting the results. First, perceived usefulness was assessed using a single-item measure; although this approach is often effective in initial investigations to reduce respondent burden, future research could further validate these findings using multi-item psychometric scales. Second, the quantitative operationalization of dialogic reflexivity relied on a frequency-based index. As suggested by the richness of the qualitative data, this metric may not fully capture the nuance of the metacognitive processes involved, highlighting the need for the development of more granular measurement tools in subsequent studies.

An immediate perspective consists of further in-depth qualitative analysis of the collected data. While the quantitative results clarified *what* predicts usefulness (feedback quality and, to a lesser extent, uptake), and the current qualitative analysis provided insights into *why* dialogic reflexivity might lack a direct impact and *how* agency manifests as a critical filtering process, additional focused analysis could yield even richer detail. Further qualitative exploration could examine the dialogues and artifacts produced to better understand specific dialogue patterns and critical adaptation practices characterizing high-agency teachers.

Secondly, future research should aim to extend the context and develop new instruments. Our sample consists of pre-service teachers; it would be of great interest to replicate the study with in-service teachers, who possess established professional experience and agency. Furthermore, the non-significance of our quantitative measure of reflexivity suggests the need to develop and validate more sophisticated measurement instruments, such as a scale for "Pragmatic Reflexivity in AI Interaction". Such a tool could better capture the instrumental and product-oriented nature that emerged from the qualitative analysis.

Disclosure of Interests.. The authors declare no conflict of interests to the content of this article.

References

1. Vinci, V., Berardi, P.: Familiarity and perception of AI in teacher education: factors influencing its acceptance and use. J. Inclusive Methodol. Technol. Learn. Teach. **5**(2) (2025). https://doi.org/10.32043/jimtlt.v5i2
2. Agrati, L.S., Beri, A.: Intelligenza artificiale e prassi didattica: Indagine esplorativa sugli atteggiamenti degli insegnanti. RTH – Educ. Philos., Bio-Educ. Cogn. **12**(1), 43 (2025). https://doi.org/10.6093/2284-0184/11563
3. Verma, G., Campbell, T., Melville, W., Park, B.-Y.: Navigating opportunities and challenges of artificial intelligence: chat GPT and generative models in science teacher education. J. Sci. Teach. Educ. **34**(8), 793–798 (2023). https://doi.org/10.1080/1046560X.2023.2263251
4. Vinci, V., Berardi, P.: Between enthusiasm and resistance: perceptions of AI in teacher education. Ital. J. Health Educ. Sports Incl. Didact. **9**(1) (2025)
5. Stenberg, C.-J., Åkerfeldt, A., Stenliden, L., McGrath, C.: Teaching with the algorithm: anticipations of AI in teacher education. Eur. J. Teach. Educ. Adv. Online Publ. **48**, 1056 (2025). https://doi.org/10.1080/02619768.2025.2540793
6. Al Nabhani, F., Bin Hamzah, M., Abuhassna, H.: The role of artificial intelligence in personalizing educational content: enhancing the learning experience and developing the teacher's role in an integrated educational environment. Contemp. Educ. Technol. **17**(2), ep573 (2025). https://doi.org/10.30935/cedtech/16089
7. Perla, L., Fabris, A.: Insegnare con l'intelligenza artificiale. Scholé (2025)
8. Lozano, A., Blanco Fontao, C.: Is the education system prepared for the irruption of artificial intelligence? A study on the perceptions of students of primary education degree from a dual perspective: current pupils and future teachers. Educ. Sci. **13**(7), 733 (2023). https://doi.org/10.3390/educsci13070733
9. Alkaissi, H., McFarlane, S.: I.: artificial hallucinations in ChatGPT: implications in scientific writing. Cureus. **15**(2), e35179 (2023). https://doi.org/10.7759/cureus.35179
10. Montenegro-Rueda, M., Fernandez-Cerero, J., Fernandez-Batanero, J.M., Lopez-Meneses, E.: Impact of the implementation of ChatGPT in education: a systematic review. Computers. **12**(8), 153 (2023). https://doi.org/10.3390/computers12080153
11. Borji, A.: A categorical archive of ChatGPT failures. arXiv (2023). https://doi.org/10.48550/arXiv.2302.03494
12. Rezende Junior, M.F., López-Simó, V.: What are the perceptions of physics teachers in Brazil about ChatGPT in school activities? J. Phys. Conf. Ser. **2693**(1), 012011 (2024). https://doi.org/10.1088/1742-6596/2693/1/012011
13. Kaplan-Rakowski, R., Grotewold, K., Hartwick, P., Papin, K.: Generative AI and teachers' perspectives on its implementation in education. J. Interact. Learn. Res. **34**(2), 313–338 (2023) https://www.learntechlib.org/primary/p/222363/
14. Nazaretsky, T., Ariely, M., Cukurova, M., Alexandron, G.: Teachers' trust in AI-powered educational technology and a professional development program to improve it. Br. J. Educ. Technol. **53**(4), 914–931 (2022). https://doi.org/10.1111/bjet.13232
15. Golinkoff, R. M., Wilson, J.: ChatGPT is a wake-up call to revamp how we teach writing. The Philadelphia Inquirer (2023). https://www.inquirer.com/opinion/commentary/chatgpt-ban-ai-education-writing-critical-thinking-20230202.html
16. Bin, Y., Mandal, D.: English teaching practice based on artificial intelligence technology. J. Intell. Fuzzy Syst. **37**(3), 3381–3391 (2019). https://doi.org/10.3233/JIFS-179141
17. Ma, L.: An immersive context teaching method for college English based on artificial intelligence and machine learning in virtual reality technology. Mob. Inf. Syst. **2021**, 2637439 (2021). https://doi.org/10.1155/2021/2637439

18. Vinci, V.: Peer review, feedback e nuovi modelli di valutazione partecipata nell'higher education: una sperimentazione presso l'Università Mediterranea di Reggio Calabria. Educ. Sci. Soc. – Open Access. **12**(2) (2021). https://doi.org/10.3280/ess2-2021oa12477
19. Evmenova, A.S., Borup, J., Shin, J.K.: Harnessing the power of generative AI to support ALL learners. Tech Trends. **68**, 820–831 (2024). https://doi.org/10.1007/s11528-024-00966-x
20. Ciampa, K., Wolfe, Z.M., Bronstein, B.: ChatGPT in education: transforming digital literacy practices. J. Adolesc. Adult Lit. **67**(3), 186–195 (2023). https://doi.org/10.1002/jaal.1310
21. Javier, D.R.C., Moorhouse, B.L.: Developing secondary school English language learners' productive and critical use of ChatGPT. TESOL J. **15**, 1 (2023). https://doi.org/10.1002/tesj.755
22. Van Wyk, M.: Integration of GenAI tools by academics to humanise pedagogical spaces: an AI humanising pedagogical perspective. J. Appl. Learn. Teach. **8**(1), 56–66 (2025). https://doi.org/10.37074/jalt.2025.8.1.24
23. Striano, M., Malacarne, C., Oliverio, S.: La riflessività in educazione: Prospettive, modelli, pratiche. Scholé (2018)
24. Davis, F.D.: Perceived usefulness, perceived ease of use, and user acceptance of information technology. MIS Q. **13**(3), 319–340 (1989). https://doi.org/10.2307/249008
25. Glover, C., Brown, E.: Written feedback for students: too much, too detailed or too incomprehensible to be effective? Biosci. Educ. **7**(1), 1–16 (2006). https://doi.org/10.3108/beej.2006.07000004
26. Hattie, J., Timperley, H.: The power of feedback. Rev. Educ. Res. **77**(1), 81–112 (2007). https://doi.org/10.3102/003465430298487
27. Merry, S., Orsmond, P.: Students' attitudes to and usage of academic feedback provided via audio files. Biosci. Educ. **11**(1), 1–11 (2008). https://doi.org/10.3108/beej.11.3
28. Serbati, A., Grion, V., Fanti, M.: Peer feedback features and evaluative judgment in a blended university course. Italian J. Educ. Res., 115–138 (2019)
29. Grion, V., Tino, C.: Toward a "sustainable assessment" in higher education: perceptions of the giving and receiving peer feedback effectiveness. Lifelong Lifewide Learn. **14**(31), 38–55 (2018)
30. Sutton, P.: Conceptualizing feedback literacy: knowing, being, and acting. Innov. Educ. Teach. Int. **49**(1), 31–40 (2012). https://doi.org/10.1080/14703297.2012.647781
31. Price, M., Handley, K., Millar, J.: Feedback: focusing attention on engagement. Stud. High. Educ. **36**(8), 879–896 (2011). https://doi.org/10.1080/03075079.2010.483513
32. Rust, C., O'Donovan, B., Price, M.: A social constructivist assessment process model: how the research literature shows us this could be best practice. Assess. Eval. High. Educ. **30**(3), 231–240 (2005). https://doi.org/10.1080/02602930500063819
33. Michelini, M. C.: Fare comunità di pensiero. Insegnamento come pratica riflessiva (2ª ristampa 2022). Franco Angeli (2016)
34. Schön, D.A.: The Reflective Practitioner: how Professionals Think in Action. Basic Books (1983)
35. Biesta, G., Tedder, M.: How is agency possible? Towards an ecological understanding of agency-as-achievement (learning lives: learning, identity, and Agency in the Life Course, working paper 5). Teach. Learn. Res. Programme. (2006)
36. Biesta, G., Tedder, M.: Agency and learning in the lifecourse: towards an ecological perspective. Stud. Educ. Adults. **39**(2), 132–149 (2007). https://doi.org/10.1080/02660830.2007.11661545
37. Mouta, A., Torrecilla-Sánchez, E.M., Pinto-Llorente, A.M.: Comprehensive professional learning for teacher agency in addressing ethical challenges of AIED: insights from educational design research. Educ. Inf. Technol. **30**, 3343–3387 (2025). https://doi.org/10.1007/s10639-024-12946-y

38. Nucci, D., Liu, A., Sun, M., Males, L.M.: The professional knowledge required for high-quality AI-generated mathematics lesson planning. Connect. (2024)
39. Aiken, L.S., West, S.G.: Multiple Regression: Testing and Interpreting Interactions. Sage Publications, Inc (1991)

AI-Driven Formative Assessment for Learning (From Research to Action)

Vilmos Vass(✉), Kinga Szálkai, and József Zoltán Málik

Budapest Metropolitan University, 1148, Nagy Lajos király útja 1–9, Budapest, Hungary
{vvass,kszalkai,jmalik}@metropolitan.hu

Abstract. The study highlighted three key themes. First, AI applications are already embedded in everyday academic practice, showing that digital tools have become an integral part of institutional routines. Second, the focus is not on "artificial intelligence" itself but on the human dimension: reflection, creativity, and critical thinking remain at the core of educational value. Third, students must be prepared to use AI consciously, critically, and creatively. This approach strongly resonates with METU's *MyBrand* program, Hungary's first portfolio-based higher education model, where students develop personal portfolios through project-based learning and authentic outputs that later support their career pathways. In this framework, AI-driven formative assessment not only enhances immediate feedback and learning outcomes but also contributes to the long-term development of students. By connecting technological innovation with reflective pedagogy, the study illustrates how AI can complement and enrich human-centered education.

To better understand how these themes emerge, the analysis adopts a qualitative, exploratory research design, grounded in interviews conducted with teachers and students at Budapest Metropolitan University (METU). So far, 10 semi-structured interviews have been completed, each lasting on average one hour. As the research is ongoing, the findings represent the first phase of data collection. While natural differences exist across disciplines and individual perspectives, the analysis also revealed clear common patterns. The coding process was carried out both manually and computationally, using NVivo, ChatGPT, and Python. Furthermore, the results were visualized through mind-mapping (thematic codes) and a dendrogram (clustering interviewees), making the emerging patterns more accessible.

Keywords: Formative assessment · Transformation · VUCA-world · FLUX-world · Information processing · Information transfer · .

1 Background and Introduction

It is a well-known fact that the period between 1760 and 1830, marked by early industrialization and technological changes, is referred to as the First Industrial Revolution. One of the most significant inventions of this era was Stephenson's locomotive. In 1825 the engine, later called Locomotion, took 450 people 25 miles from Darlington to Stockton at 15 miles per hour. This was the first outing of the world's first public passenger steam

M. Adamoli et al. (Eds.): HELMeTO 2025, CCIS 2958, pp. 337–353, 2026.
https://doi.org/10.1007/978-3-032-31850-3_21

train. By 1830 Stephenson's new locomotive, the Rocket, which could achieve a speed of 36 miles per hour, was operating on the Liverpool and Manchester. According to contemporary records, a horseman rode in front of the locomotive, warning people of the train's approach with loud shouts. During the fifth revolution, we are in a similar situation with Artificial Intelligence (AI). The pace of development is significantly faster, and fears are greater. However, alongside these fears, it is also worth noting that, AI has been used in many fields with significant results for many years. With some exaggeration, it is an integral part of our lives. Think of our online banking, our communication in the digital space, route planning, or even diagnostic imaging in health.

Nowadays, on the basis of the research findings and under the umbrella of lifelong learning, AI is reshaping higher education, fundamentally shaking up old structures from curricula to teaching methodology to assessment [1, 2]. A range of studies, articles, conferences, round tables, workshops, and projects address the links between AI and education, from ethical issues to the concept of knowledge and learning, and from the practical to the developmental [3–6]. In our paper, we are focusing on assessment, especially formative assessment. From the output view, the significant and effective starting steps of this process to change and transform the functions of assessment, especially from summative to formative assessment, come to the forefront, which affects the innovative teaching methods. As Black and Wiliam defined, "…formative assessment when the evidence is actually used to adapt the teaching to meet student needs" [7]. Higher education institutions have different strategies for personalized learning, feedback culture, and using responses and feedback for improving assessment and teaching [8–10]. This paper aims to contribute to both national and international discussions on AI-driven assessment under the umbrella of the transformational changes in higher education. Through research findings (international, national, and local) to present some practical examples using AI-driven formative assessment in practice at higher education.

Accroding to Du Preez et al. [11], transformation is a complex, fluid, open-ended process, which can refer to changes in institutional culture, especially curriculum development. No doubt, that transformative learning has enormous impact of higher education from micro (learning and teaching) to macro level (social and communication dimensions) [12]. At the micro level, under the umbrella of changing learning and teaching, the transformative process – on the one hand- has a significant impact on professional discourse about knowledge and thinking, which is greatly amplified by the use of Artificial Intelligence [13].

On the other hand, metacognitive skills, reflective and critical thinking are becoming increasingly important. Basically, this is a transformation process, which has systematic and multiple impacts in higher education [14]. In fact, this is a two-speed transformation process that incorporates both regressive and progressive elements. The first speed started thinking about thinking in the early 20th century, namely when John Dewey published his well-known book How we think about the scientific thinking in 1910.

"…this book also represents the conviction that such is not the case; that the native and unspoiled attitude of childhood, marked by ardent curiosity, fertile imagination, and love of experimental inquiry, is near, very near, to the attitude of the scientific mind." [15].

From the point of view on our topic, it is worth to emphasize the curiosity, imagination and inquiry as a part of scientific mind are significant parts of creative thinking. In some decades, scientific mind came to the front on the process of cognitive revolution, but at another point of view. In 11 September, 1956 some scholars, mainly informatics organized an "Information Theory Symposium" about the "new way of thinking" held at the Massachusetts Institute of Technology (MIT) [16, 17]. No surprisingly, they believed that human mind works as a computer. This statement is the fundamental point of the operation system on AI. Later Jerome Bruner called it computational thinking, which is based on algorithm and routinized steps. But Bruner defined the other type of thinking, which has two phenomena: culturalism and narratives. In this sense the mind works as Dewey's previous creative concept [18, 19].

Turning back to the computational thinking, this approach is related to the information processing. As Bruner wrote: *„how finite, coded, unambiguous information about the word is inscribed, sorted, stored, collated, retrieved, and generally managed by a computational device"* [20].

Nowadays, it is more and more evident that AI's computational thinking is better and faster than human mind. Luckily, narrative- and culturalism-based creative thinking gives chance to use our mind more effective e ways. Besides information processing, this way of thinking is much more complex with critical thinking with "curiosity, imagination and inquiry". Moreover, the quantity of information is growing in an unbelievable speed. According to Fabio Duarte, approximately 402.74 million terabytes of data are created each day. Around 147 zettabytes of data will be generated in 2025 [21]. Navigating in this information jungle is not simple the challenge of information processing. But after some decades of Bruner's theory this process becomes much more complex, because of fast changing world, called VUCA (Volatile, Uncertain, Complex, Ambiguous). According Paul J. LeBlanc, one of the major challenges, which we need to confront from the higher education is:

„Rethinking education and curriculum for a world of human-machine hybrid work, in which whole job categories (and thus majors) are taken over by machines, others are performed in human-machine hybrids, and others remain human only. That rethinking of work will extend to the jobs that get done within educational providers, including colleges and universities." [22].

What does it mean from the view of information processing? The complexity of this process consists of four overlapping steps, namely finding, selecting, constructing and transferring information. The search for information raises the issue of reliability, especially when using AI to access information quickly. Selecting information, firstly is based on navigation with some significant points of view, which is relevant quality of prompting using AI. Secondly, the quality of structures on mind are the fundamental pillar in selecting information. It is not surprising that Bruner was the first to write in detail about the importance of structure in learning and thinking in his early seminal work.

"*How can this exposure be made to count in their thinking for the rest of their lives? The dominant view of among men who have been engaged in preparing and teaching new curricula is that the answer to this question lies giving students an understanding of the fundamental structure of whatever subjects we choose to teach.*" [23].

But understanding fundamental structure, parallel to conscious use of AI, which is more related to constructing and transferring information. Constructing information is based on prior knowledge and learning strategies on self-directed learning in the coherent connection with intrinsic motivation. In our opinion, effective constructing information mainly is based on narrative approach of mind, creative and critical thinking turning back to Dewey and Bruner. The must challenging point is transferring information, which two types. First is a cognitive- and algorithm-based type, which is relatively the combination of computational and creative thinking in different personalized manners. Second types is an affective-based, creative information transfer, where creative thinking is a dominant factor. This is the first-speed transformation process from cognitive revolution to the end of VUCA-world.

The second-speed transformation process is started with concept of FLUX (Fast, Liquid, Uncharted, eXperimental)-world. According to Timothy Timur Tiryaki, this process is "navigating the AI Era with a New Mental Model" [24]. We think, that at this second-spe3ed transformation process, especially turning to the "New Mental Model", the functioning of the mind is essentially complex. In addition to information processing, selection, construction, and transfer, the development of critical and reflective thinking is becoming increasingly important.

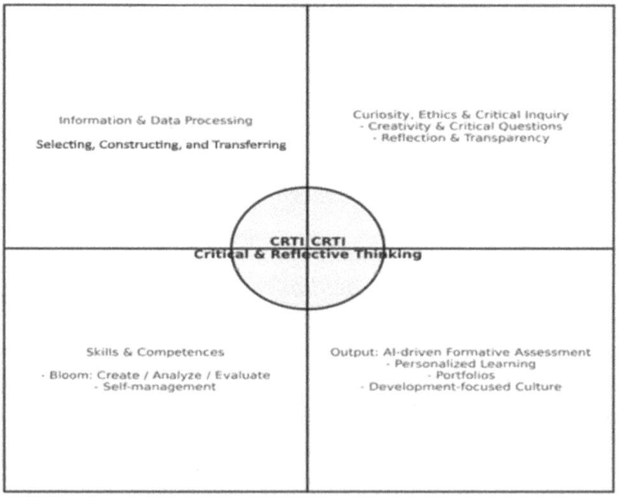

Fig. 1. The second-speed transformation process (the authors' own elaboration)

The base of the second-speed process in higher education is the information and data processing, selecting, constructing, and transferring, emphasizing the role of individual construction and creative information transfer. In higher education, this process is based on renewed Bloom taxonomy (curriculum planning), especially the requirement levels of create, analyse and evaluation under the umbrella of self-management, which is related individual information construction. Curiosity and questioning with promotion of reflections are the engine of the above-mentioned process. These are the tuning back to the Dewey's concept of scientific-based thinking [25]. The expected outcomes of the second-speed transformation process is AI-driven formative, portfolio-based assessment in the context of personalised learning.

2 Methodology

The emergence of Artificial Intelligence (AI) in higher education in recent years has radically transformed the traditional structures of learning, teaching, and assessment. Digital transformation has introduced not only technological but also conceptual and ethical challenges. The rapid spread of AI compels universities to redefine their mission, as well as the very concepts of knowledge, learning, and assessment. Higher education institutions must find a balance between efficiency, human creativity, and the responsible use of technology. In this context, it has become necessary to examine how AI influences formative assessment, i.e., a form of assessment aimed at developing rather than concluding the learning process.

The aim of the research was to explore how university and faculty leaders perceive the role and place of AI in formative assessment and how they interpret the educational, ethical, and organizational changes generated by the integration of AI. The study is part of the 2025 research program of the AI Research Group at Budapest Metropolitan University (METU) and also aligns with the professional discourse of the HELMeTO – Higher Education Learning Methodologies and Tools international research network. The study approached the integration of AI in higher education not as a technical issue but as a cultural, ethical, and pedagogical phenomenon, thus employing a qualitative, interpretive methodology.

The research was exploratory in nature and followed a qualitative design, using semi-structured interviews as the primary method. This allowed leaders to express their thoughts in their own words regarding the relationship between AI, education, and assessment. The interviews focused on experiential knowledge, professional reflections, and decision-making dilemmas. The interpretive approach did not seek generalisability but rather aimed to uncover meanings, specifically, how leaders perceive AI's impact on the overall culture of learning.

Sampling was conducted using a purposive sampling method. Ten higher education leaders were included in the study, representing various faculties and disciplines (social sciences, communication, arts, economics, and information technology). A common characteristic among participants was their active role in university management, particularly in overseeing curricular and assessment innovations. The sample did not aim for statistical representativeness but instead ensured professional diversity and experiential depth. Interviews were conducted between March and June 2025, either in person or online, each lasting approximately 40 to 60 min. Interviews were recorded with the written consent of participants, all of whom were guaranteed full anonymity. Audio recordings were transcribed verbatim and stored in a standardized format with coded identifiers.

The interview script was structured around three main dimensions. The first block addressed experiences with and attitudes toward AI use: what tools are used and what benefits or risks are perceived. The second block focused on the transformation of learning and assessment practices, including AI-based written assignments, the role of feedback, and issues related to self-directed learning. The third block explored ethical and organizational aspects, with particular attention to institutional regulations and the responsibilities of educators. The questions were open-ended and allowed space for free narrative reflections, enabling the emergence of individual interpretive patterns.

Interview analysis followed a thematic approach. The first step involved open coding, during which each interview was independently reviewed to identify meaningful segments. The codes were not based on pre-existing categories but emerged from the data. Coding was performed manually and independently by two researchers. Before resolving coding differences, intercoder reliability was assessed using Cohen's kappa ($K = 0.73$), indicating substantial agreement. The researchers then discussed discrepancies and finalised the coding framework by consensus.

In this study, manual coding was not an alternative to machine analysis but rather a complementary interpretive tool. Its purpose was to identify experiential meanings, emotional dynamics, and pedagogical reflections embedded in the interview texts—elements only partially perceptible in AI's semantic models. Manual coding operates on the level of human meaning-making, where intonation, ambiguity, intention, and tacit knowledge play a crucial role.

The methodological principle of this research was to preserve the values of the qualitative hermeneutic tradition alongside AI-based textual analysis: the researcher is not merely a data processor but an interpretive agent engaging with the participants' experiences. Manual coding thus functioned not only as a technical operation but also as a dialogue between data and researcher, where understanding evolves through an iterative process.

Following open coding, identical or similar codes were grouped into thematic categories. These resulting categories encapsulate the central meanings of the research. Throughout the process, seven key themes emerged (c.f., Fig. 2):

1. The Dual Nature of AI (as both a tool and an illusion),
2. The Paradox of Student Motivation,
3. The Dilemma of Plagiarism and Transparency,
4. The Transformation of Teaching Roles and Competencies,
5. The Need for Differentiated Regulation,
6. Issues of Labor Market Skills and Adaptability, and
7. The Transformation of University Identity and Values.

These themes consistently emerged throughout the interviews, regardless of institutional affiliation or faculty profile, which confirmed data saturation (theoretical saturation).

An innovative aspect of the research was its reliance on a combination of human and machine coding. Manual coding was complemented by AI-supported text analysis, which identified the main content nodes based on word frequency, semantic networks, and thematic coherence. The comparison of the two analytical approaches not only served to validate the data but also enabled the complementary use of human interpretation and machine pattern recognition. While AI-based analysis revealed the statistical structure of the data, manual coding focused on the implicit meanings and contextual nuances of the interviews. Together, these approaches ensured a balance between objectivity and interpretive depth.

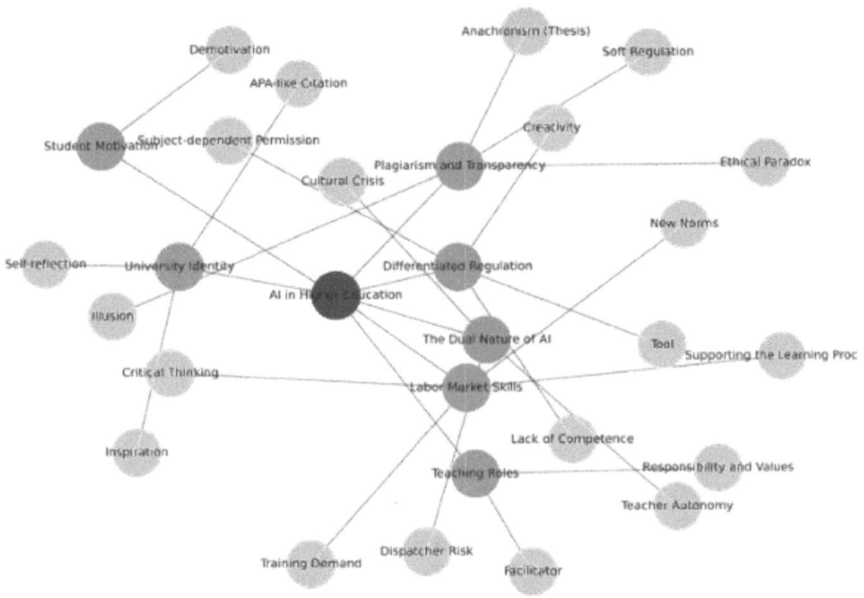

Fig. 2. The Mindmapping of the Identified Themes Based on the Hungarian Interviews (a simplified version based on the original Hungarian version, the authors' own elaboration)

During the research, we conducted a hierarchical cluster analysis based on the coded thematic units, using the Ward method (Fig. 3).

This method minimizes within-cluster variance and merges categories based on the greatest thematic similarity. The cluster analysis revealed four main groups among the leadership interviews:

1. *Student-focused cluster*, dominated by themes of motivation, self-directed learning, and creative writing;
2. *Philosophical–identity cluster*, which addressed knowledge, values, and the cultural mission of the university;
3. *Instructor–practical cluster*, which focused on the transformation of teaching roles, lack of competencies, and training needs;
4. *Labor market cluster*, which brought together themes of adaptability, skills development, and AI literacy.

The dendrogram visually illustrated the thematic distances between interviewees, aiding in the interpretation of emerging patterns.

Manual coding not only complemented but also validated the machine analysis. The two researchers worked independently and then jointly interpreted the AI-suggested categories. This methodological triangulation significantly enhanced the reliability and objectivity of the research. Through manual analysis, we were able to identify subtle, context-specific meanings that AI did not detect; for instance, the psychological dimension of students' loss of self-confidence or the identity crisis of the teaching profession.

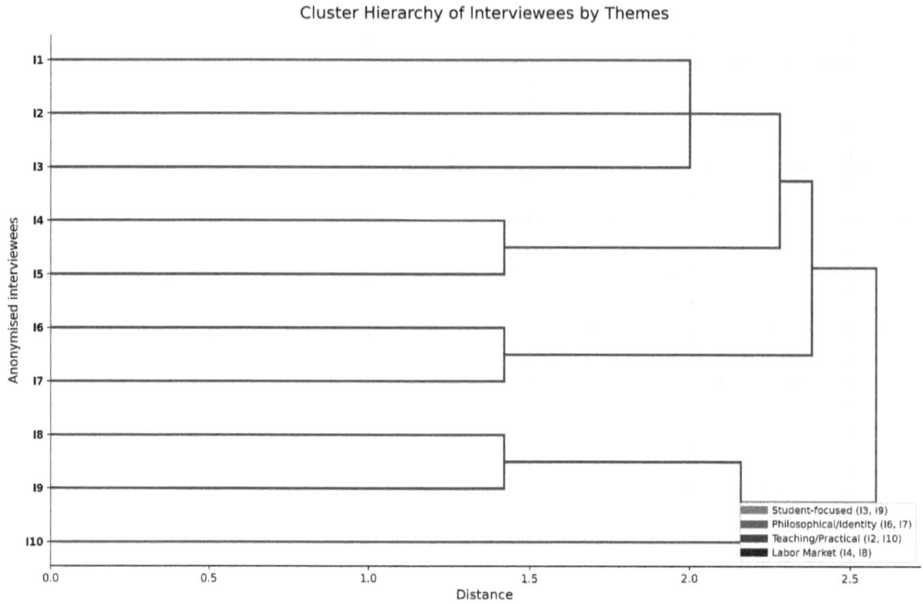

Fig. 3. Dendrogram of thematic clusters based on interview data (the authors' own elaboration)

The combination of the two levels can be interpreted as a new, reflective research model in the age of artificial intelligence.

Reliability was ensured on three levels. First, *intercoder reliability*was assessed using Cohen's kappa (K = 0.73), indicating substantial agreement between the two independent coders, we minimized researcher bias. Second, through *data triangulation*, which incorporated both machine-generated and human-coded sources. Third, through *reflexivity*: after each analysis cycle, researchers maintained reflexive memos, in which they recorded interpretive decisions and dilemmas. This continuous self-reflection helped ensure that the analysis was not merely a technical process, but a consciously interpretive one.

3 Results

3.1 Machine Coding

In the early phases of open coding, several hundred unique codes were generated, which captured specific statements, opinions or experiences based on the interviewees' formulations. These raw codes were still fragmented: they often repeated, partly overlapped, and appeared in different contexts. The second level of coding therefore aimed to merge, unify and thematically organise the codes. Codes with identical or similar content were grouped into unified thematic clusters, which no longer only showed coherence in vocabulary, but also in underlying meaning.

During the process, seven key themes emerged, which were closely interrelated and together form the conceptual map of the interviews. These themes are not artificial categories, but have organically surfaced from the interviewees' ways of thinking, their experiences and reflections. Each theme represents a critical dimension of AI's integration into higher education: technologically, pedagogically, ethically, organisationally and culturally.

The dual nature of AI: Tool and Illusion

This theme arose from the recognition that most interviewees hold an ambivalent attitude toward AI: they regard it simultaneously as an indispensable aid and a potential threat. The codes in this category often appeared in pairs – "it helps, but alienates", "accelerates, but empties out", "supports, but distorts" – which express the technology's dual aspect. The manual analysis made it clear that AI does not simply appear as a pedagogical innovation, but also raises ontological questions: what counts as knowledge when access to information is no longer the result of individual achievement, but a machine-mediated process.

In leadership discourses the motif of "illusion" frequently appeared – AI offers a kind of "appearance of knowledge" behind which no genuine understanding lies. At the same time many emphasised its nature as a "tool": if used consciously, AI can liberate human creativity by taking over repetitive, mechanical tasks. Thus the duality is not contradiction, but tension in which the future of education may be decided.

The paradox of student motivation

The second key theme uncovers the dual nature of student motivation. According to interviewees, AI on the one hand inspires students, on the other reduces independent effort. Manual coding identified subtle distinctions: inspiration often linked to creative experimentation and rapid idea generation, while demotivation stemmed from a culture of "instant results". Students increasingly view AI as a tool that "solves tasks for them", thereby the experience of effort and failure disappears from the learning process. At the same time, used within an appropriate pedagogical framework, AI allows students to experience new forms of reflective learning: by comparing their own thoughts with AI-generated responses, they can develop critical thinking. This paradox is thus not merely a psychological question but an issue of balance between self-directed learning and digital dependence.

The dilemma of plagiarism and transparency

The third thematic group is organised around ethical and regulatory questions. A recurring motif in the interviews was the re-definition of plagiarism: what does "originality" mean in an era in which texts are partly or wholly generated by AI?

The codes in this group covered several levels:

- The technical aspect (false citations, recognising generated content),
- The ethical dimension (student honesty and instructor credibility), and
- The institutional level (the lack of regulatory frameworks and control systems).

Manual analysis revealed that instructors and leaders do not merely interpret plagiarism as cheating, but as a crisis of trust: the mutual transparency between learning and assessment breaks down. Several proposed that AI-use should not be banned but documented and reflected on (e.g., "AI-usage log", "prompt citation"). This theme thus lies at the intersection of ethics, technology and culture, and clearly demonstrates that AI is not only a tool but also a normative challenge for education.

The transformation of instructor roles and competencies

The fourth theme centres on changing instructor identity. Many interviewees believe that the emergence of AI demands new pedagogical roles: the instructor must become a facilitator, mentor and guide for reflective learning. The previous instructor role—based on knowledge transmission—is gradually giving way to the role of knowledge filtration and interpretation. The coding here highlighted three key concepts: responsibility, flexibility and creative pedagogy.

The question of regulation

The fifth key theme concerned regulation. The interviews prominently revealed that AI-use cannot be uniformly regulated – each course, subject and learning situation demands a different degree of flexibility. The codes identified two extreme positions: full prohibition ("AI is dangerous, must be excluded from education") and full liberalism ("students can use it however they like"). However, most interviewees advocated a middle-way, adaptive regulation. The coding here identified not only normative statements but also pedagogical justifications. According to leaders, the aim of regulation is not control but fostering responsibility: the student should learn when, why and how to use AI. Hence this theme brings to light the dilemma of autonomy and accountability.

The question of labour-market skills and adaptation

The sixth theme interprets the labour-market implications of artificial intelligence in an educational context. Leaders unanimously argued that AI will become a basic competency, and future graduates must not only know but use AI tools meaningfully. The coding identified three main skill-groups:

1. Digital and technological literacy,
2. Critical thinking and problem-solving,
3. Creativity and adaptability.

Manual analysis revealed that leaders envisage future education as competency-based rather than content-centred. AI is not the goal but the environment: education must develop skills that algorithms cannot reproduce – human judgement, moral responsibility and collaboration.

The transformation of the university's identity and value-system

The final key theme is located on a deeper, cultural level. The interviews repeatedly presented concerns that the university as a knowledge institution is losing its previous normative role. The "anachronism of the thesis", the "crisis of values", or the "hollowing out of creativity" are all codes indicating the transformation of the university's self-identity. Manual analysis in this area went beyond empirical description: leadership remarks sketched how AI shapes not only the technology of education but also the academic ethos. The university's identity is transforming: instead of knowledge possession, the relation to knowledge becomes central. This is a paradigm shift, in which higher education must redefine itself not as a knowledge-producing machine but as an interpretive community.

3.2 Manual Coding

The manual coding process revealed several deeper layers of meaning related to the educational application of artificial intelligence (AI). These were identified not based on frequency, but on significance.

Changing Roles and Competencies

The interviews confirmed that the rapid expansion of AI is reshaping the competences developed in higher education while it is also accelerating the fundamental re-evaluation of traditional assessment practices. Interviewees often claimed that AI does not only represent a single innovation to introduce in higher education, but also a catalyst for systemic transformation, which affects what students are expected to know and how their performance and development are evaluated. In their opinion, the influence of AI challenges the very logic of knowledge acquisition and assessment that higher education has relied on for centuries. One of the experts stated explicitly *that "AI tools [are] questioning and even invalidating current norms of teaching, competences, knowledge, and evaluation methods,"* while another participant claimed, *"what may have been considered good three or four years ago may not be considered as such today by the same colleagues or institutions."*

In this context, the acquisition of knowledge, competences, and skills is no longer a linear process of learning a previously agreed content, but an ongoing negotiation between human and machine capabilities. As one interviewee argues, *"[AI is] an extremely dynamically evolving and improving partner [...] increasingly capable of being a high-quality intellectual collaborator,"* and students need to learn how to communicate and cooperate with it efficiently. Consequently, students are increasingly expected to relearn how to learn: to adjust their methods to AI-based environments, critically assess the tools they use, and maintain a reflective awareness of how knowledge is produced and validated in a world where AI systems continuously evolve. They need to know *"what [AI] is like, how to use it responsibly and carefully, how to really achieve what they want, what mistakes to watch out for, what ethical issues to pay attention to, how to avoid getting into some kind of professionally damaging situation by using it,"* as one interviewee explained.

Experimental learning was claimed to be a key component in acquiring this knowledge. According to one interviewee, identifying the specific competences that higher education needs to develop in response to the rise of AI remains an open and complex question, but *"it is essential that [students] experiment with [AI], think about it, and that it is constantly present at the university."* Related to this, another expert claimed that students have to learn *"(...) not to take anything for granted, but to experiment a lot before they claim something [based on AI], to be sure that it is correct."* Another interpretation also confirms that digital literacy in the age of AI means *"a highly diverse, interest-driven knowledge built through random experimentation."*

Interviewees widely agreed that the growing presence of AI in higher education has renewed the focus on the value of inherently human competences. As one of the experts noted, many such human competences are being reinterpreted and gaining new meaning and significance in higher education: *"For example, active learning, learning strategies, complex problem-solving, critical thinking and analysis, creativity, originality, resilience, stress management, and flexibility."* He also added that *"these are precisely the areas in which artificial intelligence does not excel."* The interviews revealed a consensus that the skills most important to develop in contemporary higher education are those that cannot be easily automated. While AI can process data, detect patterns, and even simulate reasoning, it lacks the capability for critical thinking, including independent judgment, which was mentioned as a cornerstone of human thinking. *"We need to teach and explain to [students], so that they truly understand, that AI can ease and accelerate their work, support them, and assist them, but it does not replace their ability to formulate ideas and evaluate problems. They must not lose this [ability]. AI does not replace their evaluative capability. A program, in the full sense of the word, does not do evaluation the way a human being can."* In another interpretation, *"the associations [of AI] are very mechanical or very clichéd. (...) [T]his is not the way how human thinking works, but rather a kind of instrumental functioning on products created by human thinking. (...) It cannot be called thinking; it creates its output by uniquely combining texts produced by human thinking."*

A related challenge is to ensure that AI contributes to human intellectual growth rather than replacing it with an output of different quality. Several interviewees expressed concerns about how AI may undermine students' intellectual autonomy, creativity, and originality: *"[AI] takes away students' confidence in creating their own texts, demotivating them from reading, learning, and creating their own texts or knowledge."* In their view, the appropriate way to adapt to this challenge would be to learn *"how artificial intelligence can be used to create products that also strengthen the user's personal competences. In other words, so that I do not remain a mere technical dispatcher who controls communication between different AI platforms without understanding what that communication is about."* Alongside critical thinking, the importance of flexibility, reflexivity, and continuous adaptation cannot be overstated in this new environment. These are skills that are not only essential for learning with AI in higher education, but also for navigating future labor markets and professional environments.

Alongside these competences, interviewees often highlighted the renewed and growing importance of empathy and the emotional foundations of teaching and learning. *"No one should be afraid that ChatGPT will replace teachers, because it simply does not know your students,"* claimed one interviewee. *"[Teaching with AI] feels very impersonal. (...) the essential contact between the lecturer and the students, the exchange that should be there, is missing. For example, the feedback you get from their facial expressions, or when you see that they do not understand what you are saying. That cannot be replaced. Nor can the spontaneous answers to unexpected questions, or the emotional dimension of teaching."* Interviewees observed that personal, trust-based relations and close mentoring are becoming increasingly important in higher education with the expansion of AI. Beyond this, the majority mentioned that students and professors alike are expected to develop their competences of ethical reflection: *"What we need to teach is that artificial intelligence, when used to accelerate, facilitate, or increase the quantity of human knowledge acquisition or intellectual and physical work, inevitably raises moral—and not just narrowly defined professional ethical—but broadly understood ethical and moral questions as well. These challenges are real, and they confront us constantly in new and changing forms."*

Assessment in the Age of AI

A related challenge is to ensure that AI contributes to human intellectual growth rather than replacing it with an output of different quality. Several interviewees expressed concerns about how AI may undermine students' intellectual autonomy, creativity, and originality: *"[AI] takes away students' confidence in creating their own texts, demotivating them from reading, learning, and creating their own texts or knowledge."*

As competences transform, assessment methods also need to transform accordingly. Interviewees emphasized that building a solid foundation of knowledge that remains relevant even in AI-free contexts is essential. *"There is ChatGPT, but do you know that Miklós Horthy was not a king? Because if you do not, you are in trouble,"* said one interviewee, while another claimed, *"one of the main problems is when someone does not know their fields in sufficient depth, only to the extent of running a search or generating a literature suggestion. In reality, they have never actually read these texts, not even the foundational works, and often do not even know who the key authors in the field are."* Consequently, participants suggested that testing related competences under AI-free conditions has to be a crucial part of academic evaluation. At the same time, it was emphasized that *"it would also be important to let go of what is totally irrelevant or meaningless [under the changing circumstances], things we only teach because we have always taught them. We should leave such content aside, since it makes little sense to memorize information that can be accessed or solved within seconds."*

Some participants linked this transformation to the question of whether writing a thesis should remain a requirement for obtaining a university degree, arguing that this expectation has become problematic under the changing circumstances. *"Because, frankly, if I rely entirely on artificial intelligence from start to finish, what is the point of a thesis, for example?"* asked one of the interviewees, while another expert argued, *"The thesis itself becomes something difficult to interpret, something that, in my view, causes equal frustration for those who have to read it, consult on it, and for those who actually work on it, because it often feels meaningless. The real issue is not merely how I might use AI for literature reviews or methodology. (...) Where regulations do not make it mandatory, I would personally let these go, because it is a struggle comparable to trying to train armored knights today. That was perfectly fine in the Middle Ages, and writing a thesis is still useful in contexts where the goal is to educate intellectuals. But where the aim is simply to produce well-trained professionals who enter the job market with a diploma, it is completely unnecessary and unproductive."*

The interviewees are experimenting with diverse approaches to manage AI use during their examinations. While some advocated a return to traditional paper-and-pen methods or oral presentations, others argued that "new technologies require new solutions" and are experimenting with innovative forms of assessment that integrate AI as a legitimate learning aid. *"We need to completely rethink our methods of assessment (...) [we need one that] places greater emphasis on oral communication, and assesses skills, abilities, and knowledge acquired without the use of AI tools in the classroom. Where appropriate, it may also include assessment tasks that measure performance using generative tools, but these should be kept separate."* – suggested a participant.

For many interviewees, the rise of AI has renewed interest in formative assessment: methods that focus on feedback, reflection, and process rather than solely on outcomes. *"We always ask students to explain how they constructed their work, what inspired them, and how they developed it. Within two minutes, it becomes clear if they [created the entire work with AI], as they are unable to answer these questions or describe their own creative process."* Class feedback receives additional importance with the expansion of AI. *"A good teacher can see when students' attention starts to fade and responds to it. They also notice when a more difficult example is not understood, and then they ask questions, walk around the classroom, see how everyone is progressing, and where someone got stuck."* Continuous evaluation and feedback allow educators to observe how students engage with AI, whether they use it responsibly, and how it influences their independent thinking. The process-oriented approach can help maintain a balance between fostering digital literacy and AI skills, and developing inherently human competences related to thinking, communication, and empathy.

Many interviewees highlighted that the transformation of assessment methods also necessitates a pedagogical shift. Historically, evaluation has been centered on demonstrating mastery of content, often in a quantitative sense. With the expansion of AI, as its efficient use places more emphasis on traditionally less central types of competences, assessment increasingly revolves around demonstrating understanding, critical thinking, independent judgment, and creativity. Interviewees argued that rubrics must therefore be redesigned to capture qualitative dimensions of learning built on critical thinking and reflection: the originality of argumentation, the ability to synthesize information, and the awareness of ethical implications. The majority also claimed that as the university prepares students for a labor market in which digital literacy is indispensable, they must ensure that assessment includes skills such as efficient prompting, the critical evaluation of AI outputs, and the ability to select tools appropriate to specific professional challenges.

Based on the above interview findings, it can be stated that the majority of participants agree that the adaptation to the rapid pace of technological change requires an educational culture that values experimentation, critical thinking, and reflection. This involves changing the traditional emphasis on several competences and adapting new perspectives on assessment. Nevertheless, most interviewees agreed that such a shift is difficult to achieve within existing structures, which tend to privilege stability and tradition. As one interviewee pointed out, *"How honest we can be about this, I think, is a very interesting question. Naturally, no one wants to endanger their own position or take risks that might threaten their status. In education, (...) we can observe self-justifying systems with centuries of tradition behind them—systems that inherently strive to preserve themselves. If we could distinguish ourselves by being a little more honest about what really matters, we might be able to offer students something more meaningful."*

3.3 Evaluation of the Findings

This insight illustrates how manual coding was capable of capturing the hidden human dimension absent from machine analysis. Human connection, mentorship, and personal feedback are qualities that form the foundation of higher education's identity. The relationship between the two coding methods was synergistic. Machine coding quickly and accurately identified frequently occurring words and concepts, while manual analysis unpacked their meanings and interrelations.

The combination of machine and manual coding yielded three benefits:

1. **Validation** – the alignment between the two coding methods confirmed the stability of the themes,

2. **Complementarity** – where the machine failed to detect patterns, human interpretation identified new meanings,
3. **Reflexive knowledge construction** – researchers became aware of how AI tools influence their own thinking.

Manual coding thus became not just a data processing technique but a tool for researcher self-reflection.

Throughout the manual coding process, researchers paid particular attention to ethical transparency. All identifying data from the interviews were anonymized, and researchers consciously reflected on their own values and assumptions. Reflexivity here was not only a research ethics requirement but a methodological value. Researchers documented instances where a topic affected them personally or where an interview elicited a strong emotional response. These reflexive memos were later compared to examine how the researcher's subjectivity may have influenced the coding process. This level of transparency contributed to the integrity of the analysis and aligned with the ethical principles of the HELMeTO project, which emphasize the preservation of responsibility and human interpretation in AI-related research.

4 Conclusion

Learning support AI tools (e.g., chatbot, recommender system, feedback engine), automatic assessment systems (e.g., essay improvement using AI), and the development of reflective thinking (e.g., learning diary analysis using AI, career portfolio) will make the transformation process in higher education. The current phase of our ongoing research confirms that the integration of AI in formative assessment is not only a technological issue but an educational and cultural challenge, placing students' reflective and creative development at the centre.

5 Limitations and Further Research

Despite the promising findings, this study presents several limitations. First, the relatively small sample size and the focus on a single institution limit the generalizability of the results. Second, participants' engagement with AI-driven tools varied in both depth and frequency, which may have influenced the richness and consistency of their responses. Third, given the rapid pace of AI development, the specific tools examined in this study may soon become obsolete or be replaced, underscoring the need for ongoing research and adaptation.

Future research should pursue several directions. Comparative studies across institutions and academic disciplines could offer a more comprehensive understanding of how AI is reshaping formative assessment. Longitudinal studies would be particularly valuable in examining how AI-generated feedback influences learning outcomes over time. Furthermore, interdisciplinary collaboration—particularly among pedagogy, computer science, and ethics—will be essential for designing AI tools that are not only technologically robust but also pedagogically effective and ethically aligned with human values.

Declarations.

Funding. This research received no external funding.

Data Availability. The datasets generated and analysed during the current study are available from the corresponding author on reasonable request.

Disclosure of Interests. The authors declare that they have no competing interests.

Ethical Approval. The study was conducted in accordance with the ethical guidelines of the HELMeTO project.

References

1. Vass, V.: The coherence between innovative teaching methods and formative assessment in higher education. Int. J. Adv. Corp. Learn. **17**(3), 108–116 (2024)
2. Vass, V.: The relationship between artificial intelligence and knowledge transfer in the light of changing concepts of knowledge and learning (the triangles of conscious use of AI). In: Gómez Chova, L., González Martínez, C., Lees, J. (eds.) INTED2025 Proceedings: 19th International Technology, Education and Development Conference, pp. 3818–3825. IATED, Valencia (2025)
3. Chen, L., Chen, P., Lin, Z.: Artificial intelligence in education: a review. IEEE Access. **8**, 75264–75278 (2020). https://doi.org/10.1109/ACCESS.2020.2988510
4. Robert, J., et al.: EDUCAUSE Horizon Report: Teaching and Learning Edition. EDUCAUSE, Boulder, CO (2025) https://library.educause.edu/-/media/files/library/2025/5/2025hrteachinglearning.pdf#page=3.00
5. Holmes, W., Bialik, M., & Fadel, C.: Artificial intelligence in education: Promises and implications for teaching and learning. Center for Curriculum Redesign (2019)
6. AI Index Steering Committee: The AI Index 2025 Annual Report. Institute for Human-Centered AI, Stanford University (2025) https://hai-production.s3.amazonaws.com/files/hai_ai_index_report_2025.pdf
7. Black, P., Wiliam, D.: Inside the black box: raising standards through classroom assessment. Phi Delta Kappan. **80**(2), 139–148 (1998)
8. Du Boulay, B.: Artificial intelligence as an effective classroom assistant. IEEE Intell. Syst. **31**(6), 76–81 (2016). https://doi.org/10.1109/MIS.2016.93
9. Garcia, M., et al.: Rethinking educational assessment in the age of generative AI: Actionable strategies to mitigate academic dishonesty (2024). https://ssrn.com/abstract=5250120 or https://doi.org/10.2139/ssrn.5250120
10. Guan, R., Raković, M., Chen, G., Gašević, D.: How educational chatbots support self-regulated learning? A systematic review of the literature. Educ. Inf. Technol. **30**, 4493–4518 (2025)
11. Du Preez, P., Simmonds, S., Verhoef, A.H.: Rethinking and researching transformation in higher education: a meta-study of south African trends. Transform. High. Educ. **1**(1), 1–7 (2016)
12. Smith, M.K., Vass, V.: The relationship between internationalisation, creativity and transformation: a case study of higher education in Hungary. Transform. High. Educ. **2**(1), 1 (2017)

13. Vass, V.: The relationship between artificial intelligence and knowledge transfer in the light of changing concepts of knowledge and learning (the triangles of conscious use of AI). In: Gómez Chova, L., González Martínez, C., Lees, J. (eds.) INTED2025 Proceedings: 19th International Technology, Education and Development Conference, pp. 3818–3825. IATED, Valencia (2025)
14. Fowler, D.S.: AI in higher education. J. Ethics High. Educ., 127–143 (2023)
15. Dewey, J.: How we Think. D. C. Heath (1910)
16. Gardner, H.: The mind's New Science: a History of the Cognitive Revolution. Basic Books, New York (1985)
17. Miller, G.A.: The cognitive revolution: a historical perspective. Trends Cogn. Sci. **7**(3), 141–144 (2003)
18. Bruner, J.S.: The Process of Education. Harvard University Press (1960)
19. Bruner, J.: The Culture of Education. Harvard University Press (1996)
20. Bruner, J.: The Culture of Education. Harvard University Press (1996)
21. Duarte, F.: Amount of data created daily. Exploding Topics (2025). https://explodingtopics.com/blog/data-generated-per-day
22. LeBlanc, P.J.: Higher education in a VUCA world. Change: Mag. High. Learn. **50**(3–4), 23–26 (2018)
23. Bruner, J.S.: The Process of Education. Harvard University Press (1960)
24. Tiryaki, T. T.: From VUCA to FLUX: Navigating the AI era with a new mental model. LinkedIn (2025). https://www.linkedin.com/posts/timtiryaki_vuca-flux-transformation-activity-7300892492743249921-V0LQ/
25. Dewey, J.: How we Think. D. C. Heath (1910)

Dialoguing with Hattie&TimperlAI: a Research Based AI-Feedback Coach for Math Teacher Training

Silvia Funghi[1], Marta Valentini[2], Agnese Del Zozzo[2](✉), and Alberto Montresor[2]

[1] Università di Genova, Genova, Italy
silvia.funghi@unige.it
[2] University of Trento, Trento, Italy
{marta.valentini-1,agnese.delzozzo,alberto.montresor}@unitn.it

Abstract. This paper presents Hattie&TimperlAI (H&TAI), a research-based AI agent that acts as a feedback coach for mathematics teacher education grounded in the Hattie and Timperley's model. Building on a previous version (TP-H&TAI), which generates examples of effective feedback for classroom use, we introduce TT-H&TAI, a new configuration designed to help teachers refine their own feedback during training. TT-H&TAI was implemented on three LLM platforms (ChatGPT, Gemini, and Claude) and evaluated through controlled dialogue simulations based on a standardized mathematics task. A qualitative content analysis examined how each implementation supported teachers' reflection on feedback practices. Findings show that all platforms fostered the use of the Hattie and Timperleys framework for analyzing feedback, with Claude additionally supporting the construction and reformulation of feedback. The paper discusses the differences in relation to prompt configuration and proposes a replicable, research-grounded workflow for developing AI tools for teacher education.

Keywords: AI in education · Teacher training · Formative feedback

1 Introduction

Generative AI has rapidly become a key instrument for supporting human work in areas once considered impossible to delegate to machines. As AI permeates daily life, its presence in classrooms and educational contexts is likewise contributing to the ongoing transformation of teaching and learning practices.

From a broad perspective, Holmes and Tuomi [11] offer a comprehensive survey of AI in education, outlining a taxonomy of AI-based solutions targeting students, teachers, and institutions. These systems are primarily designed to relieve teachers of repetitive or routine tasks, such as automated grading or administrative management, thereby freeing up time for human interaction and higher-level pedagogical activities. This category also includes tools that support

M. Adamoli et al. (Eds.): HELMeTO 2025, CCIS 2958, pp. 354–371, 2026.
https://doi.org/10.1007/978-3-032-31850-3_22

formative assessment, learning material development, classroom management, and, more broadly, teachers' professional practice.

Nevertheless, the literature reviewed by Holmes and Tuomi supports the view that, rather than treating AI merely as an automation tool, "the transformative effect of AI could be in augmenting human cognition in learning" (p. 543). In this view, AI is not intended to replace human activity, but to enhance and extend human cognitive processes, especially in complex tasks that continue to demand human judgment and oversight.

Even within disciplinary educational research, such as mathematics education, this broader vision of AI as a cognitive partner has begun to take shape. A growing body of work investigates both the opportunities and the risks of AI-supported instruction in this field. For example, a recent special issue [20] includes a scoping survey on ChatGPT's role in mathematics education [19]. These studies show that much of the current work conceptualizes AI primarily as a tool for teachers' professional practice. At the same time, they call for greater attention to AI's role in learning processes themselves, shifting the focus from assistance in professional tasks to support for understanding and reflection. Nevertheless, the literature warns of well-known limitations (such as hallucinations, propagated bias, and potential over-reliance on automated responses), which may undermine both the accuracy of support and learner autonomy.

The shift from using AI merely as a professional aid to exploring how it can mediate learning processes has important implications for teacher education as well. If teachers are to guide students in an AI-rich world, one of the most effective ways to prepare them is to let them experience AI as a learning partner firsthand. Recent research highlights the educational potential of AI to support both pre-service and in-service teacher development [5,15]. Specifically, AI can serve as a scaffolding tool for teachers' professional reflection, helping them articulate reasoning, confront alternative interpretations, and refine their pedagogical decisions. For instance, Noster et al. [17] investigate pre-service teachers' mathematical content knowledge while solving tasks with ChatGPT; Cheng [3] examines AI assistance in effective task formulation; and Schorcht et al. [23] study AI-mediated collaborative task design.

Among the different areas where AI can support teachers' work, formative assessment, and in particular the formulation of formative feedback, stands out as especially significant [5]. Extensive research has shown that formative feedback plays a crucial role in fostering students' learning processes [12]. At the same time, it is a demanding and delicate practice: feedback can easily lose its educational value, or even become counterproductive, when it is vague, overly evaluative, or misaligned with learning objectives [10,13]. A recent study [9] also points to the potential of AI to assist teachers in producing personalized feedback on students' work, while warning of risks such as over-praise (excessive positive evaluation) and over-inference (feedback based on inconsistent interpretations of students' actual performance).

Going beyond the general potential of AI for feedback generation, our previous work proposed a research-based approach to configure *AI agents* that embody established educational frameworks [7]. In this context, the term *AI agent* refers to a conversational chatbot based on a large language model (LLM) that is explicitly configured through dialogue guidelines and a dedicated knowledge base. This configuration allows the agent to act according to a defined pedagogical identity. Such agents differ from generic chatbots because they are designed to enact theoretical principles within the dialogue itself, turning interaction into a space for reflection rather than mere information retrieval.

Following this approach, we developed Hattie&TimperlAI (H&TAI), an AI feedback coach informed by the model of Hattie and Timperley [10]. The first version of H&TAI (TP-H&TAI, Teacher Practice H&TAI) was designed to provide teachers with examples of effective feedback to support their classroom practice.

Building on this foundation, the present paper introduces a second version of the agent TT-H&TAI (Teacher Training H&TAI), reconceived as a learning companion for teachers. Rather than producing feedback examples, TT-H&TAI engages teachers in a process of reflection and refinement of the feedback they have already produced, thereby promoting metacognitive awareness of the dimensions and levels of formative feedback. This paper outlines the design process that led to this new configuration and its implementation across different LLM platforms, and examines the learning opportunities and dialogic patterns that emerge in user–AI interaction.

It is worth clarifying that the notion of *agent* can refer to two different operational instantiations. In our prior study, the agent was deployed as a preconfigured system, with the configuration embedded in the runtime setup and not exposed to end users (e.g., custom GPTs or Gemini Gems). In the present paper, by contrast, we make the configuration explicit and portable by providing a configuration prompt that users can manually paste at the beginning of a chat to instantiate the same pedagogical behavior within a standard LLM interface.

2 Theoretical Framework

LLM-based chatbots are essentially dialogic entities that simulate human language conversations. Human languages, as used by AI, typically require a grammatical *subject*. As a result, simulating human dialogue almost inevitably takes the form of utterances that involve an "I" corresponding to the speaker. It follows that the chatbot is, in a sense, compelled to adopt some form of identity, however loosely defined it may be. In particular, Qian et al. [21] state: "*the personality of a chatbot refers to the character that the bot plays or performs during conversational interactions. In this scenario, personality can be viewed as a composite of the identity (the background and profile) that a chatbot is endowed with, linguistic style that an agent exhibits during interactions, and many more explicit and implicit cues that may portray character*" (p. 1). In this regard, the example provided by Cheng et al. [4] is especially relevant: they propose a chatbot whose identity emerges progressively through interaction with the user.

To use the terms of Qian et al. [21], the character we intended for H&TAI to embody was that of a feedback expert. As a scientific reference for shaping

H&TAI's identity, we chose the seminal work of Hattie and Timperley [10]. In their paper, feedback is defined as "*information by an agent (e.g., teacher, peer, book, parent, self, experience) regarding aspects of one's performance or understanding, given in order to fill the gap between what is understood and what is aimed to be understood*" (pp. 81–82). Through an analysis of existing literature on feedback, the authors observe that it can be a highly influential tool in students' learning process, but that its impact (positive or negative) depends greatly on how and when feedback is delivered. They note that praise, rewards, and punishments, which are typically not accompanied by information for improvement, are generally minimally effective. Conversely, feedback that highlights an error but also offers pathways for improvement can have a significant positive impact on student progress.

To better frame what constitutes effective feedback, Hattie and Timperley proposed a model in which feedback addresses three major questions:

- *Where am I going?* (feed-up dimension - FU), concerning the expected learning objectives;
- *How am I going?* (feed-back dimension - FB), concerning information about the student's progress towards the learning objectives;
- *Where to next?* (feed-forward dimension - FF), concerning guidance for the student on further steps to "close the gap".

Each question can address one of the following four levels (descriptions taken from [10], p. 87):

- *Task-level Feedback* (TF): focused on how well the task is understood or performed;
- *Process-level Feedback* (PF): focused on the main process needed to understand how to do the task;
- *Self-regulation-level Feedback* (SRF): focused on the student's self-monitoring, directing, and regulating of actions;
- *Self-level Feedback* (SF): focused on personal evaluations and affect about the learner.

Nevertheless, Hattie and Timperley highlight that feedback is most powerful when it promotes deeper understanding and self-regulation; in other words, PF and SRF are the feedback types most likely to have the greatest impact on student learning. TF can be useful when it does not merely point out an incorrect product but also invites reflection on the thought process behind that product. Finally, SF is considered the least effective type of feedback.

The other theoretical foundation that informed the H&TAI design concerns the role of the teacher's interpretation of errors in structuring an instructional intervention, i.e. a feedback response. In mathematics education research, it is widely acknowledged that handling students' errors is a fundamental teaching competence [18]. This has also been conceptualized as a specific component of teacher knowledge related to the interpretation of students' reasoning behind their productions, often referred to as interpretative knowledge [22]. However, providing students with feedback that facilitates their understanding of their own errors and fosters reflection on the underlying thought processes is far from straightforward. Zan [24], in particular, highlights that the effectiveness of a teacher's intervention (in this case, feedback) depends on its coherence with the actual difficulty that led the student to make a specific error. Zan emphasizes that teachers' actions always stem from their interpretation of the causes underlying a student's mistake–a notion consistent with Guo et al. [9] regarding AI's tendency to over-infer when generating feedback–and that teachers should have a "repertoire of interpretations" of students' behaviors.

A first version of H&TAI, hereafter TP-H&TAI (Teacher-Practice H&TAI), was developed to provide example feedback to teachers and to support them in their teaching practice. In [7], we compared the feedback produced by this agent with that generated by basic chatbots. We found that interactions with TP-H&TAI (both in its ChatGPT and Gemini implementations) were consistent with the Hattie and Timperley's framework, whereas basic chatbots tended to produce short lectures rather than coaching dialogues.

Building on these findings, we collected perspectives from in-service teachers who interacted with TP-H&TAI. Their insights guided the design of a new version, focused more specifically on fostering teachers' learning about formative feedback exchange in the context of teacher training. This paper presents this new version of H&TAI, hereafter TT-H&TAI (Teacher-Training H&TAI), obtained by modifying the previous configuration prompt to support a process of refinement of user-generated feedback rather than providing AI-generated feedback proposals.

Once the configuration prompt for TT-H&TAI was finalized, the model was implemented on ChatGPT, Gemini, and Claude. We then investigated the following research questions:

1. To what extent does the dialogue with TT-H&TAI offer teachers the opportunity to learn about formative feedback exchange?
2. Considering the implementation of TT-H&TAI on the ChatGPT, Gemini, and Claude platforms, what differences are there in the way they provide support for prompting teacher reflections?

3 Methodology

To provide a complete overview, this section describes the design of both TP-H&TAI and TT-H&TAI, with greater emphasis on the latter.

3.1 TP-H&TAI Design

In order to design H&TAI, we[1] began in April 2025 with a very first version of the AI Agent structured around Hattie and Timperley's paper. Many cycles of

[1] In all the paper, "we" refers exclusively to the author team: AI was used only to refine the formulation of prompts for H&TAI and not to support or perform any reasoning about its development.

test and refinement were set in motion by the critical analysis of early versions' behavior in dialogue simulations in the subsequent phases.

Moreover, two documents were inserted as a knowledge base for the chatbot: i) the foundational article on feedback exchange by Hattie and Timperley [10]; ii) an institutional document describing Italy's national learning goals for grades 1–8 school mathematics [16].

Phase 0 – H&TAI's *identity definition.* We created a prompt embedding the key traits of effective feedback, drawing on the framework by Hattie and Timperley [10]. The agent's role was strictly limited to providing feedback based on these theoretical principles, and it was not specified whether it was addressed to students or teachers (potentially both).

Phase 1 – Simulation of dialogue with a student. To evaluate whether H&TAI internalized its theoretical identity, we simulated a dialogue between the agent and a "student" prompted by a middle school math task. The student was played by us to control responses and elicit realistic misconceptions. This controlled setting allowed us to fine-tune the agent's behavior and assess whether its feedback aligned with Hattie and Timperley's four levels. A first revision of the configuration prompt was done after this phase, to require the AI to give different interpretations for the student's error [24].

Phase 2 – Teacher–Coach–Student Simulation. We simulated a realistic classroom scenario inspired by Cusi et al. [6], involving three roles: a teacher (played by ourselves), a student (simulated by a chatbot) and H&TAI. In this setting, the "teacher" interacted with H&TAI describing the task and the student's mistake, asking for advice. H&TAI's answer was used by the teacher to give feedback to the student, whose response was turned over again by the teacher to H&TAI to ask for new advice, and so on. This controlled setting enabled us to fine-tune the agent's behavior and to observe the agent's support in a dynamic, practice-oriented context. The prompt was structurally optimized, also with the aid of AI itself, to guide AI's internal reasoning process consistently and to emphasize references to the different levels of feedback.

Phase 3 – Field Evaluation. We involved in-service teachers, who interacted with H&TAI using examples drawn from their own classroom practice. This was done to inform the refinement of the agent's configuration and provide insight into its perceived usefulness and usability in authentic teaching contexts.

The progressive refinement process of TP-H&TAI's configuration prompt ultimately led to the last version of TP-H&TAI[2]. The design process involved several key iterations, each step building on the previous one to sharpen the agent's pedagogical and structural capabilities. Crucially, insights from teachers in the final phase led to a revision of H&TAI's objective: instead of suggesting feedback, it now offers proposals for reflection on or refinement of a feedback statement already formulated by the teacher, resulting in a new type of agent, TT-H&TAI.

[2] https://tinyurl.com/ICTMT17.

3.2 TT-H&TAI Design

Building on the final prompt revised during Phase 3 of the TP-H&TAI design process, a new round of revisions was conducted to fine-tune the agent's behavior and better support teachers' reflection. In the TP-H&TAI configuration prompt, the key rules of conduct for the agent include:

1. ask the teacher what are the learning objectives (feed-up);
2. not provide complete solutions for students;
3. ask questions one at a time (to temper the intrinsic verbosity and proactivity of generative AI);
4. propose a list of possible interpretations of the error;
5. provide PF–SRF based on the interpretation identified by the teacher;
6. give priority to PF and SRF with respect to TF, avoid SF;
7. invite the teacher to reflect on how they will use feedback with the student (feed-forward).

In configuring TT-H&TAI, this list of key rules was revised and expanded asking also to:

8. accompany the list of possible error interpretations with reflective questions, inviting the teacher to consider whether further interpretations are possible;
9. ask the teacher for spontaneously offered feedback;
10. provide a synthesis outlining the three dimensions (FU, FB, FF) and the four levels (TF, PF, SRF, SF), and ask the teacher to classify their feedback according to these descriptions;
11. provide a justified classification of the teacher's feedback in terms of levels and dimensions, and engage in dialogue with them to propose reformulations that incorporate any missing dimensions, operating at the PF/SRF levels;
12. adopt a Socratic approach and formulate a series of questions to the teacher to stimulate meaningful reflection on the construction and phrasing of feedback, and when needed facilitate a deeper comprehension of the Hattie and Timperley model.

To test the resulting configuration prompt[3], we simulated a scenario involving two roles: a teacher (played by ourselves) and TT-H&TAI. In this case as well, the "teacher" interacted with TT-H&TAI by describing the task and the student's mistake, and by providing indications related to learning objectives, chosen interpretation, and corresponding feedback.

3.3 A TT-H&TAI-Teacher Simulation

Simulations with TT-H&TAI included tests with ChatGPT (GPT-5), Gemini (Gemini 2.5 Flash), and Claude (Claude Sonnet 4.5)

[3] https://tinyurl.com/CONF-PROMPT-V7.

This paper analyzes a simulated teacher-agent interaction with TT-H&TAI, where we (the researchers) assumed the teacher role and consulted the agent to critically reflect on feedback related to an incorrect task solution. The task is derived from an item of the Italian standardized test (INVALSI) designed for Grade 8 students, which features an image of a racetrack (Fig. 1). The problem is the following: "*The figure represents the layout of a track composed of the following elements: two circular arcs, each with a radius of 50 cm; two straight segments, each 100 cm long, which are perpendicular to each other at their midpoint. What is the total length of the track? Show the calculations used to find the answer and finally state the result. Result: approximately ___ cm.*" (our translation).

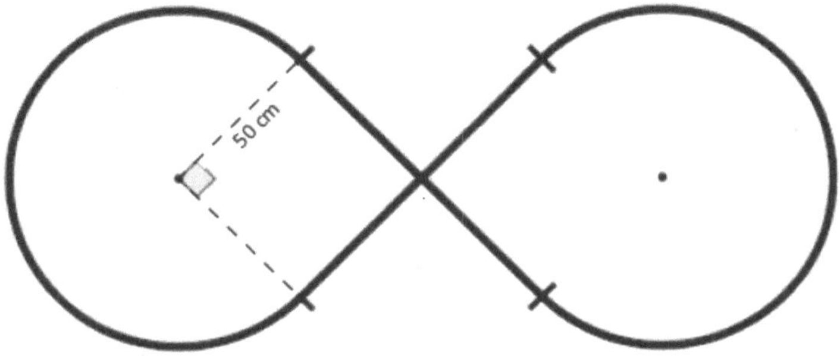

Fig. 1. The figure associated with the test problem

The specific erroneous student solution is adapted from Asenova et al. [1], who documented a student protocol consisting of the following steps: (a) $100 + 100 = 200$; (b) $\pi \times radius^2 = 7850$; (c) $7850 \div 2 = 3925$; (d) $7850 + 3925 = 11775$; with the student's final answer being approximately 11975 cm. The authors propose a possible interpretation of the reasoning underlying this solution, suggesting that step (a) corresponds to the sum of the straight segments' lengths, and step (b) to the calculation of the full circumference (although the student appears to have used the formula πr^2 instead of $2\pi r$). Steps (c) and (d) allow for the calculation of the lengths of the circular arcs, which together comprise two parts, each equivalent to $3/4$ of the full circumference. Since $3/4 + 3/4 = 3/2 = 1 + 1/2$, we can infer that the student may have computed half of the full circumference in step (c) and then added it to the full circumference in step (d). The final answer would thus correspond to the sum of the values obtained in steps (a) and (d).

Considering the INVALSI classification, which identifies problem-solving as the primary competence addressed by this task, one learning objective in proposing this problem can be defined as follows: "to solve accessible problems across all content domains, maintaining control over both the resolution process and the final results. The student can describe the procedure followed and recognize solution strategies that differ from their own" ([16], p. 61, our translation).

This item was selected because it allows for feedback formulation at all levels. A TF would address just the incorrectness of result or formula used in (b) (e.g., "the formula you used in the second step computes the area, not the circumference"). A PF would address the more general strategy selection process (e.g., "explain how you determined the length of the curvilinear parts"). A SRF could focus on strategies to check solution acceptability (e.g., "try to consider how you can check if the result is plausible within the context"). Furthermore, a teacher's management of the FF dimension will depend on their specific interpretation of the student's mistake in the formula in step (b). If the teacher considers it a minor oversight, then, in relation to the aforementioned learning objective, the emphasis should predominantly be on control processes, particularly the verification of results. Conversely, if the teacher suspects the student is conceptually confusing the perimeter and area of a figure, then they may place greater emphasis on the definitions of the two concepts and on differences between them.

Once the task was selected, we implemented TT-H&TAI across Gemini, Claude, and ChatGPT and initiated the conversation with each of them. In all cases, the first input was the configuration prompt (see Footnote 3).

4 Data Analysis

All the chats were collected and organized as transcriptions of real conversations. To facilitate comparison, we created a single table containing all three conversations together[4]. We then applied an approach inspired by qualitative content analysis [14] to these three conversations, examining the interventions of the AI acting as a coach and focusing on comparing the support modalities implemented by TT-H&TAI across the three platforms.

In general, among the three dialogues with TT-H&TAI, the one with Claude appears to be the most concise in its verbal output, whereas the other two are more verbose and analytical. The overall structure of the three conversations is very similar, apart from some supplementary "digressions" encountered with TT-H&TAI implemented on Claude before returning to the main conversational flow—which adheres to the structure of the configuration prompt. The conversational flow unfolds as follows (referring to the lines of the table):

1. Agent presentation and request for the instructional objective (lines 3–4).
2. Request for the student's production (lines 5–6).
3. Transcription of the task and the student's solution, and request for confirmation (lines 7–10).
4. Error analysis and proposal of interpretations, asking the teacher for their point of view (lines 11–12).
5. Request for feedback from the teacher (lines 13–14).
6. Synthesis of the three dimensions and four levels of Hattie and Timperley and request for the teacher to classify the feedback (lines 15–16).
7. Analysis of feedback from TT-H&TAI, accompanied by questions and, potentially, proposals for reformulation (lines 17–21).

[4] https://tinyurl.com/SIMULATION-V7.

Given general chatbots' interaction modalities and the specific structure of the configuration prompt, all three TT-H&TAIS behave consistently with the request to activate the teacher and all conclude their turns with a question.

Considering the teacher's turns, several reflective processes can be activated: reflection on learning objectives (line 4); monitoring and, if necessary, correction of the AI's response (line 8); reflection on the evidence collected to support their own interpretation, critical examination of alternative interpretations, and explicit articulation of their position (line 12); formulation of feedback (line 14); application of Hattie and Timperley's dimensions and levels as tools for feedback analysis (line 16); and further reflection on feedback (line 18 and following).

The learning opportunities related to feedback exchange therefore concern two main aspects: the dependence of the provided feedback on the chosen interpretation (a point not yet explicitly addressed in the three dialogues with TT-H&TAI), and the use of Hattie and Timperley's framework both to analyze feedback and to improve its quality. In the dialogue with TT-H&TAI in Claude, these opportunities are further enriched by the possibility of reflecting on a level not present in the initial response and of applying Hattie and Timperley's framework for feedback construction and reformulation.

The qualitative analysis of the conversations led to the identification of several categories describing differences in the dialogic behavior of the three TT-H&TAI implementations, referred to as H&TAI-GEM (Gemini), H&TAI-CLD (Claude), and H&TAI-GPT (ChatGPT).

We considered each interaction with TT-H&TAI as a unit of analysis. In the following, we refer to the lines of the table mentioned above (linked in Footnote 4), each of which corresponds to a single conversational turn between our research team and the chatbot.

The categories were constructed in two steps. First, we read all conversations and conducted an initial coding phase to describe the chatbots' actions in their turns and to identify differences between them (e.g., line 1 was coded as: "Presentation of the agent and request for indication of the learning objective. "Anticipated" request by H&TAI-CLD for the student's solution. Anticipation by H&TAI-GPT of the Hattie and Timperley model."). After this first round of coding, we observed that chatbot responses did not fully align with the intended coach behavior. In some cases, however, these issues were due to general technical limitations, such as H&TAI-CLD's difficulty in recognizing that the curvilinear parts of the track corresponded to $^3/_4$. A second round of coding allowed us to construct four categories through a process of grouping the previous open codes: consistency with the teacher's initial stated learning objective, consistency with the interpretation provided by the teacher, consistency with the Hattie and Timperley model, and consistency with interpretation relative to the configuration prompt requests. We will comment on each category in detail below.

Consistency with the Teacher's Initial Stated Learning Objective. The stated learning objective of the chosen task was "solving problems, maintaining control over both the resolution process and the final results" (line 4), in agreement with the INVALSI test guidelines. When synthesizing the three dimensions and four levels (line 15) and analyzing feedback (line 17), H&TAI-GEM and H&TAI-GPT shift focus to calculation of the track's length (e.g., *"Remember, the goal of the problem is to compute the total length of the track."*, line 17, H&TAI-GEM; *"it does not clearly state the overall objective ("finding the total length of the track")"*, line 17, H&TAI-GPT), whereas H&TAI-CLD maintains correspondence with the teacher's initially declared objective—even in the analysis of the reformulated feedback (*"How could you remind the student of the complete goal of the activity? (not just "find the answer" but also "maintain control over the resolution process")"*, line 19). It is noteworthy that despite this main trend, H&TAI-GEM recalls from time to time the initial stated objective, but not in the FU dimension (see the mention to *"key objectives (maintaining control over the process)"* when justifying why the formulated feedback lacks SRF, line 17).

Consistency with the Interpretation Provided by the Teacher. The teacher's interpretation referred to a confusion between the formula for the area of a circle and that for the circumference length (*"I believe the student incorrectly retrieved the formula for the circumference instead of the area formula from memory"*, line 12, conversation with H&TAI-GEM). In line 17, H&TAI-GPT generates a PF that is inconsistent with this interpretation (*"To improve, start again from the drawing: identify which fractions of the circumference are present and use the formula $L = fraction \times 2\pi r$"*): if the student correctly identified the curvilinear parts but simply recalled the wrong formula, asking them to start again from the drawing is unlikely to be useful. Moreover, some of the questions generated by H&TAI-GPT and H&TAI-CLD focus on the conceptual difference between area and length, rather than aligning with the teacher's initial interpretation. For instance, the self-regulation question *"Am I looking for an area or a length?"* (line 17, conversation with H&TAI-GPT) is minimally useful if the problem is a lapse in memory regarding the formula. Also process questions from H&TAI-CLD (line 19) appear slightly out of focus relative to the interpretation provided (*"How could you help the student conceptually distinguish between 'measuring a boundary' (circumference) and 'measuring a surface' (area)? What question could you ask them to make them reflect on the difference between the two measures?"*).

Consistency with Hattie and Timperley Model. In the synthesis of Hattie and Timperley's framework (line 15), H&TAI-GEM, reports also SF, while H&TAI-CLD and H&TAI-GPT do not, even if it could be helpful of SF to be explicitly stated. Despite this, the rationale for H&TAI-GPT discarding SF is unclear (*"This level should be avoided, as it is too generic (e.g., "You are intelligent", "Well done")."*). Both H&TAI-GEM and H&TAI-GPT accompany the definitions with example questions, which somewhat risks directing the teacher's feedback revision: the "quick examples" from H&TAI-GPT actually constitute the construction of feedback accordingly with Hattie and Timperley's framework (e.g., *"SRF (example): "Always check: (a) units of measurement, (b) whether you are using area or perimeter, (c) a quick estimate to check plausibility"."*, line 15).
The feedback provided by the teacher was formulated as a TF, which we deemed likely to be among those most commonly used by a teacher: *"Attention! The rea-*

soning is correct but you used the area formula instead of the circumference formula". The feedback analysis (line 17) across the three TT-H&TAIS is consistent: all of them evaluate the provided feedback as lacking FU and FF, and classify it as TF. The arguments concerning the different levels are generally coherent, except for the rationale behind FU absence (see the category *Consistency with the teacher's initial stated objective*).

It is interesting to observe that H&TAI-GEM and H&TAI-GPT explain not only why certain dimensions/levels are present in the feedback, but they also justify why they say others are *not* present (e.g., *"Absent or underexpressed dimensions: Feed-Up (FU): it does not clearly state the overall objective ("finding the total length of the track"). Feed-Forward (FF): it does not suggest concrete actions for improvement ("what to do to correct"). PF / SRF: it also does not yet address strategies or personal reflection on the error."*, line 17, conversation with H&TAI-GPT). H&TAI-CLD instead explains why the feedback lacks FU and FF dimensions, but does not motivate why the feedback is not PF or SRF: this is noteworthy, since H&TAI-GEM emphasizes the presence of a PF "nuance" (*"The feedback is predominantly situated at the Task Level (TF), but with a slight touch of the Process Level (PF)"*, line 17). In its feedback proposal (line 17), H&TAI-GEM suggests a structure consistent with the Hattie and Timperley model but classifies its feedback as PF, even though it offers the student no stimulus for personal reflection and merely instructs them to *"find the correct formula for length and recalculate"*. In the PF proposed by H&TAI-GPT (*"To improve, start again from the drawing: identify which fractions of the circumference are present and use the formula (L = fraction $\times\ 2\pi r$)"*, line 17), the formula presented (L = *fraction* $\times\ 2\pi r$) combines verbal and symbolic language and risks leading the student to memorize a new "rule" rather than reason about the process.

Consistency and Interpretation Relative to the Configuration Prompt Requests. We have observed that the general conversational flow follows the prompt's instructions. Regarding point 8 in Sect. 3.2, all three TT-H&TAIS accompany the interpretations with follow-up questions directed at the teacher (line 11). However, while H&TAI-CLD and H&TAI-GPT limit themselves to questions seemingly aimed at gathering evidence to support one or more interpretations (e.g., *"Have you noticed if the student systematically shows confusion between area and perimeter formulas?"*, line 11, conversation with H&TAI-CLD), H&TAI-GEM mixes these types of questions with those that anticipate reflection on the teacher's feedback (e.g., *"How can I help them build the habit of always writing down what each calculation step represents?"*, line 11).

Regarding point 11 in Sect. 3.2, a different interpretation of the meaning of "engage in dialogue [...] to propose reformulations of the feedback" emerges from H&TAI-CLD compared to the other two chatbots. H&TAI-GEM and H&TAI-GPT automatically generate reformulation proposals:

Reformulation Proposal (integrates TF, PF and SRF; FU-FB-FF). "The objective was to calculate the length of the track (FU). Your reasoning about combining the arcs and straight segments is correct (FB), but you applied the area formula instead of the circumference formula, so the result does not measure a length (TF). To improve, start again from the drawing: identify which fractions of the circumference are present and use the formula (L = fraction × 2πr) (PF). Before concluding a similar problem, always ask yourself: 'Am I looking for an area or a length?'—this will help you self-regulate in future exercises (SRF, FF)." (line 17, conversation with H&TAI-GPT).

H&TAI-CLD, instead, asks a question to help the interlocutor delve deeper into SRF (*"What could help the student distinguish between'when to use the area' and 'when to use the circumference' autonomously, without having to rely solely on memory?"*, line 17). In subsequent turns, it poses further questions to help the teacher add the missing feedback components (e.g., *"How could you phrase a concrete invitation to verify the reasonableness of the result?"*, line 19). Once new feedback is received from the teacher, H&TAI-CLD re-proposes an analysis against the three dimensions and four levels of Hattie and Timperley model and concludes with further probing questions (e.g., *"On the Missing Part: The student failed to explicitly state their reasoning in writing (as required by the assignment). In your feedback, you ask them to "explain in writing what each operation is for." Do you think this is sufficient guidance, or might the student need an example/model of how to articulate a step?"*, line 21).

Regarding point 12 in Sect. 3.2, once the user's feedback has been analyzed and commented on by the agent, the questions intended to stimulate further reflections on feedback are not always "Socratic":

- H&TAI-GEM proposes a generic question (*"What are your thoughts, Teacher? Do you believe this reformulation is more effective?"*, line 17) after providing its own formulation of the feedback, which, rather than triggering users' reflection, risks ending the conversation, since the goal of building complete feedback according to the Hattie and Timperley model has been achieved.
- H&TAI-GPT provides a question explicitly labeling it as 'Socratic' (*"Socratic Questions for Reflection (Step 5f). In your opinion, how might this type of reformulation help the student understand their error, instead of merely correcting it?"*, line 17), but since, also in this case, the question is asked after the agent has provided its own formulation of the feedback, it is unlikely to give rise to new reflections.
- The behavior of H&TAI-CLD, on the other hand, is more in line with the initial prompt requests: it explicitly invites the user to work on feedback formulation, without any suggestions (*"Let's Discuss Possible Reformulations. Now I would like to work with you to enrich this feedback, also including the FU and FF dimensions, and moving towards the PF and SRF levels."*, line 17). Then, H&TAI-CLD poses a question that effectively redirects the user to reflection on the initially identified problem, namely, the difficulty of remembering the correct formula. (*"Let's start with a Socratic question: What could help the student distinguish between 'when to use the area' and 'when to use the circumference' autonomously, without having to rely solely on memory?"*, line 17). In our simulation, the question actually presented us with an interesting issue that we had not yet considered, and allowed us to highlight both

"practical" strategies (checking the textbook) and metacognitive strategies (checking the plausibility of the result obtained with the formula remembered in relation to the units of measurement), which had not been made explicit until then (line 18). In the following, H&TAI-CLD is even more aligned with a Socratic approach, as in subsequent exchanges (lines 19 and 21) it continues to accompany its response with interesting questions for reflection (in line 19 on each of the FU, FB, and FF dimensions; in line 21, after the user's feedback has been classified as complete with respect to the Hattie and Timperley's framework, on other possible aspects of the feedback).

5 Results and Discussion

The analysis of the three conversations highlighted both how TT-H&TAI supports teachers' learning and how the three AI implementations differ in their dialogic support for reflection. All three versions of TT-H&TAI offer the learning opportunity to use Hattie and Timperley's framework for analyzing feedback. They could also support reflection on the consistency between feedback and error interpretation, but none of the three explicitly prompted this reflection. Only the interaction with H&TAI-CLD enabled teachers to use Hattie and Timperley's framework for constructing or reformulating feedback.

Regarding differences in the interactions with the three TT-H&TAIS, we identified several coherence issues, the most relevant of which relate to how specific parts of the configuration prompt were interpreted. In all three cases, the overall structure of the conversation proved to be quite faithful to the sequence of key rules listed within the configuration prompt (so much so that H&TAI-GEM and H&TAI-GPT explicitly refer to the points in the list of key rules in several turns). However, the synthesis of Hattie and Timperley's framework shows interesting differences: H&TAI-GEM and H&TAI-GPT generate accompanying examples related to the various dimensions and levels, which could preemptively suggest possible feedback components to the teacher, thereby diminishing the reflective potential of the interaction.

Furthermore, when analyzing the teacher's feedback, H&TAI-GEM and H&TAI-GPT not only provide their analysis but also generate a new formulation of a possible feedback; the subsequent proposal of follow-up questions might lead the interlocutor to believe that the work on the feedback is concluded, when in fact the proposed feedback is only one of the possibilities. H&TAI-CLD, on the other hand, refrains from providing reference examples throughout the conversation and prompts the teacher to reformulate the feedback, offering a reflection question consistent with the instructional objective indicated initially as support.

6 Conclusions

In this paper, we proposed a research-based approach to design AI personalized dialogical partners configurations for teacher training, exemplified by the development of H&TAI, a prototype AI feedback coach grounded in the model by Hattie and Timperley [10]. Because LLM technology evolves rapidly, our goal was not to define a *definitive* prompt for designing a scientifically grounded AI agent, but rather to develop a stable and coherent process that supports comparison and adaptation over time.

In this paper, we have sought to outline such a process, consisting of the following stages: (i) prompt definition, (ii) internal testing, (iii) internal simulations, (iv) context-based trials, and (v) public release of the configuration prompt. This process is the main contribution we wish to emphasize, as it extends beyond the specific objective for which H&TAI was designed.

This study targets the internal testing and simulation phases of the TT-H&TAI design process, with researchers acting as teachers for the simulated interactions. Here, our aim was not to present TT-H&TAI as a finished "product", but to highlight its potential and reflect on possible prompt refinements that emerged during the process. We consider this important as a second contribution, since it allowed us to present a concrete example of the refinement process within our broader AI agent development workflow.

We distinguished between TP-H&TAI, developed to assist teachers by providing AI-generated feedback proposals, and TT-H&TAI, designed to support the refinement of user-generated feedback. The design of TT-H&TAI builds on the final version of the TP-H&TAI prompt configuration, which was developed through multiple rounds of simulation and refinement. We first described how TP-H&TAI's identity was defined and what changes were introduced to shape TT-H&TAI's identity. We then conducted an internal validation of the chatbot's behavior through a simulated coaching session involving a teacher and TT-H&TAI implemented on Gemini, Claude, and ChatGPT. The coaching dialogue focused on an INVALSI item and on an interpretation of the student's solution that allowed for feedback at different levels. Finally, we transcribed and analyzed the conversations using a qualitative content analysis approach.

Regarding the first research question, namely the opportunities that TT-H&TAI offers for teachers' learning about feedback exchange, the results suggest that TT-H&TAI can serve as a metacognitive tool to support teachers' reflection, particularly with respect to the three dimensions and four levels of feedback defined by Hattie and Timperley. These constructs proved effective as structured references for feedback analysis. Only the Claude implementation of TT-H&TAI allowed us to use this structure in producing feedback. This aspect should be improved in future versions of the configuration prompt. The chatbot's tendency to generate examples or guiding questions based on Hattie and Timperley's framework should be limited, to keep teachers actively engaged in creating feedback that covers all three dimensions and higher levels. Future updates of TT-H&TAI should also include prompts that ask users to reflect on how their feedback aligns with the identified error interpretation, and mechanisms that help the AI maintain consistency throughout the dialogue, especially in relation to the learning objective, the error interpretation, and the elements of Hattie and Timperley's framework. Another improvement to the configuration prompt would be revising the key rules to avoid ambiguity or unwanted behavior (e.g., clarifying that teachers should reformulate feedback first, not AI).

Regarding the second research question, the interactions with the three TT-H&TAI implementations all showed some issues. However, the version implemented on Claude was, in this case, the closest to the desired behavior. The overall conversation flow, except for the final segment, was similar across the three implementations. This suggests that the key regulatory structure defined in the current prompt provides a certain degree of control over the trajectory of the dialogue. We hope that further refinements of the prompt will lead to interactions with stable characteristics, regardless of the implementation platform.

Future work will involve further exploration of how to improve the definition of rules of conduct, and in-field studies in two main directions. The first one is the teacher training dimension - with a field evaluation involving pre-service and in-service teachers to test TT-H&TAI in real contexts of teacher education or teacher professional development. This work is still in its preliminary stages: while initial tests have been conducted with teachers, the findings remain to be evaluated through an extensive trial. Nevertheless, it is possible to propose some initial hypotheses. Given its functional design, TT-H&TAI could prove useful in enabling teachers to familiarize themselves with the Hattie and Timperley's framework—not through a purely theoretical study of the model, but through "guided reformulation exercises" of feedback.

The fact that TT-H&TAI (the H&TAI-CLD version in particular) enabled users to reflect on how their feedback integrates across dimensions and levels is noteworthy, as it may help teachers view feedback not merely as error correction, but as a flexible tool tailored to specific instructional aims. For instance, reflecting on the possibility of providing process-oriented or self-regulatory guidance shifts the focus from the error itself to the student's stance toward a mathematical task. Furthermore, reflecting on the explicit articulation of learning objectives implicitly means to share the goal of fostering greater metacognitive awareness in students. Both of these aspects partially transcend performance on a specific task and relate to broader conceptions of the teaching-learning process. Consequently, the use of TT-H&TAI could indirectly encourage reflection on the role of the teacher. Teachers are no longer merely "judges" of task correctness, but rather, they are experts who guide each student toward reflective awareness of their own learning. The extent to which such AI-mediated reflection can reshape professional identity remains a compelling avenue for future longitudinal research.

As a second direction, we intend to embrace more recent lines of research that shift the attention from feedback formulation (which is the actual focus of both versions of H&TAI) to the feedback exchange as a process [8]. This shift requires studies that focus not only on how teachers formulate feedback, but also on how students use feedback, considering also long-term perspectives [2]. These studies would provide a clearer understanding of possible pedagogical implications of using an AI feedback coach like TT-H&TAI, not only in teacher training but also in classroom practice.

Disclosure of Interests. The authors have no competing interests to declare that are relevant to the content of this article.

References

1. Asenova, M., Del Zozzo, A., Santi, G.: Unfolding teachers' interpretative knowledge into semiotic interpretative knowledge to understand and improve mathematical learning in an inclusive perspective. Educat. Sci. **13**(1), 65 (2023)
2. Carless, D.: Feedback loops and the longer-term: towards feedback spirals. Assessment Evaluat. Higher Educat. **44**(5), 705–714 (2019)
3. Cheng, E.C.: Leveraging generative AI in science lesson study: transforming density concept instruction through ChatGPT integration. Int. J. Lesson Learn. Stud. (2025)
4. Cheng, Y., et al.: Evolving to be your soulmate: personalized dialogue agents with dynamically adapted personas. arXiv e-prints pp. arXiv–2406 (2024)
5. Chu, Z., et al.: LLM agents for education: Advances and applications (2025). https://arxiv.org/abs/2503.11733, arXiv preprint
6. Cusi, A., Morselli, F., Sabena, C.: Promuovere strategie di valutazione formativa in matematica con le nuove tecnologie: l'esperienza del progetto FaSMEd. Annali online della Didattica e della Formazione Docente **9**(14), 91–107 (2017)
7. Del Zozzo, A., Funghi, S., Montresor, A., Valentini, M.: H&TAI: Improving formative feedback through a research-driven teacher coach. In: Proceedings of the 17th International Conference on Technology in Mathematics Teaching (ICTMT17). London, UK (2026). https://discovery.ucl.ac.uk/id/eprint/10223410/
8. Grion, V., Serbati, A.: Valutazione sostenibile e feedback nei contesti universitari. Pensa Multimedia (2019)
9. Guo, S., Latif, E., Zhou, Y., Huang, X., Zhai, X.: Using generative AI and multi-agents to provide automatic feedback. arXiv preprint (2024). https://arxiv.org/abs/2411.07407v1
10. Hattie, J., Timperley, H.: The power of feedback. Rev. Educ. Res. **77**(1), 81–112 (2007)
11. Holmes, W., Tuomi, I.: State of the art and practice in AI in education. Eur. J. Educ. **57**(4), 542–570 (2022)
12. Hughes, G., Smith, H., Creese, B.: Not seeing the wood for the trees: developing a feedback analysis tool to explore feed forward in modularised programmes. Assessment Evaluat. High. Educat. **40**(8), 1079–1094 (2015)
13. Kluger, A.N., DeNisi, A.: The effects of feedback interventions on performance: a historical review, a meta-analysis, and a preliminary feedback intervention theory. Psychol. Bull. **119**(2), 254–284 (1996)
14. Kuckartz, U.: Qualitative text analysis: a systematic approach. In: Compendium for early career researchers in mathematics education, pp. 181–197. Springer International Publishing Cham (2019)
15. Lee, U., et al.: Generative agent for teacher training: Designing educational problem-solving simulations with large language model-based agents for pre-service teachers. In: NeurIPS'23 Workshop on Generative AI for Education (GAIED). Advances in Neural Information Processing Systems, Curran Associates, Inc. (2023)
16. MIUR - Ministero dell'Istruzione, dell'Università e della Ricerca: Indicazioni nazionali per il curricolo della scuola dell'infanzia e del primo ciclo d'istruzione. Annali della pubblica Istruzione (2012)

17. Noster, N., Gerber, S., Siller, H.S.: Pre-service teachers' approaches in solving mathematics tasks with ChatGPT: a qualitative analysis. Digital Experiences Math. Educat. **10**(4), 543–567 (2024)
18. Novotná, J., Moraová, H., Tatto, M.T.: Mathematics teacher education organization, curriculum, and outcomes. In: Encyclopedia of mathematics education, pp. 1–7. Springer (2018)
19. Pepin, B., Buchholtz, N., Salinas-Hernández, U.: A scoping survey of ChatGPT in mathematics education. Digital Exper. Math. Educat. **11**, 9–41 (2025)
20. Pepin, B., Buchholtz, N., Salinas-Hernández, U.: "Mathematics education in the era of ChatGPT: investigating its meaning and use for school and university education"—editorial to special issue. Digit. Exper. Mathematics Education **11**, 1–8 (2025)
21. Qian, Q., Huang, M., Zhao, H., Xu, J., Zhu, X.: Assigning personality/identity to a chatting machine for coherent conversation generation. arXiv preprint arXiv:1706.02861 (2017). https://arxiv.org/abs/1706.02861v3
22. Ribeiro, M., Mellone, M., Jakobsen, A.: Interpreting students'non-standard reasoning: insights for mathematics teacher education. Learn. Math. **36**(2), 8–13 (2016)
23. Schorcht, S., Peters, F., Kriegel, J.: Communicative AI agents in mathematical task design: a qualitative study of GPT network acting as a multi-professional team. Digit. Exper. Math. Educ. **11**(1), 77–113 (2024)
24. Zan, R.: Difficoltà in matematica: osservare, interpretare, intervenire. Springer (2007)

Peer Assessment in the Age of Artificial Intelligence: The ENGAGE Model at University

Elif Gulbay[1], Leonarda Longo[1], Vanessa Pitrella[1,2,3](✉), Martina Bruno[1,2], and Dorotea Rita Di Carlo[1]

[1] University of Palermo, Palermo, Italy
{elif.gulbay,leonarda.longo,vanessa.pitrella,martina.bruno, dorotearita.dicarlo}@unipa.it
[2] University of Modena and Reggio Emilia, Modena, Italy
[3] Institute for Educational Technology - National Research Council, Genoa, Italy

Abstract. Peer formative assessment fosters self-regulation, critical thinking, and collaboration but is often underused due to time constraints, limited confidence in applying evaluation criteria, and discomfort with mutual judgment. This study presents the ENGAGE AI-Based model, an adaptation of the ENGAGE framework, integrating artificial intelligence tools to support peer feedback processes. Conducted at the University of Palermo within the Metacognitive and Cooperative Teaching course during the academic year 2024/2025, the research involved 150 pre-service teachers engaged in project-based tasks and AI-enhanced peer review activities using ChatGPT. Students compared and integrated AI-generated feedback with their own comments, developing critical interpretation and metacognitive reflection skills. Qualitative analysis of participants' perceptions highlighted appreciation for the model's structured approach and the supportive role of AI in learning, while also revealing the need for specific training on the ethical and pedagogical use of such tools. Overall, the model demonstrated potential in promoting assessment literacy and AI awareness, emphasizing that artificial intelligence can support - but not replace - human judgment in formative assessment.

Keywords: Peer assessment · Artificial Intelligence · ENGAGE model · teacher education · formative evaluation

1 Peer Formative Assessment in Higher Education

Peer assessment is a crucial component of university teaching [1], serving multiple purposes beyond grading. It provides students with feedback on their learning progress, helping them identify strengths and areas for improvement by involving them evaluating each other's work [2]. This approach fosters critical thinking, enhances learning, and encourages collaboration among peers [3, 4]. Students provide feedback based on established criteria, which helps them develop their analytical skills and gain different perspectives on their own work [5, 6]. Additionally, engaging in discussions about assessments can deepen understanding and improve overall performance within a more interactive and participatory learning environment [7].

M. Adamoli et al. (Eds.): HELMeTO 2025, CCIS 2958, pp. 372–382, 2026.
https://doi.org/10.1007/978-3-032-31850-3_23

Students typically take on both roles of evaluator and evaluated [8]. As evaluators, they assess their peers' work and provide critical feedback to help them improve their products. As evaluated, they receive and respond to feedback from their peers to enhance their own work. Receiving feedback from multiple, sometimes conflicting perspectives, while also providing feedback, helps students adopt an active role [4, 9].

Peer assessment is integrated into the learning process, offering ongoing feedback that helps students refine their work and develop critical thinking skills [10]. According to [11], peer assessment can be described as a process where learners evaluate and articulate the level, value, or quality of a product or performance produced by their equally ranked peers. This involves providing detailed feedback and engaging in discussions about their evaluations to reach a mutually agreed-upon outcome.

Engaging in peer assessment requires students to analyze work critically, compare it against predefined criteria, and articulate meaningful feedback [1, 10]. This process deepens their understanding of the subject matter. When students assess others, they reflect on their own work, improving self-awareness and the ability to self-assess [12, 13]. Students learn how to give and receive feedback effectively, a crucial skill for academic and professional success [14, 15]. By emphasizing learning as a process rather than a final product, peer formative assessment fosters a growth mindset among students. They learn to view challenges as opportunities for growth rather than threats to their abilities.

Despite these advantages, peer assessment is not without challenges, which often hinder its effective implementation. While peer formative assessment is widely acknowledged for its benefits, several barriers prevent its full integration into university teaching. First, students sometimes perceive peer assessment as unfair or unhelpful. Concerns over reliability, peer bias, and low student motivation can hinder its adoption.

Peer marking is more controversial and less favored, and it requires structured guidance and time for training students on evaluation criteria. Ensuring the quality and usefulness of peer feedback requires instructor supervision, which can be time-consuming. Many instructors struggle to allocate the necessary time within tight course schedules [16, 17]. Some students feel uncomfortable assessing their peers, either due to fear of giving incorrect feedback or concern about receiving criticism. Peer assessment may introduce personal biases, favoritism, or a reluctance to provide honest criticism. Students may question the credibility of peer feedback compared to instructor feedback, leading to skepticism about the process.

In an era marked by rapid advancements in artificial intelligence, traditional educational practices are being redefined, particularly in higher education. The Engage Model [18] of peer assessment emerges as a progressive approach that leverages technology to foster collaborative learning and enhance student engagement. Recent scoping reviews have highlighted how AI-based educational tools, particularly those supporting personalized learning, have shown a positive impact on students' motivation and learning outcomes across different school levels, especially in K-12 education [19]. By encouraging students to evaluate and provide feedback on each other's work, this model not only cultivates critical thinking and analytical skills but also promotes a sense of community and shared responsibility among learners.

As universities adapt to the changing landscape of education, integrating AI-driven tools into the peer assessment process offers new opportunities for personalized feedback and improved learning outcomes [20]. This exploration of the Engage Model highlights its potential to transform the educational experience, preparing students for a future where adaptability and collaboration are paramount.

The study examines the phases of the ENGAGE-AI Based model, which has been applied starting from the reference model [18].

As a result, the paper aims to analyze the potential of AI in supporting peer formative assessment and adopted the Engage Model to AI-supported learning environments. It also seeks to discuss implementation strategies in university courses by evaluating the benefits and challenges of the ENGAGE-AI Based model.

This contribution presents a preliminary study that forms part of a larger research project focused on artificial intelligence and assessment in higher education.

2 The Impact of AI in Peer- Assessment and AI Literacy of Teacher Candidates

Artificial Intelligence (AI) is increasingly being integrated into higher education, offering innovative solutions to enhance peer-assessment processes.

Traditional peer assessment faces several challenges, including students' difficulties in applying evaluation criteria consistently, concerns over fairness, and the logistical burden on instructors [21]. AI-powered tools can mitigate these issues by providing automated feedback [22], ensuring consistency in evaluation, and assisting students in understanding assessment rubrics. Additionally, AI can facilitate anonymous peer reviews, reducing bias and fostering a more objective assessment environment. While AI cannot replace the critical judgment of human evaluators, its role in streamlining and supporting formative peer assessment is becoming increasingly relevant.

In order to facilitate the reliable and effective use of artificial intelligence applications in educational settings, it is necessary to determine the AI literacy of pre-service teachers before they enter the profession [23]. Ensuring that future teachers possess AI literacy can enable them to utilize AI technologies in learning environments in a correct, reliable, and ethical manner while also providing an opportunity to serve as role models for their students [24, 25]. Considering the necessity of integrating our teachers into evolving technology, it can be said that understanding pre-service teachers' levels of AI literacy and their perceptions of emerging technologies in education has become essential.

AI is also transforming peer assessment by enabling more objective, efficient, and personalized feedback. By automating aspects of the evaluation process, AI reduces biases, enhances consistency, and provides real-time insights into student performance [26]. It streamlines administrative tasks for instructors, allowing them to focus on deeper learning and mentorship.

AI tools analyze student work, offer instant feedback, and help structure peer reviews to align with assessment rubrics. They also assess an evaluator's past performance, expertise, and biases to predict the reliability of future contributions while identifying areas for improvement. By leveraging machine learning, AI enhances peer review quality, fostering deeper understanding and skill development for both assessors and assesses.

3 Methodology

3.1 Research Objectives and Participants

The research aims at investigating the perceptions of future primary and lower secondary school teachers attending a course on Metacognitive and Cooperative Teaching at the University of Palermo, regarding peer assessment practices based on the use of the Engage Model for an AI-Based.

The research was conducted at the University of Palermo. The convenience sample is composed as follows: 63.4% of future teachers are preparing for lower secondary school, while 36.6% are preparing for primary school. The majority (86.3%) are female, and 55.2% are aged 40 or older. Only 35.8% of future teachers are currently teaching.

3.2 The Engage Model for an AI-Based Peer Assessment

Pairs of students exchanged their project work and used a guideline with criteria to provide feedback to their peers. However, before offering feedback, each member of the pair had to integrate the AI-generated work with their own observations (i.e., human intelligence) to enhance the work. Each student submitted a file to their peer with three columns: one containing the original text, one with AI-generated feedback based on the criteria, and one with their own suggestions (human intelligence). In the final phase, the pairs had the opportunity to reflect on the entire assessment process.

As shown in Table 1, the ENGAGE model, already tested by [18], presents well-defined phases. At the first stage, teachers establish a supportive learning environment and clarify the aims and expectations of peer assessment so that students can understand the purpose, roles, and responsibilities of peer assessment. At the second stage, students collaborate with the teacher to co-construct marking criteria after learning the target content. They are engaged in different activities alongside teachers and peers to collaboratively develop performance indicators and weightings while refining their assessment skills. At the third stage, students develop their work based on given instructions. Projects can take various forms, including text, audio, video, images, and animations. At the fourth stage, students act as assessors, reviewing peer work and providing feedback, ideally through an online system. As suggested by [18], confidentiality is crucial to minimize peer pressure, though maintaining anonymity in face-to-face settings can be challenging. At the fifth stage, students take on the role of the assesses and they are asked to critically evaluate the feedback rather than accepting it without question. Finally, at the sixth stage, students refine their work by assessing peer feedback and deciding how to implement it for improvement. Writing a reflection on how they revised their work based on feedback can be beneficial.

The Engage Model provides a structured framework for peer formative assessment, guiding students through key phases that enhance their ability to evaluate and provide constructive feedback. However, traditional peer assessment faces several challenges, including time constraints, inconsistent feedback, and student reluctance to engage in the evaluation process. AI technologies offer potential solutions to these challenges by automating certain aspects of assessment, enhancing feedback quality, and supporting both students and instructors.

Table 1. ENGAGE – Peer Assessment Model [18]

Stage 1	E	Teacher **e**xplicates aims and expectations
Stage 2	N	Students **n**egotiate making criteria
Stage 3	G	Students **g**enerate projects
Stage 4	A	Students **a**nalyze peer work and provide feedback
Stage 5	G	Students **g**auge the value of feedback received
Stage 6	E	Students **e**nhance their own work

As mentioned in the previous paragraph, this paper presents the ENGAGE AI-Based model, designed to conduct peer reviews using AI tools based on a set of evaluation criteria identified and shared for peer assessment. The ENGAGE AI-Based model was initially tested with a small group of 10 students enrolled in the *Design, Documentation, and Evaluation* course, part of the third-year curriculum in the Bachelor's Degree program in Educational Sciences. It was later extended to 150 prospective teachers.

The ENGAGE AI-Based model, structured in six stages, was implemented during a five-hour session:

1. **E**ngagement: preparing students for peer assessment with AI;
2. Negotiation: definition of the evaluation criteria to be used through the use of AI;
3. **G**uidance: providing students with structured guidance on assessment with evaluation criteria to be used through the use of AI;
4. **A**ssessment: conducting peer reviews through AI- tools with evaluation criteria;
5. **G**eneration: refining work based on AI insights and peer feedback;
6. **E**valuation: providing a reflection on the assessment process.

The ENGAGE AI-Based model, initially required the completion of two micro-projects as an evaluative task: the first of a metacognitive nature and the second of a cooperative nature. Once the projects were completed, future primary and secondary level teachers were asked to review one anonymous work from a colleague after sharing the evaluation criteria with the instructor, allowing them to be both the evaluator and the evaluated. Before the submission, the instructor shared and explained the evaluation criteria as shown on the following table (Table 2).

Once the criteria were explained, each participant made an initial evaluation of a colleague's work using ChatGPT. They were asked to follow these steps:

- Access ChatGPT.
- Input the text to be reviewed according to the provided criteria.
- Refine their work based on AI insights and peer feedback.
- Reflect on the assessment process.

After receiving the response from ChatGPT, participants were asked to create a table with three columns in which to include the original text, the response provided by ChatGPT, and their personal suggestions and feedback regarding the work done. It was therefore necessary to refine work based on AI insights and peer feedback and to reflect on the assessment process. This last step was crucial to help future teachers understand

Table 2. Evaluation criteria for peer review submissions

Dimensions	Criteria	Indicators
CONCEPTUAL ANALYSIS RELATED TO THE TEXT CONTENT	Relevance to the topic	Explaining significant relationships between concepts.
	Lexical variety	Using a diverse range of words to articulate arguments while avoiding repetition.
	Use of Discipline-Specific Terminology	Incorporating specialized terms from the field, such as "Metacognitive and Cooperative Teaching."
ORGANIZATIONAL ASPECTS	Sequence or logical flow of considerations	Structuring sentences in a way that enhances readability and comprehension.
INTERNAL COHERENCE	First design phase	Defining specific objectives aligned with the general objective.
		Designing an activity that is consistent with both the general and specific objectives.
	Second Cooperative Design Phase	Establishing specific objectives that align with the general objective.
		Creating a cooperative learning activity that adheres to the formulated objectives.

that the evaluation of work, even among peers, cannot be solely entrusted to artificial intelligence; rather, it requires verification and revisions by human intelligence.

3.3 Focus Group

To investigate the perceptions of future primary and lower secondary school teachers enrolled in the course "Metacognitive and Cooperative Teaching" at the University of Palermo regarding peer assessment practices involving artificial intelligence, ten focus group sessions (each lasting 45 min) were conducted at the conclusion of the peer evaluation activity. The sessions were facilitated by two researchers who served as moderator and note-taker, respectively. The moderator was responsible for managing communication among the group members, while the note-taker recorded the responses provided by the participants.

The focus group agenda explored the following areas: students' perceptions of AI in peer assessment; the effectiveness of the Engage Model in improving the quality of feedback; and the challenges encountered in implementing the model. The focus group questions were designed to allow for open-ended, discursive responses.

During the discussion, the moderator aimed to address all the topics on the agenda, devoting equal time to each. The funneling strategy [27] was adopted to ensure that the most important topics were placed at the center of the discussion.

The responses collected during the focus group were organized into a set of assertions and relationships between assertions, following an approach similar to that used in text analysis and ethnographic research [28]. The analysis of the material gathered during the focus group session was carried out using specific grids and pre-designed frameworks, allowing for a structured systematization of the future teachers' opinions and positions on the topics discussed.

To ensure methodological rigor, all focus group sessions were audio-recorded, fully transcribed, and subjected to a thematic analysis [29]. This qualitative approach allowed the identification of recurring patterns and themes related to participants' perceptions of AI-supported peer assessment. Two researchers independently coded the transcripts, compared their interpretations, and discussed any discrepancies until consensus was reached. This procedure enhanced the reliability and consistency of the analysis. Thematic analysis was chosen for its flexibility and suitability in exploring participants' experiences and meanings in depth, aligning with the exploratory nature of this study.

In the following paragraph, the main outcomes of the evaluation conducted by the future teachers on the experience they underwent will be discussed, starting with the realization of the focus group session.

As examples, some statements made by the participants during the focus group activity will be included.

4 Finding and Discussions

The findings highlight a nuanced perception of AI-supported peer assessment among pre-service teachers, characterized by a balance between motivation and critical awareness. While the integration of AI was perceived as engaging and stimulating, participants did not interpret artificial intelligence as a neutral or fully objective evaluator. Instead, they consistently emphasized the need for human judgment in assessment processes, particularly when interpretative, contextual, and relational dimensions are involved. This confirms that students do not passively accept AI outputs but actively question their reliability and scope.

A recurring theme concerns the perception of AI as a *supportive partner* rather than a substitute for human evaluation. Participants valued AI-generated feedback for its structure, clarity, and capacity to stimulate reflection, especially when used as a reference point for comparison with peer feedback. At the same time, they highlighted the limits of AI in capturing contextual nuances and emotional sensitivity, which they considered central to meaningful formative assessment. This finding aligns with previous studies suggesting that AI can enhance feedback processes while remaining insufficient in addressing the qualitative and relational dimensions of assessment [30, 31].

The comparison between AI-generated feedback and human feedback played a crucial role in fostering metacognitive awareness. By engaging with multiple sources of feedback, participants were encouraged to reflect on assessment criteria, feedback quality, and their own evaluative judgments. This process supported the development of feedback literacy and critical thinking, reinforcing the metacognitive dimension of peer assessment. As noted by [32], exposure to diverse feedback perspectives can strengthen learners' ability to evaluate, justify, and improve their own judgments.

Despite these positive outcomes, the findings also reveal significant challenges related to ethical awareness and understanding of AI systems. Participants expressed uncertainty regarding how AI processes information, as well as concerns about data use, transparency, and potential algorithmic bias. Such uncertainties can undermine trust in AI-supported assessment and contribute to cognitive and emotional demands associated with the adoption of digital tools [33, 34]. These concerns indicate that effective integration of AI in assessment practices requires not only technical familiarity but also explicit pedagogical and ethical preparation.

Another critical issue relates to the authenticity of feedback. Some participants warned that excessive reliance on AI may lead to standardized and less pedagogically sensitive comments, reducing opportunities for dialogic and situated feedback. This perception is consistent with recent research showing that, although generative AI can produce coherent and linguistically accurate feedback, it often lacks the interpretative depth and relational grounding that characterize human assessment practices [35].

Finally, differences emerged based on participants' levels of digital confidence. Pre-service teachers with greater familiarity with digital technologies appeared more open and trusting toward AI-supported assessment, whereas those with less experience expressed higher levels of skepticism. This finding suggests that digital competence plays a mediating role in shaping attitudes toward AI integration in educational contexts.

Overall, the ENGAGE AI-Based model appears effective in promoting a balanced form of human–AI interaction. By positioning AI as a scaffolding tool rather than an evaluative authority, the model supports reflective judgment, peer dialogue, and critical engagement with technology, contributing to more thoughtful and informed assessment practices.

5 Conclusion

This study presents a preliminary contribution within a broader research agenda on artificial intelligence and formative assessment in higher education. Despite limitations related to the exploratory design, sample size, and qualitative focus, the findings suggest that the ENGAGE AI-Based model provides a pedagogically grounded approach to integrating AI into peer assessment practices.

The results indicate that the use of AI in peer assessment can enhance motivation, engagement, and critical reflection among pre-service teachers. Participants recognized the value of AI-generated feedback in supporting structure and clarity, while simultaneously acknowledging its limitations in ensuring objectivity and capturing the relational and contextual dimensions of assessment. The combination of AI-generated feedback and human judgment emerged as a particularly effective strategy for improving feedback quality and fostering metacognitive reflection.

From an ethical and pedagogical perspective, the findings support a model of human–AI collaboration in which artificial intelligence functions as a mediating and supportive tool rather than an autonomous evaluative authority. This approach reinforces the centrality of teacher agency and highlights the importance of developing AI literacy, ethical awareness, and critical understanding of intelligent systems within teacher education programs [34].

In line with recent literature on the transformation of the teaching profession in the AI era [36], this study contributes to ongoing debates by illustrating how AI can be integrated into assessment practices without undermining the role of human educators. Rather than replacing teachers, AI can support them as critical mediators who interpret algorithmic input, guide reflective learning processes, and uphold pedagogical and ethical values. In this sense, the challenge for education lies not in delegating assessment to intelligent systems, but in empowering educators to use them critically, responsibly, and creatively.

Disclosure of Interest. The authors declare that they have no conflict of interest.

Author Contribution. This work was carried out through a collaborative effort by all five authors. E. Gulbay drafted Sects. 1 and 5. L. Longo contributed to Sects. 3.1 and 3.2. V. Pitrella authored Sect. 4. M. Bruno prepared Sect. 2. D.R. Di Carlo wrote Sect. 3.3.

References

1. Bruschi, B.: IRIDI START: un progetto di formazione per i docenti neoassunti. In: Faculty Development e innovazione didattica universitaria, pp. 271–278. Genova University Press, Genova (2021)
2. Jongsma, M.V., Scholten, D.J., van Muijlwijk-Koezen, J.E., Meeter, M.: Online versus offline peer feedback in higher education: A meta-analysis. J. Educ. Comput. Res. **61**(2), 329–354 (2023). https://doi.org/10.1177/07356331221114181
3. Topping, K.: Peer assessment between students in colleges and universities. Rev. Educ. Res. **68**(3), 249–276 (1998)
4. La Marca, A., Di Martino, V., Gülbay, E.: Valutazione tra pari all'università: due approcci didattici a confronto. Form@re – Open J. per la formazione in rete. **20**(1), 154–171 (2020)
5. Coggi, C. (ed.): Innovare la didattica e la valutazione in Università: Il progetto IRIDI per la formazione dei docenti. FrancoAngeli, Milano (2019)
6. Coggi, C., Ricchiardi, P.: Developing effective teaching in Higher Education. Form@re – Open J. Per La Formazione in Rete. **18**(1), 23–38 (2018)
7. Senden, M., Coertjens, L.: The impact of peer assessment design on interpersonal processes: A systematic review. Stud. Educ. Eval. **83**, 101405 (2024)
8. Vegliante, R.: La valutazione tra pari per promuovere strategie collaborative: il punto di vista degli studenti. Pedagogia Oggi. **22**(1), 112–122 (2024)
9. Longo, L., Gülbay, E., Di Carlo, D.R.: Valutazione formativa e didattica a distanza all'Università. Annali online della Didattica e della Formazione Docente. **13**(21), 199–214 (2021)
10. Marzano, A.: Apprendere attraverso la valutazione tra pari nella formazione universitaria: i risultati di una esperienza didattica. Pedagogia Oggi. **21**(1), 81–88 (2023)
11. Topping, K.: Peer assessment: Learning by judging and discussing the work of other learners. Interdisc. Educ. Psychol. **1**(1), 1–17 (2017)
12. Tore, R.: La valutazione formativa come strategia di apprendimento. Formazione Insegnamento. **17**(3), 408–416 (2019)

13. Henderson, M., Ajjawi, R., Boud, D., Molloy, E. (eds.): The Impact of Feedback in Higher Education: Improving Assessment Outcomes for Learners. Palgrave Macmillan, Cham (2019)
14. Scierri, I.D.M.: Strategie e strumenti di valutazione formativa per promuovere l'apprendimento autoregolato: una rassegna ragionata delle ricerche empiriche. J. Educ., Cult. Psychol. Stud. (ECPS J.). **24**, 213–227 (2021)
15. Capperucci, D.: Uso della valutazione per l'apprendimento. In: A cosa serve la ricerca educativa? Il dato e il suo valore sociale, pp. 766–770. Pensa MultiMedia, Lecce (2024)
16. Adachi, C., Tai, J., Dawson, P.: Academics' perceptions of the benefits and challenges of self and peer assessment in higher education. Assess. Eval. High. Educ. **43**(2), 294–306 (2018). https://doi.org/10.1080/02602938.2017.1339775
17. Fleckney, P., Thompson, J., Vaz-Serra, P.: Designing effective peer assessment processes in higher education: a systematic review. High. Educ. Res. Dev. **44**(2), 386–401 (2025)
18. Li, L.: ENGAGE Students in formative peer assessment to support learning. Italian J. Educ. Res., 63–70 (2019)
19. Pitrella, V., et al.: Artificial intelligence for personalized learning in K-12 education: a scoping review. In: International Conference on Higher Education Learning Methodologies and Technologies Online, pp. 372–382. Springer, Cham (2023)
20. Falzone, Y., Leone, A., Pitrella, V., Longo, L., Di Carlo, D.R.: Integrating AI and Flipped Learning: A Modern Framework for Initial Teacher Training. In: International Conference on Higher Education Learning Methodologies and Technologies Online, pp. 124–136. Springer, Cham (2024)
21. Cain, J., Medina, M., Romanelli, F., Persky, A.: Deficiencies of traditional grading systems and recommendations for the future. Am. J. Pharm. Educ. **86**(7), 8850 (2022)
22. Gnanaprakasam, J., Lourdusamy, R.: The role of AI in automating grading: Enhancing feedback and efficiency. In: Artificial Intelligence and Education – Shaping the Future of Learning. IntechOpen (2024). https://doi.org/10.5772/intechopen.1005025
23. Erdogdu, F., Cakir, O.: Determining Teacher Candidates' Artificial Intelligence Literacy and Their Perceptions of Artificial Intelligence. TURKSOSBİLDER. **9**(2), 63–95 (2024)
24. Celebi, C., Yilmaz, F., Demir, U., Karakus, F.: Artificial intelligence literacy: An adaptation study. Instr. Technol. Lifelong Learn. **4**(2), 291–306 (2023)
25. Livberber, T., Ayvaz, S.: The impact of Artificial Intelligence in academia: Views of Turkish academics on ChatGPT. Heliyon. **9**(9), e19688 (2023). https://doi.org/10.1016/j.heliyon.2023.e19688
26. Topping, K.J., Gehringer, E., Khosravi, H., Gudipati, S., Jadhav, K., Susarla, S.: Enhancing peer assessment with artificial intelligence. Int. J. Educ. Technol. High. Educ. **22**(1), 3 (2025)
27. Frisina, A.: Focus group Una guida praticaa. Il Mulino, Bologna (2010)
28. Losito, G.: L'analisi del contenuto nella ricerca sociale. FrancoAngeli, Milano (1993)
29. Braun, V., Clarke, V.: Using thematic analysis in psychology. Qual. Res. Psychol. **3**(2), 77–101 (2006)
30. Williamson, B., Eynon, R.: Historical threads, missing links, and future directions in AI in education. Learn. Media Technol. **45**(3), 223–235 (2020)
31. Owan, V.J., Abang, K.B., Idika, D.O., Etta, E.O.: Bassey, B.A.: Exploring the potential of artificial intelligence tools in educational measurement and assessment. Eurasia Journal of Mathematics, Science and Technology. Education. **19**(8), em2307 (2023)
32. Tai, J., Ajjawi, R., Boud, D., Dawson, P., Panadero, E.: Developing evaluative judgement: enabling students to make decisions about the quality of work. High. Educ. **76**(3), 467–481 (2018)
33. Messineo, L., Tosto, C.: Evaluation of the psychometric properties of the Italian version of the 10-item perceived stress scale in a sample of teachers. Front. Psychol. **14**, 1330789 (2024)
34. Holmes, W., Porayska-Pomsta, K.: The Ethics of Artificial Intelligence in Education. Routledge, London (2023)

35. Henderson, M., et al.: Comparing Generative AI and teacher feedback: student perceptions of usefulness and trustworthiness. Assess. Eval. High. Educ., 1–16 (2025)
36. Gentile, M., Città, G., Perna, S., Allegra, M.: Do we still need teachers? Navigating the paradigm shift of the teacher's role in the AI era. In: Frontiers in Education, vol. 8, p. 1161777. Frontiers, Media SA (2023)

AI-Mediated Formative Feedback in Open-Ended Mathematics Tasks

Michele Giuliano Fiorentino(✉) and Antonella Montone

University of Bari Aldo Moro, Bari, Italy
{michele.fiorentino,antonella.montone}@uniba.it

Abstract. This study examines how AI-mediated formative feedback supports conceptual reasoning and metacognitive processes in open-ended university mathematics tasks. Conducted within the PRIN project "AI&F – Artificial Intelligence & Feedback for Effective Learning," the research analyzes how AI-generated prompts guide students from intuitive reasoning toward mathematically grounded explanations. Two open-ended tasks were implemented with pre-service primary and secondary teachers, who worked collaboratively, submitted written solutions, received AI formative feedback, and revised their responses iteratively. Qualitative analysis of interaction excerpts and written productions shows that AI feedback functioned as a dialogic trigger rather than a purely evaluative response, fostering conceptual clarification, generalization, and reflective discussion. Results indicate that pedagogically designed AI feedback, embedded in collaborative settings, can enhance formative assessment practices and support effective human–AI partnership in mathematics education.

Keywords: AI in education · Formative Assessment · Automated Feedback · Open-ended problems · Mathematics Education · Collaborative Learning

1 Introduction

The integration of Artificial Intelligence (AI) in higher education is increasingly reshaping teaching and assessment practices, offering opportunities for more personalized and scalable forms of feedback. In university mathematics courses, where large enrolments often limit timely individual support, formative assessment represents a central challenge. As highlighted by Black and Wiliam [1], feedback is most effective when it is prompt, individualized, and oriented toward improving learning processes rather than simply judging outcomes.

Within this context, open-ended problems play a particularly significant role. These tasks require students to engage in reasoning, creativity, and justification, rather than merely providing a correct answer. By allowing multiple solution paths and diverse strategies, open-ended problems create authentic opportunities for inquiry and reflection. They encourage students to explore the underlying mathematical structures, articulate their thinking, and engage in collaborative problem-solving, fostering both conceptual understanding and metacognitive awareness.

M. Adamoli et al. (Eds.): HELMeTO 2025, CCIS 2958, pp. 383–395, 2026.
https://doi.org/10.1007/978-3-032-31850-3_24

The present study is part of the PRIN project "AI&F – Artificial Intelligence & Feedback for Effective Learning" [2], which investigates how AI-based tools can support formative assessment in mathematics education. Specifically, the project examines how automated feedback can guide students in refining their reasoning, promoting iterative cycles of problem-solving, reflection, and revision. In this framework, AI is not intended to replace teacher mediation but to act as a dialogic partner that amplifies instructional support, providing timely prompts that stimulate conceptual thinking and collaborative sense-making.

By combining open-ended tasks with AI-mediated feedback, the study aims to explore both the cognitive and social dimensions of learning. Students are invited to interpret, evaluate, and act on feedback, thereby enhancing their ability to construct meaning independently and collectively. Simultaneously, these practices offer insights into the professional development of teachers, as they learn to integrate AI feedback effectively within classroom dynamics, balancing guidance and autonomy, and fostering environments where reasoning and exploration are valued.

Overall, this approach positions AI as a catalyst for deeper engagement with mathematical ideas, supporting a shift from procedural execution to conceptual understanding and reflective inquiry. By examining how students respond to AI-generated prompts within authentic problem-solving scenarios, the study seeks to illuminate the potential of AI to enhance formative assessment and promote richer, dialogic learning experiences in higher education mathematics.

Beyond its technological novelty, the integration of AI in university mathematics education responds to a long-standing pedagogical need: to make students' reasoning visible and to provide responsive feedback within complex cognitive tasks. Mathematics, as a discipline grounded in abstraction and justification, often exposes a gap between procedural proficiency and conceptual understanding. Traditional assessment systems—especially in large courses—struggle to capture the nuances of reasoning that emerge in exploratory, open-ended problem solving.

AI-based formative feedback offers a potential bridge across this gap. By analyzing students' written arguments, identifying implicit patterns of reasoning, and generating targeted prompts, AI systems can help learners engage more consciously with their own thought processes. In this sense, AI functions not only as a technological innovation but also as a cognitive partner that makes mathematical thinking traceable and discussable.

From a research perspective, this experiment aims to explore how human–AI interaction can foster cycles of reflection, dialogue, and revision, contributing to a broader rethinking of formative assessment practices in mathematics. The study therefore addresses a dual purpose: on one hand, it examines how students respond to AI-generated feedback in open-ended mathematical tasks; on the other, it investigates how these interactions can inform pedagogical design and teacher development in digital learning environments. By doing so, it contributes to the growing field of research on AI-enhanced education, situating formative feedback as a key mediating process between technology and meaningful mathematical learning.

2 Theoretical References

Open-ended problems are here understood in the sense proposed by Pehkonen [3], as mathematical situations that allow for a range of possible solutions, strategies, and lines of reasoning. Unlike traditional closed exercises that typically converge on a single correct answer, open-ended problems invite students to explore multiple pathways, formulate conjectures, and justify their conclusions through argumentation. Their educational value lies precisely in this openness: they encourage flexible thinking, creativity, and the capacity to engage in genuine mathematical inquiry.

From a pedagogical standpoint, open-ended tasks serve several purposes. They can reveal students' conceptual understanding more deeply than procedural exercises, offering insights into how learners make sense of mathematical ideas, represent problems, and communicate reasoning [4]. Furthermore, they foster a classroom culture where uncertainty and error are viewed as integral components of the learning process rather than as signs of failure. Such an environment supports the development of mathematical resilience and promotes metacognitive awareness, as students are required to plan, monitor, and reflect upon their own strategies [5].

At the same time, open-ended problems pose significant challenges for both teachers and learners. For students, they demand not only content knowledge but also autonomy, perseverance, and the ability to justify decisions and solutions. For teachers, they complicate the assessment process: evaluation can no longer rely on correctness alone, but must consider the reasoning process, the appropriateness of the strategy, and the coherence of the explanation [6]. In this sense, assessment becomes an interpretive act that requires sensitivity to the nuances of students' thinking and argumentation.

The integration of open-ended problems into everyday practice thus calls for a rethinking of classroom dynamics. Teachers must balance guidance and freedom, ensuring that students are supported while maintaining the authenticity of inquiry. Feedback, whether human or automated, plays a crucial role here, as it can help students recognize the value of their reasoning even when their final answers diverge from conventional solutions. The use of digital tools and AI-based feedback systems, in particular, may offer new opportunities to document, analyze, and respond to students' diverse approaches to open-ended tasks, although these technologies must be designed and employed with strong pedagogical awareness.

The integration of technology in mathematics education not only supports students' reasoning but also provides a context for the professional development of teachers. Previous studies highlight that teachers' engagement in collaborative problem-solving and reflective practice using digital tools can enhance their ability to mediate mathematical discussions effectively [7, 8] These frameworks underline the importance of learning in and from practice, showing how AI-supported feedback and interactive environments can inform both student and teacher growth.

Similarly, recent contributions have emphasized the role of digital technologies in promoting interdisciplinary approaches and the professional preparation of pre-service teachers in mathematics and science education [9–11]. These studies demonstrate how online and blended environments can foster reflective practice, model-based reasoning, and the integration of applied mathematical thinking within authentic learning contexts.

In sum, open-ended problems represent a powerful means to cultivate mathematical thinking that is flexible, reflective, and creative. They shift the focus from "finding the answer" to "exploring the problem," and from reproducing procedures to constructing meaning—thus aligning closely with contemporary visions of mathematics education as a dialogic and inquiry-oriented practice.

Formative assessment, conceptualized as a lever for learning [1], provides a useful framework for understanding the role of AI in this context. AI-driven analysis of written solutions may enhance formative processes by supporting teachers in identifying reasoning strategies, misconceptions, or promising directions. In this sense, AI does not replace the teacher but complements human mediation, fostering iterative cycles of feedback and revision that are central to effective learning.

Feedback plays a pivotal role in enhancing learning outcomes, as it enables students to compare their current performance with reference standards and identify ways to bridge the gap between actual and desired results [12, 13]. Initially grounded in transmissive models of teaching, educational research has progressively embraced a socio-constructivist perspective, viewing feedback not merely as information transmitted from teacher to student, but as a dialogic and interactive process that fosters active knowledge construction [14]. Within this paradigm, learners are regarded as active agents capable of interpreting, evaluating, and applying feedback to refine their understanding and performance [15, 16].

Recent technological developments have introduced new possibilities for feedback delivery. Automated feedback systems, powered by advanced digital technologies and artificial intelligence (AI), represent a promising avenue for addressing long-standing challenges of personalization and scalability in assessment, particularly in large classrooms [17]. By providing immediate and detailed responses, these tools can help students reflect independently on their work, recognize specific areas for improvement, and take greater responsibility for their own learning [18]. Furthermore, such systems may facilitate the implementation of innovative assessment practices grounded in formative and participatory approaches that actively engage students in the learning process [19]

Nevertheless, the potential of automated feedback can only be realized through pedagogically informed integration [20]. Both teachers and students need to develop the necessary competencies to interact meaningfully with these tools. Teachers, in particular, are called to rethink their instructional strategies, blending digital technologies with active learning processes, while students must cultivate critical literacy to interpret and apply the feedback effectively [20, 21].

However, the growing adoption of AI-based feedback systems also raises significant challenges. Research warns that poorly designed systems may generate feedback that is ambiguous, misleading, or even counterproductive, thus requiring careful evaluation of human–machine interaction effectiveness [22]. Moreover, the integration of AI in educational contexts prompts crucial ethical and pedagogical reflections concerning data privacy, equity of access, and the long-term sustainability of digital innovation [20]. The project explores how language models and machine learning techniques can analyze students' responses to open-ended tasks, offering immediate, individualized feedback. Such an approach holds potential to create fairer, more transparent, and scalable assessment systems, bridging the gap between automation and human interaction.

3 Research Methodology

Two open-ended problems were central to the new experiment, designed to explore how AI-supported feedback can enhance students' reasoning in authentic mathematical contexts. The first task, of a geometric nature, asked participants to determine whether a rectangular plot of land could be divided equally between two siblings by connecting an interior point of the rectangle to its vertices, thus generating four triangles. Students were invited to discuss and justify the fairness of the division, compare different strategies, and propose alternative constructions that might guarantee equality of area. This problem was intended to elicit reasoning on proportional relationships, geometric argumentation, and the role of visual representations in validating conjectures.

The second task, in the arithmetic domain, focused on exploring numerical patterns within a hundred chart (a 10×10 grid of numbers from 1 to 100). Participants selected a 2×2 square within the grid and were asked to analyze the relationships among the diagonal numbers, examining differences, sums, and products, to identify and generalize invariant properties. The problem encouraged inductive reasoning, algebraic generalization, and the articulation of mathematical explanations.

The experimentation was carried out in presence, within the regular university classroom settings of the Primary Education Sciences and Mathematics degree courses at the University of Bari. Approximately 180 pre-service primary teachers (PTs) and 40 pre-service secondary teachers participated. The authors of this paper served as course instructors and facilitators.

Each group, composed of four PTs, engaged in a collaborative problem-solving session where they produced a shared written report supported by digital tools. In this phase, an AI-based feedback system was introduced to assist the analysis and refinement of the students' written arguments. After submitting their initial solutions, the groups received automated formative feedback generated by the AI tool, focusing on aspects such as clarity of reasoning, mathematical correctness, and completeness of justification.

Subsequently, participants were asked to revise their solutions, discussing the feedback both within the group and with the instructors. This iterative process reflected the theoretical assumptions discussed in the previous section, particularly the view of feedback as a dialogic and formative process. In line with this perspective, the study sought to examine not only the outcomes of problem solving but the evolution of reasoning through human–AI interaction.

After the iterative cycles of submission, AI feedback, and group revision, all written productions and interaction logs were collected for qualitative analysis. The analysis focused on identifying how the AI prompts influenced students' reasoning processes, revisions, and collaborative dialogue. In this sense, the study aimed not only to assess the accuracy of students' final answers, but to trace how their conceptual understanding evolved through the human–AI interaction.

The AI-mediated feedback system used in the experiment was based on a large language model integrated within a structured prompting protocol developed in the AI&F project. Students' written solutions were processed through prompts that included the task description and pedagogical feedback criteria, instructing the model to generate short formative cues focused on reasoning quality, justification, and conceptual completeness rather than correctness alone. The AI was constrained to produce dialogic, non-solution-giving feedback (e.g., requests for clarification, generalization, or verification). Feedback outputs were reviewed by the instructors before release to ensure pedagogical alignment. For data analysis, a qualitative interpretive approach was adopted: written productions, AI prompts, and interaction excerpts were coded with respect to reasoning shifts, feedback uptake, and metacognitive moves. Coding was conducted by both authors and refined through iterative agreement to ensure interpretive consistency.

Building upon the theoretical framework that conceives feedback as dialogic, formative, and generative [1, 14] the experiment was guided by the following research questions:

RQ1: Can AI-generated formative feedback effectively guide students' transition from intuitive or empirical reasoning toward conceptually valid mathematical explanations?

RQ2: Does the integration of AI feedback within collaborative open-ended tasks foster reflective and metacognitive learning processes consistent with formative assessment principles?

These questions aim to explore the extent to which AI-mediated formative interactions can promote conceptual understanding and metacognitive awareness in authentic mathematical problem-solving contexts.

4 AI-Mediated Interactions: Guiding Conceptual Evolution

The collaborative sessions revealed how the AI agent functioned not merely as a provider of evaluative feedback, but as a dialogic partner that supported the progressive refinement of students' reasoning. The interaction between the pre-service teachers and the system frequently triggered productive discussions within groups, fostering a shift from procedural or intuitive reasoning to more conceptually grounded explanations.

4.1 Example 1 – The Geometric Task.

One group initially approached the rectangular land division problem by assuming that connecting any interior point to the rectangle's vertices would automatically generate four triangles of equal area. Their justification relied on the symmetry of the figure rather than on explicit geometric arguments. The AI-generated feedback highlighted that *"equal distances from the center do not necessarily imply equal areas"* and suggested verifying the equality of areas through proportional reasoning or by computing base–height relationships.

After reading the feedback, the group began to question their assumption and engaged in a short but dense exchange, recorded as follows:

- [08:42] M1: So if the point is somewhere near the center, it should divide the land fairly, right? Because it looks symmetric.
- [08:45] M2: Yes, visually it seems fair. Each triangle is kind of the same shape.
- [08:48] AI feedback (screen): "Equal distances from the center do not necessarily imply equal areas. Try comparing base–height ratios."
- [08:52] M3: Wait—so even if the point is centered, the areas might not be equal?

- [08:56] M4: Maybe we can check using coordinates. If the rectangle is 6 by 4, and we pick a point not exactly in the middle, the areas might change.
- [09:02] M2: Let's test with GeoGebra. (Opens software.) If the point is exactly at the intersection of the diagonals, it works! But if it moves a little, one triangle becomes smaller.
- [09:06] M1: Oh, so equality only holds when the point is at the intersection.
- [09:09] M3: The feedback was right, distance doesn't guarantee area. We need to prove it using base times height.
- [09:12] M4: So the condition for fairness is that the point lies at the diagonal intersection. We can express that algebraically.

This brief exchange illustrates how the AI's feedback functioned as a *cognitive trigger*, destabilizing an initial perceptual belief ("symmetry implies equality") and reorienting the group toward analytical validation. The feedback served not as a correction but as a catalyst for rethinking. The students' reasoning evolved from visual intuition to proportional reasoning and formal proof. They appropriated the AI's prompt as a *shared object of discussion*, transforming external feedback into an internalized questioning process.

The collaborative context amplified this transition: each peer contributed a different epistemic resource—one using visual intuition, another computational verification, and another symbolic reasoning. The episode demonstrates how AI-mediated feedback can sustain what Nicol [14] calls *dialogic feedback*, where learners construct meaning through collective interpretation of external cues. The digital tool's role was not to provide solutions but to *mediate* inquiry, aligning with the principles of formative assessment that emphasize feedback as a process of shared knowledge construction rather than simple evaluation.

The observed dialogue illustrates how AI prompts can scaffold productive struggle and support conceptual reasoning in alignment with Boaler's [5] framework of mathematical mindsets. The group's shift from visual intuition to proportional and algebraic validation demonstrates the capacity of AI to challenge initial assumptions without imposing solutions, fostering resilience and critical engagement. Moreover, the episode reflects aspects of AI literacy [24] students actively interpreted the AI-generated cues, evaluated their reasoning strategies, and integrated computational verification tools (e.g., GeoGebra) into their problem-solving process. This interplay highlights how learners can develop the skills to critically navigate AI-mediated feedback and use it as a cognitive resource rather than a directive authority.

4.2 Example 2 – The Arithmetic Task.

In the 100-chart problem, another group identified that in every 2×2 square the difference between the diagonal numbers was constant (equal to 9). Their report initially framed this as an empirical observation without explanation. The AI feedback noted that *"regularity has been observed but not yet generalized: can you explain why this difference is always constant?"*

The prompt initiated an exploratory discussion among the participants:

- [10:17] A1: We noticed that in any 2×2 square, the diagonals differ by 9.

- [10:19] A2: Yes, always 9. It works for every example we tried.
- [10:22] AI feedback (screen): "Regularity has been observed but not yet generalized. Can you explain why this difference is always constant?"
- [10:26] A3: So it wants an explanation... maybe we can represent the numbers algebraically.
- [10:29] A4: Let's call the top-left number *n*. Then the others are $n + 1$, $n + 10$, and $n + 11$.
- [10:32] A1: Okay, then one diagonal is *n* and $n + 11$, the other is $n + 1$ and $n + 10$.
- [10:36] A2: The difference between diagonals is $10–10 = 0$, wait no, let's compute properly.
- [10:40] A3: It's $(n + 11) – (n + 1) = 10$ and $(n + 10) – n = 10$. So both are 10, not 9!
- [10:44] A4: Ah, so our observation was close but not exact—it's 10, because of the structure of the Table.
- [10:48] A1: The feedback helped us see the need to justify with a general rule. It's not just a pattern, it's a property of how the grid is built.

Here again, the AI's role was not evaluative but *provocative*. The question "Can you explain why...?" activated a search for generality and a move from empirical pattern recognition to algebraic justification. The students' algebraization of the pattern—representing numbers symbolically—marked a transition from procedural observation to structural understanding.

The transcript reveals a subtle but powerful metacognitive shift: as the group grappled with the feedback, they began to question their own certainty, verify results, and refine conceptual precision. The process embodies Black and Wiliam's [1] notion of *closing the gap* through feedback-driven reflection. Moreover, the social negotiation of meaning—visible in self-correction and peer confirmation—suggests that AI prompts can stimulate inner feedback loops that activate both reasoning and reflection.

In the arithmetic task, the AI feedback prompted the group to move from empirical observation to symbolic reasoning, eliciting metacognitive reflection and collaborative negotiation of meaning. This transition exemplifies the principles described by Boaler [5], where engagement with uncertainty and error becomes a driver of deeper conceptual understanding. Simultaneously, the episode underscores the importance of *AI literacy* [24] as students were required to interpret algorithmic prompts, formulate algebraic representations, and validate their reasoning systematically. By navigating these interactions, learners demonstrate an emerging capacity to treat AI as a dialogic partner, capable of enhancing cognitive agency while preserving student autonomy.

Across both examples, the AI agent promoted iterative cycles of conjecture, verification, and justification that paralleled human tutoring behaviors. Rather than replacing teacher mediation, the system amplified formative dialogue by generating precise prompts that reoriented attention toward the logical structure of students' reasoning. The written traces of these interactions documented a genuine evolution of ideas—from initial intuitive beliefs toward mathematically valid conceptualizations.

The analysis of these episodes provides evidence that AI-mediated formative assessment can operate as a *semiotic and cognitive amplifier*, enabling learners to externalize thought processes, test hypotheses collaboratively, and internalize conceptual understanding through reflective dialogue.

5 Discussion

The analysis of the two episodes provides valuable insight into how AI-mediated formative assessment can reshape students' engagement with mathematical reasoning. Both cases demonstrate that the feedback generated by the AI system acted not as a static evaluation but as a dialogic impulse that prompted students to interrogate, negotiate, and reconstruct their understanding.

In relation to RQ1, the findings show that the integration of AI feedback into collaborative problem solving can sustain a gradual shift from intuitive or perceptual reasoning toward formalized, conceptual understanding. In the geometric task, the feedback questioned a perceptual assumption and initiated a process of collective validation through proportional reasoning. In the arithmetic task, it encouraged the students to move from empirical observation to algebraic generalization. These transitions suggest that AI feedback can foster epistemic agency, allowing learners to appropriate prompts as resources for self-explanation rather than mere corrections.

Concerning RQ2, the episodes illustrate that students did not passively receive the feedback but actively interpreted and discussed it, transforming the AI prompt into a shared semiotic artifact. This process gave rise to what Carless and Boud [23] describe as feedback literacy—the capacity to make sense of, and act productively upon, evaluative information. The transcripts show how the system's short, non-directive messages stimulated both cognitive and social processes of meaning-making. The resulting peer dialogues bridged the space between algorithmic suggestion and human reasoning, transforming AI interaction into a genuinely educational exchange.

The implications of these findings extend beyond the specific tasks. They point toward a model of AI-augmented formative assessment in which feedback is co-constructed through cycles of human–machine dialogue. Rather than replacing teacher mediation, the AI becomes an intermediary that enables micro-reflections, scaffolds justification, and maintains epistemic tension—the productive uncertainty that drives conceptual growth.

From a pedagogical perspective, this model situates AI as a partner in reasoning rather than an evaluator of performance. It aligns with sociocultural theories of learning that emphasize the distributed nature of cognition and the centrality of dialogue in knowledge construction. The episodes suggest that, when designed with pedagogical intentionality, AI feedback can activate the same generative mechanisms as peer discussion or teacher scaffolding—thereby contributing to a richer ecology of formative practices within mathematics education.

Recent discussions in the field of higher education have emphasized the sustainability of feedback practices, particularly in large and resource-limited contexts. In this regard, the use of AI to generate formative prompts can be viewed as a strategy for democratizing access to high-quality feedback. Rather than a substitution of human expertise, the approach illustrated here exemplifies a redistribution of pedagogical resources: AI extends teachers' capacity to provide individualized, timely, and dialogic support across wider student cohorts. This perspective aligns with ongoing efforts to design inclusive and equitable feedback systems that recognize diversity in learners' reasoning and communication styles. By combining algorithmic precision with human interpretive sensitivity,

AI-supported formative assessment could thus represent a step toward more sustainable and human-centered models of mathematics education.

6 Conclusion and Preliminary Results

The study set out to explore how AI-mediated formative feedback can foster conceptual reasoning and collaborative meaning-making in mathematics education. Through the analysis of two classroom episodes, we observed that the interaction between students and the AI agent generated productive dialogic tension: feedback messages, even when minimal, opened cognitive and social spaces for questioning, argumentation, and conceptual refinement.

With respect to RQ1, findings indicate that AI-driven feedback can successfully trigger cognitive transitions from perceptual or procedural reasoning to analytical, conceptually grounded forms of understanding. This shift was particularly visible in the geometric task, where the AI's prompt catalyzed the movement from visual symmetry to algebraic proof. Similarly, in the arithmetic task, feedback stimulated the formalization of pattern recognition into algebraic justification. In both cases, the feedback acted as a bridge between intuitive insight and mathematical generalization.

Regarding RQ2, the study demonstrates that students' interpretation of AI feedback was not individual but socially mediated. Learners appropriated the prompts through peer dialogue, negotiating meanings and constructing shared explanations. This collective engagement highlights the potential of AI as a pedagogical interlocutor—a presence that activates discussion rather than prescribes solutions. The AI's contribution, therefore, lies in its capacity to amplify formative dialogue, providing a continuous stimulus for reflection that complements rather than replaces the teacher's role.

These findings contribute to a growing body of research emphasizing the importance of human–AI partnership in educational contexts. When embedded in well-designed collaborative frameworks, AI agents can operate as mediators of metacognitive processes, sustaining cycles of feedback and reflection that are essential for deep learning. The challenge for future research lies in identifying the pedagogical conditions that maximize this potential—how feedback phrasing, timing, and adaptivity can be tuned to different stages of reasoning, and how teachers can orchestrate AI prompts within broader formative ecosystems. While the qualitative design does not aim at statistical generalization, the analytic depth of the interaction episodes provides transferable insights into AI-supported formative processes in mathematics education.

Ultimately, the study underscores a redefinition of feedback as co-constructed meaning rather than transmitted information. In this perspective, AI becomes part of a distributed network of agency, one that includes students, peers, and teachers, jointly engaged in the shared pursuit of understanding.

The study also opens important avenues for future innovation within national and international research frameworks. Within the broader context of the PRIN "AI&F" project, these findings contribute to defining models of formative interaction that can be scaled across disciplines. At the European level, they resonate with current initiatives aiming to integrate AI literacy and digital pedagogies into higher education. Embedding such approaches within mathematics education can promote both disciplinary depth and transversal digital competence, supporting the development of reflective practitioners and autonomous learners. Ultimately, this line of inquiry invites a reconsideration of how intelligence—both human and artificial—can coexist in educational practice, not in opposition but in synergy, toward the shared goal of understanding, reasoning, and learning together.

7 Implications for Practice and Future Research

The findings of this study offer several implications for both educational practice and future research in mathematics education and AI-supported learning. The evidence suggests that AI-mediated formative feedback can serve as a catalyst for conceptual reasoning when it is integrated within pedagogically rich environments that value dialogue, inquiry, and reflection.

7.1 Pedagogical Implications

From a pedagogical standpoint, the study highlights the necessity of rethinking the role of feedback as a shared interpretive space rather than a one-way transmission. Teachers are called to act as feedback orchestrators—mediating between algorithmic suggestions and students' interpretive work. This requires not only technical competence but also AI literacy [24] understood as the ability to critically interpret, adapt, and humanize AI outputs within authentic learning contexts.

Furthermore, the results reinforce the importance of cultivating productive struggle [5] moments of cognitive dissonance that stimulate reasoning rather than frustration. The AI prompts analyzed here maintained such productive tension, fostering micro-reflections and collaborative sense-making. Teachers can leverage these moments by integrating AI feedback into classroom discourse, using it as an anchor for collective reasoning rather than as an evaluative endpoint.

7.2 Design Implications

For developers and educational technologists, the study underscores the importance of pedagogically aligned AI design. Feedback systems should not aim to correct students mechanically but to sustain reasoning by posing open, generative questions. The brevity and non-directive nature of the AI prompts proved essential in eliciting deeper student thinking.

Future systems might further evolve by incorporating features that recognize not only syntactic correctness but epistemic stance, detecting when a learner is reasoning inductively, analogically, or deductively, and tailoring feedback accordingly. This approach would align with Holmes et al. [25], who argue for AI tools that augment rather than automate human cognition.

Another crucial design consideration concerns the *timing* and *tone* of feedback. As shown in the episodes, delayed or reflective feedback can encourage discussion and reduce overreliance on algorithmic authority. Designers should therefore conceptualize AI as a dialogic presence that supports metacognitive processes rather than as an immediate source of right or wrong answers.

7.3 Research Implications

Future research should extend these findings through longitudinal and mixed-method studies. The short-term analysis presented here demonstrates promising cognitive and social effects, but long-term investigations are needed to assess sustained conceptual development and transfer of metacognitive skills.

Moreover, further work should explore the triadic interaction among teacher, learner, and AI. While the present study focused primarily on learner–AI interaction, teachers' orchestration strategies, how they frame, interpret, and extend AI feedback, represent a key dimension of effectiveness.

Moreover, the study resonates with findings from recent research on teacher professional development, emphasizing the role of digital technologies in fostering reflective practice and effective facilitation of mathematical discussions [7, 8] Embedding AI-supported feedback within these frameworks could further enhance teachers' capacity to orchestrate learning environments where students engage deeply with mathematical concepts.

Finally, methodological triangulation could combine qualitative discourse analysis with learning analytics to capture both the microgenetic evolution of reasoning and broader patterns of engagement. Such a multi-layered approach would deepen our understanding of how feedback circulates and transforms within hybrid human–machine ecosystems.

Disclosure of Interests. The authors have no competing interests to declare that are relevant to the content of this article.

References

1. Black, P., Wiliam, D.: Developing the theory of formative assessment. Educ. Assess. Eval. Account. **21**(1), 5–31 (2009)
2. Foschi, L. C. et al.: AI and feedback. Assessing written tasks in Higher Education through human and artificial agent interaction. Education Sciences & Society - Open Access. 15(2) (2025). https://doi.org/10.3280/ess2-2024oa18951
3. Pehkonen, E.: Introduction to the concept "open-ended problem". In Use of open-ended problems in mathematics classroom (Issue 7) (1997). Available online: http://files.eric.ed.gov/fulltext/ED419714.pdf
4. Schoenfeld, A.H.: Mathematical Thinking and Problem Solving. Routledge (2016)
5. Boaler, J.: Mathematical Mindsets: Unleashing Students' Potential through Creative Math, Inspiring Messages and Innovative Teaching. Jossey-Bass (2016)
6. Lesh, R., Zawojewski, J.: Problem solving and modeling. In: Lester, F. (ed.) Second Handbook of Research on Mathematics Teaching and Learning, pp. 763–804. Information Age, Charlotte, NC (2007)
7. Fiorentino, M.G., Montone, A.: Learning the mathematical discussion (MD) pedagogical model in and from practice: the professional development of mathematics teachers in a technological environment. Educ. Sci. **15**(6), 653 (2025)
8. Montone, A., Fiorentino, M.G.: A learning experience in and from practice using digital technologies: the mathematical discussion. Ital. J. Pure Appl. Math. **52**, 356–369 (2024)

9. Serpe, A.: Online resources for training pre-service primary school teachers in mathematics. In: Casalino, G., et al. (eds.) Higher Education Learning Methodologies and Technologies Online. HELMeTO 2023. Communications in Computer and Information Science, vol. 2076. Springer, Cham (2024). https://doi.org/10.1007/978-3-031-67351-1_18
10. Serpe, A.: Applied mathematical modelling in the physics problem-solving classroom. In: Sergeyev, Y.D., Kvasov, D.E., Astorino, A. (eds.) Numerical Computations: Theory and Algorithms. NUMTA 2023 Lecture Notes in Computer Science, vol. 14478. Springer, Cham (2025). https://doi.org/10.1007/978-3-031-81247-7_1
11. Serpe, A.: Digital tools to enhance interdisciplinary mathematics teaching practices in high school. In: Fulantelli, G., Burgos, D., Casalino, G., Cimitile, M., Lo Bosco, G., Taibi, D. (eds.) Higher Education Learning Methodologies and Technologies Online. HELMeTO 2022. Communications in Computer and Information Science, vol. 1779. Springer, Cham (2023). https://doi.org/10.1007/978-3-031-29800-4_16
12. Nicol, D.: From monologue to dialogue: improving written feedback processes in mass higher education. Assess. Eval. High. Educ. **35**(5), 501–517 (2010)
13. Price, M., Handley, K., Millar, J., O'Donovan, B.: Feedback: all that effort, but what is the effect? Assess. Eval. High. Educ. **35**(3), 277–289 (2010)
14. Nicol, D.: Unlocking generative feedback via peer reviewing. In: Grion, V., Serbati, A. (eds.) Assessment of Learning or Assessment for Learning? Towards a Culture of Sustainable Assessment in HE, pp. 73–85. Pensa Multi Media, Lecce (2018)
15. Grion, V., Serbati, A.: Valutazione sostenibile e feedback nei contesti universitari. Prospettive emergenti, ricerche e pratiche. PensaMultiMedia, Lecce (2019)
16. Nicol, D.: Guiding learning by activating students' inner feedback. Times Higher Education (2021). https://www.timeshighereducation.com/campus/guide-learning-activating-students-inner-feedback
17. Grion, V., Cesareni, D.: Multiplicity, fluidity, dialogue and sharing: keywords to understand the complex dynamics between human learning and technology. QWERTY-Interdisc. J. Technol., Cult. Educ. **11**(1), 5–10 (2016)
18. Steiss, J., et al.: Comparing the quality of human and ChatGPT feedback of students' writing. Learn. Instr. **91**, 101894 (2024)
19. Redecker, C., Punie, Y.: European Framework for the Digital Competence of Educators: DigCompEdu. Publications Office of the European Union, Luxembourg (2017)
20. Raffaghelli, J.E.: Post Digital Scholarship. Professionalità accademica e trasformazione digitale in università. Didattiche, Tecnologie e Media Education. Frontiere per la Sostenibilità. **1**, 1–460 (2024)
21. Giannandrea, L.: Valutazione, feedback, tecnologie. In: Rivoltella, P.C., Rossi, P.G. (eds.) Tecnologie per l'educazione, pp. 69–81. Pearson, Milano (2019)
22. Facer, K., Selwyn, N.: Digital technology and the futures of education – towards 'non-stupid' optimism. Educ. Philos. Theory. **53**(3), 233–244 (2021)
23. Carless, D., Boud, D.: The development of student feedback literacy: enabling uptake of feedback. Assess. Eval. High. Educ. **43**(8), 1315–1325 (2018)
24. Luckin, R.: Towards AI literacy: a new model of teacher knowledge and professional development. Br. J. Educ. Technol. **52**(4), 1615–1628 (2021)
25. Holmes, W., Bialik, M., Fadel, C.: Artificial Intelligence in Education: Promises and Implications for Teaching and Learning. Center for Curriculum Redesign (2019)

From Anxiety to Agency: the DUE Learning Design Model for Pre-Service Teachers Facing Uncertainty

Lorenza Maria Capolla[1(✉)], Lorella Giannandrea[1], Francesca Gratani[1], Pier Giuseppe Rossi[1], Giacomo Nalli[2], Stelios Kapetanakis[3], and Georgios A. Dafoulas[2]

[1] Department of Education, Cultural Heritage and Tourism, University of Macerata, MC 62100, Italy
{l.capolla,lorella.giannandrea,f.gratani}@unimc.it

[2] Computer Science, Science and Technology, Middlesex University London, London NW4 4BT, UK
{g.nalli,g.dafoulas}@mdx.ac.uk

[3] Distributed Labs, Distributed Analytics Solutions, 30 Churchill Pl, London, E14 5RE London, UK
stelios@dstr.co.uk

Abstract. In an increasingly uncertain educational context, it is crucial to update training programs and educational tools for pre-service teachers, who must be prepared to face the unexpected and manage stress. To address these challenges, researchers at the University of Macerata (Italy) developed the Design for the Unexpected in Education (DUE) model in 2022/23. Over the past three years, the model has proven effective in helping pre-service teachers anticipate and consciously design activities that take potential unforeseen events into account, thereby improving overall lesson management. However, its potential to support anxiety and stress management during lesson implementation remains underexplored. This research, conducted in collaboration with the University of Middlesex, aims to investigate whether the DUE model provides valid support to help pre-service teachers identify and manage the unexpected events that are most anxiety-provoking for them, according to their personality. The research involved five volunteer trainees attending the third and fourth year of the Master's degree course in Primary Education. Results coming from the triangulation of biometric data, personality profiling, and direct observation of teaching activities outlined the critical moments experienced by each trainee, as well as how they differently dealt with unexpected events and stressful situations in the classroom consistently with their personalities. The study provided relevant insights and some suggestions to be used in initial teacher training, which should not only promote structured yet flexible planning models, but also encourage the development of differentiated emotional self-regulation strategies tailored to individual profiles and needs.

Keywords: Pre-service Teachers · Learning Design · Designing for the Unexpected · Uncertainty · Anxiety

M. Adamoli et al. (Eds.): HELMeTO 2025, CCIS 2958, pp. 396–411, 2026.
https://doi.org/10.1007/978-3-032-31850-3_25

1 Introduction

When speaking about contemporary society, some of the most used adjectives are complex and post-digital [1]. In particular, post-digital refers to the necessity of navigating multiple crises and rapid technological, digital, and socio-cultural changes that occur over a limited period. Post-digital society can be messy and confusing, and therefore traditional educational paradigms can quickly become outdated [2, 3].

In an increasingly uncertain educational context, it is crucial to update training programs and educational tools for pre-service teachers, who must be prepared to face the unexpected and manage stress. The unpredictable nature of modern classes, in fact, challenges both traditional and overly rigid lesson plans - unable to adapt to emerging circumstances - and those that are too flexible or based mainly on improvisation and experience, which require teachers to engage in real-time decision-making processes [4].

To address these contemporary challenges and support pre-service teachers in managing uncertainty and stress, a group of researchers at the University of Macerata in Italy has developed the Design for the Unexpected in Education (DUE) model [5] in the a.y. 2022/23. DUE is a learning design model specifically built for pre-service teachers with the aim of helping them plan activities and also redesign them or some of their aspects in the event of the emergence of something unexpected. The model has been tested with trainees from the Master's program in Primary Education over the past three years and has produced some positive and encouraging results in terms of its effectiveness in helping pre-service teachers anticipate the teaching activities, design them more consciously by considering possible unexpected events, and improve the overall management of the lessons [4, 5]. However, its potential to help them manage the stress and anxiety that often accompany the implementation phase, especially in the presence of unexpected and destabilizing events, remains under-researched.

Starting from this gap, the research narrated in this paper, conducted in collaboration with the University of Middlesex, aims to investigate whether the DUE model provides valid theoretical and operational support to help pre-service teachers identify and manage the unexpected events that are most anxiety-provoking for them. From this initial hypothesis, the following research questions were formulated:

1. Can the triangulation between biometric data, personality profile identification, and direct observation of the teaching action help to identify critical moments of stress?
2. Do the design strategies included in the DUE model support pre-service teachers in identifying and managing the unexpected events that are most anxiety-provoking for them?

2 Theoretical Framework

Teacher training is a complex process involving the development of teaching and pedagogical skills, as well as the management of emotions and challenges that could impact the well-being and effectiveness of pre-service teachers.

The link between pre-service teachers' well-being and professional anxiety has been studied by several researchers. For instance, according to van der Want and colleagues

[6], the well-being of trainee teachers is linked to two fundamental aspects. The first one being professional anxiety, defined as anxiety that is often triggered by aspects typical of the profession, such as: relationships with students, aspects related to the subject being taught, student behavior, and unexpected events in the daily routine. The second one is self-efficacy, which refers to teachers' belief in their ability to design, organize, and conduct activities that will enable them to achieve their objectives and impact their students' learning [7]. The two aspects are deeply connected [8]: the more teachers perceive themselves as effective, the more their professional anxiety tends to decrease. This states the importance of identifying the moments when pre-service teachers are most stressed in order to gain an indication of the areas in which they might need more training and support.

Moreover, anxiety is a topic of considerable importance in education because it profoundly affects teachers' well-being, the quality of their teaching, and their professional development. For this reason, it should be carefully addressed during pre-service teacher training, a period marked by a major transition from theoretical learning to practical experience. According to Veenman's concept of "reality shock" [9], new teachers experience a negative emotional impact when they realize that their expectations of the profession do not match the everyday reality of teaching. Although this transition is crucial to their growth, it can give rise to complex emotions such as insecurity and fear, as well as considerable difficulty in managing the classroom. These situations can fuel anxiety and stress. Uncertainty about their ability to cope with the daily challenges of the profession can affect the effectiveness of their teaching and their perception of themselves as competent and confident teachers.

Furthermore, anxiety in trainee teachers can manifest in various ways, including fear of judgement by colleagues and students, concern about the adequacy of their teaching methods, or an inability to handle unexpected classroom situations. Excessive anxiety can negatively affect the quality of teaching, reducing teachers' ability to manage the classroom effectively and respond flexibly to students' needs. Teachers with high levels of professional anxiety tend to experience a decline in their perception of self-efficacy, which in turn can lead to a reduced ability to adapt in teaching practice. This phenomenon is reflected in more rigid, less engaging teaching characterized by reduced interaction with students.

In addition, some studies have shown that anxious teachers may develop a more passive teaching style, avoiding situations that could expose them to the judgment of students or supervisors [10].

According to Maslach and Leiter [11], the prevention of burnout should begin during training, through interventions that promote psychological well-being and emotion management.

To tackle this major issue for prospective teachers, various researchers have engaged in studies aimed at improving their understanding of professional anxiety. In recent years, there has been a lot of research into stress monitoring using wearable devices, which offer new perspectives for understanding and managing anxiety in trainee teachers. Gjoreski and colleagues [12] have developed a stress detection system based on wrist devices and machine learning techniques, which allows moments of increased tension to be identified and provides tools for emotional management. Their studies show that continuous monitoring can help identify patterns of chronic stress and intervene with targeted strategies before anxiety compromises the teacher's well-being.

Even though traditionally, anxiety has been considered a negative factor, to be limited or eliminated, recent studies suggest that it can also have positive effects, acting as a stimulus for adaptation and professional growth [13]. In particular, students and trainee teachers who experience controlled anxiety tend to perform better, as this emotional state drives them to prepare more thoroughly and manage educational challenges more effectively [7]. That represents one more reason why future teachers' educators must identify, understand, and operate with the matter of professional anxiety. The study presented in this paper fits into this theoretical framework and attempts to add some reflections with a view to improving the identification of particularly anxiety-provoking moments for future teachers and how they can be supported in managing them.

2.1 The DUE Model

To support pre-service teachers in managing anxiety and help them develop a more neutral view of this emotional state, the teacher training courses at the University of Macerata now include specific tools and activities designed to show how anxiety can serve as a constructive factor for effective teaching, while also providing practical strategies to apply in the classroom. Among these innovative elements, the main one is the Design for the Unexpected in Education (DUE) learning design model. Unlike traditional linear models such as ADDIE [14], DUE embraces unexpected situations by intentionally introducing complexity at the early stages of the design process.

The model was inspired by Berthoz's theory of simplexity [15], from which several key principles were drawn to form its foundation. Specifically, these principles include:

1. Principle of Probabilistic Anticipation. It encourages envisioning future scenarios based both on imagination and on past experiences.
2. Principle of Deviation. It involves introducing additional complexity to better interpret and manage complex situations.
3. Principle of Cooperation and Redundancy. It promotes combining diverse perspectives, tools, and approaches to make more effective decisions in problem-solving.
4. Principle of Meaning. It emphasizes the need to attribute purpose, function, and intention to actions and choices within the simplexity framework.
5. Principle of Vicariance. It refers to the creative capacity of the brain to solve problems and make decisions by using known elements in novel ways, depending on context and needs.

From the identification of these principles, five strategies were then defined [15, 16, 17, 18, 4]:

- Modularity means that learning paths should not be a rigid sequence of activities but should be designed around adaptable strategies and content that can change according to the context, generating new meanings each time through processes of hybridization.
- Anticipation is the ability to envision and mentally rehearse future teaching scenarios, enabling reflection, adaptation, and improvement of learning design.

- Redundancy refers to designing multiple, diverse activities that lead to the same learning objectives. These activities should be context-appropriate and feasible, while ensuring that each provides an alternative pathway to achieve the same goals.
- Deviation involves deliberately departing from the initial plan to construct a new, context-responsive pathway. Deviation may concern part or all of the lesson and requires a high level of design flexibility and the ability to orchestrate multiple strategies effectively.
- Hierarchization means assigning labels during the design phase to distinguish between essential tasks and those that can be removed or replaced. This distinction allows teachers, during implementation, to make quicker and less stressful decisions, manage time more effectively, and stay aligned with the overall direction of the learning pathway.

Following the strategies proposed in the model, all students who took part in the research were asked to complete three documents that enable these strategies to be implemented. The three documents to be completed are:

1. A pre-action descriptive artefact: a holistic document containing all relevant aspects of the session (goals, spaces, materials, internal and external consistency, etc.).
2. A pre-action narrative artefact: containing the possible activities that could be implemented during the two-hour teaching session. All the activities must be anticipated and simulated by the pre-service teacher before taking action. The activities included in the pre-action sheet undergo a labelling process to establish their priority. This prioritization allows the pre-service teacher, during the action phase, to make decisions quickly without compromising the quality of the outcomes.

    - The first key distinction concerns *essential activities*, marked with an asterisk (*). These are activities that must not be omitted under any circumstances, as doing so would compromise the lesson's core meaning and objectives.
    - Activities labelled with an *X* are considered *redundant*. They differ in form but achieve the same learning goals as the essential activities, using alternative tools, languages, supports, communication channels, or teaching methods.
    - Finally, activities marked with a plus sign (+) are *additional*. They are designed to support classroom and time management, for example, by engaging students or groups who finish early. These activities may also address topics not strictly related to the current lesson.

3. A post-action narrative artefact: containing the transcriptions of the carried out activities and the post-action reflections (difficulties and unexpected events, positive aspects, emotional states, variations from the pre-action plan,...) [18].

3 Methods

3.1 The Context

The research was conducted with the voluntary participation of five trainees (four female and one male) attending the third and fourth year of the Master's degree course in Primary Education at the University of Macerata.

Each trainee was already familiar with the DUE model, having completed the *"Theories and Methods of Learning Design and Assessment"* (TeM) course and its associated mandatory workshop in the first semester of the third year. The third year is a pivotal time for trainees as they design a teaching session to be carried out in a classroom for the first time.

The TeM course explores the theoretical aspects of designing, teaching, and evaluating in today's complex society, and offers trainees the opportunity to familiarize themselves with the DUE model and its key strategies. Trainees can indeed experiment with the model under the guidance of workshop tutors and discuss its critical issues and potential with the professors of the course.

At the time of data collection, all five trainees were engaged in direct internships in some Italian primary schools. In line with the TeM course objectives, each participant was asked to design and implement a complete teaching session using the DUE model.

3.2 Data Collection and Data Analysis

The experimentation narrated in this paper focuses on the implementation phase of the lessons, conducted in primary school classrooms.

We used three tools to collect data, both before and during the lesson.

Before the lesson, each trainee was asked to complete a personality questionnaire developed by Dr. Harley Friedman [19] based on the foundational work of Isabel Briggs Myers: the MBTI (Myers-Briggs Type Indicator) personality test [20, 21, 22]. The test consists of 70 closed-ended questions with two possible answers, accessible using a dedicated website. Based on the answers given to the test, it returns one of 16 personality profiles, obtained by a combination of four pairs of opposing characteristics of each person: extraversion (E) / introversion (I), sensing (S) / intuition (N), feeling (F) / thinking (T), perceiving (P) / judging (J). The test can be used for self-reflection on personal preferences, potential, strengths, and weaknesses. In our study, it enabled us to identify some relevant personality traits of pre-service teachers and correlate them with the other data collected.

During the lesson, each trainee was equipped with a Polar OH1 optical heart rate monitor, a wearable IoT device capable of capturing 60 heart rate recordings per minute and storing them in CSV format that can be downloaded through the online Polar Flow application [23]. This device was chosen for its accuracy and non-invasiveness, allowing participants to carry out the teaching session without interruption.

In parallel, a non-participating silent observer was present in the classroom to take structured field notes, focusing on: (1) the occurrence of unexpected events (e.g. student behavior, technical problems, misunderstandings about content); (2) the teachers' responses and regulation strategies; (3) their use of planning materials (both paper and digital) to regain control or adapt the flow of the lesson, according to the DUE model.

At the end of each teaching session, the observer's notes were correlated with biometric data, interpreted in relation to individual characteristics identified through the MBTI test. This allowed the identification of moments of heightened physiological activation in response to classroom events. For each case, HR data were analyzed alongside evidence of action regulation and potential use of the DUE model's structure, as observed during the management of critical situations. The HR data collected has been analyzed by using Microsoft Excel to calculate the maximum, minimum, average, and standard deviation of the heart rate for each participant. Along with it, the same tool has also been used to create the visualizations related to the student's heart rate during the lecture. The integration of physiological-quantitative and observational-qualitative data within a mixed-methods framework [24] provided initial insights into pre-service teachers' stress responses and the DUE model's role in supporting emotional self-regulation during the action.

4 Results

To identify the critical moments of stress experienced by trainees during teaching sessions, a triangulation of biometric data, personality profiling, and direct observation of teaching activities was performed. The personality profiles have been detected by using the MBTI personality test, accessible through a website that allows for anonymous data collection, using an ID for each participant.

Each of the five participating trainees obtained a different personality profile identified by a string of letters: i) ESFJ, ii) ENTP, iii) INFJ, iv) ISTJ, v) ENFP.

Trainee A.B. was found to have a Consul personality (ESFJ), indicating that she is a "most harmonizing" person, eager to please others, and thoughtful, with good interpersonal skills. This personality type is characterized by strong practical skills and a caring attitude, as well as a strong sense of duty and an ability to organize daily routines. People with this personality have a good connection with people, although their mindset is not very flexible and they are vulnerable to criticism. However, this personality type can be overly selfless, leading to quick overwhelm by people who don't need doting attention.

Trainee D.F. was found to have an Entrepreneur personality (ENTP), meaning he is the most inventive type of person, testing the limits and enthusiastic about proposing new ideas. This personality type is characterized by quick thinking, allowing them to shift from one idea to another with little effort and often proposing original ideas. People with this personality type are energetic and very argumentative. However, they are not very tolerant of people with different ideas. Individuals with this personality type also find it difficult to focus, which means they often abandon original plans and ideas in favor of new ones.

Trainee A.M. has an Advocate personality (INFJ), meaning she is a highly contemplative, reflective, and introspective person. Creativity is one of the main features of this personality type, who are always looking for opportunities to express themselves and think outside the box. People with this personality are perfectionists, which leads them to reject the messiness of real life. They avoid the ordinary and are prone to burnout.

Trainee A.P. has a Logistician personality (ISTJ), meaning she is a highly responsible, organized, and compulsive person. People with this personality type are very disciplined, following rules strictly and respecting authority. They are also calm and practical, providing clear and rational decisions, which makes them organized and effective. They are prone to burnout and think they are responsible for failure.

Trainee V.D.S. was found to have a Campaigner personality (ENFP), indicating that she is the most optimistic and people-oriented person. Those with this personality type are highly perceptive and believe that everyone is important. They are excellent communicators, but can be unfocused, especially when involved in collaborative projects. They also have evolving interests, meaning they find it challenging to maintain discipline and focus over the long term. Disorganization is another characteristic of the Campaigner, as well as optimism.

Having obtained and analyzed the trainees' personality profiles, the next step was to analyze the heart rate data collected during the lecture to determine whether and how personality could impact stress levels [25]. Firstly, an overview was analyzed by considering the maximum, minimum, average, and standard deviation of the trainees' heart rate [26]. Then, a more detailed analysis was performed by cross-checking the trainees' heart rate data at specific timestamps with the related observations received during the lecture.

Table 1. Overview of the aggregated heart rate values collected for each trainee.

Trainee	Personality	HR max	HR min	HR avg	HR sd
A.B.	ESFJ	147	88	120	7.08
D.F.	ENTP	151	88	117	13.08
A.M.	INFJ	125	62	99	7.75
A.P.	ISTJ	130	68	93	9.22
V.D.S	ENFP	97	71	84	4.27

Analyzing Table 1, the trainees can be divided into three different categories based on levels of stress: high stress, stress, and relaxation. These categories were developed based on relevant literature, which defines a normal resting heart rate for adults as ranging between 60 and 90 beats per minute (bpm) [27].

Trainee A.B. exhibited a high level of stress, as indicated by the elevated mean and low standard deviation. The trainee showed an initial state of stress that escalated sharply in response to unexpected events. However, the minimum value of 88 corresponds to approximately the upper limit of the range typically observed in calm individuals. The low standard deviation indicates that there were no significant changes, and the heart rate remained roughly in the same range, highlighting constant stress with no actual rest. Further confirmation is provided by Fig. 1, which displays the trainee's heart rate graph throughout the lecture. The graph shows three peaks of stress. The peak observed at minute 5 corresponds to the moment immediately before the lesson begins. Consistent with the personality profile of a highly conscientious and responsible individual, this increase can be attributed to anticipatory anxiety and the desire for the lesson to proceed exactly as planned. The second peak occurs immediately at minute 17, when the children who will take part in the trainee's lesson enter the classroom. In this case, anticipatory anxiety becomes stress, causing an increase in heart rate. A third spike in heart rate at minute 30 coincides with the moment when the trainee experiences difficulties in clarifying how the proposed activity should be carried out. For a controlling personality who wants things to follow the plan strictly, this situation generates intense emotional tension.

In general, the heart rate and observation data align with the trainee's personality traits. The trainee does not seem to be very flexible when facing unexpected circumstances and tends to show an increase in her heart rate, probably due to the personality's attitude to be vulnerable to criticism. Nevertheless, the trainee demonstrates the capacity to regulate her behavior and to manage potentially critical situations through the support provided by the DUE design artifact. For instance, between minute 1:10 and 1:15, a brief episode of confusion occurs in the classroom as some pupils complete the task earlier than others. This situation is effectively managed by the trainee, who refers to an additional activity (indicated with a "+" in the pre-action artifact), namely the coloring of the laptop cover. In this case, despite the critical event, the heart rate remains relatively stable, suggesting an improved ability to cope with situational stressors.

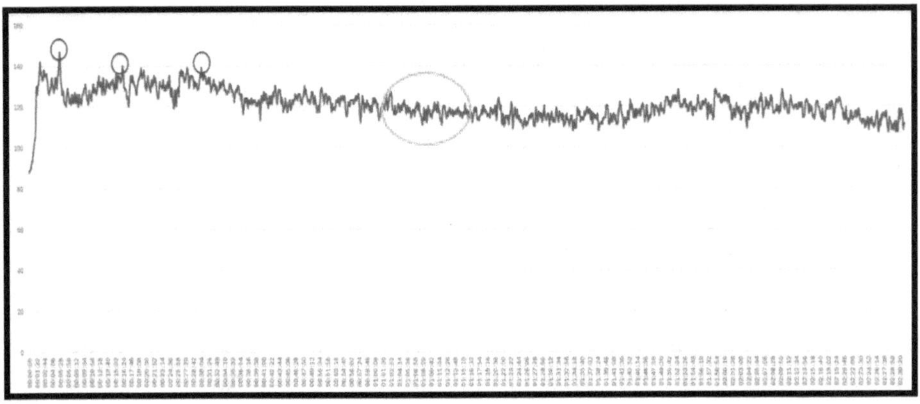

Fig. 1. Heart rate graph of Trainee A.B. during the teaching session. The dark circles show the stress peaks. The light circle shows a situation in which the trainee successfully managed an unexpected event supported by the pre-action design artifact.

Trainee D.F. has also reported a high level of stress, as indicated by the high average score. The higher standard deviation indicates greater fluctuations in heart rate, suggesting more peaks. This suggests an initial state of stress that escalates sharply in response to unexpected events. However, the minimum value of 88 corresponds to the upper limit of the range typically observed in calm individuals. Fig. 2 illustrates the trainee's heart rate fluctuations, showing three main peaks with higher values. The first peak, observed at minute 12, occurs when the trainee attempts to elicit cognitive conflict among the students. In this case, the anxiety could be linked to the fear that the conflict will not emerge as expected or will not align with what was anticipated during the planning phase, a rather common concern among prospective teachers. At minute 24 the trainee begins to move around the desks to check that everyone has the required material. He then realizes that the material prepared in advance is not sufficient for all pupils. The peak is followed by a rapid and significant decrease in heart rate, which may be related to the trainee's personality, characterized by quick thinking and the ability to identify a possible solution almost immediately. At minute 1.12 the trainee begins an activity using conventional and unconventional musical instruments, which, however, generates confusion among the learners. This high-stress condition appears to be associated with the trainee's personality profile, which tends to show lower tolerance for unexpected circumstances. Moreover, the trainee does not seem to rely on supplementary or redundant activities but rather attempts to adhere strictly to the lesson plan as initially designed. This behavioral pattern is further confirmed when, at the sound of the bell announcing the break, the trainee does not interrupt the activity and continues the ongoing discussion. Only after recognizing a decline in pupils' attention does he decide to suspend the activity and allow the break to begin.

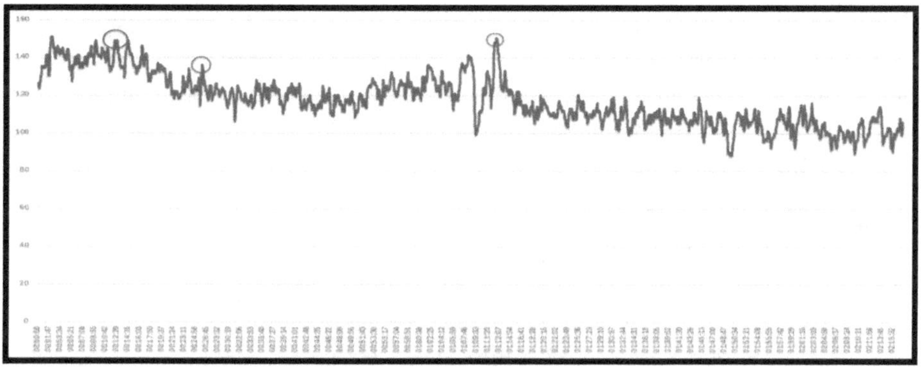

Fig. 2. Heart rate graph of Trainee D.F. during the teaching session. The circles show the stress peaks.

Trainee A.M.'s average heart rate is slightly above the typical range observed in calm individuals. Although the standard deviation is low, the significant difference between the minimum and maximum values indicates that the trainee generally remains calm under normal circumstances but experiences increased stress in response to unexpected events. During the teaching session, four distinct moments of heightened heart rate were recorded. At minute 5 the trainee projects an image on the interactive whiteboard and asks the pupils what they see. As in the previous case, this marks the moment when the trainee attempts to elicit the cognitive conflict in the classroom. This phase is generally anxiety-inducing for any pre-service teacher, as the lesson plan revolves around the identified conflict. However, the personality of trainee

A.M. justifies the spike, as her perfectionism could further intensify expectations at this stage. A second peak occurs at minute 16 when the pupils demonstrate that their prior knowledge exceeds what the trainee had anticipated during the planning phase. This situation challenges her tendency towards perfection, requiring her to adapt her lesson quickly to the real classroom context. At minute 27, the trainee moves between the desks to hand out a worksheet containing a summary map of the task. She explains that the pupils must fill in the missing information along the dotted lines. The peak that occurs at this point could be linked to the transfer of control from the trainee to the student, who has to work independently, thereby providing, even unconsciously, feedback on what has been learned up to that point. Finally, a last interesting peak appears at minute 30 when a pupil finishes before his classmates and asks the trainee what he should do next. The trainee asks him to wait a moment, and the peak is immediately followed by a significant decrease in the heart rate. The contemplative personality that characterizes the INFJ profile helps the trainee to regain calm after initial stress, especially thanks to her creative thinking, which enables her to think outside the box and make alternative decisions to continue the teaching session. Moreover, throughout the lesson, the trainee makes effective use of the DUE model, as shown at minutes 48–49 or 1:00-1:03. At minutes 48-49, the trainee, in response to pupils' loss of concentration and the resulting classroom confusion, activates a redundant activity (marked with an "X") that had been planned in advance. This activity engages the pupils in group work where they read a fairy tale and create their own comic strip. It successfully rekindles the pupils' interest and participation, while simultaneously reducing the trainee's anxiety, thanks to its anticipatory inclusion in the lesson plan within the DUE model. Similarly, between minutes 1:00 and 1:03, to manage the situation in which some groups complete their tasks earlier than others, the trainee proposes an additional activity, thereby restoring balance among the groups and maintaining the overall flow of the lesson.

These data suggest an enhanced ability to manage classroom dynamics through anticipatory planning, highlighting how the DUE model can support emotional regulation, reduce stress levels, and foster adaptive decision-making during teaching practice (Fig. 3).

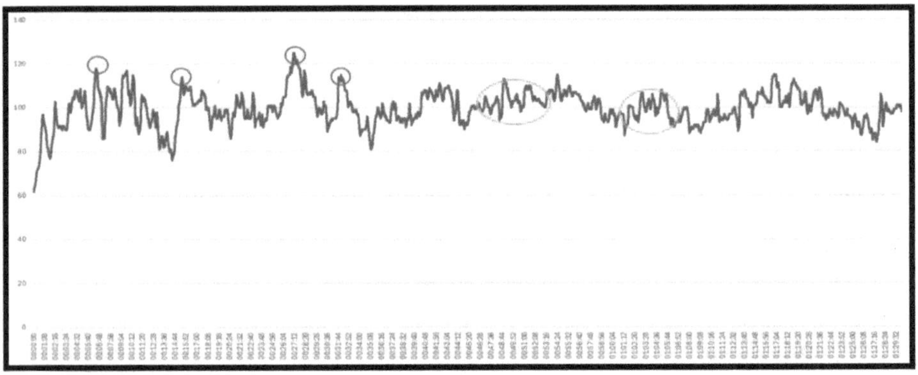

Fig. 3. Heart rate graph of Trainee A.M. during the teaching session. The dark circles show the stress peaks. The light circles show situations in which the trainee successfully managed unexpected events supported by the pre-action design artifact.

Trainee A.P. returned a state of stress, with an average heart rate higher than that typically observed in calm individuals. Although in this case the standard deviation is low, the significant difference between the minimum and maximum values indicates that the trainee remains calm under normal circumstances but experiences increased stress when faced with unexpected events. Indeed, the trainee's heart rate increases significantly when unexpected events occur. At minute 5, the interactive whiteboard switches off, and the teacher (tutor) helps the trainee reconnect it. This spike is related to an event beyond the trainee's control, and the fact that it occurred right at the beginning of the lesson justifies the stress experienced. At minute 42, while the trainee is showing a video, a new pupil arrives in the classroom. The other pupils become distracted and the trainee loses their attention. The situation is resolved and managed thanks to the intervention of the teacher (tutor). In this case, the peak of stress, in addition to being linked to the unexpected event, could also be linked to the personality of the trainee, who tends to take responsibility for issues upon herself. Finally, at minute 1:35, the bell signaling the end of the lesson rings during the final group presentations. The trainee asks the teacher if the last group of learners can finish their presentations so that the lesson can have a proper closure, completing the debriefing phase. The teacher intervenes, asking the pupils to complete their oral presentations and inviting the group leader to present. However, the pupils become distracted, and only a few listen when the teacher calls them back. In this case, the peak is strongly linked with the trainee's expectations for the development of her lesson. Moreover, the ISTJ personality aligns with her stress condition, as it may lead the trainee to experience feelings of guilt and responsibility for a potentially poor performance resulting from class interruptions.

Once again, the DUE model has shown to be effective in helping the trainee to manage unexpected events, particularly those related to pupils' lack of understanding. At minutes 46–47, for instance, one pupil did not understand the video about Napoleon. Despite this critical event, the trainee immediately proposes an alternative strategy to address the issue, having anticipated this potential difficulty during the pre-action phase (in line with the DUE model). The same situation occurs at 1:04– 1:05 (Fig. 4).

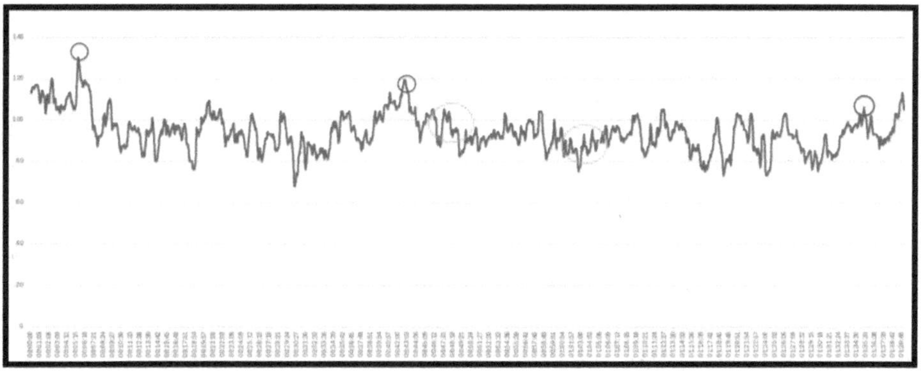

Fig. 4. Heart rate graph of Trainee A.P. during the teaching session. The dark circles show the stress peaks. The light circles show situations in which the trainee successfully managed unexpected events supported by the pre-action design artifact.

Data from trainee V.D.S. indicates that she is calm, with an average heart rate within the typical range for calm individuals (60–90) and a low standard deviation. Even during unexpected events, her stress levels do not exceed 100, demonstrating her ability to remain in control during lessons. The ability to manage the class effectively has also been confirmed by Fig. 5, particularly in terms of how she reacts to unexpected situations that don't affect the stress state, as the picks don't exceed the value of 97. One of the peaks presented by the trainee occurs as early as minute 7. In this initial phase of the lesson, the trainee struggles to manage the class and the confusion created by the pupils.

In order to start the lesson and manage the unexpected situation, she needs the support of the class teachers, both the tutor and the support teacher. At minute 53, before leaving the classroom to go to the garden for the next activity, the trainee recommends that pupils remain silent in the corridor. In any case, managing the transfer of a group of children to another location while ensuring that they keep their vivacity under control is a potentially stressful situation. In addition, the class proved to be much more chaotic than the trainee had expected, which may have contributed to a spike in stress at this time. Then, at 1.01 the ASD learner becomes nervous, so the support teacher has to take him out for a walk. This event could be particularly stressful for the trainee, as her personality leads her to be enthusiastic and eager to include everyone in her activities.

Although the trainee's personality profile (ENFP - Campaigner) describes her as a generally disorganized person, the fact that she had to follow a highly structured lesson plan, which also takes into account unexpected and potentially anxiety-inducing situations, may have helped her to maintain a general state of calm throughout the lesson.

In this case, the observer's notes show that the trainee often refers to the printed-out pre-action artefact she brought to school. Significant moments can be noted, such as at minute 1:25 when the trainee realizes that break time is about to begin. She checks the plan and decides to skip an unnecessary activity that she had included in the design in order to move directly to the debriefing phase and conclude the lesson.

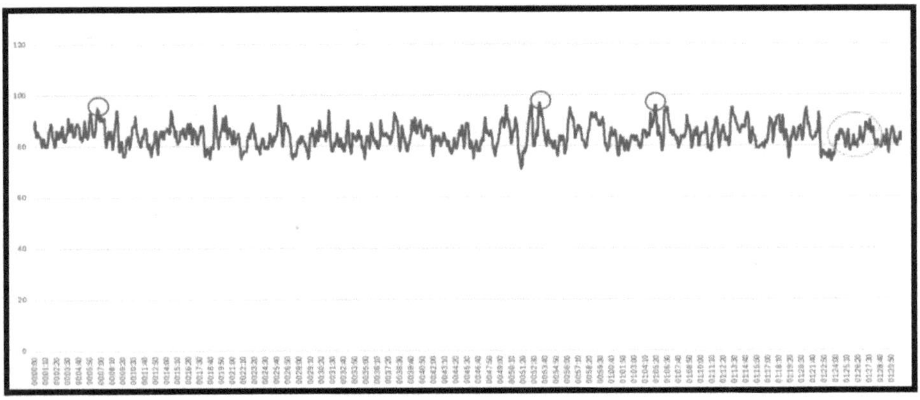

Fig. 5. Heart rate graph of trainee V.D.S. during the teaching session. The dark circles show the stress peaks. The light circle shows a situation in which the trainee successfully managed an unexpected event supported by the pre-action design artifact (Table 2).

Table 2. The comparative table shows the students' heart rate (HR) peaks during the observations.

Trainee	Personality	HR peak	Time
A.B.	ESFJ	144	0:05:33
		140	0:16:27

(*continued*)

Table 2. (*continued*)

Trainee	Personality	HR peak	Time
		139	0:30:16
D.F.	ENTP	149	0:12:33
		136	0:26:04
		150	1:12:42
A.M.	INFJ	117	0:06:39
		114	0:15:32
		123	0:27:18
		115	0:32:03
A.P.	ISTJ	130	0:05:30
		119	0:42:50
		106	1:35:19
V.D.S	ENFP	95	0:06:45
		97	0:53:11
		96	1:05:22

5 Conclusions

The comparative analysis of the five observed cases shows that all of the trainees involved experienced challenging situations and difficult moments during the lesson.

The critical moments more often experienced by the trainees included loss of control of the class, technical difficulties, time management issues, unexpected pupil requests, and interference from other actors. This confirms the most common types of unexpected events already highlighted in previous research [4, 5].

Triangulating qualitative observations, personality profiles, and HR biometric data enabled us to outline the critical moments experienced by each trainee, as well as how they dealt differently with unexpected events and stressful situations in the classroom. Considered individually, each type of data would only provide an incomplete picture. However, by correlating the three types of data, we noticed that the moments of maximum physiological activation did not always coincide with the most critical moments experienced by the trainees. This can be explained by individual personality traits, determining a different perception of the critical moments, as well as by the different use of the DUE model to manage them.

The main limitation of this study is the small number of lessons and trainees analyzed, which is partly due to the voluntary nature of participation and the sustainability of the process.

Despite its limitations, the pilot study confirms the potential of DUE in managing uncertainty, helping future teachers to deal with the emotional activation experienced during critical and unexpected moments. In particular, the study provided relevant insights into initial teacher training, which should not only promote structured yet flexible planning models, but also encourage the development of differentiated emotional self-regulation strategies tailored to individual profiles and needs.

Future developments will include the analysis of a larger and more representative sample of trainee teachers, with particular attention to data collected during lessons conducted at both the beginning and the end of the five-year program. This will allow for a comparison of the data emerging from the first and final years of their internship experience.

Disclosure of Interests. The authors have no competing interests to declare that are relevant to the content of this article.

Authors contribution. This paper stems from the collaborative work of the authors. Specifically, Lorenza Maria Capolla is the author of section 2; Lorella Giannandrea is the author of sections 1 and 5; Francesca Gratani is the author of section 3; Giacomo Nalli is the author of section 4 (statistical analysis of heart rate); Stelios Kapetanakis is the author of section 4 (visualizations) and Georgios A. Dafoulas is the author of section 4 (analysis and detection of personalities). Pier Giuseppe Rossi conceptualized and supervised the study. Abstract and references have been written collaboratively.

References

1. Jandrić, P., Knox, J., Besley, T., Ryberg, T., Suoranta, J., Hayes, S.: Postdigital science and education. Educational Philosophy and Theory. **50**(10), 893–899 (2018)
2. Eriksen, T.H.: Overheating: An Anthropology of Accelerated Change. Pluto, London (2016)
3. Lawrence, M., Homer-Dixon, T., Janzwood, S., Rockström, J., Renn, O., Donges, J.F.: Global polycrisis: The causal mechanisms of crisis entanglement. Global Sustainability. **7**, e6 (2024)
4. Capolla, L.M.: DUE. Design for the Unexpected in Education [PhD dissertation, Università degli Studi di Macerata]. UNIMC IRIS (2025)
5. Capolla, L.M., Giannandrea, L., Gratani, F., Pentucci, M., Rossi, P.G.: Rethinking and formalizing initial teacher training on learning design for and in uncertainty. Frontiers in Education. **9**, 1268936 (2024)
6. van der Want, A.C., den Brok, P., Beijaard, D., Brekelmans, M., Claessens, L.C.A., Pennings, H.J.M.: Teachers' interpersonal role identity. Scandinavian Journal of Educational Research. **59**(4), 424–442 (2014)
7. Skaalvik, E.M., Skaalvik, S.: Dimensions of teacher self-efficacy and relations with strain factors, perceived collective teacher efficacy, and teacher burnout. Journal of Educational Psychology. **99**(3), 611–625 (2007)
8. Bandura, A.: Self-efficacy: Toward a unifying theory of behavioral change. Psychological Review. **84**(2), 191–215 (1977)
9. Veenman, S.: Perceived problems of beginning teachers. Review of Educational Research. **54**(2), 143–178 (1984)
10. Popov, S., Popov, B., Damjanović, R.: The role of stressors at work and irrational beliefs in the prediction of teachers' stress. Primenjena Psihologija. **8**(1), 5–15 (2015)
11. Maslach, C., Leiter, M.P.: Understanding the burnout experience: Recent research and its implications for psychiatry. World Psychiatry. **15**(2), 103–111 (2016)
12. Gjoreski, M., Luštrek, M., Gams, M., Gjoreski, H.: Monitoring stress with a wrist device using context. Journal of Biomedical Informatics. **73**, 159–170 (2017)

13. Al Majali, S.: Positive anxiety and its role in motivation and achievements among university students. International Journal of Instruction. **13**, 975–986 (2020)
14. Molenda, M.: In search of the elusive ADDIE model. Performance Improvement. **42**(5), 34–37 (2003)
15. Berthoz, A.: La semplessità. Codice Edizioni, Torino (2011)
16. Gero, J.S.: Design prototypes: A knowledge representation schema for design. AI Magazine. **11**(4), 26–36 (1990)
17. Gero, J.S., Kannengiesser, U.: The situated function–behaviour–structure framework. In: Gero, J.S. (ed.) Artificial Intelligence in Design '02, pp. 89–104. Kluwer Academic Publishers, Dordrecht (2002)
18. Rossi, P.G., Pentucci, M.: Progettazione come azione simulata. Didattica dei processi e degli ecosistemi. Franco Angeli, Milano (2021)
19. Friedman, H.: MBTI Personality Test. Dartmouth College. https://www.maximusveritas.com/wp-content/uploads/2017/07/MBTI-Personality-Type-Te st.pdf (last Accessed 20 Oct 2025)
20. Myers, I.B., Briggs, K.: Gifts Differing: Understanding Personality Type. Nicolas-Hays, York Beach (2014)
21. Briggs-Myers, I., Briggs, K.C.: Myers-Briggs Type Indicator (MBTI). Consulting Psychologists Press, Palo Alto, CA (1985)
22. Bharadwaj, S., Sridhar, S., Choudhary, R., Srinath, R.: Persona traits identification based on Myers-Briggs Type Indicator (MBTI) – a text classification approach. In: 2018 International Conference on Advances in Computing, Communications and Informatics (ICACCI), pp. 1076–1082. IEEE (2018)
23. Mandal, S., Ghosh, B., Naskar, R.: A photoplethysmography (PPG) sensor-based stress level monitoring system for undergraduate students of technical education. In: 2023 IEEE 20th India Council International Conference (INDICON), pp. 197–202. IEEE (2023)
24. Creswell, J.W., Creswell, J.D.: Research Design: Qualitative, Quantitative, and Mixed Methods Approaches. Sage Publications, Thousand Oaks (2017)
25. Trotman, G.P., Veldhuijzen van Zanten, J.J., Davies, J., Möller, C., Ginty, A.T., Williams, S.E.: Associations between heart rate, perceived heart rate, and anxiety during acute psychological stress. Anxiety, Stress, & Coping. **32**(6), 711–727 (2019)
26. Giannandrea, L., Capolla, L.M., Gratani, F., Nalli, G., Kapetanakis, S.: Pre-service teachers and public speaking anxiety. Insights and possible interventions through AI and IoT. In: International Conference on Higher Education Learning Methodologies and Technologies Online, pp. 120–133 (2024)
27. Mason, J.W., Ramseth, D.J., Chanter, D.O., et al.: Electrocardiographic reference ranges derived from 79,743 ambulatory subjects. Journal of Electrocardiology. **40**(3), 228–234 (2007)

Model, Mine, Mentor: AI for UML Modeling

Pasquale Ardimento[1(✉)], Mario Luca Bernardi[2], Marta Cimitile[3], Melanie Scalera[4], and Michele Scalera[1]

[1] Department of Informatics, University of Bari Aldo Moro, Bari, Italy
{pasquale.ardimento,michele.scalera}@uniba.it
[2] Department of Engineering, University of Sannio, Benevento, Italy
bernardi@unisannio.it
[3] Department of Law and Digital Society, UnitelmaSapienza University, Rome, Italy
marta.cimitile@unitelmasapienza.it
[4] University of Guelph, Guelph, ON, Canada
mscalera@uoguelph.ca

Abstract. This paper describes *UML Miner*, a learner-centered platform for UML modeling education that operationalizes Vygotsky's Zone of Proximal Development and Cognitive Load Theory through an *observe–compare–explain* loop. Implemented as a Visual Paradigm plugin, the system logs modeling actions, applies declarative process discovery and conformance checking to locate strengths and misconceptions, and turns these findings into transparent, context-sensitive feedback via Retrieval-Augmented Generation with Large Language Models. The contribution is conceptual/system: we articulate the pedagogical rationale and architecture; show how process analytics are distilled into instructional descriptors; and outline guidance policies (minimal sufficient hints, pacing, and fading) that reduce extraneous load and foster autonomy. We also sketch a roadmap toward reliable and inclusive tutoring, including lightweight quality checks and evidence-tagged explanations for generative outputs, adaptive learner modeling for next-step selection, and coordinated (distributed) scaffolding delivered in a single concise voice. The approach supports metacognition and provides instructors with concise diagnostic indicators, and we outline an evaluation plan across distinct learner populations.

Keywords: UML modeling · Scaffolding · Process mining · Retrieval-Augmented Generation · Large Language Models · Intelligent Tutoring Systems

1 Introduction

We describe *UML Miner* [1–4], a Visual Paradigm plugin that combines process discovery and conformance checking techniques and Retrieval-Augmented Generation (RAG) with Large Language Models to provide reflective, adaptive

M. Adamoli et al. (Eds.): HELMeTO 2025, CCIS 2958, pp. 412–423, 2026.
https://doi.org/10.1007/978-3-032-31850-3_26

feedback during UML modeling. Implemented as a plugin for Visual Paradigm, UML Miner analyzes learner software modeling actions in real time to deliver reflective, adaptive, and context-sensitive feedback on ongoing modeling tasks.

The design of UML Miner is based on *Zone of Proximal Development* (ZPD) and *Cognitive Load Theory* (CLT), which guide the scaffolding strategies and the presentation of information; detailed theoretical foundations are discussed in Sect. 2.

This is a conceptual/system paper; it does not include an empirical evaluation, which is left for future work. Our contributions are as follows.

- a transparent and adaptive scaffolding framework for UML modeling that integrates process discovery, conformance checking and RAG-LLM;
- the rationale used to design UML Miner;
- the pedagogical alignment to ZPD/CLT into concrete scaffolding policies;
- a roadmap of extensions and research directions (e.g., reliability of generative support, learner modeling, and predictive analytics).

The remainder of the paper is organized as follows. Section 2 presents the theoretical foundations on which the system is based. Section 3 briefly describes the architecture and functionalities of UML Miner, while Sect. 4 explores innovative trends and extensions. Finally, Sect. 5 outlines future research directions and Sect. 6 concludes the paper.

2 Theoretical Foundations

This section introduces the pedagogical foundations that guide *UML Miner*. We first outline the *Zone of Proximal Development* and *Cognitive Load Theory*, then synthesize them into actionable principles for AI-enhanced scaffolding. Finally, we translate these principles into design implications for the platform, establishing a clear bridge to the architecture in Sect. 3.

Zone of Proximal Development (ZPD). The *Zone of Proximal Development* (ZPD) introduced by Vygotsky [26] denotes the range between what a learner can accomplish independently and what becomes achievable with guidance from a more knowledgeable other [21]. Within this dynamic range, *scaffolding*, temporary supports adapted to the learner's current level, is most effective [9]. Classic scaffolding strategies include task modeling, prompting and questioning, feedback calibrated to the learner's state, and the gradual release of responsibility [27]. In digital learning environments, these strategies translate into just-in-time, context-sensitive supports that align assistance with the learner's proximal needs while progressively fostering autonomy.

Cognitive Load Theory (CLT). CLT [23] starts from two simple facts: 1) working memory is narrow, meaning that working memory has limited capacity; 2) long-term memory, instead, stores knowledge as organized *schemas*. Good teaching, therefore, (a) matches task difficulty to prior knowledge, (b) avoids needless effort, and (c) invests effort where it helps schema building. In a software modeling course this means, for example: introduce one UML element (e.g., class, relationship) at a time on a diagram, avoid crowded notations and long digressions, and use short worked examples (e.g., when to prefer composition over inheritance). The aim is to keep attention on the idea being learned, not on fighting the interface or the explanation.

ZPD and CLT: Working Heuristics. In practice, we follow a few plain heuristics rather than a rigid recipe. We first locate the *next* obstacle by looking at the most recent edits and at simple conformance cues (for example, the learner is already refining attributes of two related classes, but the relationship between them has not been created yet). Our idea is to provide a single, short hint tied to the exact place where the student is working with no further hints, one step at a time. Multistep goals are staged into small moves (name the class → choose the relation → add the attribute), so the challenge matches prior knowledge. Each hint carries a brief reason or a micro-self-check ("Does this generalization really remove duplicated attributes?") to encourage reflection. Once the pattern stabilizes, the help is reduced quickly: from concrete hints to light nudges to silence.

These heuristics guide the design in Sect. 3. Conformance checking tells us *where* that process building could be improved by timely, concrete detections; the RAG-LLM component turns those detections into short messages anchored to the current action, so the attention stays on the modeling decision and the students progressively improve their way to build a diagram.

Recent work has compared the performance of LLMs with that of students in online university courses, showing that ChatGPT-3.5 can match or even surpass learners' results, although with occasional hallucinations in contextual tasks [12]. Complementary studies have emphasized the importance of explainability in educational AI, with XAI methods and tools helping to increase trust and informed adoption in learning settings [8]. More recently, LLMs have also been applied to directly support instructors, for example, in rubric-based code classification, where they provide contextualized feedback aligned with pedagogical criteria while preserving instructor oversight [11]. Together, these findings underscore both the potential and the risks of deploying AI in education. In contrast, our approach does not focus on outcome comparison or grading support, but rather on process-oriented scaffolding, where the LLM is integrated to provide adaptive and transparent guidance during modeling activities.

3 Platform Architecture and Functionalities

Following the pedagogical principles presented in Sect. 2, this section explains *how UML Miner* turns these concepts into practice. We describe the platform from a learner-centered viewpoint, focusing on what the system observes, how it compares learner actions to meaningful references, and how it explains the next small step through adaptive scaffolding. UML Miner operates through three coordinated components. These are behavior tracking, process-aware analysis, and RAG-LLM feedback:

1. **Behavior tracking** (event logs inside Visual Paradigm), which captures the learner's significant actions in software modeling.
2. **Process-aware analysis** (process discovery and conformance checking), which compares the observed behavior with reference models (e.g., models built by instructors) to detect misconceptions and strengths.
3. **RAG-LLM feedback**, which turns findings into short, transparent, and context-sensitive suggestions aligned with the learner's current proximal needs.

These components work together to deliver timely, transparent support and gradually fade guidance as competence grows. This layered architecture allows the system to detect misconceptions early, interpret student actions meaningfully, and provide timely, targeted guidance.

Figure 1 shows the observe–compare–explain loop implemented by UML Miner, which turns process traces into transparent, context-sensitive feedback. It observes learner actions, compares them to meaningful reference models to identify strengths and misconceptions, then explains the next small step through adaptive scaffolding aligned with ZPD and CLT.

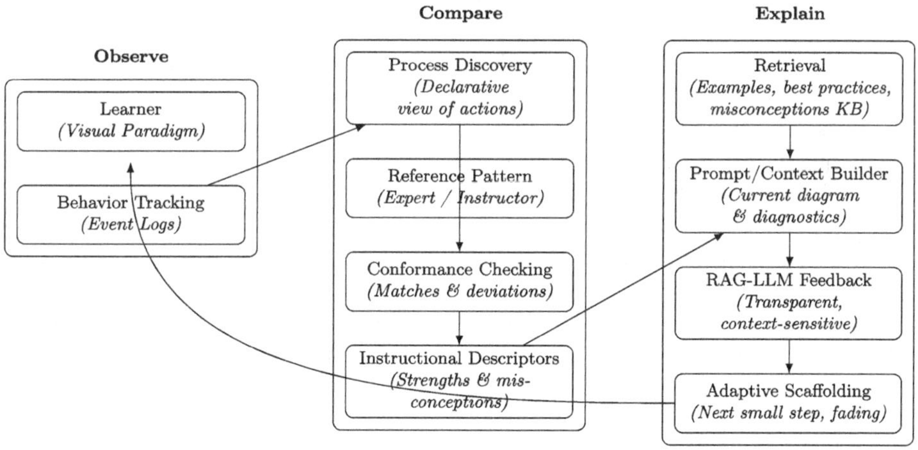

Fig. 1. Didactic overview of the *UML Miner* architecture.

3.1 Process Discovery: What the System "sees"

UML Miner reconstructs a readable picture of the learner's *actual* modeling path. To do so, it uses established declarative discovery techniques (e.g., Declare Miner [6] and MINERful [10]) to identify constraints that typically govern effective modeling (for instance, whether certain actions usually precede or follow others, or how often an action should occur). The discovery step returns a compact description of how the modeling unfolded. We keep it in two simple forms:

- **Diagram view:** an MP-Declare model (Multi-Perspective Declare), i.e., a constraint-based representation (not a prescriptive control flow) where templates such as PRECEDENCE(A, B), RESPONSE(A, B), or EXISTENCE(A) are instantiated on observed activities (e.g., PRECEDENCE(*CreateAssociation*, *RefineAttributes*)). This artifact is *used internally* as the reference for conformance checking and is *not* shown to learners. It can be exported for instructor/research inspection or visualized in external tools (e.g., RuM).
- **Textual rendering:** an instructor-facing, controlled-language rendering derived one-to-one from the same constraint set C (e.g., "Create the association before refining attributes."), intended for quick review and discussion without prior knowledge of Declare.

At runtime, students see only the short feedback messages produced downstream; neither the MP-Declare diagram nor the textual constraint list is part of the student UI.

3.2 Conformance Checking: Comparing Work with a Reference

When a reference is available (an expert solution or an instructor-defined pattern), *UML Miner* examines how the current process fits that reference. We rely on established methods, Declare Analyzer [7] and Declare Replayer [16], to know where the learner's behavior follows the reference behavior and where it departs from it. Typical signals concern, for example, creating an association before refining attributes, introducing generalization only after duplication is observable, or respecting cardinalities implied by the task. For instance, in `Order--OrderLine`, the line side typically carries multiplicity 1..∗.

The results can be reported at several different granularities (log, single trace, single constraint). We then translate them into short labels that are easy to discuss with the learner, such as *"add the association before attribute refinement"* or *"generalize after spotting duplication"*. The aim is not merely to point out an error, but to make clear why the behavior matters for the quality and readability of the final class diagram.

3.3 Feedback Generated with Retrieval and an LLM

The feedback component combines RAG with a LLM. Instead of generic feedback, it:

- generates a few concrete examples and brief rules relevant to class diagrams (naming, relationships, generalization);
- customizes the message in the *current* situation (what the student just did and what the conformance check highlighted);

- proposes the next small step and a one-sentence reason, rather than a full rewrite.

This keeps messages short and local to the ongoing action, prevents overload, and, when appropriate, adds a quick self-check (e.g., "Does this generalization remove duplicated attributes?"). As performance stabilizes, the tone shifts from directive hints to lighter cues and, eventually, to silence.

A Short Walk-Through. A typical cycle is as follows: (1) the student edits the diagram in Visual Paradigm, and events are logged; (2) the system reconstructs a simple declarative view of the process so far; (3) alignment with the chosen reference is checked and a few salient issues or strengths are selected; (4) the RAG component explains why each item matters and suggests exactly one next move; (5) as the learner improves the diagram, the amount of guidance decreases, and the prompts become more reflective. Figure 2 shows two examples of how UML Miner uses the software modeling actions captured during diagram building to generate informed feedback. Additional materials (video, source code, installation) are available on the UML Miner website.

4 Innovative Trends to Integrate Into UML Miner

Anchored in the pedagogical principles of Sect. 2 and the platform loop described in Sect. 3, this section outlines the future directions of UML Miner. For each trend, we explain in simple terms what it is, why it matters for ZPD/CLT-aligned scaffolding, and how it will translate into learner-centered features. The focus is on instructional value rather than technical detail.

4.1 Reliable Generative Feedback for Self-Regulated Learning

Recent work explores ways to *check* AI-generated feedback before showing it to learners (e.g., "LLM-as-a-Judge" and multi-agent reliability), mitigating hallucinations and increasing trust [3,17,19]. UML Miner will include a lightweight *verification* phase that validates feedback against an expert knowledge base and pedagogical rules, promoting accuracy and relevance prior to delivery. In this sense, it is our intention to improve:

- **Trust and transparency:** show concise *evidence tags* (e.g.,"based on rule X / example Y") to explain the rationale.
- **ZPD alignment:** release only the *minimal* hint needed now; queue deeper guidance if required.
- **Safe fallback:** when validation is uncertain, prefer templates or worked examples over speculative advice.

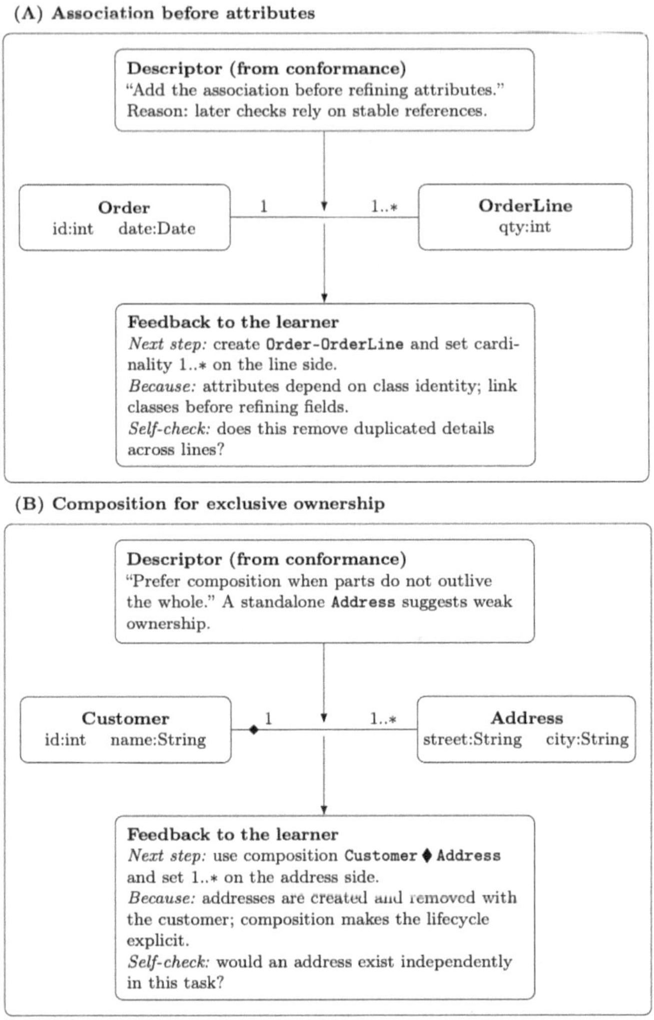

Fig. 2. Two conceptual examples of how feedback is built.

4.2 Balancing Support and Autonomy (Enhanced Cognitive Scaffolding)

Addressing the comfort–growth paradox: too much help hinders growth; too little stalls progress. The idea is to *fade* support as competence rises while managing cognitive load [13,20]. Start with clearer, more directive hints; move to shorter, reflective prompts as the learner improves; adapt the *pace* of tasks to avoid overload and dependency. Key improvements include:

- **CLT:** keep messages short and local (reduce extraneous load); adjust task granularity (manage intrinsic load); add reflection prompts (germane load).

- **Fading:** shift from "do this now" to "why does this pattern help?" fostering metacognition and autonomy.

4.3 Adaptive Learner Modeling

Adaptive models estimate proficiency and detect transitions from difficulty to fluency using learning analytics and, when appropriate, IRT-style profiling [5,15, 24]. This enables real-time estimates of *skill-by-skill* proficiency for class-diagram modeling (e.g., relationships, generalization, naming), supporting better *next-step* selection. This will include:

- **Personalization:** offer worked examples when difficulty is detected; reduce hints during fluent performance.
- **Early warning:** simple predictors flag emerging misconceptions to intervene before they ossify.
- **Fairness:** keep models interpretable; allow instructors to review and override recommendations.

4.4 Distributed Scaffolding via Multi-source Support

Scaffolding can come from multiple sources (e.g., tools, examples, peers, and instructors), coordinated so that responsibility gradually shifts to the learner [14]. The system orchestrates *one* concise message that blends a targeted hint, a relevant example, and (when available) an instructor note, so learners are not overwhelmed by fragmented cues. This requires:

- **One-voice policy:** unify sources into a single, short prompt to minimize extraneous load.
- **Progressive autonomy:** reduce tool-driven cues and increase self-check lists as competence grows.

4.5 Towards an Intelligent Tutoring System (ITS)

ITS emulates one-to-one tutoring through student modeling, error detection, and adaptive tasking [18,22,25]. More *responsive* tutor behavior will be reached by monitoring errors, pace, and attention signals to adapt difficulty and keep participation within the proximal zone of the learner.

Practical Settings and Teacher Oversight. Some learners progress better with short hints and small steps, others prefer to see more at once. *UML Miner* lets them trim the interface (fewer panels, shorter messages) and adjust the step size. Each recommendation ends with a one-line 'because' that points to a concrete rule or example, for example, choosing composition when parts do not outlive the whole. Instructors remain in charge: they decide how strict checks should be, how often messages appear, and how quickly support fades.

These directions deepen the observe–compare–explain loop: messages become more reliable, adaptivity is finer, and access improves for diverse learners. We now set out what we plan to build and how we will check that it helps.

5 Future Work and Evaluation Roadmap

We outline the next steps and the way we will test them, aiming for small, verifiable changes that keep ZPD in view and avoid unnecessary cognitive load.

5.1 Trustworthy Feedback, Checked and Concise

Before a message reaches the learner, two quick validation checks will be performed. First, the suggestion must match a small rule base and a handful of worked examples (e.g., aggregation vs. composition; generalization only when it removes duplication). Second, we ask the generator for a paraphrase and require agreement on the key point; if agreement is weak, we fall back to a short worked example. A few symbolic validations also run on the current class diagram (e.g., naming collisions, cycles in generalization, dangling associations), so advice never contradicts basic semantics. Each hint closes with a brief rationale that cites the rule or example used. We keep these validations symbolic and deterministic—unique naming, acyclic inheritance, and well-formed associations are checked on the class-graph—because LLM judgements are non-deterministic and may miss edge cases. The LLM then turns the outcomes into concise, pedagogically grounded hints ("because ...") with a single next step.

Trial Runs with Two Learner Groups. We will conduct short, timed activities with two cohorts: undergraduates in software engineering and post-diploma ITS students. Both work on class-diagram tasks; we compare a baseline toolset with the version that includes the reliability layer above. We track targeted skills (relationships, generalization, naming), time on task, deviation patterns, and a short rating of effort and usefulness. Open comments from students and instructors guide tone, pacing, and when to fade help.

Inclusive, Tutor-Like Support. Adaptivity will expand to serve learners who struggle with attention or pace. Step size and hint frequency adjust to recent performance; when a learner is ready, guidance can switch to a compact checklist that supports self-checks. Repeated patterns, for example, late renaming of classes, trigger early warnings, and instructors can override any automated choice.

First, we add the reliability gates and the short rationale, then pilot them in one course. Next, we introduce adaptive pacing and the checklist mode and run the two-cohort study. Finally, we extend symbolic checks, grow the example set, and refine instructor controls (strictness, hint frequency, pacing). For instructors, a compact panel will surface a few signals: which deviation types occur most and how quickly they are resolved; how often hints are accepted or ignored; and the share of reflective ("why-focused") messages versus directive ones—enough to tune strictness and pacing without adding extra load for students.

6 Conclusions

This paper described *UML Miner*, a learner-centered platform that operationalizes Vygotsky's ZPD and Sweller's CLT through an *observe–compare–explain* loop: it observes modeling actions, compares them with meaningful references via process mining, and explains the next small step through transparent, context-sensitive feedback. The work offers a conceptual/system contribution along four complementary dimensions:

1. **Framework and architecture.** We articulate a design that combines real-time behavioral traces, declarative process discovery and conformance checking and RAG-LLM explanations to implement adaptive scaffolding with a clear fading policy.
2. **Process-aware, transparent feedback.** We outline how conformance results can be distilled into *instructional descriptors* and turned into concise advice grounded in a curated knowledge base, paving the way for reliability checks and short, evidence-tagged rationales.
3. **Pedagogical alignment.** We translate ZPD/CLT into concrete guidance policies: minimal sufficient hints, pacing to manage intrinsic load, concise messages to reduce extraneous load, and reflective prompts to foster germane load and autonomy.
4. **Roadmap and evaluation.** We specify near-term steps to increase reliability and inclusiveness (quality gates, explanation templates, adaptive pacing) and a plan to evaluate effectiveness across learner populations.

This is a conceptual/system paper; empirical validation, scalability studies, and broader domain coverage remain open. The planned roadmap focuses on (i) strengthening trustworthiness through lightweight validation and explainable rationales, (ii) assessing learning gains and cognitive load across distinct cohorts, and (iii) refining inclusive, ITS-oriented support that keeps learners within their proximal zone while promoting autonomy.
UML Miner contributes a pedagogically grounded and process-aware approach to AI-assisted modeling education. By coupling process mining with RAG-LLM under ZPD/CLT principles, it lays a clear foundation for reliable, adaptive scaffolding and a rigorous evaluation agenda.

Disclosure of Interests. The authors have no competing interests to declare that are relevant to the content of this article.

References

1. Ardimento, P., Aversano, L., Bernardi, M.L., Carella, V.A., Cimitile, M., Scalera, M.: UML miner: a tool for mining UML diagrams. In: ACM/IEEE International Conference on Model Driven Engineering Languages and Systems, MODELS 2023 Companion, Västerås, Sweden, October 1-6, 2023, pp. 30–34. IEEE (2023). https://doi.org/10.1109/MODELS-C59198.2023.00014
2. Ardimento, P., Bernardi, M.L., Cimitile, M.: Teaching UML using a RAG-based LLM. In: International Joint Conference on Neural Networks, IJCNN 2024, Yokohama, Japan, June 30 - July 5, 2024, pp. 1–8. IEEE (2024). https://doi.org/10.1109/IJCNN60899.2024.10651492

3. Ardimento, P., Bernardi, M.L., Cimitile, M., Scalera, M.: Enhancing software modeling learning with AI-powered scaffolding. In: Proceedings of the ACM/IEEE 27th International Conference on Model Driven Engineering Languages and Systems, pp. 103–106. ACM (2024). https://doi.org/10.1145/3652620.3687776
4. Ardimento, P., Bernardi, M.L., Cimitile, M., Scalera, M.: Back to the model: UML miner and the power of process mining. In: Mecella, M., Rensink, A., Maciaszek, L.A. (eds.) Proceedings of the 20th International Conference on Software Technologies, ICSOFT 2025, Bilbao, Spain, June 10-12, 2025, pp. 207–214. SCITEPRESS (2025). https://doi.org/10.5220/0013500100003964
5. Bai, Z.: Variable incremental adaptive learning model based on knowledge graph and its application in online learning system. Int. J. Comput. Appl. **44** (2022). https://doi.org/10.1080/1206212X.2021.1878419
6. Bernardi, M.L., Cimitile, M., Di Francescomarino, C., Maggi, F.M.: Using discriminative rule mining to discover declarative process models with non-atomic activities, pp. 281–295 (2014). https://doi.org/10.1007/978-3-319-09870-8_21
7. Burattin, A., Maggi, F.M., Sperduti, A.: Conformance checking based on multi-perspective declarative process models. Expert Syst. Appl. **65**, 194–211 (2016). https://doi.org/10.1016/j.eswa.2016.08.040
8. Casalino, G., Castellano, G., Ducange, P., Fazzolari, M., Pecori, R., Zaza, G.: Leveraging explainable AI methods and tools for educational data. In: Casalino, G., et al. (eds.) Higher Education Learning Methodologies and Technologies Online, pp. 95–111. Springer Nature Switzerland, Cham (2024). https://doi.org/10.1007/978-3-031-67351-1_7
9. Chaiklin, S.: The zone of proximal development in Vygotsky's analysis of learning and instruction, pp. 39–64 (2003).https://doi.org/10.1017/CBO9780511840975.004
10. Ciccio, C.D., Mecella, M.: On the discovery of declarative control flows for artful processes. ACM Trans. Manage. Inf. Syst. **5**(4) (2015). https://doi.org/10.1145/2629447
11. Cipriano, E., Ferrato, A., Limongelli, C., Schicchi, D., Taibi, D.: Leveraging large language models to assist teachers in code grading. In: Cristea, A.I., Walker, E., Lu, Y., Santos, O.C., Isotani, S. (eds.) Artificial Intelligence in Education, pp. 204–217. Springer Nature Switzerland, Cham (2025). https://doi.org/10.1007/978-3-031-98459-4_15
12. Denaro, F., Ducange, P., Pecori, R., Tradigo, G., Veltri, L.: Comparative evaluation of chatgpt and students in the outcomes of online learning courses related to security. In: Ardimento, P.,et al. (eds.) Higher Education Learning Methodologies and Technologies Online, pp. 61–73. Springer Nature Switzerland, Cham (2025).https://doi.org/10.1007/978-3-031-94002-6_5
13. for Faculty Development, C.C.C., Innovation, T.: Consider scaffolding (2023). https://ecampusontario.pressbooks.pub/ccgenerativeai/chapter/consider-scaffolding/
14. Henning, E., der Westhuizen, D.V.: Crossing the digital divide safely and trustingly: how ecologies of learning scaffold the journey. Comput. Educat. **42** (2004). https://doi.org/10.1016/j.compedu.2003.08.006
15. Lee, Y.J., Palazzo, D.J., Warnakulasooriya, R., Pritchard, D.E.: Measuring student learning with item response theory. Phys. Rev. ST Phys. Educ. Res. **4**, 10102 (2008). https://doi.org/10.1103/PhysRevSTPER.4.010102
16. de Leoni, M., Maggi, F.M., van der Aalst, W.M.P.: Aligning event logs and declarative process models for conformance checking, pp. 82–97 (2012). https://doi.org/10.1007/978-3-642-32885-5_6

17. Li, T., Nath, D., Cheng, Y., Fan, Y., Li, X., Raković, M., Khosravi, H., Swiecki, Z., Tsai, Y.S., Gašević, D.: Turning real-time analytics into adaptive scaffolds for self-regulated learning using generative artificial intelligence. In: Proceedings of the 15th International Learning Analytics and Knowledge Conference, pp. 667–679. LAK '25, Association for Computing Machinery, New York, NY, USA (2025). https://doi.org/10.1145/3706468.3706559
18. Liu, S., et al.: Hyperbolic embedding of discrete evolution graphs for intelligent tutoring systems. Expert Syst. Appl. **241** (2024). https://doi.org/10.1016/j.eswa.2023.122451
19. Qian, K., et al.: Towards reliable generative ai-driven scaffolding: reducing hallucinations and enhancing quality in self-regulated learning support (2025). https://arxiv.org/abs/2508.05929
20. Riva, G.: The architecture of cognitive amplification: enhanced cognitive scaffolding as a resolution to the comfort-growth paradox in human-AI cognitive integration (2025). https://arxiv.org/abs/2507.19483
21. Shabani, K., Khatib, M., Ebadi, S.: Vygotsky's zone of proximal development: instructional implications and teachers' professional development. Engl. Lang. Teach. **3**(4), 237–248 (2010). https://doi.org/10.5539/elt.v3n4p237
22. Sharma, P., Harkishan, M.: Designing an intelligent tutoring system for computer programing in the pacific. Educat. Info. Technol. **27** (2022). https://doi.org/10.1007/s10639-021-10882-9
23. Sweller, J.: Cognitive load during problem solving: effects on learning. Cogn. Sci. **12**(2), 257–285 (1988). https://doi.org/10.1016/0364-0213(88)90023-7
24. Uesaka, Y., Suzuki, M., Ichikawa, S.: Analyzing students' learning strategies using item response theory: toward assessment and instruction for self-regulated learning. Front. Educat. **7** (8 2022). https://doi.org/10.3389/feduc.2022.921844
25. vanLehn, K.: The relative effectiveness of human tutoring, intelligent tutoring systems, and other tutoring systems (2011). https://doi.org/10.1080/00461520.2011.611369
26. Vygotsky, L.S., Cole, M.: Mind in Society: Development of Higher Psychological Processes, Harvard University Press (1978)
27. Wood, D., Bruner, J.S., Ross, G.: The role of tutoring in problem solving. J. Child Psychol. Psych. **17**(2), 89–100 (1976). https://doi.org/10.1111/j.1469-7610.1976.tb00381.x

Learning by Editing: Teaching Scholarly Digital Methods Through Fifteenth-Century Historical Account Books

Antonella Ambrosio[1], Giuseppe Consolo[1,2(✉)], and Maria Pia Tiseo[1,3]

[1] University of Naples, Federico II, Naples, Italy
antonella.ambrosio@unina.it, giuseppe.consolo@uni-graz.at, mariapia.tiseo@unibas.it
[2] University of Graz, Graz, Austria
[3] University of Basilicata, Potenza, Italy

Abstract. This paper presents a multidisciplinary Digital Humanities training project focused on the Scholarly Digital Edition (SDE) of fifteenth-century historical account books. Developed by the Laboratory of Historical Documents on the Web (DSW Lab) at the University of Naples Federico II, the program integrates the disciplinary traditions of Palaeography and Diplomatics with a structured ecosystem of digital tools and procedures. Its goal is to make interpretive decisions in historical research explicit, verifiable, and debatable, moving beyond implicit practices. The curriculum, designed for Master's students, adopted a constructivist pedagogical model based on authentic tasks and collaborative problem-solving. It developed through three interconnected stages: an internship, a Master Class, and a seminar series aimed at building core competences and connecting local learning to an international scholarly context. Students employed specialized software within a coordinated workflow: Transkribus for layout analysis, segmentation, and transcription, treating layout decisions as interpretive acts; Oxygen XML Editor for semantic encoding, using a customized TEI bookkeeping ontology from the University of Graz; and FRAT (Fast Rectangle Annotation Tool) for detailed palaeographic and graphemic analysis of scribal hands.

This approach transformed technical operations into scholarly interpretation, making digital competence essential for transparent disciplinary reasoning. The focus on shared lexicon, peer review, and continuous documentation fostered a community of practice within the international ICARUS network. The resulting TEI-compliant digital edition, prepared for publication on the DEPCHA platform, demonstrates how the SDE can function simultaneously as a research object and a training environment for critical and collaborative scholarship.

Keywords: Scholarly Digital Editions · Digital Humanities Pedagogy · Digital Palaeography and Diplomatics

1 Introduction: Digital Competences for Historical Sources

During our teaching activities, while examining a fifteenth-century account register, a student raised the question of how to distinguish between the entry written by the *scriptor* responsible for drafting the document and the notes visible in the margins or

M. Adamoli et al. (Eds.): HELMeTO 2025, CCIS 2958, pp. 424–455, 2026.
https://doi.org/10.1007/978-3-032-31850-3_27

at the lower edge of the folio, written by other hands. That question, seemingly minor, marked the starting point of our project. The goal is not to use digital tools to work more quickly, but to observe with greater awareness, making interpretive decisions explicit, and therefore debatable, verifiable, and improvable, that in the historian's practice often remain implicit.

In this case, the distinction between the original entry and later interventions is not merely a problem of palaeographic or diplomatic analysis: it affects the historical interpretation of the source and, at the same time, guides the editorial choices for its digital representation, where each decision of transcription or markup conveys a critical reading in computable form.

Starting from the academic year 2023–24, these needs shaped a training project of the Laboratory of Historical Documents on the Web (DSW Lab) of the University of Naples Federico II, addressed to students of the Master's degree in Historical Sciences. The program intertwined the disciplinary tradition of Palaeography and Diplomatics with an ecosystem of tools and procedures designed to translate historical-documentary intuition into computable representation: observing the page, segmenting its layout, discussing hypotheses, transcribing, encoding according to the Text Encoding Initiative (TEI) standard,[1] [2]reviewing, releasing a new version, and documenting the rationale for each decision. This was therefore not a simple methodological exercise but a genuine research workflow accompanying the transition from the archival object to its digital counterpart.

The process unfolded in three connected stages, conceived as parts of a single educational design.

The first phase, an internship in Palaeography, Diplomatics, and Digital Humanities, constituted the operational core: small stable groups worked on original sources, a fifteenth-century administrative register from the archive of the Neapolitan monastery of SS. Pietro e Sebastiano, with shared responsibilities and rotating roles (transcription, encoding, revision) to produce a scholarly digital edition, that is, a scientific representation of the document realized with digital tools, which makes explicit and verifiable the editor's interpretive choices, such as transcription, variant selection, apparatus use, and contextual reconstruction, and connects them to structured and navigable data. Here the common foundations were built: shared lexicon, procedures, quality criteria, and documentation habits [24].

The second phase, the Master Class *The Scholarly Digital Edition of the Account Books and Registers* (Naples and online, 3–4 May 2024), involved mainly the same students, with a few additional participants, and served as a threshold experience: confrontation with an international context, external validation of the practices initiated, and reflection on the relationship between automation and human control. It was the theme introduced in the keynote lecture by Georg Vogeler (University of Graz), a leading European figure in the field, as a criterion of editorial responsibility.

[1] Paragraphs 1–3.1 were written by Antonella Ambrosio, paragraphs 4–4.1 by Maria Pia Tiseo, and paragraphs 4.2–5.1 by Giuseppe Consolo. The conclusion (paragraph 6) represents a synthesis of the reflections shared by all the authors. All the websites mentioned were active as of October 20, 2025.

[2] *TEI,* https://tei-c.org/

The third phase, the seminar series *Hands that Count* (November 2024–February 2025), represented the moment of consolidation and reflective recomposition: the students, mostly the same from the previous phases, traversed the entire path from diplomatic description to Scholarly Digital Edition, up to the first interpretation of the data generated by the editorial process. At this stage, the experimental procedures became stable practices; the artefacts produced (transcriptions, XML-TEI files, decision logs) were organized as editorial prototypes, and choices were argued and revised in light of shared criteria.

In summary: the internship built basic competences and methodological unity; the Master Class offered an international perspective; the seminars established standards and evaluation tools, transforming the work carried out into reusable outputs and professional awareness consistent with the objectives of the program.[3]

In greater detail the program adopted a distributed model, structuring learning over time (synchronous meetings, progressively provided materials), roles (trainer, tutor, evaluator, discussion community), and contexts (in person and online). It followed a blended approach, combining archive-based activities to foster situated knowledge with a strong online component. On Microsoft Teams,[4] students took part in collaborative workshops, material sharing, revision monitoring, and tutor interaction. Training included Transkribus[5] for layout analysis, XML/TEI encoding with an ontology from the University of Graz, and graphemic annotation with the open-source tool FRAT.[6] Each microgroup transcribed, marked up, and edited a section of a historical account book. The results were integrated into a collective digital edition, now in final review on the international platform DEPCHA, Digital Edition Publishing Cooperative for Historical Accounts.[7]

In this framework, learning appeared as research in progress. The folio of the archival register became a laboratory of thought: not a source to be normalized, but each page presents itself as a stratified field of writing practices: the hand that writes, the one that corrects or adds, the ductus and morphology of letters, abbreviations, text layout, and marginal notes of reference or administrative checking. In this context, every decision of reading or editing requires a conscious act of interpretation and explicit documentation: distinguishing the original writing from later interventions, identifying a marginal note as correction or index of use, deciding whether to normalize a spelling or preserve variation.

Digital competence, in this perspective, is not a mere instrumental addition but the very condition for making disciplinary reasoning transparent: the palaeographic or diplomatic hypothesis takes form in coherent markup, where every element, the presence of hands, text structure, graphic phenomena, or formulae, becomes a traceable and verifiable decision. The digital does not replace expert judgment but exposes it, rendering it public, debatable, and improvable over time through cycles of review and peer comparison.

---

[3] *SS. Pietro e Sebastiano Monastery project,* https://www.coop-unina.org/ss-pietro-e-sebastiano-monastery-project/

[4] *Teams,* https://www.microsoft.com/en-us/microsoft-teams/group-chat-software

[5] *Transkribus,* https://www.transkribus.org/it

[6] *FRAT*, https://github.com/anguelos/frat

[7] *DEPCHA*, https://gams.uni-graz.at/context:depcha

To understand how this approach was translated into the didactic design, we now make explicit the methodological lens that guided it: an operative constructivism, centred on authentic tasks and on editorial decisions made public and discussed collectively within a transparent scholarly environment [3, 6, 7].

2 Constructivist Framework

When we asked students to segment the layout of an account book using the software Transkribus, the goal was not simply to introduce a new technical tool, but to place them in a position to critically question their own mental categories regarding what a document is, how it produces meaning, and how it can be represented in digital form.

From this perspective, constructivism, from a theoretical principle, becomes a laboratory practice: knowledge is not transmitted but constructed through the shared solution of real problems that admit no univocal answers and require reasoned decisions [17, 36].

A typical scene from classroom work illustrates the meaning of this approach: one group identifies three text regions in a folio of the register, another distinguishes five, separating the heading, the body of the entries, and the marginalia. Rather than intervening from above to "correct," we encourage dialogue: we let hypotheses, arguments, and material references emerge, lines, text alignments, changes of hand or ink, until we connect these observations to the graphic forms and to the diplomatic forms and functions, and to their editorial implications in TEI. This is the moment when that process of assimilation and accommodation described by Piaget becomes active: the initial interpretive categories are put to the test, and, when they are no longer sufficient, they are restructured in light of experience [28]. This transformation is not a mere methodological detail but the core of the educational process.

The traditional concept of the document as a linear flow of text gives way to a stratified and functional conception: the document as a complex object in which its structure, the hands that produced, laid out, and used it, interact and must be represented in an explicit and traceable way. Following the theory-theory of Gopnik and Meltzoff, we regard students as "little theorists": they advance hypotheses, verify them on the basis of graphic and structural evidence, and reformulate them when necessary [15, 16, 22]. We do not eliminate uncertainty; we design it as a productive part of the learning process.

Operationally, the activity unfolds through a sequence of decisions: observe, describe, transcribe, formulate an editorial hypothesis, verify it in light of disciplinary conventions, make it explicit in markup, and submit it to peer review. Each phase involves a different mode of thinking: perceptual ("what do I see?"), conceptual ("what does marginal mean here?"), operational ("what level of TEI granularity is coherent?"), and argumentative ("can I justify my choice?"). In this way, the traditional lecture becomes a research workshop, where theoretical reflection is intertwined with technical practice.

A constructivist approach also requires scaffolding, that is, a structured support that accompanies the transition between what the student already knows and what still needs to be learned. We provide students with standards for markup execution, annotated examples, and quality checklists, thus guiding the transition from individual interpretive hypotheses to a coherent and verifiable formal representation. In this way, the digital environment does not merely host the work but structures its processes and documents its editorial quality. Assessment is not reduced to a judgment on the final outcome but documents the cognitive path: "How did you reason? Which alternatives did you discard? Why is this solution more reproducible?" [36].

At the same time, we avoid the misunderstanding of a purely individual constructivism.

Learning takes place among people and objects, within small working groups that rotate roles (transcriber, encoder, reviewer), document their choices, and discuss them through shared artefacts (images, XML files, different editorial versions). Knowledge emerges as the outcome of a dialogical process among the materiality of the source, the formal models of representation (markup standards, descriptive conventions, criteria of interoperability), and the interpreting community which, through negotiation and shared revision, transforms empirical observation into disciplinary knowledge. In this sense, the collaborative dimension is not an accessory but the natural condition of knowledge construction [17].

Finally, there remains the question of translatability: how can the observation of a historical-documentary feature become a structured and queryable piece of information? Here constructivism meets the discipline itself. Understanding that a marginal note functions as an accounting correction is an interpretive act; deciding how to represent it in TEI so that it becomes searchable and interoperable is an act of formalization that transforms understanding into a verifiable model. Asking students to make their criteria explicit in editorial notes means teaching them to stabilize their reasoning in a technical artefact that others can examine and reuse. This approach is not useful only to historians or diplomatics scholars working in digital environments, but to anyone training for research in the humanities: it makes visible the transferable competences most required today – analysis, design, justification, negotiation, documentation.

At the same time, it shows how an ancient disciplinary tradition such as the palaeographic and diplomatic approach and the digital domain meet on common ground: turning the historical source into a laboratory of thought rather than merely a corpus to be edited.

Within this framework, the transition to the next theme becomes clear: in an environment that makes choices traceable and public, evaluation ceases to be a final act and becomes an integral part of the process. Decisions become common goods, and sharing, beyond being a collaborative gesture, transforms into a genuine research method.

3 Sharing: Learning Communities and Communities of Practice

In our laboratory, sharing is neither an accessory gesture nor a simple act of "uploading a file." It is a way of organizing collective intelligence: intermediate products, transcriptions, markups, versions, decision notes, do not remain the property of those who created them but become common goods to be revisited, discussed, and improved. In this sense, the classroom is no longer the place where a student submits an assignment to the instructor; it becomes a public workspace in which every step is visible and reasoned.

A typical scene is as follows: two groups have proposed different solutions for the text regions of a complex page. Before "choosing" which one is best, we open the shared repository, scroll through the versions, and read the comments. What we are looking for is not who has "guessed right," but how the idea has evolved through hypotheses and evidence. This is the logic of knowledge building: the unit of measurement is not individual learning but the progressive improvement of shared ideas [11].

Each artefact, from the definition of a region to the selection of a TEI element, is treated as a hypothesis that grows stronger because it is supported by arguments, examples, and comparisons. Teams, with its timelines and file diffs, becomes the collective notebook where disciplinary reasoning leaves its traces. This publicity of work functions because it is inhabited by roles. Undergraduates, doctoral students, tutors, and teachers co-design activities ranging from layout analysis to editorial revision; the entry point is guided, but autonomy grows along the way. This is what we call a learning community: it is not merely a matter of "helping one another," but of experiencing that the context, the archive with its rules, the platform with its constraints, the standards with their affordances, is not a neutral background. It shapes questions and answers, compels the clarification of vocabulary, and trains participants to negotiate meanings. Learning, in short, is situated within things and among people [31, 32]. Gradually, this mode of working takes on the shape of a community of practice.

The shared enterprise is clear: to produce a sound digital edition.

Mutual engagement becomes visible in daily exchanges, in rotating shifts among transcription, encoding, and revision, and in recurring requests for clarification that circulate until equilibrium is found. Most importantly, a shared repertoire is consolidated: glossaries that fix terminology, markup guides that prevent inconsistency, quality checklists that safeguard coherence, model examples and export templates that enable everyone to proceed. Those entering for the first time do not merely "observe": they participate immediately, in tasks of increasing complexity, while internalizing the language and practices of the DSW Lab–ICARUS community [47].

To ensure that all this does not remain a statement of intent, we have given sharing a ritual form. Editorial decisions are public and open to comment, not to expose errors, but to build scientific accountability and accelerate peer learning. Issue logs and decision logs serve as boundary objects, connecting different subgroups without erasing their technical specificities. Review meetings, short stand-ups for updates, milestone reviews for synthesis, mark a recognizable cycle: propose, discuss, revise, release. Revision is not punitive; it is formative. It traces the evolution of ideas, not merely the correction of errors. The repertoire, too, is alive: it is updated whenever a recurring case (a type of abbreviation, an ambiguous marginal note, an irregular table) is convincingly resolved.

That case then enters the cookbook as an annotated example, ready to be reused by the entire community.

It is in these moments that the transformation becomes visible: from a collection of individual works to a collective operational memory, which makes subsequent processes faster and responsibilities clearer.

Ultimately, "sharing" ceases to be a moral invitation and becomes a method. It generates professional identity, as participants recognize themselves within a disciplinary community that speaks the same language and follows shared rules; it produces editorial quality, because standards are not declarations but practices maintained through peer control; and it ensures sustainability, since procedures and materials are reused, adapted, and passed on. Thus, our path moves from "teaching tools" to doing research together: communities, when they work on shared and improvable objects, generate knowledge—and they do so by leaving traces that others can build upon. However, for this kind of sharing to acquire scientific weight, it needs a home and a network that recognize and sustain it.

This home is ICARUS: an ecosystem where local hypotheses enter into dialogue with international repertoires and standards [46].

3.1 The Scholarly Community: ICARUS as an Ecosystem of Practice

The effectiveness of this part of the training pathway did not arise by chance, but from the context in which it took shape.

It developed within ICARUS, the International Centre for Archival Research, a network that brings together around 200 archives and research institutions across Europe, which for over twenty years has promoted a collaborative vision of the description and accessibility of documentary sources, as well as a culture of sharing based on common infrastructures, interoperable standards, and shared technical languages.

Working in this environment means entering an ecosystem in which research, teaching, and scholarly production are parts of the same process: the act of editing becomes a collective enterprise, and digital tools such as Monasterium.net, MOM-CA, and DEPCHA are not merely repositories for depositing results but spaces for elaboration, experimentation, and dialogue.

Within this framework, DEPCHA was not used as a final platform for "uploading results," but as an active construction laboratory: within it we negotiated terminologies, verified the coherence of our descriptive schemes, adapted pre-existing models, and incorporated good practices tested in previous projects.

In this sense, ICARUS has represented an operational bridge between the university classroom and a broad, international scholarly community that shares a technical lexicon, quality criteria, and a value system centred on openness, traceability, and peer review.

The impact of this affiliation is visible in everyday practice.

When a student proposes a markup solution for a marginal note of difficult interpretation, the discussion does not end within the local working group: it is enriched through comparison with repertoires, examples, and guidelines circulating within the ICARUS network or already published on its platforms.

The discussion, therefore, does not take the form of a dialogue between teacher and student, but rather of an exchange among disciplinary artefacts: what is produced in the laboratory is situated in continuity with what others have already elaborated and can, in turn, become a model or reference for future work.

It is in this process of recursivity and accumulation that the notion of the scholarly community acquires tangible meaning: not merely an institutional framework, but a device for validation and cumulative growth of knowledge [47].

This orientation also affects the quality and purpose of the work carried out.

Students know that they are not preparing an exercise destined only for internal assessment, but a public editorial prototype, developed through successive versions, each one documented and traceable so as to make the process of revision and improvement transparent and interrogable, and aligned with international standards.

The awareness of operating within a real publication context shifts attention from performance to responsibility: documenting decisions, justifying choices, and checking coherence become integral components of the group's collective scientific reputation.

Thus, the passage from a learning community to a professional community occurs almost naturally: a doctoral student assumes the role of associate editor; a student corrects an inconsistency in the markup guide; a tutor proposes a new export template for data. Everything remains traceable, reusable, and improvable. In this context, peer review is not an appendix or a concluding ritual but an integrated practice. Each version, each annotation in the decision log, becomes an opportunity for learning and mutual verification. Digital tools—from Teams to shared repositories—make the review process visible, transforming the act of correction into a moment of metacognitive reflection.

The same principle underlies participation in networks such as DEPCHA, platforms that promote the public review of didactic and editorial designs through usage metrics, structured comments, and improved releases. In this sense, technology has not merely accelerated the work: it has given it a public and verifiable form.

Looking back at the previous experiences of the DSW Lab, we can recognize that this method is rooted in a historical continuity of practices. The digitized collections uploaded to Monasterium, the experiments on the edition of the Santa Maria della Grotta documents, the collections built over time, and the manuals and glossaries collaboratively compiled have gradually consolidated a corpus of operational knowledge. Each project has left a useful trace for the next, each solution has generated a fragment of repertoire, and each corrected error has refined a methodological criterion [1, 2, 4, 5].

When today's students work on a new register, they do not start from scratch: they enter a flow of shared practices and knowledge, contributing to its renewal. From this perspective, the scholarly community functions because it possesses a home (ICARUS and the platforms of its member institutions across Europe), a shared craft: the construction of robust, interoperable, and reusable digital editions and an operational memory that grows through use.

In the didactic context, this has meant moving beyond the logic of "teaching tools" toward the shared production of research: products are not mere assignments but disciplinary commons; evaluations are not grades but reasoned reviews; learning is not only individual progress but the collective improvement of ideas and practices.

The following case studies are therefore not secondary examples but proofs of concept: they demonstrate how the university classroom can become part of a real scholarly community, capable of integrating technical infrastructure, methodological rigour, and a culture of collaboration—producing at once impact, sustainability, and reuse.

4 Tools

Within the methodological framework outlined above, the following section will concretely illustrate the process that guided the students from the visual analysis of the source using Transkribus, through structural and semantic encoding with Oxygen, to the examination of the materiality and handwriting using FRAT.

4.1 Transkribus as a Critical-Pedagogical Tool for Historical Account Books

The historical-administrative source chosen for the training activities presents Diplomatics challenges due to its highly formalized and complex structure: introductions, entries in tabular form, *marginalia* [13, 14]. Analyzing and managing such a complex layout is not a merely technical activity, but represents a critical interpretive exercise in which students must confront core disciplinary questions. For example: how many meaningful regions can I identify in this *folio*? How do I handle the *marginalia*? What meaning was a given text region meant to acquire for the medieval *scriptor*? Which export format allows me to preserve the analyses carried out and ensure interoperability of the data? These questions, prompted by the source itself, guided the students in defining and explicating the document's structure. Notably, layout analysis constituted the first phase of the workflow outlined for producing the Scholarly Digital Edition, the phase where students moved from observing the physical document to formally representing it. In this context, a digital tool like Transkribus appeared suitable for experimenting with layout management through the integration of human and machine activity. Using Transkribus was not about speeding up work, but it was about amplifying observation: the platform provided a digital means to test hypotheses about the document's structure and to make explicit, and thus discussable, the interpretative decisions often tacitly made.

The Transkribus Graphic User Interface (Transkribus GUI) platform was launched in 2015 with European funds from the 7th Framework Program (7FP), within the framework of the tranScriptorium project (2013–2015) [35, 45].[8] It is a Java-based client program, downloadable locally but connected to the central server hosted by the University of Innsbruck, under the responsibility of the Digitisation and Electronic Archiving (DEA) of the same University. Transkribus GUI stabilized with the initial version 1.0 starting in 2017, representing for users the only access route to the platform until 2021, the year in which the web version was launched [41]. However, the maintenance, development, and promotion of the platform were made possible thanks to the subsequent Recognition and Enrichment of Archival Documents READ project (2016–2019), funded with European Horizon 2020 resources and coordinated by the University of Innsbruck, in collaboration with other European universities and research institutions.[9] The platform is currently managed by READ-COOP-SCE (societas cooperativa Europaea), founded in 2019 to ensure the project's sustainability after European public funding ended, covering ongoing costs for maintenance, updates, and other needs required by a digital infrastructure [38]. Having grown in just a few years, the cooperative today has more

[8] The project, funded by the EU with approximately €2.4 million, was managed by a consortium coordinated by the Polytechnic University of Valencia, which was responsible for implementing the system. For more info see the European Commission's web page on the project, at the link https://cordis.europa.eu/project/id/600707/factsheet.

[9] Grant agreement ID: 674943, with funding of approximately €8.2 million. For beneficiaries, see the dedicated European Commission webpage at https://cordis.europa.eu/project/id/674943. The essential components of the Transkribus infrastructure were provided by the University of Rostock and the Polytechnic University of Valencia.

than 200 members, both institutions and individuals, from more than 30 countries.[10] The platform is currently used by a diverse group of users: archivists, humanists, computer scientists, and the general public. Each can contribute to the development of the platform and, at the same time, benefit from it [23, 25]. The success of Transkribus probably lies in this aspect: a system that has automatically transcribed over 100 million images [40] and counts over 300.000 registered users.[11] In fact, the cooperative society is perceived as a co-creation system. In this system, the surplus is reinvested in infrastructures made available for the common good, based on artificial intelligence systems perceived as reliable and transparent [40]. For teaching, it translates into easy access and support, clear data-handling policies, and reproducible workflows suitable for classroom and laboratory use. A significant benefit of Transkribus is that it offers layout analysis and handwritten text recognition service without users having to provide their own technological infrastructures. All data and documents entered into Transkribus are stored centrally, leveraging 1.2 PB of gross storage capacity, including backups.[12] To cover the costs associated with the services just mentioned, Transkribus offers various subscription plans that provide more credits and grant access to certain features, including priority in job processing, credit sharing, export in all formats, and greater storage capacity.[13] However, Transkribus allows users to test the platform's features free of charge, by granting 50 credits per month. Moreover, during the training, the team chose workflows that minimized credit use, as discussed below, ensuring that cost was not a barrier for student participation.

By adopting Transkribus, the students worked in a realistic digital research setting: they had to negotiate user roles, data management, and system limitations much like a research team, all while focusing on interpreting the source in diplomatics key. In this way, the students were able to engage in collaborative discussions with the entire team about the work carried out, critically address ambiguous cases, and learn to argue their thesis regarding the forms and functions of the analyzed source. The students learned more from this knowledge-building process than from corrections, in line with the methodological framework outlined in the previous paragraphs.

Layout Analysis, Transcription and XML–TEI Export with Transkribus

The integration of Transkribus into the training program presented here followed a carefully designed procedure intended to introduce students to the organized management of the account books' structure, aligning with the constructivist, learning-by-doing philosophy described earlier. Before the hands-on work, students were provided with a tutorial video showing every step, from uploading images to exporting the text in XML-TEI format. This preparatory step gave the class a common reference point and set expectations for how the digital tool would be used in conjunction with traditional analysis. The process of using Transkribus began with the free registration of an account on the

[10] READ-COOP-SCE website at https://readcoop.org/en. For up-to-date information on the cooperative's ever-expanding membership, see the dedicated section of the website at https://readcoop.org/members.

[11] *Transkribus – Text Recognition*, https://www.transkribus.org/ai-text-recognition

[12] Petabyte (PB): 10^{15} byte (=1.000.000.000.000.000 byte)

[13] *Transkribus – Plans,* https://www.transkribus.org/plans

dedicated web page and verification of the email address. For these training activities, the eXpert client version (the desktop application)[14] was chosen because it allowed offline work with periodic synchronization, meaning students could work simultaneously on the shared project without needing continuous internet connectivity and all edits would be merged into central collection when online. Another advantage was pragmatic: the desktop software at that time offered a more complete feature set and stability. For instance, it enabled local layout analysis runs without consuming any credit quota, and it bypassed some performance bugs that the early web version had. To start the eXpert version, after downloading the installation files, it was necessary to run the specific file based on the operating system of one's PC.[15] After logging in with their previously chosen credentials, students gained access to the Transkribus eXpert interface. The organization of the data digitally replicates the archival structure: a dedicated *Collection* was created and, within it, a *Document* for the account book under examination. This step of defining *Collections* and *Documents* represented a teaching moment to discuss how physical archives are organized and how those principles translate into digital platforms. With the project space set up, the digitized material[16] was imported simply and intuitively through the steps *Document → Import document to server → Upload single document*, selecting the local folder where the images had been stored (accepted in various formats, including png, jpg, tif, pdf, etc.), and then selecting the destination *Collection*. Once the images had been imported, everyone in the shared collection could see the sequence of pages on their screens, replicating the experience of leafing through the register, but now in a virtual workspace where annotations and segmentations could be added collaboratively. The core exercise began with the layout analysis phase, that is, the identification of parts of the document with a specific function, through the creation of text regions – rectangular areas encompassing all text, and baselines – polylines running along the bottom of each line of written text (Fig. 1).

Guided by tutors and PhD students, the participants examined the document and reflected on its mise en page, such as text alignment, changes in handwriting, presence of ruled lines, and marginal annotations. To perform layout segmentation in Transkribus, they explored Transkribus's two layout analysis modes: manual segmentation and automatic segmentation. Working in groups, they took turns creating text regions and baselines manually, using the desktop version's shortcuts: TR for text regions and BL for baselines. By manually marking these, students literally outlined their interpretation of how the document is structured – for instance, deciding to put a separate text region around a marginal note indicates they considered it functionally distinct from the main register entries. After manually segmenting one page, they tested the automatic mode, comparing the two approaches as part of the exercise. In the automatic mode, they selected in the *Tools* section the options *Find text regions* and *Find lines*, finally starting the *Run* operation. The results, while impressively fast, were not perfect: the algorithm correctly outlined large text blocks and many lines, but it struggled with the

[14] *Transkribus Expert Client* v1.26.0, https://transkribus.eu/TranskribusX/releases/?__hstc=48127928.b3429fa7f60d70e15f8b0bba995ce330.1760365021434.1760709535822.1760801691715.7&__hssc=48127928.1.1760801691715&__hsfp=2679447906

[15] Windows: Transkribus.bat; Mac OS - Apple: Transkribus.command; Linux: Transkribus.sh

[16] For image digitisation, see Sect. 4.3 below.

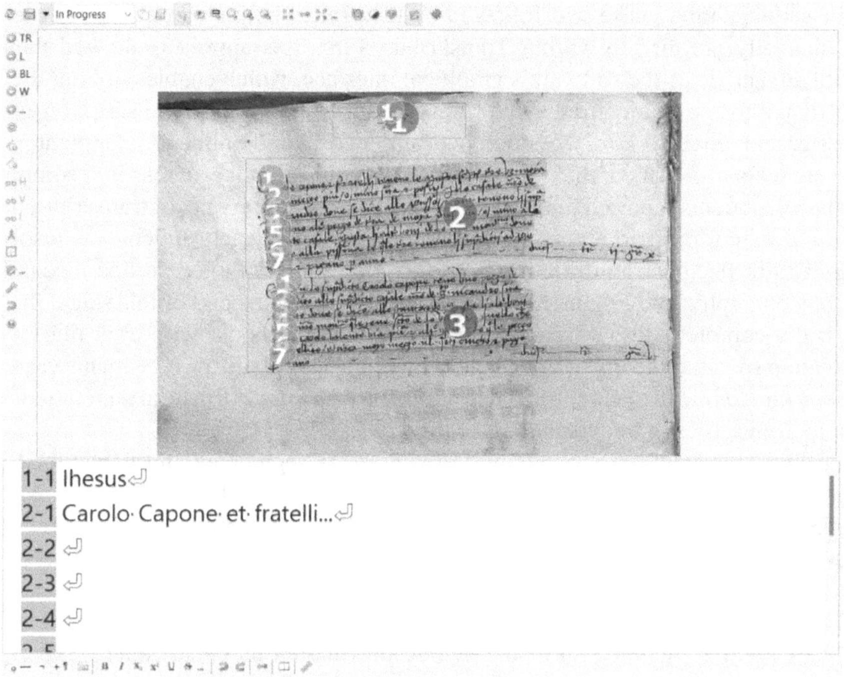

Fig. 1. Transkribus client version – Region and Line

idiosyncrasies of source. For instance, it sometimes merged a marginal annotation with the main text region or missed lines where the ink was faded or overlapping.

The two approaches were then discussed collectively: why did certain differences occur, and what did that say about the document's features versus the tool's assumptions? Crucially, instead of the instructors supplying answers, the students debated and reasoned together, citing evidence from the images. Through this dialogue, a direct application of the course's constructivist approach, the group concluded that, for this particular handwriting and structure, the most effective solution was a hybrid method: creating the writing areas manually – also to enable the identification of distinct text regions relating to headings, accounting entries or *marginalia* – but using automatic detection for the baselines. As specified above, the automatic outcome of layout analysis for recognizing the baselines did not yield completely correct results, given the presence of overwritten words, marginal notes, and gaps due to the preservation state of the source. Therefore, digital diplomatics learning also took shape in the phase of manual review and correction: it prompted discussions about why the software misinterpreted certain layouts, leading back to diplomatic concepts. For instance, an overwritten word might confuse the algorithm, but a student recognizing the diplomatic significance of that insertion (for instance, a later correction by the scribe) understood why it should be marked distinctly. In essence, the students were learning to "read" the document's physical evidence and encode it explicitly. This step embodies the human checks on automated procedures promoted by the didactic framework presented here.

The segmentation phase was followed by text transcription, carried out by the students manually but directly within Transkribus. First, this approach allowed them to take full advantage of the software's graphical interface, which enables linking the line of the image to the line of transcription at a glance, making the transcription operation easier and reducing errors. Second, working in a shared online environment meant that as students transcribed, their peers and tutors could watch progress in a communal workspace. Students reported that this made the usually solitary act of transcription feel collaborative and transparent: everyone could observe how each student was resolving ambiguities or deciphering difficult characters, and this prompted ad-hoc discussions about palaeographic and linguistic issues encountered. By the end of this stage, the students had a complete digital transcription of the account book, with each line of text mapped to a specific line on an image, all within a single platform. The manuscript had thus been turned into a machine-readable form, enriched with structural annotations that reflect their interpretive understanding of the source.

The final step with Transkribus was to export the segmented and transcribed data for subsequent encoding in Oxygen. Transkribus offers several export options (METS, PDF, TEI, Docx, TXT, XLSX), but for the digital edition, the preference fell on the TEI format, a format suited to guaranteeing interoperability and scholarly value, essential for creating a Scholarly Digital Edition.

Through the Transkribus export interface, the students learned how to generate an XML-TEI file that included all of the layout information they had added. Export can be performed through two options: Server export and Client export. In the first case, export occurs through the dedicated server, which sends a link to the email address used for registration. In the second case, the user exports the data directly to their own PC, choosing the destination folder in which to save them. Data export is also very intuitive: one must click on the icon with the folder and a right-pointing arrow in the *Main Bar (Export document)* and choose the export format best suited to one's needs. In the specific case, to export the transcription in TEI so as to preserve the information entered in Transkribus's metadata section and all the baselines and text regions identified, user must click on *Export document*, select TEI and the checkboxes *Zone per region, Zone per line, Line breaks (<lb/>), Export all tags in doc.* Once exported, the generated file presents a structure compliant with TEI standards, articulated into essential macro-elements: the <TEI> root, the <teiHeader> for contextual and descriptive metadata, the <facsimile> that creates the hyperlink between image and transcription, and the <text> element that encloses the content of the transcription itself.

Seeing this output was significant for the class: the once intimidating TEI encoding appeared less abstract, because they realized they had already been encoding the document's structure through the layout work in Transkribus. This set the stage for the next steps of the course, since students were no longer starting from a blank XML document, but rather editing and enhancing a machine-generated draft that reflected their own prior decisions.

From a pedagogical perspective, the Transkribus module achieved several important outcomes in line with our course framework. First, the logical structuring of documents into Collections and Documents represented an initial teaching moment to link the principles of traditional archival cataloging with the practice of digital data management.

Second, the manual segmentation of text regions and correction of baselines enabled students to critically and actively interpret the diplomatic structure of the document before proceeding to transcription. This approach ensured that the digital representation reflected the formal intent of the document's producer, providing a structured basis indispensable for the subsequent encoding phase. The use of Transkribus thus took shape as a collaborative mediation tool that facilitates the transition from diplomatic analysis to the structural encoding of the source. Third, Transkribus has helped to create a community learning experience: students made decisions together, shared the labor of correction and transcription, and immediately saw each other's contributions. This aligns with the above-mentioned *community of practice*: knowledge was constructed through peer discussion and shared tasks, not just individual work. Finally, by completing the visual and textual encoding in Transkribus and exporting it, the students created a concrete product, the TEI file, that served as a starting point for the next steps. The entire experience with Transkribus confirmed that a thoughtfully implemented blend of traditional diplomatics and digital tools can significantly enhance learning. The students did not simply learn to use software, but they learned through the software. With the manuscript now available in a structured digital form, we were ready to shift our focus from how the document was written and organized (form) to what it contains (content), as discussed in the following sections.

4.2 Oxygen: From Encoding to Critical Reflection on the Document

The transition from the analysis of form to that of content marks the beginning of the second phase of the workshop, made possible through the use of a specific tool: Oxygen XML Editor.[17] In this phase, the educational dimension assumes a central role: encoding is no longer understood as a mere act of transcription or textual formalization, but as a cognitive and reflective process in which technical learning becomes an opportunity for critical awareness and methodological growth. Encoding thus ceases to be a purely technical operation. It transforms into an experience of active and collaborative learning, where students come to read the digital structure as an expression of the diplomatic structure of the document.

Oxygen provides a wide range of features and tools for the creation, modification, and publication of XML documents, allowing the application of various encoding schemes that comply with international standards such as TEI. Within the context of the internship, these features were not simply demonstrated but explored in a hands-on manner. Each student was able to directly experiment with the relationship between markup choices and the requirements of diplomatic representation in the register, thereby learning to *read* code as a form of critical interpretation.

This software, now in version 27.1,[18] is not open source but offers a simple and intuitive user interface that makes it accessible to both expert and novice users alike. In addition to enabling XML editing in any schema, such as TEI, or transforming it via XSLT from a pre-structured template, Oxygen allows for collaborative project development. It includes an integrated error validator that suggests the most effective corrections through

[17] *Oxygen,* https://www.oxygenxml.com/xml_editor.html

[18] *Oxygen 27.1, https://www.oxygenxml.com/xml_editor/whats_new.html*

built-in assistance functions. This validation feature was also used as a learning tool: errors were not perceived as failures but as opportunities to understand the logic of the TEI standard and to improve the precision of encoding. Automated checking thus acquired pedagogical value, providing immediate feedback that facilitated students' comprehension of the structural rules governing the XML language. The version used for this work was 24.1,[19] which, compared to earlier releases, introduced several improvements for working with XSLT transformation sheets and XQuery queries, offering a more efficient and powerful experience in handling these languages. These functions were presented to the students not as purely technical aspects but as instruments for understanding the logic of data transformation and the transition between different levels of digital text representation.

Furthermore, to make the software more accessible to less experienced users, general usability enhancements were introduced. Most notably, the *Author* mode was made smoother and easier to use, proving to be an effective aid for visualizing the results of markup choices immediately and intuitively. This function, in fact, provides a snapshot of the ongoing work, a sort of *beta phase* of the output which, in this specific case, corresponds to a draft of the edition that can also be exported as a printable PDF. Within the educational context, this feature carried significant reflective value: seeing their own work take shape made the connection between the logical structure of the code and the final editorial product tangible, enhancing motivation and reinforcing the sense of individual contribution. The current version, 27.1, has improved the user experience of the Oxygen AI Positron Assistant extension.[20] This add-on enables the use of artificial intelligence for tasks such as text revision, translation, and certain forms of automated code annotation. Since an earlier version of the software was used in our project, this feature was not employed; however, it was introduced as a topic for critical discussion on the role of AI in digital diplomatics through a lecture delivered via Teams by Dr. Mario Tartaglia of the San Bonaventura Foundation.[21] This collective reflection focused on how artificial intelligence should be used *ethically* as a tool to support rather than replace human judgment in the encoding of sources. Oxygen thus stands out as one of the most powerful tools for tag management and implementation, offering functionalities that streamline editing and making it a crucial instrument for preparing documents for digital editions. Its introduction into the internship had a dual purpose: to provide participants with applicable technical skills and, at the same time, to foster critical awareness of their own representational choices. The group discussions on the use of tags, the meaning of attributes, and the coherence of encoding transformed each activity into an exercise in methodological reflection, promoting cooperative and interdisciplinary learning.

Having explored the characteristics and potential of this software, we can now turn to how tags are specifically used in accounting registers, highlighting how encoding becomes not merely an act of description but also a means of understanding the economic and social phenomena underlying the documents.

---

[19] *Oxygen 24.1*, https://www.oxygenxml.com/xml_editor/whatisnew24.1.html

[20] *Oxygen AI Positron*, https://www.oxygenxml.com/ai_positron_assistant.html

[21] *San Bonaventura*, https://fondazionesanbonaventura.it/

TEI as a Language for Representing Medieval Accounting Books

The model used during this experience is the result of a customized adaptation of the TEI encoding schema, specifically designed to describe this type of documentation and already employed for this purpose in the course of a doctoral research project. The schema used is that of the bookkeeping ontology,[22] developed at the Institut für Digitale Geisteswissenschaften, Austrian Department of Digital Humanities of the Karl-Franzens-Universität Graz,[23] directed by Professor Georg Vogeler, and freely available in a repository on GitHub.[24] The encoding activity was conceived and conducted with a didactic purpose, as an opportunity to apply, within a guided learning context, the methodological principles of digital diplomatics. Each phase was approached collectively, transforming the technical process into an exercise in critical reflection and scholarly collaboration.

The work presented below was completed collaboratively by the students throughout the entire internship experience. The XML file exported from Transkribus, once opened, was composed of three macro-sections, which were then enriched with all the information necessary for the description of the document and the text. The analysis of this structure became the object of collective exercises aimed at understanding the hierarchical logic of XML language and its application to the description of historical sources (Fig. 2).

```
<?xml version='1.0' encoding='UTF-8'?>
<?xml-model href="http://www.tei-c.org/release/xml/tei/custom/schema/relaxng/tei_all.rng"
type="application/xml" schematypens="http://relaxng.org/ns/structure/1.0"?>
<TEI xmlns='http://www.tei-c.org/ns/1.0'>
    <teiHeader> [166 lines]
     <standOff> [544 lines]
    <facsimile> [2898 lines]
    <text> [2465 lines]
</TEI>
```

Fig. 2. Oxygen – TEI

The first step in producing the edition concerned the drafting of the <teiHeader>,[25] which represents the section containing all the information regarding the source and the electronic document. The compilation of this section was guided step by step through a learning by doing approach, allowing each participant to understand the function of metadata and their importance for transparency and traceability in the editorial process.

The standards of the TEI Consortium establish the structure and compilation criteria of the header. For this XML-based metalanguage, specific guidelines have been developed to ensure coherence and interoperability among digital edition projects.[26] Students were encouraged to compare their encoding choices with these guidelines, gaining awareness of the necessity to adhere to common standards in order to ensure scientific validity and data reusability.

---

22 *Bookkeeping Ontology for Historical Accounts*, https://gams.uni-graz.at/archive/objects/o:depcha.bookkeeping/methods/sdef:Ontology/get

23 *Department of DH*, https://digital-humanities.uni-graz.at/en/

24 *GVogeler*, https://github.com/GVogeler/bookkeeping

25 *<teiHeader>*, https://tei-c.org/release/doc/tei-p5-doc/en/html/ref-teiHeader.html

26 *Tei Guide*, https://tei-c.org/guidelines/

The elements contained in TEI schemas allow for a high degree of customization, enabling adaptation to the specific characteristics of each text or to the needs of the editors. Within it, there are essential and optional modules. The former, which include the header module,[27] textstructure,[28] and core,[29] represent the header of the file containing the information related to the TEI/XML document, the structural elements of the texts, and the descriptive elements common to all types of documentation. The distinction between mandatory and optional modules was used as an opportunity to clarify the difference between structure and content, encouraging a deeper understanding of the relationship between digital representation and the documentary phenomenon.

Through the optional modules, it is then possible to customize the text encoding for the creation of Scholarly Digital Edition that take into account all levels of the document, both diplomatic and critical [33, 44]. In the educational context, this freedom of choice stimulated a project-oriented approach: students learned to justify every encoding decision, making it part of a shared methodological reasoning.

The most recent version of the TEI is version 5 (TEI P5), which also includes a lite version that less experienced users can use.[30] In the TEI P5 version, modules for manuscript description, for the rendering of non-standard characters, and for the encoding of the critical apparatus were introduced. During the internship, the comparative study of these versions offered an opportunity to discuss the principles of data interoperability and sustainability, fundamental topics in Digital Humanities education.

The drafting of a text in XML/TEI, as already mentioned, cannot overlook the composition of the <teiHeader>, which consists of the sub-elements <fileDesc>,[31] <encodingDesc>,[32] and < profileDesc>.[33] Each section was treated as a distinct work module, allowing students to alternate between moments of theoretical explanation and phases of practical exercises (Fig. 3).

<fileDesc>, the only mandatory element among the three mentioned above, contains the complete bibliographic description of the electronic file and was completed through the use of the elements <titleStmt>,[34] <publicationStmt>,[35] and < sourceDesc>.[36] The compilation of these fields was carried out collectively, encouraging reflection on the correct attribution of scholarly roles, the transparency of contributions, and the editorial responsibility within a collaborative project.

The first of these included the project title, the names of the editors, the university that enabled this project, and the names of the final reviewers of the edition. The discussion

---

27 *Organization of the TEI Header,* https://www.tei-c.org/release/doc/tei-p5-doc/en/html/HD.html

28 *Default Text Structure,* https://www.tei-c.org/release/doc/tei-p5-doc/en/html/DS.html

29 *Overview of the Core Module*, https://www.tei-c.org/release/doc/tei-p5-doc/en/html/CO.html#COOV

30 *Tei Lite*, https://tei-c.org/Vault/P5/1.0.1/doc/tei-p4-lite/teiu5_it.html

31 *FileDesc,* https://www.tei-c.org/release/doc/tei-p5-doc/en/html/ref-fileDesc.html

32 *EncodingDesc,* https://tei-c.org/release/doc/tei-p5-doc/de/html/ref-encodingDesc.html

33 *ProfileDesc,* https://www.tei-c.org/release/doc/tei-p5-doc/en/html/ref-profileDesc.html

34 *TitleStmt,* https://www.tei-c.org/release/doc/tei-p5-doc/it/html/ref-titleStmt.html

35 *PublicationStmt,* https://www.tei-c.org/release/doc/tei-p5-doc/it/html/ref-publicationStmt.html

36 *SourceDesc,* https://www.tei-c.org/release/doc/tei-p5-doc/it/html/ref-sourceDesc.html

```
<TEI xmlns='http://www.tei-c.org/ns/1.0'>
    <teiHeader>
        <fileDesc> [82 lines]
        <encodingDesc> [65 lines]
        <profileDesc> [5 lines]
        <revisionDesc> [9 lines]
    </teiHeader>
     <standOff> [544 lines]
    <facsimile> [2898 lines]
    <text> [2465 lines]
</TEI>
```

Fig. 3. Oxygen – teiHeader composition

of these elements promoted a direct understanding of the editorial chain of a digital project and of the value of academic attribution.

The element <publicationStmt> contains the information related to the publication and distribution of the electronic text. Within it, we find, for instance, elements such as <publisher>[37] and < idno>,[38] which allow the unique identification of the publication venue of the edition. This step served as a teaching opportunity to introduce the concepts of persistent identifier, usage license, and open access, all essential aspects of contemporary scientific research.

The third and final element of which <fileDesc> is composed is <sourceDesc>. This allows for a detailed description of the source, which in turn includes the sub-elements <listBibl>[39] and < msDesc>.[40] In this case as well, the workshop approach enabled students to work in small groups, comparing descriptions and verifying the coherence of the data entered.

In <listBibl>, which contains a list of bibliographic citations of any kind, students entered those texts that proved essential for the description of one or more elements of the source. The bibliographic sources were discussed collectively, and students learned to assess secondary sources critically and to select the most relevant bibliographic resources, developing analytical and evaluative skills typical of scholarly research.

In <msDesc>, the intrinsic and extrinsic characteristics that define the type of document and its place of preservation were described. This work fostered observational skills and the translation of material data (support, dimensions, script) into formal encoding elements, reinforcing the connection between palaeographic analysis and digital representation.

---

[37] *Publisher*, https://tei-c.org/release/doc/tei-p5-doc/it/html/ref-publisher.html
[38] *IDNO*, https://tei-c.org/release/doc/tei-p5-doc/en/html/ref-idno.html
[39] *Citation list*, https://tei-c.org/release/doc/tei-p5-doc/en/html/ref-listBibl.html
[40] *Manuscript description*, https://tei-c.org/release/doc/tei-p5-doc/en/html/refmsDesc.html

The <encodingDesc>, which in digital editions corresponds to the definition of editorial criteria in print editions, allows one to define the objectives of the project (projectDesc),[41] the tags used for text description (tagsDecl),[42] the editorial choices made during transcription (editorialDecl),[43] and the definition of taxonomies (classDecl),[44] in this case, those concerning categories of goods or agricultural products. It also allows the definition of a list of URI prefixes for referencing external resources in the TEI document (listPrefixDef),[45] and the declaration of the units of measurement that may be used within the document (unitDecl).[46] Understanding this section enabled students to recognize the importance of editorial documentation as an integral part of the scientific method, and not merely as a technical requirement.

The third element of the <teiHeader> is <profileDesc>, which describes the non-bibliographic aspects of the source, thereby enriching the text. For this edition, it was decided to include the elements <calendarDesc>[47] and < langUsage>[48] to highlight the use of the indictional dating system and the presence of a mixture of Latin, Italian, and Neapolitan vernacular in the source.

Following the header is the element <standOff>.[49] Although not part of the mandatory modules, this element is of fundamental importance when aiming to provide the most complete and detailed edition possible. This element, which in analogue editions corresponds to the indices of notable entities, became the core of collective reflection. Here, students built lists of entities and relationships, learning to manage the complexity of historical data in a structured and interoperable manner. Specifically, indices were created for people, organizations, and places, corresponding respectively to <listPerson>, <listOrg>, and < listPlace>. Students thus found themselves in a real context of shared micro-research, in which constructing the lists required consulting historical sources, toponymic repertoires, and specialized bibliography, leading them to experience a complete investigative process: from observation to verification, and finally to data modelling.

Each group of students took responsibility for a specific list (people, places, or organizations), developing teamwork, coordination, and peer-review skills. The constant exchange with tutors fostered an ongoing methodological dialogue, transforming academic guidance into true scientific mentoring.

Students, for instance, identified certain localities in the Campanian countryside mentioned in the documents that have changed their names over time. This search for

[41] *project description*, https://tei-c.org/release/doc/tei-p5-doc/en/html/refprojectDesc.html

[42] *tagging declaration*, https://tei-c.org/release/doc/tei-p5-doc/en/html/reftagsDecl.html

[43] *editorial practice declaration*, https://tei-c.org/release/doc/tei-p5-doc/en/html/refeditorialDecl.html

[44] *classification declarations*, https://www.tei-c.org/release/doc/tei-p5-doc/en/html/ref-classDecl.html

[45] *list of prefix definitions*, https://tei-c.org/release/doc/tei-p5-doc/en/html/ref-listPrefixDef.html

[46] *unit declarations*, https://tei-c.org/release/doc/tei-p5-doc/it/html/ref-unitDecl.html

[47] *calendar description*, https://www.tei-c.org/release/doc/tei-p5-doc/de/html/ref-calendarDesc.html

[48] *language usage*, https://tei-c.org/release/doc/tei-p5-doc/en/html/ref-langUsage.html

[49] *standOff*, https://tei-c.org/release/doc/tei-p5-doc/en/html/ref-standOff.html

historical correspondences had an extremely high educational value, as it demonstrated that digital analysis cannot exist apart from critical engagement with both territory and sources. Students thus experienced the importance of historical geography and toponymy in constructing coherent datasets, and they came to understand the dynamic and historical dimension of data itself.

Each entity within the <standOff> was assigned a unique xml:id, which allowed the linking of each specific person, place, or organization to the corresponding element within the text. Constructing these connections made clear to students the value of semantic relationships, showing how digital encoding makes possible a networked representation of historical knowledge (Fig. 4).

```
<TEI xmlns='http://www.tei-c.org/ns/1.0'>
    <teiHeader> [166 lines]
    <standOff>
      <listPerson ana="depcha:index"> [381 lines]
      <listPlace ana="depcha:index"> [153 lines]
      <listOrg ana="depcha:index"> [6 lines]
   </standOff>
    <facsimile> [2898 lines]
    <text> [2465 lines]
</TEI>
```

Fig. 4. Oxygen – standoff composition

Before the <text> element, which contains the transcription, there is the <facsimile> element,[50] which allows each encoded folio of the register to correspond to its respective image. When exporting data from Transkribus to XML, the software assigned each <surface> element – that is, each subdivision of <facsimile> – a unique xml:id that allows this element to be recalled within the text through the @facs attribute (Fig. 5).

```
<TEI xmlns='http://www.tei-c.org/ns/1.0'>
    <teiHeader> [166 lines]
     <standOff> [544 lines]
    <facsimile>
        <surface xml:id='facs_1' ulx='0' uly='0' lrx='919' lry='1235'> [5 lines]
        <surface xml:id='facs_2' ulx='0' uly='0' lrx='933' lry='1226'> [23 lines]
        <surface xml:id='facs_3' ulx='0' uly='0' lrx='880' lry='1220'> [5 lines]
        <surface xml:id='facs_4' ulx='0' uly='0' lrx='925' lry='1258'> [5 lines]
        <surface xml:id='facs_5' ulx='0' uly='0' lrx='915' lry='1322'> [26 lines]
```

Fig. 5. Oxygen – facsimile composition

50 *Facsimile*, https://tei-c.org/release/doc/tei-p5-doc/en/html/ref-facsimile.html

The XML file thus concludes with the <text> module, in which the transcription was enriched with all the <tags> necessary to highlight the key aspects of the source examined in this work. The discussion on tagging practices allowed for the development of a shared vocabulary and encouraged a critical approach to data categorization, transforming encoding into a proper exercise in collective interpretation.

The tags employed for the encoding were the following:

- <persName>, used to identify personal names;
- <placeName>, to indicate both micro and macro toponyms;
- <orgName>, for the names of organizations;
- <measure>/<measureGrp>, to mark economic elements such as coins and goods;
- <seg>, to highlight specific diplomatic aspects;
- <date>, for the chronological date;
- <div>, to divide the text into sections;
- <head>, used in conjunction with <div> to identify section titles;
- <note>, to separate marginalia from the main text and to insert editorial elements;
- <term>, to identify different agricultural products;
- <del>, used to mark erasures and deletions; <p>, for paragraphs.

Each tag employed, except for <div>, <head>, and < del>, is accompanied by attributes that further specify its function. Attributes, in fact, play a central role within the bookkeeping ontology, as depending on the tag to which they are attached, they allow for the specification of the role of a person, organization, or place in relation to the economic action described. The joint analysis of tags and their corresponding attributes encouraged in students a deep understanding of the ontological logic of the model, showing how encoding can become a representational language for medieval economic dynamics (Fig. 6).

The application phase of these tags constituted one of the most significant moments from a pedagogical perspective: each element was discussed, tested, and verified collectively, within a cooperative learning process that transformed encoding into a genuine exercise in shared interpretation of the document. Students learned not only to recognize the formal structures of the source but also to translate them into a coherent and interoperable digital language.

The entire process described was the subject of a collective concluding reflection during the *lectio magistralis* delivered by Professor Georg Vogeler at the State Archives of Naples, where the register under study is preserved.[51] The meeting offered an opportunity to critically reconsider the work carried out, highlighting both the scholarly and educational dimensions of the project and reinforcing the dialogue between traditional diplomatics and digital methodologies. From this moment of synthesis emerged the subsequent phase of experimentation with FRAT, a tool designed to deepen the paleographic and graphemic observation of documents, thereby continuing the trajectory of laboratory-based learning.

[51] *Lectio Magistralis Vogeler*, https://www.coop-unina.org/wp-content/uploads/2022/02/Naples-and-online_May-4–2024.pdf

```
<div>
    <head facs="#facs_5_region_1713208876523_145">
        <lb facs="#facs_5_line_1713208881089_148" n="N001"/><seg type="invocatio"
            >Ihesus</seg>
    </head>
    <p facs="#facs_5_region_1713208915508_163" ana="bk:entry bk:debit">
        <lb facs="#facs_5_line_1713208938157_168" n="N001"/><seg ana="bk:from"><persName
                ref="#p1">Carolo Capone</persName> et <rs ref="p2">fratelli</rs></seg>
        teneno le infrascripte terre videlicet moya <lb
            facs="#facs_5_line_1713208947035_173" n="N002"/>dui et meczo più o mino sita
        et positi illo casale nostro de <lb facs="#facs_5_line_1713208952578_178"
            n="N003"/><placeName ref="#San_Nicandro">Sancto Nicandro</placeName> dove se
        dice allo <placeName ref="#Russo">Russo</placeName> et più teneno li supra <lb
            facs="#facs_5_line_1713208956176_183" n="N004"/>dicti uno altro peczo de
        terra de moya dui più o mino alo <lb facs="#facs_5_line_1713208959637_188"
            n="N005"/>supradicto casale iusta li altri boni de lo nostro monasterio dove
            <lb facs="#facs_5_line_1713208962038_193" n="N006"/>se dice alla <placeName
            ref="#Pissina">Pissina</placeName> le quale terre teneno li supradicti ad re
            <lb facs="#facs_5_line_1713208977117_198" n="N007"/>ndito et pagano per anno
                <measureGrp><measure ana="bk:money" quantity="0" unitRef="#duc."
                >duc.</measure>
            <measure ana="bk:money" quantity="2" unitRef="#tr.">tr. 2</measure>
            <measure ana="bk:money" quantity="10" unitRef="#gr.">gr.
            10</measure></measureGrp>
```

Fig. 6. Oxygen – Text with part of the tags

4.3 FRAT - (F)ast (R)ectangle (A)nnotation (T)ool[52]

Within the same internship program dedicated to the digital edition of the accounting registers of the monastery of SS. Pietro e Sebastiano in Naples, a second line of research was developed, focused on the palaeographic and graphemic analysis of the scribal hands [8]. The educational goal was to provide students with an approach complementary to the one already explored through Oxygen: whereas TEI encoding had promoted the structural and semantic understanding of the document, the use of FRAT aimed to bring out its material and scriptural dimension. The activity thus made it possible to combine diplomatic practice, palaeographic observation, and digital skills, offering students an integrated vision of editorial and research work.

FRAT (Fast Rectangle Annotation Tool) is a lightweight image annotation software developed by Anguelos Nicolaou (University of Graz). It is a web-based tool, written in Python and JavaScript, available for Linux and Mac OS X, and usable in a Windows environment through Docker. The file format is based on JSON, and the user interface (UI) is lightweight, fast, and intuitive, making it suitable even for users without advanced technical expertise [26]. FRAT enables users to focus on the scientific content of annotation rather than on technical aspects, providing an immediate and accessible working environment. Through simple rectangles and predefined classes, students can select text

52 The author wishes to express his gratitude to Desire Di Donato, currently a graduate student in the Master's Degree Program in Historical Sciences, for creating the images included in this paragraph. The images were produced as part of her internship activities, which later formed the basis of her master's thesis entitled *"I registri del monastero femminile domenicano dei SS. Pietro e Sebastiano di Napoli del XV secolo. Il digital turn nell'approccio paleografico ai documenti storici a carattere amministrativo e contabile attraverso il software FRAT"* (tutor: prof.ssa Antonella Ambrosio).

portions, associate transcriptions or comments, and create datasets to be used for the study of handwriting and, potentially, for training machine learning models. The use of the software was therefore conceived as a starting point for a shared palaeographic study, aimed at investigating the different scribal hands found in the registers and creating an initial sample of annotated digital data. The work combined practical exercises and scholarly research: each annotation was discussed with the tutors and collectively verified, turning the activity into a workshop of discussion and critical validation.

Since FRAT operates directly on images, the quality of the source material proved decisive both for the scientific precision and for the educational success of the project. The digitization of the registers was carried out through collaboration between the State Archives of Naples and the Photographic Laboratory of the Department of Humanities at the University of Naples "Federico II".[53] This partnership offered students the opportunity to learn about the technical stages of digitization and to understand the link between archival photography and humanistic research.

After obtaining authorization from the Archives, the operations were carried out at a carefully prepared workstation, which was also used as a teaching opportunity to raise awareness among participants about the correct handling of original materials. The register was placed on a black background, covered with protective glass, and illuminated under controlled lighting conditions to ensure chromatic uniformity and sharpness. The photographs were taken with a Nikon D850 camera. At the same time, post-production and data acquisition were managed using the METIS EDS GAMMA A1 planetary scanner, which allows for manual corrections and precise image sequencing. Each digitized register was organized into a dedicated folder, named according to the year and type of register (e.g., 1398_00001, 1398_00046, etc.), with a progressive numbering independent of the original foliation. No additional elements such as loose sheets, notes, receipts, or later inserts were excluded, as their presence represents an important object of study and a valuable pedagogical reflection on the concept of the "complex document" [9, 10, 43] (Fig. 7).

Fig. 7. Example of viewing images in a folder

[53] *Laboratorio foto/grafico – Studi Umanistici,* https://www.studiumanistici.unina.it/dipartimento/strutture-dipartimento/laboratori-e-archivi/laboratorio-fotografico/

The images thus produced, in TIF format, constitute a high-resolution digital archive that can be used for subsequent analyses. Once the digitization process was completed, the students were able to work directly with FRAT in an Ubuntu environment, which had been installed to ensure full software compatibility. The students engaged in the FRAT activity were provided with a practical guide that enabled them to operate autonomously throughout the work process. In fact, after installation, it is necessary to open the Ubuntu terminal and type the command *cd frat* (Fig. 8).

Fig. 8. Ubuntu Terminal

This command allows the user to open the folder containing the program. Subsequently, still within the terminal, one can paste the "folder path" where the previously digitized images have been saved. At that point, the system automatically loads the images and generates a link that can be copied and pasted into the Google Chrome browser (Fig. 9).

The FRAT interface displays, at the top, a numbered list of images and, in the center, the working area. By selecting a page, users can begin annotation by drawing rectangles ("TextBlocks") over the lines of text. Each rectangle identifies a possible scribal hand (Figs. 10, 11, 12).

The annotation work had a dual purpose:

- scientific, as it enables the creation of datasets for training algorithms for automatic handwriting recognition;
- educational, as it stimulates observation skills and the ability to distinguish different hands through direct engagement with the digital image.

Each rectangle was labeled according to a shared convention consisting of four elements:

- the number of the register,
- the indication M or F (male/female),

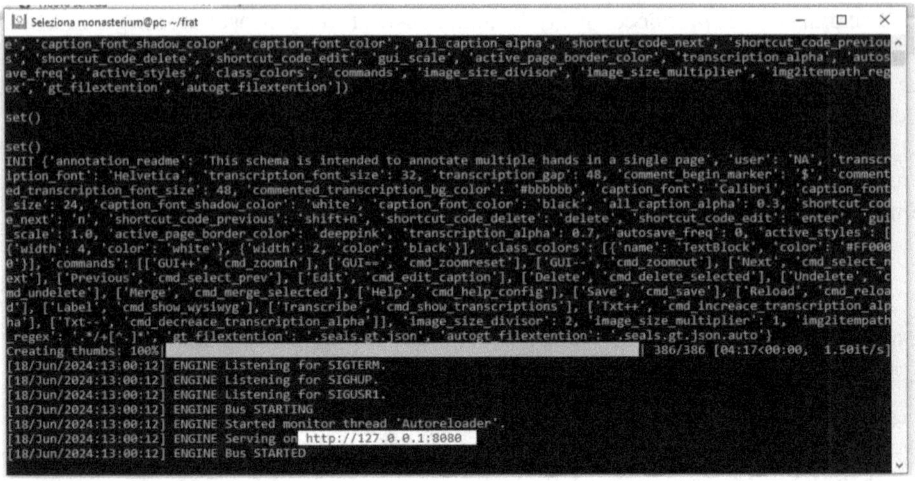

Fig. 9. Ubuntu terminal - Images correctly loaded in FRAT - Link view

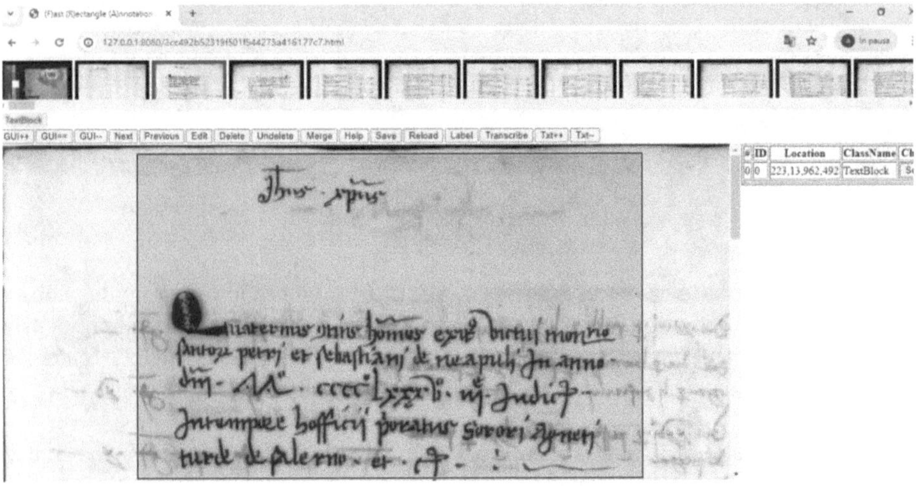

Fig. 10. FRAT -Text Block creation

- the abbreviation H for "hand,"
- and a progressive capital letter (A, B, C …).

For example, the first female hand in the 1401 register was annotated as "1401_FHA."

This system made the process clear and replicable, strengthening participants' awareness of the importance of data standardization and methodological rigor.

During the laboratory sessions, each annotation was discussed collectively in order to minimize errors and harmonize evaluation criteria. The ongoing interaction among tutors, doctoral students, and participants transformed the work into a process of peer learning, in which assessment was reflective rather than punitive.

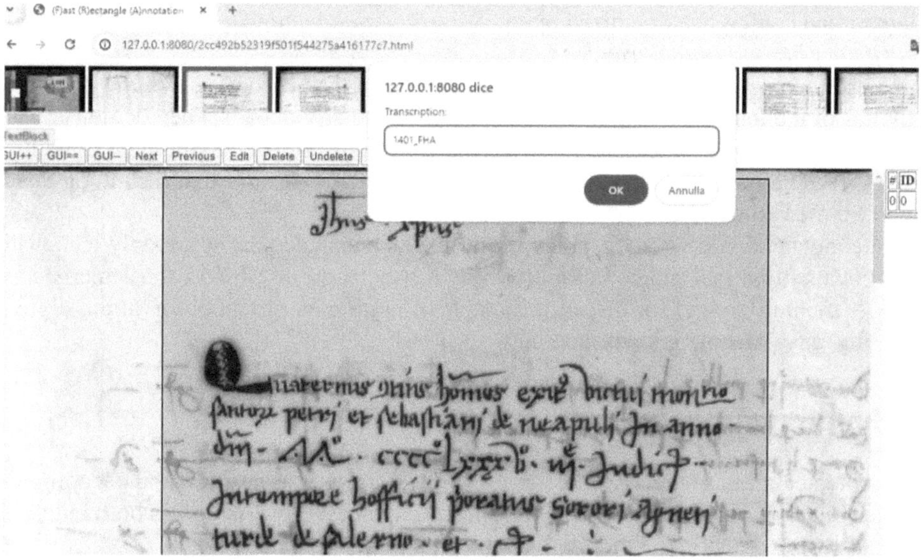

Fig. 11. FRAT - Insert Metadata

Fig. 12. FRAT - Metadata Visualization

The preliminary results of this experimentation were presented at the International Medieval Congress (IMC) in Leeds, in a paper entitled *Learning to Write in Medieval Female Monasteries: An Interdisciplinary Study of SS. Pietro e Sebastiano in Naples, Italy.*[54] The experience was also discussed in a seminar series at the University of Naples "Federico II," entitled *Can automatic methods hint the gender of unknown scribes in Neapolitan monasteries?*, attended by the software's author, Anguelos Nicolaou, and in a panel session entitled *Hands that Matter. Unveiling, Identifying, and Studying Female Writing in the European Late Middle Ages* (coordinator: Antonella Ambrosio) during the

[54] *IMC*, https://imc-leeds.confex.com/imc/2025/meetingapp.cgi/Paper/12169

International conference organized by the *Società italiana delle Storiche* (SIS), *Gender and History beyond Boundaries.*[55]

These moments of exchange had great educational value: they placed the practical activities of the internship within an international scholarly debate. They demonstrated to students that digital research is now an integral part of historical and palaeographic inquiry. From a pedagogical standpoint, the use of FRAT showed that technology can become a mediator of learning.

To annotate, discuss, verify, and present results meant acquiring not only technical skills but also a critical and collaborative research methodology. FRAT thus emerged as a proper training ground for research, capable of uniting empirical observation, digital modeling, and palaeographic reflection.

5 Results and Pedagogical Impact

The implementation of the digital edition workflow, from transcription and encoding in Oxygen to graphical annotation in FRAT, produced measurable outcomes both in terms of skills acquired and in the quality of the digital objects created.

Students completed the encoding and validation of multiple folios, produced structured metadata compliant with the TEI standard, and contributed to the construction of lists of entities within the standOff section (persons, places, and organizations).

On the quantitative level, assessment rubrics documented a steady improvement across the primary evaluation criteria, such as the accuracy of transcription, markup consistency, semantic tagging, and validation autonomy. Each validation cycle corresponded to a visible decrease in technical errors and an increase in collaborative problem-solving capacity. However, the most relevant results emerged on the qualitative and pedagogical level. The progressive mastering of the TEI vocabulary and the ability to justify encoding choices marked a shift from procedural competence to reflective awareness.

Through continuous feedback and tutor-guided review, students developed an understanding that digital representation is not a neutral operation but a scholarly interpretation of the source (Fig. 13).

Learning, therefore, moved from execution to conceptualization: the act of encoding, annotation, and validation became an instrument for reasoning about the structure of medieval documents, their transmission, and their material features. This process reinforced key educational dimensions such as collaboration and peer learning. Participants developed cross-cutting skills for research and communication, from transcription to XML coding, workflow management, and open access publishing. The final edition, soon to be published on the DEPCHA infrastructure, will turn the educational experience into a concrete act of scholarly dissemination.

5.1 DEPCHA

The final phase of the training pathway was devoted to preparing the digital edition for integration into DEPCHA (Digital Edition Publishing Cooperative for Historical

[55] *Panel Session,* https://societadellestoriche.it/wp-content/uploads/2024/06/Abstract-degli-interventi.pdf

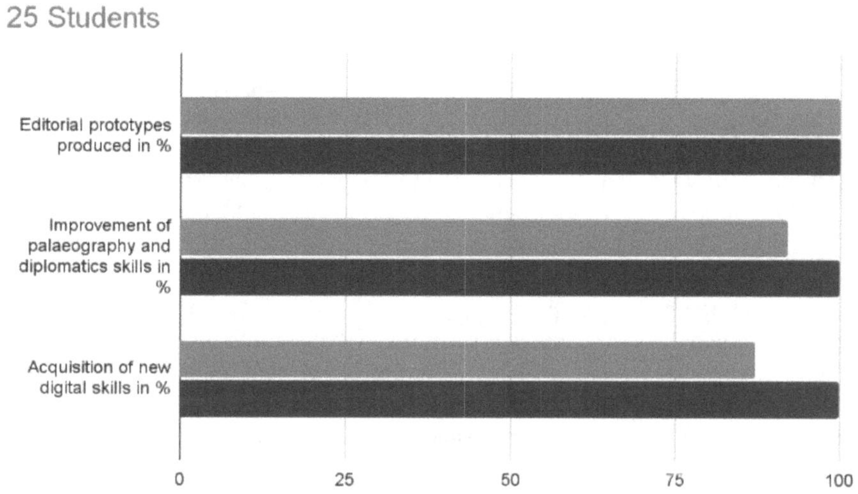

Fig. 13. Summary of experience in data

Accounts), a publishing infrastructure hosted on the GAMS platform at the Department of Digital Humanities, University of Graz.

Developed by Georg Vogeler and Christopher Pollin, DEPCHA extends the Bookkeeping Ontology to support the semantic description and publication of medieval and early modern accounting records. It enables the encoding, visualization, and querying of documents through interoperable standards such as TEI-XML and RDF, providing a shared environment for research on administrative and financial sources. In the context of this project, the DEPCHA phase did not yet result in a public release of the edition, which is currently under revision and internal validation. However, its inclusion in the workflow marked an essential pedagogical step, transforming the conclusion of the internship into a simulation of a real editorial process.

Students learned to prepare XML packages for submission, to validate metadata and file structures, and to document encoding practices according to DEPCHA's publication standards. Through this activity, they experienced the editorial dimension of digital scholarship, understanding how a digital edition progresses from a local dataset to an interoperable, reusable scholarly resource [29, 30].

Pedagogically, this phase served as a bridge between learning and dissemination.

While the edition remains in revision, the process of aligning the project with DEPCHA's ontology and technical requirements fostered reflective awareness and a sense of scholarly responsibility.

The project also strengthened cooperation between the Universities of Naples and Graz. Although rooted in the historical-documentary field, the model is transferable to other corpora, such as notarial records, administrative documentation, or literary sources in digital philological editions. The experience highlights the educational potential of a blended, feedback-based approach that combines archival and philological dimensions with digital tools. Preserving the centrality of sources and student authorship, it fosters an active, participatory, and conscious learning model.

6 Conclusion

This experience demonstrates that teaching can become living research and that digital tools, when framed within a constructivist and collaborative model, can generate authentic scholarly outcomes. Throughout the process, from transcription and layout analysis in Transkribus, through semantic encoding in Oxygen, to palaeographic annotation in FRAT, and the preparation of the digital edition for DEPCHA, students were not passive recipients of knowledge but active co-authors in a genuine editorial and interpretive enterprise [20]. The historical sources remained at the center of the process, yet the way of engaging with them changed profoundly.

Students learned that every technical operation, whether defining a text region, choosing a tag, or annotating a hand, is also an interpretive act that requires justification and transparency. In doing so, they moved from procedural learning to reflective understanding and from individual exercises to a shared form of knowledge creation. Learning became research, and the classroom became a scholarly workshop where the logic of palaeography and diplomatics met the logic of markup and data modeling. The educational value of this pathway lies not only in the acquisition of digital skills but in the development of meta-competences such as critical reasoning, teamwork, and awareness of how scholarly knowledge is constructed, validated, and disseminated. The integration of feedback cycles, peer review, and documentation practices fostered a culture of openness and reproducibility that aligns with the principles of open science. The collaboration between the Universities of Naples and Graz further demonstrated that such a model is both scalable and transferable, providing a bridge between local academic training and the international research ecosystem fostered by ICARUS and its infrastructures. The outcomes suggest that the Scholarly Digital Edition can serve simultaneously as a research object, a pedagogical device, and a training environment for critical thinking. Students learned to act as editors, researchers, and responsible users of digital heritage, understanding that the digital representation of a source is not a copy but a critical model, open to revision and dialogue.

Thus, the educational process mirrored the scholarly one, both cyclical, collaborative, and cumulative. This model, tested within the fields of palaeography and diplomatics, can be extended to other domains that deal with complex textual and visual sources, such as notarial, administrative, literary, or artistic materials, and even to the broader field of digital civic education. Its reproducibility lies in its simplicity: observe, encode, share, and reflect. In this way, students not only learn to read medieval documents but also to build knowledge together with scientific rigor, methodological transparency, and an international perspective.

This approach redefines the relationship between teaching, research, and technology. By preserving the centrality of sources and student authorship, it turns education into an act of scholarship and scholarship into a collective act of learning [19].

Through this dialogue, both the discipline and its new generations gain renewed vitality, as hands that count online become minds that think together.

Disclosure of Interests. The authors have no competing interests to declare that are relevant to the content of this article.

References

1. Ambrosio, A., Schwarz-Ricci, V.I.: Un'esperienza al di fuori di EVT. L'edizione digitale dei documenti dell'abbazia di S. Maria della Grotta sul portale internazionale Monasterium.Net. In: Fonti archivistiche medievali nel digitale. La sfida di trattare e visualizzare dati semi-strutturati, Umanistica Digitale. **10**, 359–371 (2021) ISSN 2532–8816
2. Ambrosio, A.: La Diplomatica e il digitale. Il Fondo della Biblioteca della Società Napoletana di Storia Patria online. In: Research Trends in Humanities Education & Philosophy, pp. 1–15 (2020) ISSN 2284–0184. http://www.serena.unina.it/index.php/rth/article/view/8912
3. Ambrosio, A.: Can online European documents be a valuable resource for the informal learning of adults? The cases of the Monasterium.Net and Topotheque portals in the coop project. In: Research Trends in Humanities Education & Philosophy 6, Quaderno Think Tank Immersive University Education, a cura di F. Santoianni, pp. 22–30. ISSN 2284–0184 (2019). http://www.serena.unina.it/index.php/rth/article/view/6016
4. Ambrosio, A.: Digital critical editions of medieval documents on monasterium.Net. In: Balouzat-Loubet, C. (ed.) Digitizing Medieval Sources. L'édition en ligne de documents d'archives médiévaux. Challenges and Methodologies. Enjeux, méthodologie et défis, Atelier de recherche sur les textes médiévaux (ARTEM) 27, pp. 69–84. Brepols Publishers, Turnhout (2020) ISBN 978-2-503-58413-3
5. Ambrosio, A.: L'edizione critica digitale dei documenti medievali. Le forme degli atti di Octavianus notarius. In: Figliuolo, B., Di Meglio, R., Ambrosio, A. (eds.) Ingenita curiositas. Studi sull'Italia medievale per Giovanni Vitolo, vol. 3, pp. 1153–1173. Laveglia & Carlone, Battipaglia. ISBN 978-88-86854-68-9 (2018)
6. Ambrosio, A.: Insegnare la diplomatica con le tecnologie digitali. Potenzialità e spunti di riflessione. In: Cherubini, P., Nicolaj, G. (eds.) Sit liber gratus, quem servulus est operatus. Studi in onore di Alessandro Pratesi per il suo 90° compleanno, Littera Antiqua 19, pp. 1315–1326. Scuola Vaticana di Paleografia, Diplomatica e Archivistica, Città del Vaticano (2012). ISBN 978–88–85054-25-7
7. Ambrosio, A.: Towards the creation of a learning environment within the Monasterium project: teaching experiences of diplomatics. In: Aigner, T., Hoenbruck, S., Just, T., Kemper, J. (eds.) Archive im Web. Erfahrungen, Herausforderungen, Forderungen, Visionen / Archives on the Web. Experiences, Challenges, Visions, vol. 1, pp. 202–214. Medieninhaber und Herausgeber Diözesanarchiv St. Pölten / St. Pölten Episcopal Archives, St. Pölten (2011). ISBN 978-3-901863-39-4
8. Ambrosio, A.: Literacy in Neapolitan Women's convents: an example of female handwriting in a late fifteenth-century accounts ledger. In: Blanton, V., O'Mara, V., Stoop, P. (eds.) Nuns' Literacies in Medieval Europe. The Kansas City Dialogue, pp. 88–108, Brepols, Turnhout (2015) (Medieval Women: Texts and Contexts, 27)
9. Ambrosio, A.: Alla rota. Scrivere e documentare il quotidiano in un monastero femminile a Napoli, dal foglio di un registro d'archivio al Web semantico. In: Pogliani, P., Rava, E. (eds.) Microstorie e storie di vita quotidiana nei monasteri di clausura femminili (XV–XIX secc.), pp. 85–92. Edizioni di Storia e Letteratura, Roma (2023) (Temi e testi – Donne e culture)
10. Ambrosio, A., Consolo, G.: Dai registri medievali alle tecnologie digitali: un'edizione critica per nuove prospettive di ricerca. In: Atti del convegno "Topografia delle attività economiche nelle città campane del basso Medioevo" Napoli, 4–5 aprile, in stampa (2024)
11. Bereiter, C.: Education and Mind in the Knowledge Age. Lawrence Erlbaum Associates, Mahwah, NJ (2002)
12. Bookkeeping Ontology for Historical Accounts, https://gams.uni-graz.at/archive/objects/o:depcha.bookkeeping/methods/sdef:Ontology/get, last Accessed 2025/10

13. Consolo, G.: La digitalizzazione dei registri del monastero dei SS. Pietro e Sebastiano: identità e memoria attraverso l'edizione digitale. In: I Convegno internazionale dei dottorandi e dottori di ricerca, Tracce d'identità: espressioni, manipolazioni e persistenze dall'Antichità all'Età contemporanea, in stampa
14. Consolo, G.: L'edizione critica digitale della documentazione del monastero dei SS. Pietro e Sebastiano di Napoli nel medioevo. PhD Thesis, Università degli Studi di Napoli Federico II, Dottorato di ricerca in Scienze Storiche, Archeologiche e Storico-Artistiche (XXXVII ciclo), pp. 9–13, notes 7–16 (2025)
15. Carey, S.: Conceptual Change in Childhood. MIT Press, Cambridge, MA (1985)
16. Carey, S., Gelman, R. (eds.): The Epigenesis of Mind: Essays on Biology and Cognition. Lawrence Erlbaum Associates, Hillsdale, NJ (1991)
17. Carletti, A., Varani, A.: Didattica costruttivista. Erickson, Trento (2005)
18. DEPCHA, https://gams.uni-graz.at/context:depcha, last Accessed 10 2025
19. Forino, G.: La prof.ssa Ambrosio: per gli studenti "un percorso formativo stimolante". Atenapoli 8, p. 19 (2024). https://ateneapoli.it/atenei/federico-ii/la-prof-ssa-ambrosio-per-gli-studenti-un-percorso-formativo-stimolante/, last Accessed 26 May 2025
20. Forino, G.: Digitalizzazione degli archivi e valorizzazione del patrimonio culturale: gli studenti partecipano alla convention di Icarus. Atenapoli. **17**, 19 (2024)
21. FRAT, https://github.com/anguelos/frat, last Accessed 10 2025
22. Gopnik, A., Meltzoff, A.N.: Costruire il mondo Una teoria dello sviluppo cognitivo. McGraw-Hill, Milano (2000)
23. Kahle, P., Colutto, S., Hackl, G., Mühlberger, G.: Transkribus – a service platform for transcription, recognition and retrieval of historical documents. In: Proceedings of the 14th IAPR International Conference on Document Analysis and Recognition (ICDAR 2017), pp. 19–24. IEEE, Kyoto (2017)
24. Mancinelli, T., Pierazzo, E.: Che cos'è un'edizione scientifica digitale. Carocci, Roma (2021)
25. Muehlberger, G., et al.: Transforming scholarship in the archives through handwritten text recognition: Transkribus as a case study. J. Doc. **75**(5), 954–976 (2019). https://doi.org/10.1108/JD-07-2018-0114
26. Nicolaou, A., Luger, D., Decker, F., Renet, N., Christlein, V., Vogeler, G.: Efficient Annotation of Medieval Charters. arXiv preprint (2023). https://arxiv.org/abs/2306.14071
27. Oxygen, https://www.oxygenxml.com/xml_editor.html, last Accessed 10 2025
28. Piaget, J.: Lo sviluppo mentale del bambino. Einaudi, Torino (1967)
29. Pollin, C., Vogeler, G.: Semantically Enriched Historical Data. Drawing on the Example of the Digital Edition of the "Urfehdebücher der Stadt Basel". Presented at the 2nd Workshop on Humanities in the Semantic Web (WHiSe 2017) (2017)
30. Pollin, C.: Digital edition publishing cooperative for historical accounts and the bookkeeping ontology. In: Riechert, T., Beretta, F., Bruseker, G. (eds.) RODBH 2019, Proceedings of the Doctoral Symposium on Research on Online Databases in History 2019, vol. 2019, pp. 7–14
31. Retallick, J., Cocklin, B., Coombe, K. (eds.): Learning Communities in Education: Issues. Strategies and Contexts. Routledge, London (1999)
32. Rogoff, B., Turkanis, C.G., Bartlett, L. (eds.): Learning Together: Children and Adults in a School Community. Oxford University Press, Oxford (2003)
33. Sahle, P.: Digitale Editionsformen. Zum Umgang mit der Überlieferung unter den Bedingungen des Medienwandels, pp. 45–81. BoD, Norderstedt (2013)
34. San Bonaventura, https://fondazionesanbonaventura.it/, last Accessed 10 2025
35. Sánchez, J.A., Bosch, V., Romero, V., et al.: Handwritten text recognition for historical documents in the Transcriptorium project. In: Proceedings of the First International Conference on Digital Access to Textual Cultural Heritage (DATeCH '14), pp. 111–117 (2014) https://cordis.europa.eu/project/id/600707

36. Santoianni, F.: Modelli e strumenti di insegnamento. Carocci, Roma (2010)
37. SS. Pietro e Sebastiano Monastery project, https://www.coop-unina.org/ss-pietro-e-sebastiano-monastery-project/, last Accessed 10 2025
38. Stuermer, M., Abu-Tayeh, G., Myrach, T.: Digital sustainability: basic conditions for sustainable digital artifacts and their ecosystems. Sustain. Sci. **12**(2), 247–262 (2017)
39. TEI, https://tei-c.org/, last Accessed 10 2025
40. Terras, M., et al.: READ-COOP and Transkribus: A Cooperative Model for Responsible Technology. Poster presented at Digital Humanities Benelux, Amsterdam, Netherlands (2025). https://www.research.ed.ac.uk/en/publications/read-coop-and-transkribus-a-cooperative-model-for-responsible-tec
41. Terras, M., Anzinger, B., Gooding, P., et al.: The artificial intelligence cooperative: READ-COOP, Transkribus, and the benefits of shared community infrastructure for automated text recognition. [version 2; peer review: 1 approved with reservations, 1 not approved]. Open Res. Europe. **5**, 16 (2025). https://doi.org/10.12688/openreseurope.18747.2
42. Transkribus AI Text Recognition Homepage. https://www.transkribus.org/ai-text-recognition, last accessed 2025/10
43. Vogeler, G.: The content of accounts and registers in their digital edition. XML/TEI, spreadsheets, and semantic web technologies. In: Sarnowsky, J. (ed.) Konzeptionelle Überlegungen zur Edition von Rechnungen und Amtsbüchern des späten Mittelalters, pp. 13–42. V&R Unipress, Göttingen (2016)
44. Vogeler, G.: Die konzentrische Edition. Auswertungspotentiale von digitaler Tiefenerschließung und Proto-Editionen. In: Vogeler, G., Kolnberger, T., Kraxner, M. (eds.) Digitale Methoden in der Geschichtswissenschaft. Eine Standortbestimmung, pp. 63–86. Böhlau, Köln–Wien–Weimar. (Historisch-kulturwissenschaftliche Kommunikationsforschung) (2025)
45. Vukčević, M.: The Transkribus automated tool for recognition, transcription and translation of handwritten historical documents. Babel. **66**(2), 294–310 (2020)
46. Wenger, E.: Communities of Practice: Learning, Meaning, and Identity. Cambridge University Press, Cambridge (1998)
47. Wenger, E., McDermott, R., Snyder, W.M.: Cultivating Communities of Practice: a Guide to Managing Knowledge. Harvard Business School Press, Boston, MA (2002)

Educator as Co-pilot: Advancing Presentation Training with Teacher-Guided Systems

Daniele Di Mitri[1,2(✉)] and Talha Burak Onat[3]

[1] German University of Digital Science, Potsdam, Germany
daniele.dimitri@german-uds.de
[2] DIPF | Leibniz Institute for Research and Information in Education, Frankfurt/Main, Germany
[3] Goethe University Frankfurt, Frankfurt/Main, Germany
s0577804@stud.uni-frankfurt.de

Abstract. This study addresses the limitations of current presentation training software, which provide automated, multimodal feedback on presentation skills but often exclude teachers from the feedback process. We designed, implemented, and evaluated a teacher-driven feedback feature for Presentable, a new web-based presentation training software. The teacher-driven feedback feature enables educators to supplement automated analytics with contextual, actionable feedback. The tool supports rich text comments, feedback templates, timestamped and transcript-linked annotations, and automated feedback validation. A qualitative study with teachers and tutors found the tool intuitive and effective, highlighting the value of structured, dialogic feedback alongside AI - generated feedback. The results of this study reinforce the idea that integrating teacher-driven feedback in AI-driven tutors can enhance the quality and pedagogical impact of presentation training software, supporting more meaningful learning experiences and closing the feedback loop between students and instructors.

Keywords: teacher-driven feedback · multimodal learning analytics · presentation training software · educational technology · formative assessment · AI-based feedback

1 Introduction

The ability to communicate effectively is a cornerstone of modern education and professional development. Together with creativity, critical thinking, and collaboration, it is recognised as one of the essential "4 Cs" for twenty-first-century skills and a fundamental competence required by professionals [25]. In educational contexts, oral presentation skills form a key component of effective communication and are best developed through frequent practice and the provision of meaningful feedback [26]. Feedback plays a crucial role in learning by

M. Adamoli et al. (Eds.): HELMeTO 2025, CCIS 2958, pp. 456–472, 2026.
https://doi.org/10.1007/978-3-032-31850-3_28

helping students identify mistakes, understand their causes, and improve their future performance [7].

In the context of oral presentation skills training, advances in educational technology have led to the emergence of presentation training software systems, technically known as *Oral Presentation Automated Feedback* systems (OPAFs), that capture, analyse, and evaluate multimodal data such as speech, body language, and visual focus to generate performance feedback for presenters [18]. These systems enable students to rehearse on their own and receive immediate automated insights into their presentation performance. However, while automation supports self-paced and repeated practice, OPAFs often exclude the valuable pedagogical input of teachers, thereby limiting opportunities for personalised and dialogic feedback [22].

This gap highlights the need for a teacher-driven feedback mechanism that complements automated feedback with human judgment and pedagogical expertise. A teacher-driven feedback system can strengthen students' learning experiences by allowing instructors to deliver personalised, targeted comments and by enabling students to ask follow-up questions, ensuring that the feedback is understood and acted upon [16,24]. Such two-way interaction not only enhances student engagement but can also increase motivation and learning outcomes [6]. Considering that teachers typically have limited time to provide extensive individual feedback [13], the design of such a system must prioritise efficiency, clarity, and usability while maintaining feedback quality [2].

The work presented in this study extends an existing presentation training tool named *Presentable* [4], a web-based software application that provides automated feedback on users' oral presentation rehearsals, focusing on both non-verbal and verbal communication. While *Presentable* currently offers automated analysis and a teacher dashboard for data management, at the time this research was conducted, it lacked mechanisms for teachers to actively engage with student presentations. To address this limitation, two new features were investigated: (1) *teacher-driven feedback* component that allows instructors to add personalised comments and guidance, and (2) a *validation feature* that enables instructors to validate or reject automated feedback, ensuring that incorrect feedback messages are properly marked to the users.

The study described in paper aimed therefore to design, implement, and evaluate a teacher-driven feedback system to enhance the overall quality and pedagogical value of automated feedback in presentation training contexts. The study was driven by the following central research question:

How can a teacher-driven feedback system be effectively integrated into presentation training software to enhance the quality and efficiency of feedback provision?

To address this question, three sub-questions were formulated:

RQ1 *What core functionalities are required to enable teachers to provide contextual and personalised feedback?*

RQ2 *How should these functionalities be designed to support usability, clarity, time efficiency, and pedagogical effectiveness?*
RQ3 *How should feedback data be structured and integrated into the software architecture?*

This paper is structured as follows. Section 2 reviews related work on automated feedback systems and teacher involvement in presentation training. Section 3 details the methodology and technical implementation of the teacher-driven feedback system. Section 4 presents the evaluation results based on interview data from educators. Section 5 discusses the findings, limitations, and implications for future development. Section 6 provides concluding remarks and highlights directions for further research and feature expansion.

2 Background

2.1 Presentation Training Software

In recent years, presentation training systems, often referred to as *Oral Presentation Automated Feedback* systems (OPAFs), have become an important application area within the educational technologies and learning analytics research fields. Their goal is to support the acquisition and practice of oral presentation skills through automated, data-driven feedback [18]. These systems integrate software and hardware to capture multimodal data during presentations, such as body posture, gaze direction, vocal modulation, articulation speed, and visual aid usage. Based on these recordings, they provide immediate or delayed alerts, recommendations, or summary reports to presenters. This capability offers scalable solutions to one of education's key challenges, providing regular, formative feedback to learners when instructor time is limited [20].

Automated feedback systems such as presentation training software can be categorised according to the depth and actionability of their feedback [3]. Level 1 systems capture raw performance metrics; Level 2 systems generate alerts when presenters deviate from expected performance norms; Level 3 systems deliver targeted evaluations of aspects such as structure, voice, or delivery; and Level 4 systems provide formative, actionable feedback and explicit improvement guidance. Level 4 systems, though rare, represent the most pedagogically valuable design, as they move beyond quantitative analytics to genuine performance enhancement through adaptive and contextualised feedback [10]. Despite technical advances, many existing systems remain research prototypes with limited real-world validation and often neglect the pedagogical dimension of feedback design [27].

2.2 Teacher Dashboards

To enhance the pedagogical validity of automated feedback systems, several systems have incorporated teacher dashboards or supervisory components that allow educators to review, interpret, and comment on automated results [1,19]. These dashboards typically provide user management, access to student artefacts, and aggregated performance data. However, they are frequently restricted to monitoring rather than active engagement [11], lacking mechanisms that enable teachers to insert personalised comments, validate automated analyses, or engage in asynchronous discussion with students.

Designing such teacher-facing components introduces unique challenges [12]. Effective presentation feedback tools must balance automation with human pedagogical judgement. As studies on feedback authoring tools have shown [2,8], teachers favour interfaces that minimise unnecessary steps and cognitive load while allowing targeted, contextual comments. Henderson et al. [8] identify the use of structured feedback templates as a key condition for effective, actionable feedback, as such templates reduce teachers' administrative burden and allow them to concentrate on substantive comments rather than formatting. Feedback systems should therefore include accessible layouts, visual clarity, and features such as automated reminders.

Furthermore, timing and interactivity are particularly significant aspects of feedback design. While immediate feedback supports performance correction during practice, delayed feedback promotes deeper reflection and long-term knowledge retention [14]. Additionally, feedback is not purely unidirectional: it functions most effectively as a dialogic process, involving both teacher guidance and student response [16,24]. This principle of two-way engagement underpins modern views of feedback as a dynamic, constructive dialogue rather than a static correction [5].

2.3 Presentable

Presentable is a research-oriented, web-based presentation training platform developed using participatory, human-centred design methods to directly address the limitations of earlier OPAFs [4]. Its core design emerged from interviews with experienced presentation instructors, systematic analyses of existing OPAFs [10], iterative user testing, and integration of expert feedback at each stage. The resulting tool supports students through key stages of presentation development: message composition, rehearsal, and reflection.

Presentable guides users in structuring their presentation content, prompting them to define their target audience, clarify communication goals, and develop a logical message structure [15]. This is followed by video-based presentation practice, where students receive immediate, automated feedback on both verbal and non-verbal elements, including speech pacing, clarity, posture, and gestures [9] (see example in Fig. 1). Computer vision and speech technologies, utilised with accessible tools such as webcam video and browser-based pose estimation, offer constructive feedback to help users identify and correct common presentation mistakes in real time.

A distinguishing feature of *Presentable* is its focus on iterative practice and self-reflection. After each rehearsal, students review recordings and are guided through self-assessment prompts addressing both strengths and areas for improvement. The platform's teacher dashboard enables educators to monitor student progress and review shared presentation data.

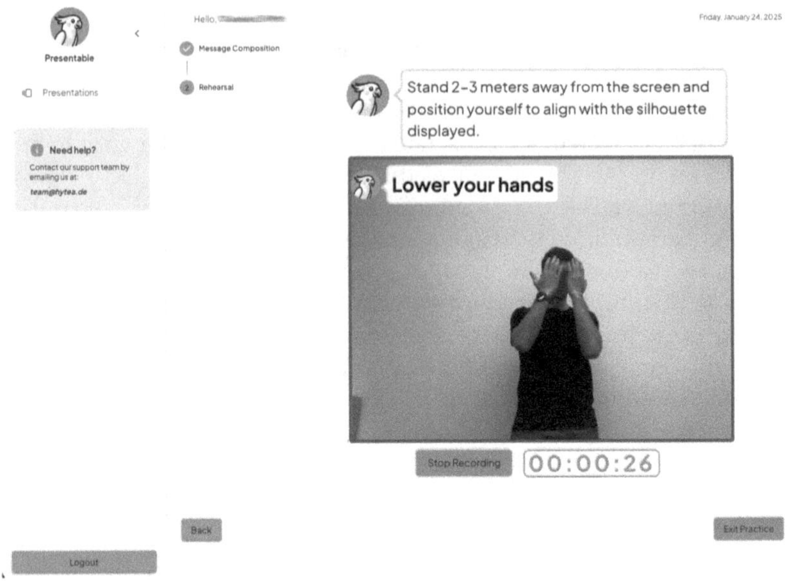

Fig. 1. Example of the automated feedback given by *Presentable* during the video-based presentation practice.

Presentable operates between Levels 2 and 3 of the automated feedback classification system. It moves beyond simple alerts by offering system-generated recommendations and visual feedback, but (at the time this research was conducted) lacks features for comprehensive evaluation and teacher feedback.

The pedagogical foundation for this extension draws on the feedback model proposed by Hattie and Timperley [7], which distinguishes between *Feed Up* (clarifying learning objectives), *Feed Back* (evaluating progress), and *Feed Forward* (guiding future effort). Research shows that written, structured feedback that incorporates all three elements leads to significantly improved learning outcomes compared with informal verbal comments [21]. Recent studies comparing AI-only feedback with teacher-supported AI feedback have demonstrated that teacher involvement significantly enhances students' presentation performance, particularly when educators provide interpretive commentary alongside automated analytics [23].

Integrating a teacher-driven feedback component into Presentable could extends its functionality, creating opportunities for educators to offer contextualised feedback. This feature could close the feedback loop between automated analytics and human pedagogy, transforming presentation training into a more interactive and reflective learning process.

3 Method

To conduct this study *Presentable* was used as environment to collect presentation training sessions and automated feedback. The study started by first deciding on a set of functional and non-functional requirements based on scientific literature and discussion with the *Presentable* research team. At this stage, it was envisioned that the teacher-driven feedback tool could enable teachers write rich text comments, apply feedback templates, annotate transcripts, and validate automated feedback messages. Later, the implementation of the took placed based on Presentable technology stack. However, to minimise interdependency, the teacher-driven feedback tool was developed and evaluated stand-alone from Presentable. A qualitative evaluation was conducted with two secondary school teachers and two university-level tutors to assess the tool's usability and effectiveness.

3.1 Functional Requirements

The core functional requirements (FR) define the application's essential capabilities, with each feature developed based on pedagogical relevance and usability considerations.

FR1 *Rich text feedback for presentations.* Teachers can provide structured feedback using a rich text editor that supports formatting options such as bold, italics, bullet points, and headers. This ensures that feedback is readable and visually organised, helping students interpret and apply comments effectively.

FR2 *Default and custom feedback templates.* The tool includes a default feedback template based on the Hattie and Timperley model [7], while also allowing teachers to create and reuse their own templates. Templates promote efficiency by reducing repetitive tasks and aligning feedback with pedagogical frameworks [13].

FR3 *Comment section on feedback.* Each feedback section includes an interactive comment thread where teachers and students can exchange messages, ask clarifying questions, and respond to feedback. This supports dialogic, two-way feedback processes.

FR4 *Timestamp links in feedback messages.* Teachers can insert clickable timestamps in feedback comments to reference specific moments in a video. This contextualises feedback, linking it directly to observable performance features and minimising ambiguity.

FR5 *Video transcription.* If available, transcripts are displayed alongside the video. Clicking on a segment of the transcript navigates directly to the corresponding section of the presentation, enhancing accessibility and comprehension of the spoken language.

FR6 *Transcription comments.* Teachers can highlight text within the transcript and attach comments to specific sections, enabling fine-grained feedback on verbal delivery and content quality.

FR7 *Relevant event navigation.* Automated feedback messages provided by *Presentable*, such as gestures or posture suggestions, are displayed as clickable items. Selecting an event directs the video to that exact point, helping students visualise specific moments.

FR8 *Event validation.* Teachers can validate or reject the automated feedback messages. Only validated messages are visible to students, ensuring accuracy and providing a layer of pedagogical oversight.

3.2 Nonfunctional Requirements

In addition to functional aspects, several nonfunctional requirements (NFR) ensure that the tool is robust, usable, and inclusive.

NFR1 *Modular database structure.* The database follows a modular relational design enabling easy integration with other educational systems. This supports long-term flexibility.

NFR2 *Minimised distractions for time efficiency.* The interface prioritises clarity and simplicity, reducing visual clutter. This design consideration supports teachers who often operate under time constraints and helps students focus on core feedback.

NFR3 *User-friendly workflow.* The application adopts an intuitive workflow, reducing the learning curve for new users. Tasks can be executed with minimal procedural steps.

NFR4 *Accessibility compliance.* The tool follows accessibility guidelines, including proper contrast ratios, screen reader compatibility, and keyboard navigation, ensuring equal access for users with disabilities.

NFR5 *Mobile support.* All core functionalities are optimised for use on mobile devices, allowing teachers and students to access feedback flexibly and asynchronously.

3.3 System Architecture

The teacher-driven feedback tool follows a classic web-based architecture, separating the frontend and backend layers for flexibility and maintainability. The backend, implemented in Django and Django REST Framework, exposes a RESTful API to manage entities such as users, courses, presentations, feedback, and comments. Key endpoints include *Users*, *Courses*, *Presentations*, and *Feedbacks*. Authentication is managed using JSON Web Tokens (*JWT*), secured through the *rest_framework_simplejwt* library.

The database uses MySQL in a relational structure. Major entities include *User*, *Course*, *Presentation*, *Feedback*, and *FeedbackComment*. Each model corresponds to a logical component of the feedback process. For example, the *FeedbackComment* model allows nested, hierarchical comments, preserving discussion threads between teachers and students.

The frontend, in line with *Presentable*, is built with Next.js and TypeScript, and uses React Query in combination with Axios for handling API communication, caching, and state updates. This approach ensures responsive interfaces and reduces redundant server requests. Tailwind CSS and Material UI provide consistent visual styling and responsive layout design for both desktop and mobile environments.

3.4 Frontend Implementation

The frontend is component-based, with reusable units combined into page-level structures. The feedback editor, based on the Tiptap framework, allows teachers to create feedback with full formatting control, including lists, headings, and code text formatting. Additional extensions provide Markdown conversion for backend compatibility and reactive feedback rendering through the *react-markdown* library.

Timestamp Links. Timestamps of the automated feedback by *Presentable* are automatically converted into clickable hyperlinks (see on the bottom of the video in Fig. 2). When clicked, the tool synchronises with the video playback, jumping to the corresponding moment. This is implemented using a custom React hook (*useVideoTimestamp*) that ensures smooth playback transitions while maintaining state.

Templates and Comments. Feedback templates are saved locally in the browser's storage for quick reuse (see Fig. 3). The comment section on each feedback page allows hierarchical threading, enabling replies and animations for smooth interactions using the Motion library. Deleted comments remain visible if they contain replies, preserving conversation context.

Transcript and Event Integration. The transcript view enables quick navigation and text-based comments on spoken content. Highlighted transcript sections can be annotated, visually embedding teacher comments within the text. The automated feedback messages given by *Presentable* are listed alongside the transcript and marked on a video timeline (see Fig. 2). Through event validation, teachers ensure that only contextually relevant and pedagogically accurate information reaches the student, while students retain the option to flag uncertain cases for review.

4 Results

4.1 Interview Procedure

The evaluation was conducted through semi-structured interviews designed to explore participants' perceptions of the usability, effectiveness, and pedagogical value of the teacher-driven feedback tool. Participants were informed that the study aimed to assess a new system for supporting feedback on student presentations. Still, they were not provided with detailed descriptions of the

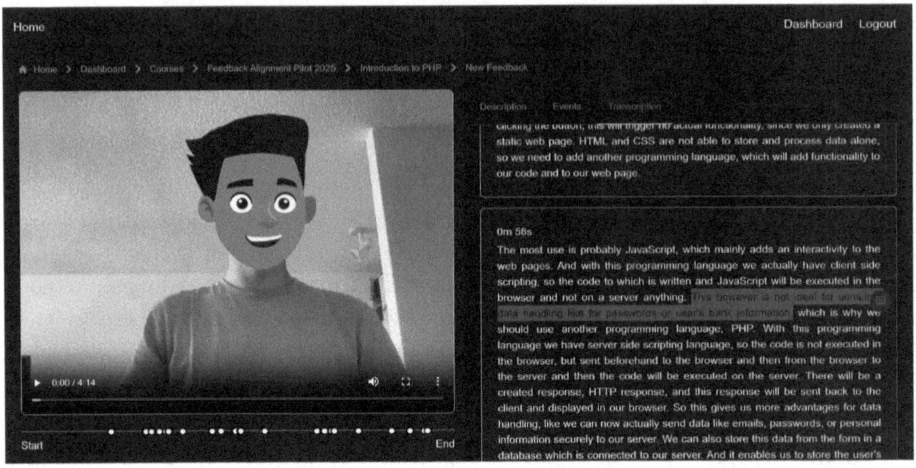

Fig. 2. Transcript commenting feature of the teacher-driven feedback tool.

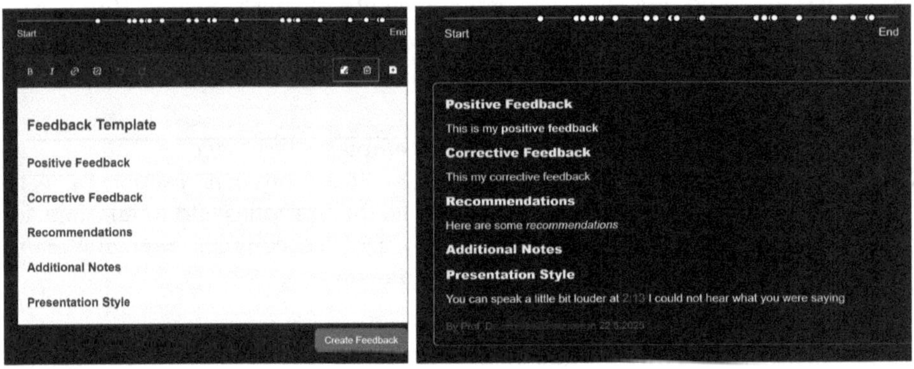

Fig. 3. Left: the feedback template to be edited by the teacher; Right: the student view of the feedback.

tool's features beforehand to minimise response bias. The interview followed a consistent thematic structure, beginning with general questions about the participants' teaching practices and approaches to providing feedback. The main part of the interview focused on hands-on experiences with the tool, including its usability, intuitiveness, and the perceived effectiveness of individual features such as the feedback editor, the automated feedback flagging mechanism, and the comment section. The interviews concluded with a comparison to traditional feedback methods and an invitation for participants to suggest improvements or additional functionalities.

4.2 Data Collection and Participants

To create a realistic testing context, short presentation videos were collected from volunteer students using the *Presentable* platform. These recordings provided the material for participants to work with while testing the feedback tool. In total, four educators participated in the evaluation: two secondary school teachers and two university tutors. The secondary school teachers, both from Gymnasia in the German state of Hesse, had extensive teaching experience (11 and 25 years respectively). At the same time, the university participants were a doctoral researcher and a teaching assistant, each with one to two years of supervisory experience in higher education.

All interviews were conducted remotely via video conferencing and lasted between 30 and 45 min. Participants were asked to use the feedback tool to evaluate at least one student presentation, validate automated feedback messages, and explore the available functions. The interviews were recorded, transcribed, and translated into English. A qualitative thematic analysis identified recurring themes and patterns relating to usability, effectiveness, and opportunities for improvement.

4.3 General Experience with Feedback

Before discussing the feedback tool itself, participants described their general approaches to assessing student presentations. Across all interviews, the content-related quality of the presentation was identified as the primary concern, including logical structure, argument clarity, and coherence between visual elements and spoken delivery. A clear narrative thread and appropriate timing were commonly cited as hallmarks of strong performance.

Non-verbal aspects such as body language, eye contact, and vocal expressiveness were usually observed but played a secondary role compared to content and structure. Three of the four participants reported relying on handwritten or typed notes taken during live presentations to support their evaluations. Feedback was typically provided orally immediately after the presentation and occasionally supplemented with written summaries or standardised rubrics.

Participants noted several consistent challenges, primarily limited time for preparation and follow-up. This time pressure constrained both the level of detail provided in feedback and opportunities for dialogue with students. Some participants also reflected on the difficulty of finding a balance between evaluative and constructive feedback, aiming not only to identify weaknesses but also to guide concrete improvement strategies.

4.4 Experience with the Feedback Tool

Overall, participants described the feedback tool as user-friendly, logically organised, and generally well aligned with their preferred feedback practices. The clear separation into functional sections (presentation details, automated feedback messages, and transcript) was highlighted as particularly helpful. Features such as timestamp-based comments and transcript-linked annotations were considered intuitive and realistic, reflecting how teachers naturally refer to specific presentation moments when giving feedback.

The Rich Text Feedback Editor received positive feedback for its clarity and ease of use. Teachers appreciated the ability to structure feedback visually and to rely on predefined templates, which allowed them to focus more on the content of their comments than on formatting. The permanent documentation of written feedback was seen as a valuable improvement over purely oral feedback, as it provided students with accessible records for future self-improvement.

The asynchronous comment section was also viewed favourably, as it enables ongoing interaction between teachers and students outside the classroom. This function was seen as especially relevant in school contexts with limited contact hours. Nonetheless, participants identified some usability issues. The transcript comment feature was not immediately visible, leading to confusion during initial use. Additionally, the tool did not allow editing of submitted feedback without deleting it entirely.

The usefulness of automated feedback messages prompted mixed reactions. While some participants acknowledged their potential to draw attention to non-verbal aspects, others felt the automated feedback messages were sometimes trivial or irrelevant to assessment criteria. Teachers suggested that AI feedback should evolve to include constructive advice rather than simple detection. Additionally, the English-only interface was perceived as a potential barrier for teachers who are less comfortable with the language or digital technology, suggesting that multilingual support is a necessary enhancement.

4.5 Suggestions for Improvement

Participants proposed a range of refinements and additional features aimed at improving accessibility, workflow flexibility, and pedagogical value. A commonly requested enhancement was a draft mode for saving in-progress feedback privately before submission, allowing teachers to return to unfinished evaluations later. They also emphasised the need for an autosave function to prevent data loss from technical interruptions or session timeouts.

From a design perspective, teachers suggested integrating transcript comments directly within the transcript view to improve visibility and context. Additional formatting options in the feedback editor, such as extended colour palettes or custom text styles, were recommended to make feedback more structured and visually differentiated.

Participants also expressed interest in expanding automated analysis functionalities. They suggested that the AI should prioritise detecting more meaningful presentation behaviours and potentially identify filler words in transcripts to support assessments of fluency. Other proposals included integrating a grading module, enabling the recording and upload of voice feedback, and introducing peer-feedback capabilities so that students could learn by evaluating one another's presentations.

While the feedback tool was generally received with enthusiasm, the recurring emphasis across interviews was the need for enhanced flexibility, better feedback integration, and continued alignment with authentic teaching workflows. The inclusion of both structured and conversational features was seen as particularly valuable for bridging the gap between human insight and automated analysis.

5 Discussion

This study aimed to explore how a teacher-driven feedback tool can be integrated into a presentation training software to enhance the quality and efficiency of feedback provision. To answer this overarching question, three sub-questions were addressed: (1) identifying the core functionalities required to enable teachers to provide contextual and personalised feedback, (2) determining how these functionalities should be designed to maximise usability, clarity, time efficiency, and pedagogical soundness, and (3) defining how feedback data should be structured and integrated into the software architecture.

5.1 RQ1: Core Functionalities for Teacher-Driven Feedback

The first research question focused on identifying the core functional requirements (FRs) that enable teachers to deliver high-quality, contextualised feedback. The responses confirmed the relevance of the eight functional requirements established during design. Teachers particularly valued features such as the rich text feedback editor (FR1), which allowed structured and expressive feedback, and the use of predefined or custom templates (FR2), which increased consistency and saved time. Timestamp linking (FR4) and transcript commenting (FR6) were described as vital for contextual feedback that ties comments directly to specific segments of a presentation. Automated feedback validation (FR8) was also widely appreciated, as it provided teachers with control over the visibility of automated feedback messages provided by *Presentable* and ensured that only pedagogically relevant feedback was shown to students. Collectively, these findings reaffirm that effective feedback systems must combine precision with flexibility, enabling teachers to modulate depth and focus according to students' needs.

5.2 RQ2: Designing for Usability and Pedagogical Effectiveness

The second question addressed how these functionalities should be designed to balance usability and pedagogical value while minimising cognitive load. This aspect relates directly to the non-functional requirements (NFRs) established for the tool. Participants described the user interface as clear, logically structured, and aligned with teachers' workflows, which supports NFR3 (user-friendly workflow). They also emphasised the importance of efficiency and minimal distractions (NFR2), highlighting that streamlined navigation and simple visual design enabled them to provide feedback quickly and effectively. Accessibility across devices (NFR5) was perceived as essential to adapt the tool to diverse teaching environments, including mobile and hybrid learning contexts. Furthermore, teachers recommended enhancements such as draft-saving, richer text styling, and better integration between transcript and feedback views: improvements that reinforce NFR1 (modularity) and promote a more holistic and fluent feedback process. Pedagogically, participants reported that the clear structure and contextualised nature of the feedback encouraged more reflective learning, supporting a shift from corrective to developmental feedback practices.

5.3 RQ3: Structuring and Integrating Feedback Into the Architecture

The third research question examined how feedback data should be structured and integrated with the system's architecture to support scalability and future expansion. The modular client-server design using Django REST Framework and Next.js was found to provide sufficient flexibility for storing and connecting multiple data types, including presentation videos, transcripts, comments, and automated feedback messages. Participants' suggestions for future development (such as peer feedback functionality, notification systems, and Learning Management System (LMS) integration) point directly to the need for adaptable data schemas and API endpoints that can accommodate additional feedback layers without disrupting existing workflows. These structural design considerations will be central as the *Presentable* evolves toward broader institutional adoption and interoperability.

5.4 Synthesis and Implications

Overall, the study demonstrates that the integration of teacher-driven feedback within automated presentation training systems is both feasible and pedagogically advantageous. The evaluation confirmed that the combination of automated analytics with human oversight reduces ambiguity, increases interactivity, and supports sustained reflection. While the study involved a small group of teachers and tutors, the insights gathered have clear implications for scaling and iterative design. Future evaluations should include larger, more diverse samples and combine qualitative insights with learning analytics to examine how teacher feedback translates into measurable improvements in student performance over time.

The research validates the original design concept: that a teacher-driven feedback tool, guided by well-defined functional and non-functional requirements, can significantly enhance the quality, precision, and educational value of feedback within presentation training environments. The findings lay a robust foundation for the next development phase, which aims to expand integration of the teacher-driven feedback tool into *Presentable*, streamline interaction, and contribute to transform *Presentable* into a fully collaborative platform that supports both automated and human-centred feedback at scale.

6 Conclusions

The exploratory methodology adopted in this study enabled the identification of both usability considerations and pedagogical requirements for a teacher-driven feedback tool in presentation training. Although the small sample size limits the generalisability of the findings, the results offer clear and actionable directions for further development. Participant feedback was instrumental in refining existing features and prioritising enhancements that address authentic teaching needs. Key recommendations for future iterations include implementing draft-saving functionality, expanding formatting options in the feedback editor, improving the visibility and integration of transcript-linked comments, and increasing the contextual relevance of automated feedback messages provided by *Presentable*.

The teacher-driven feedback feature developed in this work significantly extends the capabilities of the *Presentable* presentation training system by enabling educators to close the feedback loop in AI-supported tutoring [17]. The positive reception among school teachers and university-level tutors demonstrates its potential to raise the quality and accessibility of feedback in educational contexts. In particular, functions such as timestamp-linked comments, transcript annotation, and asynchronous dialogue reflect established feedback practices while using technology to support clarity, engagement, and iterative improvement.

Future development should be aligned with priorities identified in both the evaluation and the additional feature roadmap. The introduction of a robust notification system is recommended to maintain user engagement and ensure that students and teachers are promptly informed about new feedback, comments, or updates. This could be implemented through in-app alerts, push notifications, and email updates, allowing users to control the type and frequency of notifications they receive based on their preferences. Such functionality would foster timely interaction and strengthen feedback as an ongoing process.

Integration with institutional Learning Management Systems (LMS) such as Moodle, Google Classroom, or Microsoft Teams would provide seamless access to the tool within familiar teaching environments. LMS integration would centralise presentation resources, feedback records, and evaluation metrics, streamline workflows, and enable improved tracking of student progress. Leveraging built-in LMS grading capabilities could also reduce manual workload, thereby increasing efficiency for instructors.

The incorporation of structured peer feedback, including anonymous options, has strong potential to enhance learning outcomes by building analytical skills, promoting reflection, and supporting collaborative learning environments. Peer feedback would diversify perspectives available to presenters and could reduce the evaluation workload for teachers, allowing them to focus on specific developmental priorities. Such interaction can improve communication skills for all participants and encourage greater student ownership of the learning process.

In conclusion, this project demonstrates that even at an early stage of design and implementation, meaningful and constructive user input can be collected and transformed into tangible improvements. The tool can provide richer, more relevant, and more interactive learning experiences. Continued development guided by educational best practices and practical usage data will help ensure that the tool meets the demands of real-world teaching while supporting the cultivation of communication competence in students across diverse educational settings.

Acknowledgements. The authors would like to thank the teachers and tutors who participated in the evaluation study for their time and valuable insights. This work originated from the Master's thesis of Talha Burak Onat, conducted at Goethe University Frankfurt in collaboration with the DIPF Leibniz Institute for Research and Information in Education.

Disclosure of Interests. The authors declare no financial or personal conflicts of interest that could have inappropriately influenced the design, conduct, or reporting of this study. The Presentable platform described in this paper is a research prototype developed within the authors' affiliated institutions and is not a commercial product.

References

1. Banihashem, S.K., Noroozi, O., Van Ginkel, S., Macfadyen, L.P., Biemans, H.J.: A systematic review of the role of learning analytics in enhancing feedback practices in higher education. Educ. Res. Rev. **37**, 100489 (2022). https://doi.org/10.1016/j.edurev.2022.100489
2. Carless, D., Boud, D.: The development of student feedback literacy: enabling uptake of feedback. Assess. Eval. High. Educ. **43**(8), 1315–1325 (2018). https://doi.org/10.1080/02602938.2018.1463354
3. Deeva, G., Bogdanova, D., Serral, E., Snoeck, M., De Weerdt, J.: A review of automated feedback systems for learners: classification framework, challenges and opportunities. Comput. Educ. **162**, 104094 (2021). https://doi.org/10.1016/j.compedu.2020.104094
4. Mitri, D., et al.: Enhance your presentation skills with presentable. In: Companion Proceedings of the 15th International Learning Analytics and Knowledge Conference (LAK 2025), Dublin, Ireland, p. 285. Society for Learning Analytics Research (SoLAR) (2025)
5. Er, E., Yannis, D., Gašević, D.: A collaborative learning approach to dialogic peer feedback: a theoretical framework. Assess. Eval. High. Educ. **46**(4), 586–600 (2021). https://doi.org/10.1080/02602938.2020.1786497. Publisher: SRHE Website _eprint: 10(1080/02602938), pp. 1786497, 2020
6. Evans, C.: Making sense of assessment feedback in higher education. Rev. Educ. Res. (2013). https://doi.org/10.3102/0034654312474350
7. Hattie, J., Timperley, H.: The power of feedback. Rev. Educ. Res. **77**(1), 16–7 (2007). https://doi.org/10.3102/003465430298487
8. Henderson, M., et al.: Conditions that enable effective feedback. High. Educ. Res. Dev. **38**(7), 1401–1416 (2019). https://doi.org/10.1080/07294360.2019.1657807
9. Hummel, S., Alomari, M., Schneider, J., Mouhammad, N., Klemke, R., Di Mitri, D.: Evaluating WEBPOSE, a posture feedback system for oral presentations. In: European Conference on e-Learning, vol. 24, no. 1, pp. 162–169 (2025). https://doi.org/10.34190/ecel.24.1.4285

10. Hummel, S., Schneider, J., Mouhammad, N., Klemke, R., Di Mitri, D.: Enhancing presentation skills: key technical features of automated feedback systems - a systematic feature analysis. Int. J. Technol. Enhanc. Learn. **17**(6), 1–25 (2025). https://doi.org/10.1504/IJTEL.2025.148593
11. Kaliisa, R., Dolonen, J.A.: CADA: a teacher-facing learning analytics dashboard to foster teachers' awareness of students' participation and discourse patterns in online discussions. In: Technology, Knowledge and Learning, pp. 1–22 (2022). https://doi.org/10.1007/s10758-022-09598-7
12. Karademir, O., Ahmad, A., Schneider, J., Di Mitri, D., Jivet, I., Drachsler, H.: Designing the learning analytics cockpit - a dashboard that enables interventions. In: De la Prieta, F., et al. (eds.) Methodologies and Intelligent Systems for Technology Enhanced Learning, 11th International Conference. LNNS, pp. 95–104. Springer, Cham (2022). https://doi.org/10.1007/978-3-030-86618-1_10
13. Karademir, O., et al.: I don't have time! But keep me in the loop: co-designing requirements for a learning analytics cockpit with teachers. J. Comput. Assist. Learn. **40**(6), 2681–2699 (2024). https://doi.org/10.1111/jcal.12997
14. Metcalfe, J.: Learning from errors. Ann. Rev. Psychol. **68**, 465–489 (2017). https://doi.org/10.1146/annurev-psych-010416-044022
15. Mouhammad, N., Schneider, J., Klemke, R., Di Mitri, D.: From nervous to noteworthy: evaluating SPEAKS, an educational software for speech content. In: European Conference on e-Learning, vol. 24, no. 1, pp. 271–280 (2025). https://doi.org/10.34190/ecel.24.1.4104
16. Nicol, D.J., Macfarlane-Dick, D.: Formative assessment and self- regulated learning: a model and seven principles of good feedback practice. Stud. High. Educ. **31**(2), 199–218 (2006). https://doi.org/10.1080/03075070600572090
17. Ninaus, M., Sailer, M.: Closing the loop – The human role in artificial intelligence for education. Front. Psychol. **13** (2022). https://doi.org/10.3389/fpsyg.2022.956798
18. Ochoa, X.: Multimodal systems for automated oral presentation feedback: a comparative analysis. In: Giannakos, M., Spikol, D., Di Mitri, D., Sharma, K., Ochoa, X., Hammad, R. (eds.) The Multimodal Learning Analytics Handbook, pp. 53–78. Springer, Cham (2022). https://doi.org/10.1007/978-3-031-08076-0_3
19. Pardo, A., Jovanovic, J., Dawson, S., Gašević, D., Mirriahi, N.: Using learning analytics to scale the provision of personalised feedback. Br. J. Edu. Technol. **50**(1), 128–138 (2019). https://doi.org/10.1111/bjet.12592
20. Schneider, J., Borner, D., Van Rosmalen, P., Specht, M.: Can you help me with my pitch? Studying a tool for real-time automated feedback. IEEE Trans. Learn. Technol. **9**(4), 318–327 (2016). https://doi.org/10.1109/TLT.2016.2627043
21. Shute, V.J.: Focus on formative feedback. Rev. Educ. Res. **78**(1), 153–189 (2008). https://doi.org/10.3102/0034654307313795
22. Shvets, O., Murtazin, K., Piho, G.: Providing feedback for students in E-learning systems: a literature review, based on IEEE explore digital library. In: 2020 IEEE Global Engineering Education Conference (EDUCON), pp. 284–289 (2020). https://doi.org/10.1109/EDUCON45650.2020.9125344. ISSN 2165-9567
23. Sichterman, B., et al.: Can AI feedback stand alone for fostering students' presentation performance? A comparison of AI-only versus teacher-supported AI feedback. Interact. Learn. Environ., 1–18 (2025). https://doi.org/10.1080/10494820.2025.2521338
24. Steen-Utheim, A., Wittek, A.L.: Dialogic feedback and potentialities for student learning. Learn. Cult. Soc. Interact. **15**, 18–30 (2017). https://doi.org/10.1016/j.lcsi.2017.06.002

25. Trilling, B., Fadel, C.: 21st Century Skills: Learning for Life in Our Times, 1st edn. Wiley (2012)
26. Van Ginkel, S., Gulikers, J., Biemans, H., Mulder, M.: Towards a set of design principles for developing oral presentation competence: a synthesis of research in higher education. Educ. Res. Rev. **14**, 62–80 (2015). https://doi.org/10.1016/j.edurev.2015.02.002
27. Van Ginkel, S., et al.: Fostering oral presentation competence through a virtual reality-based task for delivering feedback. Comput. Educ. **134**, 78–97 (2019). https://doi.org/10.1016/j.compedu.2019.02.006

A Narrative Review of the Role of Artificial Intelligence and Machine Learning in Physical Activity

Mariasole Antonietta Guerriero[1(✉)], Angelo Basta[2], Maria Ruberto[2], Fiorenzo Moscatelli[2], Nicola Mancini[2], Marcellino Monda[3], Giovanni Messina[3], Rita Polito[4], and Francesco Paolo Colecchia[3]

[1] Department of Humanistic Studies, University of Foggia, Foggia 71121, Italy
mariasole.guerriero@unifg.it

[2] Department of Education and Sport Sciences, Pegaso Telematic University, 80143 Naples, Italy

[3] Department of Experimental Medicine, Section of Human Physiology and Unit of Dietetics and Sports Medicine, University of Campania "Luigi Vanvitelli", 80138 Naples, Italy

[4] Department of Psychology and Health Sciences, Pegaso Telematic University, 80143 Naples, Italy

Abstract. Physical inactivity remains a major global health concern, despite ample evidence linking regular physical activity to reduced risk of chronic diseases and improved mental wellbeing. Advances in artificial intelligence (AI) and machine learning (ML) have introduced new opportunities to promote and encourage active lifestyles through intelligent monitoring, adaptive feedback, and predictive analytics. **Aim:** This systematic narrative review aimed to synthesise recent evidence (2020–2025) on the use of AI and ML in the promotion, monitoring, and evaluation of physical activity and sports performance, as well as to identify methodological trends, current gaps, and future directions for research. **Methods:** Following the PRISMA 2020 and SWiM guidelines, a comprehensive search was conducted on PubMed and Scopus. Sixteen studies were included and analysed narratively according to five areas of intervention: activity monitoring and recognition, feedback and behavioural support, prediction and data analysis, virtual coaching and interactive systems, and integration and multimodal systems. **Results:** AI applications consistently demonstrated improvements in terms of accuracy, personalisation, and adaptability of interventions. The clear upward trend in publications since 2022 highlights the growing interest in AI-based physical activity research. Despite promising results, the heterogeneity of study designs and the absence of standardised protocols limit their generalisability. **Conclusions:** Future research should prioritise multimodal integration, methodological standardisation, and ethical implementation to translate AI innovations into effective tools for public health and exercise science.

Keywords: Artificial Intelligence · Physical activity · Machine Learning

M. Adamoli et al. (Eds.): HELMeTO 2025, CCIS 2958, pp. 473–489, 2026.
https://doi.org/10.1007/978-3-032-31850-3_29

1 Introduction

Physical activity (PA) is a fundamental determinant of health and wellbeing, associated with reduced risks of cardiovascular disease, diabetes, and mental health disorders. Despite these benefits, global inactivity rates remain high—over one in four adults worldwide do not meet the World Health Organization (WHO) recommendations for weekly PA [1]. Conventional interventions have often struggled to achieve sustainable behavioral change, largely due to their limited ability to provide continuous, personalized, and data-driven feedback.

Recent advances in digital health technologies and artificial intelligence (AI) have transformed how PA is measured, understood, and promoted. The proliferation of wearable devices, smartphones, and connected sensors has generated large volumes of behavioral data, while machine learning (ML) algorithms can process these data to detect patterns, predict engagement, and personalize interventions [2, 3]. AI-powered systems are increasingly being used to enhance real-time monitoring, goal setting, and adaptive feedback through just-in-time adaptive interventions (JITAIs). These tools can deliver individualized recommendations, improve adherence, and support health-related behavior change at scale [4, 5].

Recent studies have further demonstrated that AI-driven applications can extend beyond performance optimization to encompass psychological and behavioral wellbeing. For instance, Guerriero et al. (2024) [6] highlighted how AI-based tools—such as chatbots and digital coaching platforms—can mitigate stress and sedentary behavior by integrating personalized activity prompts and emotional feedback mechanisms. Similarly, Bruno et al. (2024) [7] emphasized the role of AI and ML in improving physical activity engagement through motion recognition, adaptive learning, and predictive analytics, underscoring their potential to enhance motivation and participation in health-promoting behaviors. In a related framework, Guerriero et al. (2024) [6, 8] demonstrated how AI-supported monitoring systems provide continuous and adaptive support, combining physical and psychological parameters to foster holistic wellbeing. Together, these findings indicate a growing convergence between technological innovation and preventive health strategies, where AI functions not only as an analytical tool but also as a behavioral facilitator.

Nevertheless, despite this rapid expansion, the existing evidence remains methodologically fragmented. Research varies widely in its objectives, populations, and AI approaches—ranging from motion detection and classification to behavior prediction and virtual coaching. Previous reviews have largely focused on niche domains such as elite sports or wearable device validation [9, 10] leaving a gap in understanding how AI and ML are systematically applied across diverse PA contexts. Moreover, the lack of standardized outcomes and transparent reporting limits the comparability and scalability of findings across studies.

The present systematic review aimed to provide an updated synthesis of recent evidence on the use of Artificial Intelligence (AI) and Machine Learning (ML) in the field of physical activity and sport promotion. Based on the PICOS framework and the defined search strategy, this review addressed the following research questions:

RQ1: What is the current evidence (2020–2025) on the use of Artificial Intelligence (AI) and Machine Learning (ML) to promote, monitor, or evaluate physical activity and sport performance in humans aged 14 years and older?

RQ2: Are there standardized intervention protocols using AI or ML to promote, monitor, or evaluate physical activity and sport performance in humans aged 14 years and older?

RQ3: What are the main outcomes reported across studies regarding accuracy, behavioral adherence, performance improvement, or health indicators?

Accordingly, the main objectives of this review were:

- to identify and categorize current applications of AI and ML related to physical activity and sport;
- to analyze the effectiveness and methodological trends of such interventions according to study design, population, and technological approach; and
- to summarize the main outcomes and knowledge gaps to inform future research and implementation in health promotion, sport sciences, and digital health contexts.

This review followed the Preferred Reporting Items for Systematic Reviews and Meta-Analyses (PRISMA 2020) guidelines [11] and the Synthesis Without Meta-analysis (SWiM) approach [12] . The search was conducted in PubMed and Scopus (2020–2025), applying predefined filters (English, humans, free full text, excluding COVID-19), and eligibility criteria defined through the PICOS model. A total of 16 studies meeting all inclusion criteria were identified and analyzed in the final qualitative synthesis.

2 Materials and Methods

This systematic review followed the Preferred Reporting Items for Systematic Reviews and Meta-Analyses (PRISMA 2020) guidelines [11] and the Synthesis Without Meta-analysis (SWiM) recommendations [12]. A comprehensive literature search was conducted in PubMed and Scopus databases for studies published between 2020 and 2025. The research phase of the following review was conducted between July and September 2025.

The following Boolean search string was applied to both databases:

("artificial intelligence" [Title/Abstract] OR "AI" [Title/Abstract]) AND ("machine learning" [Title/Abstract]) AND ("physical activity" [Title/Abstract] OR "sport" [Title/Abstract]) AND NOT ("COVID-19" [Title/Abstract])

Filters were applied to restrict results to English-language, human, and free full-text publications. Reference lists of eligible studies and relevant reviews were also screened manually to ensure comprehensive coverage.

2.1 Eligibility Criteria (PICOS Framework)

Studies were included if they met all predefined criteria structured according to the PICOS model:

- **Population (P):** Adolescents (14–18 years), young adults (≥19 years), and older adults (65+). Only human participants engaged in physical activity, exercise, or sport were included.
- **Intervention (I):** Application of Artificial Intelligence (AI) or Machine Learning (ML) techniques for the purpose of promoting, monitoring, or analyzing physical activity or sport-related behaviors.
- **Comparison (C):** Traditional or non-AI/ML interventions, usual care, or other digital technologies without AI/ML components.
- **Outcomes (O):** Primary outcomes related to physical activity behavior, adherence, movement recognition, performance, or associated health indicators. Secondary outcomes were considered when relevant to the research question.
- **Study design (S):** All peer-reviewed human studies, including randomized controlled trials (RCTs), quasi-experimental, observational, mixed-methods, pilot, and qualitative studies, as well as secondary reviews with explicit AI/ML applications.

The PICOS framework points are also shown in the table below (Table 1).

Table 1. Summary of PICOS framework

Element	Description
P – Population	Adolescents (14–18 years), young adults (≥19 years) up to older adults (65+). Humans only, engaged in physical activity or sport.
I – Intervention	Artificial Intelligence (AI) and Machine Learning (ML) applications: digital coaching, chatbots, predictive models, wearable sensors with AI/ML algorithms.
C – Comparison	Traditional interventions (non-AI/ML), no intervention/usual care, or other digital technologies not based on AI/ML.
O – Outcomes	Primary: levels of physical activity, sport performance, adherence to exercise programs. Secondary: usability, acceptability, related health indicators (e.g., weight, VO_2max, sleep quality).
S – Study design	All peer-reviewed study types on humans: RCTs, quasi-experimental, observational, qualitative, mixed-methods, pilot trials, and pertinent secondary reviews.

Exclusion criteria were:

- studies not involving human participants;
- papers focused solely on algorithm development without behavioral or health outcomes;
- non-English publications;
- conference abstracts, commentaries, or editorials without primary data;
- studies primarily addressing COVID-19–related topics.

2.2 Study Selection

All retrieved records were exported to a structured Excel database for duplicate removal and screening.

A total of 76 records were identified across databases (PubMed = 32, Scopus = 44). No duplicates were detected. Titles and abstracts were independently screened by two reviewers based on the PICOS criteria, resulting in the exclusion of 52 records (46 not focused on physical activity or sport, and 6 primarily related to COVID-19 and mental health).

a. Following the first screening phase, 24 full-text articles were assessed for eligibility. Of these, 8 studies were excluded due to the following reasons:
   not AI/ML-based (n = 4).
b. Outcome limited to mental health (n = 1).
c. Not focused on physical activity or sport (n = 2).
d. Lack of measurable outcomes (n = 1).

Ultimately, 16 studies fulfilled all inclusion criteria and were retained for qualitative synthesis. The detailed selection process is depicted in the PRISMA 2020 flow diagram described in Fig. 1 [11].

2.3 Data Extraction and Management

Data from the included studies were systematically extracted using standardized Excel forms developed for this review as well as the management of search results, screening and inclusion of papers, and analysis of results, was done using Zotero.

The extracted information included:

- study authors, publication year, and country;
- study design and sample characteristics;
- AI/ML technique or model employed;
- type of intervention or monitoring system;
- primary and secondary outcomes relevant to physical activity, adherence, or performance.

Two reviewers independently verified all entries for accuracy and completeness. Discrepancies were resolved through discussion until consensus was achieved.

3 Results

Due to the heterogeneity in study design, participant characteristics, AI/ML applications, and measured outcomes, a quantitative meta-analysis was not feasible. Instead, a narrative synthesis was conducted in accordance with the SWiM guideline [12].

The studies included were grouped and analyzed according to two dimensions:

1. **Area of intervention**: distinguishing AI/ML applications aimed at monitoring, feedback, prediction, performance assessment, or digital coaching;

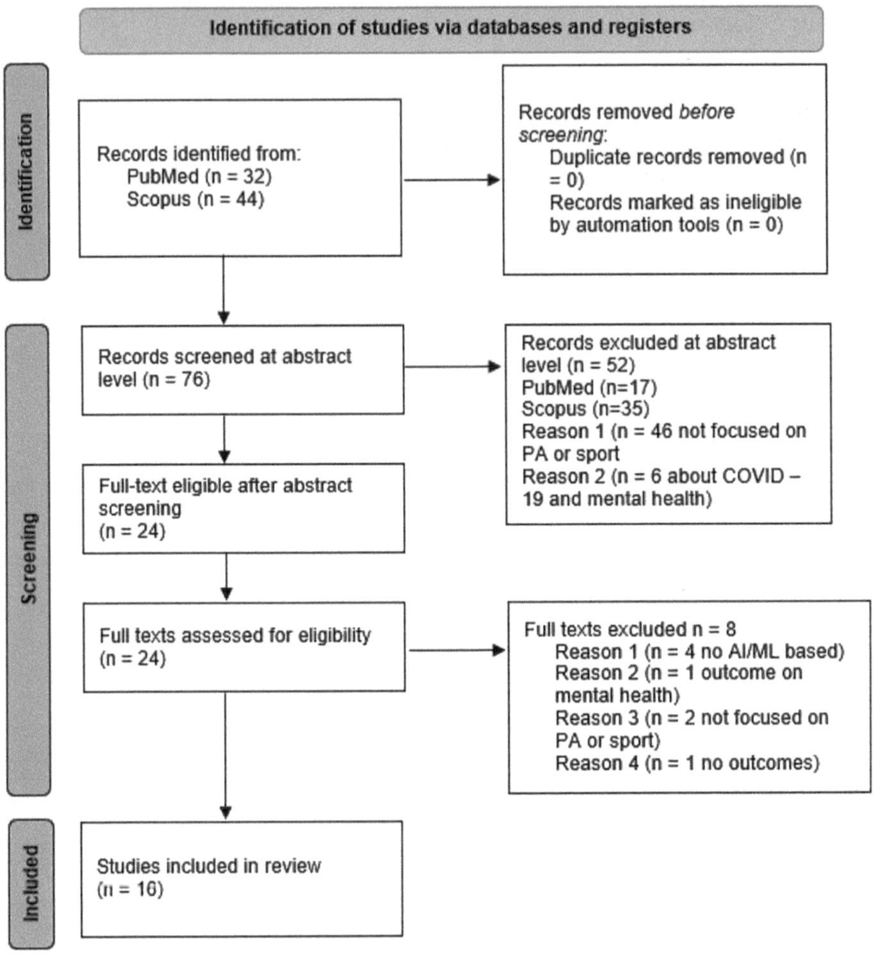

Fig. 1. .

2. **Type of AI/ML technology:** categorizing methods such as supervised learning, deep learning, reinforcement learning, computer vision, and natural language processing (NLP).

Results were summarized descriptively, emphasizing methodological trends, direction and consistency of effects, and implications for future research and practice.

The areas of intervention identified following the screening and inclusion of papers are as follows:

1. Monitoring & Activity Recognition
2. Feedback & Behaviour Support
3. Prediction & Data Analytics
4. Virtual Coaching & Interactive Systems
5. Integration & Multimodal Systems (Table 2)

Table 2. Summary of papers assigned by area of intervention

Area	Studies	Authors by first name
Monitoring & Activity Recognition	4	Lincke, Vanstrum, Peimankar, Wesely
Feedback & Behavior Support	3	Forman, Mohammadi, Canzone
Prediction & Data Analytics	4	Fan, Zheng, Kumar, Choe
Virtual Coaching & Interactive Systems	2	Korn, Suryanto
Integration & Multimodal Systems	3	Anaya, Li, Köhler

A total of 16 studies met all inclusion criteria and were included in the final synthesis.The studies varied in design, population, and purpose but consistently explored the application of Artificial Intelligence (AI) and Machine Learning (ML) techniques to promote, monitor, or evaluate physical activity and sport performance in humans aged 14 years and older. Table 3 provides a concise overview of the included studies, detailing for each the study design, type of AI/ML technique employed, target population, main objectives, and the primary outcomes reported.

The synthesis revealed five major functional domains of AI/ML application: (1) monitoring and activity recognition, (2) feedback and behavior support, (3) prediction and data analytics, (4) virtual coaching and interactive systems, and (5) integration and multimodal frameworks.

Studies were narratively analyzed within these domains to identify common approaches, methodological trends, and emerging challenges.

3.1 Monitoring and Activity Recognition

Studies included in this area demonstrate how artificial intelligence and machine learning can be effectively applied to objectively recognise and monitor motor activity across different populations and settings, ranging from clinical assessment to sport performance.

Lincke et al. (2023) [13] compared 2D and 3D skeleton avatar technologies for assessing physical activity and functional performance in healthy older adults. While 3D systems showed overall higher accuracy, the 2D approach achieved comparable results for accelerometer-based physical activity outcomes, with a mean absolute error of approximately 7%, and no significant differences for selected functional tests such as the Timed Up and Go and the 30-s chair stand test. These findings highlight the potential of low-cost, camera-based AI solutions for physical activity monitoring in clinical and home-based contexts.

Sensor-based approaches were further explored by Peimankar et al. (2023) [14], who developed machine learning models to classify walking activity in older adults with gait disorders using a single accelerometer placed on the back. By combining feature selection through particle swarm optimisation with ensemble learning methods, the proposed models achieved classification accuracies of up to 93%, with strong sensitivity and F1-scores, despite the challenging population and non-standard sensor placement. This supports the feasibility of continuous activity monitoring in vulnerable groups using minimally invasive wearable technologies.

Table 3. Summary of results

Author (Year)	Study Design	AI/ML Technique	Population	Main Objective	Main Outcome(s)
Lincke et al. (2023)	Experimental comparative	2D/3D Skeleton Avatar (Pose Estimation)	Older adults (healthy)	Compare accuracy of 2D vs. 3D motion capture for PA assessment.	2D pose estimation achieved accuracy comparable to 3D models for physical activity evaluation.
Peimankar et al. (2023)	Experimental	kNN, RF, XGBoost with PSO feature selection	20 older adults with gait disorders	Classify gait activities using ML on accelerometer data.	Reached ~93% classification accuracy with strong sensitivity and F1-score.
Wesely et al. (2025)	Experimental	Supervised ML on IMU sensor data	16 cheerleading athletes	Recognize acrobatic movements from wearable sensors.	ML models accurately detected acrobatic elements and generalized across athletes.
Vanstrum et al. (2023)	Observational analytical	SVM, XGBoost, Gradient Boosting	1625 adults (NHANES dataset)	Classify postural dysfunction using ML applied to PA data.	ML models effectively classified postural dysfunction; age and moderate PA intensity were key features.
Forman et al. (2023)	RCT protocol	Reinforcement Learning (cluster-optimized)	336 adults with overweight/obesity	Develop adaptive behavioral weight loss intervention using RL.	Protocol described RL-based adaptive feedback; outcome results pending.
Mohammadi et al. (2020)	Observational + algorithm development	Supervised Neural Network	20 adults with BMI $\geq$25	Adapt PA goals from wearable tracker data.	Low MAE prediction error and satisfactory adherence to adaptive goal recommendations.
Canzone et al. (2025)	Narrative review	ML, DL, RL (various applications)	15 RCTs (mixed populations)	Summarize AI/ML use in exercise and PA programs.	AI-enabled interventions improved PA adherence and performance in several RCTs.
Fan et al. (2024)	Cross-sectional	Random Forest, Gradient Boosting	400+ older adults	Predict functional status using accelerometer-based features.	ML models accurately predicted physical function and identified key digital biomarkers.
Zheng et al. (2025)	Cross-sectional	XGBoost with SHAP (Explainable AI)	51 older adults (mean age $\approx$85)	Identify frailty status using wearable accelerometer data.	Model accurately classified frailty; SHAP explained influence of dynamic gait features.
Kumar et al. (2025)	Longitudinal observational	Supervised ML with feature selection (EMA data)	43 healthy adults	Predict short-term PA patterns for JITAI optimization.	Prediction achieved AUC $\approx$ 0.87; stress and self-efficacy emerged as strongest predictors.
Choe et al. (2025)	Cross-sectional	Decision Tree, RF, SVM, XGBoost	11,638 adults (NHANES, USA)	Predict adherence to PA guidelines via ML models.	AUC ranged 0.54–0.70; age, sex, and sedentary behavior were major predictors.
Korn et al. (2025)	Bibliometric review	NLP, LLMs, text mining	540 studies (2001–2024)	Map virtual coaching research using AI-based text analysis.	Identified thematic clusters and emerging research trends in AI virtual coaching.

(continued)

Table 3. *(continued)*

Author (Year)	Study Design	AI/ML Technique	Population	Main Objective	Main Outcome(s)
Suryanto et al. (2023)	Systematic review	Transformer-based NLP (BERT, GPT)	Not applicable	Examine AI chatbot approaches across domains.	Classified NLP chatbot models and discussed ethical and bias-related implications.
Anaya et al. (2024)	Consensus + narrative review	Data harmonization + integrative ML	Adults in population-based studies	Identify optimal tools to measure PA, diet, and sleep behaviors.	Proposed integrative ML framework for behavioral data and outlined research gaps.
Li et al. (2025)	Predictive quantitative	Seq2Seq LSTM + attention (Deep Learning)	384 adults (training program)	Predict health improvement trajectories from multimodal data.	Deep learning model achieved low MAE/RMSE and high predictive precision (R^2).
Köhler et al. (2024)	Conceptual viewpoint	Supervised ML on wearable signals	Smartwatch users (conceptual framework)	Define functional framework for smartwatch-based AI analytics.	Proposed monitoring–nudging–predicting model with ethical and clinical implications.

In a sport-specific context, Wesely et al. (2025) [15], applied supervised machine learning algorithms to inertial measurement unit data collected from 16 collegiate cheerleaders, analysing over 1100 tumbling elements. Using a single sensor positioned at the pelvis, the models were able to accurately recognise different acrobatic movements, demonstrating robustness to inter-individual variability and movement complexity. These results suggest that AI-based monitoring systems can provide objective performance assessment even in highly dynamic and technical sports environments.

At a population level, Vanstrum et al. (2023) [16], analysed accelerometer-derived physical activity data from 1625 adults included in the NHANES dataset to classify postural dysfunction. Machine learning models, particularly support vector machines and gradient-boosted algorithms, achieved area under the curve values up to 0.73, with age and moderate-intensity physical activity emerging as key predictive features. This study illustrates how routinely collected physical activity data can be leveraged to identify balance impairments in real-world settings.

Overall, studies within this cluster consistently report good to high classification performance across heterogeneous populations and technologies. Together, they indicate that AI-driven monitoring and activity recognition systems can provide accurate, scalable, and objective measures of movement, supporting their application in both preventive health and sport science contexts.

3.2 Feedback and Behaviour Support

Studies included in this cluster highlight the role of artificial intelligence in delivering personalized feedback and behavioural support to enhance engagement and adherence to physical activity interventions. Rather than focusing solely on activity recognition, these approaches leverage AI-driven decision-making to dynamically adapt goals, feedback intensity, and intervention delivery based on individual behaviour patterns.

Mohammadi et al. (2020) [17] developed a neural network–based model to predict achievable weekly step targets using wearable activity tracker data combined with behavioural and environmental variables. In a cohort of 30 adults with overweight, data from 20 participants were used to train and test the model over an eight-week observation period. The proposed approach achieved a mean absolute error of approximately 1,545 steps when predicting weekly activity targets, demonstrating the feasibility of AI-driven goal adjustment to sustain engagement with activity trackers and reduce goal attrition over time.

A more complex adaptive intervention strategy was proposed by Forman et al. (2023) [18], who introduced a reinforcement learning–based system to optimise the delivery of behavioural weight loss treatment. In this ongoing randomized controlled trial involving 336 adults with overweight or obesity, the AI system dynamically selects the most appropriate intervention modality each week (e.g., group sessions, individual calls, or automated messages) based on continuously monitored digital data, including physical activity. Preliminary evidence from earlier pilot work indicated that AI-optimised interventions achieved weight loss outcomes comparable to standard behavioural treatment while requiring approximately one-third of the coaching contact time, suggesting substantial gains in efficiency and scalability.

Finally, Canzone et al. (2025) [19], provided a comprehensive overview of AI applications in exercise and physical activity programmes, with particular emphasis on automated messaging systems and adaptive feedback mechanisms. According to the studies included in their review, AI-driven feedback was associated with improvements in motivation, adherence, and self-management behaviours in diverse populations, ranging from healthy adults to individuals with chronic conditions. These findings reinforce the potential of AI-based behavioural support systems to complement traditional physical activity interventions by offering scalable, personalized, and context-aware feedback.

Collectively, studies in this cluster indicate that artificial intelligence can effectively enhance behavioural support strategies by tailoring feedback and intervention intensity to individual needs. Such approaches appear particularly promising for improving long-term adherence and engagement in physical activity programmes, addressing one of the main limitations of conventional behaviour change interventions.

3.3 Prediction and Data Analytics

Studies within this cluster focus on the use of machine learning models to predict physical activity behaviours and functional health outcomes by leveraging large-scale datasets, wearable sensor data, and advanced feature engineering techniques. Unlike activity recognition approaches, these studies primarily aim to identify individuals at risk of insufficient physical activity or functional decline through predictive analytics.

Choe et al. (2025) [20] developed multiple machine learning classification models to predict adherence to physical activity guidelines using nationally representative data from the National Health and Nutrition Examination Survey, including 11,638 adults. Among the evaluated algorithms, decision tree models achieved the best performance, with an accuracy of 0.705, an F1-score of 0.819, and an area under the curve of 0.54. Permutation feature importance analysis revealed sedentary behaviour, age, gender, and educational status as the strongest predictors of guideline adherence, highlighting the relevance of lifestyle and sociodemographic factors in population-level physical activity prediction.

A more granular and temporally sensitive predictive approach was proposed by Kumar et al. (2025) [21], who applied machine learning techniques to ecological momentary assessment data collected from 43 adults over a three-week period. Using a reduced set of motivational and volitional EMA features, including self-efficacy, stress, planning, and perceived barriers, the best-performing models achieved a mean area under the curve of 0.87 in cross-validation. These findings demonstrate that short-term physical activity engagement can be predicted with high accuracy using a limited number of self-reported contextual variables, supporting the development of just-in-time adaptive interventions.

Zheng et al. (2025) [22] focused on predicting frailty status among older adults living in long-term care facilities using accelerometer-derived gait and physical activity data. Machine learning models trained on dynamic gait features and daily activity patterns achieved high classification performance, with the extreme gradient boosting model reaching an accuracy of 86.3% and an area under the curve of 0.92. Explainable artificial intelligence analyses identified gait variability, symmetry, and complexity as the most influential predictors, suggesting that dynamic gait characteristics may provide more sensitive indicators of frailty than traditional spatial-temporal metrics.

Similarly, Fan et al. (2024) [23], investigated the prediction of physical function impairment in older adults using wrist-worn accelerometer data from 747 participants in the National Health and Aging Trends Study. By combining engineered digital biomarkers derived from time-series analysis with demographic variables, the best-performing gradient boosting model achieved an accuracy of 81.5% and an area under the curve of 85.9%. The results showed that temporal and frequency-domain features outperformed conventional cumulative physical activity metrics, emphasizing the importance of capturing multidimensional activity patterns for functional health prediction.

Overall, studies in this cluster consistently demonstrate that machine learning-based predictive models can effectively identify individuals at risk of physical inactivity, frailty, or functional impairment. The integration of wearable sensor data, contextual self-reports, and explainable artificial intelligence techniques appears particularly promising for supporting early detection, personalized interventions, and scalable public health strategies in physical activity promotion.

3.4 Virtual Coaching and Interactive Systems

Studies included in this cluster explore the role of artificial intelligence–driven virtual coaching and interactive systems in supporting behaviour change, user engagement, and long-term interaction. Rather than focusing exclusively on physical activity outcomes, these works address the broader technological and conceptual foundations that enable scalable, personalized, and adaptive coaching solutions.

Korn et al. (2025) [24] conducted a large-scale bibliometric analysis of virtual coach research, examining 540 publications published between 2001 and 2024. Their analysis highlights the rapid growth and strong interdisciplinarity of the field, with virtual coaching applications spanning physical fitness, health promotion, mental health, education, and professional development. The authors identify artificial intelligence, conversational agents, personalization, and behaviour change as central research themes, while also emphasizing emerging trends such as explainable AI, multimodal interaction, and ethical design. Importantly, the study underlines that virtual coaches increasingly move beyond simple rule-based systems toward autonomous, context-aware coaching systems capable of sustained user interaction.

Complementing this macro-level perspective, Suryanto et al. (2023) [25] provided a systematic literature review of chatbot-based interactive systems using PRISMA guidelines, analysing over 300 studies across multiple application domains. Their findings show that advances in natural language processing, particularly transformer-based models such as BERT, GPT, and T5, have significantly improved conversational quality, user engagement, and contextual understanding. In health- and coaching-related applications, chatbots were frequently used to deliver guidance, motivation, and self-management support, although challenges related to empathy, ethical concerns, and data privacy remain prominent.

Together, these studies indicate that virtual coaching systems represent a key enabling technology for future physical activity and health promotion interventions. By combining conversational AI, adaptive feedback mechanisms, and scalable system architectures, virtual coaches have the potential to support personalized behaviour change at scale. However, both studies emphasize the need for rigorous evaluation, ethical frameworks, and user-centred design to ensure effectiveness and long-term adoption.

3.5 Integration and Multimodal Systems

Studies grouped within this cluster emphasize the integration of heterogeneous data sources to capture the multidimensional nature of physical activity and health-related behaviours. Rather than relying on single-modality inputs, these approaches combine wearable sensor data, self-reported measures, and contextual information to support more comprehensive monitoring, prediction, and decision-making processes.

Anaya et al. (2024) [26] provided a consensus-based framework derived from a National Heart, Lung, and Blood Institute workshop focused on optimal instruments for measuring dietary intake, physical activity, and sleep in population-based studies. The authors highlighted the necessity of integrating report-based methods with device-based assessments, such as wearables and physiological biomarkers, to create harmonized, time-stamped behavioural phenotypes. The study emphasizes that standardized data collection protocols, interoperable infrastructures, and access to raw time-series data are essential prerequisites for the effective application of artificial intelligence and machine learning techniques in large-scale multimodal health research.

A system-level perspective on multimodal integration was presented by Köhler et al. (2024) [27], who proposed a conceptual framework categorizing smartwatch use into monitoring, nudging, and predicting domains. Their analysis underscores how smartwatches act as integrative hubs by combining physiological signals, activity metrics, and contextual data, which can be leveraged for machine learning–based prediction of health outcomes. The authors further highlight interoperability challenges, data quality issues, and ethical considerations, particularly when integrating consumer-grade wearable data into clinical and public health workflows.

At the methodological level, Li (2025) [28] demonstrated the potential of deep learning architectures to integrate heterogeneous time-series data for personalized health prediction. The proposed sequence-to-sequence LSTM model with an attention mechanism fused physiological parameters, activity metrics, sleep features, and body measurements collected from 384 participants over 32 days. Compared to traditional machine learning models, the multimodal deep learning approach achieved substantially lower prediction errors (22.8% reduction in MAE and 19.3% reduction in RMSE) and higher explained variance, illustrating the added value of multimodal data fusion and temporal attention mechanisms for modeling complex health improvement trajectories.

Collectively, these studies demonstrate that multimodal integration represents a critical advancement in the application of artificial intelligence and machine learning to physical activity research. By combining diverse data streams across behavioural, physiological, and contextual domains, integrated systems enable more accurate predictions, richer behavioural phenotyping, and more personalized interventions. However, the effectiveness of such systems remains contingent on data harmonization, transparency, and ethical governance to ensure scalability and real-world applicability.

4 Discussions

This narrative systematic review summarised the most recent evidence on the application of Artificial Intelligence (AI) and Machine Learning (ML) in the promotion, monitoring and assessment of physical activity in different contexts and populations. The 16 studies included showed a consistent trend towards the integration of intelligent systems in exercise monitoring processes, behavioural support and predictive analyses. Although the approaches and technologies adopted were very heterogeneous, ranging from single-sensor recognition models to multimodal and conversational systems, AI applications demonstrated a consistent ability to improve the accuracy, personalisation, and adaptability of physical activity interventions.

Within the five areas of intervention identified, some converging directions emerged. Studies related to Monitoring and Activity Recognition highlighted the use of wearable sensors and artificial vision systems for the objective detection of movement, with good levels of accuracy in identifying walking patterns, postural deficits or specific gestures. Research in Feedback and Behaviour Support confirmed the effectiveness of adaptive feedback systems, often based on supervised or reinforcement learning algorithms, capable of sustaining motivation and adherence by modulating goals and messages based on individual progress. The Prediction and Data Analytics area has shown how AI models can predict health or behavioural outcomes — such as frailty, adherence or functional decline — based on sensory or self-reported data, offering valuable insights for prevention. Finally, the Virtual Coaching and Integration and Multimodal Systems areas represent the next step in technological evolution, combining conversational interfaces, emotional intelligence and heterogeneous data flows into interactive, context-sensitive digital assistants.

Significantly, scientific output in this field has increased markedly since 2022, signalling growing research interest in the potential of AI and ML in movement and health sciences. Recent bibliometric analyses confirm a steady upward trend in publications on digital interventions and AI-supported technologies for physical activity, wearable devices and predictive health analysis. This increase appears to be driven by the greater availability of data from consumer devices, the spread of large language models (LLMs) and the growing focus on personalised and preventive healthcare.

From an application perspective, this evidence highlights the transformative potential of AI in the shift from reactive to proactive physical activity promotion. The integration of wearable technologies, predictive models, and adaptive feedback mechanisms can support healthcare professionals in defining personalised prescriptions and maintaining long-term adherence. However, the actual implementation of such systems requires interoperable data management infrastructures, validated algorithms, and careful consideration of the ethical implications related to privacy, transparency, and bias.

Limitations and Potential Biases

This review has some limitations that should be acknowledged. Firstly, the literature search was conducted exclusively in two databases (PubMed and Scopus), which may have resulted in the exclusion of relevant studies indexed elsewhere. Furthermore, the application of predefined filters — such as language, full-text availability, and age range — may have led to the exclusion of additional potentially relevant studies. Secondly, the number of eligible studies was limited, and the experimental designs were highly heterogeneous, including qualitative, quantitative, and mixed approaches. This variability reduces the generalizability of the results and made a meta-analytic evaluation impossible. A further limitation concerns the lack of standardised tools and protocols across studies, which also represents an important future direction for research: the development of shared frameworks and validated metrics for AI-based physical activity studies. Finally, possible biases may arise from the choice of a descriptive synthesis instead of a meta-analysis, although this decision was methodologically justified by the high heterogeneity of the included studies.

Future Perspectives

Overall, this is a rapidly expanding field, and the integration of AI, ML and Natural Language Processing (NLP) technologies is set to play an increasingly central role in tackling physical inactivity and sedentary lifestyles, issues which, as highlighted in the introduction, remain a global public health priority. Future research should focus on identifying and validating digital tools that can prevent and reduce sedentary behavior, promote health and motivation, and support long-term adherence to active behaviors. The most advanced AI systems will need to enhance the predictive and feedback capabilities of health technologies, offering personalized and adaptive experiences that simplify access to movement and help increase the population's levels of physical activity and well-being. Such developments will be essential to translate the growing potential of AI into concrete benefits for public health.

5 Conclusions

This narrative systematic review provides an up-to-date summary of the use of Artificial Intelligence and Machine Learning in promoting and monitoring physical activity. The evidence gathered indicates that AI can effectively support the recognition of movement patterns, the provision of personalised feedback, the prediction of health outcomes, and the creation of interactive virtual coaching systems. Taken together, these approaches mark a shift towards more adaptive, data-driven, and user-centred models of health promotion.

The growth trend in publications since 2022 highlights the growing scientific and clinical interest in these technologies. This expansion reflects the broader integration of AI into digital health ecosystems, where predictive analytics and adaptive feedback are increasingly recognised as key elements of prevention and personalised care.

Despite progress, the literature still appears fragmented, and further efforts are needed to define shared metrics, interoperability standards, and ethical guidelines that ensure reliability and fairness in AI-based applications. Future research should focus on multimodal integration, longitudinal evaluation, and interdisciplinary collaboration to strengthen evidence and facilitate the translation of AI technologies into real-world health and sports contexts. Looking ahead, the development of increasingly accessible, motivating and inclusive AI and NLP systems is key to facilitating access to exercise, reducing sedentary lifestyles and promoting the well-being of the entire population.

Disclosure of Interests. The authors have no competing interests to declare that are relevant to the content of this article.

References

1. World Health Organization (WHO): Global status report on physical activity 2023. Geneva, WHO (2023)
2. Bucher, A., Blazek, E.S., Symons, C.T.: How are machine learning and artificial intelligence used in digital behavior change interventions? A scoping review. Mayo Clinic Proc. Digit. Health **2**(3), 375–404 (2024). https://doi.org/10.1016/j.mcpdig.2024.05.007
3. Farrahi, V., Clare, P.: Artificial intelligence and machine learning-powerful yet underutilized tools and algorithms in physical activity and sedentary behavior research. J. Phys. Act. Health **21**(4), 320–322 (2024). https://doi.org/10.1123/jpah.2024-0021
4. Mateus, N., Abade, E., Coutinho, D., Gómez, M.-Á., Peñas, C.L., Sampaio, J.: Empowering the sports scientist with artificial intelligence in training, performance, and health management. Sensors **25**(1), 139 (2025). https://doi.org/10.3390/s25010139
5. Goh, Y.S., Ow Yong, J.Q.Y., Chee, B.Q.H., Kuek, J.H.L., Ho, C.S.H.: Machine learning in health promotion and behavioral change: scoping review. J. Med. Internet Res. **24**(6), e35831 (2022). https://doi.org/10.2196/35831
6. Guerriero, M.A., Moscatelli, F., di Padova, M.: Integrating the use of artificial intelligence (ai) to promote physical activity: the effects on lifestyle and academic performance of university students. A literature review. Giornale Italiano di Educazione alla Salute, Sport e Didattica Inclusiva. **8**(2) Edizioni Universitarie Romane (2024). https://doi.org/10.32043/gsd.v8i2.1194
7. Bruno, A., Guerriero, M., Basta, A., Moscatelli, F.: Artificial intelligence, a useful ally in physical education at school. Ital. J. Health Educ. Sports Inclusive Didactics **8**(2) Edizioni Universitarie Romane (2024). https://doi.org/10.32043/gsd.v8i2.1198
8. Guerriero, M.A., di Padova, M., Moscatelli, F., Bellantonio, S., Dipace, A., Basta, A.: Stress in the university population: a literature review of the positive role of physical activity to improve the wellbeing of students. In: Ardimento, P., et al. (eds.) Higher Education Learning Methodologies and Technologies Online. HELMeTO 2024. Communications in Computer and Information Science, vol. 2468. Springer, Cham (2025). https://doi.org/10.1007/978-3-031-93999-0_7

9. Souaifi, M., et al.: Artificial intelligence in sports biomechanics: a scoping review on wearable technology, motion analysis, and injury prevention. Bioengineering **12**(8), 887 (2025). https://doi.org/10.3390/bioengineering12080887
10. Yousefi, F., et al.: Artificial intelligence in health promotion and disease reduction: rapid review. J. Med. Internet Res. **27**, e70381 (2025). https://doi.org/10.2196/70381
11. Page, M.J., et al.: The PRISMA 2020 statement: an updated guideline for reporting systematic reviews. BMJ (Clin. Res. ed.) **372**, n71 (2021). https://doi.org/10.1136/bmj.n71
12. Campbell, M., McKenzie, J.E., Sowden, A., Katikireddi, S.V., Brennan, S.E., Ellis, S., et al.: Synthesis without meta-analysis (SWiM) in systematic reviews: reporting guideline. BMJ **368**, l6890 (2020). https://doi.org/10.1136/bmj.l6890
13. Lincke, A., Fagerström, C., Ekstedt, M., Löwe, W., Backåberg, S.: A comparative study of the 2D- and 3D-based skeleton avatar technology for assessing physical activity and functioning among healthy older adults. Health Inf. J. **29**(4) (2023). https://doi.org/10.1177/14604582231214589
14. Peimankar, A., Winther, T.S., Ebrahimi, A., Wiil, U.K.: A machine learning approach for walking classification in elderly people with gait disorders. Sensors **23**(2), 679 (2023). https://doi.org/10.3390/s23020679
15. Wesely, S., et al.: Artificial intelligence for objective assessment of acrobatic movements: applying machine learning for identifying tumbling elements in cheer sports. Sensors **25**(7), 2260 (2025). https://doi.org/10.3390/s25072260
16. Vanstrum, E.B., Choi, J.S., Bensoussan, Y., Bassett, A.M., Crowson, M.G., Chiarelli, P.A.: Machine learning analysis of physical activity data to classify postural dysfunction. Laryngoscope **133**(12), 3529–3533 (2023). https://doi.org/10.1002/lary.30698
17. Mohammadi, R., et al.: Neural network-based algorithm for adjusting activity targets to sustain exercise engagement among people using activity trackers: retrospective observation and algorithm development study. JMIR Mhealth Uhealth. **8**(9), e18142 (2020). https://doi.org/10.2196/18142
18. Forman, E.M., et al.: Using artificial intelligence to optimize delivery of weight loss treatment: protocol for an efficacy and cost-effectiveness trial. Contemp. Clin. Trials **124**, 107029 (2023). https://doi.org/10.1016/j.cct.2022.107029
19. Canzone, A., et al.: The multiple uses of artificial intelligence in exercise programs: a narrative review. Front. Public Health **13**, 1510801 (2025). https://doi.org/10.3389/fpubh.2025.1510801
20. Choe, J.P., Lee, S., Kang, M.: Machine learning modeling for predicting adherence to physical activity guideline. Sci. Rep. **15**(1), 5650 (2025). https://doi.org/10.1038/s41598-025-90077-1
21. Kumar, D., Haag, D., Blechert, J., Niebauer, J., Smeddinck, J.D.: Feature selection for physical activity prediction using ecological momentary assessments to personalize intervention timing: longitudinal observational study. JMIR Mhealth Uhealth. **13**, e57255 (2025). https://doi.org/10.2196/57255
22. Zheng, X., Zeng, Z., S van Schooten, K., Yang, Y.: Machine learning approach for frailty detection in long-term care using accelerometer-measured gait and daily physical activity: model development and validation study. JMIR Aging **8**, e77140 (2025). https://doi.org/10.2196/77140
23. Fan, L., et al.: Predicting physical functioning status in older adults: insights from wrist accelerometer sensors and derived digital biomarkers of physical activity. J. Am. Med. Inform. Assoc. **31**(11), 2571–2582 (2024). https://doi.org/10.1093/jamia/ocae224
24. Korn, F., Karger, E., Ahlemann, F.: Mapping the research landscape of virtual coaches: what is to come? IEEE Access 1–1 (2025). https://doi.org/10.1109/ACCESS.2025.3581440
25. Suryanto, T., Wibawa, A., Hariyono, H., Nafalski, A.: Evolving conversations: a review of Chatbots and implications in natural language processing for cultural heritage ecosystems. Int. J. Robot. Control Syst. **3**(4), 955–1006 (2023). https://doi.org/10.31763/ijrcs.v3i4.1195

26. Anaya, G., et al.: Optimal instruments for measurement of dietary intake, physical activity, and sleep among adults in population-based studies: report of a National Heart, Lung, and Blood Institute workshop. J. Am. Heart Assoc. **13**(21), e035818 (2024). https://doi.org/10.1161/JAHA.124.035818
27. Köhler, C., Bartschke, A., Fürstenau, D., Schaaf, T., Salgado-Baez, E.: The value of smartwatches in the health care sector for monitoring, nudging, and predicting: viewpoint on 25 years of research. J. Med. Internet Res. **26**, e58936 (2024). https://doi.org/10.2196/58936
28. Li, X.: Deep learning to promote health through sports and physical training. Front. Public Health **13**, 1583581 (2025). https://doi.org/10.3389/fpubh.2025.1583581
29. Wibawa, A., Hariyono, H., Nafalski, A.: Evolving conversations: a review of Chatbots and implications in natural language processing for cultural heritage ecosystems. Int. J. Robot. Control Syst. **3**, 955–1006 (2023). https://doi.org/10.31763/ijrcs.v3i4.1195

Evaluating the Application of the SPIRAL Model: Mapping Macro Learning Outcomes for Curriculum Coherence and Design Validation

Francesco Floris[1](✉), Sorana Cimpan[2], Marina Marchisio Conte[1], and Sergio Rabellino[1]

[1] Univerisity of Turin, Turin, Italy
{francesco.floris,marina.marchisio,sergio.rabellino}@unito.it
[2] University of Savoie Mont-Blanc, Chambery, France
sorana.cimpan@univ-smb.fr

Abstract. Higher education is undergoing a profound transformation shaped by competence-based paradigms, digitalization, and the growing integration of artificial intelligence and learning analytics. While numerous initiatives have sought to model curricula around measurable competencies, few approaches provide structural coherence and data-informed validation across programs. Within this landscape, the SPIRAL model offers an integrative framework that unites pedagogical, technological, and analytical dimensions of personalization. It formalizes the relationships among competences, Learning Outcomes (LOs), and learning paths through a graph-based architecture capable of representing inclusion, equivalence, and progression. In this study, the SPIRAL model is applied to the *Bâtiment Écoconstruction Énergie* programme (Polytech Annecy–Chambéry, 2021–2025) to examine its capacity to represent macro-level outcomes and validate curricular coherence. The methodology combines automatic transcription, translation, Bloom-level classification (via BloomBERT), and semantic similarity computation (via Sentence-BERT) to construct a graph of interconnected LOs. Network indicators such as degree distribution, clustering coefficient, and average path length were used to assess internal organization and progression. Results reveal a well-connected and hierarchically coherent structure, highlighting linguistic competences as transversal anchors. These findings demonstrate the potential of SPIRAL to support data-driven curriculum auditing and to inform adaptive, transparent, and sustainable learning design.

Keywords: Adaptive learning · Competence-based education · Curriculum analytics · Graph theory · Learning outcomes · SPIRAL model

M. Adamoli et al. (Eds.): HELMeTO 2025, CCIS 2958, pp. 490–511, 2026.
https://doi.org/10.1007/978-3-032-31850-3_30

1 Introduction

Higher education is undergoing a structural and epistemological transformation driven by three converging forces: the global shift toward competence-based education, the digital transformation of teaching and learning, and the rapid development of artificial intelligence and learning analytics. Together, these factors are reshaping how institutions conceive, design, and evaluate learning. The traditional linear and content-driven paradigm is gradually giving way to data-informed, student-centered approaches that prioritize adaptability, personalization, and coherence across programs ([8,23]). This change has been further accelerated by the pandemic, which forced universities to adopt hybrid and online modalities and to reflect on the sustainability and transparency of their curricula ([17]).

The need to structure and visualize competence progression in a measurable and transferable form has become increasingly critical for both learners and institutions. Competency-based education (CBE) highlights the challenge of translating intended outcomes into operational curricular structures that support authentic learning, assessment, and professional relevance ([5]). As argued by Curry and Docherty, the successful implementation of CBE requires not only the definition of endpoint competencies but also their systematic articulation across courses, programs, and real-world experiences. This process depends on the alignment of learning goals, assessment practices, and institutional frameworks that ensure transparency and continuous improvement ([5]).

From this perspective, curriculum modeling must be understood as a dynamic and iterative process rather than a static representation. It evolves through feedback, analytics, and adaptive design, allowing educators to identify redundancies, gaps, and misalignments in the learning progression. Despite widespread interest in competence-based approaches and their endorsement by accreditation agencies and qualification frameworks such as the EQF, many curricula are still expressed only in textual or tabular formats, limiting their analytical and developmental potential. A structured, data-informed representation of competencies and outcomes thus becomes essential to ensure curricular coherence, accountability, and adaptability.

In parallel, the literature on personalized learning provides a strong theoretical foundation for these systemic changes. Bernacki, Greene, and Lobczowski ([2]) note that personalized learning research has expanded rapidly but remains fragmented, often lacking a shared conceptual framework that connects learner characteristics, instructional design, and measurable outcomes. Their review calls for integrated models capable of bridging the gap between individualized pedagogy and curricular structure. Major et al. ([15]) complement this view through a meta-analysis of 58 studies, demonstrating that technology-supported personalization leads to moderate but consistent improvements in student achievement, particularly in blended and adaptive environments. These findings validate the pedagogical relevance of personalization while emphasizing the need for models that ensure its coherence at the curricular level.

Recent research on adaptive and AI-enhanced learning further supports this direction. Jing et al. ([13]), in their large-scale bibliometric study of adaptive learning from 2000 to 2022, identify four major research clusters: deep learning for educational data analysis, AI-based adaptive modeling, intelligent tutoring systems, and computational modeling for knowledge tracing. Their analysis confirms that adaptive learning has become a mature interdisciplinary domain bridging computer science and education, yet still lacks frameworks capable of connecting micro-level adaptivity to macro-level curricular design. This gap - between technological personalization and pedagogical coherence - represents one of the most critical challenges in contemporary higher education.

At the same time, pedagogical approaches such as student-centered and blended learning provide operational strategies for integrating personalization into everyday teaching practice. Islam et al. ([12]) propose a student-centered blended learning model that emphasizes collaboration, autonomy, adaptability, and integration of digital technologies. Similarly, Soubra et al. ([20]) demonstrate that problem-based learning (PBL) and just-in-time teaching (JiTT) significantly enhance students' problem-solving skills, motivation, and critical thinking in online contexts. These findings illustrate that personalization is not limited to technological adaptation, but also to the design of flexible learning ecosystems where students can navigate pathways that align with their competences, interests, and learning pace.

Within this evolving context, the SPIRAL model (Student-centered Personalization of Individual education through Reusable and Autonomous Learning units, [3]) emerges as an integrative framework that unites the pedagogical, technological, and structural dimensions of personalization. Building on previous research in adaptive learning, graph theory, and digital curriculum modeling, SPIRAL formalizes the relationships among learning outcomes, competencies, and learning paths in a graph-based representation. This representation allows for human and computational interpretation, supports transparency in curricular design, and enables analytics for progression mapping. The model seeks to address three recurring challenges identified in the literature:

1. the lack of structural coherence among learning outcomes across courses;
2. the absence of tools to visualize learning paths;
3. the difficulty of validating curricular design through data.

The present study applies the SPIRAL model to a real curricular framework: the *Référentiel des compétences de la spécialité Bâtiment Écoconstruction Énergie* (2021–2025). The goal is to evaluate whether SPIRAL can effectively represent macro-level learning outcomes, identify implicit relationships, and assess the overall coherence of the curriculum through graph-based analysis. By integrating theoretical insights from personalized learning, adaptive education, and digital transformation, this work aims to contribute to the development of data-informed methods for curricular design and to support the broader transition toward competence-based and sustainable higher education systems.

2 State of the Art

The transformation of higher education in the last two decades has been deeply influenced by the convergence of digitalization, competence-based design, and artificial intelligence. These dynamics have progressively redefined the logic of curriculum planning and delivery, moving from teacher-centered transmission models to ecosystems characterized by adaptability, personalization, and data-informed governance. This section reviews the main lines of development in the current literature, focusing on three interrelated areas:

1. the evolution of competence-based and outcome-oriented education;
2. the emergence of AI-driven adaptive learning and learning analytics;
3. integrative frameworks aiming to connect personalization and curriculum coherence.

2.1 From Competence-Based Education to Personalization

The competence-based turn in higher education has profoundly transformed the epistemology of teaching and learning. Rooted in frameworks such as the European Qualifications Framework (EQF) and national accreditation systems, competence-based education (CBE) advocates a shift from content transmission to demonstrable skills and measurable learning outcomes. The effective implementation of this paradigm depends on the alignment between institutional governance, faculty development, and competence-oriented curricula, as well as the creation of transparent mechanisms that connect intended learning outcomes with authentic assessment and progression (see [5]). However, while CBE provides an essential foundation for learning design, its implementation often remains descriptive rather than analytical. Curricular documents frequently present lists of competences and learning outcomes but fail to represent the logical and hierarchical relationships among them - such as dependency, progression, or equivalence. This lack of structural modeling limits the potential for adaptive learning, cross-course coherence, and data-informed evaluation of curricular integrity. Recent debates have also questioned the broader implications of student-centered and personalized learning approaches, warning that an uncritical emphasis on individual autonomy may reproduce forms of ontological individualism that undermine collective and sustainable educational goals (see [14]). This perspective highlights the need for systemic models - such as SPIRAL - that balance personalization with curricular coherence and social responsibility.

Universities increasingly rely on digital platforms for content delivery, yet few exploit their analytical potential to assess coherence and progression within programs, resulting in outcomes that are often isolated and redundancies across modules that remain undetected ([17]). This rigidity contradicts the needs of post-pandemic universities, which require flexibility, personalization, and responsiveness to evolving contexts ([23]). In particular, Whalley et al. (in [23]) describe a model of "flexible personalization" in which curricula operate as adaptive ecosystems capable of responding dynamically to individual and collective needs, a vision that resonates with the broader shift toward lifelong and self-directed learning. They identify several challenges that must be addressed to realize flexible personalized learning:

- Institutional inertia: universities are often slow to embrace systemic change due to rigid policies and assessment standards.
- Digital inequality: not all students have equal access to devices, connectivity, or digital competences.
- Faculty readiness: teachers require professional development to design and manage flexible and personalized experiences.
- Data ethics and governance: personalization requires responsible use of learning analytics and transparent data policies.

Pedagogical research provides several models that attempt to operationalize such flexibility. A blended learning framework emphasizing collaboration, autonomy, and technology integration demonstrates that personalization is effective only within coherent instructional designs ([12]). This view is further supported by studies showing that Problem-Based Learning (PBL) and Just-in-Time Teaching (JiTT) methods promote both cognitive depth and learner agency in online education ([20]). Together, these studies indicate that personalization must be understood not as a purely technical adaptation but as a pedagogical principle of orchestration, where structure supports autonomy and coherence fosters engagement.

A systematic review of personalized learning research reinforces this perspective, revealing that the field remains conceptually fragmented ([2]). Many studies interpret personalization as a technological function - algorithmic adjustment of content - rather than as a pedagogical process involving learner identity, motivation, and metacognition. A meta-analysis of technology-supported personalization further confirms that such approaches improve achievement only when supported by coherent instructional alignment ([15]). Both contributions highlight a critical gap: the need for formal frameworks connecting pedagogical design, technological affordances, and measurable learning outcomes.

2.2 AI, Adaptivity, and Learning Analytics

Parallel to pedagogical reform, artificial intelligence (AI) and learning analytics have driven the emergence of adaptive learning as a multidisciplinary field bridging computer science, psychology, and education. A comprehensive bibliometric analysis of 900 publications from 2000 to 2022 identified four dominant clusters: deep learning for educational data mining, adaptive modeling for tutoring systems, AI-based knowledge tracing, and computational personalization models ([13]). The results reveal a shift from deterministic, rule-based systems to probabilistic, data-driven architectures capable of representing complex learner profiles. Despite this progress, Jing et al. ([13]) highlight several limitations in current adaptive learning research. Most studies remain focused on *reactive personalization*, that is, real-time adaptation based solely on behavioral data. Few consider the vertical alignment between micro-level adaptivity and macro-level curriculum design, including learning outcomes, competences, and overall program coherence. Moreover, the systemic and institutional dimensions of adaptive learning are often overlooked.

To address these gaps, Jing et al. ([13]) advocate for the development of multi-level adaptive models in which data collected at the micro level can inform pedagogical decisions at the course level (meso) and support structural improvements in curriculum design (macro). In this view, micro-level personalization refers to the capacity to adjust the learning experience to the individual student in real time, but its potential remains limited unless integrated within a meso and macro curricular perspective (the same kind of integration pursued by the SPIRAL model).

Within this context, AI serves not only as a personalization engine but also as a mechanism of reflection and inclusion. Personality-based learner modeling in Moodle environments has been shown to enhance adaptive feedback and engagement ([22]). Artificial Intelligence in Education (AIEd) has also been conceptualized as a foundation for constructing dynamic, data-informed learning pathways that reflect both cognitive and affective dimensions ([21]). Recent syntheses of AI applications in e-learning further emphasize the need to balance algorithmic adaptivity with human oversight to preserve pedagogical transparency and interpretability ([11]). Collectively, these studies indicate that AI-driven personalization can improve motivation, equity, and engagement when appropriately integrated into instructional design.

The interaction between adaptivity and human learning design has also been widely investigated in studies on motivation and cognition. Student-centered digital tools have been found to foster metacognitive awareness and cognitive performance, especially when implemented in collaborative contexts ([6]). Additional evidence suggests that personalized learning strategies enhance academic performance and motivation, particularly for low-performing students, provided that feedback mechanisms remain coherent and formative ([16]; [10]). These findings reinforce the view that adaptivity should be conceived as a property of the entire learning environment - an emergent dynamic between technology, pedagogy, and learner agency - rather than as a static system function.

2.3 Integrative Frameworks and Open Challenges

Despite the progress in both pedagogical and technological research, the literature reveals a persistent fragmentation between theory and practice. Most adaptive frameworks remain isolated prototypes, emphasizing technical innovation over theoretical coherence or empirical validation ([7]). This limitation reduces their applicability in institutional contexts, where personalization must coexist with accountability and curricular integrity.

Graph-based frameworks have recently emerged as potential solutions to this problem. The SPIRAL model proposes a formal representation of learning outcomes and competences as interconnected nodes within a directed graph ([3]). Relationships such as inclusion, equivalence, and progression are expressed as weighted links, enabling both human interpretation and computational analysis. This structure allows educators to identify redundancies and gaps, while data scientists can evaluate the consistency and coherence of curricular progression. SPIRAL therefore translates the abstract goals of competence-based and personalized learning into an operational, data-driven framework.

This integration resonates with the systemic vision of sustainable higher education that emphasizes the role of technology in supporting - rather than replacing - pedagogical decision-making and in fostering transparent and adaptable systems ([23]). Similarly, the *Horizon Report* identifies AI-based curriculum design and adaptive learning ecosystems as strategic priorities for the coming decade ([8]). Within this context, models like SPIRAL provide a methodological bridge between personalization and quality assurance, enabling institutions to visualize, analyze, and validate the internal coherence of their programs. In conclusion, the state of the art demonstrates a convergence of three trajectories:

- competence-based and outcome-oriented education providing institutional legitimacy;
- adaptive and AI-supported learning offering technological sophistication;
- integrative frameworks proposing structural and analytical coherence.

However, the integration of these domains remains incomplete. The SPIRAL model try to responds to this gap by offering a unified, graph-based approach capable of mapping and validating learning outcomes across the curriculum. Building on this foundation, the next section presents the methodology adopted to apply and evaluate the SPIRAL framework within a real-world educational context.

3 The SPIRAL Model

The SPIRAL model (*Student-centered Personalization of Individual education through Reusable and Autonomous Learning units*, [3]) represents an innovative approach to structuring, visualizing, and managing learning outcomes in education. Designed as both a pedagogical and computational framework, it formalizes the relationships between learning outcomes progression within a graph-based environment. Each component of the model plays a distinct role in ensuring transparency, adaptability, and coherence across different levels (meso and micro).

At the core of the SPIRAL model lies the concept of the *Learning Unit* (LU), which serves as the smallest autonomous building block of learning design. A Learning Unit is not equivalent to a lesson or activity; instead, it encapsulates a coherent micro-structure of knowledge, skills, and attitudes that can be reused, recombined, and adapted across different courses or programs. Each LU is defined by one and only one Learning Outcomes (LO), representing what the student is expected to know, understand, or be able to do upon completion. Through this modularity, the SPIRAL model supports scalability and reusability: Learning Units can be aggregated to form modules, courses, or entire programs, while maintaining traceability of intended outcomes.

Learning outcomes form the semantic backbone of the model. They express the cognitive, procedural and affective dimensions of learning in measurable terms and are aligned with Bloom's Taxonomy and competence frameworks. In SPIRAL, LOs are treated as nodes within a directed graph, connected by relationships that describe their logical or pedagogical dependencies. These relationships - such as 'includes', 'is equivalent to', or 'prerequisite' - are important for both human interpretability and computational analysis of curricular coherence. The model enables educators and institutions to visualise how knowledge and skills evolve within and across learning units, ensuring that each outcome meaningfully contributes to the overall competence structure. What the SPIRAL model proposes is not only a framework for representing learning coherence but also a methodological approach for *standardizing the creation of Learning Outcomes* (LOs). Formalising LOs in structured, comparable and analysable terms enables educational institutions to overcome a major challenge in competence-based and personalised learning: the variability and lack of interoperability of outcome descriptions across programmes and institutions ([3]). This standardization has strategic relevance in the context of transnational collaborations and university alliances. By defining Learning Outcomes through shared descriptors, semantic consistency, and graph-based relations, SPIRAL enables the comparison, reuse, and integration of curricular elements such as courses and micro-credentials. In this way, the model helps to develop a shared digital language for higher education, promoting transparency, portability, and co-certification within European University Alliances.

From an analytical perspective, this graph-based architecture transforms curriculum design into a dynamic, data-informed process. It allows identification of redundancies, gaps, or inconsistencies among Learning Outcomes and provides a foundation for adaptive learning pathways. The SPIRAL model can integrate with learning analytics systems to monitor student achievement at the level of specific Learning Units, thus enabling continuous improvement and personalization. By formalizing the relationship between Learning Outcomes and competences, SPIRAL operationalizes the principles of competence-based education and sustainability, ensuring that personalization occurs within a coherent and transparent curricular structure.

In essence, SPIRAL connects the micro-level precision of Learning Outcomes with the macro-level coherence of institutional curricula. Its modular and graph-based nature provides a methodological bridge between pedagogical design, data analytics, and quality assurance, positioning it as a powerful framework for structuring adaptive, transparent, and evidence-based learning ecosystems.

4 Methodology

4.1 Research Questions

Building on the theoretical background discussed in the previous section, this study shifts focus from conceptual considerations of competence-based and adaptive education to the practical implementation of these principles within a specific curriculum. As introduced earlier, the SPIRAL model offers a structured, data-driven approach to representing curricular coherence through graph-based modelling of learning outcomes (LOs) and competences. While existing literature and projects have addressed competence mapping and visualisation, this study extends this work by systematically analysing Learning Outcomes and focusing on how they can be represented, connected and validated through the SPIRAL framework. This study aims to investigate how the SPIRAL model can effectively support the representation, validation and enhancement of curriculum coherence in competence-based higher education. The following research questions guide the study:

1. **RQ1:** How can Learning Outcomes (LOs) be modeled as interconnected elements within a graph-based structure to represent inclusion, equivalence, and progression relationships between competences and curricular components?
2. **RQ2:** To what extent can the SPIRAL model contribute to identifying and validating coherence, redundancy, and progression within competence-based curricula?
3. **RQ3:** How can the standardization of Learning Outcomes foster interoperability and transparency across institutional and transnational educational frameworks, such as European University Alliances and micro-credential systems?

These research questions aim to bridge theoretical and practical dimensions: they explore how SPIRAL can serve both as an analytical tool for validating curricular coherence and as a methodological framework for promoting sustainable, interoperable, and data-informed educational design.

4.2 Research Design

The research is structured as a case study focused on the *Référentiel des compétences de la spécialité Bâtiment Écoconstruction Énergie* (2021–2025), developed at Polytech Annecy-Chambéry. This reference framework defines the expected competences and learning outcomes for the Building Engineering specialization, with explicit articulation between transversal and specific competences. Each competence is decomposed into essential components (e.g., BAT-1.1, BAT-1.2, BAT-2.1, TC-1.1, etc.), reflecting the professional, technical, and sustainable dimensions of the training pathway.

The primary document analyzed is the official *Référentiel des compétences de la spécialité Bâtiment Écoconstruction Énergie* (2021–2025), which provides a detailed mapping of competences, associated learning outcomes, and their levels of mastery (Notion, Application, Mastery, Expertise). Complementary information about program structure and course distribution was drawn from the *Programme du diplôme Bâtiment Écoconstruction Énergie*. The program follows a coherent sequence of learning units distributed across ten semesters, each defined by specific *Unités d'Enseignement* (UE) and *Eléments Constitutifs* (EC). This organization ensures vertical alignment between competences, courses, and learning outcomes - a structure conceptually consistent with the SPIRAL model, which emphasizes modularity, progression, and data-informed coherence. The work conducted with Cimpan et colleagues ([19]) has so far concentrated on the competence dimension, emphasizing the formal mapping, visualization, and validation of competence networks (see [19]). In contrast, the present application of the SPIRAL model aims to shift the analytical focus from competences to *Learning Outcomes* (LOs). While competences are explicitly coded and hierarchically structured in the BAT framework, Learning Outcomes are expressed in natural language, without standardized identifiers or taxonomic classification. This makes their systematic analysis and cross-course alignment significantly more complex. At present, the available data allow analysis at the *macro level* only, as the framework specifies competences and their associated macro-learning outcomes but does not yet include detailed subdivisions into micro-learning units. For this reason, the analysis has been intentionally truncated at the macro-outcome level. Such a focus remains meaningful for several reasons:

- macro-level outcomes capture the institutional vision and transversal competences that define program identity;
- they provide a stable and standardized foundation for cross-program comparison and competence alignment;
- they enable validation of coherence and coverage before introducing micro-level modularization.

In summary, this macro-level analytical approach serves as a preliminary but essential phase in implementing the SPIRAL model, acting as a bridge between the competence-centered representation achieved in [19] and the outcome-centered analysis proposed by SPIRAL. It ensures that the subsequent graph-based representation of learning outcomes and competences is grounded in validated curricular structures, paving the way for the integration of semantic, linguistic, and structural dimensions in data-driven curriculum design.

4.3 Graph Rappresentation of BAT Program

4.4 Preliminary Operations

Before graph construction, a series of preprocessing steps were conducted to ensure data consistency, linguistic uniformity, and analytical readiness. All operations were performed in Python using dedicated scripts for parsing, translation, classification, and similarity computation.

Data transcription and preparation. The information extracted from the *Référentiel des compétences Bâtiment Écoconstruction Énergie (2021–2025)* was manually transcribed from PDF format into a structured CSV file. Each record corresponds to a macro-level Learning Outcome (LO). Since the original framework was written in French, all Learning Outcomes were translated into English using the `GoogleTranslator` module from the `deep-translator` Python library. A new column (`LO_EN`) was appended to the dataset to store the English version of each Learning Outcome. The translation process aimed to maintain terminological consistency, particularly for technical and pedagogical expressions, to facilitate the subsequent application of NLP-based similarity and classification algorithms. Each translated Learning Outcome was automatically classified according to Bloom's taxonomy using the *BloomBERT* algorithm ([9]). This transformer-based model predicts the cognitive level of an outcome across the six Bloom categories - *Remember*, *Understand*, *Apply*, *Analyze*, *Evaluate*, and *Create*. For each LO, the model outputs both the predicted level and the associated confidence percentages for all six categories. These values were added as new attributes in the dataset (`bloom_level`, `prob_category`, `prob_Bloom`, etc.), providing a quantitative foundation for comparative analysis.

4.5 The Similarity Function

This study builds upon the SPIRAL model by investigating the semantic similarity between learning outcomes. To this end, we developed a dedicated computational pipeline designed to calculate pairwise similarity scores between LO statements. The algorithm is based on a transformer-based language model (Sentence-BERT, model `all-mpnet-base-v2`), which generates high-dimensional semantic embeddings for each English learning outcome statement. These embeddings encode contextual meaning beyond surface lexical similarity, enabling a more reliable comparison between pedagogical statements written in natural language.

Each pair of learning outcomes is compared by computing the *cosine similarity* between their embedding vectors, according to the formula:

$$\text{sim}(A, B) = \frac{A \cdot B}{||A||\,||B||}$$

where A and B are the embedding vectors corresponding to two learning outcome sentences. The cosine similarity ranges from 0 (no semantic correlation) to 1 (maximum semantic similarity).

This metric was used to determine the weight of the relationships within the graph, representing the degree of semantic inclusion or equivalence between two outcomes. To avoid the creation of redundant or meaningless edges, we set a semantic similarity threshold of 0.5 as the minimum value required for an edge to be created between two nodes. The resulting weighted graph allows identifying clusters of conceptually related learning outcomes, detecting redundant or overlapping formulations, and quantifying progression patterns across levels of cognitive complexity.

To compute the semantic proximity between learning outcome embeddings, we used the `cos_sim()` utility provided by the `sentence-transformers` library. This function directly operates on PyTorch tensors, returning a similarity matrix where each element (i, j) represents the cosine similarity between two embeddings. Internally, the operation is fully vectorized and optimized for GPU acceleration, allowing the comparison of all pairs of outcomes simultaneously. This ensures both computational efficiency and numerical precision without requiring explicit loops or conversions to external numerical formats.

Summary of preprocessing workflow. In summary, the preprocessing pipeline included:

- transcription of Learning Outcomes from PDF to CSV;
- automatic LO translation from French to English;
- Bloom level classification using *BloomBERT*;
- computation of pairwise semantic similarity.

4.6 Data Representation

The data were modeled as a directed labeled graph in Neo4j, using Python scripts to parse and import the information extracted from the CSV dataset. Each entity in the dataset corresponds to a specific node type, allowing a clear hierarchical and semantic organization of the learning structure within the BAT programme.

The model includes the following node types:

- **Programme**: representing the academic programme (`BALT`).
- **Semester**: corresponding to the semester in which the courses are offered (e.g., `S5`, `S6`).
- **Didactic-cluster**: representing each didactic unit (column `UE`).
- **Course**: corresponding to the courses listed in the column `EC`, characterized by a unique `code` and a descriptive `name`.
- **Learning-outcome**: representing each macro learning outcome, defined by its `sentence-en`, `sentence-fr`, `level-bloom`, `category-bloom`, and `Niveau`.
- **Competence**: representing the transversal or technical competences associated with the learning outcomes.

The relationships were defined to reflect the hierarchical and semantic dependencies among entities:

- `HAS_SEMESTER`: links the **Programme** node to its **Semester** nodes.
- `HAS_DC`: connects each **Semester** to its **Didactic-cluster**.
- `HAS_COURSE`: associates each **Didactic-cluster** with its **Course** nodes.
- `HAS_MACRO_OUTCOME`: connects each **Course** to its corresponding **Learning-outcome**.
- `ASSOCIATED_COMPETENCE`: links each **Learning-outcome** to the **Competence** nodes listed in the same row of the dataset.
- `Equivalent_to`: a bidirectional relation between learning outcomes having the same Bloom level, with a weight proportional to their similarity computed through a similarity function.
- `Include`: a directed relation from a learning outcome of higher Bloom level to one of lower level, with a weight proportional to their similarity computed through a similarity function.

4.7 Evaluation Metrics

To assess the internal structure and consistency of the Learning Outcomes (LO) network, we computed a set of topological indicators adapted from network theory and curriculum analysis frameworks ([18]). These indicators provide quantitative insights into the coherence, progression, and robustness of the curriculum structure when represented as a directed graph. Importantly, in this study, competences were not included as nodes, allowing the analysis to focus exclusively on the internal organization of the Learning Outcomes and their semantic and cognitive interrelations.

- **Degree Distribution (DD)** - measures the number of connections incident to each node, reflecting the hierarchical organization of Learning Outcomes. Nodes with high degree act as conceptual anchors within the curriculum, indicating key outcomes that integrate multiple cognitive or thematic elements. A heterogeneous degree distribution, where few nodes exhibit high connectivity, suggests a well-structured hierarchy consistent with principles of cumulative knowledge building.
- **Clustering Coefficient (CC)** - evaluates the local density of connections among neighboring Learning Outcomes, quantifying the degree of local coherence within thematic or cognitive clusters. A high CC value indicates the presence of cohesive micro-modules in which Learning Outcomes are mutually reinforcing, potentially corresponding to self-contained conceptual domains or Bloom-level substructures.
- **Average Path Length (APL)** - measures the average number of edges along the shortest paths connecting all pairs of Learning Outcomes. This metric reflects the efficiency of conceptual progression across the graph. Lower APL values correspond to smoother pedagogical transitions between outcomes, whereas higher values may signal fragmentation or cognitive distance between key concepts. An optimal APL balance suggests both conceptual depth and navigability.
- **Hub Centrality (H)** - quantifies the systemic importance of nodes that act as bridges across distinct regions of the network. In the absence of competence nodes, hub centrality identifies Learning Outcomes that mediate transitions between different Bloom levels or cognitive domains, thus functioning as cross-level or integrative anchors. These hubs contribute to vertical coherence and ensure continuity between knowledge acquisition, application, and higher-order reasoning skills.

Collectively, these indicators allow a multidimensional evaluation of the curriculum's structural properties. In the present context, they serve as proxies for four higher-order dimensions of curricular quality:

- *Structure* (DD, H): the degree of hierarchical differentiation and integration among Learning Outcomes.
- *Coherence* (CC): the extent to which local clusters of outcomes form thematically consistent modules.

- *Continuity* (APL): the smoothness of conceptual progression and cognitive sequencing.

This network-based evaluation framework enables an analytical comparison between different curricular configurations or modules, supporting the identification of imbalances - such as excessive linearity, fragmentation, or overdependence on single outcomes - and guiding iterative refinement of the learning design in alignment with personalized learning paradigms and graph-based instructional models like SPIRAL.

Furthermore, the use of network indicators aligns with recent research on *learning coherence* and *adaptive learning analytics* ([2,7,11]). In this perspective, metrics such as CC and APL are not only descriptive of the structural topology but can also be interpreted as proxies for cognitive load distribution and knowledge integration across Bloom levels. Similarly, Hub Centrality correspond to the concepts of *adaptive flexibility* in personalized learning ecosystems, highlighting the degree to which a curriculum can dynamically support differentiated learning paths without compromising overall integrity. This approach positions the graph model as a tool for both analytical evaluation and pedagogical design within data-informed frameworks for higher education.

5 Results

5.1 Descriptive Overview

The graph extracted from the dataset (Fig. 1) comprises 60 courses and 157 distinct Learning Outcomes (LOs). The distribution of LOs across Bloom's taxonomy levels is reported in Fig. 2. The majority of the outcomes are positioned in the intermediate cognitive levels: 83 outcomes (52.9%) correspond to the *Apply* category (Level 2), followed by 22 outcomes (14.0%) at the *Create* level (Level 5), and 17 outcomes (10.8%) at the *Understand* level (Level 1).

Lower-order levels such as *Remember* (Level 0) account for 13 outcomes (8.3%), while higher-order categories such as *Analyze* (Level 3) and *Evaluate* (Level 4) comprise 14 (8.9%) and 8 (5.1%) outcomes respectively. From a pedagogical standpoint, the distribution of Bloom levels suggests that the curriculum is predominantly skill-oriented rather than concept-oriented. More than half of the Learning Outcomes (52.9%) are situated at the *Apply* level, emphasizing procedural knowledge and the ability to transfer concepts into practice. Conversely, higher-order cognitive levels such as *Analyze*, *Evaluate*, and *Create* together account for only 28.0% of the total, indicating that reflective and critical thinking skills are represented but not dominant within the current structure. This profile is consistent with a curriculum that prioritizes operational competencies and performance-based learning objectives over abstract reasoning and conceptual synthesis.

From a structural perspective, the network in Fig. 1 includes 270 unique `Equivalent_to` relationships (or 135 bidirectional pairs) and 152 `Include` relationships. The average semantic weight associated with the equivalence edges is

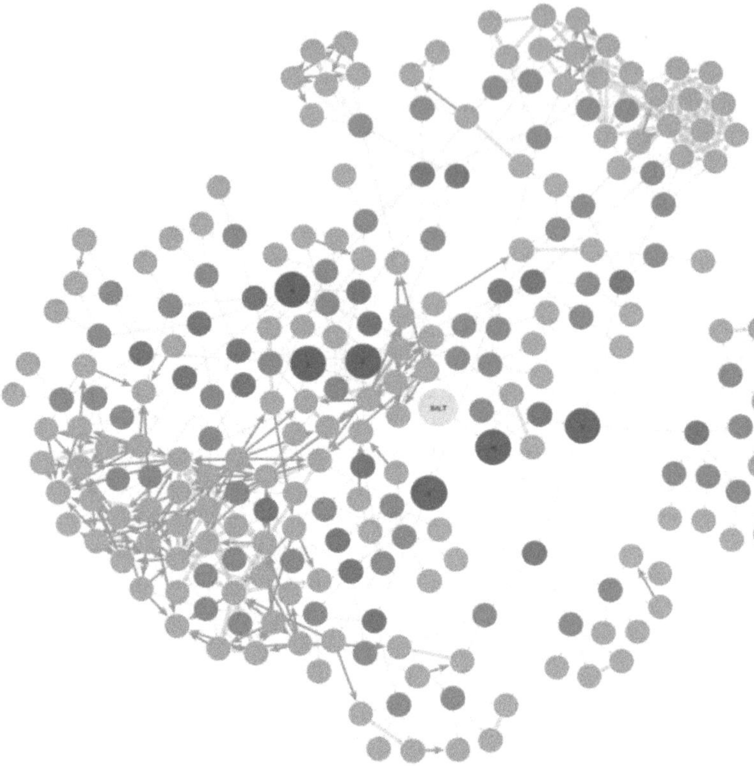

Fig. 1. Graph-based representation illustrating the structure and interconnections within the BAT programme.

0.66, suggesting a moderate-to-high degree of conceptual overlap among certain outcomes. In contrast, the average inclusion weight of 0.57 reflects the presence of hierarchical or progressive relations in which one outcome partially implies another, but with weaker semantic similarity overall. These values collectively outline a moderately connected and hierarchically organized curriculum graph, where equivalence clusters coexist with directional learning progressions.

As shown in Fig. 1, a bird-eye analisys reveals that the overall structure of the graph is divided into some *main subgraphs*, clearly distinguishable in terms of internal density and degree of connectivity. In the upper-right part of the graph presentend in Fig. 1 (and detailed in Fig. 3a), a subgraph emerges with a high number of *equivalent Learning Outcomes* (in the Fig. 3a the labels inside the DOT are the values of the Bloom's level of each LO.). In this area, the connected courses are mostly related to language learning, while their links to the rest of the network appear weaker and less frequent. Several isolated subgraphs can also be observed, corresponding to groups of outcomes characterized by a relatively low *Degree Density (DD)*, indicating limited internal interconnections.

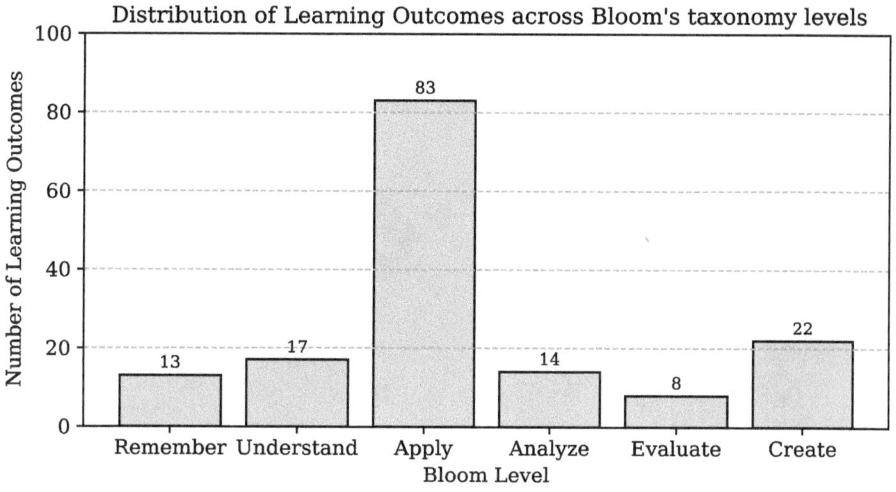

Fig. 2. Distribution of Learning Outcomes across Bloom's taxonomy levels.

Conversely, in the lower-left part of the graph in Fig. 1 (and detailed in Fig. 3b), a much more connected region is visible. This represents the *main subgraph* (the largest strongly connected component, meaning the biggest subset of vertices where each vertex can reach every other through directed paths), which includes the nodes used for the subsequent analyses on *Average Path Length (APL)* and *Network Diameter*.

5.2 Graph Analysis

Degree Distribution. The degree distribution provides a first structural insight into the topology of the Learning Outcomes (LO) network. This metric quantifies the number of direct relationships incident to each node, reflecting the extent to which an outcome is semantically or hierarchically linked to others within the curriculum graph [18]. Nodes with a higher degree can be interpreted as conceptual anchors or hubs ([1]), which play a pivotal role in connecting multiple cognitive domains and maintaining overall curricular coherence.

Table 1 summarizes the main descriptive statistics of the network. The graph comprises 157 nodes, corresponding to individual Learning Outcomes, with an average degree of 5.38 and a median degree of 3. The maximum observed degree is 31, indicating the presence of a few highly connected nodes acting as conceptual hubs, while the minimum value of 0 reveals isolated or weakly connected outcomes.

The distribution of degree values across intervals (Table 2) highlights a strongly right-skewed pattern. Approximately one-third of the nodes (34%) fall within the lowest interval (0–1), corresponding to Learning Outcomes that are marginal or highly specific. At the opposite end, around one quarter (24%) of the

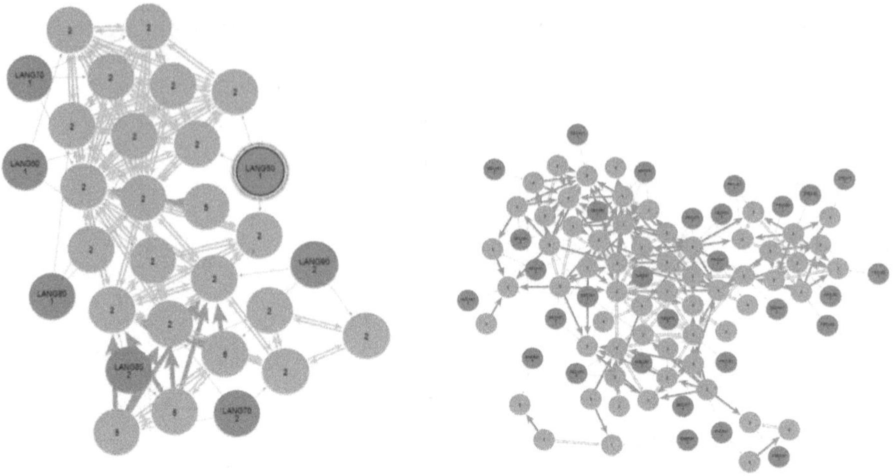

(a) Language subgraph. (b) Zoom on the main subgraph.

Fig. 3. (a) subgraph of language courses and (b) main subgraph.

Table 1. Degree distribution statistics for the Learning Outcomes network.

Metric	Value
Number of nodes (N)	157
Minimum degree	0
Median degree	3
Average degree	5.38
Maximum degree	31

nodes exhibit more than nine connections, forming a limited number of hubs that integrate multiple relations of equivalence and inclusion. This asymmetric shape is consistent with the properties of *scale-free* networks, where a small number of highly connected nodes sustain the overall structure, while the majority of nodes maintain a limited local influence.

From an educational perspective, the observed pattern indicates a hierarchical organization of Learning Outcomes: many outcomes are peripheral and locally connected, whereas a few act as integrative anchors that link distinct thematic or cognitive clusters. Such a topology suggests that curricular coherence is not uniformly distributed but concentrated around central Learning Outcomes that mediate conceptual progression and cross-level integration. This aligns with the findings of O'Meara and Vaidya [18], who interpret highly connected nodes as key components for maintaining curricular consistency and knowledge transfer across levels of complexity.

Table 2. Frequency distribution of node degrees (binned).

Degree interval	Number of nodes (n)	Percentage (%)
0–1	54	34.4
2–3	32	20.4
4–5	15	9.6
6–8	19	12.1
9+	37	23.6

Hub and Eigenvector Centrality. The analysis of hub nodes confirms the presence of a highly connected core within the curriculum graph. According to degree centrality, the most connected Learning Outcomes (LOs) belong to the *Apply* level of Bloom's taxonomy. The two statements "*intervene in writing and orally, always aiming for inter-activity of operational communication*" reach the maximum degree value (31), followed by "*apply scientific and technical knowledge to meet construction specifications*" and other procedural outcomes related to design and implementation tasks. These nodes act as quantitative hubs, sharing strong semantic similarity with a large portion of the graph. Eigenvector centrality refines this picture by highlighting not only the most connected, but the most *influential* outcomes -those linked to other central nodes. The same linguistic LOs ("*intervene in writing and orally*", "*understand written and audio documents and express oneself*") achieve the highest eigenvector scores (≈ 0.36), forming a dense and self-reinforcing cluster at the *Apply* level. This suggests that communicative and language-related outcomes constitute the structural core of the curriculum network, acting as conceptual anchors that integrate the procedural, technical, and reflective dimensions of the program. This is also consistent with the competencies included in the BAT framework, which places significant emphasis on the development of communicative and language-related skills.

Average Path Length (APL) and Network Diameter. To assess the efficiency of conceptual progression across the network, we computed the *Average Path Length* (APL) and the *network diameter* within the largest connected component (LCC) of the undirected graph. The LCC (`loGraphLCC`) was isolated by means of a weakly connected components procedure, retaining only the subgraph corresponding to the largest component. The analysis yielded an APL value of 2.04, with a minimum distance of 1 and a maximum distance (diameter) of 5. This indicates that, on average, any learning outcome can be reached from another in slightly more than two conceptual transitions, demonstrating a compact and highly navigable topology. The density of the LCC is 0.12, and the average node degree is 7.3, meaning that each LO is connected, on average, to seven others. This reflects a well-connected but non-redundant topology, indicating a balanced level of conceptual overlap among outcomes.

Clustering Coefficient. The local clustering analysis, computed on the LCC with 61 nodes, yielded an average coefficient of $\overline{C} = 0.44$ (median 0.42, range $[0, 1]$, sd $= 0.33$). This value indicates a moderate degree of triadic closure, meaning that many learning outcomes form locally coherent clusters in which connected nodes are also linked to each other. Such a pattern is consistent with the presence of a few dense semantic cores interconnected through more linear, bridging nodes. This structure reflects the internal organization of the curriculum, where practical and evaluative competences (*Apply*, *Evaluate*) act as highly clustered hubs connecting more theoretical outcomes.

6 Discussion and Conclusions

The structural analysis of the Learning Outcome (LO) network, built following the SPIRAL model, provides an integrated view of how learning objectives interrelate within the curriculum. By applying SPIRAL's computational framework for deriving semantic and hierarchical relations among LOs, the resulting graph captures both equivalence (conceptual similarity) and inclusion (developmental progression) relations. This graph-based approach makes explicit the latent structure of the curriculum, supporting a deeper understanding of how cognitive and operational competencies evolve across LOs. The analysis reveals a curriculum that is both operationally coherent and hierarchically organized, yet only partially balanced across Bloom's levels. The predominance of outcomes situated at the *Apply* level (Level 2) highlights a strong focus on procedural and performance-based competencies, confirming that the program prioritizes actionable knowledge and professional skills over abstract conceptualization. This profile aligns with Zheng's [24] implementation-oriented model of technology-facilitated learning, in which learners are guided towards concrete application rather than theoretical reflection. From a network analytic perspective, a visual analisys reveal that the topology of the SPIRAL-generated graph exhibits features of a *scale-free structure*: a small number of highly connected nodes (hubs) link otherwise sparse and locally cohesive clusters. Such an organization supports both efficiency and resilience, as conceptual connectivity is maintained through a limited set of integrative outcomes. The hubs identified - mainly linguistic and communicative LOs - serve as transversal mediators between technical and reflective domains. Their centrality suggests that communicative competence functions as a connective tissue across disciplinary boundaries. Similar findings are reported by Bernacki *et al.* [2], who note that personalization and adaptivity in learning environments are most effective when they leverage cross-domain constructs that unify otherwise isolated learning components. The moderate clustering coefficient ($\overline{C} = 0.44$) and compact average path length (APL $= 2.04$) indicate that the SPIRAL-based LO network is locally dense but globally navigable - a desirable configuration for adaptive curriculum design. Pedagogically, this structure facilitates multiple personalized trajectories through the curriculum, supporting differentiated learning paths without compromising overall coherence. This mirrors the principles of personalized adaptive learning described by du Plooy *et al.* [7], who emphasize that adaptability depends on the interplay between *semantic proximity* (to ensure local relevance) and *structural distance* (to sustain progression) within a learning network. The coexistence of strong equivalence clusters and directional inclusion relations, as derived from SPIRAL's relational rules, can be interpreted as an emergent *adaptive hierarchy*. Equivalence relations delineate conceptually redundant or overlapping LOs that could be recognized by intelligent recommender systems, while inclusion relations define prerequisite chains that guide the sequencing of learning experiences. This dual structure mirrors the logic of adaptive learning tools such as those analyzed by Contrino *et al.* [4], in which diagnostic assessments and feedback loops dynamically adjust the order and complexity of learning tasks. From a design perspective, the SPIRAL model demonstrates the potential of *graph-based curriculum analytics* as a foundation for personalized learning ecosystems. The resulting network provides both a cognitive map and a computational framework that can inform the dynamic alignment between learning outcomes, activities, and assessment strategies. In this sense, the SPIRAL-generated graph can evolve into an adaptive layer capable of recommending optimal pathways through the curriculum, consistent with evidence from meta-analyses showing that technology-facilitated personalized learning produces medium-to-large gains in achievement [24]. Nonetheless, certain limitations emerge. The overrepresentation of procedural LOs suggests limited scaffolding toward higher-order thinking skills such as evaluation and creation. In this study, higher levels of Bloom's taxonomy were only marginally represented; therefore, future applications of the SPIRAL network could focus on contexts featuring a greater number of higher-level learning outcomes, to explore how the model performs when addressing tasks that require critical reasoning, metacognition, and creativity - dimensions identified in the literature as key for sustaining engagement and motivation in adaptive learning environments [7,24]. Furthermore, the hub-dependent structure of the network may entail a degree of fragility: changes in a few central LOs could disproportionately affect the overall coherence of the graph. In conclusion, the SPIRAL-based graph analysis provides quantitative evidence of curricular coherence and highlights the central role of communicative competences as structural anchors of the program. These findings reinforce the pedagogical value of network analytics as a diagnostic and design instrument within adaptive and personalized learning environments. Integrating SPIRAL's graph metrics with learning analytics and AI-driven personalization engines could thus support the transition from static curriculum design to a *data-driven, dynamically adaptive learning ecosystem*, where outcomes, activities, and assessments are continuously aligned to individual learner profiles.

Disclosure of Interests. The authors have no competing interests to declare that are relevant to the content of this article.

References

1. Barabási, A.L., Frangos, J.: Linked: How everything is connected to everything else and what it means for business, science, and everyday life (2014). Basic books
2. Bernacki, M.L., Greene, M.J., Lobczowski, N.G.: A systematic review of research on personalized learning: personalized by whom, to what, how, and for what purpose (s)? Educ. Psychol. Rev. **33**(4), 1675–1715 (2021)
3. Cimpan, S., Floris, F., Marchisio Conte, M., Rabellino, S.: Student-centered personalization of individual education through reusable and autonomous learning units-the spiral model. In: Proceedings of International Conferences e-Learning and Digital Learning 2024 and Sustainability, Technology and Education 2024, pp. 75–82. IADIS Press (2024)
4. Contrino, M.F., Reyes-Millán, M., Vázquez-Villegas, P., Membrillo-Hernández, J.: Using an adaptive learning tool to improve student performance and satisfaction in online and face-to-face education for a more personalized approach. Smart Learn. Environ. **11**(1), 6 (2024)
5. Curry, L., Docherty, M.: Implementing competency-based education. Collected Essays Lear. Teach. **10**, 61–73 (2017)
6. Dada, D., Laseinde, O.T., Tartibu, L.: Student-centered learning tool for cognitive enhancement in the learning environment. Proc. Comput. Sci. **217**, 507–512 (2023)
7. Du Plooy, E., Casteleijn, D., Franzsen, D.: Personalized adaptive learning in higher education: a scoping review of key characteristics and impact on academic performance and engagement. Heliyon **10**, e39630 (2024). https://doi.org/10.1016/j.heliyon.2024.e39630
8. EDUCAUSE Learning Initiative: Educause horizon report: Teaching and learning edition 2021 (2021). https://library.educause.edu/resources/2021/4/2021-horizon-report-teaching-and-learning-edition
9. F., R.L.Q.: Bloombert: A task complexity classifier. https://github.com/RyanLauQF/BloomBERT (2025)
10. Fariani, R.I., Junus, K., Santoso, H.B.: A systematic literature review on personalised learning in the higher education context. Technol. Knowl. Learn. **28**(2), 449–476 (2023)
11. Gligorea, I., Cioca, M., Oancea, R., Gorski, A.T., Gorski, H., Tudorache, P.: Adaptive learning using artificial intelligence in e-learning: a literature review. Educat. Sci. **13**(12), 1216 (2023)
12. Islam, M.K., Sarker, M.F.H., Islam, M.S.: Promoting student-centred blended learning in higher education: a model. E-learn. Digit. Media **19**(1), 36–54 (2022)
13. Jing, Y., Zhao, L., Zhu, K., Wang, H., Wang, C., Xia, Q.: Research landscape of adaptive learning in education: a bibliometric study on research publications from 2000 to 2022. Sustainability **15**(4), 3115 (2023)
14. Komatsu, H., Rappleye, J., Silova, I.: Student-centered learning and sustainability: solution or problem? Comp. Educ. Rev. **65**(1), 6–33 (2021)
15. Major, L., Francis, G.A., Tsapali, M.: The effectiveness of technology-supported personalised learning in low-and middle-income countries: a meta-analysis. Br. J. Edu. Technol. **52**(5), 1935–1964 (2021)
16. Makhambetova, A., Zhiyenbayeva, N., Ergesheva, E.: Personalized learning strategy as a tool to improve academic performance and motivation of students. Int. J. Web-Based Learn. Teach. Technol. (IJWLTT) **16**(6), 1–17 (2021)
17. Otto, S., Bertel, L.B., Lyngdorf, N.E.R., Markman, A.O., Andersen, T., Ryberg, T.: Emerging digital practices supporting student-centered learning environments

in higher education: A review of literature and lessons learned from the covid-19 pandemic. Educ. Inf. Technol. **29**(2), 1673–1696 (2024)
18. O'meara, J., Vaidya, A.: A network theory approach to curriculum design. Entropy **23**(10), 1346 (2021)
19. Sorana, C., Ferrer, R., Hinata, Y.: Forested : interactive tool for competency centered curriculum visualization. In: 19th International Conference on e-Learning and Digital Learning. IADIS, Lisbonne, Portugal (2025). https://hal.science/hal-05227339
20. Soubra, L., Al-Ghouti, M.A., Abu-Dieyeh, M., Crovella, S., Abou-Saleh, H.: Impacts on student learning and skills and implementation challenges of two student-centered learning methods applied in online education. Sustainability **14**(15), 9625 (2022)
21. Tapalova, O., Zhiyenbayeva, N.: Artificial intelligence in education: AIEd for personalised learning pathways. Electron. J. e-Learn. **20**(5), 639–653 (2022)
22. Tlili, A., Denden, M., Essalmi, F., Jemni, M., Chang, M., Kinshuk, Chen, N.S.: Automatic modeling learner's personality using learning analytics approach in an intelligent moodle learning platform. Interact. Learn. Environ. **31**(5), 2529–2543 (2023). https://doi.org/10.1080/10494820.2019.1636084
23. Whalley, B., France, D., Park, J., Mauchline, A., Welsh, K.: Towards flexible personalized learning and the future educational system in the fourth industrial revolution in the wake of covid-19. Higher Educat. Pedagog. **6**(1), 79–99 (2021)
24. Zheng, L., Long, M., Zhong, L., Gyasi, J.F.: The effectiveness of technology-facilitated personalized learning on learning achievements and learning perceptions: a meta-analysis. Educ. Inf. Technol. **27**(8), 11807–11830 (2022)

Assessment Perception in Blended Learning Pathway: An Exploratory Study in Secondary School Teacher Training

Andrea Garavaglia[1], Ilaria Terrenghi[2](✉), and Livia Petti[3]

[1] Pegaso University, Naples, Italy
andrea.garavaglia@unipegaso.it
[2] eCampus University, Novedrate, Italy
ilaria.terrenghi@uniecampus.it
[3] University of Molise, Campobasso, Italy
livia.petti@unimol.it

Abstract. This study explores the perceptions of secondary school teacher trainees regarding assessment practices in blended learning programs. The research was conducted with participants from two Italian universities, the University of Milan and the University of Molise, who were enrolled in initial training courses that combine online theoretical lectures with in-person laboratory and internship activities. The purpose of this research was to understand how participants perceive the assessment practices in these programs, which, according to ministerial decree, include only a final written test and a simulated lesson. An exploratory study was carried out using an anonymous, semi-structured questionnaire distributed online thanks to Computer-Assisted Web Interviewing (CAWI) methodology. The questionnaire collected 614 validated responses and the analysis we propose concerns four key areas: the ideal timing for assessment, preferred assessment methods, the value of specific assessment features, and participants' motivational orientation toward the training. Results indicate that while many students favored final assessments, a significant portion also advocated for continuous assessment. Reasons included cognitive benefits, better workload management, and formative feedback opportunities. Participants considered practical simulations and oral exams most effective for developing competencies. They also highly valued feedback and self-assessment, rating them as more beneficial for learning than the final exam grade. These findings reveal a wide range of motivations among trainees, from a desire for quick completion to a focus on in-depth professional development. Significant correlations exist between motivational orientation and preference for certain assessment types, such as project development.

Keywords: Assessment · blended learning · higher education

M. Adamoli et al. (Eds.): HELMeTO 2025, CCIS 2958, pp. 512–524, 2026.
https://doi.org/10.1007/978-3-032-31850-3_31

1 Introduction

In higher education, assessment is a fundamental component of improving student learning outcomes. In an increasingly global educational landscape, quality assessment is essential for promoting educational innovation [1].

The effectiveness of assessment largely depends on teachers' ability to choose appropriate timing, methods and tools, as assessment significantly influences students' perceptions of and approaches to learning [2].

Although there is currently growing interest in international research on assessment as a tool for improving learning, and this is widely developed, at the design and implementation level, insufficient attention is still being paid to an aspect that should be considered a key element for any post-secondary education institution [3]. Furthermore, the assessment process is not always applied systematically, especially in higher education contexts, despite being considered and implemented as a means of improvement.

These two issues are particularly relevant to the impact that different moments and modes of assessment have on learners' experience of university in an academic field [4].

Considering the importance of these issues, a study on assessment processes was conducted within the initial training programs for secondary school teachers (Percorsi Abilitanti established under the Decree DPCM of August 4, 2023). These programs were implemented across all universities in a blended learning format, with a significant portion of teaching hours delivered online and the remaining in-person sessions devoted primarily to laboratory work and internship activities. The entire pathway was completed within a relatively short time frame, only a few months, in order to promptly meet the requirements set by the ministerial educational mandate.

According to Article 9, Paragraph 1 of the Decree, the final assessment consists of two distinct components: a written test and a simulated lesson. Together, these are designed to verify the achievement of professional competencies as specified in Annex A of the same Decree. As a result, assessment takes place exclusively at the end of the program, without any explicit provision for the assessment of the individual courses or laboratories included in the curriculum.

In consideration of these factors, the purpose of this research was to survey the perceptions of participants enrolled in two Italian universities, the University of Milan and the University of Molise, regarding assessment practices within these initial teacher training courses. To achieve this aim, an exploratory study was carried out through the administration of an anonymous semi-structured questionnaire.

2 The Assessment Role in Training Courses

Assessment plays a fundamental role in any training programme because it regulates the teaching-learning process while also improving the quality of training activities.

Assessment can be described as an activity aimed at producing feedback on an action or event [5]. For Ausubel [6], assessment means expressing a judgement of value or merit that makes it clear to the learner how close or far they are from achieving their goal.

As Benvenuto [7 , p. 60] aptly describes, "assessment is an intrinsic part of the teaching process and consists of a deliberate and planned process of gathering elements/information aimed at expressing a judgement (descriptive, comparative, progress, certifying) on the learning progress of individuals or groups of learners".

Effective assessment requires the use of appropriate methods and tools and can be used to improve teaching practices [8]. An essential condition for starting an assessment procedure is to define the object to be assessed, which is useful for avoiding the risks of arbitrariness and bias. It is then necessary to establish how to assess and what types of tests to use in order to carry out a valid and reliable measurement [9]. Subsequently, it is necessary to carry out the actual assessment, i.e. interpret the data collected. The assessment usually reflects the teacher's appreciation of the test taken by the student and, in expressing it, various elements are usually considered: progress made, commitment shown, interest, etc. It is also important to establish the timing of the assessment. With regard to this last point, during a training course, it is possible to assess at different times: at the beginning (ex-ante), during the course (interim assessment), and at the end (ex-post).

The initial assessment is used to review the knowledge, skills and competences that the trainee possesses at the beginning of a given course of study in order to understand whether there are any gaps to be filled and, if necessary, to take action.

Ongoing assessment, also known as interim or formative assessment, allows any learning difficulties experienced by trainees to be identified (diagnostic assessment) and considered as opportunities to make the training more flexible and more precisely targeted towards the learning objectives [10, 11]. Formative assessment can be considered a tool that regulates teaching activity [12]. "The function of formative assessment is to create a dense network of information, such as to determine the appropriate differentiation of teaching interventions according to the needs of each individual" [13 , p. 19].

Final assessment, also known as summative assessment (assessment of learning), takes place at the end of a training activity of varying length. It is used to make a final assessment of the objectives achieved by the trainees. This assessment becomes increasingly definitive and final as the course draws to a close, because the final assessment can provide the trainee with certifications that definitively determine the extent to which the objectives have been achieved. This assessment does not always take into account the time needed to assimilate the learning.

Since it is necessary to have an assessment that makes the trainee aware of their learning, their cognitive process and the objectives to be achieved, it does not make sense to carry out the assessment only at the end of the training activities [14]: this data, in fact, allows information on the learning achieved by the trainee to be collected only when the teaching programme has been completed. In that case, it is only possible to record whether or not learning has taken place without being able to use the data acquired during the process to improve the quality of learning outcomes through appropriate interventions. Formative assessment, on the other hand, takes place during the learning process and allows teachers to implement targeted, even individualised, interventions, acting on the learning and difficulties encountered by the learner.

In fact, formative assessment (assessment for learning) allows the trainer to check the learner's performance during the training course, which is extremely useful for the development of learning: thanks to feedback, it becomes possible to work on mistakes, redesign and plan learning support activities.

Feedback strategies have been shown to improve students' assessment skills and planning abilities [15, 16]. These participatory and formative assessment methods, implemented throughout the course of study, improve learning, support study, promote educational success and develop students' assessment skills [17, 18]. For feedback to be truly effective, it is essential that it be formulated in a timely manner and provided on an ongoing basis throughout the learning process, so as to support learners in redirecting their efforts and progressively improving their performance.

Hadji [8] goes beyond formative assessment by talking about assessment as learning, which consists of assessing students during the learning activity, without them being aware of it: in this way, any activity can be assessed. The advantages of this type of assessment are considerable, as performance anxiety is reduced and assessment regains its original purpose, which is learning.

3 Method

In this contribution, we present an exploration survey of the assessment processes within the initial training programs for secondary school teachers. Specifically, the objective of this study was to examine the perceptions of trainees enrolled at two Italian universities, the University of Milan and the University of Molise, concerning the topic of assessment adopted.

In accordance with the provisions outlined in the relevant Ministerial Decree, universities delivered these qualification programs in a blended learning format. The online components were primarily organized as theoretical lectures delivered in a transmissive format, while in-person sessions were dedicated to laboratory activities and internship experiences.

The final assessment was administered at the conclusion of the program and consisted of two main components: a written examination and a simulated teaching lesson. These were designed to evaluate the acquisition of professional competencies, as defined in Annex A of the Ministerial Decree.

The exploratory study was conducted through the administration of a semi-structured anonymous questionnaire [19], developed based on a review of the relevant literature [20–22] and adapted to the specific aims of the study and the target population. The questionnaire was distributed online via Google Forms between April and May 2025, at the end of the training program. The methodology employed was the Computer-Assisted Web Interviewing (CAWI) approach.

The questionnaire was composed of seven sections, each focusing on 7 different areas of investigation, respectively:

1. socio-demographic characteristics (D1, 7 items);
2. employment status (D2, 5 items);
3. prior experience in other teacher qualification pathways (D3, 2 items);
4. evaluation of the training model attended (D4, 4 items);

5. compatibility and preference levels regarding an ideal training model (D5, 10 items);
6. a specific focus on assessment in the qualification experience (D6, 3 items);
7. overall evaluation of the training experience (D7, 1 item).

A total of 614 responses were collected. In this paper, we focus specifically on the analysis and discussion of the data gathered in Sects. D6 and D7, particularly the responses provided by trainees enrolled in the 30–36-60 CFU qualification pathways.

We therefore present the main findings related to four key questions:

1. timing of Assessment: trainees were asked to indicate when, during the course experience, they believed assessment should ideally occur. This question was accompanied by an open-ended prompt (first question), inviting participants to explain the reasons behind their selected response (second question);
2. assessment methods: the second question explored which assessment methods trainees considered most effective in supporting the development of teaching competencies. Various types of methods were proposed (e.g., written tests, oral exams, peer review, practical simulations), and respondents were asked to rate each method on a 6-point Likert scale;
3. assessment features: the third question focused on specific aspects of assessment, such feedback and comments, or the grades students received. Again, participants rated each aspect using a 6-point Likert scale;
4. motivational orientation toward the training experience: the final question invited trainees to position themselves along a continuum between two opposing motivations; on one end, the desire to complete the training as quickly as possible; on the other, a willingness to engage with the course in-depth for the purposes of professional development and competence-building.

4 Results and Discussion

In this section, we present and briefly discuss the main findings that emerged from the analysis of the four questions presented. Analysis of the sample data revealed no significant differences between the responses provided by students from the two universities with regard to the aspects investigated in this study. For this reason, the data are treated as a whole, without distinguishing between the educational programs of the two universities. This homogeneity highlights that the constraints of ministerial regulations probably have a direct impact on the implementation of the programs of the various universities, effectively making the programs homogeneous in terms of assessment methods.

4.1 Timing of Assessment

In response to the first question (Q1, Sect. D6), the largest proportion of students (around 43%) said that assessments should be carried out at the end of the training course. Another significant proportion (about 18%) suggested that assessment should take place at the end of each phase or activity. Additionally, a considerable number of participants selected both options, advocating a combination of final and ongoing assessment throughout the programme (Table 1). The data also show few cases of students thinking about assessment before starting the course (about 1%), before and at the end of the course

(4.2%), or throughout the training period, i.e., before, during, and at the end of the course (almost 2% of cases).

Table 1. Students' perception of the moment in the educational process at which it is useful to assess.

	N	%
At the end of the training course	265	43,2%
At the end of each teaching activity included in the training course	110	17,9%
At the end of each teaching activity included in the training course + At the end of the training course	50	8,1%
At the end of each teaching activity included in the training course + During specific periods dedicated to assessment tests	15	2,4%
During specific periods dedicated to assessment tests	43	7,0%
During specific periods dedicated to assessment tests + At the end of the training course	63	10,3%
Before starting the training course	7	1,1%
Before starting the training course + At the end of the training course	26	4,2%
Before starting the training course + During specific periods dedicated to assessment tests + At the end of the training course	11	1,8%

In this section an open-ended question was also included (Q2, Sect. D6), inviting respondents to elaborate on their choices. A thematic analysis of the 215 open responses yielded several noteworthy categories. We believe it is particularly important to present three of them.

The first category, which includes 146 occurrences, comprises participants who mentioned a form of assessment that can be described as continuous and/or integrated [23, 24]. The central idea is that assessment should be a frequent event, closely connected to the conclusion of individual teaching units, whether lectures, modules, or workshops [25]. The reasons given can be grouped into three main areas. The first is cognitive in nature: assessing topics while they are still "fresh" is seen as a way to promote memory and consolidate knowledge ("to better consolidate learning"). This approach makes it possible to "anchor the proposed content" before moving on to new topics, preventing the "dispersion of information" that may occur over time. The second area relates to workload management. Many teachers emphasize that modular assessment allows for the distribution of study throughout the course, avoiding cognitive overload and the stress associated with preparing for a single final exam on an extensive syllabus ("*to avoid the accumulation of content to memorize*" "*less cognitive load*"). This strategy is seen as a way to make learning more sustainable and less anxiety-inducing, especially for those who must balance study with work commitments. The third area concerns formative and metacognitive aspects. Continuous assessment offers the opportunity to receive immediate feedback, which helps to "*monitor progress gradually*" and "*understand whether the necessary competencies have been acquired*". This close feedback cycle transforms assessment from a simple judgment tool into an integral part of the learning process, fostering awareness and self-evaluation.

The second category, with 35 occurrences, includes those who support a final summative assessment, useful for verifying the competencies acquired [26]. The underlying logic is that only at the end of the course is it possible to have an "*overall view*"of all the content covered. Some responses imply that "*at the end of the course, the necessary competencies are acquired*" suggesting that such competencies are progressively built and can only be fully assessed at the end of the process. This model reflects a more traditional approach to assessment, focused on the final certification of learning objectives achieved.

The third category, with 22 occurrences, refers to logistical and organizational considerations [27], which are equally important for fully understanding participants' perceptions, as they concern aspects that influence the sustainability of the entire process. A strong need emerges for clear and realistic planning, considering that many participants are working professionals and/or have family responsibilities. The main requests include the establishment of "*specific periods dedicated to assessment*" in order to avoid overlapping study for exams with the continuation of lectures. There is a clear demand for "*more time for preparation*" and for scheduling that allows students to better organize their study. These concerns highlight a crucial aspect of adult education: the need for flexibility and for course design that respects the external constraints faced by participants.

4.2 Preferred Assessment Methods

In this second question (Q2, Sect. D6), we presented the trainees with a list of assessment types, including written exams with multiple-choice and open-ended questions, oral test, practical simulation, written reports, project work and competency test-skill-assessment.

Among these, practical simulation received the highest number of top scores (5 and 6 on the Likert scale), followed by the oral examination. The prominence of the simulation is noteworthy, as it also forms part of the official final assessment.

Open-ended written assignments also received relatively high average scores (typically between 3 and 4). In contrast, written tests with closed or open questions were rated lower, indicating that they are perceived as less effective in promoting competency development, as shown in the respective data (Fig. 1).

4.3 Assessment Features

When examining specific assessment-related elements (Q3, Sect. D6), students clearly demonstrated a strong appreciation for feedback. This component of assessment is regarded as crucial for guiding learning and supporting the regulation of cognitive processes.

In fact, the feedback and comments category received the highest frequency of top scores (5 and 6). Moreover, when aggregating responses in the 4–6 range, self-assessment also emerged as a valuable component, followed closely by peer assessment. By contrast, the final exam grade ranked lowest, suggesting that it is considered less informative or beneficial for the learning process (Fig. 2).

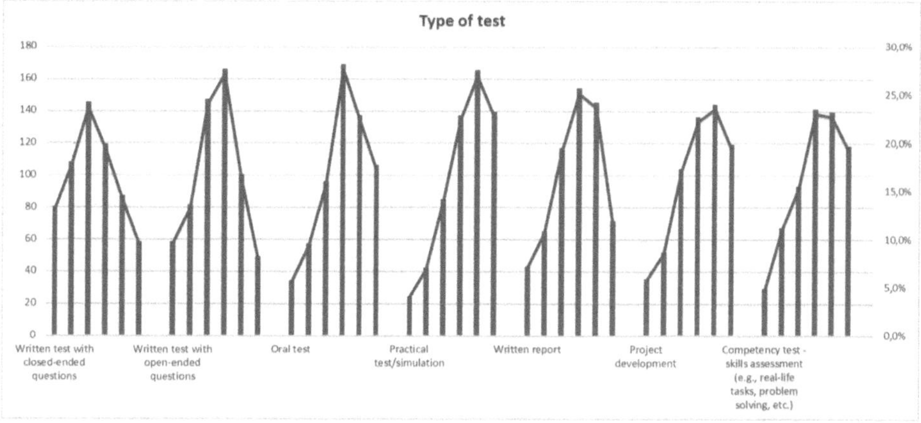

Fig. 1. Students' perception of the usefulness of assessment methods.

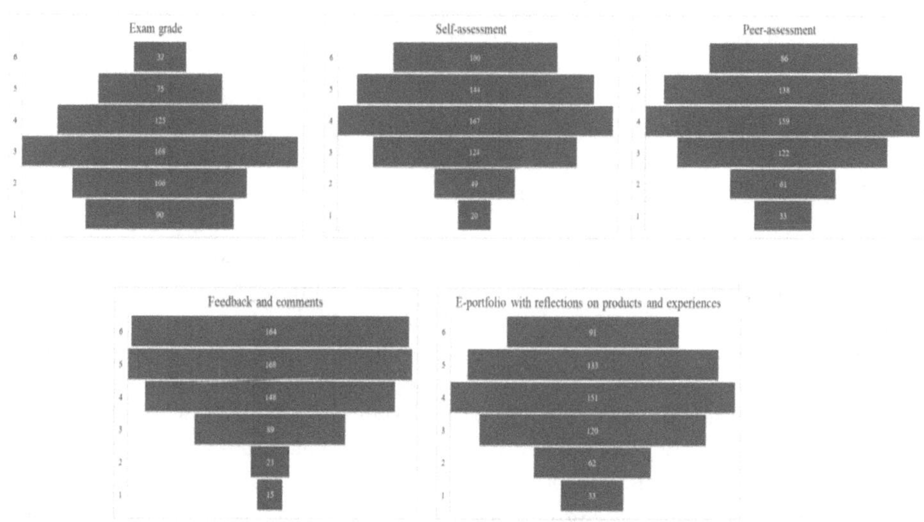

Fig. 2. Students' perception of the usefulness of assessment elements.

4.4 Motivational Orientation toward the Training Experience

In this question we asked participants to indicate their motivational orientation for attending the course by positioning themselves on a continuum between two statements: at one end (score = 1) "I prefer to keep the training course as short as possible" and at the opposite end (score = 6) "I prefer to focus on developing my skills to the best of my ability".

The resulting distribution was quite varied, with many participants placing themselves in the middle of the continuum. However, we also observed a notable number of responses at both extremes, indicating a range of motivations (Fig. 3). This diversity reflects differing expectations and attitudes toward professional development among participants in enabling pathways.

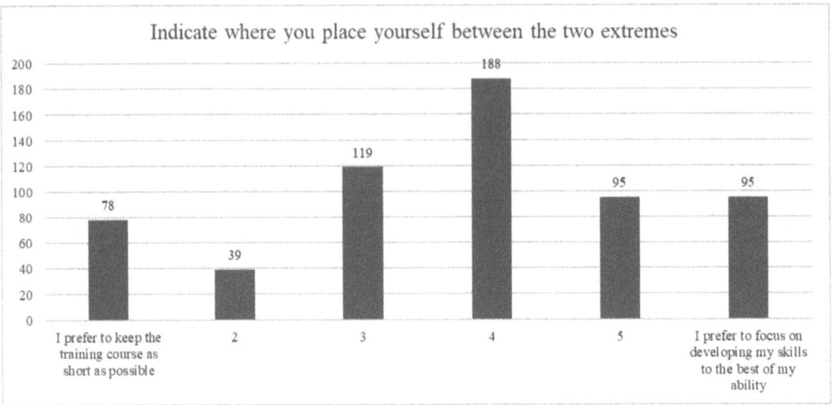

Fig. 3. The positioning of students along the continuum.

This question, which allowed us to study the orientation with respect to the training experience, also presents some rather interesting correlations related precisely to the methods of assessing and verifying learning.

First of all, it is worth mentioning which assessment methods show the least correlation with this approach (see Fig. 1 for the overall results). First of all, written tests with closed-ended questions, which are often used in these courses given the large number of students to be assessed in short sessions. This method does not differ greatly from the different gradients of the poles, as is the case with written tests with open-ended questions and written reports.

Oral tests are slightly more popular among those who are oriented towards developing skills to the fullest (25.3% respond '6 = completely adequate' compared to 12.8% who prefer the course to last as little as possible).

There are three types of learning assessment methods that show a significant correlation with the student's orientation, presented below:

1) The weakest correlation ($r = 0.222$) is linked to competency-based assessments (such as authentic tasks, real-life tasks, or problem solving). 19.2% of students who are totally focused on completing the course in a short time consider this assessment method "6 = completely adequate." The percentage rises to 31.6% for students focused on developing their skills to the fullest.
2) The practical test and simulations show a similar correlation ($r = 0.235$). In this case, the cumulative percentages of those who answer "5" and "6 = completely adequate" is 28.2% for those who are totally focused on completing the course in the shortest time possible, while it rises to 63.2% for those who aim to develop their skills to the fullest.
3) The highest correlation ($r = 0.267$) is linked to assessment through project development (see Table 2). There is an almost linear association whereby those who are

focused on completing the course in the shortest possible time consider this assessment method to be "1 not at all adequate" in 21.8% of cases. The response percentages shift as the gradient rises, reaching 34.7% of those who respond "6 = completely adequate" among course participants oriented towards developing their skills to the fullest. This latter cluster has the highest values of "5" and "6" at 54.7%, with only 5.3% for '1' and "2."

Table 2. Association between learning assessment methods (rows) and motivational orientation (columns).

	1 = I prefer to make the training course last as little as possible	2	3	4	5	6 = I prefer to aim to develop skills in the best possible way
Learning assessment method: Elaboration of a project	% of cases per column	% of cases per column	% of cases per column	% of cases per column	% of cases per column	% of cases per column
1 = not at all	21,8%	2,6%	6,7%	2,1%	4,2%	1,1%
2	14,1%	12,8%	13,4%	6,9%	3,2%	4,2%
3	16,7%	28,2%	21,0%	16,0%	15,8%	10,5%
4	15,4%	28,2%	19,3%	24,5%	22,1%	24,2%
5	14,1%	20,5%	18,5%	29,3%	30,5%	20,0%
6 = Completely adequate	9,0%	7,7%	17,6%	18,1%	22,1%	34,7%
I don't know	9,0%	0,0%	3,4%	3,2%	2,1%	5,3%

5 Conclusion

Despite the limitations of the study, we can draw some conclusions from the presented research that may be relevant to discuss. However, before proceeding, it is important to clarify some of these limitations.

A first limitation concerns the fact that this study was carried out in only two Italian universities and is therefore not representative of the overall situation. With a view to future development, it would be interesting to select training courses from universities in different geographical areas (e.g., central Italy and the islands, which are not currently represented) and of different types (e.g., at least one online university). Furthermore, we emphasize that, at the methodological level, the exploration was carried out through the administration of self-report questionnaires, thus tracking the student's statements without triangulating different points of view. Nevertheless, we emphasize the optional and anonymous nature of the data collection tool.

A second limitation concerns the possibility that some of the responses may be linked to subjective perceptions and specific characteristics of the training course that may have influenced the students to perceive certain assessment methods or teaching proposals differently. Although no differences were found between universities in relation to the aspects covered by this study, the correlation analysis revealed some significant differences in the assessment of the teaching system, which may have had undetected effects.

It is interesting to revisit some aspects that emerged from the analysis, with a view to making further considerations.

The first consideration concerns the moment in which to propose the assessments. Although the ministerial decree only requires a final assessment, less than half of the course participants (43.2%) indicated this as the ideal assessment moment. However, there is no clear consensus on an alternative moment, which means that there are multiple factors and personal needs that can affect the perceived effectiveness of the assessment period.

However, we should consider that some students (around 7%) find it useful for assessment to take place at specific points during the course, rather than only at the end or at the end of each activity (around 18%). Combined with the strong preference for ongoing feedback, this fact seems to support the importance of a type of assessment that can be defined as formative, as Scriven [28] states. In this way, assessment can focus on students and give them a decisive role in their own educational process [29]. Finally, the development of an educational project was considered the most time-consuming type of assessment test by the respondents: those who did not prefer this type of test wanted the educational process to be completed as quickly as possible. Developing skills takes time, and working on authentic tasks can facilitate this process [30]. Those who prefer to complete the training course quickly are likely to be less interested in developing their skills and more focused on obtaining certification.

Authorship Attribution. The article is the result of the authors' joint work and reflections. The overall structure was collaboratively agreed upon by all authors. Specifically:

- AG, IT, and LP jointly wrote paragraphs 1 (*Introduction*) and 5 (*Conclusion*);
- AG and IT jointly wrote paragraph 4 (*Results and Discussion*);
- LP wrote paragraph 2 (The Assessment Role in Training Courses);
- IT wrote paragraph 3 (*Method*).

Disclosure of Interests.. The authors have no competing interests to declare that are relevant to the content of this article. It is also declared that Author 2 (IT) is a member of Publicity and Communication Chairs of the seventh International Conference on Higher Education Learning Methodologies and Technologies Online.

References

1. Sawand, F.A., Chandio, B.A., Bilal, M., Rasheed, M.R., Raza, M.A., Ahmad, N.: Quality assessment in higher education. Int. Lett. Soc. Humanistic Sci. **50**, 162–171 (2015)
2. Hatamli, S.: Understanding assessment and feedback in higher education. Int. Sci. J. **17**(4), 45–48 (2023)
3. Bevitt, S.: Assessment innovation and student experience: a new assessment challenge and call for a multi-perspective approach to assessment research. Assess. Eval. High. Educ. **40**(1), 103–119 (2015)
4. Bartram, B., Bailey, C.: Assessment preferences: a comparison of UK/international students at an English university. Res. Post-Compuls. Educ. **15**(2), 177–187 (2010)
5. Alessandrini, G.: Manuale per l'esperto dei processi formativi. Carocci, Roma (1998)
6. Ausubel, D.P.: Educazione e processi cognitivi. Francoangeli, Milano (1978)
7. Benvenuto, G.: Mettere i voti a scuola. Introduzione alla docimologia. Carocci, Roma (2013)
8. Hadji, C.: The Evaluation of Training Actions. Morcelliana Scholè, Brescia (1992)
9. Visalberghi, A.: Misurazione e valutazione nel processo educativo. Edizioni di Comunità, Milano (1955)
10. Grandi, G.: Misurazione e valutazione. La Nuova Italia, Firenze (1977)
11. Garavaglia, A.: L'agire valutativo. In: Rivoltella, P.C., Bochicchio, F. (eds.) L'agire organizzativo. Manuale per i professionisti della formazione, pp. 183–197. La Scuola, Brescia (2017)
12. Vannini, I.: La qualità nella didattica. Metodologie e strumenti di progettazione e valutazione. Erickson, Trento (2009)
13. Vertecchi, B.: Valutazione formativa. Loescher, Torino (1976)
14. Vertecchi, B.: Manuale della valutazione: analisi degli apprendimenti e dei contesti. Francoangeli, Milano (2003)
15. Vinci, V.: Peer review, feedback and new models of participatory assessment in higher education: an experiment at the Mediterranea University of Reggio Calabria. Educ. Sci. Soc. **12**(2) (2021). https://doi.org/10.3280/ess2-2021oa1247
16. Triacca, S., Petti, L.: Digital written feedback to promote motivation and engagement. A case study in higher education. In: Helmeto Conference 2023 Book of Abstract, pp. 24–25. Edizioni STUDIORUM (2023)
17. Hattie, J., Timperley, H.: The power of feedback. Rev. Educ. Res. **77**(1), 81–112 (2007)
18. Grion, V., Serbati, A.: Sustainable assessment and feedback in university contexts: emerging perspectives, research and practices. Pensa Multimedia, Lecce (2019)
19. Zammuner, V.L.: Tecniche dell'Intervista e del Questionario. Il Mulino, Bologna (1998).
20. Appiah, M., Van Tonder, F.: E-assessment in higher education: a review. Int. J. Bus. Manag. Econ. Res. **9**(6) (2018)
21. Heil, J., Ifenthaler, D.: Online assessment in higher education: a systematic review. Online Learn. **27**(1), 187–218 (2023)
22. Morris, R., Perry, T., Wardle, L.: Formative assessment and feedback for learning in higher education: a systematic review. Rev. Educ. **9**(3) (2021)
23. Hadji, C.: La valutazione delle azioni educative. La Scuola, Brescia (1992)
24. Rivoltella, P.C.: Valutare (con) gli EAS. In: Rivoltella, P.C. (ed.) Fare didattica con gli EAS. Editrice La Scuola, Brescia (2013)
25. Coggi, C., Emanuel, F.: La valutazione inclusiva degli studenti universitari. L'integrazione scolastica e sociale 20(4), 67–83 (2021)
26. Iannotta, I.S., Tammaro, R.: Uno studio esplorativo sulle pratiche di valutazione sommativa all'Università. Pedagogia Oggi 23(1), 137–143 (2025)

27. Garavaglia, A., Terrenghi, I.: Didattica emergenziale universitaria e post pandemia: analisi di caso dell'esperienza degli studenti di un corso di laurea. In: Dipace, A., Panciroli, C., Rivoltella, P.C. (eds.) Apprendere con le tecnologie tra presenza e distanza, pp. 407–423. Morcelliana Scholé, Brescia (2024)
28. Scriven, M.: Methodology of evaluation. In: Tyler, R., Gagné, R.M., Scriven, M. (eds.) Perspectives of Curriculum Evaluation, pp. 39–83. Rand McNally & Co., Chicago (1967)
29. Sambell, K., McDowell, L., Montgomery, C.: Assessment for learning in higher education. Routledge, London (2012)
30. De Vecchi, G., Carmona-Magnaldi, N.: Aiutare a costruire le conoscenze. La Nuova Italia, Firenze (1999)

RiProVapp and the New Frontiers of AI Formative Feedback*

Delio De Martino(✉), Marilena di Padova, Andrea Tinterri, and Anna Dipace

Department of Education and Sport Sciences, Pegaso Telematic University, 80143 Naples, Italy
{delio.demartino,marilena.dipadova,andrea.tinterri, anna.dipace}@unipegaso.it

Abstract. Starting from the evolution of formative feedback during the XX century, from a behavioral approach to a dialogic one, the contribution analyzes the RiProVapp. It is an AI based app that provides personalized feedback from a document (Word, Pdf, PowerPoint, ODP or audio file) also based on specific rubrics. It is an example of AI apps that could be developed by a teacher with no code skills to improve the formative feedback also beyond the limits of the classic classroom. Formative feedback apps such as RiProVapp could fit in a new paradigm oriented to enhance the possibility of the human feedback in direction to even more feedback centred and learner entered learning process.

Keywords: Formative feedback · Artificial Intelligence · app

1 The Effective Feedback: Human or Digital?

1.1 The Relevance of the Feedback

In the last century the feedback has become increasingly central to the learning process. The feedback has gained importance attracting the attention of pedagogists and teachers and becoming one of the most important elements to obtain deep learning. Starting from John Dewey's educational philosophy to contemporary pedagogy the formative feedback has slowly replaced also the old concepts of reward, punishment and reinforcement [1] and it is currently a key to go beyond the culture of scholar marks to make the learning visible [2, 3].

The sign of this evolution is the addition of the adjective "formative" to the term "feedback" and the expression "formative feedback" is now a key instrument to enhance learning. Feedback is formative insofar as it significantly enhances the learning process [4]. It is also the key instrument for the inclusive management of the classroom [5] and to promote inclusiveness.

The feedback can be defined as the mechanism by which a student receives information about his learning and his product and obtains a comparison about the gap between his performance and the expected standard.

Nowadays, despite the digital revolution, the feedback at the same time is something that has traditionally been seen in the global imagination as a typically human element.

M. Adamoli et al. (Eds.): HELMeTO 2025, CCIS 2958, pp. 525–538, 2026.
https://doi.org/10.1007/978-3-032-31850-3_32

High quality formative feedback is connected to the human teacher and to his high-profile skills.

Only the skill of the human teacher allows a conscious, deep, and significant feedback, able to improve the student learning with all human capabilities, as deep assessment skill, assessment of the zone of proximal development, empathy, capability of adaptation of the communication to the singular and special student, in a learned centred perspective. In current educational theory, feedback is conceived as a complex and high-level pedagogical process. In some way the formative feedback could also bring deep meanings and personal values into play. Feedback may also incorporate the storytelling, engaging the learner's whole personality and values and his existential meaning [6].

Even the Pygmalion effect, also known as the Rosenthal effect, is linked to the formative assessment: the high value human formative feedback has the capability to improve the learning through the transformation of the formative feedback in motivational feedback [7].

The reflexive and metacognitive skill is a feedback skill that a good trained human teacher looks like able to have [8]: an expert teacher knows how to give feedback that helps students to progress [9] and that's why the human feedback appears hard to be replaced by a digital tool.

The current feedback theory views the feedback as a core factor to guide the student. Indeed, the correct feedback is something linked to a modern pedagogy view of learning and that spreads only in the second half of the '900 century.

In the traditional transmissive teaching, typical of the nineteenth century, the content of the teaching, as well the feedback, is given in one way direction from the teacher to the learner from a monologic perspective. The framework was essentially behaviorist and delivery, but following the pedagogical evolution a more sociocostructivist vision of the feedback emerged [10].

So, the focus has switched from a content-centred perspective, where the subject was the focus, to a more process-centred perspective, where instead the focal point is the process and its usefulness. In this framework the role of the learner is more and more important, because he is a critical actor of the process, as well his self-consciousness, his deep "weltanschauung".

1.2 The Feedback as Dialogic Process

In the modern framework the feedback is a dialogic process, more Socratic and complex (in an etymological sense of woven together), result of a continuous interchange of information, data, but also emotions, points of view, embodied elements in a more co-built process that is given in a dialogic texture. There is a continuous communication, both cognitive and emotional, from student to teacher, from teacher to student and from student to student [11].

It's just for this dialogicity and complexity, made of a texture of different elements all interrelated and guided by the formative feedback, it is seen as an element almost irreplaceable by a machine in the collective imagination.

However, the global diffusion of AI technologies, beginning in 2021 with the emergence of large language models (LLLMs), appears as a new frontier both for students and for the teachers that with a new approach could build more modern, dialogic, flexible and adaptable instruments to improve the formative feedback in and of the classroom.

The new AI-driven feedback apps could enrich the third space of the learning with a real innovative perspective, giving to the automated feedback a more human shape. Both teachers and students are more likely to rethink the feedback in an innovative way and to explore the new frontiers of the formative feedback in order to enhance the entire learning process. Just AI could be the key to rejuvenate the practices that usually are too much anchored to outdated but consolidated teacher *modus operandi* [10].

To better understand this historical shift in the concept of feedback, it is useful to examine the evolution of educational technology and its links to formative feedback.

The first vision of feedback in the past century was connected to behavioral theory. In this traditional didactic framework, feedback followed a stimulus-response model. Just for cause-effect mechanisms in early-mid'900 the feedback was seen as easier to be replaced by a machine.

1.3 Automatic Feedback: from the Learning Machine to the Digital Revolution

The history of automatic feedback is the story of a progressive attempt of psychologists, pedagogists and informatics to reproduce mechanically first and digitally then the complexness of the human feedback, a challenge that just now in the era of AI appears more challenging [12].

In the history of education, the first attempt to automatize the learning process and formative feedback dates back to the 1920s and it is linked to the psychologist Sidney Leavitt Pressey. His learning machine released in 1926 represented the first dream to replace human feedback with a machine. The learning machine was conceived as a device that proposed multiple choice test and counter the right answer in order to give results and feedback to the students in a more efficient way than a human teacher.

As Stephen Petrina [13] explains recalling the Pressey words [14]:

Pressey claimed that the machine simulated teaching by providing individual instruction and feedback. "The average teacher," he asserted, "is woefully burdened by such routine drill and information-fixing." The Automatic Teacher "automatically gives and scores a test," and "will automatically, teach—and teach informational and drill material more efficiently, in certain respects, than the 'human machine' [...]".

After this first tool in the 1950s was released another notorious learning machine based on the principle of immediate and automatic feedback. But the most known learning machine is that one of the fathers of behaviorism, Burrhus Skinner, the most famous psychologist and pedagogist to try to build a feedback machine ideally able to automatize and to entirely replace the teacher in the feedback process.

The teaching machine actually was the first automatized device that used the just in time automated feedback to teach without the teacher. The feedback related to the principle of "operant conditioning in which characteristic learning is controlled by rewarding the student after he has made the correct response" [15].

The problem of this learning machine was clarified by the same Skinner in an article of 1963 [16], a decade after the introduction of the teaching machine. In that age the learning machine was spreading but the efficacy was questioned: "Some of the so-called computer-based teaching machines are designed simply to duplicate the behavior of teachers. To automate education with mechanical teachers is like automating banking with mechanical tellers and bookkeepers".

But this automatization was not easy because of the complexity of the learning process that the behaviorism approach did not consider sufficiently.

A turning point for the automated feedback was the Plato (Programmed Logic for Automatic Teaching Operations) of the University of Illinois, held by Daniel Alpert and Don Bitzer in 1960, that brought to the creation of the first digital distance learning courses and software for digital education.

With the emergence of the first experiments of distance learning as Plato and of the first digital distance learning nets (third generation of distance learning according to the Nipper classification), also the automated feedback changed dramatically [17].

In the digital era the automated feedback, linked to the structure of the digital net and after the internet, was more socio-constructivist.

In Plato and in 1960s systems first feedback was linked to the earliest digital instruments as quiz, test, forum, message board, chatrooms and elemental software that allowed the initial forms of branching (depending of the student response the system created a different learning path).

After the digital revolution of the internet in'900 and the spreading of third generation of Distance learning, the tools for feedback evolved, becoming increasingly complex and efficient. The evolution of learning analytics helped the automated feedback also in collaborative learning digital environments [18].

The digital distance learning LMS (Learning Management Systems) offered the possibility to give feedback in a natural and totally integrated way through, for instance, alert systems and dashboard. The feedback system, more and more evolved, also spread in different educational software: from classic LMS to gamification platform as Kahoot! or Mentimeter, offering the possibility to integrate feedback in gamification [19, 20], but also in mobile learning and Adaptive learning systems.

During the Covid era many teachers had difficulties providing online feedback [21] and had the opportunity to test digital feedback tools.

Before the Covid most of the attention of educational research was paid to the AR/VR and Metaverse applications, that seemed the starting point of a new educational revolution (regarding also the feedback). Instead, just in the period of the return to normality after Covid another new technology deeply changed the digital paradigm: the Artificial Intelligence.

1.4 AI and the New Frontiers of the Digital

Just in these years we are witnessing a new digital revolution that regards also the educational field. The spreading of Artificial Intelligence started with the release of the public beta of ChatGPT on October the 30th of 2022. In these years the massive use of ChatGPT and of other tools of generative AI is changing the digital context. The AI, between apocalyptic and integrated ones, to cite Umberto Eco [22], is providing new possibilities to feedback.

Liquid dialogic feedback managed and tailor-made by the teacher, even if he is not an expert in educational technologies, is emerging thanks to the use of natural language.

Indeed, a revolution regards just the feedback because "ChatGPT harnesses the power of Reinforcement Learning from Human Feedback (RLHF), a technique that has shown immense promise in aligning Large Language Models (LLMs) with human intent" [23]. More personalized feedback can be given to the student in a more efficient way and all the previous instruments powered by AI are improving their effectiveness.

But a great revolution could be a more efficient integration in the daily practice of the teacher. Thanks to the ease of the app creation by the teacher without the need of knowing the coding, the possibility for the teacher to build a feedback application tailored to the specific need of the teacher and of the specific learning environment opens new possibilities to enhance the feedback.

Beyond the debate between the risks of AI and the apocalyptic scenario of the replacement of teachers by machines (similar to that one exposed in 1950s with the Skinner machine), the new AI feedback tools allow new modality of use of the feedback apps.

For instance, thanks to AI the teacher could create a specific feedback app based on assessment rubrics or with personalized characteristics. A teacher by natural language could profile a feedback app to be more or less empathetic for specific targets of students and could create feedback to leverage for instance the Pygmalion effect or to mitigate some cognitive bias.

These specific and personalized feedback app could be useful both in person and in distance learning environment, in a new more liquid framework that blends distance and presential learning. In a liquid education that could be provided in presence and in distance the feedback became even more important to link all the pieces of the educational mosaic.

Not only the teacher could be protagonists in these new scenarios but also the students, according to the more and more learner centred feedback framework. AI could open new frontiers related to the new paradigms as the peer feedback [24] and the auto-assessment.

The feedback app RiProVapp, created by the app creation AI software Lovable, just fits in this evolving educational context and it's a first step to what could become the future of digital feedback in the near future.

2 RiProVapp, an App for Giving Feedback

As part of the research, RiProVapp (https://aiedu-formative-feedback-hub.lovable.app/) was developed, an application designed to integrate and enhance formative assessment processes for the development of a text or speech. The application represents a Proof of Concept (PoC) designed and implemented, intended to be validated and tested in an educational context (Fig. 1).

The tool allows tests and activities to be prepared digitally, providing immediate, targeted and adaptive feedback that helps students understand their mistakes and consciously rework their knowledge [25].

The logic behind RiProVapp is not merely corrective, but acts as a metacognitive and reflective lever, accompanying learners on a path of progressive and personalized

Fig. 1. RiProVapp application QR code.

improvement. In this sense, the application is a digital environment that promotes inclusion and accessibility, offering concrete support for innovative, person-centred teaching [26].

One of the sectors in which Artificial Intelligence applications based on no-code/low-code platforms are attracting growing interest is education [27]. In schools and universities, these solutions enable teachers, administrators and even students to create customized tools to support learning and manage teaching activities, without the need for programming skills.

This makes it possible to create study support chatbots, automated assessment and feedback systems, adaptive learning platforms that tailor content to individual needs, and predictive models that can be used to monitor academic performance and even take preventive action to reduce the risk of dropouts. Thanks to these technologies, educational innovation becomes immediately accessible, transforming pedagogical ideas into concrete and operational tools in just a few steps.

This is the context in which RiProVapp was developed, using the Lovable platform (https://lovable.dev/), a no-code environment that uses Artificial Intelligence to simplify and enhance the application creation process. The choice of Lovable made it possible to translate the RiProVa method [5], adapted by John Hattie and recognized in literature for the effectiveness of its formative feedback, into a flexible and customizable digital tool.

Teachers can use their own assessment rubrics or generate new ones with the support of integrated AI, obtaining targeted comments, specific suggestions and assessments tailored to the needs of each student. The application also allows you to enter work in different formats and quickly receive detailed reports, saving time on repetitive tasks while improving the quality of feedback. The use of Lovable has made it possible to develop an application that is accessible even to those without IT skills, with an intuitive web interface that allows teachers and students to directly experience personalized assessment paths. RiProVapp integrates progress monitoring features and produces reports that are useful for both teachers and students, with the option of including gamification elements – such as digital badges and dynamic quizzes – to increase motivation and engagement.

This experience shows how AI-based no-code platforms are not just technical tools, but real catalysts for pedagogical innovation: they allow assessment to be adapted to different educational contexts, promote the inclusion of students with special educational needs, and develop more effective and sustainable teaching practices. The architecture of RiProVapp has been designed to go beyond purely corrective feedback, acting as a metacognitive and reflective lever that guides students towards progressive and personalized improvement [28]. The application is configured as a digital environment that promotes inclusion and accessibility, offering concrete support for innovative and person-centered teaching [29]. The effectiveness of RiProVapp lies in its ability to process work in multiple formats (typed text, PDF, Word, presentations, or audio files) to generate targeted feedback based on the RiProVa model. The system allows users to select the desired area of analysis—linguistic, argumentative, or content—ensuring an extremely flexible review process tailored to specific needs. In addition, teachers can leverage the integrated Ai not only to quickly obtain specific comments and suggestions, but also to generate or customize assessment rubrics, ensuring transparency and consistency in formative assessment. This ability to adapt and customize transforms even a complex task into a structured learning process.

The integration of these features into a no-code platform maximizes RiProVapp's potential as a catalyst for innovation. From an operational standpoint, the application saves teachers considerable time on repetitive tasks while improving the quality of the feedback provided. From a more pedagogical perspective, RiProVapp integrates progress monitoring features and produces downloadable reports that encourage self-assessment and awareness of the learning process, increasing student motivation and engagement. Its simple and intuitive design helps to make assessment a tool for growth, adaptable to different educational contexts and useful for the inclusion of students with special educational needs (Table 1).

To use the app, in the first step, users are guided through the process of uploading their work, choosing from several options: directly entering typed or pasted text, uploading a file in one of the most common formats (Pdf, Word), uploading a presentation (PowerPoint or ODP), or recording or attaching an audio file. Once the format has been selected, the analysis can begin (Fig. 2).

In the second step, the user is asked to choose the type of feedback they want, selecting the area they wish to receive analysis on. The available options include: linguistic feedback, focusing on grammar, syntax, vocabulary and style; argumentative feedback, dedicated to evaluating the thesis, arguments and logical structure; and content feedback, aimed at verifying the accuracy, completeness and relevance of the information. This choice allows the revision process to be tailored to the specific needs of each user, making RiProVapp an extremely flexible and adaptive learning tool (Fig. 3).

In the third phase, RiProVapp offers the possibility to select or create an assessment rubric, making feedback even more specific and structured. Users can choose not to use any rubric, select a standard rubric divided into linguistic and argumentative categories, or generate a new one with the support of Artificial Intelligence. This feature allows for further customization of the assessment based on learning objectives and skills to be developed, ensuring consistent and transparent analysis. Thanks to rubrics, feedback

Table 1. Features and capabilities of the RiProVapp application.

Topic	Features	Educational opportunities
Technological base	App based on Artificial Intelligence (AI). Developed using the Lovable platform, a no-code environment.	It makes educational innovation accessible to teachers without programming skills, allowing the creation of customized tools.
Input	Provides feedback from documents (Word, PDF, PowerPoint, ODP) or audio files, as well as typed or pasted text.	Flexibility and accessibility, supporting the analysis of different types of work and learning contexts.
Feedback customization	Generates personalised and adaptive feedback. Allows users to select the desired area of analysis: linguistic, argumentative or content.	Adapt the review process to the specific needs of each user. Create a progressive and personalised improvement process.
Assessment tools	Option to use specific assessment rubrics. Integrated AI supports the generation or customisation of rubrics.	Ensures transparency and consistency in formative assessment, making feedback more detailed and structured.
Output	Produces a structured, downloadable Final Report (PDF). The report is divided into sections: Student Results, Learning Process and Self-Regulation (RiProVa model). Includes Questions for Reflection and Final Suggestions.	Transforms assessment into a tool for growth and self-evaluation. Provides immediately actionable feedback for work review and teaching planning.

becomes more detailed and targeted, facilitating both the understanding of strengths and weaknesses and the planning of improvement strategies [30] (Fig. 4).

The final stage of the assessment process is the Final Report, a structured, downloadable document that summarizes the analysis in a comprehensive manner.

Fig. 2. RiProVapp main menu.

Fig. 3. RiProVapp feedback selection.

This structure ensures that the feedback is immediately actionable, transforming the report into a concrete tool for self-assessment and for teachers to plan their teaching activities. The report concludes with a section devoted to student reflection questions, designed to promote self-regulation and critical analysis of their work. Finally, the Final Suggestions section proposes concrete actions, such as adding details, checking logical consistency, or exploring alternative points of view, providing a clear roadmap for revising the work. The report, which can be downloaded in Pdf format, thus becomes

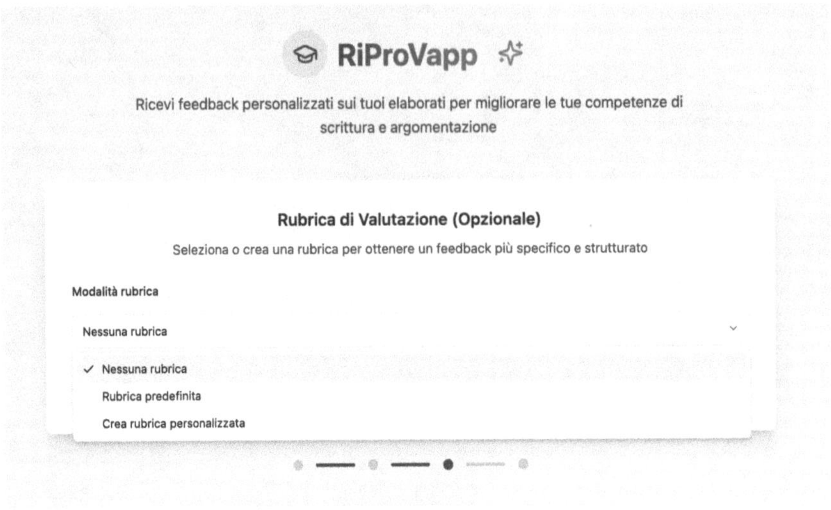

Fig. 4. Rubric selection.

a concrete tool to guide both teachers' teaching activities and students' learning paths, reinforcing the pedagogical value of the entire process.

The architecture of RiProVapp is explicitly designed to operationalize Hattie and Timperley's theoretical framework. As visually demonstrated by the application's report structure (Fig. 5), the interface is organized into four distinct sections, each corresponding to one of the four levels of feedback:

1. Task Level: The 'Student Results' (Risultati degli studenti) section addresses the specific product, highlighting strengths and errors.
2. Process Level: The 'Learning Process' (Processo di apprendimento) section focuses on the strategies employed and difficulties encountered.
3. Self Level: The 'Self-evaluation' (Auto-valutazione) section addresses the student's personal reaction and satisfaction, channeling the Self dimension constructively.
4. Self-Regulation Level: The 'Reflection Questions' (Domande di Riflessione) section at the bottom acts as the lever for self-regulation.

Crucially, this structural organization is driven by the three guiding questions: Where am I going? (Feed Up), How am I doing? (Feed Back), and Where to next? (Feed Forward). While the first three sections primarily provide the system's answer to 'How am I doing?' across different domains, the final Self-Regulation section explicitly prompts the student to answer all three questions personally (e.g., by asking 'What was the goal?', 'How did I work?', and 'What is the next step?'), thus closing the feedback loop and fostering active metacognition. Unlike generic interactions with Large Language Models (LLMs), which often function as unstructured 'black boxes' dependent solely on user prompting, RiProVapp is characterized by the structural integration of the pedagogical model during the development phase. The RiProVa framework was not applied ex-post but was embedded into the application's logic to guide the generative process. This

Fig. 5. Feedback report.

'pedagogy-by-design' approach acts as a structural constraint that forces the AI to operate within the validated four-level taxonomy (Task, Process, Self, Self-regulation), mitigating hallucinations and ensuring consistency. Consequently, the teacher's pedagogical agency is preserved: rather than delegating assessment to a neutral algorithm, the educator utilizes a tool where the pedagogical method is technically embedded, combining the efficiency of AI with a transparent, teacher-directed educational framework.

Alongside these opportunities, ethical issues related to the use of AI in education remain crucial. It is not only a question of ensuring algorithmic transparency, personal data protection and reducing possible bias in assessments, but also of questioning the relationship between technology and pedagogical responsibility [31]. It is essential that teachers and students are able to understand how the tools they use work, so that AI is not reduced to a "black box". Addressing these challenges therefore requires integrated strategies: promoting structured digital education pathways, introducing clear and shared regulations, and encouraging ethical and inclusive design practices [32]. Only through this critical awareness and a responsibility-oriented approach can applications such as RiProVapp truly contribute to educational innovation that is fair, sustainable and respectful of educational values.

3 Conclusions

This essay presents the features of RiproVapp as a proof of concept of the new tools of AI based formative feedback apps that are spreading in education after the milestone ChatGPT release in November 2022.

In particular this contribution is conceived as a first step in direction of further studies on this typology of formative feedback AI tools [33]. Indeed, apps such as RiProvApp, in accordance with the principles of new emerging paradigms of the learning process, could constitute a precious piece of the mosaic of the technology enhanced learning experiences [34] with an anthropocentric perspective [35]. But more studies are needed to prove the effectiveness in concrete educational contexts.

While this paper presents RiProVapp primarily as a Proof of Concept, the next phase of research will focus on rigorous empirical validation. Future studies will employ a mixed-method approach to measure the app's impact on students' revision capabilities and metacognitive awareness compared to traditional feedback methods. Specifically, data will be collected to verify if the structured nature of RiProVapp leads to a statistically significant improvement in the 'Process' and 'Self-regulation' levels of learning, validating the theoretical alignment with Hattie's model in a real-world classroom setting.

So, an evidence-based approach with quantitative and qualitative analysis could go into detail of the pros and cons of these apps and verify the most effective ways to use formative feedback AI based tools in concrete and more specific contexts also focusing on the perspective of teachers and students.

*Although all the authors have collaborated on the article, D. De Martino has written §1.1, 1.3, M. di Padova § 2, A. Tinterri the § 3 and Anna Dipace § 1.2 and 1.4.

Disclosure of Interests. The authors have no competing interests to declare that are relevant to the content of this article.

References

1. Still, A., d'Inverno, M.: Creative feedback: a manifesto for social learning. In: Educational Data Mining, London, United Kingdom (2014)
2. Hattie, J., Clarke, S.: Visible Learning: Feedback. Routledge, London and New York (2019)
3. Hattie, J. & Clarke, S.: Il feedback in classe. Oltre la cultura del voto. Erickson, Trento (2025)
4. Irons, A., Elkington, S.: Enhancing Learning through Formative Assessment and Feedback. Routledge, London (2021)
5. Tacconi, G., Gentile, M.: Il feedback formativo come strategia di gestione inclusiva della classe. CNOS-FAP-Il CFP si rinnova (2017)
6. Pellerey, M.: Il potere del feedback nei processi formativi e nell'attività lavorativa. Rev. Psychol., 543–568 (2010)
7. Geis, G.L.: Formative feedback: the receiving side. Perform.+ Instr. **25**(5), 3–6 (1986). https://doi.org/10.1002/pfi.4150250503
8. Fabbri, M.: Dare e ricevere feedback: stimolare la competenza riflessiva dei futuri docenti in un corso universitario. In: Sistemi educativi, Orientamento, Lavoro, pp. 725–729. Pensa MultiMedia, Lecce (2023)
9. Wisniewski, B., Zierer, K., Hattie, J.: The power of feedback revisited: a meta-analysis of educational feedback research. Front. Psychol. **10** (2020). https://doi.org/10.3389/fpsyg.2019.03087

10. Doria, B., Foschi, L.C., Slaviero, G., Zaggia, C., Grion, V.: Feedback e feedback automatizzato: Pratiche e percezioni dei docenti universitari. Res. Trends Humanit. Educ. Philos. **12**(1), 25–42 (2025)
11. Bonaiuti, G., Dipace, A.: Insegnare e apprendere in aula e in rete: Per una didattica blended efficace. Carocci, Roma (2021)
12. Watters, A.: Teaching Machines: the History of Personalized Learning. Mit Press Cambridge, Massachusetts (2023)
13. Petrina, S.: Sidney Pressey and the automation of education, 1924–1934. Technol. Cult. **45**(2), 305–330 (2004). https://doi.org/10.1353/tech.2004.0085
14. Pressey, S.: A simple apparatus which gives and scores tests – and teaches. Sch. Soc. **23** (1926)
15. Fly, E.: Teaching machine dichotomy: Skynner vs Pressey. Psychol. Rep. **6**, 11–14 (1960)
16. Skinner, B.F.: Reflections on a decade of teaching machines. Teach. Coll. Rec. **65**(2), 1–9 (1963)
17. De Martino, D.: Storia dell'e-learning in Italia, Progedit, Bari (2022)
18. Yan, L., et al.: Evidence-based multimodal learning analytics for feedback and reflection in collaborative learning. Br. J. Educ. Technol. **55**(5), 1900–1925 (2024). https://doi.org/10.1111/bjet.13498
19. Martino, D., Dipace, A., Tinterri, A.: Mentimeter e valutazione: una sperimentazione di gamification. Education. Sci. Soc. **1**, 59–68 (2023a)
20. De Martino, D., Guerriero, M., Annoscia, S., Basta, A., Tinterri, A., Dipace, A.: Kahoot! And student-generated formative assessment. A pilot study. In: International Conference on Higher Education Learning Methodologies and Technologies Online, pp. 483–501. Springer, Cham (2023)
21. Pereira, Í.S.P., Fernandes, E.L., Flores, M.A.: Teacher education during the COVID-19 lockdown: insights from a formative intervention approach involving online feedback. Educ. Sci. **11**(8), 400 (2021). https://doi.org/10.3390/educsci11080400
22. Eco, U.: Apocalittici e integrati. Comunicazioni di massa e teorie della cultura di massa. La nave di Teseo, Milano (First edition 1962)
23. Al-Smadi, M.: ChatGPT and Beyond: The Generative AI Revolution in Education (2023). arXiv preprint https://arxiv.org/abs/2311.15198. https://doi.org/10.48550/arXiv.2311.15198
24. Aprilianti, B.D.A., Widyantoro, A.: Digital peer feedback and students critical thinking: what correlation and to what extent? J. Lang. Lang. Teach. **12**(2), 629–644 (2024). https://doi.org/10.33394/jollt.v12i2.10264
25. Meyer, J., et al.: Using LLMs to bring evidence-based feedback into the classroom: AI-generated feedback increases secondary students' text revision, motivation, and positive emotions. Comput. Educ. Artif. Intell. **6**, 100199 (2024). https://doi.org/10.1016/j.caeai.2023.100199
26. Alsaiari, O., Baghaei, N., Lahza, H., Lodge, J.M., Boden, M., Khosravi, H.: Emotionally enriched AI-generated feedback: supporting student Well-being without compromising learning. Comput. Educ. **105363** (2025). https://doi.org/10.1016/j.compedu.2025.105363
27. Abahussain, O., Al-Ammary, J.: Low-code/no-code platforms: impact and concerns. In: 2024 International Conference on IT Innovation and Knowledge Discovery (ITIKD), pp. 1–6. IEEE (2025)
28. Yaseen, H., Mohammad, A.S., Ashal, N., Abusaimeh, H., Ali, A., Sharabati, A.A.A.: The impact of adaptive learning technologies, personalized feedback, and interactive AI tools on student engagement: the moderating role of digital literacy. Sustainability **17**(3), 1133 (2025). https://doi.org/10.3390/su17031133

29. Vashishth, T.K., Sharma, V., Sharma, K.K., Kumar, B., Panwar, R., Chaudhary, S.: AI-driven learning analytics for personalized feedback and assessment in higher education. In: Using Traditional Design Methods to Enhance AI-Driven Decision Making, pp. 206–230. IGI Global Scientific Publishing (2024). https://doi.org/10.4018/979-8-3693-0639-0.ch009
30. Anderson, N., Browning, J., Stewart, D., McGowan, A., Galway, L.: Transforming feedback with AI: a smarter way to support student learning. In: EDULEARN25 Proceedings, pp. 6–12. IATED (2025). https://doi.org/10.21125/edulearn.2025.0004
31. Eden, C.A., Chisom, O.N., Adeniyi, I.S.: Integrating AI in education: opportunities, challenges, and ethical considerations. Magna Sci. Adv. Res. Rev. **10**(2), 006–013 (2024). https://doi.org/10.30574/msarr.2024.10.2.0039
32. Deng, X., Joshi, K.D.: Promoting ethical use of generative AI in education. ACM SIGMIS Database: DATABASE Adv. Inf. Syst. **55**(3), 6–11 (2024). https://doi.org/10.1145/3685235.3685237
33. Arsena, A., Basta, A., Dipace, A.: Il digitale a scuola. Dimensioni culturali, pedagogico-didattiche ed organizzative. Edizioni Studium, Roma (2024)
34. De Martino, D.: Oltre l'antinomia "in presenza" e "a distanza": verso un ambiente di apprendimento sociale e liquido. IUL Res. **2**(3), 141–151 (2021). https://doi.org/10.57568/iulres.v2i3.95
35. De Martino, D., di Padova, M., Di Cataldo, M.C., Dipace, A.: AI act: a Quanti-qualitative analysis. In: Ardimento, P., Di Fuccio, R., Fulantelli, G., Limone, P., Pecori, R., Raviolo, P., Rondonotti, M., Schicchi, D., Taibi, D., Zaza, G. (eds.) Higher Education Learning Methodologies and Technologies Online: 6th International Conference HELMeTO 2024, Rome, Italy, September 25–27, 2024. Revised Selected Papers, Part II (Communications in Computer and Information Science). Springer, Cham (2025)

X-IDEA: A Framework for Explainable, Inclusive, and Equitable Code-Learning Assistants

Nadia Di Leo(✉) and Luigi Traetta

Department of Humanities, University of Foggia, 71121 Foggia, Italy
{nadia.dileo,luigi.traetta}@unifg.it

Abstract. First-year programming courses are plagued by high attrition rates, a problem that disproportionately affects students from groups historically excluded from computing [1]. While Large Language Models (LLMs) like GitHub Copilot and ChatGPT offer promising avenues for scalable feedback, their adoption is hampered by significant concerns regarding inscrutability, academic integrity, and data privacy. This paper introduces X-IDEA, a design framework for developing code-learning assistants that are explainable, privacy-aware, and governed by educators. The framework is organized into five interacting layers: learning objectives, learner modelling, generative support, explainable AI, and teacher-in-the-loop governance. Each layer is associated with a core Design Principle (DP1-DP5). Its design principles are directly informed by a qualitative analysis of community discussions on Reddit, ensuring that the proposed solutions address genuine learner and instructor anxieties. The framework is presented as a theoretical contribution, offering a set of constructs and research propositions to guide the future empirical development and evaluation of more transparent, inclusive, and equitable educational technologies for programming.

Keywords: Programming Education · AI in Education · Large Language Models

1 Introduction

The challenge of teaching introductory programming is a persistent and well-documented issue within computer science education. CS1 is commonly described as difficult with high dropout [1, 3], but the strongest survey evidence reports about 28–33% failure/withdrawal on average, with wide variability [2]. This phenomenon, often termed the "CS1 attrition problem", not only represents a significant pedagogical hurdle but also has profound social implications. Attrition is demonstrably heavier among students who enter academic probation, and socioeconomic factors like mental health and insufficient pre-college preparation can increase a pattern that actively constrains workforce diversity and limits pathways to social mobility for many talented individuals [4].

The recent emergence of powerful, publicly accessible Large Language Model (LLM) assistants, such as GitHub Copilot and OpenAI's ChatGPT, presents a paradigm

M. Adamoli et al. (Eds.): HELMeTO 2025, CCIS 2958, pp. 539–551, 2026.
https://doi.org/10.1007/978-3-032-31850-3_33

shift in the educational landscape. These tools can provide learners with instantaneous feedback, generate abundant worked examples, and offer step-by-step explanations for complex code. For instructors facing overcrowded classrooms and limited resources, the potential of such systems to offer personalized, scalable support seems immensely attractive. They promise to offload repetitive instructional tasks and empower students to overcome minor hurdles independently, thereby freeing up educator time for more substantive pedagogical interactions [5].

However, empirical work and community discourse reveal a deep-seated ambivalence toward these technologies. While students and educators alike express enthusiasm for the rapid assistance LLMs can provide, this is matched by significant anxiety. Learners often perceive the systems as inscrutable "black boxes" whose reasoning is opaque, while instructors voice legitimate concerns about the erosion of academic integrity, the potential for baked-in algorithmic bias, and the challenge of navigating institutional privacy regulations when student data is processed by third-party services [6].

This tension was starkly illustrated in a recent qualitative content analysis of 156 Reddit posts and 3,512 comments from the r/learnprogramming community[1] [16]. The study revealed that negative and mixed feelings toward AI in learning programming were the most prevalent categories of discussion. Forum participants repeatedly raised concerns about developing an unhealthy over-reliance on AI, the unreliability of generated code, and the ethical gray areas of using AI for academic assignments. These "forum voices" expressed a clear need for tools that do not simply provide answers but actively support the learning process, for systems that are transparent, and for educational environments where instructors can "step in and set boundaries".

In response to this complex interplay of opportunity and risk, the present contribution introduces X-IDEA, a design framework for building explainable, privacy-aware, and teacher-governed code-learning assistants. X-IDEA (Explainable, Inclusive, Equitable, Data-Aware) is not a specific software implementation but rather a conceptual model intended to guide researchers and practitioners. It offers a set of principles and constructs for creating educational tools that harness the power of generative AI while proactively mitigating its pedagogical and ethical pitfalls. The framework is theoretical in nature, proposing a structure that can be operationalised and examined in future empirical studies.

2 Background and Related Work

The design of the X-IDEA framework is situated at the intersection of three distinct but related fields of inquiry: the pedagogy of introductory programming, the application of artificial intelligence in education, and the growing discipline of explainable AI (XAI).

2.1 The Enduring Challenges of Introductory Programming

Learning to program involves a complex synthesis of skills, including mastering abstract concepts, understanding formal syntax, developing problem-solving strategies, and

[1] The full Dataset is retrievable at: https://github.com/debugginglearningloop/Dataset%2D%2D-Debugging-the-learning-loop

engaging in metacognitive practices like debugging [7–10]. Novices often struggle with the high cognitive load imposed by these simultaneous demands [11]. This challenge is compounded by what Risko and Gilbert [17] term "cognitive offloading", the tendency to use external tools to reduce internal cognitive demands. Over-reliance on AI assistants may prevent learners from developing the mental representations necessary for independent problem-solving. The disconnect between a student's mental model of a program's execution and its actual behaviour is a frequent source of frustration and a primary reason for the high attrition rates observed by Bidlake and colleagues [12].

Traditional pedagogical interventions, such as peer instruction, pair programming, and intensive tutoring, have proven effective but are difficult to scale. The concept of scaffolding, originally articulated by Wood, Bruner, and Ross [18] as a process whereby an expert supports a novice within their Zone of Proximal Development [19], provides the theoretical foundation for adaptive educational support. The advent of AI-driven tools has long been seen as a potential solution for providing individualized support at scale [5]. Early intelligent tutoring systems focused on rule-based feedback for specific programming exercises. The current generation of LLM-based assistants represents a quantum leap in capability, moving beyond simple feedback to generative, conversational, and context-aware support [13].

2.2 Large Language Models as Educational co-Pilots

LLMs offer several affordances highly relevant to programming education. Their ability to generate code snippets on demand provides learners with worked examples that can illustrate abstract concepts, and they can rephrase complex error messages in natural language, helping novices overcome the cryptic output of compilers and interpreters. Furthermore, their conversational nature allows students to ask follow-up questions, creating a dynamic learning environment that simulates a one-on-one tutoring session [6].

This potential, however, is met with significant apprehension from both learners and educators, a tension vividly captured in community discourse. A large-scale qualitative analysis of the r/learnprogramming community was conducted, and provided substantial empirical grounding for these concerns. The study, which examined 156 posts and 3,512 comments on the use of AI, revealed that negative (19.66%) and mixed (16.14%) sentiments were the most prevalent categories of discussion, far outweighing purely positive views. Figure 1 presents the distribution of coded categories across all posts and comments. The coding scheme was developed iteratively through a conventional content analysis approach [20], wherein codes emerged inductively from the data rather than being imposed a priori. Two coders independently analysed a subset of 50 posts to establish initial categories, then refined these through discussion until consensus was reached. The resulting taxonomy comprises 20 categories, ranging from sentiment-based codes (e.g., "Negative feelings towards AI use in learning programming") to functional codes (e.g., "Technical advice", "Ethical question"). The high prevalence of negative (19.66%) and mixed (16.14%) sentiment categories, compared to positive feelings (10.25%), indicates substantial community ambivalence toward AI in programming education.

A dominant community concern, echoed throughout the data, was that unguided LLM use fosters a dangerous over-reliance that prevents the development of core

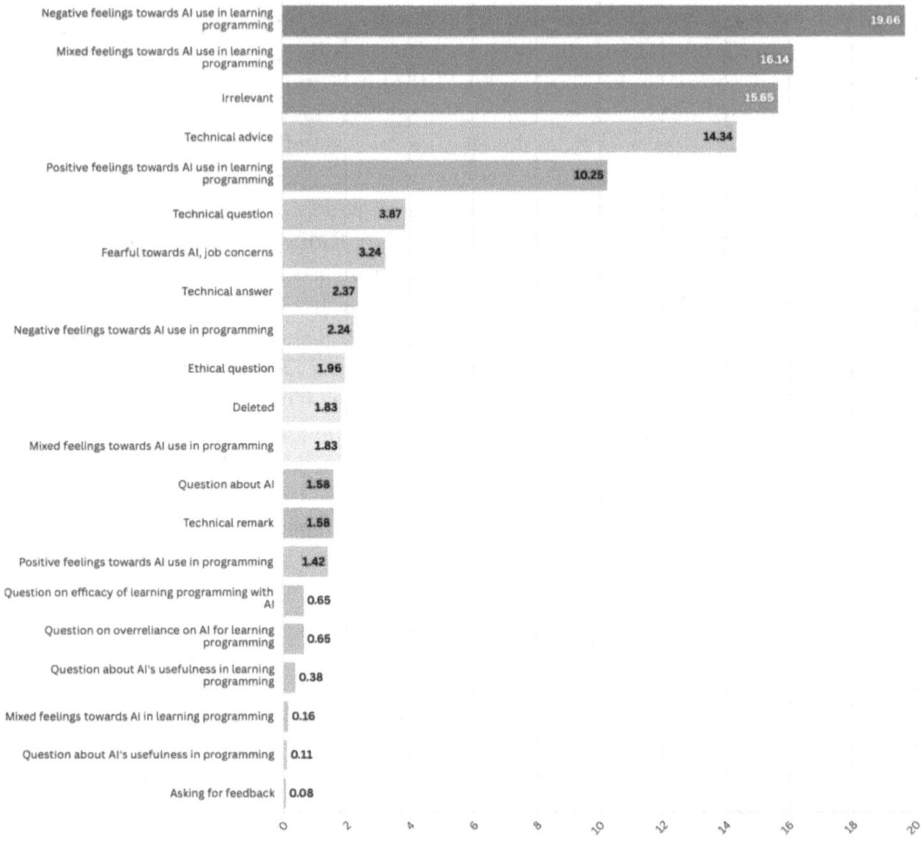

Fig. 1. Distribution of categories across post and comments as a percentage.

problem-solving skills. One user lamented that such tools create an "illusion of competence" that shatters under the pressure of an exam or technical interview; others described the technology as a "crutch" that, while occasionally helpful, ultimately hinders the ability to learn independently.

Consequently, the unguided use of these tools can be counterproductive. This aligns with pedagogical theories that stress the importance of "productive failure" and desirable difficulties in fostering robust, long-term learning [14].

Simply providing a correct answer could circumvent the cognitive processes involved in diagnosing a problem and constructing a solution from first principles, a shortcut that the learning community itself appears to deeply distrust.

The full dataset was used to create a word cloud with the most frequent terms in posts and comments (Fig. 2). This visualization serves to illustrate the central preoccupations of the learning community. The prominence of terms such as "use", "ChatGPT", "code", "learn", "work", and "help" reflects the pragmatic orientation of discussions, users are primarily concerned with how AI tools function in practice and whether they genuinely support learning. The co-occurrence of "understand" alongside "answer" and "problem" suggests a tension between seeking quick solutions and developing genuine comprehension. While word frequency alone cannot establish causal relationships, this pattern is consistent with the qualitative findings regarding learner ambivalence discussed above.

Fig. 2. Word cloud of the most frequent terms in posts and comments.

2.3 The Need for Explainability, Privacy, and Governance

The "black box" nature of many LLMs is a central barrier to their educational adoption [6]. When a student receives a piece of code from an assistant, they often have no insight into why that code is correct or how it relates to the concepts they are meant to be learning. This lack of transparency undermines trust and impedes self-regulated learning. Zimmerman [21] defines self-regulated learning as self-generated thoughts, feelings, and actions planned and cyclically adapted to the attainment of personal goals; when AI systems are opaque, learners cannot effectively monitor their own understanding or adjust their learning strategies accordingly. The field of Explainable AI seeks to address this by developing techniques to make AI decision-making processes more transparent to human users [15].

For an educational context, explanations must be tailored for pedagogical value as well as for correctness.

Privacy is another critical concern. Many commercial AI tools require sending student code and interaction data to external servers, raising significant issues for educational institutions bound by data protection regulation. Tsai, Perrotta, and Gašević [22] argue that educational technologies must balance personalisation with learner agency and data protection, noting that transparency about data use is essential for maintaining trust. A framework for educational AI must therefore consider architectures that protect student privacy by design [15].

Finally, the role of the educator cannot be overlooked. Holstein, McLaren, and Aleven [23] demonstrated that teachers require "orchestration tools" to effectively integrate AI systems into their practice, including dashboards that provide actionable insights without overwhelming cognitive demands. Unfettered AI assistants can undermine an instructor's pedagogical strategy and create an adversarial dynamic centered on policing plagiarism. The findings from the Reddit analysis make this need explicit. The discussions frequently featured pleas from learners for instructors to provide clear guidelines on AI use, indicating a strong desire for governance structures that place educators "in the loop". This community-driven demand calls for systems that allow teachers to shape how AI assistants are used in their classrooms, monitor student progress, and intervene when necessary. X-IDEA is designed specifically to address these three well-documented needs: explainability, privacy, and governance.

3 Methodology: Framework Development Process

The X-IDEA framework did not emerge in a vacuum. Its principles were derived through a design-science research methodology, which integrates problem identification and solution design in an iterative process. This process unfolded in three distinct stages.

The first stage involved a comprehensive review of literature on programming pedagogy, AI in education, and AI ethics. This review identified the foundational challenges and the primary risks of AI adoption. This academic understanding was then triangulated against the insights from the Reddit corpus study, which provided a rich, grounded perspective on the lived experiences of learners and educators.

In the second stage, the extracted requirements were used to sketch low-fidelity prototypes of user interfaces and interaction flows embodying the five design principles. These prototypes, in turn, informed the creation of AI prompts for students, carefully constructed to help them circumvent the previously discussed challenges of programming with AI. This stage was particularly useful in strengthening the emphasis on teacher dashboards and the human override mechanism to maintain pedagogical control.

The third stage involved synthesizing the refined principles into a coherent theoretical framework.

To move from a purely theoretical construct to a practically grounded one, an initial feasibility study was conducted in the form of a hands-on workshop. This study involved 225 participants from master's and bachelor's degree programs in Pedagogical Sciences and Educational Design, Education and Training Sciences, and Primary Education Sciences. In this case, students possessed no prior experience in programming. The task, conducted in small groups, was to create a simple HTML landing page. The intervention consisted of using a commercial LLM (Google's Gemini 2.5 via AI Studio) guided by a custom system prompt developed by the researchers. This prompt was carefully engineered to operationalize key X-IDEA principles (DP1 and DP3, formally defined in Sect. 4), instructing the AI to act as a Socratic tutor that scaffolds information, provides clear concept-linked explanations, and avoids simply giving away the final code. The preliminary results were encouraging: all 45 groups successfully produced functional HTML pages that met the specified requirements (e.g., including headings, paragraphs, images, and hyperlinks). Post-workshop interviews indicated that most of the participants agreed or strongly agreed that the AI's explanations helped them understand HTML concepts. However, these findings should be interpreted cautiously, as the study lacked a control group, employed no standardised assessment of learning outcomes, and relied on self-reported measures. A rigorous evaluation awaits future controlled studies as outlined in the roadmap (Sect. 5). This initial study provides early exploratory evidence that the framework's principles may be viable and warrants further investigation.

3.1 Research Propositions

Building on the theoretical development and these encouraging preliminary findings, the following propositions are intended to guide future empirical research. These propositions are offered as testable hypotheses for the broader research community; the authors intend to examine selected propositions in subsequent studies, but validation will require collaborative effort across multiple research groups and contexts. The following propositions are intended to guide a more formal and rigorous empirical evaluation of systems built according to the X-IDEA framework and its Design Principles (DP), which are formally defined in Sect. 4 (DP1-DP5).

P1: Transparency fosters trust. Systems that provide concept-level explanations for their suggestions (DP1, DP4) will lead to higher levels of perceived trust among student users. This increased trust is expected to mediate a positive effect on measures of self-regulated learning, as students will feel more confident in using the tool as a legitimate learning partner rather than a simple answer key. This proposition is grounded in research demonstrating that transparency in algorithmic systems increases user trust and engagement [24], and that trust is a necessary condition for productive use of educational technologies [25].

P2: Scaffold depth predicts learning gain. The pedagogical effectiveness of the assistant is directly related to its scaffolding strategy (DP3). We hypothesize that an intervention group using an X-IDEA assistant that progresses from Socratic questions to micro-hints to partial code will demonstrate significantly higher learning gains on post-tests compared to a group receiving immediate, complete solutions or a control group with no AI assistance. This proposition draws on extensive evidence that scaffolded instruction produces superior learning outcomes compared to direct instruction, particularly for complex problem-solving tasks [26, 27].

P3: Governance engagement affects equity. The teacher-in-the-loop governance layer is crucial for ensuring equitable outcomes (DP5). We propose that in classrooms where instructors frequently interact with the governance dashboard, customizing hints, overriding suggestions, and monitoring for bias, achievement gaps across demographic groups will narrow over the course of a semester compared to classrooms where the AI assistant operates with minimal teacher oversight. Holstein et al. [23] found that teacher awareness of individual student difficulties, facilitated by AI dashboards, enabled more targeted interventions; we extend this finding to hypothesize effects on equity.

P4: Privacy architecture shapes adoption. The institutional adoption of AI learning tools is not solely a function of their pedagogical effectiveness but is also constrained by practical and ethical considerations. We predict that educational institutions, particularly those with limited connectivity or stringent data privacy mandates, will declare a higher intent to adopt systems based on a minimal-intrusion data architecture (DP2), even if the on-premise models demonstrate slightly lower accuracy than cloud-based alternatives. Empirical surveys of institutional technology adoption consistently identify data privacy as a primary concern [24], suggesting that privacy-preserving architectures may overcome adoption barriers.

P5: Explainability has an optimum. While transparency is a core goal (DP4), the cognitive load of explanations must be considered. We propose that the relationship between the level of detail in an explanation and its pedagogical utility is non-linear. An optimal middle ground exists; excessive detail can overload a novice learner, while overly brief explanations may be unhelpful. This proposition is consistent with cognitive load theory [28], which posits that instructional materials must be designed to manage intrinsic, extraneous, and germane load. Kalyuga's [29] expertise reversal effect further suggests that optimal explanation complexity varies with learner proficiency. This proposition suggests the need for adaptive explanation strategies that are personalized based on the learner's current level of mastery (Layer 2).

4 Discussions

X-IDEA is organized into five interacting layers. Each layer is designed to address a pressing opportunity presented by generative AI while simultaneously confronting a key technical or ethical challenge identified in the literature and in community forums. Each layer is associated with a core Design Principle (DP).

4.1 Layer 1: Learning Objectives and Concept Alignment

The first layer establishes the pedagogical foundation of the system. It consists of a graph of core concepts that span the programming curriculum, covering syntax (e.g., for loops, conditional statements), semantics (e.g., variable scope, pointers), and common problem-solving patterns (e.g., searching, sorting). Each concept node in this graph can be indexed to a specific level of cognitive mastery, such as those defined by Bloom's Taxonomy (e.g., remember, understand, apply, analyze).

DP1: In this case, the concept alignment is that every AI action carries a pointer to a concept node, which later enables transparent assessment.

This principle directly counters the inscrutability of generic LLMs. When the assistant suggests a code correction, generates an example, or provides an explanation, that output is explicitly linked to one or more concepts in the knowledge graph. For the student, this means every interaction is contextualized within their learning journey. For the instructor, it creates a transparent audit trail of the skills a student has practiced, allowing for more precise and meaningful assessment.

Implementation of DP1 may proceed through several technical approaches. First, the concept graph can be constructed by mapping existing curriculum standards (e.g., ACM/IEEE CS2013 guidelines) or institutional learning outcomes onto a hierarchical ontology of programming concepts. Second, AI-generated outputs can be tagged with concept identifiers through post-generation classification models, fine-tuned on expert-labelled examples of code-to-concept mappings. Third, prompt engineering techniques can instruct the LLM to explicitly reference concepts in its outputs. Finally, the user interface should visually display concept tags alongside AI suggestions, enabling learners to see the pedagogical purpose of each interaction. Existing work on knowledge tracing

[30] and curriculum sequencing in intelligent tutoring systems provides precedents for such concept-aligned architectures.

4.2 Layer 2: Learner Modelling and Minimal-Intrusion Data

This layer is responsible for personalizing the learning experience. The system maintains a model of each learner's progress by logging interactions within their local development environment. These logs include telemetry such as compilation outcomes (successes and failures), traces from unit tests, and debugging paths taken. This data provides a rich, evidence-based picture of a student's evolving understanding and persistent misconceptions.

DP2: Only telemetry created inside the development environment is stored, and all raw code remains on institutional servers.

This principle addresses the profound privacy concerns associated with third-party AI services. By restricting data collection to anonymized interaction metadata and ensuring that the student's actual source code never leaves the institution's control, this design respects learner privacy and helps institutions comply with data protection regulations. This architecture fosters trust among all stakeholders, students, educators, and administrators, by ensuring that the educational mission is not compromised by commercial data extraction practices.

4.3 Layer 3: Scaffolding-First Generative Support

This layer governs the behavior of the generative model itself. X-IDEA advocates for the use of several smaller, specialized, and potentially light-weight language models rather than a single monolithic one. These models can be fine-tuned for specific tasks, such as synthesizing hints, generating partial solutions, or creating culturally localized storylines for programming problems to enhance inclusivity. The core interaction design is governed by a principle of progressive assistance.

DP3: The default output is a question or micro-hint; direct code appears only when earlier prompts were exhausted.

This principle is a direct response to the most common fear expressed in the Reddit forums: that AI tools make it too easy to get the answer without learning. The finding from the Reddit analysis that users complain "Copilot gives you code before you know what it does" is the central motivation for this design. Instead of providing a solution, the X-IDEA assistant first prompts the student with a question (e.g., "What happens to the loop counter when the array is empty?"). If the student still struggles, it might offer a micro-hint or a partial piece of code. A complete solution is offered only as a last resort, and its delivery is logged for the instructor's review. This scaffolding approach keeps the student in a state of active problem-solving, using the AI as a guide rather than a crutch.

4.4 Layer 4: Dual-Audience Explainable AI

This layer focuses on making the AI's reasoning transparent to both learners and educators. To achieve this, the framework proposes two primary explanation modalities:

token-level concept labels, which annotate generated code with pointers to the concept graph from Layer 1, and counter-factual test simulations, where the system shows what would happen if a different (incorrect) approach were taken.

DP4: In this case, novice-friendly text expands, on demand, into a technical rationale that teachers can audit.

This principle recognizes that students and teachers have different explanatory needs. A student might need a simple, intuitive explanation, whereas an instructor may need to verify the technical and pedagogical soundness of the AI's suggestion. In an X-IDEA system, a concise explanation provided to a student would be accompanied by an option to "see more detail". Clicking this would reveal a more thorough rationale, including confidence scores and references to the underlying models, allowing the teacher to audit the system's behavior and build trust in its recommendations.

4.5 Layer 5: Teacher-in-the-Loop Governance

The final layer ensures that human educators retain ultimate authority over the learning environment. This is achieved through dashboards that provide both aggregate and individualized views of student progress, AI assistant performance, and emerging patterns of difficulty. The dashboard would visualize common misconceptions, highlight potential indicators of bias in the AI's suggestions, and show the accuracy of the model's alignment with the curriculum's learning objectives.

DP5: Every override is logged and feeds back into the learner model and bias detector.

This principle operationalizes the idea of teacher governance. From the dashboard, an instructor can review, approve, edit, or even block suggestions made by the AI. For instance, if the assistant offers a hint that uses a concept not yet taught, the teacher can block it for the entire class. If it provides a suboptimal explanation, the teacher can edit it. Every such intervention is logged, creating a valuable feedback loop that can be used to fine-tune the AI models and improve the overall system over time. This transforms the AI from a potential source of unvetted information into a true assistant that operates under the direct supervision of the professional educator, responding directly to the community's call for instructors to set clear boundaries.

4.6 Limitations, Barriers, Risks

The X-IDEA framework, while theoretically grounded, faces several limitations that must be acknowledged. First, the framework's reliance on smaller, specialised language models (Layer 3) presupposes technical infrastructure and expertise that may not be available at under-resourced institutions. Running on-premise models requires computational resources and technical staff that many schools and universities lack, potentially creating a new form of digital divide.

Second, the teacher-in-the-loop governance model (Layer 5) assumes that educators have sufficient time and training to engage meaningfully with AI dashboards. In practice, teachers already face substantial workload pressures; adding AI oversight responsibilities without corresponding support could lead to superficial engagement or rejection of the system altogether. Professional development and institutional support structures are prerequisites for effective implementation.

Third, the framework's emphasis on scaffolding over direct solutions (DP3) may create friction with learner expectations. Students accustomed to instant answers from commercial AI tools may perceive X-IDEA-compliant assistants as unhelpful or frustrating, particularly under time pressure. Managing these expectations requires explicit communication about pedagogical rationale.

Fourth, the qualitative evidence base, while valuable, has limitations. The Reddit dataset represents a self-selected population of English-speaking users willing to discuss AI publicly; their concerns may not generalise to all learner populations. Cultural contexts, educational traditions, and attitudes toward technology vary substantially across regions.

Fifth, the propositions (P1-P5) remain untested. While grounded in relevant theory, empirical validation is essential before the framework can be recommended for widespread adoption. The proposed roadmap (Sect. 5) addresses this need, but the timeline for generating robust evidence may span several years.

Finally, there is a risk that any educational AI system, regardless of design intentions, may be co-opted for surveillance or punitive purposes. The logging mechanisms intended for pedagogical feedback could, if misused, become tools for excessive monitoring. Institutional policies and ethical guidelines must accompany technical implementations to prevent such misuse.

5 Roadmap and Conclusion

The X-IDEA framework is presented here as a conceptual model, and its true value can only be determined through rigorous empirical research. To this end, we propose a three-phase roadmap for its validation and refinement.

- Phase 1: Design Validation. This initial phase will focus on validating the core design principles against the community concerns that motivated them. The twenty-topic taxonomy of learner and educator concerns developed from the Reddit analysis will be used as a validation instrument. A panel of experienced programmers will perform expert walkthroughs of an X-IDEA prototype, judging whether each design principle adequately and robustly addresses the specific anxieties and needs voiced by the community.
- Phase 2: Pilot Deployment. Following the design validation, an early prototype of an X-IDEA assistant will be deployed with a small group of programming students. This pilot study will employ a mixed-methods approach. Quantitative logs of student interactions with the assistant will be collected to analyze usage patterns and their correlation with performance metrics. Concurrently, qualitative data will be gathered through semi-structured interviews and focus groups with both students and experts to gain rich insights into their perceptions of the tool's usability, trustworthiness, and pedagogical impact.
- Phase 3: Multi-Site Studies. The final phase will involve scaling up the evaluation to test the research propositions (P1-P5) across multiple institutions. Quasi-experimental trials will be conducted in diverse settings, encompassing different types of institutions (e.g., research universities, community colleges), a variety of curricular approaches, and varying levels of infrastructural capacity. This multi-site

approach will be essential for assessing the generalizability of the framework and understanding how its effectiveness is moderated by local context.

The X-IDEA framework offers a structured response to the dual promise and peril of integrating Large Language Models into programming education. By deliberately weaving together principles of personalized tutoring, privacy-aware deployment, robust explainability, and meaningful teacher governance, it provides a comprehensive conceptual model for moving forward. It seeks to reframe the role of AI from that of an omniscient, inscrutable oracle to that of a transparent, customizable, and pedagogically-aligned learning assistant. The framework is intended as a compass for researchers and practitioners who share the goal of steering coding education toward a future that is not only more technologically advanced but also fundamentally more clear, inclusive, and equitable.

References

1. Álvarez, C., Samary, M., Wise, A.: Modularization for mastery learning in CS1: a 4-year action research study. J. Comput. High. Educ., 1–44 (2023). https://doi.org/10.1007/s12528-023-09366-1
2. Bennedsen, J., Caspersen, M.E.: Failure rates in introductory programming. ACM SIGcSE Bulletin. **39**(2), 32–36 (2007)
3. Robins, A., Rountree, J., Rountree, N.: Learning and teaching programming: a review and discussion. Comput. Sci. Educ. **13**(2), 137–172 (2003)
4. Neda, B., Morales, F., Juarez, K., Wong-Ma, J., Masagué, S.: Investigating the role of socioeconomic factors on CS1 performance. In: 2024 IEEE Global Engineering Education Conference (EDUCON), pp. 1–8 (2024). https://doi.org/10.1109/EDUCON60312.2024.10578863
5. Major, L., Francis, G., Tsapali, M.: The effectiveness of technology-supported personalised learning in low- and middle-income countries: a meta-analysis. Br. J. Educ. Technol. **52**, 1935–1964 (2021). https://doi.org/10.1111/BJET.13116
6. Wang, S., et al.: Large Language Models for Education: A Survey and Outlook. ArXiv, abs/2403.18105 (2024). https://doi.org/10.48550/arXiv.2403.18105.
7. Xie, B., et al.: A theory of instruction for introductory programming skills. Comput. Sci. Educ. **29**, 205–253 (2019). https://doi.org/10.1080/08993408.2019.1565235
8. Medeiros, R., Ramalho, G., Falcão, T.: A systematic literature review on teaching and learning introductory programming in higher education. IEEE Trans. Educ. **62**, 77–90 (2019). https://doi.org/10.1109/TE.2018.2864133
9. Nouri, J., Zhang, L., Mannila, L., Norén, E.: Development of computational thinking, digital competence and 21st century skills when learning programming in K-9. Educ. Inq. **11**, 1–17 (2019). https://doi.org/10.1080/20004508.2019.1627844
10. Hu, L.: Programming and 21st century skill development in K-12 schools: a multidimensional meta-analysis. J. Comput. Assist. Learn. **40**, 610–636 (2023). https://doi.org/10.1111/jcal.12904
11. Quintero-Manes, R., Vieira, C.: Differentiated measurement of cognitive loads in computer programming. J. Comput. High. Educ. (2024). https://doi.org/10.1007/s12528-024-09411-7
12. Bidlake, L., Aubanel, E., Voyer, D.: Investigating the progression of the mental models formed by programmers learning parallel programming. ACM Trans. Comput. Educ. **25**, 1–31 (2025). https://doi.org/10.1145/3712707

13. Yan, W., Nakajima, T., Sawada, R.: Benefits and challenges of collaboration between students and conversational generative artificial intelligence in programming learning: an empirical case study. Educ. Sci. **14**(4), 433 (2024)
14. Steenhof, N., Woods, N., Van Gerven, P., Mylopoulos, M.: Productive failure as an instructional approach to promote future learning. Adv. Health Sci. Educ. **24**, 739–749 (2019). https://doi.org/10.1007/s10459-019-09895-4
15. Felzmann, H., Fosch-Villaronga, E., Lutz, C., Tamò-Larrieux, A.: Towards transparency by Design for Artificial Intelligence. Sci. Eng. Ethics **26**, 3333–3361 (2020). https://doi.org/10.1007/s11948-020-00276-4
16. Di Leo, N.: Programmare l'inclusione con l'Intelligenza Artificiale: un'indagine sulle percezioni degli studenti di coding online. Ital. J. Spec. Educ. Incl. **13**(1), 231–243 (2025)
17. Risko, E.F., Gilbert, S.J.: Cognitive offloading. Trends Cogn. Sci. **20**(9), 676–688 (2016)
18. Wood, D., Bruner, J.S., Ross, G.: The role of tutoring in problem solving. J. Child Psychol. Psychiatry **17**(2), 89–100 (1976)
19. Vygotsky, L.S.: Mind in Society: the Development of Higher Psychological Processes, vol. 86. Harvard university press (1978)
20. Hsieh, H.F., Shannon, S.E.: Three approaches to qualitative content analysis. Qual. Health Res. **15**(9), 1277–1288 (2005)
21. Zimmerman, B.J.: Becoming a self-regulated learner: an overview. Theory Pract. **41**(2), 64–70 (2002)
22. Tsai, Y.S., Perrotta, C., Gašević, D.: Empowering learners with personalised learning approaches? Agency, equity and transparency in the context of learning analytics. Assess. Eval. High. Educ. **45**(4), 554–567 (2020)
23. Holstein, K., McLaren, B.M., Aleven, V.: Designing for complementarity: teacher and student needs for orchestration support in AI-enhanced classrooms. In: International Conference on Artificial Intelligence in Education, pp. 157–171. Springer International Publishing, Cham (2019)
24. Guo, Y., Zhang, X.: The impact mechanism of algorithmic transparency on user Trust in Intelligent Recommendation Systems of internet platforms. J. Comput. (2025). https://doi.org/10.63367/199115992025063603022
25. Nazaretsky, T., Mejia-Domenzain, P., Swamy, V., Frej, J., Käser, T.: The critical role of trust in adopting AI-powered educational technology for learning: an instrument for measuring student perceptions. Comput. Educ. Artif. Intell. **8**, 100368 (2025). https://doi.org/10.1016/j.caeai.2025.100368
26. Hmelo-Silver, C.E., Duncan, R.G., Chinn, C.A.: Scaffolding and achievement in problem-based and inquiry learning: a response to Kirschner, Sweller, and Clark. Educ. Psychol. **42**(2), 99–107 (2007)
27. Belland, B.R.: Scaffolding: definition, current debates, and future directions. In: Handbook of Research on Educational Communications and Technology, pp. 505–518. New York, NY, Springer New York (2013)
28. Sweller, J.: Cognitive load theory. In: Psychology of Learning and Motivation, vol. 55, pp. 37–76. Academic (2011)
29. Kalyuga, S.: Expertise reversal effect and its implications for learner-tailored instruction. Educ. Psychol. Rev. **19**(4), 509–539 (2007)
30. Corbett, A.T., Anderson, J.R.: Knowledge tracing: modeling the acquisition of procedural knowledge. User Model. User-Adap. Inter. **4**(4), 253–278 (1994)

Memes in Higher Education: Exploration of Participatory Learning and Neuroeducational Practices

Giuseppe Liverano and Marianna Liparoti(✉)

University of study "G. d'Annunzio" Chieti-Pescara, via dei vestini 31, 66013 Chieti, Italy
marianna.liparoti@unich.it

Abstract. The research explores the educational potential of digital memes as tools for learning and cultural mediation in educational contexts. The study aims to verify how memes can be integrated into teaching as tools for reflection and knowledge construction; which transversal and disciplinary skills are activated during their collaborative production; and how the use of digital languages affects students' motivation, participation and ethical awareness.

Seventy-two university students (64 women and 8 men) participated in the study, which was divided into eight phases, including: media literacy training, design and production of memes on the theme of early school leaving, presentation of results, and evaluation with shared rubrics and peer feedback.

The qualitative and observational methodological approach made it possible to analyse both the cooperation processes and the products generated, highlighting the relational and metacognitive dynamics activated.

Findings show how the conscious use of digital languages mediated by shared assessment practices can be an effective tool for multimodal and inclusive learning. The experience confirms the pedagogical value of memes as a resource for educational innovation, motivation, inclusion and participatory knowledge construction, while recognising the limitations associated with the exploratory nature of the study.

Keywords: neuroeducation · early school leaving · innovative didactic

1 Introduction

Current education is undergoing a profound transformation in the communication languages that characterise the new generations [1]. The latter interact mainly through digital tools in media environments, which convey symbols that constitute genuine emerging cultural codes [2]. In this scenario, internet memes emerge as one of the dominant languages: highly iconic, synthetic cultural artefacts, often characterised by critical humour, capable of condensing complex meanings, emotions, opinions and social representations within an immediate and accessible visual structure [3, 4]. Meme concept was introduced by Richard Dawkins [5], who outlined an evolutionary definition based on the concept of a unit of cultural transmission that spreads through imitation, analogous to genetic

M. Adamoli et al. (Eds.): HELMeTO 2025, CCIS 2958, pp. 552–565, 2026.
https://doi.org/10.1007/978-3-032-31850-3_34

replication. In this perspective, memes take the form of an idea, a behaviour, or a symbol that replicates through social interaction. Subsequently, Daniel Dennett [6] expanded on this insight, arguing that memes are cognitive structures capable of influencing human thought and culture, acting as true "mind viruses", in other words, active mental agents. Finally, Kate Distin [7], reworked the concept of memes, emphasising their transformative nature, according to which, in cultural transmission, memes are not simply replicated but actively reinterpreted by those who receive them, thus becoming cognitive tools involved in learning processes and the construction of meaning. In this direction, Quinal [8] observed how memes on the internet are not only entertainment tools, but are actual cultural artefacts that contribute to the dissemination of knowledge, beliefs and values within a community. In fact, they reflect and at the same time shape the way people interpret social and cultural reality, playing a central role in the processes of collective identity construction. They operate as instruments of cultural mediation, simultaneously challenging and consolidating the stereotypes that structure the social imagination [9]. The definition of "meme" is a useful starting point for understanding broader cultural and communicative phenomena, as these products act as spaces for symbolic mediation through which knowledge, experience and culture are continuously reinterpreted and shared [10]. In other words, every time a meme is created, modified or disseminated, a communicative act takes place that renews and transforms its original meaning. In this sense, memes are distinguished by their ability to attract attention, spread rapidly and adapt to different contexts, while maintaining a strong social and emotional dimension that guarantees their communicative dynamism and constant redefinition of meaning [11].

Current research shows that the phenomenon of memes is an area of growing interest to the scientific community, involving multiple disciplines, from sociology to communication, cultural psychology to media and digital culture studies [12]. In the field of education, following the rapid expansion of virtual learning environments, which has forced a profound rethinking of teaching and assessment practices, a line of research has been initiated to explore the educational and formative potential of memes, particularly in relation to the processes of knowledge acquisition and practice through participatory, narrative and intertextual methods. However, the results that have emerged so far appear to be limited and not yet fully consolidated, leaving open the need for further empirical and theoretical research to understand more systematically the impact of memes in educational contexts and knowledge- construction processes.

Hence, this explorative study aims to explore the possibility of transforming the ambivalence of memes into a significant educational opportunity, investigating how they can be leveraged in teaching and learning processes. The ambivalence of memes, oscillating between entertainment and critical reflection, between spontaneous communication and intentional expression, suggests a teaching potential that has yet to be fully explored, which could help stimulate active participation, creativity, and critical thinking among students. In this perspective, the theoretical hypothesis of reference falls within the framework of participatory culture outlined by Henry Jenkins [13], who believe that the contemporary digital ecosystem favors forms of horizontal and collaborative communication, in which individuals take an active role in the production and sharing of content. By transferring this paradigm to the educational context, we aim to verify whether and to what extent memes can be considered cultural artifacts capable of promoting participatory, narrative, and intertextual learning methods. In this sense, the exploratory study aims to understand whether memes can really contribute to making teaching more inclusive, dialogical, and culturally relevant, responding to the languages and communication practices of the younger generations. In line with these premises, the research questions are:

RQ 1. How can memes contribute to the development of transversal skills within educational contexts?

RQ 2. What assessment practices emerge from the educational use of memes, and to what extent can these practices make participatory and reflective learning processes visible and enhance them?

RQ 3. What theoretical and pedagogical constructs can support the integration of memes into educational design?

The overall objective is therefore to explore whether and how memes can be significant resources for didactic innovation, contributing to a rethinking of the relationship between digital culture, learning, and training.

2 Methods and Materials

The exploratory study involved 72 students enrolled in the Philosophy and Education Sciences degree program (64 female and 8 male; average age = 20.5 ± 0.5 years), characterized by homogeneous socio-cultural backgrounds. At enrollment, participants gave their informed consent. The research was conducted in person over five days of workshop activities scheduled as part of the university program, for a total of 15 h. To ensure a collaborative learning perspective consistent with the research objectives, the entire student population was divided into six groups of twelve participants each. Within each group, six students took on an *operational role*, dealing with the design and production of memes, while the other six took on an *observational role*, dedicating themselves to the documentation and collaborative analysis of the design and implementation processes. Students were also asked to continue their individual reflection on the work carried out outside of laboratory hours, to consolidate the processes of analysis and conceptual reworking activated during the collective sessions.

2.1 Materials

Research made use of a set of teaching, digital, and assessment tools designed to support participatory learning and systematically document the educational and communication processes activated during the workshop. A central role was played by the assessment rubric (Table 1), conceived as a training and assessment tool [14]. It was designed by the teacher, based on theoretical content of Rivoltella [15] and Castoldi [14], It was designed by the teacher, based on the theoretical content of Rivoltella and Castoldi, which highlights the function of authentic and reflective assessment as an integrated process of learning and awareness. The rubric was designed to guide the planning of activities, monitor processes, and evaluate final products, but also to offer students a reference point for metacognitive reflection and self-assessment. The rubric is divided into six dimensions (creativity, critical thinking, digital competence, participation and collaboration, motivation, and knowledge of the subject) that represent the main areas of competence mobilized during the course. For each dimension, five levels of mastery have been defined, from basic to advanced, which describe the progression of observable performance. The use of the rubric has made the quality criteria of the products transparent and allowed for a consistent assessment of the integration between content, processes, and skills. The rubric was designed as a formative and evaluative tool with a dual function: on the one hand, to guide the design and production processes of the memes, and on the other, to encourage metacognitive reflection and self-assessment by students.

Logbooks were also used [16], in which students with an observational role noted down personal reflections, observations on the processes, and self-perceived assessments in relation to the six dimensions of the rubric. For students with an operational role, the diary provided a space to analyse the design and communication choices made; for students with an observational role, it served as a tool for systematic documentation and qualitative analysis of group processes.

Open-source digital tools were also used for the design and creation of memes (including applications for image creation and text and layout management), selected based on their accessibility and consistency with the educational objectives. Finally, PowerPoint presentations, descriptive group reports, and observation sheets were additional tools for data collection and qualitative analysis, useful for understanding both the productive and reflective dimensions of the experience.

Finally, the teacher used an assessment grid based on the same dimensions and levels of mastery as the assessment rubric but used for analytical and certification purposes. This grid made it possible to systematize the observations that emerged during the workshop, ensuring consistency between the ongoing formative assessment and the summative assessment of the results achieved.

Table 1. Multidimensional assessment rubric.

Dimensions\ Criteria	Level 1 Basic	Level 2 Adequate	Level 3 Good	Level 4 Very good	Level 5 Excellent
Creativity	Unoriginal memes, poor consistency and visual impact.	A few original elements, a simple and straightforward message.	Good creative ability, clear irony and effective message.	Original and well-developed ideas, creative use of visual language.	Maximum originality, strong communicative impact, innovative and engaging synthesis.

(continued)

Table 1. (*continued*)

Dimensions\ Criteria	Level 1 Basic	Level 2 Adequate	Level 3 Good	Level 4 Very good	Level 5 Excellent
Critical Thinking	No reflection on the subject, superficial approach.	Partial analysis, limited cause-effect connections.	Appropriate analysis, clear messages with relevant reflections.	Advanced critical thinking, articulate and well-argued interpretations.	In-depth critical re-examination, multiple perspectives, independent and sound assessments.
Digital literacy	Serious difficulties in using the tools, frequent errors.	Basic use of tools, poor graphics. Basic use of tools, poor graphics.	Correct and independent use, appropriate graphics.	Master digital tools, aesthetic and functional attention.	Expert, creative and informed use of graphics, tools and digital language.
Participation and Collaboration	Low participation, unresolved conflicts, work not shared.	Discontinuous collaboration, unbalanced contributions.	Regular participation, constructive interaction and appropriate distribution of roles.	Effective collaboration, clear team synergy, inclusion of members.	Excellent collaboration, strong team spirit, shared leadership, everyone involved.
Motivation and angagement	Lack of interest, activity carried out with little commitment.	Fluctuating interest, inconsistent participation.	Good motivation, active participation in most stages.	Strong motivation, enthusiasm and constant participation.	Maximum involvement, infectious enthusiasm, proactive and independent commitment.
Knowledge of meme topic	Incomplete or incorrect information, lack of understanding.	Superficial understanding, scarce or inaccurate references.	Adequate knowledge, correct use of data and basic concepts.	In-depth knowledge, good ability to connect data, causes and effects.	Complete mastery of the topic, complex analysis and ability to relate the topic to broader social contexts.

2.2 Procedure

The study was divided into nine phases, each aimed at exploring specific aspects of the process of creating, analyzing, and interpreting memes in an educational context. The different phases, described below, outline the methodological path through which the entire workshop was developed.

1. *Training and media literacy.* In the initial phase, the teacher, recognizing the value of media literacy as a fundamental cross-cutting skill for lifelong learning and for the exercise of informed digital citizenship [17, 18], organized informative and formative sessions aimed at exploring the concept of memes, the main techniques for producing them, and their educational potential. This process was accompanied by the definition of ethical guidelines [19, 20], considered essential for guiding students toward responsible use of digital languages, preventing the reproduction of stereotypes and the dissemination of inappropriate or offensive content. At the same time, all students conducted preliminary research aimed at collecting sources, examples, and digital tools related to memes, also developing technical skills in the use of the main university search engines and databases, learning how to select, evaluate, and critically interpret the quality and reliability of the information found.

- *Choice of meme topic.* Upon discussion between the teacher and students, the central theme for the meme production emerged: early school leaving [21]. The choice of topic was the result of a collective discussion aimed at identifying a socially and educationally relevant issue capable of stimulating critical reflection and personal involvement. This decision reinforced the educational value of the course, allowing the theoretical content covered during the lessons to be linked to concrete experiences that were recognizable in the students' everyday lives.
- *Definition of working groups.* A The total population of 72 students was divided into six working groups of twelve participants each. This organization ensured numerical balance and promoted effective collaborative learning within manageable units. Each group was then divided into two subgroups, which were assigned complementary but interdependent functions. In each group, six students took on an operational role, dedicating themselves to the design, creation, and revision of the memes, while the other six took on an observational role, engaging in the documentation and qualitative analysis of the work processes. The students with an operational role oversaw the entire production cycle: analysis of the theme, definition of the concept, selection of cultural references, design of the key message, choice of formats and expressive registers, graphic and textual creation using open-source software, and subsequent revision considering the feedback received. Students with an observational role systematically monitored group processes, paying particular attention to collaborative dynamics (roles, interactions, negotiation of choices), the quality of the creative process (clarity and consistency between objectives and expressive solutions), and compliance with ethical and evaluative guidelines. Structured observation sheets and logbooks were used to collect data. At the end of each session, the observers wrote a summary report containing evidence, critical issues, and suggestions for improvement, which was shared with the operational subgroup during the review phase.

4. *Meme design.* At this stage, the meme design process began. Students with an operational role developed the meme concepts, defining key messages, communication tones, and visual solutions, while those with an observational role documented the design choices, analysed the collaborative dynamics, and monitored consistency with ethical and methodological guidelines. Both groups referred to the evaluation rubric

(Table 1) as a guidance tool, analysing its dimensions and discussing the quality criteria of the memetic product.

5. *Meme creation.* With the help of previously selected open-source digital tools and applications, students with operational roles began the meme production phase, translating the ideas developed in the design phase into visual and textual form. The goal was to create communication products that balanced creativity, ethical rigor, and consistency with the theme of early school leaving. The main challenge was to combine the expressive effectiveness typical of memetic language with the complexity and sensitivity of the topic, avoiding any trivialization or distortion of the educational message. Students with an observational role monitored the production process, collecting data on technical choices, time management, problem-solving strategies, and relational dynamics within the groups.
6. *Preparation of a presentation and report.* In this phase, the groups organized the material produced into a PowerPoint presentation and a descriptive report, with the aim of systematically documenting the process of designing and implementing the memes. This phase served a dual purpose: on the one hand, to facilitate the reconstruction and visibility of work processes, role distribution, and collaborative dynamics; on the other hand, to promote critical reflection on the learning that had taken place. In this sense, the production of summary materials represented not only a moment of verification, but also an opportunity for reflective learning, oriented towards the shared construction of meaning and the valorization of processes as well as products. Specifically, students with an operational role were responsible for selecting materials and constructing the visual and textual message, while those with an observational role wrote analytical sections dedicated to processes, interactions, and decisions.
7. *Meme presentation.* During the plenary session, students presented the memes they had created, illustrating not only the final products but also the process that had guided their design choices. For each group, the students with operational roles described their working method, the difficulties encountered, the solutions adopted, and the reasons behind their creative decisions. The presentation encouraged peer comparison and gave rise to a constructive debate, which was useful for discussing critical aspects related to the interpretation of messages, in particular the risk of ambiguity or provocative readings of the content produced.
8. *Evaluation phase.* The evaluation phase was based on the dimensions identified in the evaluation rubric (Table 1). The teacher used these dimensions as reference criteria, applying a five-level Likert scale (from 'basic' to 'advanced') and accompanying the evaluation with qualitative observations and constructive comments aimed at highlighting strengths and identifying possible areas for improvement. At the same time, the students carried out an individual reflection activity, documented by the students acting as observers in their logbooks, in which they expressed personal assessments and self-observations in relation to the same dimensions provided for in the rubric.
9. *Final brainstorming.* Brainstorming served a dual purpose: it was used as a cross-cutting tool at various stages of the experiment, particularly during the design and review of memes, to stimulate the generation of original ideas, encourage collective

discussion, and select the most relevant proposals from an educational, communicative, and creative perspective; it was organized as the concluding part of the program, aimed at promoting shared reflection on the overall experience.

The qualitative analysis covered the entire body of documents produced during the workshop. The analytical framework consisted of the six dimensions of the multidimensional rubric, defined before the start of the experiment. These dimensions were used as analytical categories for the systematic examination of the data. The materials were subjected to an analytical and comparative reading, aimed at identifying evidence attributable to each dimension. For each category, both the manifestations related to the processes (collaborative dynamics, negotiation of choices, role management, project strategies) and the characteristics of the final products (communicative coherence, conceptual quality, integration between disciplinary content and multimodal expression) were considered. The interpretation was based on a cross-comparison of the various documentary sources, relating systematic observations, individual reflections contained in the logbooks, and memes created. This procedure made it possible to verify the consistency between the reflective dimension, the process dimension, and the productive dimension.

3 Results

The workshop activity led to the production of a set of memes on the theme of early school leaving. All groups created at least two final products, using visual formats commonly found in digital communication and combining iconic and textual elements. The memes feature concise and highly symbolic language, in line with the typical characteristics of the genre. In most cases, the students chose to represent situations related to everyday school life, alternating between ironic and critical tones. Fig. 1 shows two examples of memes produced, chosen as representative of the work carried out by the groups. The first (Fig. 1, left) uses the format of the game "UNO" to express, through a parodic structure, the tension between the obligation to address the problem of early school leaving and the tendency to avoid it. The second (Fig. 1, right) contrasts two symbolic representations of school: a positive one, associated with construction and pleasure, and a negative one, connected to states of anxiety and discomfort. Both products demonstrate the students' ability to synthesize complex content into simple and immediate forms of communication, while maintaining consistency with the theme and respecting the ethical guidelines defined during the design phase.

The semiotic analysis of products, aimed at exploring rhetorical structures, visual elements, and underlying cultural meanings in greater depth, will be the subject of a subsequent dedicated study.

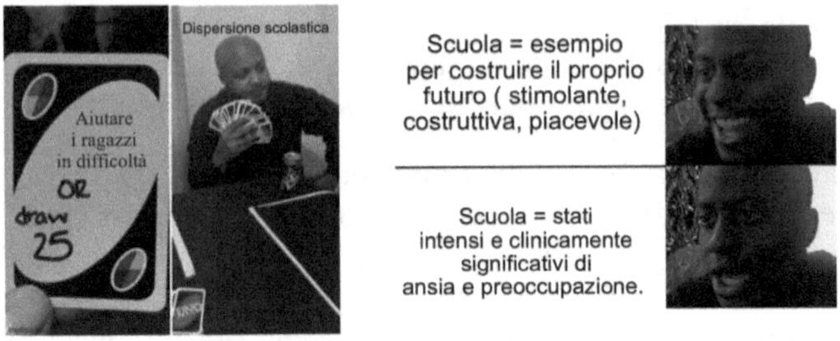

Fig. 1. Meme. Examples of memes produced, chosen as representative of the overall work carried out by the groups.

Qualitative analysis of the logbooks revealed students' perceptions of the educational value of the workshop experience. The texts collected reveal reflections that highlight an evolution in critical awareness and a sense of ethical responsibility in the use of digital languages.

Some students emphasized the complexity of the relationship between memetic language and inclusion, recognizing the ambivalent potential of memes as educational tools. The course has fostered the development of a more mature and critical view of digital media:

«During our discussions, we spent a lot of time debating whether memes could be considered an inclusive teaching method. We recognized that, as they are often linked to satire, memes can carry risks, such as misuse in contexts of cyberbullying or denigration. However, this awareness was not a limitation for us, but rather an opportunity to reflect deeply on the ethical and educational value of digital languages».

Other groups described the relational value of the experience, emphasizing how the collaborative nature of the workshop contributed to building a climate of trust and cohesion:

«At the end of the course, what stands out most is not the initial difficulty, but the atmosphere of camaraderie and trust that developed among us. The light-heartedness, satisfaction, and pride in the work accomplished testify to the positive outcome of the activity, not only in terms of content production, but above all in terms of collective growth and awareness of ourselves as a group».

These excerpts show how the workshop activity not only promoted the acquisition of technical and communication skills, but also triggered reflective, metacognitive, and relational processes, which can be traced back to forms of meaningful and conscious learning.

In parallel with the production of memes, the teacher conducted an assessment based on the assessment rubric. The scores assigned were represented in summary form using a radar chart (Fig. 2), which was useful for visualizing the average performance profile obtained in each dimension.

The chart shows a differentiated distribution of results among the groups. Groups 2 and 4 have the highest scores, with maximum values in the dimensions of creativity and motivation. Group 3 shows a regular profile, with average scores in all areas, while groups 1 and 5 show a more uneven trend, characterized by lower values in the dimensions of critical thinking and participation. Group 6 ranks at an intermediate level, with higher results in digital competence and knowledge of the subject, but lower in creativity.

Overall, the scores recorded are concentrated in the middle and upper-middle levels of the scale (from 1 to 5), with an overall average between 3 and 4. The dimensions with the highest average values are creativity, motivation, participation, and collaboration, while critical thinking and knowledge of the subject are more variable and tend to be lower. The radar chart therefore shows overall balanced profiles, but with differences in amplitude that reflect the different levels of development of the transversal skills activated during the workshop.

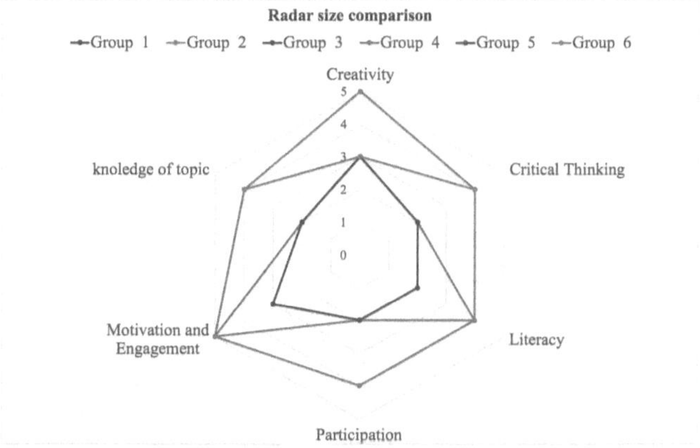

Fig. 2. Comparative radar chart of participating groups. relating to the assessment of skills developed during the activity. The figure illustrates the distribution of assessment data across the six areas analysed (creativity, critical thinking, digital competence, collaboration, motivation and knowledge of the subject) highlighting the differences in the learning profiles.

4 Discussion

Findings offer a detailed interpretation of the potential of memes as educational tools, supported by three main theoretical constructs: situated learning [15], cultural participation [13] and integrated neuroeducational approach [22, 23]. The theme of early school leaving allowed the work to be anchored to a real issue, activating processes of civic awareness and social responsibility. This choice reinforced the educational value of the activity, allowing the theoretical content covered to be linked to concrete experiences that are recognizable in everyday life. From a neuroeducational perspective, this corresponds to situated, emotionally relevant, and contextualized learning, which promotes the connection between memory, emotion, and meaning. At the same time, the participatory and collaborative nature of the workshop echoes the principles of participatory culture described by Jenkins. This approach has fostered processes of shared attention and co-construction of knowledge, supported by mechanisms of social learning and cooperative motivation.

Finally, the neuroeducational perspective has made it possible to interpret memetic production as a multimodal and integrated learning activity [15], capable of simultaneously activating cognitive, emotional, and social dimensions. In this view, the meme is not only a communicative object, but a complex cognitive device that stimulates processes of abstraction, analogy, and symbolization, laying the foundations for learning that is deeply connected to experience and relationships.

Product and assessment analysis showed that the workshop significantly promoted the development of cross-cutting skills, particularly creativity, motivation, and collaboration. In neuroeducational terms, these outcomes are consistent with the activation of processes related to reward, curiosity, and participation, which are the foundation of intrinsic learning. Furthermore, analysis, synthesis, and evaluation required students to process complex concepts through concise and culturally recognizable forms of communication, encouraging not only creativity but also critical thinking. The integration of textual and iconic elements promoted multichannel learning, which, according to neuroeducational literature, strengthens working memory and deep understanding thanks to the simultaneous involvement of different perceptual channels and associative networks [24].

From a socio-cognitive perspective, group work and the distinction between operational and observational functions generated a condition of functional interdependence. The subgroups cooperated through structured moments of discussion and feedback, developing communication skills, negotiation of meanings, and collective self-regulation. The logbooks show how this organization facilitated the development of metacognitive awareness and reflection on one's role within the learning process.

Regarding the evaluative dimension, this was addressed through an integrated model based on rubrics, logbooks, and systematic observations. The assessment rubric made it possible to transparently document levels of mastery in the six dimensions identified, highlighting both expressive and digital skills, as well as processes of reflection and collaboration. At the same time, the logbooks provided direct evidence of the metacognitive strategies adopted by the students. The reflections reveal a shift from an aesthetic and superficial perception of memes to a deeper understanding of their ethical, communicative, and educational value. These results confirm the effectiveness of assessment practices oriented towards reflective learning, which neuroeducation interprets as the ability to plan, exercise cognitive control, and self-regulate, to build autonomous and conscious competence.

These findings are not only consistent with the theoretical framework but are also confirmed by the results of other empirical studies on the educational use of memes. In the higher educational setting, it has been shown that the creative production of memes can promote the development of critical thinking through processes of conceptual selection, synthesis, and argumentative reinterpretation [25]. Similarly, the results of this study indicate that the transformation of complex content into concise and culturally recognizable forms of communication required students to critically and consciously process meanings. In the field of linguistic disciplines, the integration and production of memes, as multisensory tools, seems to support lexical acquisition and linguistic awareness [26, 27]. In this study, the integration of textual and iconic elements promoted multichannel learning which, according to neuroeducational literature, reinforces deep understanding of content. In the field of mathematics, the creation of memes seems to facilitate conceptual reworking and reflection on recurring errors [28–30]. In line with these contributions, the laboratory experience described here suggests that memetic production can be configured as a space for the co-construction of knowledge, capable of activating processes of negotiation of meanings and collective self-regulation. Analysis of the products and evaluation practices showed that the workshop promoted the development of transversal skills, in particular creativity, motivation, and collaboration. These results appear consistent with the evidence in the literature that recognizes memes as a teaching tool capable of integrating cognitive, emotional, and social dimensions. However, in line with the exploratory nature of the study, these results should be interpreted as indicative and contextually situated, offering a contribution that is part of an emerging line of research still in the process of empirical consolidation. To this end, several limitations of the study are explained in the paper. First, the exploratory nature of the research and its configuration as a single-case study conducted within a specific university workshop context limit the transferability of the results. The sample was relatively small and socio-culturally homogeneous, which does not allow for statistical generalization. Furthermore, the intervention was limited in duration, preventing systematic observation of long-term effects related to skill consolidation and transfer. The study therefore provides a contextually situated analysis rather than evidence of stable or longitudinal impact. An additional limitation concerns the teacher's multiple roles as instructional designer, facilitator, observer, and evaluator. This may have influenced data collection and interpretation. The evaluation of memetic products was based on qualitative criteria anchored in the multidimensional rubric and on the teacher's interpretative judgment. While structured descriptors were employed to reduce discretionary interpretation, the absence of external evaluators represents a potential source of bias that future research could address through independent or triangulated assessment procedures. Moreover, the study did not include direct measurements of neurocognitive processes, and therefore any connections between meme-based learning and neuroeducational mechanisms remain inferential and theoretically grounded rather than empirically measured. For these reasons, the results provide promising indications for the development of further research aimed at empirically validating the connections between digital languages, neuroeducational processes, and participatory learning.

5 Conclusion

The use of memes in a higher educational setting could be configured as an integrated learning practice, capable of critical re-elaboration, collaborative participation, and metacognitive reflection. However, these findings must be interpreted considering the exploratory nature of the study and the specific context in which it was conducted. The paper offers preliminary and contextually situated indications about the educational potential of memes as a multimodal teaching tool, which are useful for further theoretical and empirical research in the future.

Acknowledgments. We would like to thank all the students who contributed to this study.

Disclosure of Interests The authors have no competing interests to declare that are relevant to the content of this article.

Author Contributions.. All authors had full access to all the data in the study and take responsibility for the integrity of the data and the accuracy of the data analysis. *Conceptualization*, G.L.; *Methodology*, G.L.; *Investigation*, G.L.; *Formal Analysis*, G.L.and M.L.; *Writing – Original Draft*, M.L.; *Writing –Review & Editing*, M.L.; *Project Administration*, M.L.;

References

1. Lütge, C.: Foreign Language Learning in the Digital Age: Theory and Pedagogy for Developing Literacies. Taylor & Francis (2022)
2. Antón-Sancho, Á., Nieto-Sobrino, M., Fernández-Arias, P., Vergara-Rodríguez, D.: Usability of memes and humorous resources in virtual learning environments. Educ. Sci. **12**(3), 208 (2022)
3. Masek, A., Hashim, S., Ismail, A.: Integration of the humour approach with student's engagement in teaching and learning sessions. J. Educ. Teach. **45**(2), 228–233 (2019)
4. Aunger, R.: The Electric Meme: a New Theory of how we Think. Simon and Schuster (2002)
5. J. R. Baylis: The selfish gene: By Richard Dawkins. New York and Oxford: Oxford University Press (1976). Pp. 224. $8.95, hard cover; $2· 95 paperback, (1978)
6. D. C. Dennett, Darwin's Dangerous Idea: Evolution and the Meanins of Life, 39. Simon and Schuster, (1996)
7. Distin, K.: The Selfish Meme: a Critical Reassessment. Cambridge University Press (2005)
8. K. Quinal: Philippines vs. America: Filipino Generated Memes as Stimuli for Xenocentrism (2019)
9. Vickery, J.R.: The curious case of confession bear: the reappropriation of online macro-image memes. Inf. Commun. Soc. **17**(3), 301–325 (2014)
10. Nowak, J.: Internet meme as meaningful discourse: towards a theory of multiparticipant popular online content. Cent. Eur. J. Commun. **9**(16), 73–89 (2016)
11. Xie, C.: Internet memes we live by (and die by). Internet Pragmat. **3**(2), 145–173 (2020)
12. R. Brodie, Virus of the mind: The new science of the meme. Hay House, Inc (2009)
13. Jenkins, H., Ito, M.: Participatory Culture in a Networked Era: a Conversation on Youth, Learning, Commerce, and Politics. John Wiley & Sons (2015)
14. Castoldi, M.: Rubriche valutative: guidare l'espressione del giudizio. UTET università (2019)
15. Rivoltella, P.C., et al.: Fare didattica con gli EAS. Episodi di Apprendimento Situato, La scuola (2013)
16. Batini, F.: Il diario di bordo. In: Artisti dell'educazione La professionalità educativa tra necessità e possibilità, vol. 1, pp. 135–152. ARACNE EDITRICE Srl (2012)
17. Rivoltella, P., Rossi, P.G.: Tecnologie per l'educazione. Pearson (2024)
18. Potter, J., McDougall, J.: Digital Media, Culture and Education: Theorising Third Space Literacies. Springer (2017)
19. Decreto Ministeriale n.35 del 22 giugno 2020 - Decreto Ministeriale n.35 del 22 giugno 2020: Mi - Ministero dell'istruzione. Consultato: (2025). Disponibile su: https://www.mim.gov.it/-/decreto-ministeriale-n-35-del-22-giugno-2020?
20. Romero, E.D., Bobkina, J.: Exploring critical and visual literacy needs in digital learning environments: the use of memes in the EFL/ESL university classroom. Think. Ski. Creat. **40**, 100783 (2021). https://doi.org/10.1016/j.tsc.2020.100783
21. Liverano, G.: La dispersione scolastica come criticità educativa di sistema: tra prevenzione e intervento. NON SOLO SCUOLA, 1–176 (2023)

22. Liparoti, M.: Neuroeducation: the importance of training to become agents of change in the school setting. Ital. J. Health Educ. SPORT Incl. Didact. **7**(2_sup) (2023)
23. Rivoltella, P.C.: Neurodidattica. Insegnare al cervello che apprende, Raffaello Cortina (2012)
24. Jolles, J., Jolles, D.D.: On neuroeducation: why and how to improve neuroscientific literacy in educational professionals. Front. Psychol. **12**, 752151 (2021)
25. C. Petrucco: Sviluppare le abilità di Critical Thinking attraverso l'uso creativo dei meme: una esperienza in un corso Universitario. Q-TIMES WEBMAGAZINE, **1**, (3), pp. 264–277, (2023)
26. P. Ortolano: La "grammematica", o grammatica dei meme: insegnare la grammatica attraverso i meme. DIDIT Didattica Dell'italiano Studi Appl. Lingua E Lett. 04, pp. 11–30, 2024.
27. Kayali, N.K., Altuntas, A.: Using memes in the language classroom. Shanlax Int. J. Educ. **9**(3), 155–160 (2021)
28. Friske, A., Rosa, M.: Memes, Matemática e formação com professores/professoras: uma perspectiva sociopolítica. Rev. Educ. Matemática. (18), 14 (2021)
29. G. Bini: MatheMemeThon: Una esperienza di didattica a distanza con i meme matematici. In: Apprendimento Laboratoriale in Matematica e Fisica in presenza ea distanza, pp. 116–124. Università di Torino (2022)
30. Bini, G., Montagnani, M.: Comprendere, creare e utilizzare in classe i meme matematici. In: Matematica e Fisica nella cultura e nella società, pp. 339–346. Università di Torino (2020)

Assessment to Learn: Practice and Perception of Assessment and Self-assessment in Teacher Education

Maria Luisa Boninelli[1] (✉) and Susanna Piacenza[2]

[1] Dipartimento di Scienze della Formazione, Università degli Studi di Catania, Catania, Italy
marialuisa.boninelli@unict.it
[2] CREDDI, Università telematica eCampus, Novedrate, Italy
susanna.piacenza@uniecampus.it

Abstract. This article presents the findings of a survey investigating assessment and self- assessment practices among trainee teachers in Italy, with a focus on the development of metacognitive skills, professional self-efficacy, and the facilitation of cognitive, emotional, and relational learning outcomes. The study draws on quantitative and qualitative data from 1,100 participants enrolled in qualifying ("*Percorsi Abilitanti*") and specialized support ("*Tfa Sostegno*") teacher training pathways at two Italian universities during the 2024–2025 academic year. The research employs the Questionnaire for Self-Analysis of Teaching Practices (QAPD), assessing frequency of instructional and evaluative practices, self-efficacy beliefs, and perceived challenges. The theoretical framework integrates perspectives from self-efficacy theory, Feuerstein's structural cognitive modifiability, and assessment for learning, emphasizing the multifaceted and dynamic nature of contemporary teaching, which is understood as an interaction of cognitive, socio-emotional, relational, and identity-building functions. The results advocate for robust initial and ongoing professional development that systematically enhances trainee teachers' assessment skills, self-efficacy, and adaptive expertise, supporting effective and inclusive educational practices responsive to both cognitive and emotional learner needs.

Keywords: Teacher effectiveness · Student achievement · Assessment

1 Introduction

Contemporary educational research consistently emphasises the transformative potential of assessment for learning in developing students' metacognitive abilities, enhancing engagement in learning processes, and fostering self-regulated learning behaviours. By incorporating strategies such as self-assessment and peer assessment, students develop a deeper awareness of their own progress, strengthen their metacognitive monitoring, control processes, and contribute to cooperative and interactive classroom environments characterised by shared responsibility for learning.

The pedagogical landscape has shifted from product-oriented evaluation, which focuses on summative assessment, towards process-oriented perspectives that put on

M. Adamoli et al. (Eds.): HELMeTO 2025, CCIS 2958, pp. 566–580, 2026.
https://doi.org/10.1007/978-3-032-31850-3_35

evidence the ongoing analysis of learning processes, continuous feedback loops, and the seamless integration of assessment practices within instruction. This transformation requires teachers to possess technical competence in assessment design and implementation, as well as a refined understanding of how assessment practices influence learning trajectories, cognitive development, socio-emotional growth, and student identity as learners. Furthermore, teachers should develop what [12] refers to as 'assessment literacy': the ability to design valid assessments, interpret results meaningfully, provide actionable feedback, and modify instruction based on assessment outcomes. Contemporary conceptions of assessment literacy extend beyond psychometric knowledge to encompass ethical considerations, contextual sensitivity, and the alignment of assessment practices with core professional values. Teacher self-efficacy [1; 4; 14]; educators' beliefs about their ability to influence desired outcomes in student engagement and learning, emerges as a critical mediator between theoretical knowledge and classroom implementation. Research demonstrates that teachers with higher levels of self-efficacy in formative assessment report more frequent use of these practices and greater persistence when implementation proves challenging. However, the relationship between self-efficacy and objectively measured practice quality is complex and mediated by contextual factors. The main goal is to understand how trainee teachers develop assessment competencies, self-efficacy beliefs, and professional identities as assessors during initial qualification programmes.

2 Theoretical Perspectives on Teacher Efficacy, Cognitive Modifiability and Formative Assessment

The theoretical framework of this study integrates various complementary perspectives, including self-efficacy theory, Feuerstein's theory of structural cognitive modifiability, and assessment for learning.

This integration reflects the multifaceted nature of teaching as cognitive, socio-emotional, relational, and identity-constructing work. Indeed, teacher effectiveness research has demonstrated [1, 4, 5] that educators' beliefs about their professional capabilities significantly influence instructional decisions, persistence in the face of challenges and, ultimately, student outcomes. At the same time, self-efficacy theory, based on Ban- dura's social cognitive framework, suggests that people's beliefs about their ability to plan and carry out actions influence their effort, resilience when facing difficulties, emotional responses to challenges, and ultimate performance levels.

In educational contexts, teacher self-efficacy encompasses beliefs about the capacity t organise content effectively, manage a diverse classroom, engage all students (including those who present challenges) and positively influence their learning outcomes, even among students with significant needs. Evidence consistently demonstrates a positive relationship between teacher self-efficacy and various indicators of teaching quality, including the use of innovative instructional strategies, the provision of emotional and academic support to students, persistence with struggling learners and open- ness to professional development. Studies specifically examining formative assessment self-efficacy reveal that mastery experiences and the successful implementation of assessment strategies in a supportive environment are the most influential sources of efficacy beliefs for most assessment tasks. However, for complex or novel formative assessment practices that require substantial pedagogical reasoning and adaptive expertise, social persuasion from colleagues, administrators and teacher educators be- comes more important. Meanwhile, Feuerstein's theory of Structural Cognitive Modifiability (SCM) offers a profoundly optimistic perspective on human potential. It asserts that cognitive functioning can be modified at any age through appropriate mediation, regardless of the cause, severity, or timing of cognitive difficulties. This represents a radical departure from traditional psychometric perspectives that view intelligence as largely fixed and measurable through static, standardised tests.

The Romanian author's emphasis on cognitive functions and dysfunctions provides teachers with a 'diagnostic' lens through which to understand learning difficulties as modifiable inefficiencies in specific cognitive operations. This functional analysis facilitates a fundamental shift in teachers' perspectives, encouraging them to view learning difficulties as indicative of the need for targeted cognitive mediation rather than immutable limitations, thereby strengthening their sense of efficacy and sustaining their commitment to supporting students who present significant challenges [6]. This shift from static to dynamic conceptions of learning capacity finds parallel expression in formative assessment theory, which similarly challenges traditional assessment paradigms by reconceptualising assessment as a tool for learning rather than merely measurement.

Assessment for learning [2] involves using evidence of student understanding to adapt instruction, clarify learning intentions and success criteria, provide actionable feedback, activate students as instructional resources for peers and activate students as owners of their learning. This conception requires teachers to view assessment as an integral, ongoing component of the teaching-learning cycle that informs instructional decisions, rather than as an endpoint that measures achievement for reporting purposes. All these strategies emphasise responsive teaching, whereby instructional decisions are continuously informed by evidence of student understanding. It is also important to note that these strategies are interdependent and mutually reinforcing, rather than being discrete techniques applied in isolation. Contemporary investigations reveal persistent discrepancies between teachers' professed beliefs about formative assessment and their actual classroom practices. While many educators endorse the improvement function of assessment, using it to enhance learning rather than merely measuring it for accountability purposes, their practices often remain dominated by summative orientations focused on grading, ranking, and reporting. This disconnection reflects the complexity of assessment conceptions, which are multifaceted and interconnected, and are shaped by institutional cultures, accountability policies, parental expectations, and broader societal values.

The cognitive demands of effective formative assessment present challenges for teacher learning and practice. Implementing the five key strategies requires teachers to continuously gather, interpret and act upon evidence of student thinking. This process demands substantial pedagogical content knowledge, assessment literacy, adaptive expertise, and the capacity to make real-time decisions. Teachers must discern not only what students know, but also how they are thinking, where misconceptions arise, which instructional approaches will most effectively advance learning and how to differentiate support for different learners. This interpretative and responsive capacity develops gradually through cycles of practice, reflection, feedback, and refinement, rather than through the mere transmission of declarative knowledge. Effective formative assessment involves several complementary strategies that work together to support student learning. The process begins with clarifying learning intentions and success criteria, making explicit what students are expected to learn and what achievement looks like, thus enabling students to understand the learning goals and systematically evaluate their own progress.

Teachers then plan interesting class talks, jobs and activities to check what the students know. These talks show what the students are thinking, find out what they don't under- stand and show what they do understand, and are better than just getting the answers right or wrong. Feedback is a key component of formative assessment, with teachers providing information related to learning objectives and actionable suggestions for improvement, emphasising developmental guidance over merely assigning grades or making evaluative judgements. Another crucial practice is activating students as instructional resources for each other through peer assessment, peer tutoring and collaborative work, fostering a supportive learning community and mutual assistance.

Finally, formative assessment empowers students to take ownership of their learning by nurturing their self-assessment, self-regulation, and metacognitive monitoring abilities, which are essential for independent and autonomous learning.

Even though assessment for learning emphasises teachers' use of assessment evidence to improve instruction, assessment as learning foregrounds students' active engagement with assessment processes to develop metacognitive awareness, self-regulation, and ownership of learning. It conceptualises assessment itself as a vehicle for learning, rather than merely a measurement tool, and positions students as active participants in generating, interpreting, and acting upon assessment information. Research demonstrates a significant positive relationship between the implementation of formative assessment and the development of students' self-regulated learning behaviours [9]. When teachers clearly communicate their learning intentions, model self-assessment strategies, provide descriptive feedback and create opportunities for revision, students develop stronger metacognitive awareness, more effective learning strategies, greater persistence and improved academic performance. Conversely, assessment environments that are dominated by grades, social comparison, and the idea of fixed ability undermine self-regulation by focusing attention on performance in relation to others rather than on the learning process and personal growth. Students must understand learning goals, apply success criteria to their work, identify strengths and areas for improvement, and plan next steps, including cognitive activities that are central to self- regulation. However, research indicates that students often struggle with self-assessment without explicit instruction, structured support, and guided practice.

3 Research Design and Epistemological Stance

This study integrates quantitative survey data with qualitative analysis of open-ended responses to develop a comprehensive understanding of trainee teachers' assessment practise, self-efficacy beliefs, perceived challenges, and professional identity development. The convergent design collects quantitative and qualitative data con- currently, analyzes each dataset independently using appropriate methods, and then merges findings to generate integrative interpretations leveraging the strengths of both approaches.

Data collection occurred between second April and 25th June 2025 at two Italian institutions: eCampus University (online university) and University of Catania. The research context reflects recent Italian legislative reforms restricting initial teacher training through the establishment of "*Percorsi Abilitanti*" and "*Tfa Sostegno*" pathways. The first "*Percorsi Abilitanti*" intends to prepare candidates for teaching specific curricula in subject areas in the secondary school. The second, "*Tfa Sostegno*" provides specialization in support activities for students with disabilities and special education needs at specific school levels.

The sample consisted of 1.100 trainee teachers from pre-school through secondary education enrolled in qualifying pathways and specialized support courses during the 2024–2025 academic year. It is divided into two distinct sub-sample based on training pathway:

a) **Sub-sample 1:** "*Percorsi Abilitanti" eCampus* University: 451 participants enrolled in qualifying pathways for secondary school teachers across various disciplinary areas. Data analysis revealed that 72% possessed current teaching experience distributed across various contract types: annual curricular assignments (28%), temporary or short-term curricular substitute teaching (22%), annual support teaching assignments (6%), temporary support teaching (5%), tenured curricular teachers (3%), and other teaching assignments including private language schools (approximately 8%). The remaining 28% reported not currently teaching, but most had prior teaching experience. This sub-sample demonstrated substantial prior classroom experience, with most participants working as teachers on temporary or fixed-term contracts while pursuing formal qualifications to improve employment stability and career prospects. School level distribution showed predominance of upper secondary school, divided among "Licei" (classic/scientific secondary school, 6%, technical institute (12%), and professional schools (14%)
b) **Sub-sample 2**: "*Tfa Sostegno*", University of Catania: 252 participants from University of Catania enrolled in specialized support training courses across different levels: pre-school, primary, lower secondary, upper secondary. Only 34% reported current teaching experience, with 66% indicating they were not currently teaching. School-level distribution showed particularly significant presence in primary schools (21%), followed by pre-schools (12%), with various secondary school levels represented and no private language school representation (0%).

These two sub-samples differed markedly in teaching experience levels, professional contexts, training objectives, and likely career trajectories. These differences necessitated a comparative analysis examining how training pathway and prior experience influenced practise, perceptions, and professional identity development.

3.1 Research Instrument and Data Collection Procedures

The research employed the Questionnaire for Self-Analysis of Teaching Practices (QAPD) developed by Trinchero and Piacenza in 2022. This comprehensive instrument was previously applied in a 2022 pilot study with Italian in-service teachers, providing preliminary validation evidence regarding reliability and construct validity. It comprises 149 closed-response items plus two open-ended tasks, organized into five different sections:

1) *Section 1*: Personal data. It refers to demographic information, including cur- rent position, school level, years of teaching experience, educational back- ground, and professional development participation.
2) *Section 2:* Teaching and Assessment Practices. It is constituted by 120 items whose goal is to measure the frequency of specific instructional and evaluative practices using eight-point Likert-type scales (Once a month, once a week, two to three times a week, every day). Items address diverse practice domains, including lesson planning, instructional methods, assessment, classroom management, use of technologies, attention to cognitive and socioemotional development, and cooperation with colleagues and families.
3) *Section 3*: Self-efficacy and challenges. Items assessing perceived competence for various teaching tasks, challenged encountered in implementation, and re- sources needed for improvement.
4) *Section 4:* Summary description. Two open-ended reflection prompting participants to describe their teaching philosophy, perceived strengths, challenges, and professional goals.
5) Presentation of a typical lesson. Structured description of a representative instructional sequence, including learning objectives, activities, assessment methods, and reflections on effectiveness

Data collection procedures employed online survey administration using online platforms, enabling anonymous participation and automated data storage. Quantitative data analysis employed JsStat v.2.01 statistical analysis software [10].

4 The Variables Investigated

The study analyzes pedagogical, didactic, and evaluative aspects that are relevant in initial and in-service teacher training programs, as they provide the necessary tools to promote meaningful learning for students, based on cognitive, emotional, and relational components. Each question is examined in three ways: a closed question about what teachers claim to do, a closed question about their perceived self-efficacy regarding these evaluative and didactic practices, and an open question about the difficulties encountered in these practices.

4.1 Univariate Analysis of the eCampus Telematic University Sub-Sample: Background Variables and Items

A total of 593 responses were received for the background variable 'Current job position'. Of these, 72% of course participants have current teaching experience, 28% of whom hold an annual contract. The background variable 'School level where they work' received 459 responses. The frequency distribution shows that secondary school teachers are particularly well represented (51%), with the majority working in technical institutes (21%), high schools (16%), and vocational institutes (11%). Only 8% of course participants teach in primary schools, while 4% teach in nursery schools (Table 1).

4.1.1 Item: "Define Learning Objectives Capable of Stimulating Specific Cognitive Processes in Students"

Table 1. Sub-sample "*Percorsi Abilitanti*" eCampus University, Item "Define learning objectives capable of stimulating specific cognitive processes in students."

Number of cases: 454		
Central tendency indices	Mode	Once a week
	Median	Once a week
Indici di disper-sione	Skewness	0.2
	Range	7
	Interquartile Range	1

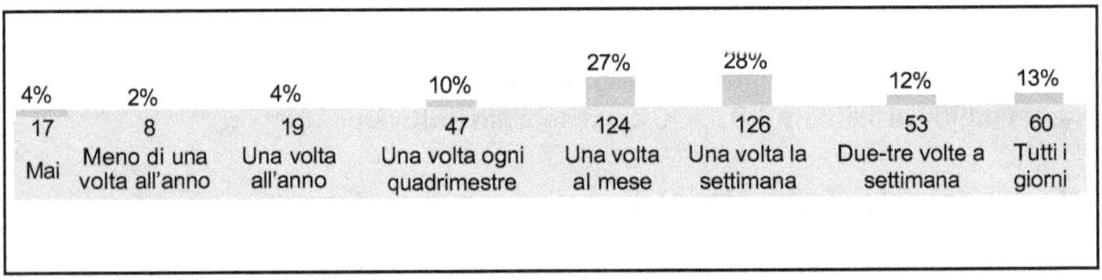

Graph 1. Sub-sample "*Percorsi Abilitanti*" eCampus University. Item "Define learning objectives capable of stimulating specific cognitive processes in student".

The question on self-efficacy perception, represented in the bar graph, was answered by 521 course participants. These data show that the most frequently reported practice by teachers is "once a week" (28%), followed by "once a month" (27%). Lower per- centages are distributed among "every day" (13%) and "two to three times a week" (12%). Even more marginal is "once every four months" (10%), "once a year" (4%), "less than once a year" (2%), and "never" (4%). In this case, both the mode and the median coincide with "once a week", indicating a more balanced distribution centered on this frequency. The interquartile range confirms relatively limited internal variability compared to other

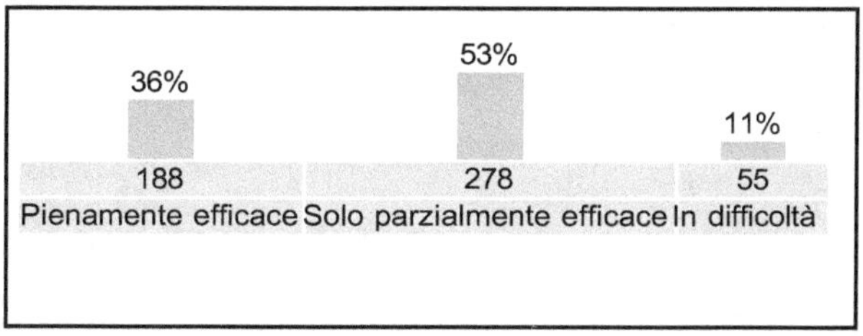

Graph 2. Sub-sample "*Percorsi Abilitanti*", eCampus University. Item "Perception of self-efficacy.

items, suggesting a pattern shared by most of the sample. The Skewness is minor (0.2), indicating a homogeneous distribution without strong polarization. While 55 individuals reported feeling ineffective, n = 196 people described experiencing difficulties in the open-ended responses. These difficulties were categorized as: challenges in identifying cognitive processes, lack of experience and specific training, lack of time, and problems in engaging students. A lack of awareness regarding the cognitive processes underlying learning is noted, as almost no respondents mention them in their answers (Table 2).

4.1.2 Item: "Propose Specific Activities to Improve Students' Emotional and Relational Skills"

Table 2. Sub-sample "*Percorsi Abilitanti*", eCampus University. Item "Propose specific activities to improve students' emotional and relational skills".

Number of cases: 448		
Central tendency indices	Mode	Once a month
	Median	Once a month
Dispersion indices	Skewness	0.17
	Range	7
	Interquartile Range	3

The data for this item indicate that the most frequent practices are "one a month" (23%) and "every day" (22%), followed by "once a week2 (16%) and "two to three time a week" (13%). A significant portion of responses falls within the lower frequency categories: "never" (12%), "once every four months" (10%), "once a year" (4%), and "less than once a year" (1%). The mode and median both coincide, indicating a more balanced distribution centered around these frequencies; the interquartile range of 3 reflects a rather marked degree of internal variability. The imbalance index (0.17) suggests a distribution without pronounced polarization. In response to the question regarding self-efficacy perception, which is presented in the following graph, n = 495 participants responded.

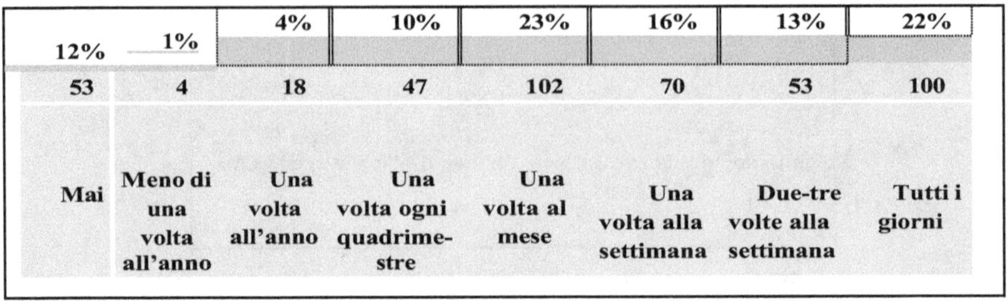

Graph 3. Sub-sample *"Percorsi Abilitanti"*, eCampus University. Item "Propose specific activities to improve students' emotional and relational skills."

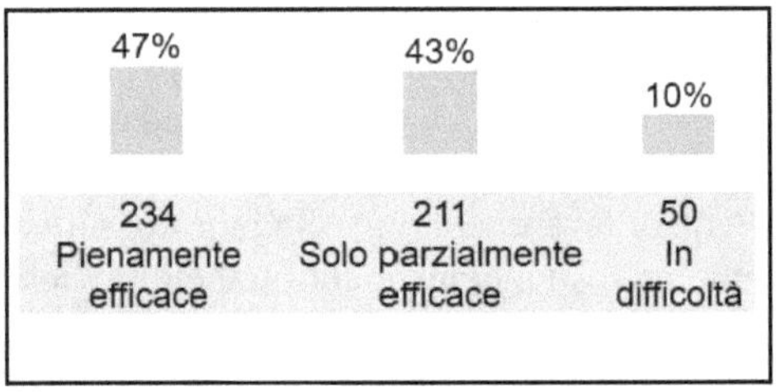

Graph 4. Sub-sample *"Percorsi Abilitanti"*, eCampus University. Item "Perception of self-efficacy in proposing specific activities to improve students' emotional and relational skills."

It is observed that, although 50 individuals report difficulties regarding their sense of efficacy, 143 cases emerge through open-ended responses. In this case, the difficul- ties identified can be categorized as follows: relational-emotional issues among stu- dents, lack of experience, student disengagement, and lack of time.

4.2 Univariate Analysis of the Sub-Sample University of Catania: Background Variables and Items

For the background variable "Current Occupation," 555 participants responded, of whom 34% indicated that they are currently teaching. The distribution of the variable "Type of school in which they work" is based on 244 responses and shows a clear prevalence of teachers from upper secondary schools, accounting for 28%; among these, vocational institutes are the most represented, followed by technical institutes and, finally, high schools (Licei). The proportion of those teaching in primary schools is 12% (Table 3).

4.2.1 Item "Define Learning Objectives Capable of Stimulating Specific Cognitive Processes in Students"

The analysis of the data for this item shows that the most frequent practice is "once a week" (25%), followed by "every day" (22%), "once a month" (19%), and "two to three times a week" (18%). Lower percentages are recorded for "once every four months" (8%), "never" (5%), "once a year" (2%), and "less than once a year" (0%). Bothe the

Table 3. Sub-sample "*Tfa Sostegno*", University of Catania. Item "Define learning objec- tives that stimulate specific cognitive processes in students".

Number of cases: 249		
Central tendency indices	Mode	Once a week
	Median	Once a week
Dispersion indices	Skewness	0.19
	Range	7
	Interquartile Range	2

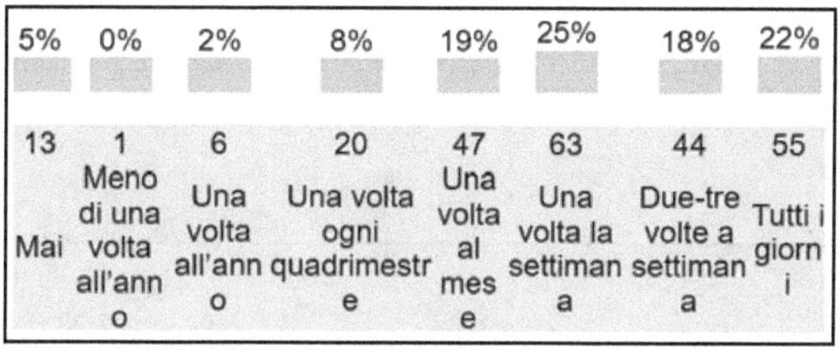

Graph 5. Sub-sample "*Tfa Sostegno*", University of Catania. Item "Propose specific activities to improve students' emotional and relational skills".

mode and median coincide with "once a week", indicating a more balanced distribution centered around this frequency. The interquartile range, equal to 2, reflects a moderate level of internal variability [14]. Regarding the question about self-efficacy perception, represented in the following graph, n = 459 participants responded.

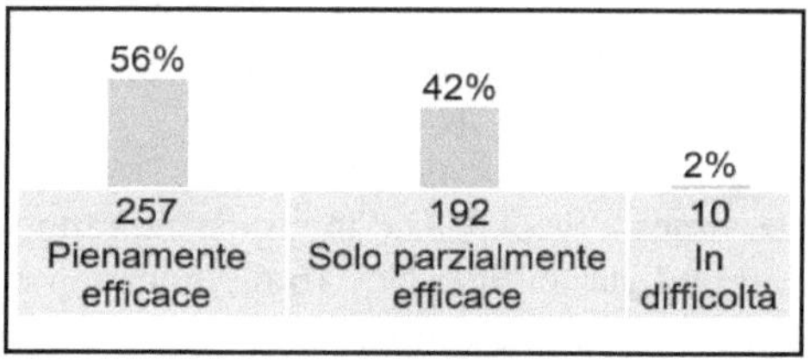

Graph 6. Sub-sample "*Tfa Sostegno*", University of Catania. Item "Perception of self-efficacy in proposing specific activities to improve students 'emotional and relational skills".

Although 10 people report feeling challenged in terms of efficacy, analysis of the open-ended responses reveals that, in fact, 105 individuals indicate difficulties, which can be categorized as follows: lack of experience on the part of the teacher, challenges in setting appropriate objectives, limited collaboration with colleagues, activities that are too difficult for some students, and lack of time (Table 4).

4.2.2 Item "Propose Specific Activities to Enhance Students' Emotional and Relational Skills"

Table 4. Sub-sample "*Tfa Sostegno*" University of Catania. Item "Propose specific activities to improve students' emotional and relational skills."

Numero di casi: 254		
Central tendency indices	Mode	Every day
	Median	Two to three times a week
Dispersion indices	Skewness	0.27
	Range	7
	Interquartile Range	3

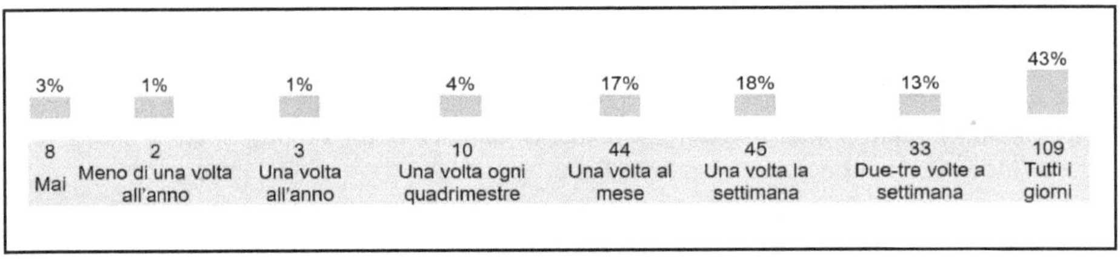

Graph 7. Sub-sample "*Tfa Sostegno*", University of Catania. Item "Propose specific activi- ties to improve students' emotional and relational skills".

The analysis of the data for this item shows that the most frequent modality is "every day" (43%), followed by "two to three times a week" (13%), "once a week" (18%), and "once a month" (17%). Lower percentages are observed for "once every four months" (4%), "once a year" (1%), "less than once a year" (1%), and "never" (3%). The mode and median values do not coincide: the mode is "every day," while the median is located at "two to three times a week." The interquartile range, equal to 3, reflects a rather marked level of internal variability [14]. To the question regarding self-efficacy perception, represented in the following graph, 465 course participants responded.

Although 7 individuals report feeling challenged in terms of efficacy, analysis of the open-ended responses reveals that 77 people indicate difficulties, which can be categorized as follows: students' difficulty in "exposing themselves," lack of experience on the part of the teacher, poor emotional management skills of teachers toward students, and time management within teaching.

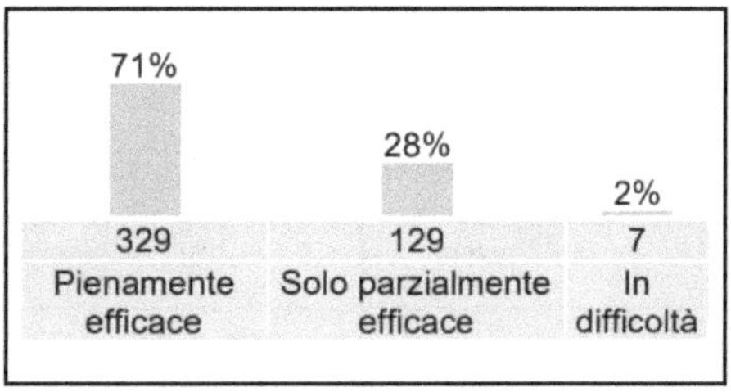

Graph 8. Sub-sample "*Tfa Sostegno*", University of Catania. Item "Perception of self-effi- cacy in proposing specific activities to improve students' emotional and relational skills."

4.3 Comparison Between the Data of the Sub-samples

4.3.1 Item: "Define Learning Objectives that Stimulate Specific Cognitive Processes in Students"

Regarding the responses related to implementation, 28% of the participants in the qualifying program at eCampus University (sub-sample A) report "once a week" and 27% report "once a month", totaling n = 454 responses. Among the TFA participants from the University of Catania (sub-sample B), 25% report "once a week", and 22% report "every day", with a total of n = 249 responses for the same item. Concerning efficacy, 53% of sub-sample A participants feel "partially effective", and 36% feel "fully effective", with 55 individuals reporting difficulties out of 521. Conversely, 56% of sub-sample B participants feel "fully effective", 42% "partially effective", and only 10 individuals report difficulties out of a total of 459. The efficacy data are more inconsistent among sub-sample B; n = 249 individuals report performing the activity, but 449 (459 minus 10) feel very or partially effective, implying they feel capable of performing the activity but do not actually do so. This inconsistency is also present in the questionnaire responses from sub-sample A, but with a smaller numerical discrepancy.

The analysis of open-ended questions includes responses from 196 individuals in sub-sample A and 105 in sub-sample B. The categories of difficulties have already been presented in the previous subsections. However, a comparison between the two groups reveals that both the inexperience of teachers and the lack of time are reported in both groups (Table 5).

4.3.2 Item "Propose Specific Activities to Enhance Students' Emotional and Relational Skills"

Regarding responses concerning implementation, 23% of participants in sub-sample A reported "once a month" and 22% "every day", for a total of 448 responses. For the same item, 43% of participants in sub-sample B indicated implementing the activities "every day" and 18% "once a week", giving a total of 254 responses. Regarding perceived efficacy, 47% of sub-sample A participants reported feeling "partially effective", while 42% indicated they felt "fully effective"; n = 58 responses signaled difficulties out of n = 501 total responses. In contrast, 71% of participants from sub-sample B reported feeling "fully effective", 28% "partially effective", and only 7 individuals re- ported difficulties out of 464 total responses.

Table 5. Comparison of results between the sub-sample "*Percorsi Abilitanti*", eCampus University, and "*Tfa Sostegno*, University of Catania on two items

	Never		Less than one a year		Onc e a year		Once every four months		Once a month		Once a week		Two-three times		Every day	
	A	B	A	B	A	B	A	B	A	B	A	B	A	B	A	B
	4	5	2	0	4	2	10	8	27	19	28	25	12	18	13	22
	12	3	1	1	4	1	10	4	23	17	16	18	13	13	22	43

Define learning objectives to elicit specific cognitive processes.

Propose specific activities to enhance emotional-relational skills.

Notably, the efficacy data are more incongruent in the responses from sub-sample B; 254 individuals reported carrying out the activity, yet 458 (465–7) consider themselves highly or partially effective. This suggests that participants feel capable of carrying out the activities, but do not, in fact, do so.

Moreover, open-ended responses from sub-sample B only report 7 individuals experiencing difficulties, while 77 affirmatively identified difficulties in open-ended responses. This pattern of incongruence also appears in the responses from sub-sample A, though, again, with lower numerical discrepancies. The analysis of open-ended responses shows 147 respondents for sub-sample A and 77 for sub-sample B; in both subgroups, organizational difficulties and teacher inexperience consistently emerge.

5 Conclusions

The principal goal of this paper is to present some components of a broader survey conducted by University Telematic eCampus and University of Catania between April and June 2025. The study aimed to investigate the assessment and instructional practices of trainee teachers, as well as their beliefs regarding self-efficacy. Among the items examined were "setting learning objectives that stimulate cognitive processes" and "proposing specific activities to enhance students' emotional and relational skills". Each item was assessed in three ways: a closed question regarding self-reported teacher practices; a closed question reflecting perceived self-efficacy; and an open-ended question concerning the difficulties encountered in the teaching and assessment practices under review.

Given the distinct composition of the sub-samples, followed by a comparative analysis. Results showed that higher values were observed among TFA respondents for both items, where trainee teachers reported implementing relevant instructional and assessment practices more frequently. Similar trends emerged concerning perceived effectiveness, with TFA participants reporting greater effectiveness in the application of those practices. The overall mean for the TFA sub-sample was 63% compared to 41% eCampus ones. Additionally, mean values indicated a lower perception of inefficacy within the Tfa sub-sample (2%) compared to the other group (10.5%). However, triangulation with open-ended responses on experienced difficulties revealed notable discrepancies. In these responses, a much higher proportion of teachers in both sub-samples reported facing various challenges. The divergence was especially pronounced among TFA participants. These differences can be attributed to the contrasting sample compositions: most TFA participants (66%) reported no previous teaching experience, whereas only 28% of the eCamps group lacked teaching experience. This difference probably makes it more difficult for respondents to evaluate their own practice in relation to the perceived need for such practices and their self-efficacy, as indicated in the questionnaire.

The survey invited teachers to focus on essential instructional elements, such as setting objectives, integrating cognitive processes and learning content, which is critical to instructional effectiveness and ensures alignment between planning and assessment [3, 13].

Equally important is the purposeful design of activities that foster students' emotional and relational skills. As highlighted in a recent European survey, many children and adolescents arrive at school burdened by significant social and emotional challenges that hinder learning and psychological well-being [11]. If formal education is to enhance cognitive functions [7], it cannot disregard the emotional components that directly shape behavioral traits in learning contexts, including self-regulation, perseverance, frustration tolerance, motivation, flexibility, and responsiveness [8]. Finally, the survey was designed to prompt reflection on the complexities inherent in teaching and assessment, and to provide future teachers with a comprehensive overview of the factors involved in effective practice.

Authors' Contribution. The contribution represents a joint work of the authors.

However, Maria Luisa Boninelli wrote the introduction and paragraphs §2, §3, §3.1, §4.2;

§4.2.1; §4.2.2. while Susanna Piacenza wrote the following paragraphs §4; § 4.1; §4.1.1; §4.1.2;§4.3.1.; §4.3.2 and conclusion.

References

1. Bardach, L., et al.: Smart teachers, successful students? A systematic review of teachers' cognitive abilities and student achievement. Teach. Teach. Educ. **92**, 2020 (2020). https://doi.org/10.1016/j.edurev.2020.100312
2. Black, P., William, D.: Assessment and classroom learning. Assess. Educ. Principles, Policy Pract. **5**(1) (1998). https://doi.org/10.1080/0969595980050102
3. Calonghi, L., Coggi, C.: Didattica e sviluppo dell'intelligenza. Tirrenia, Torino (1993)
4. Dacholfany, M.I., et al.: The effectiveness of teacher professional development program on classroom and behavior management: a systematic review. J. Educ. Cult. Soc. **15**(2), 451–470 (2024). https://doi.org/10.15503/jecs2024.2.451.470

5. Feuerstein, R.: Mediated Learning Experience: International Practices and Advances, **2**(1) (2024). https://feuerstein-institute.org/wp-content/uploads/2024/09/Me-diated-Learning-Experience-Vol-2-FINAL-2.pdf
6. Haywood, H.C.: Cognitive Early Education. Education is published online, Oxford Research Encyclopedias (2020)
7. Haywood, H.C., Lidz, C.S.: Dynamic Assessment in Practice: Clinical and Educational Applications. Cambridge University Press (2006)
8. Maulana, R.: The value of assessing the generic teaching quality: a review of teacher effectiveness research. Eur. J. Teach. Educ. **48**(3), 401–418 (2025). https://doi.org/10.1080/09243453.2025.2527742
9. Mitchell, D., Sutherland, D.: Cosa funziona nella didattica speciale e inclusiva. Le strategie basate sull'evidenza (a cura di D. Ianes). Edizioni Erickson, Trento (2022)
10. Pastore, S.: A feasible balance? The Italian teachers' standpoint on assessment literacy and practice. Eur. J. Teach. Educ. (2024). https://doi.org/10.1080/0261968.2024.2338853
11. Trinchero, R.: JsStat (2015)
12. Trinchero, R.: Manuale di ricerca educativa. Franco Angeli, Milano (2002)
13. Trinchero, R.: Penso dunque imparo. Pearson, Guida al potenziamento cognitivo. Milano (2022)
14. Tschannen-Moran, M., Hoy, A.W.: Teacher efficacy: capturing elusive construct. Teach. Teach. Educ. **17**(7), 783–805 (2001)

Learning Technologies e Data Analytics

Designing for Retention: Mixed Reality Strategies to Support Learning

Matteo Baggetto[1], Matteo Saglimbeni[1], Matteo Di Marco[2], Nicoletta Di Blas[1](✉), and Matteo Valoriani[2]

[1] Politecnico di Milano, Piazza Leonardo da Vinci 32, 20133 Milan, Italy
{matteo.baggetto,matteo.saglimbeni}@mail.polimi.it, nicoletta.diblas@polimi.it
[2] FifthIngenium, Viale Romagna 46, 20131 Milan, Italy
{matteo.dimarco,matteo.valoriani}@fifthingenium.com

Abstract. Mixed Reality (MR) in education has largely followed an object-centred paradigm, privileging visualization of "content" (e.g. complex artefacts) over the design of learning activities. This paper explores an activity-centred use of MR through two higher-education case studies aimed at strengthening conceptual processing and long-term retention. The first adapts the Ciceronian method of loci ("memory palace") to MR: learners anchor multimedia "concepts" (i.e., the content to be memorized) to familiar physical loci and engage in guided, gamified retrieval to build durable knowledge structures, individually or collaboratively. The second activity uses MR to consolidate learning after the study visit: photos, videos, notes, and 3D scans collected in the field are transformed into in-class MR quizzes and 2D/3D puzzles designed to prompt recollection. Preliminary evaluations comprised an Open Day trial (n = 63) with short activities and a classroom study (n = 7) with extended tasks, combining questionnaires and a focus group. Participants reported high comfort and ease of use (means >4.5/5) and strong perceived usefulness (>4.4/5), highlighting engagement, smooth interaction, and the motivational role of gamification. Reported limitations include occasional spatial-anchoring instability, headset fatigue for prolonged sessions, and the need for adjustable difficulty in the loci activity. Findings support MR's potential to shift from content display to pedagogically meaningful activity design. Future work will assess learning outcomes longitudinally and involve instructors to evaluate the didactic impact.

Keywords: Mixed Reality (MR) · Activity-centered learning · Memory palace (method of loci) · Study visit reinforcement · Higher education

1 Introduction

Mixed Reality (MR)—as well as Augmented Reality (AR) and, to some extent, Virtual Reality (VR)—has traditionally been employed in educational contexts primarily as a tool for visualizing tangible objects or environments that would otherwise be inaccessible, complex, or hazardous to interact with in real life. Typical examples include the

M. Adamoli et al. (Eds.): HELMeTO 2025, CCIS 2958, pp. 583–595, 2026.
https://doi.org/10.1007/978-3-032-31850-3_36

three-dimensional reconstruction of mechanical components, anatomical structures, or archaeological artifacts [7, 8, 24]. In such applications, MR is used to embed virtual representations within the physical environment, thereby creating hybrid spaces where learners can perceive and manipulate digital objects as if they were part of the real world. This "object-centered" approach represents the predominant paradigm [3, 4].

While this paradigm has enabled remarkable progress in making objects—such as complex mechanisms, artifacts, or biological organs—"tangible", it also risks narrowing the role of MR to a primarily demonstrative function. Moreover, such uses tend to privilege the technological novelty of the medium over the pedagogical design that sustains effective learning. In any well-designed learning experience, content alone is not enough: educational effectiveness also relies on the activities that allow learners to process, apply, and consolidate that content. Reducing MR to content display and manipulation would be like assuming that teaching can happen through textbooks alone, without the wide array of didactic strategies that bring knowledge to life. In fact, just as textbooks become meaningful when integrated into lectures, discussions, group projects, or problem-based scenarios, MR environments realize their full potential when they are embedded within purposeful learning tasks. This shift of focus—from the mere presentation of objects to the orchestration of interactive and collaborative activities—marks a necessary evolution in the educational use of MR.

For several years, a research group at Politecnico di Milano, in collaboration with FifthIngenium and Vodafone, has been exploring a different approach: using MR not to replicate content, but to design and deliver learning activities [9]. This paper focuses on two such activities developed within higher education contexts.

2 State of the Art

In recent years, research on Mixed Reality (MR) in education has evolved from initial proof-of-concept prototypes to more systematic explorations of its pedagogical potential. Early projects demonstrated the feasibility of embedding virtual content into real-world environments, but they often remained confined to highly specific domains such as medicine, engineering, or cultural heritage [6–8, 20, 24]. While these initiatives confirmed that MR can effectively enhance the visualization of complex or inaccessible objects, they also revealed a set of persistent limitations. Many applications were designed as stand-alone solutions, which made them difficult to adapt or reuse across curricular contexts [1, 12]. Usability issues—such as discomfort during prolonged sessions, steep learning curves, and cognitive overload—further limited accessibility and effectiveness [2, 19]. Most critically, the majority of MR experiences prioritized technological novelty or visual fidelity over pedagogical intent [3, 4]. As a result, MR has often been successful in capturing learners' attention, but less effective in supporting deeper learning processes such as reflection, conceptual engagement, and long-term retention.

A recent trend in the literature underscores the importance of shifting from content-centered to activity-centered uses of MR. Rather than serving primarily as a tool for displaying digital objects, MR can provide structured learning activities that integrate inquiry, collaboration, and reflection, and that can be embedded within wider didactic sequences [9]. This pedagogical shift reframes MR not as a showcase for digital representations, but as a medium for designing interactions that promote engagement and support knowledge consolidation.

In this paper, we present two case studies that move in this direction: one connected to the mnemonic technique of the Ciceronian *method of loci* and the other focused on the consolidation of concepts acquired during a study visit.

The Ciceronian *method of loci*—also known as the memory palace—is rooted in classical rhetoric and relies on associating information with spatial locations that can be mentally "walked through" to support recall [12]. A substantial body of research has confirmed its efficacy in enhancing memory and organizing knowledge into durable structures [14, 21]. More recently, efforts have been made to transpose this technique into extended reality (XR). Most of these studies have focused on virtual reality, through the design of so-called "Virtual Memory Palaces," which demonstrate that immersive environments can improve memory performance but cannot fully exploit the affordances of familiar, real settings [13, 18]. Augmented reality applications are even more experimental: while early results appear promising, they remain inconclusive and limited in scope. Eventually, no mature implementations of the loci technique within Mixed Reality environments have been documented in the literature—a gap that this work seeks to address by adapting the method for structured higher education use.

With regard to study visits, a small but growing line of research has explored the integration of MR into field trips and other forms of experiential learning. Most of these applications have concentrated on the "during-visit" phase, enriching students' exploration of real environments through contextual information, gamified activities, and data collection. Examples include EcoMOBILE [12], which combined AR and probeware in ecological field trips; Hwang's AR-based ecological game [11], designed to stimulate inquiry-based learning; and MacCallum and Parsons' work on landfill sites [16], which blended mobile MR with science education. Collectively, these projects illustrate the added value of linking curricular content with lived experiences, showing how digital augmentation can foster both engagement and inquiry. Yet, a critical limitation persists: the post-visit phase, which is essential for reflection, consolidation, and long-term retention of knowledge, remains largely neglected. Most MR applications are conceived as one-off experiences, with little opportunity for customization, reuse, or integration into broader pedagogical designs. Only a few studies have suggested extending MR into the classroom after the visit, for instance through student-generated tours or collaborative reflection activities. However, systematic investigation into how MR can be employed to reinforce and "make memories stick" is still lacking.

It is within this underexplored space that the two MR activities presented in this paper are situated: both move beyond the immediate excitement of on-site immersion, leveraging MR as a medium for structured reinforcement and durable memory consolidation.

3 The Case-Studies

To illustrate how MR can be employed not only for content visualization but also for the design of learning activities aimed at strengthening memorization, this paper presents two case studies developed at Politecnico di Milano within the context of higher education.

Both were conceived as part of structured learning sequences, with the objective of fostering active processing and concepts' retention. The first case study investigates the use of the loci method—a classical mnemonic technique—reinterpreted through MR, while the second focuses on the design of MR activities to reinforce learning after a study visit.

3.1 The Ciceronian Loci Application

The first activity is inspired by the ancient Ciceronian *method of loci*, a mnemonic technique that supports memorization through spatial association. Known also as the "memory palace," this method involves mentally mapping a sequence of familiar places and linking them with concepts or information to be recalled. By mentally walking through the chosen environment, the learner retrieves the stored information in a structured and durable way.

The application brings this ancient technique into the domain of MR, thereby combining the cognitive strengths of mnemonic strategies with the immersive affordances of contemporary technology. Students can construct personal memory palaces by placing virtual markers (Fig. 1) on physical objects within their environment. These markers can then be enriched with multimedia content—images, videos, audio, or 3D models—serving as anchors for knowledge retrieval. The memorization process is reinforced through guided repetition and gamified features, such as scoring systems and shared leaderboards, which add a collaborative and competitive dimension [10]. This approach not only updates a classical technique for modern learners but also overcomes a key limitation of many educational MR tools, namely their reliance on fixed, prepackaged content. Instead, students are empowered to design highly personalized and adaptable knowledge structures that can evolve over time.

To illustrate how the application functions in practice, consider a scenario in which university students are studying the key events of the 1929 economic crisis. After scanning their own study room with the MR headset, each student selects familiar reference points within the environment—for instance, a doorknob, a radiator, a window, or a lamp. These places need to be selected with a chosen order and criterion, in fact they mark the path to follow in the memory palace. Virtual markers (called "magnets") are then anchored to these real-world objects.

Each magnet is associated with a specific historical event or concept. For example, a 3D fridge can be linked to the doorknob to symbolize the industrial expansion of the 1920s, while a historical photograph of people at a bank may be placed on the radiator to represent the financial collapse. A picture of a snow avalanche can be attached to the window to illustrate the global spread of the crisis, and a video of Roosevelt delivering a speech can be anchored to the lamp to signify the New Deal. Finally, a 3D radio model can be positioned to emphasize the role of mass communication in Roosevelt's policies (Fig. 2).

Once the system is set up—with loci selected, magnets anchored to real objects in the room, and digital content attached to them—the application engages learners in gamified activities. For instance, objects may "fall" to the ground, requiring students to return each concept to its correct location. Such activities can be configured with varying levels of difficulty, time constraints, and other mechanics that encourage active recall.

Fig. 1. A "magnet" (a virtual marker) is being placed on the room's doorknob, on top of which the concept to be remembered will be set

Fig. 2. Setting a concept (in this case, an AI-made image on the 1929 crisis) on a magnet

The memorization of associations is crucial, as during the MR session the content to be learned is visually accessible, but later knowledge retrieval must occur purely in the mind—learners should be able to mentally walk through their memory palace and recall associations using imagination alone. If the student wishes to review the same concepts on the following day, the entire memory palace can be reloaded, ensuring persistence across sessions. Beyond the individual scenario, in which each learner designs and uses their own memory palace, the system also supports collaborative use. A student may share a palace with peers, or a teacher may create a shared memory palace and assign it to the entire class. In this latter case, both collaborative and competitive dynamics can be introduced, for example through leaderboards comparing student performance. This scenario illustrates how Mixed Reality can transform the ancient mnemonic strategy of the Ciceronian method of loci into an interactive, customizable, and socially engaging educational tool.

Technological Development

From a technological perspective, the application was developed using the Unity 3D engine and C#, building on the Mixed Reality Toolkit 2 (MRTK2) and the Mixed Reality Utility Kit (MRUK) provided by Meta. The system was designed for Meta Quest 3 and 3S devices, selected for their support of inside-out tracking, real-time spatial mapping, and both hand- and controller-based interactions. Development followed the standards and best practices of FifthIngenium, which also provided the TINALP platform—a no-code, web-based system for authoring, managing, and synchronizing educational content across devices.

TINALP represents a core component of the ecosystem. Through a web interface, instructors can create "decks" of educational materials, including texts, images, videos, and 3D models, and distribute them directly to the MR application. At runtime, the application parses these decks and dynamically instantiates the corresponding virtual elements within the learner's physical environment. This architecture allows instructors to design and modify activities without programming skills, while maintaining a persistent link between the web-authored content and the mixed-reality experience executed on the headset.

Several technical challenges emerged during development. A primary challenge concerned the reliable recognition and reconstruction of heterogeneous environments, as students were expected to build their memory palaces in everyday spaces. To ensure stability and persistence, virtual loci ("magnets") needed to be accurately anchored to real-world objects and restored across sessions. This was achieved through spatial anchors managed via Meta's SDKs and supported by the MRUK scene model, which stores structural information about the physical environment.

Interaction design represented another key challenge. The system needed to be intuitive for first-time users while supporting actions such as placing, selecting, and manipulating virtual content. To this end, ray-casting was implemented for object interaction, combined with visual feedback and haptic responses to support precision and reduce user effort. MRTK2 provided a stable framework for managing spatial interactions and user interface components in line with established usability guidelines.

Content flexibility was also a central requirement. The application supports multiple types of educational resources—textual, visual, audio, and 3D—without requiring technical expertise. Automatic adaptation mechanisms, such as dynamic scaling of 3D models and aspect-ratio adjustments for media elements, were implemented to ensure visual consistency.

Finally, persistence, shareability, and performance were critical aspects of the system. Learners needed to revisit and expand their memory palaces over multiple sessions and devices, while instructors required mechanisms to reuse and distribute content across classes. These features were supported through TINALP's synchronization layer, which associates each user's content with their account and restores spatial anchors and linked media at login. Performance optimization focused on maintaining stable frame rates and low latency through optimized rendering pipelines, lightweight 3D assets, and calibration routines, supporting user comfort and sustained engagement.

3.2 The Study Visit Application

The second case study focuses on the design of a Mixed Reality (MR) application aimed at reinforcing the learning outcomes of study visits once students return to the classroom. Study visits represent highly valuable pedagogical opportunities in higher education, as they provide direct immersion in professional, cultural, or scientific environments that complement theoretical instruction. However, research consistently shows that without structured follow-up activities, much of the knowledge acquired during such experiences risks fading quickly [12, 16]. This application was conceived to address precisely this gap by offering students interactive tools to recall knowledge gained during visits.

The application is organized around a set of modular challenges—such as quizzes and 2D/3D puzzles—constructed from multimedia materials collected during the visit itself. Photographs, short videos, scanned 3D models, and textual notes serve as the raw material for these activities. Once back in the classroom, this content is uploaded to the platform and transformed into interactive tasks that foster collaborative retrieval and reflection. In this way, the emphasis is not placed on the content per se—which can be easily provided by educators or students—but rather on the learning activity structured around it.

An education use case illustrates this potential. Consider a group of students engaged in a field study exploring the local cultural heritage of Milan. During the visit, students document historical buildings but also community spaces, cultural associations, and other expressions of the city's living heritage through photos, short videos, and 3D scans of façades, interiors, and urban details. Back on campus, these materials are uploaded to the MR platform, where instructors design interactive activities: reconstructing a fragmented 3D model of a civic building façade as a puzzle, solving quizzes on architectural features observed on site, and analyzing video fragments that recall principles of urban transformation in Milan. Within the MR environment, students work in small groups to complete these activities, combining disciplinary knowledge with the sensory and cultural impressions collected during the visit. The process transforms passive documentation into an active, collaborative exercise of interpretation and memory reinforcement, directly tied to the curriculum of their degree program (Fig. 3).

Technological Development

From a technological standpoint, this second application builds on the same core infrastructure adopted for the Ciceronian loci system, reusing the established MR pipeline for deployment on Meta Quest 3 and 3S headsets. As in the first case, FifthIngenium's TINALP platform supported no-code content authoring and session synchronization, while MRTK2 and MRUK provided stable spatial anchoring, interface components, and persistence across sessions.

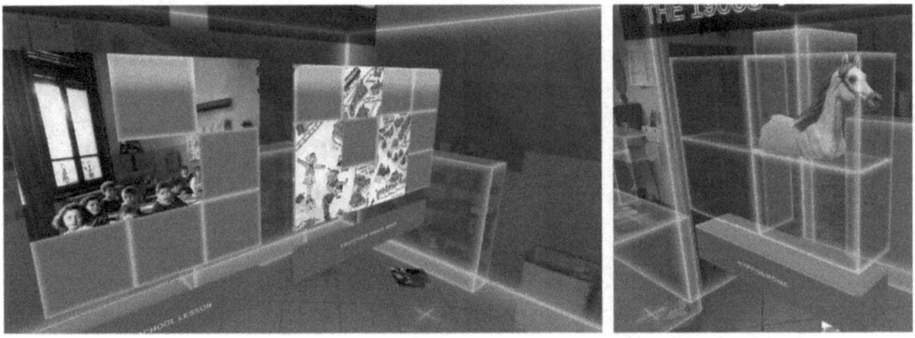

Fig. 3. A 2D and a 3D puzzle in the "study visit" application

Unlike the loci application, which focused on the creation of personal memory palaces anchored to real environments, this system introduced a different pedagogical and technical focus: the post-experience reinforcement of learning through modular and reusable activities, including 2D/3D puzzles and quizzes. This shift required a distinct implementation pipeline. Puzzle generation relied on the automatic subdivision of images or 3D meshes into grid-based interactive fragments, each instantiated with physics properties and optimized colliders. To ensure smooth performance, mesh slicing routines and adaptive level-of-detail techniques were employed to balance visual fidelity and computational efficiency.

Interaction design also presented specific challenges. While ray-casting was retained for object manipulation, the activities required continuous grabbing, rotation, and alignment of virtual elements, demanding more responsive feedback and refined collision handling. The quiz component further extended the application logic, introducing dynamic question–answer modules capable of handling text-, image-, and video-based content through TINALP's configuration files.

Persistence mechanisms were expanded beyond the first system to support content reuse and rapid iteration. Instructors could modify activities directly through TINALP, with updated configurations automatically reflected at runtime without rebuilding the Unity application. This separation between the MR runtime and the web-based authoring layer increased scalability and long-term usability.

Finally, particular attention was devoted to user comfort and session duration. Activities were designed to remain short and lightweight in rendering, informed by usability evaluations, to reduce fatigue and support accessibility for first-time headset users. Overall, while sharing the same technological backbone as the Ciceronian loci system, this implementation extends it toward a modular, activity-based architecture aimed at collective learning reinforcement and post-experience reflection.

4 Evaluation

Both applications have undergone preliminary testing with student cohorts, with particular attention to usability, user comfort—an especially critical dimension in the context of Mixed Reality—and perceived educational value. These dimensions can be considered necessary preconditions for any potential pedagogical impact. In other words, unless the applications are usable, comfortable, and positively received as useful by learners, they cannot realistically progress to the subsequent stage: serving as the foundation for effective and sustainable learning experiences.

During the Politecnico di Milano Open Day (an outreach event open to prospective students) the applications were tested on a voluntary basis with **63 participants.** These included high-school students visiting the campus as well as university students exploring options for their master's degree. Most participants were between 17 and 24 years old. Volunteers interacted with the two prototypes: in the method of loci application, they created short associative sequences linking digital objects to familiar loci in their surroundings, while in the study visit application, they reconstructed images and solved quizzes based on historical materials from Milan's Trotter Park. Each session lasted between five and ten minutes, depending on the participant's problem-solving pace (Fig. 4).

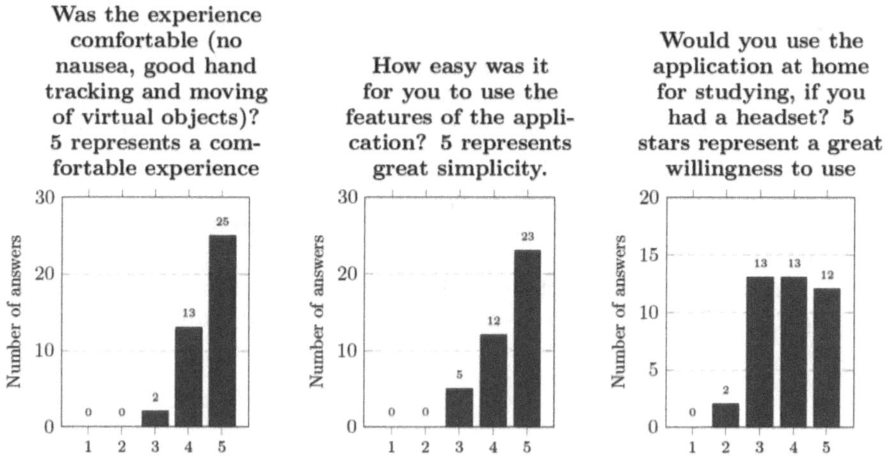

Fig. 4. The data on comfort, usability, and perceived usefulness are positive (data from the loci application)

Despite the brevity of the sessions, the majority reported very high comfort levels (mean score > 4.5/5), ease of use (> 4.6/5), and perceived educational usefulness (> 4.4/5). All respondents evaluated the experience positively, frequently describing it as "new," "fun," and "engaging".

The classroom-based evaluation, conducted with a smaller group of seven students enrolled in a higher-education design course, provided more nuanced insights into both usability and pedagogical relevance. In this setting, participants engaged with extended scenarios that included more complex tasks—12–15-piece puzzles, sequences of multimodal quizzes, and short recall activities based on materials from previous study visits. The evaluation design combined a structured questionnaire with a semi-structured focus group, allowing triangulation between quantitative and qualitative evidence. Quantitative results confirmed the usability and pedagogical potential of the applications, with mean comfort and ease-of-use scores consistently above 4.5 out of 5, in line with the Open Day findings. Qualitative feedback added further depth to these results. Students emphasized the smoothness and intuitiveness of interactions, describing the ray-casting mechanism as "like Spider-Man's web shooter," and praised the sense of immersion achieved through precise spatial anchoring and dynamic feedback. Several participants highlighted the motivational effect of gamified features—scoring systems, timers, and leaderboards—which contributed to a sense of challenge without causing frustration. Others valued the opportunity to explore and manipulate 3D objects in space, perceiving this as an engaging alternative to traditional review activities.

Across both settings, findings point to a strong motivational impact of MR activities. These results align with previous research emphasizing how immersive and gamified environments can enhance learner engagement and support retention [2, 11]. Nevertheless, users also reported a number of limitations. In the case of the Ciceronian loci application, some participants felt that the association tasks were initially difficult to manage without clear guidance. Concerns were also raised about the stability of spatial anchoring in environments with limited lighting or clutter, which occasionally led to misalignment between virtual markers and physical objects. Similarly, in the study visit application, students highlighted the need for greater flexibility in puzzle difficulty and time constraints, as some activities were perceived as either too simple or too demanding. A few participants also noted that prolonged use of the headset could become uncomfortable, limiting the feasibility of extended sessions.

In summary, preliminary evaluations demonstrate that MR can effectively support both mnemonic strategies (through the adaptation of the Ciceronian loci method) and the consolidation of experiential learning (through study visit reinforcement). At the same time, they also indicate directions for future refinement, including more complex collaborative features, adjustable activity levels, and extended testing with larger and more diverse samples.

5 Theoretical Implications

From the perspective of Cognitive Load Theory (CLT), the proposed MR activities can be interpreted as supporting learning by distributing information across multiple modalities and by grounding abstract concepts in situated, perceptual experiences [22, 17]. In particular, CLT distinguishes between *extraneous cognitive load*, which is imposed by the way information is presented and does not directly contribute to learning, and *germane cognitive load*, which reflects the mental effort devoted to schema construction and conceptual understanding [23].

In both case studies, specific design choices may have contributed to reducing extraneous load by externalizing information that would otherwise need to be mentally integrated. For instance, spatially aligned visual cues and interactive overlays allowed learners to directly perceive relationships between concepts and their physical or procedural context, minimizing the need for split attention or abstract mental transformations. At the same time, the requirement to actively manipulate virtual elements and to perform task-relevant actions within the MR environment may have fostered germane cognitive load by encouraging learners to engage more deeply with the underlying concepts and procedures. By leveraging perceptual and spatial channels, the MR interactions supported sense-making processes that are central to learning complex content. Nevertheless, these interpretations remain exploratory and warrant further investigation through studies explicitly measuring different types of cognitive load.

These findings can also be discussed through the lens of embodied learning and embodied cognition, which stress the role of bodily action and sensorimotor engagement in cognitive processes [25, 5]. By requiring learners to physically interact with digital content in spatially meaningful ways, the MR activities may have supported learning through the coupling of movement, perception, and conceptual understanding. Such embodied interactions can facilitate meaning-making by linking abstract concepts to concrete actions and spatial experiences, extending representational learning to include the body as an active component of cognition [15]. Given the preliminary nature of the evaluation, these theoretical interpretations remain indicative and call for further empirical investigations explicitly examining cognitive load and embodied interaction patterns in MR-based learning activities.

6 Limitations

Although preliminary results are promising, several limitations must be acknowledged. First, both applications were tested with relatively small and homogeneous samples, composed mainly of volunteers. This constrains the generalizability of the findings and calls for larger-scale studies involving more diverse student populations and academic disciplines. Second, the evaluations took place in controlled contexts—an Open Day demonstration and a structured classroom session—that cannot fully reproduce the complexity and variability of authentic learning environments over extended periods. Future studies should therefore investigate how these tools perform when integrated into full courses, where repeated use and instructor mediation may shape engagement differently.

A third limitation concerns the novelty effect commonly associated with emerging technologies. The immersive and interactive nature of MR likely amplified students' initial enthusiasm, potentially leading to inflated perceptions of usefulness and engagement. Longitudinal investigations would help to determine whether such motivation is sustained once the novelty diminishes. Finally, several technical constraints persist, including device comfort, session duration, and the reliability of spatial recognition across heterogeneous physical environments. These aspects directly affect usability and scalability, especially in higher education settings where classroom conditions, hardware availability, and instructor readiness vary widely. Addressing these issues will be essential to ensuring that MR can transition from promising prototypes to stable, pedagogically effective tools for everyday teaching and learning.

7 Conclusions

This work builds on a growing body of research that seeks to shift the focus of Mixed Reality (MR) in education from mere object visualization to conceptual engagement, promoting active learning, reflection, and social interaction [6]. The two case studies presented—the reinterpretation of the Ciceronian *method of loci* and the design of post-study visit reinforcement activities—illustrate how MR can be leveraged not merely as a medium for rendering otherwise inaccessible content, but as a platform for designing pedagogically meaningful and embodied learning experiences. Both cases demonstrate the feasibility of combining ancient mnemonic strategies and contemporary gamification principles with immersive technologies to foster knowledge retention, conceptual understanding, and collaborative learning in higher education.

At the same time, the findings underscore significant challenges that must be addressed before such approaches can achieve broader institutional adoption. Beyond preliminary evidence of usability and engagement, further research is needed to assess long-term learning outcomes, particularly regarding the durability of memory traces and the depth of conceptual understanding supported by MR-based activities. Equally crucial is the exploration of how these tools can be embedded into regular curricula in ways that align with existing assessment practices and teaching rhythms, ensuring that they complement rather than remain peripheral to mainstream instruction. Questions of scalability, cross-disciplinary adaptability, infrastructure requirements, and the workload demanded of instructors remain open and warrant systematic investigation.

Future work will focus on expanding collaboration with educators to refine the pedagogical design of MR activities and to examine their sustained use in authentic classroom contexts. Building on the strong positive feedback from students, forthcoming studies will emphasize co-design processes with teachers, the integration of advanced collaborative and feedback features, and the evaluation of MR interventions with larger, more diverse samples. In doing so, this line of inquiry seeks to foster a broader pedagogical shift in the use of immersive technologies in education, from applications centered on content reproduction to those that place learning activities at the core, positioning MR as a mature and pedagogically grounded component of the learning process.

Acknowledgements. This work has received funding from the European Union's Connecting Europe Facility programme under grant agreement No. 101181117 – 5G-CRESCA project. Views and opinions expressed are however those of the author(s) only and do not necessarily reflect those of the European Union or HADEA. Neither the European Union nor the granting authority can be held responsible for them.

Disclosure of Interests. The authors have no competing interests to declare that are relevant to the content of this article.

References

1. Akçayır, M., Akçayır, G.: Advantages and challenges associated with augmented reality for education: a systematic review of the literature. Educ. Res. Rev. **20**, 1–11 (2017)
2. Allcoat, D., Hatchard, T., Azmat, F., Stansfield, K., Watson, D., von Mühlenen, A.: Education in the digital age: learning experience in virtual and mixed realities. J. Educ. Comput. Res. **59**(4), 795–818 (2021)
3. Avila-Garzon, C., Bacca-Acosta, J., Duarte, J., Betancourt, J.: Augmented reality in education: an overview of twenty-five years of research. Contemp. Educ. Technol. **13**(3), 1–21 (2021)
4. Bacca Acosta, J.L., Baldiris Navarro, S.M., Fabregat Gesa, R., Graf, S.: Augmented reality trends in education: a systematic review of research and applications. J. Educ. Technol. Soc. **17**(4), 133–149 (2014)

5. Barsalou, L.W.: Grounded cognition. Annu. Rev. Psychol. **59**, 617–645 (2008)
6. Bauro, S., et al.: Mixed reality in education: towards a new paradigm. In: SITE 2022 Conference, pp. 1–13. Association for the Advancement of Computing in Education (AACE), San Diego (2022)
7. Cercenelli, L., et al.: AEducaAR, anatomical education in augmented reality: a pilot experience of an innovative educational tool combining AR technology and 3D printing. Int. J. Environ. Res. Public Health. **19**(3), 1024 (2022)
8. Chen, Y.C., Chi, H.L., Hung, W.H., Kang, S.C.: Use of tangible and augmented reality models in engineering graphics courses. J. Professional Issues Eng. Educ. Pract. **137**(4), 267–276 (2011)
9. Deterding, S., Dixon, D., Khaled, R., Nacke, L.: From game design elements to gamefulness: defining "gamification.". In: Proceedings of the 15th International Academic MindTrek Conference, pp. 9–15. ACM, New York (2011)
10. Fonseca, D., Martí, N., Redondo, E., Navarro, I., Sánchez, A.: Relationship between student profile, tool use, participation, and academic performance with the use of augmented reality technology for visualized architecture models. Comput. Hum. Behav. **31**, 434–445 (2015)
11. Hwang, G.J., Wu, P.H., Chen, C.C., Tu, N.T.: Effects of an augmented reality-based educational game on students' learning achievements and attitudes in real-world observations. Interact. Learn. Environ. **24**(8), 1895–1906 (2016)
12. Kamarainen, A.M., et al.: EcoMOBILE: integrating augmented reality and probeware with environmental education field trips. Comput. Educ. **68**, 545–556 (2013)
13. Krokos, E., Plaisant, C., Varshney, A.: Virtual memory palaces: immersion aids recall. Virtual Reality. **23**(1), 1–15 (2019)
14. Legge, E.L.G., Madan, C.R., Ng, E.T., Caplan, J.B.: Building a memory palace in minutes: equivalent memory performance using virtual versus conventional environments. PLoS One **7**(9), e 53130 (2012)
15. Lindgren, R., Johnson-Glenberg, M.: Emboldened by embodiment: six precepts for research on embodied learning and mixed reality. Educ. Res. **42**(8), 445–452 (2013)
16. MacCallum, K., Parsons, D.: Integrating mobile mixed reality to enhance learning before, during, and after physical field trips. Int. J. Mob. Blended Learn. **14**(2), 1–11 (2022)
17. Mayer, R.E.: Multimedia Learning, 2nd edn. Cambridge University Press, Cambridge (2009)
18. Qureshi, A.W., Rizvi, S.M.H., Syed, T.M., Rana, M.A., Malik, A.S.: The method of loci: a new tool for recall improvement in students. J. Behav. Brain Sci. **7**, 1–7 (2017)
19. Radianti, J., Majchrzak, T.A., Fromm, J., Wohlgenannt, I.: A systematic review of immersive virtual reality applications for higher education: design elements, lessons learned, and research agenda. Comput. Educ. **147**, 103778 (2020)
20. Renda, P.I.: Transforming Learning at Pitt Pharmacy with Augmented and Virtual Reality. University of Pittsburgh (2023). https://www.health.pitt.edu/news/transforming-learning-pitt-pharmacy-augmented-and-virtual-reality
21. Roediger, H.L., Butler, A.C.: The critical role of retrieval practice in long-term retention. Trends Cogn. Sci. **15**(1), 20–27 (2011)
22. Sweller, J.: Cognitive load during problem solving: effects on learning. Cogn. Sci. **12**(2), 257–285 (1988)
23. Sweller, J., Ayres, P., Kalyuga, S.: Cognitive Load Theory. Springer, New York (2011)
24. Wiley, B., Schulze, J.P.: ArchAR: an archaeological augmented reality experience. In: The Engineering Reality of Virtual Reality 2015, vol. 9392, pp. 15–23. SPIE, Bellingham (2015)
25. Wilson, M.: Six views of embodied cognition. Psychon. Bull. Rev. **9**(4), 625–636 (2002)

The Challenge of Corporeality in Digital and Immersive Teacher Education: An Embodied and Motor-Expressive Perspective

Maria Virginia Marchesano[1,2(✉)], Lucia Pallonetto[2], Valeria Minghelli[2], Mariateresa Ingino[2], and Carmen Palumbo[2]

[1] University of Verona, 37129 Verona, Italy
mmarchesano@unisa.it
[2] University of Salerno, 84084 Fisciano (SA), Italy
{lpallonetto,vminghelli,mingino,capalumbo}@unisa.it

Abstract. The implementation of teaching practices within immersive environments is producing a significant paradigmatic shift in pedagogy, redefining the relationship with oneself and with others. The emergence of the digital Self requires new forms of community and a reconceptualization of identity as situated, conscious, and ecologically grounded presence. In this context, it becomes essential to identify pedagogical strategies capable of fostering critical and reflective engagement with immersive technologies, preserving expressive and relational corporeality, and avoiding the reduction of embodied experience to the mere digital Self. This study proposes a training program for secondary school teachers, with implications for university-based initial teacher education, based on the integration of theoretical components and motor-expressive activities. The aim is to foster situated presence, affective engagement, and empathic communication in digital educational environments, promoting an "on-life" professional identity that integrates physical and virtual dimensions. The training unfolds in three phases: exploratory, immersive, and reflective, focused on developing motor awareness, transposition into AR/MR environments, and pedagogical elaboration of the experience. The complexity of digital learning requires strategies integrating sensory, bodily, and cognitive dimensions, fostering motivated and active participation. This work delineates an innovative approach replicable in university curricula, combining pedagogical experimentation with embodied reflection, and encouraging future experimental research on immersive environments in teacher education.

Keywords: Corporeality · Digital Education · Pre-service Teacher Education

1 The Challenge of Corporeality in Digital Education

The speed, extensiveness, and immediacy of modern mass media, combined with the pervasiveness of digital technologies and artificial intelligence systems [1], exert a profound and far-reaching influence on the contemporary socio-cultural landscape. On the

M. Adamoli et al. (Eds.): HELMeTO 2025, CCIS 2958, pp. 596–609, 2026.
https://doi.org/10.1007/978-3-032-31850-3_37

one hand, basic literacy processes are clearly facilitated, simplifying and multiplying educational practices and learning opportunities; on the other hand, a social process is unfolding, immersing individuals in a heterogeneous and dynamic ecosystem marked by the meta-category of an increasingly multifaceted and multidimensional complexity [2]. Within this context, the global market, the compression of space and time, and the growing fragmentation of communication and information flows call for a critical redefinition of individual competencies, which are called upon to face the original challenges of the digital-virtual revolution [3], a transformation defined by plasticity, versatility, and the continuous emergence of new horizons of meaning. The school system, as a space for learning and personal identity development, is increasingly regarded as an ideal setting for observation, experimentation, and pedagogical planning, both theoretically and empirically, aimed at investigating educational problems and formulating potential solutions. Schools represent the microcosmic arenas in which the dynamics of the broader social system are rearticulated, placing on educational experts the responsibility to monitor their effects and results. The advent of digital technologies is prompting a profound redefinition of teaching paradigms, transforming the times, spaces and methods of teaching. Interactive devices, digital learning environments, collaborative platforms, and multimedia resources have contributed to the emergence of an open, networked model of schooling, in which educational processes unfold across multiple communicative and cognitive layers [4]. Within this framework, the metaverse paradigm emerges as a promising prospect for generating new forms of experience and learning. However, for its potential to translate into genuine educational innovation, it must move beyond a mere digital transposition of content, instead fostering a structural transformation of teaching practices and pedagogical architecture. This transformation entails a reconceptualization of the teacher's role not as a mere transmitter of knowledge, but as a facilitator, mediator, and guide within emerging learning environments [5, 6]. From this perspective, without adequate teacher training, intentional instructional design, and critical reflection, there is a risk of a technocentric bias [7], in which innovation is reduced to a merely instrumental use of technology, without producing any substantive qualitative impact on educational practice or experience. The mere introduction of immersive environments does not, in itself, guarantee an improvement in teaching practices, unless accompanied by a critical reconceptualization of pedagogical models. An uncritical adoption of digital technologies may also lead to the progressive marginalization of the physical dimension of education, promoting disembodied, abstract, and two-dimensional learning models in which the learner's body becomes a passive medium for content consumption. Such an approach carries far-reaching implications for education, which risks losing part of its sensory, affective, and relational richness. An effective learning environment, whether physical or virtual [8], should be conceived as an adaptive system that leverages the potential of technology while fostering innovative forms of knowledge construction, dialogic and inclusive educational relationships, as well as the development of autonomy, critical thinking, and active learner participation. From this perspective, adaptive technological systems can foster not only greater access to knowledge but also the enhancement of cognitive processes through digital media and artificial intelligence, nurturing what Lévy defines as collective intelligence, a form of distributed cognition emerging from cooperation among individuals within an interconnected ecosystem. Far from promoting mass standardization, such a form of collective intelligence could serve as a driver of socio-cultural emancipation, enabling individuals to exercise expressive and participatory agency while also accessing the community's cognitive resources and relational capital, thereby generating a dynamic process of cooperative culture [9]. The notion of a hybrid educational setting finds paradigmatic expression in Extended Reality (XR), a conceptual category encompassing Virtual Reality (VR), Augmented Reality (AR), and Mixed Reality (MR) [10]. XR is not merely the sum of technological environments but rather an experiential *continuum* that connects and intertwines physical and digital spaces, generating forms of interdependence and simultaneity that redefine the traditional boundaries between reality and representation. From an epistemological point of view, this configuration redefines the concept of immersion: shifting from mere perceptual simulation within three-dimensional environments to the embodied and relational dimension of lived experience. Specifically, in AR and MR, the dynamic integration of environment, body, and technological mediation engenders a process of embodiment that engages the totality of subjectivity, activating cognitive, affective, and social dimensions. In this sense, the immersive experience acquires the features of situated learning, consistent with constructivist and sociocultural perspectives, where knowledge is not merely transmitted but constructed through interaction with the environment and with other participants in the educational process. This perspective calls for a reconceptualization of teaching within the ecology of learning, in which technology is not merely a tool but a medium capable of co-determining educational processes, expanding opportunities for the shared construction of meaning, and promoting learner agency and active participation. Conversely, the everyday reality of educational practice reveals concrete difficulties in ensuring effective conditions for students' learning, participation, and well-being. Among the three core dimensions defining the European teacher profile - attitudes, knowledge, and skills - the attitudinal dimension, encompassing teachers' perceptions and beliefs, appears particularly resistant to change, which makes it difficult to transform through conventional teacher education programs. Such rigidity negatively affects both the promotion of intentional, systematic, and assessable learning and the activation of authentic and meaningful student participation. The post-media educational system is therefore called upon to identify which teaching strategies and techniques are most effective in promoting educational practices that preserve a didactic and expressive physical dimension, without reducing it to the digital confines of a body deprived of spatial and temporal depth [11]. In this regard, a humanizing pedagogy [12, 13], which affirms the value of experience, dialogue, slowness, encounter, and physicality, can transcend the boundaries of the screen to foster the harmonious and integrated development of the human being in all its dimensions: cognitive, affective, physical, relational, and ethical.

Teaching should adhere to a principle of methodological flexibility, that is, the capacity to operate in a multimodal way from a pedagogical perspective in order to avoid the risk of sterile instructional *routines* [14]. This entails designing teaching–learning processes oriented toward the continuous exploration of learners' educational needs and grounded in the principle of non-linearity as a key element for engaging with the originality and uniqueness of each learner across diverse educational environments, including those of so-called "augmented learning" [15]. This theoretical contribution pursues two main objectives. First, it seeks to promote the acquisition of relational and empathic skills through an experiential path involving motor-expressive activities, designed to help teachers develop the ability to design participatory and immersive online lessons that foster meaningful learning. Second, it aims to outline the course's methodological approach, describing tools and procedures capable of responding flexibly, functionally, and effectively to teachers' professional development needs. Recent research in neuroscience and cognitive psychology has highlighted the profound significance of embodied pedagogy [16] in teaching and learning processes, recognizing it as a genuinely cross-disciplinary educational approach, a novel epistemological stance characterized by discovery, sensory openness, and the integrated engagement of thought, body, and emotion. This perspective not only challenges the traditional mind–body dualism by embracing the dimensions of intelligence and bodily memory but also transforms and integrates learning methodologies and the interconnections between space and knowledge. In this perspective, the notion of presence requires a deeper pedagogical redefinition. Presence cannot be reduced to mere online connection or visual participation, but should be understood as a situated, intentional, and embodied condition. Educational presence emerges from the interplay between perception, attention, movement, and relational attunement, all of which are grounded in bodily experience. When digital learning environments privilege cognitive interaction alone, the risk is not only a fragmentation of learning processes, but also a progressive weakening of students' capacity to inhabit educational situations with awareness and responsibility. Reconsidering presence as an embodied phenomenon thus becomes a central pedagogical challenge in contemporary higher education. The educational challenge is both compelling and demanding, as it requires the teaching profession to reconfigure its conventional methodological practices by constructing a multidimensional bridge between physical experience and learning processes in light of the complexity paradigm [17]. The goal is to cultivate forms of intelligence that transcend the limitations of fragmented or reductionist knowledge, functioning as bio-psycho-social entities [18] in which body, emotion, and cognition are dynamically interconnected. Motor-expressive activities can be situated within this context as a privileged medium for operationalizing these principles in educational practice. They represent a valuable opportunity to harness the expressive potential of the body, fostering educational practices that are more flexible and responsive to the diverse needs of individual learners. From this perspective, recent pedagogical scholarship has emphasized that the bodily dimension cannot be reduced to a mere functional support for teaching but rather represents a foundational principle of the educational experience. Recent studies [19] have highlighted that the body, understood as a relational and expressive mediator, represents the primary space for encounter and mutual recognition, particularly within inclusive contexts and situations of vulnerability. The body enables the preservation of continuity between personal experience and the learning process, thereby avoiding the risk of an exclusively cognitive or technocentric approach. This perspective, rooted in the pedagogy of listening and the centrality of lived experience, invites educators and researchers to re-conceptualize online educational practices through a multimodal lens, positioning the body as a dynamic "bridge" between physical presence and virtual environments. This underscores the need for initial teacher training programs that establish embodiment workshops as epistemic environments for designing and validating practices transferable to school contexts. Although the pathway is primarily oriented toward secondary school teachers, it is discussed here within a university-based pre-service teacher education perspective, as initial training represents a strategic context for developing embodied and reflective professional competencies.

2 New Training Scenarios for Teachers

In light of these considerations, this paper proposes the integration of embodied and expressive teaching methods into university-level pre-service teacher education programs [20, 21]. This perspective aligns with pedagogical research highlighting that the body is not merely a functional support for action, but rather an authentic and privileged mediator of knowledge, relationships, and meaning [22, 23]. In this framework, physicality functions not only as an object but also as an instrument of teacher training: it represents an epistemic and educational principle capable of fostering situated and experiential learning processes within the framework of embodied cognition, a paradigm widely supported by research in neuroscience and educational science [24, 25]. The introduction of theoretical–practical workshops focused on the expressive dimension of the body therefore appears to be a strategic element in developing professional teaching competence, combining disciplinary and transversal skills with affective awareness, self-presence management, and empathic communication abilities [21]. These workshops can be configured as transformative pedagogical spaces, in which future teachers experiment with physicality as a resource for teaching mediation and for the construction of inclusive and participatory learning environments [26]. From this perspective, the adopted methodology comprises reflective and experiential activities, including motor improvisation, individual and collective expressive practices, role-play, and educational simulations, stimulating processes of self-observation and embodied metacognition [27]. This embodied approach enables a re-conceptualization of the workshop beyond a mere supplementary activity, recognizing it instead as an epistemic context in which cognition, affectivity, and action are integrated and deliberately positioned as the focus of educational design. Within this pedagogical horizon, body language functions not only as a primal mode of communication but also as a fundamental educational resource: gestures, postures, and facial expressions serve as immediate indicators of attention, participation, and engagement, allowing teachers to adjust their instructional actions in real time. The systematic incorporation of these dimensions into teacher education is therefore crucial for cultivating bodily awareness, shifting teaching from mere content delivery to an embodied pedagogical relationship capable of fostering meaningful and inclusive learning. In this context, teacher education is guided by the construct of the on-life teacher [28], who can integrate and critically navigate both analogue and digital, as well as bodily and virtual dimensions. Within this framework, the concept of the on-life teacher represents a crucial theoretical shift. Rather than referring to a professional capable of managing digital tools, the on-life teacher embodies an integrated pedagogical identity in which physical, relational, and digital dimensions continuously interact. Teaching in on-life contexts requires the ability to navigate hybrid educational spaces, where learning unfolds through simultaneous bodily presence, mediated interaction, and reflective intentionality. This perspective calls for a reconceptualization of teaching competence, no longer limited to methodological efficiency, but extended to embodied awareness, ethical responsibility, and sensitivity to the relational dynamics generated by digital mediation. The centrality of expressive physicality contributes to defining professional teaching competence, which is not limited to navigating diverse educational contexts but is also capable of overseeing the pedagogical relationship in all its complexity, enhancing embodied experience even in immersive and technologically mediated scenarios. The resulting professional profile, through embodied practice, integrates reflexivity, situated presence, and empathic communication, exercising an educational function that is grounded in the body while critically extending into digital and hybrid learning environments. The integration of practices involving conscious breathing, eye contact, and interpersonal interaction, combined with individual and group body exploration activities, represents a methodological approach effective in activating the affective-embodied dimensions of learners. These practices promote an experiential journey that enables participants to explore bodily vitality and develop awareness of their potential and expressive, creative, and communicative tools, both explicit and latent. The aim of these experiences is to enhance awareness, fostering full self-awareness and self-determination. From this perspective, the risk of alienation can be mitigated, creating a shared experiential space grounded in resonance and empathy [29]. The experience of a training program through motor-expressive activities thus constitutes a performative, interactive, and multimodal pedagogical approach, facilitating an embodied cognitive process of didactic transposition. In this sense, physicality not only enriches teaching methods but also functions as an integral component of the didactic transposition process [30].

2.1 A Bio-Psycho-Social Perspective

The scientific literature has long demonstrated that teachers' professional quality is closely associated with student outcomes, both academic and behavioral [31], thereby influencing learners' well-being and their prospects for a good quality of life. Nevertheless, education systems today face a growing obsolescence, as many educators remain anchored to outdated methodologies and cultural frameworks, limiting schools' capacity to adapt to the rapid social, cultural, and economic transformations of contemporary society. Within the broader educational and cultural transformations of recent decades, schools and pedagogical research are increasingly called upon to critically examine the strategies and tools most effective in promoting genuinely inclusive and participatory education. This process requires rethinking the educational relationship as a dynamic and embodied space, particularly within immersive learning environments, capable of engaging students in meaningful, manipulative, and reflective experiences in which knowledge is not merely transmitted but enacted, experienced, and shared. From this perspective, the body is not merely the locus of action and expression, but constitutes the epistemic matrix of learning, a generative principle that interconnects mind, emotion, and movement within an experiential continuum [32, 33]. Within this interpretative framework, motor-expressive practices integrated into teacher education play a crucial role in constructing inclusive and meaningful learning environments, as they foster holistic human development. The methodological foundation of these activities draws on the constructs of the bio-psycho-social paradigm [34, 35], which provides a robust theoretical basis for overcoming the traditional dichotomies between body and mind, theory and practice, cognition and affectivity, thereby restoring an integrated and systemic conception of the human being. This paradigm, when placed in dialogue with the ecological-dynamic perspective [36, 37], the neuroscience of embodied simulation [38], and embodied cognition theories [39] supports the adoption of motor-expressive activities as a privileged pedagogical instrument in response to the contemporary need to conceive education as a situated, interactive, expressive, and relational process. Furthermore, in line with the principles of physical literacy [40] and lifelong learning [41, 42], this vision promotes a lifelong model of teacher and individual development that recognizes physicality as an educational, critical, and reflective resource, capable of counteracting the disembodied and fragmented tendencies produced by unmediated digitalization. The restoration of the educational value of the body and gesture, conceived as a complement rather than an alternative to the digitalization of school experience, enables the activation of integrated learning pathways in which body, emotion, and thought interact in a continuous and transformative dialogue [43]. From an operational point of view, the bio-psycho-social foundations of motor-expressive activities necessitate a profound reorganization of educational contexts and pedagogical methodologies. In this perspective, bodily and motor practices are no longer ancillary or marginal, but become privileged means for observing, assessing, and mediating learning processes. By encouraging expressive physicality, teachers can identify signs of attention, participation, or discomfort, design tailored interventions and foster genuinely inclusive learning environments. Gestures, posture, and the rhythm of teaching thus become qualitative indicators of the relational and cognitive dynamics of the classroom, enabling a form of "reflective practice" [44] grounded in the teacher's embodied presence. The bio-psycho-social paradigm, therefore, does not merely constitute a change in the assessment model, but an authentic epistemological stance: situated, dialogical, and embodied. It invites a redefinition of the evaluative criteria of contemporary schooling, foregrounding the quality of experience, relational intensity, and the capacity to consciously inhabit the educational gesture. Motor-expressive practices thus become authentic spaces of emergence and possibility, where elements that elude measurement-emotion, unpredictability, bodily resonance-contribute decisively to the educational process [43]. This challenge directly implicates both initial and in-service teacher education, who are called for the development of observational and reflective competences capable of apprehending the complexity of bodily and relational processes. From this perspective, teachers are no longer mere transmitters of knowledge or neutral observers, but artisans of observation [45]: professionals capable of decoding gestures as signs, interpreting physicality as language, and transforming each context into a pedagogical opportunity. In practical terms, the workshops integrated into pre-service teacher education programs foster the development of embodied professional competences, essential for addressing the challenges of immersive and digital schooling. They provide a meaningful horizon that bridges the divides between mind and body, knowing and doing, technology and presence. The overarching goal is to reorient the school's anthropological vocation, directing it towards a pedagogy grounded in embodied relationships and situated awareness. Only training that successfully integrates the biological, psychological, and social dimensions of experience can cultivate teachers who are self-aware, reflective, and capable of inhabiting the body as an educational space, thus humanizing the complexity of contemporary educational contexts.

3 Structure of the Path

The training project is structured in three interdependent phases, aiming to integrate the motor-expressive dimension with the affordances of immersive digital environments. In the first exploratory phase, teachers engage in activities designed to enhance body awareness, motor-expressive sensitivity, and the capacity to interpret non-verbal communication. Conscious breathing exercises, physical improvisation, motor games, and educational yoga practices aim to cultivate skills in self-perception and interpersonal interaction, highlighting the role of intentional actions and bodily choices as markers of self-determination and educational development [46]. The second, immersive phase involves the transposition of these practices into immersive digital contexts, such as augmented and mixed reality environments, to foster critical reflection on the interplay between embodied physicality and virtual representation. In this step, these physical experiences are mapped onto digital environments via augmented and mixed reality technologies. Teachers engage with the co-presence of the physical body and its virtual representation, analyzing gestural transformations and the associated mediation processes. The objective extends beyond technical proficiency to a critical-reflective understanding of the potential and limitations of immersive tools in pedagogical practice.

The body is conceived as an epistemological device and mediator of multisensory experiences, capable of activating cognitive and relational processes, which are powerfully catalyzed through performative languages. Finally, the third, reflective phase constitutes a space for pedagogical reflection and re-elaboration, in which experiences are analyzed and translated into novel teaching scenarios, with the aim of outlining educational strategies transferable to classroom practice. This phase focuses on the pedagogical re-elaboration of the experience, employing debriefing, critical analysis, and collaborative planning. Building on the activities experienced, teachers design prototypes of teaching units integrating motor-expressive activities with immersive technologies, developing educational strategies applicable in authentic school settings. The expected outcomes include situated awareness of transformations of gesture between presence and representation; technological selection criteria aligned with educational objectives; and the design of authentic learning tasks demanding motor coordination, emotional regulation, and collaborative engagement. This perspective aligns with evidence from the scientific literature [47], which suggests that the valorization of the body as an epistemic mediator and pedagogical instrument enables the development of innovative educational practices capable of addressing the complexity of contemporary educational contexts. Through this structure, the course aims to foster the development of professional skills oriented toward the conscious and critical use of immersive technologies, while acknowledging the body as a central epistemic and pedagogical instrument. In this sense, the proposal is situated within the contemporary discourse on methodological innovation in higher education, contributing to the discussion on teacher education through an integrated, transdisciplinary lens grounded in corporeality. The articulation of the training pathway into exploratory, immersive, and reflective phases should not be interpreted as a linear sequence of activities, but as a pedagogically intentional structure. Each phase addresses a specific educational function, while remaining interdependent with the others. The proposed pathway is conceived as a theoretical–methodological framework rather than as an empirically validated model. Its purpose is to offer a pedagogical structure capable of guiding future experimental implementations and research developments in embodied and immersive teacher education.

Table 1 summarizes the alignment between the training phases, the proposed activities, and the study objectives.

Table 1. Training pathway phases

Training phases	Main activities	Related objectives
Exploratory phase	Motor-expressive activities focused on body awareness, breathing, and non-verbal communication.	Development of relational and empathic skills; enhancement of situated presence
Immersive phase	Transposition of motor-expressive experience into augmented and mixed reality environments; guided reflection on gesture mediation.	Design of participatory online learning activities; integration of physical and virtual dimensions
Reflective phase	Debriefing, collective discussion, and pedagogical re-elaboration of experience.	Construction of an on-life professional identity; pedagogical translation of embodied experience

Table 1 clarifies the pedagogical architecture of the proposed teacher-education pathway by making explicit the alignment between training phases, types of activities, and educational objectives. Rather than functioning as a schematic repetition of the program structure, the table supports interpretation of the design logic underlying the proposal. Within this framework, the exploratory phase plays a foundational role, oriented toward reactivating bodily awareness and attention to perceptual dimensions that precede intentional action. Particular emphasis is placed on proprioceptive processes, understood as the capacity to perceive the body from within and to recognize relationships between posture, tone, movement, and emotional states. Motor-expressive activities and embodied listening practices foster perceptual availability, presence, and openness to educational relationships, without focusing on performance or technical accuracy. The immersive phase represents a transitional space in which bodily experience is brought into dialogue with augmented and mixed reality environments. Participants are encouraged to reflect on changes in perceptual coordinates as digitally mediated visual information intersects with proprioceptive and kinesthetic signals. Immersive technologies are thus treated not as ends in themselves, but as pedagogical mediators supporting critical exploration of gesture, presence, and interaction in online learning contexts. The reflective phase completes the pathway through structured moments of dialogue, narration, and guided debriefing. At this stage, embodied and immersive experiences are progressively transformed into professional knowledge, enabling connections between lived experience and pedagogical intentionality. Reflection functions as a space of pedagogical translation, in which the body becomes an object of educational thought and design. Overall, the pathway is conceived not as a rigid linear sequence, but as a dynamic and recursive process in which exploration, immersion, and reflection continuously inform one another.

From a methodological perspective, the model is intended as a flexible and transferable framework, adaptable to different higher education contexts and technological infrastructures, while maintaining the centrality of embodied experience as a guiding pedagogical principle. Immersive technologies are situated within an experiential and reflective continuum, supporting a meaningful and non-technocentric integration of digital tools in teacher education. From this perspective, the value of the proposed model does not lie in the definition of specific activities or tools, but in the identification of pedagogical conditions that can support meaningful embodied learning across different educational contexts. The pathway is therefore intended as a flexible framework, adaptable to diverse institutional settings and technological infrastructures.

4 Conclusions

The theoretical and methodological considerations presented in this study, situated within the contemporary discourse on digital and immersive technologies in schools, underscore that the integration of motor-expressive activities into initial teacher education represents not merely a curricular enrichment, but a fundamental prerequisite for critically engaging with the challenges of immersive and digital pedagogy. While the benefits in terms of innovation and enhancement of educational practices are widely acknowledged, contemporary pedagogical discourse highlights the risk of a disembodied pedagogy, in which the bodily dimension is gradually marginalized and relegated to a purely instrumental function, with significant repercussions for the relational and experiential dimensions of learning [48]. Physicality, conceived as an epistemic and relational mediator, helps maintain the integration of cognition, emotion, and action, thus preventing learning from being reduced to a solely cognitive experience. In this perspective, the vicarious abilities of the teacher [14] find in the physical dimension and in movement a privileged terrain of expression and mediation, represented by a sort of vicariousness of gesture, which is not limited to supporting verbal communication, but becomes a cognitive and educational tool capable of conveying meanings, stimulating attention and facilitating learning. From a practical point of view, based on the notion that the individual is not a pre-existing entity but is constituted through context [18], teaching-learning processes are thus intimately linked to the physical dimension and the affordances provided by diverse educational environments. From this perspective, the integration of experiential workshops centered on motor-expressive activities into pre-service teacher education reflects the recognition that teacher training cannot neglect bodily and emotional channels, nor the capacity for reflection on these, or the development of intersubjectivity and intentional consonance [49]. This reflection aligns with recent research, which underscores that educational quality, even within immersive and digital environments, is inseparable from a grounding in physicality and embodied relationships [19]. From this perspective, the body functions not merely as a "medium" of transmission, but as a genuine epistemic device capable of integrating emotion, cognition, and action. Furthermore, recent international studies [49, 50] emphasize the importance of pedagogy that cultivates soft skills and socio-emotional competencies, confirming that the centrality of physicality extends beyond initial teacher education to constitute a foundational element for building resilient and inclusive educational systems. Consequently, both initial and in-service teacher training must acknowledge the bodily dimension not as a supplementary element, but as a core dimension of professional teaching practice. The integration of motor-expressive education courses into teacher education ultimately provides tools for constructing genuinely inclusive and humanizing learning environments, in which digital and physical dimensions are mutually reinforcing rather than mutually exclusive. From a policy perspective, this entails the formal integration of mandatory motor-expressive modules into both initial teacher education and continuing professional development, with established quality standards encompassing measurable indicators of teaching presence, non-verbal communication, and the management of embodied interactions. The originality of the proposed contribution lies in the integration of motor-expressive pedagogy, embodied cognition, and immersive learning environments within a non-technocentric framework. Rather than proposing new technological solutions, the paper advances an epistemological repositioning of the body as a central mediator of meaning-making in digitally enhanced teacher education. From a research perspective, this work provides a basis for future empirical investigations, which may emphasize process-oriented analysis rather than exclusively outcome-focused metrics, adopting qualitative methodologies such as in situ observation, narrative reporting, and guided reflective sessions. Such approaches could support a more comprehensive examination of the role of motor-expressive experiences in facilitating meaningful learning, student engagement, and the development of relational dynamics within university settings. Further empirical research is needed to evaluate the impact of such approaches within authentic educational settings, thus laying the groundwork for an international research agenda integrating body pedagogy, immersive technologies, and inclusive schooling. These considerations highlight the relevance of embodied approaches not only for initial teacher education, but also for continuous professional development in higher education. In contexts increasingly characterized by hybrid and digitally mediated forms of teaching, fostering bodily awareness, relational sensitivity, and reflective presence becomes a strategic dimension of educational quality. Within this perspective, immersive technologies acquire pedagogical value only when embedded within coherent experiential and reflective trajectories, capable of supporting teachers in developing an on-life professional identity grounded in responsibility, awareness, and educational intentionality.

This perspective represents one of the pedagogical imperatives of the 21st century: only educational approaches that transcend the boundaries of the screen can foster critical, creative, and participatory individuals capable of navigating both physical and virtual environments.

Disclosure of Interests. The authors have no competing interests to declare that are relevant to the content of this article.

References

1. Orgilés, M., Morales, A., Delvecchio, E., Mazzeschi, C., Espada, J.P.: Immediate psychological effects of the COVID-19 quarantine in youth from Italy and Spain. Front. Psychol. **11**, 579038 (2020). https://doi.org/10.31234/osf.io/5bpfz
2. Acone, G.: L'orizzonte teorico della pedagogia contemporanea. Fondamenti e prospettive. Edisud, Salerno (2005). (in Italian)
3. Lévy, P.: Il virtuale. Cortina, Milano (1995). (in Italian)

4. Mena-Guacas, A.F., López-Catalán, L., Bernal-Bravo, C., Ballesteros-Regaña, C.: Educational transformation through emerging technologies: critical review of scientific impact on learning. Educ. Sci. **15**(3), 368 (2025). https://doi.org/10.3390/educsci15030368
5. Laurillard, D.: Teaching as a Design Science: Building Pedagogical Patterns for Learning and Technology. Routledge, New York (2012)
6. Trentin, G.: Dalla formazione a distanza all'apprendimento in rete. FrancoAngeli, Milano (2001). (in Italian)
7. Selwyn, N.: Education and Technology: Key Issues and Debates. Bloomsbury Publishing, London (2021)
8. UNESCO: Leveraging Information and Communication Technology to Achieve Education 2030: Report of the UNESCO 2017 International Forum on ICT and Education 2030. UNESCO, Paris (2017). https://unesdoc.unesco.org/ark:/48223/pf0000260445
9. Lévy, P.: L'intelligence collective. Pour une anthropologie du cyberespace. La Découverte, Paris (1994) (in French). Trad. it.: L'intelligenza collettiva. Feltrinelli, Milano (1996)
10. Accoto, C.: Il mondo in sintesi: Cinque brevi lezioni di filosofia della simulazione. EGEA, Milano (2022). (in Italian)
11. Milani, L.: Educational emergency and the teaching body. Pedagogia Oggi. **19**(1), 35–41 (2021)
12. Motta, S., Bennett, A.: Pedagogies of care, care-full epistemological practice and 'other' caring subjectivities in enabling education. Teach. High. Educ. **23**(5), 631–646 (2008)
13. Freire, P.: Cultural action and conscientization. Harv. Educ. Rev. **40**(3), 452–477 (1970)
14. Sibilio, M.: Corpo e cognizione nella didattica. In: Rivoltella, P.C., Rossi, P.G. (eds.) L'agire didattico. Manuale per l'insegnante, pp. 329–348. La Scuola, Brescia (2017) (in Italian)
15. Rossi, M.: Realtà virtuale aumentata per la promozione di una didattica inclusiva. In: Peconio, G. (ed.) Quality Learning: Prospettive per una didattica efficace. Progedit, Bari (2022) (in Italian)
16. Gamelli, I.: Pedagogia del corpo. Meltemi, Sesto San Giovanni (2006). (in Italian)
17. Morin, E.: La testa ben fatta. Riforma dell'insegnamento e riforma del pensiero. Raffaello Cortina, Milano (2000). (in Italian)
18. Gibson, J.J.: The Ecological Approach to Visual Perception. Psychology Press, Hove (2014)
19. Stella, D., Pallonetto, L., Palumbo, C.: Sentire oltre il corpo: duplicità e prospettive pedagogiche per una didattica del movimento. Corpo, Società, Educazione 1(1), 119–134 (2024). https://doi.org/10.14605/CSE112407
20. Sibilio, M.: Vicarianza e didattica: Corpo, cognizione, insegnamento. La Scuola, Brescia (2017). (in Italian)
21. Damiani, P., Minghelli, V., D'Anna, C., Paloma, F.G.: L'approccio embodied cognition based nella formazione docenti. Annali Online della Didattica e della Formazione Docente 13(21), 106–128 (2021). (in Italian)
22. Merleau-Ponty, M.: Phénoménologie de la perception. Gallimard, Paris (1945) (in French)
23. Dewey, J.: Experience and Education. Kappa Delta Pi, New York (1938)
24. Gallagher, S.: Phenomenology and embodied cognition. In: The Routledge Handbook of Embodied Cognition, pp. 9–18. Routledge, London/New York (2014)
25. Johnson, M.: Embodied understanding. Front. Psychol. **6**, 875 (2015)
26. Rivoltella, P.C.: Corpi in situ-azione: presupposti neuroscientifici e drammaturgici per una nuova formazione degli insegnanti. In: La professionalità degli insegnanti. La ricerca e le pratiche, pp. 89–99. Pensa Multimedia, Lecce (2017) (in Italian)
27. Parlebas, P.: Giochi, sport e società: Lessico di prasseologia motoria. INSEP, Paris (1999). (in Italian)
28. Floridi, L.: The Onlife Manifesto: Being Human in a Hyperconnected Era. Springer, Heidelberg (2014)

29. Carlomagno, N., Minghelli, V.: Insegnamento a distanza come esperienza performativa. In: Ricerche in Neuroscienze Educative. Scuola, Sport e Società, pp. 28–30. Edizioni Universitarie Romane, Roma (2021) (in Italian)
30. Chevallard, Y.: La transposition didactique. La Pensée Sauvage, Grenoble (1985). [2nd augmented edition: 1991]
31. Perrenoud, P.: Dieci nuove competenze per insegnare. Anicia, Roma (2002) (in Italian)
32. Rivoltella, P.C., Rossi, P.G. (eds.): L'agire didattico. Manuale per l'insegnante. La Scuola, Brescia (2017). (in Italian)
33. Sibilio, M.: Didattica e corpo. La prospettiva embodied nella formazione degli insegnanti. FrancoAngeli, Milano (2020). (in Italian)
34. Engel, G.L.: The need for a new medical model: a challenge for biomedicine. Science **196**(4286), 129–136 (1977). https://doi.org/10.1126/science.847460
35. Engel, G.L.: The clinical application of the biopsychosocial model. Am. J. Psychiatry **137**(5), 535–544 (1980). https://doi.org/10.1176/ajp.137.5.535
36. Newell, K.M.: Constraints on the development of coordination. In: Wade, M.G., Whiting, H.T.A. (eds.) Motor Development in Children: Aspects of Coordination and Control, pp. 341–360. Martinus Nijhoff, Dordrecht (1986)
37. Rizzolatti, G., Sinigaglia, C.: So quel che fai. Il cervello che agisce e i neuroni specchio. Raffaello Cortina, Milano (2006). (in Italian)
38. Gomez Paloma, F., Damiani, P.: Educational and inclusive process: towards the embodied cognition method of teaching, learning and training. In: Gomez Paloma, F. (ed.) Embodied Cognition. Theories and Applications in Education Science, pp. 201–210. Nova Science Publishers, New York (2017)
39. Whiting, H.T.A. (ed.): Motor Development in Children: Aspects of Coordination and Control. Martinus Nijhoff, Dordrecht (1986)
40. Nutbeam, D.: Health education and health promotion revisited. Health Educ. J. **78**(6), 705–709 (2019)
41. UNESCO: Quality Physical Education: Guidelines for Policy-makers. UNESCO Publishing, Paris (2015). https://unesdoc.unesco.org/ark:/48223/pf0000231341
42. Marchesano, M.V., Pallonetto, L., Minghelli, V., Palumbo, C.: Il corpo in gioco: verso un modello educativo integrato per lo sviluppo dell'espressività e dell'autodeterminazione. Mizar, 150–162 (2025). (in Italian)
43. Schön, D.A.: The Reflective Practitioner: how Professionals Think in Action. Basic Books, New York (1983)
44. Minghelli, V., Pallonetto, L., Palumbo, C.: Spontaneous motor investment in the biopsychosocial perspective: video modeling for an inclusive embodied training. J. Inclusive Methodol. Technol. Learn. Teach. **5**(2) (2025)
45. Minghelli, V., Palumbo, C.: Verso un apprendimento personalizzato: l'investimento motorio spontaneo in prospettiva biopsicosociale. Nuova Secondaria Ricerca 10, 305–317 (2024). (in Italian)
46. Minghelli, V.: Corporeità e inclusione. Scenari normativi, bisogni formativi e prospettive di ricerca. Pensa Multimedia, Lecce (2023). (in Italian)
47. Sacristano, A.: Ecologie dell'attenzione nella scuola digitale: ripensare la formazione tra iperconnessione, cura e silenzio. J. Inclusive Methodol. Technol. Learn. Teach. **5**(2) (2025) (in Italian)

48. Gallese, V.: The roots of empathy: the shared manifold hypothesis and the neural basis of intersubjectivity. Psychopathology **36**(4), 171–180 (2003)
49. UNESCO: Global Education Monitoring Report 2023: Technology in Education – A Tool on Whose Terms? UNESCO, Paris (2023). https://unesdoc.unesco.org/ark:/48223/pf0000385723
50. OECD: Education at a Glance 2022: OECD Indicators. OECD Publishing, Paris (2022). https://doi.org/10.1787/3197152b-en

The BotBid Project: Data Education at Work

Giorgio Delzanno[1(✉)], Giovanna Guerrini[1], Enrica Roccotiello[2], Angela Sugliano[1], Daniele Grosso[3], and Giovanni Zanone[1]

[1] Dipartimento di Informatica, Bioingegneria, Robotica e Ingegneria dei Sistemi, Università degli Studi di Genova, Genova, Italy
{giorgio.delzanno,giovanna.guerrini}@dibris.unige.it, angela.sugliano@unige.it

[2] Dipartimento di Scienze della Terra, dell'Ambiente e della Vita, Università degli Studi di Genova, Genova, Italy
enrica.roccotiello@distav.unige.it

[3] Dipartimento di Fisica, Università degli Studi di Genova, Genova, Italy
daniele.grosso@difi.unige.it

Abstract. The BotBid (From Botany to Big Data) project is an educational initiative designed to promote data literacy, scientific inquiry, research methodologies, and participatory science through a network of sustainable and smart school gardens. The project has been included among the dissemination activities of the Robotics and Artificial Intelligence for Socio-economic Empowerment Ecosystem, a National Recovery and Resilience Plan initiative funded by the Italian Ministry of University and Research. This paper presents the overall structure of the initiative, the methods and technologies adopted across its different phases, and the results of the 2024–25 edition, with a particular focus on the project's contribution to data education.

Keywords: Data Literacy · Data Education · Biomonitoring · Citizen Science · Internet of Things · Edge Computing

1 Introduction

Growing attention to environmental sustainability and climate change, together with the widespread adoption of big data technologies, is reshaping practices across many domains. At the same time, there is increasing recognition of the crucial role that data education plays in the life of every citizen [2,12]. Within this framework, the BotBid (From Botany to Big Data) project is an educational initiative aimed at designing innovative and sustainable school gardens to foster data literacy, scientific and research methodologies, and citizen science practices [3].

Developed by an interdisciplinary research group at the University of Genoa, the BotBid project was launched in May 2022 with the aim of supporting schools

M. Adamoli et al. (Eds.): HELMeTO 2025, CCIS 2958, pp. 610–621, 2026.
https://doi.org/10.1007/978-3-032-31850-3_38

selected through the Edugreen program[1] promoted by the Italian Ministry of Education, which focuses on the creation of innovative and sustainable educational gardens. Since July 2023, BotBid become part of the dissemination activities of the STACY Community[2] of Spoke 5 of the Robotic and AI for Socio-economic Empowerment (RAISE) Ecosystem, Investment 1.5 (M4C2) of the Italian National Recovery and Resilience Plan (NRRP)[3].

The goal of BotBid is to provide teachers, and consequently their students, with perspectives and tools that transform the school garden into an opportunity to develop a broad set of STEM-related skills. The project is closely connected to the themes of digital and ecological transition, supporting the transformation of each school garden into a geographically distributed biomonitoring experiment. In this sense, BotBid can also be viewed as a starting point for the development of a citizen science network that involves schools at different educational levels. More specifically, the experimental setup consists of establishing, in each participating school, a garden with thirty control plants and thirty treated plants subjected to stressful soil conditions, along with kits for collecting and transmitting environmental data. The project relies on an Internet of Things and Big Data infrastructure that gathers observational data—such as plant biomass, plant growth, soil pH, and temperature—from school gardens into a central repository. The platform acts as a digital accelerator, enabling the sharing of data and knowledge among domain experts and project participants, and provides dashboards for data visualization and aggregation.

Engagement is fostered through hands-on use of digital tools and data analysis methodologies, which help transform the school garden into a living laboratory and encourage participants to become active contributors to a citizen science experience. The initiative is therefore not only an educational proposal for teachers and students, but also a community-building experiment involving multiple schools across a wide geographical area. The increasingly participatory educational approach, supported by digital tools such as web and cloud platforms, encompasses several learning outcomes: (1) understanding the fundamentals of environmental and applied botany; (2) acquiring scientific inquiry skills through participation in a citizen science project; (3) learning to use digital devices and applications; and (4) developing the ability to process, interpret, and visually represent observational data. Through the project web portal, teachers have access to all the resources needed to carry out the activities in their schools, including in-depth materials, video tutorials, and recordings of seminars. These resources guide schools in collaborative research activities throughout the entire school year.

The BotBid WebApp has been developed to support the collection of environmental parameters and plant growth data. The WebApp provides multiple func-

[1] Edugreen: sustainability laboratories for the first cycle of education, funded by the European Regional Development Fund (ERDF), Axis V, green transition and resilience.

[2] https://www.stacy-community.it/.

[3] https://www.raiseliguria.it/en/.

tionalities, including different types of visualizations for data related to control and treated plants; expert guidelines for simulating soil stress conditions (e.g., increased soil salinity); and comparative and aggregated analyses of data from different schools using business intelligence tools. These features offer concrete examples for educating participants about the importance of data collection, manipulation, and interpretation [6,8]. Worksheets are also provided to support classroom activities, fostering the pedagogical use of digital technologies in line with the DigCompEdu framework.

From a data education perspective, BotBid represents a particularly rich training environment to develop data literacy skills. The learning pathway begins with hands-on activities and gradually introduces more abstract concepts, covering the entire data lifecycle—from data acquisition and cleaning to analysis and interpretation of results.

The 2025 edition of the project was launched through online meetings with teachers between November and December 2024 and involved ten classes from five secondary schools in Liguria and one secondary school in Sardinia. In parallel, nine first-cycle classes participated using simplified tools and methodologies. In February 2025, the BotBid project was selected by the University of Genoa among 14 outreach knowledge enhancement case studies as part of the Research Quality Evaluation exercise of the Italian Agency for the evaluation of universities and research[4]. Including previous editions, BotBid has reached more than 3,000 students and approximately 200 STEM teachers to date. A digital credential, issued through the RAISE Liguria training program, is currently awarded to university students upon completion of an online asynchronous course (worth 1 academic credit/CFU) covering themes and methodologies related to the BotBid project.

Plan of the Paper

In this paper, Sect. 2 discusses related work. Section 3 presents the overall organization of the initiative. In Sect. 4, we describe the methodology and tools adopted in the 2024–2025 edition, along with the results obtained so far, with a particular emphasis on the educational value of the project from a data literacy perspective. Section 5 focuses on the digital certificate developed for higher education students, aligned with the main themes of the project. Finally, Sect. 6 summarizes the conclusions and outlines directions for future work.

2 Background and Related Work

Citizen science [13] can enhance both engagement with science and the perceived relevance of scientific topics, thereby supporting earlier and more effective learning in formal science education. It has been shown to improve pupils' motivation, interest, knowledge, and their scientific and communication skills. High

[4] https://www.anvur.it/en/research/evaluation-research-quality.

levels of student involvement are particularly promising for achieving learning objectives [18]. In formal K–12 settings, participatory science—often referred to as school-based participatory science (SBPS)—offers the opportunity to engage teachers and students authentically in the scientific enterprise, making learning more meaningful [17]. Additional benefits include increased confidence in scientific abilities and a stronger sense of belonging to the scientific community [21]. Concerning environmental science education, several studies [9,11] highlight the critical role of lettuce in biomonitoring programs aimed at assessing soil contamination and its potential impact on human health. When integrated into citizen science frameworks, such programs not only generate valuable environmental data but also empower communities and students to engage directly with issues related to urban sustainability and public health.

Data education initiatives aim to improve data literacy and data skills within educational contexts, including data handling, data analysis, and the principles of data science. Although data literacy education is still in its early stages and is rarely integrated into school curricula [14,20], several teaching units using programming languages or software tools for data science have been developed in recent years. Examples include:

- Bootstrap: Data Science [16], a secondary-school curriculum based on Pyret, a Python-like educational language with optional static typing and native support for tabular and image data;
- IDS[5], a year-long high-school course using R for statistical computing;
- Berkeley Data8[6], an introductory Python-based course;
- A survey-based unit using the CODAP online tool[7] [5];
- School 21[8] and Tableau's official data literacy courses[9];
- An innovative curriculum where secondary school students learn about big data and its societal impact using real multivariate datasets [6].

A competency model for data literacy, along with an exemplary lesson sequence to foster these competences, is proposed in [7]. The potential of using authentic research data to support student data literacy is further explored in [10], demonstrating that data literacy develops through practicing quantitative reasoning and data science in the context of real-world data. These teaching units, the competency model, and the principle of engaging students with authentic data they collect themselves form the foundation of the BotBid data education proposal.

Related initiatives with different structures but similar goals include the GLOBE Project on earth observation[10] and the Open Case Studies (OCS)

[5] https://www.idsucla.org.
[6] http://data8.org.
[7] https://codap.concord.org.
[8] https://www.tableau.com/community/blog/2021/8/tableau-brings-data-literacy-classroom-school-21.
[9] https://www.tableau.com/it-it/learn/data-literacy.
[10] https://www.globe.gov/about/learn/program-overview.

project [19], which provides guides to real-world datasets to illustrate data analysis techniques. For soil monitoring projects not strictly focused on education, the Grow Observatory EU project is also noteworthy[11].

3 Project Structure and Management

BotBid is designed as a citizen science educational initiative tailored for schools. In this setting, citizen scientists—students and teachers—actively contribute to scientific research by collecting data, making observations, or performing other tasks defined by the project. Participants follow standardized protocols provided by scientists to ensure reliability and consistency of the data. Citizen science initiatives aim to make scientific research more accessible, allowing individuals without formal scientific training to contribute meaningfully. BotBid further incorporates an educational component, providing participants with opportunities to learn about the scientific method, data analysis, and the specific scientific focus of the project.

3.1 Timeline and Workflow

The general structure and timeline of the project are shown in Table 1. The initial phase focuses on forming a network of schools and classes through teacher contacts and online launch meetings. Once the network is established, a training phase follows, consisting of a series of online meetings to present the goals, principles, methods, and tools of the project. The training sessions include:

- **Methodology meeting:** Introduces best practices for designing a biomonitoring experiment according to the scientific method. Participants receive detailed guidelines from a domain expert on setting up a monitoring laboratory, consisting of thirty control plants and thirty plants subjected to salt stress. This setup allows multiple observations per repetition, providing robust data for statistical analysis. The domain expert also presents the hypothesis to be experimentally validated—in this case, evaluating plant responses to soil stress by measuring growth parameters such as leaf and root length and biomass over time.
- **Data acquisition meeting:** Covers the use of edge components for automating data collection and processing, with a focus on the biomonitoring case study. Participants learn how environmental sensors (e.g., pH meters) can be integrated within an Internet of Things (IoT) architecture to interconnect network nodes and support data acquisition through the IoT platform.
- **Data education meeting:** Introduces core concepts of data education, emphasizing data quality, preparation, visualization techniques, and tools for interpreting data once downloaded for local analysis.
- **Data analysis meeting:** Focuses on analyzing the collected data during and at the end of the experiment. Participants are introduced to data exploration tools and statistical tests to validate the experimental hypothesis.

[11] https://cordis.europa.eu/project/id/690199.

Table 1. Methodology and project schedule.

Phase	Goal	Contents	Timing
Network	Creation of the network of schools, classes and teachers	Call for participation Online launch of the project	October–November
	Methodology	Introduction to the scientific method; Biomonitoring best practices; Setup of the experiment	December
Training	Methods and digital tools for data acquisition	Introduction to edge components and IoT platforms with a focus on biomonitoring case-study (e.g., environmental sensors)	January
	Basics of data education	How to organize, prepare, and interpret data	February
	Main concepts of data analysis	How to validate the experiment hypothesis through statistical methods	March
Monitoring	Data collection	Use the BIoTdi platform to collect data: for 12 weeks, once a week	March–May
Restitution	Data analysis	Use of statistical analysis to validate the experimental hypothesis, compare data across different nodes, and identify correlations	June

In the third phase, participants collect data weekly for twelve weeks, corresponding to the typical growth period of the tested species (lettuce). Data collection is supported by the BotBid platform, which provides a WebApp where measurements can be entered for each monitored plant. To simplify the process, the WebApp creates a digital twin of the physical laboratory, allowing students and teachers to track each plant's growth digitally. The platform also supports automated data acquisition from BotBid edge devices.

The final phase focuses on presenting the experiment results using data visualization and statistical tools. The BotBid platform provides a self-service approach to business intelligence, enabling participants to explore and interpret the collective data.

3.2 The BotBid WebApp

Data from the various network nodes are aggregated in a shared dashboard through an IoT architecture comprising edge computing devices, a WebApp, and cloud services for data storage. The edge component consists of an Arduino R4 WiFi board, a multifunctional environmental sensor (temperature, humidity, light intensity, ultraviolet light), and a soil pH probe.

The BotBid WebApp[12] guides users throughout the experiment workflow. After registration and login, users can set up a digital twin of their smart school garden by specifying the experiment name, plant species, number of plants, group type (control/treatment), cultivation type (soil or pot), and experiment start date. Once set up, the workflow guides users through sequential sections:

1. Creating a digital twin that mirrors the physical arrangement of plants in the garden.
2. Entering observational data for each plant.
3. Monitoring progress through a dashboard once initial data are available.
4. Visualizing and analyzing experiment results at the conclusion of the monitoring phase.

Each plant can be positioned digitally to reflect the physical garden configuration. The WebApp also provides instructions and source code to configure the BotBid Arduino kit. Users can download the C code to program the controller to collect data from the sensors and send it to the Firebase cloud platform. Manual data entry is also supported via a dedicated form.

At every stage, data can be entered through a graphical card associated with each plant. The WebApp offers multiple visualization tools for monitoring each participant's experiment, including querying historical data by date range, plant ID, or value range. Weekly data are displayed using boxplots to identify potential outliers. Data can also be exported in various formats for further analysis using external tools.

4 The 2025 Edition

The 2025 edition of the BotBid project was launched together with the STACY Community on March 20, 2024[13]. The first online meeting with teachers took place on November 28, 2024, with 19 participating teachers: 9 from the first cycle (primary and lower secondary schools) and 10 from the second cycle (upper secondary schools) across six different schools from two Italian Regions, namely Liguria and Sardegna. Subsequently, we organized initial online meetings with all students[14] to introduce the project, the experiments, and the relevant scientific concepts.

[12] https://botbid.dibris.unige.it.

[13] https://www.raiseliguria.it/2024/03/14/raise-training-community-stacy/.

[14] Two separate meetings were held: one for high school students and one for first-cycle students.

Between January and March 2025, three additional online meetings with teachers were conducted to guide the setup of the physical experiment in school gardens. After these preparatory sessions, the ten registered schools began using the BotBid WebApp to collect growth data for the two groups of thirty plants. Four schools opted to integrate the Arduino kit for automated data acquisition. During the experiment, each participant had access to a private dashboard to monitor data for control and treated plants.

Preliminary analyses indicated that the assumption of normal data distribution was not valid, even when considering a single observation point. Therefore, to test the experimental hypothesis—comparing the growth of control and treated plants—we employed the non-parametric Mann–Whitney U-test. This test is appropriate for comparing differences between two independent groups when the dependent variable is ordinal or continuous. The BotBid WebApp applies the U-test to each batch of collected data, displaying the resulting Z-score, P-value, and an indication of whether the null hypothesis is accepted or rejected, allowing identification of trends and forecasting outcomes. The U-test results are also presented in tabular form for each data collection.

The experiment concluded at the end of May 2025. The hypothesis that control plants exhibit a higher growth rate was confirmed in all schools that followed the recommended monitoring protocol and instructions provided in the WebApp. After the experiment, collected data were analyzed and discussed in two closing meetings. The first, restricted to teachers, addressed methodological and technical challenges encountered during data collection, and used the visualization tools to compare experimental results across schools.

The WebApp also provides a comparative dashboard[15], which was used during student meetings to evaluate and discuss best practices adopted by different schools. Environmental data were validated against meteorological data from external sources to assess the impact of weather conditions on plant growth in the geographic areas of the participating schools.

In addition to the WebApp, Google Colab's Data Science Agent was employed to guide the creation of data analysis plans and reports from raw CSV datasets. These exercises proved valuable in providing a preliminary assessment of the potential role of generative AI tools in interdisciplinary educational projects such as BotBid. The second closing meeting involved students, where the results were discussed and interpreted collectively[16].

4.1 Data Literacy Topics and Competencies

Data literacy encompasses the fundamental skills of gathering, storing, processing, and visualizing data—skills considered essential for scientists today. In this context, data education can be seen as the structured process through which data literacy is acquired. BotBid adopts a learning-by-doing approach inspired

[15] https://botbid.dibris.unige.it/showExperiments.

[16] As in the initial meetings, two separate sessions were held for high school and first-cycle students.

by [10], which emphasizes that the strongest learning experiences occur when students work with authentic data from scientific research.

Students are not exposed to traditional lectures; instead, two interactive plenary meetings are organized for different school levels. During the kick-off meeting, students are introduced to essential data concepts via wooclap[17] polls, which prompt them to consider: what data are needed to address the research question, why replicates are necessary, how to aggregate measurements across replicates, how to compare growth between plant groups, and which visualizations are most appropriate. In the final closing meeting, each class discusses its findings, with results interpreted collectively using the WebApp visualizations.

Following the syllabus of the Bootstrap: Data Literacy curriculum [16] (and the corresponding Bootstrap: Data Science curriculum for younger students), the main topics include:

1. Introduction to data science, simple data types, and charts;
2. The data cycle, careful data collection, and handling of dirty datasets;
3. Measures of center, boxplots, and data spread;
4. Correlations;
5. Threats to validity.

According to the competency model proposed in [7], competencies are organized along two dimensions: (i) a *process area*, which includes practices reflecting how individuals interact with, handle, and process data; and (ii) a *content area*, which encompasses the theoretical background and underlying scientific concepts that must be understood.

The specific competencies exercised in BotBid (varying in depth depending on school level) are summarized in Table 2. Due to the nature of the data, content related to data ethics and protection is not covered, although topics on data storage and access may be introduced, particularly in high schools with computer science curricula.

Table 2. Data literacy competencies [7] promoted by BotBid.

	P1 Gathering, Modeling, and Cleaning	P3 Analyzing, Visualizing, and Interpreting
C1 – Data & Information	✓	✓
C3 – Data Analysis	✓	✓

Though we have no qualitative data on the learning effect via questionnaires, the quality of the discussions in the closing meeting and the content of the final reports produced by classes provide evidence that the educational goals concerning data literacy have been successfully met.

[17] https://www.wooclap.com/.

5 Open Badge for University Students

The digital credential issued through the RAISE Liguria training program, entitled "RAISE – Dalla Botanica ai Big Data: Data Education at Work"[18], is an Open Badge that certifies the acquisition of foundational competencies in data education within environmental and scientific contexts. The credential is awarded upon successful completion of an online asynchronous course and the passing of a final assessment[19]. The course introduces participants to the integration of botanical observation, environmental monitoring, and data-driven methodologies, with particular emphasis on data literacy, citizen science practices, and the use of digital tools for data collection, analysis, and interpretation. Through a combination of theoretical content and applied examples drawn from the BotBid project, learners develop skills related to the scientific method, basic data analytics, and the pedagogical use of data in educational and interdisciplinary settings. As an Open Badge, the credential provides verifiable and portable certification of learning outcomes, making the acquired competencies transparent and shareable across academic and professional contexts. Due to its interdisciplinary nature, the course is designed at a basic level and has no entry requirements. It consists of 8 h of asynchronous lessons, delivered by four authors of this paper, 17 h of independent study, and is worth 1 academic credit (CFU).

The course consists of four main parts: 1) an introduction to the design and implementation of a distributed biomonitoring experiment, 2) guidelines for acquiring experimental data (environmental and biomass), 3) best practices for sharing data via IoT platforms, 4) fundamental principles for analyzing experimental data.

Constructive learning approaches are applied through a web portal that provides H5P widgets for creating interactive exercises[20]. Assessment is conducted through a final multiple-choice test. Quality assurance of assessment validity is ensured by an examination committee composed of subject-matter experts. The Open Badge is endorsed by the Italian Institute of Technology (IIT)[21] and the National Research Council (CNR)[22]. As of February 2026, 13 examinations taken by university students from different disciplines have been recorded.

6 Conclusions and Future Work

The BotBid project effectively combines data and scientific education, technological innovation, and active participation. Through a citizen science approach, it involved students and teachers in all phases of scientific research, from hypothesis formulation to data collection and analysis. The modular structure of the project, supported by an advanced IoT infrastructure and an interactive Web

[18] https://app.myopenbadge.com/search/BotBID.
[19] https://corsi.unige.it/off.f/2023/ins/74255.
[20] https://h5p.org/content-types-and-applications.
[21] https://www.iit.it/.
[22] https://www.cnr.it/.

platform, allowed participants to engage in a hands-on research experience. The educational path emphasized active learning, promoting skills in science, technology, and statistics. Moreover, the creation of a "digital twin" of the school garden helped participants grasp the concept of digitizing physical environments. The results show how a well-designed platform can stimulate interest in science, encourage critical thinking, and enhance scientific literacy. BotBid has thus demonstrated the transformative potential of citizen science within school education.

Based on these characteristics, the project provides learning experiences aligned with the following DigCompEdu competence areas[23]: Digital Resources: 2.1–3; Teaching and Learning: 3.1–4; Assessment: 4.1–3; Empowering Learners: 5.1 and 5.3; Facilitating Learners' Digital Competence: 6.1–4.

Future developments of BotBid include expanding the network of participating schools at both national and international levels, fostering a growing community of "citizen scientists". From a technological standpoint, future improvements may involve the integration of new types of sensors and enhanced platform functionalities using artificial intelligence to detect patterns in the collected data. Educationally, the project aims to strengthen collaboration with teachers and researchers to co-design interdisciplinary lab experiences, where real data and digital tools become an integral part of the curriculum. Additionally, the analysis of aggregated data on a territorial scale could provide valuable insights for urban environmental monitoring, creating a tangible link between schools, scientific research, and civic engagement. Finally, the potential of the use of generative AI as a tool to enhance data education [4] will also be considered.

Acknowledgments. Funded by the European Union - NextGenerationEU and by the Ministry of University and Research (MUR), National Recovery and Resilience Plan (NRRP), Mission 4, Component 2, Investment 1.5, project "RAISE - Robotics and AI for Socio-economic Empowerment" (ECS00000035).

Disclosure of Interests. The authors declare that they have no conflict of interest.

References

1. Bonney, R., Phillips, T.B., Ballard, H.L., Enck, J.W.: Can citizen science enhance public understanding of science? Public Underst. Sci. **25**(1), 2–16 (2016)
2. Danyluk, A., Leidig, P., Cassel, L., Servin, C.: ACM task force on data science education: draft report and opportunity for feedback. In: Proceedings of the 50th ACM Technical Symposium on Computer Science Education, pp. 496–497 (2019)
3. Delzanno, G., et al.: BotBid - from botany to big data: combining citizen science and innovative teaching methodologies. In: Higher Education Learning Methodologies and Technologies Online (HELMeTO). CCIS, vol. 2076, pp. 112–127 (2023)
4. Ellis, A.R., Slade, E.: A new era of learning: considerations for ChatGPT as a tool to enhance statistics and data science education. J. Stat. Data Sci. Educ. **31**(2), 128–133 (2023)

[23] https://joint-research-centre.ec.europa.eu/digcompedu/digcompedu-framework_en.

5. Frischemeier, D., Biehler, R., Podworny, S., Budde, L.: A first introduction to data science education in secondary schools: teaching and learning about data exploration with CODAP using survey data. Teach. Stat. **43**(S1), S182-189 (2021)
6. Gil, E., Gibbs, A.L.: Introducing secondary school students to big data and its social impact: a study within an innovative learning environment. Promoting understanding of statistics about society. In: Proceedings of the Roundtable Conference of the International Association for Statistics Education (IASE) (2016)
7. Grillenberger, A., Romeike, R.: Developing a theoretically founded data literacy competency model. In: Proceedings of the 13th Workshop in Primary and Secondary Computing Education (Potsdam, Germany) (WiPSCE), pp. 1–10 (2018)
8. Guerrini, G., Traversaro, D.: Two introductory data-driven activities for secondary schools. In: Proceedings of the 31st Symposium of Advanced Database Systems, vol. 3478, pp. 641–664. CEUR Workshop Proceedings (2023) (2023)
9. Izquierdo-Díaz, M., Hansen, V., Barrio-Parra, F., De Miguel, E., You, Y., Magid, J.: Assessment of lettuces grown in urban areas for human consumption and as bioindicators of atmospheric pollution. Ecotoxicol. Environ. Saf. **256** (2023)
10. Kjelvik, M.K., Schultheis, E.H.: Getting messy with authentic data: Exploring the potential of using data from scientific research to support student data literacy. CBE—Life Sci. Educ. **18**(2), es2 (2019)
11. Kováts, N., Hubai, K., Sainnokhoi, T.A., et al.: Biomonitoring of polyaromatic hydrocarbon accumulation in rural gardens using lettuce plants. J. Soils Sediments **21**, 106–117 (2021)
12. Krishnamurthi, S., Fisler, K.: Data-centricity: a challenge and opportunity for computing education. Commun. ACM **63**, 24–26 (2020)
13. Lüsse, M., Brockhage, F., Beeken, M., Pietzner, V.: Citizen science and its potential for science education. Int. J. Sci. Educ. **44**(7), 1120–1142 (2022)
14. Mike, K., Ragonis, N., Rosenberg-Kima, R.B., Hazzan, O.: Computational thinking in the era of data science. Commun. ACM **65**(8), 33–35 (2022)
15. Monteiro, A., Torres, A.C., Clavero, S.B.: Digital technologies and school gardens: possibilities for transformative pedagogies and sustainable development. Issues Educ. Res. **34**(1), 123–144 (2024)
16. Schanzer, E., et al.: Integrated data science for secondary schools: design and assessment of a curriculum. In: Proceedings of the 53rd ACM Technical Symposium on Computer Science Education (SIGCSE), vol. 1 (2022)
17. Smith, P.S., Goforth, C.L., Carrier, S.J., Hayes, M.L., Safley, S.E.: An emerging theory of school-based participatory science. Citiz. Sci. Theory Pract. **10**(1), 1–10 (2025)
18. Tsivitanidou, O., Andri, I.: Citizen Science, K-12 science education and use of technology: a synthesis of empirical research. J. Sci. Commun. **19**(4), 1–22 (2020)
19. Wright, C., et al.: Open case studies: statistics and data science education through real-world applications. J. Stat. Data Sci. Educ. **32**(4), 331–344 (2024)
20. Van Audenhove, L., Van den Broeck, W., Mariën, I.: Data literacy and education: introduction and the challenges for our field. J. Media Lit. Educ. **12**(3), 1–5 (2020)
21. Zhang, E.Y., et al.: Learning by doing: a multi-level analysis of the impact of citizen science education. Sci. Educ. **107**(5), 1324–1351 (2023)

Learning *IN / WITH / ABOUT* Motion: The 3D-IWA Motion-for-Learning Model for Personalized Support Based on Human Motion Computing and its Application to Online Higher Education

Olga C. Santos(✉)

PhyUM Research Center, Artificial Intelligence Department Computer Science School, UNED, Madrid, Spain
ocsantos@dia.uned.es

Abstract. This paper provides insights into how online learning environments can be enriched with information about the movements learners perform, enabling motion-driven personalized support to improve the learning experience. To illustrate how learning can be informed by human motion computing based on artificial intelligence (AI) techniques, the 3D-IWA motion-for-learning model was conceptualized for the invited keynote talk at the HELMeTO 2025 conference. The model articulates three complementary dimensions and goes beyond treating motor skill acquisition as the sole focus of motion-driven learning: 1) learning ***in*** motion (learning while moving), 2) learning ***with*** motion (learning supported by motion as a pedagogical resource), and 3) learning ***about*** motion (learning the motion itself as a psychomotor skill). After presenting the model as a general framework applicable across educational contexts, this paper discusses its application to online higher education, examining how motion-driven guidance can be delivered within learning management systems through its inclusion in the course instructional design, addressing the challenge of moving from screen-based learning to motion-driven learning. By addressing learning *in*, *with* and *about* motion, the proposed model highlights how AI-based human motion computing can open new paths for personalization and engagement in online higher education, positioning learning management systems as integrators of motion-aware learning outcomes, linking motion capture through wearable sensors, image-based keypoint detection and immersive technologies with modeling and feedback.

Keywords: Artificial Intelligence · Motion-driven learning · Human motion computing · Psychomotor learning · Embodied learning · Learning in open spaces · Physically active learning · Online higher education · Personalized learning · Learning management systems

M. Adamoli et al. (Eds.): HELMeTO 2025, CCIS 2958, pp. 622–639, 2026.
https://doi.org/10.1007/978-3-032-31850-3_39

1 Introduction

Traditionally, personalized online learning environments such as intelligent tutoring systems have focused mainly on the cognitive aspects of learning, adapting course contents according to learning goals and student progress [1]. However, educational researchers such as Bloom (widely known for his taxonomy of learning objectives) already stressed that the psychomotor domain also needs to be considered in the learning process [2]. This domain deals with the acquisition of motor skills, such as performing surgery, speaking with sign language, playing a musical instrument, dancing, or practicing a sport technique. The learning objectives in this domain can also be classified into levels of complexity and specificity according to several taxonomies [3–7]. They all describe a progression from low-level performance (where the learner can hardly recognize the movement) to high-level performance (where the learner has internalized the movement).

In order to develop intelligent systems to learn motor skills, the **SMDD framework** has already been proposed [8]. This framework comprises four stages for human motion computing in educational scenarios using artificial intelligence (AI) techniques: 1) **Sensing** the learner's movement as specific motor skills are acquired, and the context in which this movement takes place; 2) **Modeling** the interactions to allow comparison of the learner's movement, for instance with the accurate movement (how an expert would perform it) or with previous executions of the same learner (to assess individual progression along time); 3) **Designing** the feedback to be provided (what kind of support, and when and how to provide it); and 4) **Delivering** the feedback in an effective, non-intrusive way that advises the learner on how to move to achieve the motor learning goal.

Following this research gap, in the past recent years, there have been several reviews that show an emerging research direction on developing intelligent psychomotor systems such as [9–13]. One interesting research direction within human motion computing in education -already introduced in [11]-, is to go beyond learning motor skills and explore the computing of motion for other learning purposes, such as: 1) embodied cognition (where sensorimotor experiences can affect and enhance the cognitive learning process, thus supporting the learning of cognitive skills through the learning of motor skills that have the cognitive skills implicit in their practice); 2) psychomotor learning in the open space (where learning activities require moving in open spaces, such as classrooms or fields), and 3) online psychomotor learning (where learners can practice the movements at home with system support and without continuous instructor supervision).

While many challenges still exist when learning is motion-driven, these challenges expand when motion-driven personalized support is considered within online higher education. Thus, this paper presents insights into how the future of online higher education can be shaped through human motion computing. In particular, this position paper, presented as an invited talk at the HELMeTO 2025 conference[1], introduces a conceptual model that articulates three complementary dimensions of motion in learning: learning *in* motion, learning *with* motion and learning *about* motion.

The contribution is grounded in an extensive body of prior research on human motion computing, psychomotor learning, embodied cognition, adaptive learning environments

[1] https://www.helmeto.it/2025-edition/program/keynotes/

and ethical AI in education, as well as in the research experience of the PhyUM (Physical User Modeling) research center at UNED, the Spanish national university for distance education. The model is called 3D-IWA (from IN, WITH, ABOUT). It is important to note that the three dimensions of the 3D-IWA model are not intended to be equally mature from a technological or empirical standpoint. While *learning-about-motion* is currently the most developed dimension due to the existence of established psychomotor systems, *learning-in-motion* and *learning-with-motion* are presented as emerging and underexplored dimensions that require further conceptualization and systematic research. The model is therefore proposed with conceptual balance rather than empirical symmetry and aims to ground future research on the possibilities of motion-driven learning. In addition, rather than introducing a new technical solution, the contribution of the 3D-IWA model lies in providing a unifying conceptual lens that makes explicit the different roles motion can play in learning and helps avoid reducing motion-driven learning to psychomotor skill acquisition alone.

The contents of the paper are structured as follows. First, some background on the interrelation of motion and learning from related works is presented. After that, the 3D-IWA motion-for-learning model is introduced and exemplified with research carried out in PhyUM. After that, its applicability for online higher education is discussed and finally some conclusions are outlined.

2 Background

There is growing recognition that human motion constitutes a critical yet underexplored dimension of the learning process. While traditional personalized online learning environments have primarily focused on cognitive and, to some extent, affective aspects of learning, the use of motion data to inform learning processes remains limited.

The idea of personalizing education to meet different learner needs goes back to the 60 s [14]. Soon after, AI was explored to deliver customized instruction [15], planting the seed of adaptive learning. Nowadays, see for instance [16], adaptive online learning environments are usually described in terms of the following components: i) the adaptive source ("to what will it be adapted"), consisting in the **learner model** (i.e., what a student knows and does, including affective, behavioral and cognitive characteristics) and ii) the adaptive target ("what will be adapted"), consisting in the content/domain/ **expert model** (the course knowledge base) and the instructional/pedagogical/**adaptation model** (the algorithm that assists in adapting the instruction based on the expert and learner model, and defines what, when and how adaptation can occur). The latter requires an adaptive engine that implements AI techniques and combines the three aforementioned models to identify and deliver the appropriate personalized instruction. Although none of the 61 systems reviewed by [16] considered motion in the learning process, more recent reviews [9–13], as mentioned in the introduction, have identified a small but growing set of psychomotor systems that leverage motion data for personalization. This shows an emergent line of work where **further exploration is needed to extend adaptive learning environments with motion data**, enriching the learner and expert model and informing the adaptation model.

Moreover, in the context of intelligent systems for movement-based learning, it is also crucial to consider the ethical challenges inherent to any kind of education based on AI. Reviews highlight the need for privacy, fairness, accountability, transparency and attention to bias in data and algorithms to avoid discrimination and to build trust [37]. The principle of human-in-the-loop is also increasingly proposed to keep meaningful human control and oversight in adaptive systems, combining human judgment with machine inference [38]. In parallel, explainable AI is necessary so that decisions made by the system can be understood and trusted by teachers and learners [39]. These challenges are also evident in human motion computing and **require embedding human-centered principles in the design of motion computing systems**, to ensure that the solutions developed for movement-enhanced learning are ethically robust and trustworthy.

Recent advances in human motion computing offer opportunities to capture, model and interpret movement. Beyond traditional wearables and motion capture systems [17], deep learning now enables motion modeling from video and images through keypoint extraction and pose estimation [18]. Human activity recognition has matured, and while much of the field has focused on classifying which activity is being performed [19], new approaches are beginning to address how well motion is performed, a crucial step toward skill assessment and personalized feedback [20]. In this sense, [21] reviewed 88 papers on motion assessment with machine learning in healthcare, sports and wellness, but none considered the educational perspective. A more recent review of 45 systems based on deep learning algorithms for human pose estimation [22] also did not include education, although it examined assessment methods (identifying mathematical formulae and rule-based approaches, in addition to machine learning models) and user feedback to improve motor skills. Importantly, that review highlighted the lack of standardization in feedback description in terms of content, format and timing, which limits replication, comparison and knowledge building in motor skills learning. It also found that feedback was usually presented visually and concluded that further studies about feedback are still needed, especially regarding feedback prioritization and erroneous feedback. Thus, **an education-aware computational framework is needed to generate adaptive feedback driven by progressing in motor skills acquisition,** which requires that motion information of the users' interactions is stored in the corresponding models.

Some recent works in physical education can provide useful insights regarding how to approach human motion computing with an educational perspective. For example, some of these works explore training methods to ensure correct exercise execution without physical supervision [23] or propose quantitative and qualitative motion assessment models that can provide educators with practical guidance to design feedback for their students [24]. At the same time, they highlight the need for advanced technologies such as activity monitors, videography, virtual reality (VR) or augmented reality (AR), exergames, online platforms, social media [25] and clear methodological frameworks regarding data security and technological sustainability [26]. The COVID-19 pandemic further accelerated the adoption of AI-driven tools in physical education, showing the potential of virtual environments and remote monitoring systems to sustain educational continuity and enabling personalized learning, although the integration of AI in university physical education is still emerging and requires researching on how to address the practical concerns that arise [27]. Similarly, [28] suggest that video feedback can enhance motor skill learning in online physical education, but optimal guidance strategies must still be identified. Building on these insights, **future work needs to explore**

how AI-based innovations in physical education could be deployed in online settings using advanced technologies, ensuring that motion data and feedback become part of online learning environments capable of supporting diverse learning contexts.

Although motion-enhanced learning has mainly focused on developing intelligent psychomotor systems to support the acquisition of motor skills, other strands of research suggest that motion can enrich learning in higher education in additional ways. On the one hand, the integration of active breaks (i.e., short intervals of physical activity during learning) has been shown to improve students' attention, mood and stress management, especially around high cognitive load situations, and even at university level [29]. In addition, a systematic review on classroom movement breaks and physically active learning concluded that these interventions increase focus and attention, and do not harm academic performance, encouraging their adoption in higher education [30], although there is still a need to research how technology can be used to provide support for these motion interventions [31]. On the other hand, the theory of embodied cognition [32] emphasizes the role of the body in cognitive processes, arguing that neural systems controlling the body are central to the cognitive functions. In particular, object manipulation, bodily interaction and spatial exploration can shape abstract thinking [33]. However, [34] have detected that existing AI-based educational systems overlook the essential role of movement and physical engagement in concept formation, and potentially undermine motivation, attention and deep understanding. To illustrate the potential of combining embodied cognition and technology, [35] have explored how theatre-based bodily training combined with online tools enhance the sensory perception. In turn, [36] have also explored immersive environments and highlighted the need of integrating physical and virtual dimensions to produce meaningful immersive environments capable of ensuring attention, motivation and active participation. From the perspective of adaptive learning environments, these embodied approaches are particularly relevant because motion-related information can be modeled as learner features (e.g., engagement through movement, motor fluency, spatial interaction patterns) that inform personalization decisions regarding pacing, feedback modality, instructional sequencing and task design. Thus, it is worth **exploring how to incorporate these motion perspectives when extending adaptive online learning environments for enriched motion-based personalized support**, going beyond personalized systems focused only on the acquisition of motor skills.

Finally, challenges exist not only in computing human motion to support diverse motion-driven educational approaches, but also in embedding them within online higher education. Learning management systems such as Moodle have become de facto platforms for managing teaching and learning processes in higher education. These systems provide robust support for instructional design, assessment and orchestration at scale, enabling instructors to design, deploy and manage learning activities addressing cognitive issues [40, 41], but they do not provide support for activities where motion is involved. Thus, there is a need to **ensure that the diverse types of motion data can be integrated into learning management systems** (i.e., the online learning platforms used in universities) and embedded in the course workflow defined in the instructional design.

Therefore, this vision paper proposes to generate new theoretical insights into the integration of motion into adaptive online learning environments, emphasizing how physical activity can reinforce learning processes while addressing the specific challenges of remote contexts. Figure 1 presents a visual overview of how the three main aspects involved (AI in education, human motion computing and physical education) can intersect to support the development of the 3D-IWA model proposed, which is described in detail in the next section, and also expands its applicability in the online higher education context.

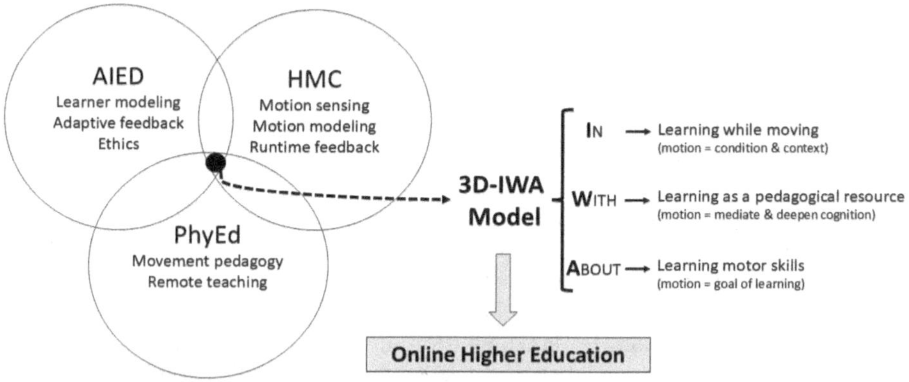

Fig. 1. The 3D-IWA model emerges from the intersection of Artificial Intelligence in Education (AIED), Human Motion Computing (HCM) and Physical Education (PhyEd) as a general motion-for-learning framework that can be instantiated in different educational contexts, including online higher education.

Figure 1 does not merely illustrate a thematic overlap between research areas, but highlights the need for an integrative model capable of translating advances in human motion computing and physical education into adaptive, motion-aware learning support in online higher education. The rationale behind is to foster online higher education to support learning activities involving physical movement, rather than remaining limited to cognitive tasks. And this should be done in a personalized way, so that adapted motion-aware learning support is provided to each learner. In this sense, research needs to move forward shaping a new line of research that integrates AI-based human motion computing into adaptive learning environments that expand the scope of current online education. As a result, human motion should not be seen only as support for psychomotor skills acquisition but also as a driver of other motion-based learning processes, such as embodied cognition and physically active learning in the open space. Crucially, this requires embedding motion data and feedback into adaptive online learning environments, ensuring that SMDD stages of motion sensing and modeling and feedback design and delivery, are integrated into the course instructional design. This will contribute to a deeper understanding of the interplay between movement and learning, advance knowledge on how motion can be effectively computed, and lay the foundations for a new generation of adaptive online learning environments in which motion becomes a central component of personalization.

3 The 3D-IWA Motion-for-Learning Model

The 3D-IWA motion-for-learning model (from IN, WITH, ABOUT) is a conceptual model that has been defined to understand the different ways in which motion can influence learning processes and guide the development of AI-based human computing approaches to support personalized motion-driven learning. It is articulated around three complementary dimensions: 1) learning-*in*-motion, that is, learning while physically moving; 2) learning-*with*-motion, that is, using motion as a pedagogical resource for learning, and 3) learning-*about*-motion, that is, learning the motion itself as a psychomotor skill. These three dimensions are described next, followed by illustrative examples drawn from research conducted at the PhyUM research center.

- **Learning IN Motion.** In this dimension, motion is not the learning goal itself, but motion is a condition and context under which learning takes place. This learning happens while physically moving, for instance by walking, exercising or taking active breaks. According to neuroscience, physical activity can stimulate the brain, creating an active bodily state that can enhance cognitive processes such as attention, memory, engagement and creativity, as well as contribute to mental well-being. This dimension also includes learning situations where learners must think and act while moving through space, reinforcing situational awareness.
- **Learning WITH motion.** In this dimension, motion is neither the goal itself, but a pedagogical resource to mediate and deepen cognition. This learning uses motion to anchor learning through physical experience and active learning methodologies. This includes embodied learning approaches where physical actions (such as gestures or bodily postures) are used to reinforce abstract knowledge. This dimension also encompasses learning by constructing and manipulating physical objects (e.g., building devices) as a way to ground and internalize conceptual understanding. It can also focus on analyzing motion patterns that can be used in data science courses. While movement plays a central mediating role, the quality of the motion itself is not the target of assessment.
- **Learning ABOUT motion.** In this dimension, motion is the goal of learning. This learning focuses on the acquisition, refinement and assessment of psychomotor skills, involving the execution, coordination and control of bodily movements in real or simulated environments. Beyond performing movements accurately and efficiently, this dimension also emphasizes the development of body awareness and spatial orientation. Here, motion quality is explicitly modeled, assessed and used to provide personalized feedback.

The dimension *learning-in-motion* can be seen as the most disruptive and innovative from the perspective of computing human motion, as research in this field has hardly explored the modeling of the motion from the data collected in the activities involved.

At the PhyUM research center, this dimension has been explored in collaboration with other researchers through the analysis of a dataset collected from undergraduate Nursing and Midwifery students at the University of Technology Sydney, capturing their movements while interacting with patients during emergency room training simulations [42]. The learning activity consisted in training future nurses how to treat the patients in that situation. However, we focused mainly on the physiological data in relation to the displacement in the room rather than on understanding motion patterns within the learning activity [43]. In any case, motion was not treated as a skill to be learned or assessed, but as contextual information accompanying the learning activity, which aligns with the *learning-in-motion* dimension.

From an educational perspective, *learning-with-motion* is intuitive as often learners and teachers use gestures to reinforce abstract concepts or define activities involving the building of physical objects to understand theory, using the physical experience of performing the movements to learn from them. At PhyUM we have explored this dimension with the system Phy + Aik [44], where we used body movements when performing some techniques from Aikido martial arts to reinforce some concepts of Physics, such as the angular momentum [45]. Here, the movements themselves are not evaluated as motor skills, but intentionally used as embodied representations to support conceptual understanding.

Finally, *learning-about-motion* is the most technically developed dimension, existing diverse psychomotor systems to support the acquisition of motor skills in diverse domains, as the reviews mentioned in the introduction [9–13] can show. In fact, at PhyUM we have already implemented several intelligent psychomotor systems for martial arts learning. Martial arts have been chosen as a key research domain in PhyUM for the particularities and opportunities for human motion computing that this application domain can offer for computing the progress in the acquisition of motor skills [46].

Thus, the following martial arts psychomotor systems, developed in the context of research activities involving the PhyUM research center, serve as representative examples of the *learning-about-motion* dimension, which focuses on psychomotor skill acquisition and is currently the most technically mature dimension within the 3D-IWA model:

- *KSAS*, a mobile application to learn the first blocking set of American Kenpo Karate with multimodal feedback (vibration, sound and visual explanations) from data gathered with the inertial sensors of the mobile [47].
- *KLS*, a virtual reality environment to also learn the first blocking set of American Kenpo Karate, which in addition takes into account affective and cognitive outcomes and delivers personalized immersive feedback using the keypoint information collected with an external synchronized camera [48].
- *KUMITRON*, a multimodal system combining information from synchronized sensors and cameras to support the practice of Karate combats [49], delivering feedback to both learners simultaneously [50].
- *MITAICHI*, a VR environment to learn Tai Chi movements guiding the learner with multimodal feedback, combining visual information in the immersive environment and haptic feedback offered through hand controllers, which also serve as motion sensing devices [51].

In addition, developments have also been carried out at PhyUM to support psychomotor learning beyond martial arts. In this context, we have explored motion-aware approaches to basketball skill development through the initial design and exploratory pilots of the psychomotor system *iBAID* (intelligent Basketball AID) [52], focusing on specific exercises: free-throw practice supported by a wrist-worn sensor with haptic feedback [53], and displacement drills monitored through keypoint extraction from video recordings, enabling post-hoc reflection (e.g., via dashboards integrated into the learning environment, as discussed in the next section) [54]. Furthermore, a computer-vision-based system called *myWORKOUT* has been developed to support movement learning in gym exercises, relying on keypoint analysis to deliver multisensorial feedback through visual and auditory cues [55].

These system-level developments have been accompanied by the formulation of broader conceptual and methodological frameworks within the *learning-about-motion* dimension, extending beyond SMDD:

- *iELA*, a feature modeling approach based on signal processing and coordinates transformations to model learners' expertise levels during the acquisition of psychomotor skills using data obtained from inertial sensors, which has been applied to classify the expertise level in the practice of the Aikido martial art [56].
- *MoRTE-Laban*, an ontology-based framework that allows semantic descriptions of motion data and also supports inverse mapping [57].
- *mCMARR* and *PsyLearn* frameworks to develop intelligent systems for psychomotor learning [48].
- *CARAIX* to develop human centric psychomotor systems that comply with the hybrid intelligence paradigm so that the personalized support delivered by the system is ethically responsible [58] following the need to define ethical frameworks for intelligent educational systems suggested previously [59].

While the *learning-about-motion* dimension is well established in terms of system development, the 3D-IWA model explicitly situates it alongside *learning-in-motion* and *learning-with-motion*, rather than treating psychomotor learning as the sole focus of motion-driven learning.

4 Human Motion Computing and Online Higher Education

Traditionally, learning in higher education focuses on cognitive processes: learners remain physically stationary, sitting at their desks, listening to the teachers in the classroom, and then, at home or in the library, they memorize the contents and do written exercises to learn them in practice. Internet and mobile devices facilitate online learning and make it possible to move the study place anywhere; they can also remove time limitations, supporting learning at any time by delivering educational material in an asynchronous manner. For this, learning management systems are usually used to join in a virtual space (i) the educational support provided by the instructors and (ii) the learning experience carried out by the learners. When doing this digital transformation, online education has kept the focus on cognitive processes. However, we have seen that movement can be a driver for learning. However, integrating physical activities in online higher education can be even more challenging than in traditional higher education, as **motion has a physical component that needs to be accommodated in a virtual learning context**.

Today, most online higher education is still built around content delivery, quizzes, and discussion in forums that take place in learning management systems, and when available, the synchronous online part is provided through videoconference systems.

While these tools are valuable, they often reduce learning to something purely cognitive, mediated through a screen, and forget that learners are not just minds in front of screens, but bodies in motion.

So, the research question that can be posed in this context is:

"How can online higher education pedagogically integrate motion-driven learning in order to inform the design of personalized support within adaptive online learning environments?"

To answer this question, let us first consider the four phases that can be identified to deliver adaptive online instruction [60]. According to the **e-learning lifecycle**, first in the **design phase**, educators have to design the course with contents, activities, services and plan their usage by the learners (considering their individual characteristics and progress in the course) to achieve the educational goals. Then, in the **publication phase** these resources and the planning have to be deployed in the learning management system together with the learners' enrollment in the course, so that learners can access them and carry out the proposed activities during the **use phase**. Afterwards, in the **auditing phase**, the execution of the course is analyzed to improve the course design, so that the cycle can start again for the next edition of the course.

To integrate motion into online higher education within an adaptive online learning environment, the dimensions of the 3D-IWA model need to be addressed within the SMDD framework for AI-based human motion computing, in the context of the e-learning lifecycle, as depicted in Fig. 2. As shown, the 3D-IWA model can be deployed within the SMDD framework during the use phase to provide motion-aware support at runtime. This focus on the use phase is intentional, as it is during this phase that motion data can be sensed, modeled and acted upon in real time.

Nevertheless, the integration of motion-aware activities also has implications for the design phase, where instructional decisions must anticipate motion-based tasks. In addition, the publication phase plays a critical mediating role, as it is at this stage that courses designed to support motion-driven learning are instantiated within the learning management system and learners are enrolled, enabling subsequent runtime interaction and motion-aware support during the use phase. Decisions made during publication, such as the configuration of tools, permissions and integrations with external sensing technologies, directly condition the extent to which motion-driven learning can be supported at runtime. Finally, the auditing phase allows motion data to support reflective course improvement. It is important to note that traditional learning management systems do not natively support the sensing, modeling and interpretation of learners' physical motion. In the context of this work, the integration illustrated in Fig. 2 assumes an extension of existing learning management systems with motion data acquisition and adaptive capabilities. Such an extension gives rise to adaptive online learning environments, in which human motion computing can be leveraged at runtime to support motion-driven personalization, while still relying on learning management systems as the backbone to instantiate instructional design and support course delivery and auditing.

In the MOODTION project we are currently exploring this integration using an authoring tool called LA-ReflecT [61] that allows to create learning tasks that can use external data collected from sensors into learning management systems using the IMS

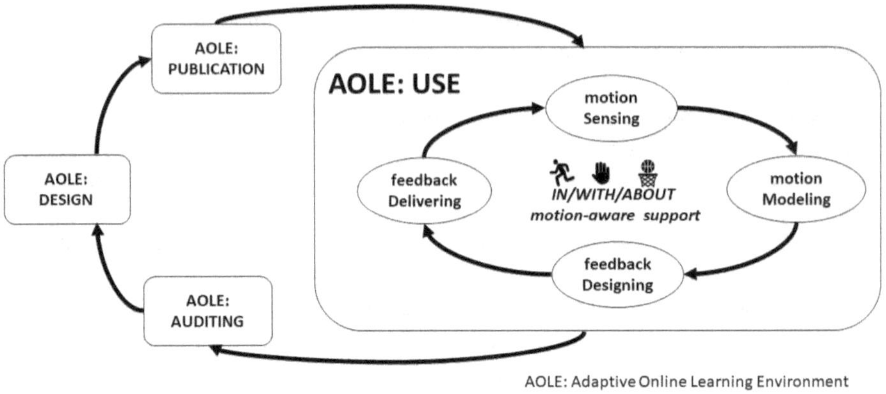

Fig. 2. Integration of the SMDD framework [8] and the three dimensions of the 3D-IWA motion-for-learning model within the use phase of the e-learning lifecycle [60]. This integration assumes learning management systems extended with motion sensing, modeling and adaptive capabilities, resulting in adaptive online learning environments that support motion-driven personalization, with implications for course design, publication and auditing.

Learning Tool Interoperability specification[2]. This information is passed into the learning design of the course and can be used to deliver feedback in the dashboard of the course space. A prototype integrating KLS psychomotor system in Moodle learning management system has already been developed as proof of concept that implements body-tracking feedback in an immersive virtual environment [62]. In a similar way, other motion-based interactions such as the reflection on the drill practice suggested in [54] can be deployed in an online context, illustrating how online platforms can move beyond sole cognitive learning.

In order to provide some insights that can contribute to answer the research question posed, Table 1 suggests several motion-based learning activities framed within the 3D-IWA motion-for-learning model dimensions that can be deployed in diverse online higher education scenarios.

Following the MOODTION approach for online higher education, learning activities addressing the different dimensions of the 3D-IWA model can be incorporated into course learning design and deployed through a learning management system extended with motion sensing and adaptive capabilities. As an illustration, three representative examples per dimension are presented next.

Regarding *learning-in-motion*, course design can include activities that support attention, creativity and engagement while studying at a distance, by encouraging learners to move as part of the learning context. Examples include:

- **Active breaks:** the integration of short guided physical activities (e.g., stretching, breathing, or walking) into long online sessions to help maintain attention and improve retention.

[2] https://www.imsglobal.org/spec/lti/v1p3

Table 1. Suggestions of motion-based-activities for online higher education following the dimensions defined by the 3D-IWA motion-for-learning model.

Dimension of the 3D-IWA motion-for-learning model	Description of the dimension of the 3D-IWA model	Suggestions for online higher education
Learning **IN** Motion: condition for learning	Learning occurs while physically moving, creating an active state where motion itself can enhance cognition, creativity, engagement, attention, memory and mental well-being. It also includes learning situations where learners must think and act while moving through space, reinforcing situational awareness. In this dimension, movement is not modeled or assessed as a skill but provides the bodily context in which learning activities take place.	Design courses that include active breaks, mindful movement by walking and listening, or online collaborative discussion walking tasks, helping students stay focused, creative and engaged while studying at a distance.
Learning **WITH** Motion: support for learning	Motion is used as a pedagogical resource to support understanding of other concepts. This includes embodied learning and constructing physical objects as a way to ground and internalize conceptual understanding. Motion is not the learning goal itself, but rather a means to mediate and deepen cognition. Although motion plays a central mediating role, the quality of the movement itself is not the learning objective nor the focus of assessment.	Design course activities that involve embodied learning applied through gesture-based video explanations, maker projects at home, or analysis of motion data as a means to learn and apply analytical techniques, where the body becomes a resource to anchor and deepen abstract learning while studying at a distance.
Learning **ABOUT** Motion: goal of learning	Learning focuses on the acquisition and improvement of psychomotor skills. This involves not only executing precise movements, but also coordinating body positioning and spatial orientation in real or simulated environments. Technology plays a central role for motion modeling and personalized runtime psychomotor guidance. This dimension explicitly focuses on psychomotor skill acquisition and assessment.	Design course activities that allow students record and share skill demonstrations, practice in VR/AR labs, or use wearables for feedback, focusing on developing and refining psychomotor and spatial competencies while studying at a distance.

- **Mindful walking and listening activities:** podcasts or micro-lectures designed for mobile use, which students listen to individually while walking, supporting creativity and focus during theoretical learning.
- **Online collaborative walking discussions:** activities in which learners walk individually while participating in synchronous audio-based discussions (indoors or outdoors), and later consolidate their reflections through a shared document submitted in the course space.

With respect to *learning-with-motion*, course design can include activities in which the body is intentionally used as a pedagogical resource to anchor and deepen abstract learning while studying at a distance. Examples include:

- **Embodied explanations:** students create short video recordings using gestures or whole-body movements to explain abstract concepts (e.g., illustrating physics formulas through martial arts–inspired movements), reinforcing conceptual understanding through embodied representation.
- **Maker projects and remote labs:** learners work individually or in teams to build physical artifacts or conduct experiments, either at home or through remote laboratories, documenting and discussing the process collaboratively to better understand the underlying theoretical principles.
- **Motion-data assignments:** students analyze motion-related datasets (e.g., wrist acceleration during basketball free throws) as a means to apply analytical or computational techniques studied in the course, with motion serving as input data rather than as a skill to be learned.

Finally, in *learning-about-motion*, course design can include activities that focus on the development, refinement and assessment of psychomotor and spatial competencies while studying at a distance. Examples include:

- **Skill demonstration videos:** students in domains such as nursing, sports, or music record themselves performing a technique, and receive peer or instructor feedback supported by structured rubrics.
- **VR/AR-based practice:** learners practice psychomotor tasks (e.g., medical procedures or engineering simulations) in immersive environments integrated into the learning management system, allowing repeated practice and guided feedback.
- **Motion-based assessment:** motion capture technologies, such as wearable sensors or computer vision techniques, are used to track movement performance (e.g., posture, gestures, or skill execution), enabling learning management system plugins to provide personalized feedback on accuracy, coordination, positioning, and progress.

In this way, motion-driven guidance can be effectively delivered in online learning environments by embedding motion-based learning activities into course instructional design following the dimensions of the 3D-IWA model.

5 Conclusions

By addressing learning *in*, *with* and *about* motion, AI-based human motion computing opens new paths for personalization and engagement across educational contexts. In this paper, these opportunities are discussed in the specific context of online higher education, where learning management systems can be envisioned as integrators of motion-aware learning outcomes, addressing the challenge of moving from screen-based learning to motion-driven learning.

As the examples presented in this paper illustrate, motion can be integrated into online higher education through familiar digital tools such as audio conferencing systems, video recordings, mobile devices, sensors, cameras and immersive technologies, going far beyond reading PDFs or participating in forums. In this way, learners can move, build, practice and improve motor skills even in virtual learning environments, provided that instructors design online courses that explicitly incorporate learning activities involving physical movement.

This shift implies a paradigm change: moving from viewing learners as minds in front of screens to understanding them as bodies whose movements can meaningfully contribute to learning. The 3D-IWA model constitutes a conceptual framework grounded in prior research carried out at the PhyUM research center. Further large-scale empirical studies are needed to validate its applicability and impact across diverse educational scenarios.

Acknowledgements. The MOODTION project has received funding from the UNED Vice-Rectorate for Educational Innovation within the Teaching Innovation Projects program for the academic years 2024–2025 and 2025–2026.

Disclosure of Interests. The author has no competing interests to declare that are relevant to the content of this article.

References

1. Rismanchian, S., Doroudi, S.: The evolution of research on AI and education across four decades: insights from the AIxEd framework. Int. J. Artif. Intell. Educ. (2025). https://doi.org/10.1007/s40593-025-00483-9
2. Bloom, B.S., Engelhart, M.D., Furst, E.J., Hill, W.H., Krathwohl, D.R.: Taxonomy of Educational Objectives: the Classification of Educational Goals. Cognitive Domain. David McKay Co., New York, Handbook I (1956)
3. Dave, R.: Psychomotor levels. In: Armstrong, R.J. (ed.) Developing and Writing Behavioral Objectives. Educational Innovators Press, Tucson, AZ (1970)
4. Harrow, A.J.: A Taxonomy of the Psychomotor Domain. David McKay Co., New York (1972)
5. Simpson, E.J.: The Classification of Educational Objectives in the Psychomotor Domain. Gryphon House, Washington, DC (1972)
6. Thomas, K.: Learning Taxonomies in the Cognitive, Affective, and Psychomotor Domain (2004). http://www.rockymountainalchemy.com/whitePapers/rma-wp-learning-taxonomies.pdf
7. Ferris, T.L.J., Aziz, S.M.: A psychomotor skills extension to Bloom's taxonomy of educational objectives for engineering education. In: Proceedings of iCEER: Exploring Innovation in Education and Research (2005) http://slo.sbcc.edu/wp-content/uploads/bloom-psychomotor.pdf
8. Santos, O.C.: Training the body: the potential of AIED to support personalized motor skills learning. Int. J. Artif. Intell. Educ. **26**(2), 730–755 (2016). https://doi.org/10.1007/s40593-016-0103-2

9. Santos, O.C.: Artificial intelligence in psychomotor learning: modeling human motion from inertial sensor data. Int. J. Artif. Intell. Tools. **28**(4), 1940006 (2019). https://doi.org/10.1142/S0218213019400062
10. Neagu, L.M., Rigaud, E., Travadel, S., Dascalu, M., Rughinis, R.V.: Intelligent tutoring systems for psychomotor training – a systematic literature review. In: Kumar, V., Troussas, C. (eds.) Intelligent Tutoring Systems. ITS 2020. LNCS, vol. 12149. Springer, Cham (2020)
11. Casas-Ortiz, A., Echeverria, J., Santos, O.C.: Intelligent systems for psychomotor learning: a systematic review and two cases of study. In: du Boulay, B., Mitrovic, A., Yacef, J. (eds.) Handbook of Artificial Intelligence in Education, chap. 18. Edward Elgar Publishing (2023). https://doi.org/10.4337/9781800375413.00030
12. Romano, G., Schneider, J., Di Mitri, D., Drachsler, H.: Through the telescope: a systematic review of intelligent tutoring systems and their applications in psychomotor skill learning. Int. J. Artif. Intell. Educ. **35**, 2756–2796 (2025)
13. Casas-Ortiz, A., Portaz, M., Echeverria, J., Santos, O.C.: Intelligent systems for psychomotor learning: an updated systematic review and the role of generative AI. In: du Boulay, B., Mitrovic, A., Yacef, J. (eds.) Handbook of Artificial Intelligence in Education. Edward Elgar Publishing, in preparation (2027)
14. Epstein, S., Epstein, B.: The First Book of Teaching Machines. Franklin Watts, Danbury (1961)
15. Carbonell, J.R.: AI in CAI: an artificial intelligence approach to computer aided instruction. IEEE Trans. Man-Mach. Syst. **11**(4), 190–202 (1970)
16. Martin, F., Chen, Y., Moore, R.L.M., Westine, C.D.: Systematic review of adaptive learning research designs, context, strategies, and technologies from 2009 to 2018. Educ. Technol. Res. Dev. **68**, 1903–1929 (2020)
17. Lara, O.D., Labrador, M.A.: A survey on human activity recognition using wearable sensors. IEEE Commun Surv Tutor. **15**(3), 1192–1209 (2013)
18. Gao, Z., Chen, J., Liu, Y., et al.: A systematic survey on human pose estimation: upstream and downstream tasks, approaches, lightweight models, and prospects. Artif. Intell. Rev. **58**, 68 (2025)
19. Kumar, P., Chauhan, S., Awasthi, L.K.: Human activity recognition (HAR) using deep learning: review, methodologies, progress and future research directions. Arch. Comput. Methods Eng. **31**, 179–219 (2024)
20. Khan, A., et al.: Generalized and efficient skill assessment from IMU data with applications in gymnastics and medical training. ACM trans. Comput. Healthc. **2**(1), 2 (2021)
21. Frangoudes, F., Matsangidou, M., Schiza, E.C., Neokleous, K., Pattichis, C.S.: Assessing human motion during exercise using machine learning: a literature review. IEEE Access **10**, 86874–86903 (2022)
22. Tharatipyakula, A., Srikaewsiew, T., Pongnumkul, S.: Deep learning-based human body pose estimation in providing feedback for physical movement: a review. Heliyon **10**(17), e36589 (2024)
23. Nurlan, O., et al.: Deep learning enabled exercise monitoring system for sustainable online education of future teacher-trainers. Front. Educ. **9**, 1385205 (2024). https://doi.org/10.3389/feduc.2024.1385205
24. Liang, H., Liang, H.: Deep learning based multi-attribute evaluation for holistic student assessment in physical education. Sci. Rep. **15**, 17698 (2025)
25. Krause, J.M., Franks, H., Lynch, B.: Current technology trends and issues among health and physical education professionals. Phys. Educ. **74**(1), 164–185 (2017)
26. Jastrow, F., Greve, S., Thumel, M., Diekhoff, H., Süßenbach, J.: Digital technology in physical education: a systematic review of research from 2009 to 2020. Ger. J. Exerc. Sport Res. **52**(4), 504–528 (2022)

27. Guerriero, M., et al.: Artificial intelligence and machine learning in physical education and sports. In: Book of Abstracts of the 7th International Conference on Higher Education Learning Methodologies and Technologies Online (HELMeTO 2025), pp. 260–262. STUDIUM s.r.l. (2025)
28. Adams, A., Belcher, D., Jenkins, A., Goad, T.: Utilizing video feedback for effective motor skill learning in online physical education. Int. J. Kinesiol. High. Educ. **9**(1), 14–30 (2024)
29. Sorrentino, C.: Moving breaks: perceptions of the effectiveness of active breaks in university teaching. In: Book of Abstracts of the 7th International Conference on Higher Education Learning Methodologies and Technologies Online (HELMeTO 2025), pp. 153–155. STUDIUM s.r.l. (2025)
30. Lynch, J., O'Donoghue, G., Peiris, C.L.: Classroom movement breaks and physically active learning are feasible, reduce sedentary behaviour and fatigue, and may increase focus in university students: a systematic review and meta-analysis. Int. J. Environ. Res. Public Health **19**, 7775 (2022)
31. Gulbay, E., La Marca, A., De Franches, G.R., Mercer, S.O.: Innovative approaches in teacher education: active breaks and technology integration. In: Proceedings of the 6th International Conference on Higher Education Learning Methodologies and Technologies Online (HELMeTO 2024), pp. 76–87. Springer Nature Switzerland, Cham (2024)
32. Fincher-Kiefer, R.: An introduction to the theory of embodied cognition. In: Fincher-Kiefer, R. How the Body Shapes Knowledge: Empirical Support for Embodied Cognition, pp. 3–12. American Psychological Association (2019). https://doi.org/10.1037/0000136-001
33. Barsalou, L.W.: Grounded cognition. Annu. Rev. Psychol. **59**, 617–645 (2008)
34. Lavazza, A., D'Ascenzo, A., Sasanelli, L.D., Di Fuccio, R.: Embodied cognition, adaptive AI and universal design for learning: towards hybrid educational models for inclusive learning. In: Book of Abstracts of the 7th International Conference on Higher Education Learning Methodologies and Technologies Online (HELMeTO 2025), pp. 257–259. STUDIUM s.r.l. (2025)
35. Carlomagno, N., Vadalá, V., Ricciardi, A.: Connected bodies: theatre and digital technologies in the training of future teachers. In: Book of Abstracts of the 7th International Conference on Higher Education Learning Methodologies and Technologies Online (HELMeTO 2025), pp. 193–195. STUDIUM s.r.l. (2025)
36. Marchesano, M.V., Pallonetto, L., Minghelli, V., Ingino, M., Palumbo, C.: The body beyond the screen: motor-expressive activities and online learning. In: Book of Abstracts of the 7th International Conference on Higher Education Learning Methodologies and Technologies Online (HELMeTO 2025), pp. 190–192. STUDIUM s.r.l. (2025)
37. Fu, Y., Weng, Z.: Navigating the ethical terrain of AI in education: a systematic review on framing responsible human-centered AI practices. Comput. Educ. AI. **7**, 100306 (2024)
38. Memarian, B., Doleck, T.: Human-in-the-loop in artificial intelligence in education: a review and entity-relationship (ER) analysis. Comput. Hum. Behav. Artif. Humans **2**(1), 100053 (2024)
39. Khosravi, H., et al.: Explainable artificial intelligence in education. Comput. Educ. Artif. Intell. **3**, 100074 (2022)
40. Coates, H., James, R., Baldwin, G.: A critical examination of the effects of learning management systems on university teaching and learning. Tert. Educ. Manag. **11**(1), 19–36 (2005)
41. Dillenbourg, P.: Design for classroom orchestration. Comput. Educ. **69**, 485–492 (2013). https://doi.org/10.1016/j.compedu.2013.04.013
42. Martinez-Maldonado, R., et al.: Towards proximity tracking and sensemaking for supporting teamwork and learning. In: Proceedings of the IEEE 17th International Conference on Advanced Learning Technologies (ICALT), pp. 89–91. IEEE (2017). https://doi.org/10.1109/ICALT.2017.79

43. Ronda-Carracao, M.A., Santos, O.C., Fernández-Nieto, G., Martinez-Maldonado, R.: Towards exploring stress reactions in teamwork using multimodal physiological data. In: Proceedings of MAIED@AIED 2021. CEUR Workshop Proceedings, vol. 2902, (2021)
44. Corbi, A., Santos, O.C., Burgos, D.: Intelligent framework for learning physics with aikido (martial art) and registered sensors. Sensors. **19**(17), 3681 (2019). https://doi.org/10.3390/s19173681
45. Santos, O.C., Corbi, A.: Can aikido help with the comprehension of physics? A first step towards the design of intelligent psychomotor systems for STEAM kinesthetic learning scenarios. IEEE Access **7**, 176458–176469 (2019). https://doi.org/10.1109/ACCESS.2019.2957947
46. Santos, O.C.: Psychomotor learning in martial arts: an opportunity for user modeling, adaptation and personalization. In: Adjunct Proceedings of the 25th Conference on User Modeling, Adaptation and Personalization (UMAP 2017), pp. 89–92 (2017). https://doi.org/10.1145/3099023.3099107
47. Casas-Ortiz, A., Santos, O.C.: KSAS: a mobile app with neural networks to guide the learning of motor skills. In: Proceedings of the XIX Conferencia de la Asociación Española para la Inteligencia Artificial (CAEPIA 20/21), pp. 997–1000 (2021)
48. Casas-Ortiz, A., Jimenez-Tellez, N., Portaz, M., Santos, O.C.: A holistic framework to create intelligent systems for psychomotor learning: a systematic review and insights from the virtual reality Kenpo learning simulator. Virtual Reality, **30**(72) (2026). https://doi.org/10.1007/s10055-026-01326-1
49. Echeverria, J., Santos, O.C.: KUMITRON: artificial intelligence system to monitor karate fights that synchronize aerial images with physiological and inertial signals. In: Companion Proceedings of the 26th International Conference on Intelligent User Interfaces (IUI 2021), pp. 37–39 (2021). https://doi.org/10.1145/3397482.3450730
50. Echeverría, J., Santos, O.C.: Towards analyzing psychomotor group activity for collaborative teaching using neural networks. In: Artificial Intelligence in Education. Posters and Late Breaking Results, Workshops and Tutorials, Industry and Innovation Tracks, Practitioners, Doctoral Consortium and Blue Sky. AIED 2023. CCIS, vol. 1831, pp. 403–408. Springer, Cham (2023). https://doi.org/10.1007/978-3-031-36336-8_63
51. Barbarelli, A., et al.: Participatory elicitation of user model dimensions for active ageing: the EMERGE methodology. In: Proceedings of the 34th ACM International Conference on User Modeling, Adaptation and Personalization (UMAP '26), pp. 418–423. Association for Computing Machinery, New York, NY, USA (2026). https://doi.org/10.1145/3774935.3806152
52. Portaz, M., Manjarrés, A., Santos, O.C.: Towards human-centric psychomotor recommender systems. In: Adjunct Proceedings of the 31st ACM Conference on User Modeling, Adaptation and Personalization (UMAP 2023 Adjunct), pp. 337–342 (2023). https://doi.org/10.1145/3563359.3596993
53. Portaz, M., Cabestrero, R., Quirós, P., Santos, O.C.: AI-powered psychomotor learning through basketball practice: opportunities and challenges. In: Santoianni, F., Giannini, G., Ciasullo, A. (eds.) Mind, Body, and Digital Brains. Integrated Science, vol. 20. Springer, Cham (2024). https://doi.org/10.1007/978-3-031-58363-6_13
54. Portaz, M., Majumdar, R., Santos, O.C.: Exploring cognitive engagement in AI-driven adaptive psychomotor sport training. In: Proceedings of the 32nd International Conference on Computers in Education (ICCE 2024) (2024). https://doi.org/10.58459/icce.2024.4903
55. Zarza, M., Portaz, M., Santos, O.C.: MyWorkout: a motion-aware learning system for integrating psychomotor skills into online education. In: Proceedings of the 21st European Conference on Technology Enhanced Learning (EC-TEL 2026), under Review (2026)

56. Portaz, M., Corbi, A., Casas-Ortiz, A., Santos, O.C.: Exploring raw data transformations on inertial sensor data to model user expertise when learning psychomotor skills. User Model. User-Adapt. Interact. **34**, 1283–1325 (2024). https://doi.org/10.1007/s11257-024-09393-2
57. Perez-Martinez, R., Casas-Ortiz, A., Santos, O.C.: MoRTELaban: a neurosymbolic framework for motion representation and analysis based on labanotation and Laban movement analysis. In: Adjunct Proceedings of the 33rd ACM Conference on User Modeling, Adaptation and Personalization (UMAP 2025), pp. 353–359 (2025). https://doi.org/10.1145/3708319.3734180
58. Portaz, M., Manjarrés, A., Santos, O.C.: Human-centered recommender systems. In: Germanakos, P., Juhasz, M., Kongot, A., Marathe, D., Sacharidis, D. (eds.) Human-Centered AI: a Visual Scientific Quest. Springer, Cham (2024). https://doi.org/10.1007/978-3-031-61375-3_11
59. Holmes, W., et al.: Ethics of AI in education: towards a community-wide framework. Int. J. Artif. Intell. Educ. **32**, 504–526 (2022). https://doi.org/10.1007/s40593-021-00239-1
60. Van Rosmalen, P., Boticario, J.G., Santos, O.C.: The full life cycle of adaptation in aLFanet eLearning environment. Learn. Technol. Newsl. **4**, 59–61 (2004)
61. Majumdar, R., Prasad, P., Kadam, K., Gatare, K., Warriem, J.M.: LA-ReflecT: a platform facilitating micro-learning and its multimodal learning analytics. In: Proceedings of the 18th European Conference on Technology Enhanced Learning (EC-TEL 2023), pp. 731–735 (2023)
62. Majumdar, R., Casas-Ortiz, A., Portaz, M., Santos, O.C.: Bringing psychomotor learning to online learning platforms: the Kenpo learning simulator in LA-ReflecT. Interactive event. In: Proceedings of the 26th International Conference on Artificial Intelligence in Education (AIED 2025) (2025)

Author Index

M. Adamoli et al. (Eds.): HELMeTO 2025, CCIS 2958, pp. 641–643, 2026.
https://doi.org/10.1007/978-3-032-31850-3

Kolibri 360 GmbH
Ferdinand-Jühlke-Straße 7
99095 Erfurt, Deutschland
produktsicherheit@kolibri360.de